𝔐𝔲𝔰𝔦𝔠
IN THE
MIDDLE AGES

𝔐usic
IN THE
MIDDLE AGES

WITH AN INTRODUCTION ON THE
MUSIC OF ANCIENT TIMES

by

GUSTAVE REESE

New York: W · W · NORTON & COMPANY

H69:7
11591
780.9

PRINTED IN THE UNITED STATES OF AMERICA
FOR THE PUBLISHERS BY THE VAIL-BALLOU PRESS
123456789

TO MY WIFE

Contents

Contents

APPENDICES

Since this book first appeared, a publication has been issued that may be used as a supplement to it: *Examples of Music before 1400,* selected and edited by Harold Gleason, 1942.

List of Plates

Preface

THE BEST of the music discussed in this book does not consist of mere museum pieces. Gregorian Chant, even if its melodies were sung in corrupt form for centuries before the recent restoration, has never been wholly dead in its history of some thirteen hundred years. Today it flourishes with renewed vigor, thanks largely to the successful research of a group of earnest scholars. The efforts of musicologists have made available a considerable repertoire of other medieval music. If by doing this they had furnished us only with a fuller knowledge of the course that our Western culture has taken in its development, they would have been justified. But, actually, they have given us much more than that, in bringing to light again and transcribing into modern notation many early compositions that are capable of arousing a deeper interest than mere curiosity in the mind of the modern listener. There is much, for example, in 13th-century polyphony that is especially in harmony with present-day taste and that may well fire the imagination of contemporary composers.

For the purposes of this book the Middle Ages close with the year 1453. Its contents are concerned mainly with style-analysis of the music itself rather than with environmental and cultural determinants, which will be treated of fully in Paul Henry Láng's forthcoming book, *Music in Western Civilization*. The present volume has given special attention to the results of recent research, and has provided many musical examples (a few not previously published) and occasional new interpretations of old facts. It also provides copious bibliographical references, making it easy for the student to learn details concerning the various developments here necessarily described in little more than outline. (Peter Wagner's Introduction to the single subject of Gregorian Chant, for example, fills three volumes, each about the size of this one.)

The book is an outgrowth of a course of lectures on Medieval and Renaissance Music that I gave for a number of years in the Washington Square College and Graduate School of New York University. At first it was intended to deal with the music of the Renaissance as well as with that of earlier times. But as chapter after chapter exceeded the length originally planned, it became clear that progress beyond the Middle Ages could not be made within the present volume (except here and there to tie up what would otherwise be loose ends) and that, if I was to deal with Renaissance music, I would have to do so in a possible second volume.

In my teaching I often felt the need for a new general textbook in English to use in orienting the student of our older music. Volume I of the *Oxford History of Music* was a splendid contribution when it first appeared, in 1901. But a fine opportunity was missed in 1929, when the second edition was published; for, while it brought some passages in line with what was then recent investigation, it left untouched other passages that badly needed revision. This is not the place to write a criticism of that edition, especially since its shortcomings have by no means gone unrecognized. Suffice it to say that the student without advance knowledge cannot tell which statements he may rely upon as representing up-to-date information and which he may not. For the trained reader the volume in question remains an invaluable tool, as do portions of it for the properly guided student. But it does not supply, in general serviceability, an equivalent of the earlier portion of Heinrich Besseler's substantial and scholarly *Die Musik des Mittelalters und der Renaissance* or of Théodore Gérold's neatly organized *Histoire de la musique des origines à la fin du XIVe siècle* (which appeared when the present work was already well under way).

Since this book is intended primarily for the American student, original sources, not as accessible to him as to his European colleagues, figure less than in certain foreign publications of a similar nature (though the books and articles to which references are made frequently enable him to trace original sources if he wishes to). The original material within easy reach of American students may be found catalogued in the *Census of Medieval and Renaissance Manuscripts in the United States and Canada* by Seymour de Ricci and W. J. Wilson. Thanks to the building up of microfilm archives, there is another body of similarly useful material available that is rapidly growing in size.

The footnotes frequently cite several different transcriptions of a single piece. This is done not only because of the interest that attaches to comparing dissimilar transcriptions where more than one interpretation of the rhythm is possible, but also as an aid to students in smaller centers, who may find one transcription at hand but not another. Consideration of this point has seemed especially desirable in view of the rapid spread—since the first chair of Musicology in this country was founded in 1930 for Dr. Otto Kinkeldey—of courses dealing with at least some phases of musicology in American colleges a number of which have only limited library facilities. In certain places the will has been in advance of the physical equipment—not necessarily a bad sign.

Since some readers are likely to consult this book for special subjects only, it has been provided with many cross references in an effort to render each major section, with the passages to which it makes reference, a reasonably well-rounded unit.

There is no point in pretending that a chapter such as the second, devoted mostly to Greek music, is easy reading. It could be made so, I fear, only by sidestepping the main problems discussed. (The same is true of some other, but shorter, divisions of the book.) The fairly self-sufficient character of each major section, however, will make it possible for the reader not especially interested in the music of Antiquity to begin with Chapter 3, though this will inevitably weaken somewhat his comprehension of the section on the Church Modes.

No extended acknowledgment need be made here of my indebtedness to the great scholars of the past and present who have enabled the music of Antiquity and the Middle Ages to assume a place in our culture analogous to that occupied by the literature and visual arts of the same periods. The debt is too obvious. Without the work of Gerbert, Coussemaker, Gevaert, Ludwig, Peter Wagner, Johannes Wolf, Pierre Aubry, Dom Ferretti, W. H. Frere, Wooldridge, Curt Sachs, Higini Anglès, Jacques Handschin—to name only a few—, whole aspects of one or both of these many-sided subjects would probably appear otherwise to us today, or perhaps would not be known at all. It should be clear that one of the purposes of this book—in which the magnitude of their achievements will become evident—is to lead the reader on to their writings in the interest of a better understanding of the music itself.

For permission to use transcriptions into modern notation and other copyrighted material from books and periodicals, grateful acknowledgment is made to the following publishers:

Akademische Verlagsgesellschaft Athenaion, Potsdam: Heinrich Besseler, *Die Musik des Mittelalters und der Renaissance* (our Exx. 91, 103); Robert Haas, *Aufführungspraxis der Musik* (Ex. 30); Curt Sachs, *Die Musik der Antike* (Ex. 2).

D. Appleton-Century Co., Inc., New York: George Grant MacCurdy, *Human Origins,* Vol. II (picture of bone flute in Plate II).

Associated Music Publishers, Inc., New York, as agents for Breitkopf & Härtel, Leipzig: Friedrich Ludwig, *Guillaume de Machaut: Musikalische Werke* (Exx. 105–9); Paul Runge, *Die Lieder und Melodien der Geissler des Jahres 1349* (Ex. 61); Peter Wagner, *Gregorianische Formenlehre* (Exx. 40, 41, 43); Johannes Wolf, *Geschichte der Mensural-Notation* (Exx. 104, 113); articles by Friedrich Gennrich, A. Z. Idelsohn, Friedrich Ludwig, Helmut Schmidt, and Marius Schneider, in the *Zeitschrift für Musikwissenschaft* (Exx. 23, 49, 62, 83–6, 88, 93).

Associated Music Publishers, Inc., New York, as agents for the Universal Edition, Vienna: *Denkmäler der Tonkunst in Oesterreich* (Exx. 120, 126).

Biblioteca Central de la Diputación (formerly the Biblioteca de Catalunya), Barcelona: Higini Anglès, *El Còdex musical de las Huelgas* (Ex. 90), *La Musica a Catalunya fins al segle XIII* (Ex. 47); Casiano Rojo and German Prado, *El Canto Mozárabe* (Exx. 21, 22).

Librairie Honoré Champion, Paris: Pierre Aubry, *La Musique et les musiciens d'église en Normandie au 13e siècle* (Ex. 44).

Chatto and Windus, London: translations from J. A. Symonds, *Wine, Women and Song,* and Barbara Smythe, *Trobador Poets* (both books in the Mediaeval Library, published in the U. S. A. by the Oxford University Press), here printed on pp. 200, 214, and 215.

Clarendon Press, Oxford: translations from E. K. Chambers, *The Mediaeval Stage;* E. S. Forster, *The Works of Aristotle,* Vol. VII (Oxford Translation of Aristotle, ed. by W. D. Ross); and H. S. Macran, *The Harmonics of Aristoxenus,* here printed on pp. 194f, 47, and 46.

Desclée et Cie., Tournai: *Antiphonale missarum juxta ritum Sanctae Ecclesiae Mediolanensis* (Ex. 19); *Antiphonale Sacrosanctae Romanae Ecclesiae pro diurnis horis* (Ex. 36); *Compendium Gradualis et Antiphonalis* (Ex. 29c); *Graduale Romanum* (Ex. 42); *Liber Usualis* (Exx. 32, 33a, 35, 38, 39); *Liber Usualis . . . in recentioris musicae notulas . . .* (Ex. 25); *Paléographie musicale* (Ex. 20 and the chart on p. 139).

Librairie Paul Geuthner, Paris: Pierre Aubry, *Le Chansonnier de l'Arsenal* (Ex. 54).

Harvard University Press, Cambridge, Mass.: quotation, on p. 12, from R. G. Bury's translation of Plato's *Laws,* as published in Vol. 187 of the Loeb Classical Library.

Hebrew Union College, Cincinnati: quotation on p. 5 from Sol Baruch Finesinger, *Musical Instruments in the Old Testament.*

Max Hesses Verlag, Berlin: Guido Adler, *Handbuch der Musikgeschichte* (Exx. 57, 70, 71, and 92, all being transcriptions by Friedrich Ludwig).

Henry Holt and Company, New York: quotations, in Chapter 1, from A. Z. Idelsohn, *Jewish Music.*

Fr. Kistner & C. F. Siegel, Leipzig: Exx. 98 and 102 and the chart on p. 333 from articles by Heinrich Besseler, and Ex. 111 from an article by Johannes Wolf, published in the *Archiv für Musikwissenschaft.*

Alfred A. Knopf, Inc., New York: quotation on p. 3 from C. F. Atkinson's translation of Oswald Spengler's *Decline of the West.*

E. M. Lohmann Company, Saint Paul, Minn.: translation of Ex. 42, from Dom Gaspar Lefebvre, *Daily Missal.*

Council of the Musical Association, London: quotations from papers by Wilfrid Perrett, Egon Wellesz, and Johannes Wolf, read before the Association and published in its Proceedings, the extracts being here printed on pp. 20, 71, 81, 86f, 365, and 369 (Exx. 116, 117).

Max Niemeyer Verlag, Halle-an-der-Saale: Friedrich Gennrich, *Die altfranzösische Rotrouenge* (Ex. 51), *Grundriss einer Formenlehre des mittelalterlichen Liedes* (Exx. 48, 55, 72), *Rondeaux, Virelais und Balladen* (Exx. 52, 53, 94, 96).

Editions de l'Oiseau-Lyre (Louise B. M. Dyer), Paris: Yvonne Rokseth, *Polyphonies du XIII⁰ siècle* (Ex. 95); Egon Wellesz, *Trésor de musique byzantine* (Ex. 11).

Leo S. Olschki, Florence: Ex. 60, from an article by Fernando Liuzzi, published in *Archivum Romanicum.*

Plainsong & Mediaeval Music Society, London: Alexander Ramsbotham et al., *The Old Hall Manuscript* (Ex. 125); quotations from Dom Anselm Hughes,

Anglo-French Sequelae and *Worcester Mediaeval Harmony* on pp. 251 and 274; a number of quotations from the Society's translation of Peter Wagner's *Einführung in die gregorianischen Melodien,* Vol. I.

Friedrich Pustet, Regensburg: Ex. 24, from an article by C. Vivell in the *Kirchenmusikalisches Jahrbuch.*

Charles Scribner's Sons, New York: a number of quotations from *The Ante-Nicene Fathers. Translations of the Writings of the Fathers down to A. D. 325* and *A Select Library of the Nicene Fathers of the Christian Church.*

G. Schirmer, Inc., New York: quotations from articles by Victor Belaiev, Ludwig Bonvin, Leonard Ellinwood, Rudolf Ficker, and H. J. W. Tillyard, published in *The Musical Quarterly,* here reprinted on pp. 249, 67, 372, 339, and 77 (Ex. 9), and J. M. Gibbon's translation of Ex. 53, taken from J. B. Beck, *The Play of Robin and Marion.*

University of California Press, Berkeley: extract, on p. 326, from L. J. Paetow, *The Battle of the Seven Arts.*

To Desclée et Cie. I am indebted also for permission to apply the Solesmes rhythmic signs to Exx. 19–22.

It has been my very good fortune to receive help in a variety of ways from many friends. I extend my sincere thanks to all of them, even if I can single out only some of them for special mention here. Acknowledgments to certain of the others are made in the course of the book.

To several I wish to express my sincere gratitude (without imputing to them responsibility for such errors as may be present) for having read the book in typescript or proof, in whole or in part. Professor Curt Sachs, despite a heavy schedule of lectures and although himself at work on a new *History of Musical Instruments,* had the extraordinary kindness to read the entire work and to give me the benefit of several most valuable suggestions. Between them, Dr. Otto Gombosi and Dr. Manfred Bukofzer gave the book another complete reading and they also were the sources of most helpful recommendations. Professor Egon Wellesz generously read and approved the section on Byzantine Chant as it stood in 1938, before the publication of more recent matter, taken into account in its present form. Dr. Oliver Strunk, besides providing the transcription printed as Example 10, made some useful suggestions affecting passages in Chapters 3, 10 and 12.

An acknowledgment must be made to the man who headed the Music Department of New York University when, during the winter of 1932-33, work on the book first got seriously under way and whose friendly interest, at that time and since, has provided most helpful encouragement—Percy Aldridge Grainger.

I am indebted to Professor Jacques Handschin of Basle for having graciously provided me with a generous selection of offprints of his articles; to Mr. Arthur Mendel for a number of valuable suggestions; and to Miss Rosemary Hughes of London for help of various kinds.

Although acknowledgments are made to Mr. Willis Wager in the course of the book, I wish to express my thanks here for the hours he spent in helping me correct the final proofs.

An acknowledgment is made in the book, also, to Mr. Igor Buketoff for having provided the section on Russian Chant. I sought his assistance, since I have only a little knowledge of this body of music and do not share his ability to read Russian. It is only fair to him to state that I have taken the liberty of making a few insertions in this section, in order to render it more useful to readers suffering from my handicap and wishing to obtain fuller information from sources in English, French, and German.

To Mr. Roland Partridge and Mr. Julius Keil I am indebted for summaries of material printed in Catalan and Polish respectively.

During a portion of 1938, Mr. Frederick W. Sternfeld and Dr. Hans Tischler acted as my assistants and were most helpful, the former chiefly in connection with part of Chapter 6 and the latter chiefly in connection with Chapter 11. They gave me ungrudgingly of their time in aiding me in library work at the British Museum and in various other ways.

To Mrs. M. D. Herter Norton I owe a very special acknowledgment. It was at her prompting that this book was undertaken, and without her interest it would probably never have been written. From time to time while work was in progress on it, she was the source of many valuable suggestions.

I am thankful also for the help that has been granted me by the libraries whose riches have enlarged my knowledge of Renaissance as well as Medieval music. The Vatican Library, the Biblioteca Medicea-Laurenziana in Florence, and the British Museum are especially entitled to my gratitude among libraries abroad. Most of my library work in America has been done at the New York Public Library, and I deeply appreciate the many courtesies extended to me by the splendid staff of its Music Room. To the excellent staff of the Music Division of the Library of Congress, I am likewise indebted for many courtesies.

Finally, I must express my appreciation to Mr. Nathan Broder, who has assisted me in many different ways since the autumn of 1936. He has at times supplied me with abstracts; at others, joined me in planning the organization of a chapter. He has aided me in library work and in the correcting of galley proofs. In certain portions of the book—notably the section in Chapter 5 on the Notation of Intervals and the section in Chapter 6 on the Gregorian Forms—he has been a collaborator. It is certain that without his help the work on the book would have lasted much longer and would have been considerably less pleasant.

AUGUST 1940   *Gustave Reese*

NOTE

Some evidence remains of the effort to save space wherever possible, made when it was still thought that the period embraced by this book would include the Renaissance, this evidence taking form chiefly in the occasional excessive abbreviations of authors' names in the symbols used in the bibliographical references—Tre for Trend, Hugh for Hughes, Schlec for Schlecht, etc. There was no opportunity, without further delaying the appearance of a book originally announced for publication in 1935, to overhaul the typescript in an effort to track down all these abbreviations and change them.

In line with some of the writing of J. F. Mountford, I have not followed the usual English custom of latinizing Greek proper names. I have refrained from doing so in order to adhere to the practice adopted in a large part of the better bibliographical material to which reference is made, thus to some degree reducing lack of uniformity in what the interested student is likely to read. (Where, however, an English form such as Ptolemy exists, or where such Latin forms as Aeschylus and Byzantium have become English, these forms are of course used.) What forms to adopt for medieval proper names is a question that has not been consistently answered—again, though this may at first seem paradoxical, in the interests of uniformity. The aim has simply been to use the forms most commonly employed by modern writers. "Johannes de Grocheo," the Latin name of the Frenchman Jean de Grouchy, is more frequently encountered than his French name; the English "Franco of Cologne" is, in writing in English, more usual than the Latin "Franco de Colonia" or the German "Franko von Köln"; the Italian "Guido d'Arezzo" designates the great Italian theorist more often than does the Latin "Guido Aretinus."

The words of refrains are underscored in musical examples. Where additional text follows an example (and in translations), such words are, in accordance with the usual custom, given in italics. (This, of course, has nothing to do with the style that has been adopted in the printing of this book, of presenting lengthy quotations in italics also.) Such additional text does not always, in the original, immediately follow the first stanza: I have at times felt prompted to give later stanzas that impressed me as attractive. For instance, in Example 65 (as the Roman numerals indicate), the stanzas given are the first and fourth.

Occasionally terms are defined without further use being made of them here, the purpose being to forearm the student proceeding to the study of special literature on this or that topic.

The term "pentatonic" is used in this book in the sense of "pentatonic without semitones."

A special effort has been made to direct the student's attention, by footnote references and actual quotations, to such translations of treatises and of other relevant writings as are available in English, French, and German.

Part One: INTRODUCTION: THE MUSIC OF
ANCIENT TIMES

Chapter 1: SOUTHWEST ASIA AND EGYPT

I HEARD, about midnight, a furious clamor. I asked what it was. 'Vocal exercises,' was the answer." This passage from a letter [1] written by Seneca (c. 4 B.C.–A.D. 65) has a strangely undated ring. Some similar incident lies within the experience of most of us. But whether the pieces in this vocalist's repertoire, if recovered, would also sound contemporary today, is open to question.

Spengler would have us believe the artistic expression in the music of the ancients too alien spiritually for our grasp. A similarity between the aural equipment of one people and another places some common limits upon the range and intensity of tone they are both able to perceive. But it will not alone suffice to enable either people to comprehend the underlying emotional and intellectual impulse that generates the outer expression of the other. For that, the two peoples must, in the broad sense, have a common culture. While technical material may survive from one culture to another, each new cycle—which does not necessarily start life wholly unprovided—invests with a new significance any material it takes over. In Spengler's words: [2]

> It may be that the Doric column was, as a matter of workmanship, borrowed from the Egyptian temples of the New Empire, or the late-Roman domical construction from the Etruscans, or the Florentine court from the North-African Moors. Nevertheless the Doric peripteros, the Pantheon, and the Palazzo Farnese belong to wholly different worlds—they subserve the artistic expression of the prime-symbol in three different Cultures.

According to Spengler, then, the survival of a mere technical medium does not denote a *causal* connection between the real basis of one culture and another—a view that serves his main thesis that each culture has its own life-span: youth, maturity, decay. But the complete break Spengler would thus have us see, for example, between the real essence of the Greek, or "Apollinian," culture and that of its successor, the "Magian"—to which he assigns Gregorian Chant—, is by no means universally recognized. The title of Vivell's *Direkte Entwicklung des römischen Kirchengesanges aus der vorchristlichen Musik* indicates the attitude of one investigator. This, to be sure, appeared before

[1] Letter CXXII.
[2] As translated by C. F. Atkinson. For a discussion of Spengler's views as they affect music, see MendS.

3

Spengler's great work. But the publication of the latter did not prevent an-other investigator, in subsequent notes on pre-medieval music, from contend-ing that "No barrier exists between Antiquity and the Middle Ages, the latter being . . . but a progressive adaptation, ethnic and regional, of the former." [3]

There is, indeed, a body of technical material in medieval music that medieval musicians themselves thought they had derived from ancient Greece. But even where there was, roughly, an external resemblance between the ancient and medieval forms of some of this material, the meanings attached to it by the ancients and the later musicians seem to have been quite different, a fact that tends to support Spengler's theory. Nevertheless, a brief survey of ancient music and its background may—indeed, we believe, will—furnish a helpful introduction to the music of the Middle Ages. It will at least shed a little light on why medieval musicians set out on certain attempts, however much these may have missed their mark. Moreover, even though some of the material of Antiquity was destined to be misunderstood in the succeeding pe-riods, its influence did survive. For the misunderstanding caused musical thinking to assume certain forms it would quite likely never have taken if the particular things that were misconstrued had not existed, and these forms were not without importance in determining the course of medieval music. Survivals, if they are heeded at all, help in some degree to limit the direction taken by a new development. And a misunderstanding of them may very well prove more fruitful than a correct interpretation.

The earliest bodies of music of which we have any contemporaneously notated examples are those of the Greeks and the still older Sumerians, and it is highly probable that oral tradition has preserved some music of the an-cient Hebrews also. Of some peoples of greater or similar antiquity, who have left no notated examples, we have instruments or reproductions of instru-ments on reliefs [4] etc., and from these a few not very satisfactory deductions may be made about the music itself.

Thus, it is interesting, and even surprising—but not very informative—to know that a Neolithic bone-flute unearthed in Switzerland supplies evidence that our ancestors of sometime between 7000 and 2500 B. c. found some use for a wind instrument with three holes. What may be a flute—dating from about 25,000 years ago—has been discovered in a Magdalenian site at Charente, France.[5] Other specimens, definitely identified as flutes, were dug up in France in 1925 and are said to be Magdalenian.

Leaping not centuries but millennia, we come to several bone-pipes of about

---

[3] MaN, 277.   [4] For a generous number of reproductions, see SachsA.

[5] See MacH II, 140. Further concerning prehistoric instruments, see SeeB or, in English, WilP (not up to date, but good for its time). See also SachsGW, which correlates pre-medieval and medieval instruments with those of primitive cultures and grades them according to chronological and geographical "strata."

6000 years ago, found in 1937 at Tepe Gawra in Northern Iraq; [6] and to a more considerable fund of instruments, as well as to an actual piece of music, yielded by Mesopotamia, the land controlled, beginning about 3000 B. C., by the Sumerians, and, from about 2000 B. C. until 538 B. C., mainly by their successors, the Babylonians and Assyrians. The Sumerians had an imposing array of instruments.

In this book we shall employ the instrument-classification of Hornbostel and Sachs (first presented in HornS). The instruments to be discussed fall into four main groups: idiophones, i. e. instruments the material of which is able to vibrate without any special tension; membranophones, or skin-vibrators; chordophones, or string-vibrators; and aerophones, or air-vibrators.

Sumerian idiophones included dancing sticks and rattles, among the latter being the type known as the *sistrum,* of which there is evidence in the earlier part of the 3rd millennium B. C.—that is, sooner than it is thus far known to have appeared in Egypt where, in a somewhat different shape, it became particularly popular (see the illustration on Plate II for a reproduction of an Egyptian example); it seems that bells and cymbals did not sound in this area until considerably later: it has been suggested that a mention of a copper temple instrument, appearing on a tablet of *c.* 1500 B. C., refers to the former, while the latter are shown on Assyrian reliefs of the 7th century B. C.

The vertical flute is among the several aerophones that the Sumerians played upon, as is the wooden horn.

Chordophones in early Mesopotamia included the harp, lute, and, representing the lyre-type, the kithara. Not before the Greeks do we find tangible evidence of the lyre proper [7] (hereinafter to be called the *lyra,* while *lyre* will be used as a generic term for the type—quotations, of course, being subject to exception). The harp is regarded by Galpin, who has done the most comprehensive investigating of the music of the Sumerians, as their most characteristic instrument. The well-known "Sumerian harp of Ur" (the city whence came Abraham), a restored specimen—dating from *c.* 2700 B. C.—at the British Museum, has eleven strings; other examples have been found with as many as fifteen. The oldest Sumerian harps were bow-shaped and strung crosswise; those especially favored by the Assyrians were upright and strung vertically. Both, like nearly all Asiatic and related types, lacked a fore-pillar.[8] It is of

---

[6] Concerning these, see SpeiR, No. 64, 8; No. 65, 8; No. 66, 19.   [7] *Cf.* GuilS, 118.

[8] FineM, 13, suggests the following as an explanation of the later widespread preference of the lyra and kithara to the harp: ". . . all ancient harps differ . . . from the harps in use since the 8th century. . . . Modern harps have the so-called fore-pillar, which serves to prevent the two ends of the frame from moving towards one another when the strings are tensed. None of the ancient harps possess the fore-pillar. We can well imagine that the Assyrian or Egyptian musician suffered considerable annoyance, for when he tightened one string of the harp, the frame would bend, thereby loosening the other strings. In the instruments of the lyre-type this difficulty did not exist. This may account for the greater popularity of the lyre and cithara."

some interest to observe that the number of strings on an instrument may not always have been determined for specifically musical reasons. Thus, it has been pointed out by Sachs, in connection with a Babylonian vase showing two harps with five and seven strings respectively, that these numbers were regarded as specially significant—the former warded off suffering; the latter sanctified—and that both were destined to play rôles in Europe far into the Middle Ages. The kitharas of the Sumerians were highly developed in structure, but were not as characteristic of these people as of the neighboring Semites, from whom the type, in a less advanced stage, was probably borrowed. The primitive lute is found in Mesopotamia early in the 2nd millennium B. c.: a lute with two strings, apparently the standard number, is shown on a plaque of about 1900 B. c.—that is, during the Babylonian rule; the lute appears in Egypt about the 15th century B. c. The presence of the psaltery in Southwest Asia around the 9th century B. c.—eleven centuries after its known existence in China—is attested by a carving on part of a Phoenician ivory box found in Mesopotamia.

An actual Sumerian hymn on the creation of man has come down to us with both words and music, and offers us the oldest example of musical notation known. It survives on a table, dating from about 800 B. c., but the piece itself is apparently older. Attempts have been made to decipher this notation,[9] which employs cuneiform characters, but Sachs has concluded,[10] sixteen years after first studying it, that each of the symbols constituting the notation represents not a single note but a short melodic pattern, the nature of which is no longer known, and that the notation is therefore definitely undecipherable.

Galpin places the Classical Age of Sumerian art within the period 2500–1500 B. c.; a renaissance took place about 500 B. c., under the Assyrian and Babylonian Empires.

The plastic arts of the Iranians and Hittites furnish evidence of an instrumental apparatus much like that of the Babylonians. But, rich as this apparatus was, there is no trace of bowed instruments among the relics of these or other ancient peoples.

The total impression made by the musical remains from ancient Southwest Asia brings to mind so forcibly what we know concerning ancient Chinese music that a Chinese influence—or a mother culture common to China and the Southwest, but stemming from nearer Central Asia—has been postulated.[11]

The Egyptian "orchestra" came to resemble the Asian. While, during the

---

[9] E. g. on pp. 99–104 of GalpS.

[10] In SachsB. Sachs's first detailed study of the notation appeared in AfMW, VII (1925), 1. This prompted a controversial article by Benno Landsberger, in *Festschrift für Max Freiherr von Oppenheim, Archiv für Orientforschung, Beiband I* (1933), 170.

[11] See SachsA, 2.

fourth dynasty (3rd millennium B. C.), instruments appear from reproductions to have been incapable of great sonority and must have produced a mild and quiet music, there was apparently a change to noisier instruments, *c.* 1700–1500 B. C., showing, according to some authorities, the influx of Asiatic culture. The infiltration seems to have been accompanied by changes in the social standing of musicians. Under the Old Empire, the upper ranks practiced the art; under the New, it became associated chiefly with professionals of no great personal repute. Doubtless the upper-class native conservatives of the new age, finding that—then as now—noisy music won more general popularity than quiet music, and being perhaps somewhat nationalistically inclined, retired into their shell, artificially prolonged the life of the old Egyptian music in temple and school, and left the foreign novelties to the possession of the masses. The resulting split in Egyptian culture may supply the explanation of the apparent contradictions between various accounts, such as Plato's report that only "good" music—designated as such by the priests—was taught to Egyptian youths, and the statement of Diodoros the Sicilian (a good deal later, to be sure) that it was not the custom of the Egyptians to study music—that, in fact, they were convinced not only of its uselessness but of its feminizing harmfulness. The instruments developed or adopted by the Egyptians included lyras (during the Hellenistic period), kitharas, lutes, harps, flute-, clarinet-, and oboe-types, castanets, cymbals, bells, drums, and rattles including sistra. Apparently attempts to construct trumpets were not very successful. (Plutarch, early in the Christian Era, in his *Concerning Isis and Osiris* likened the Egyptian trumpets to the braying of an ass.) It has been deduced, especially from the wind instruments (of which we have about 50 in museums at Brussels, Berlin, Florence, Leyden, London, Paris, Turin, etc.), that the old Egyptian native music was probably devoid of semitones, while at least some of that imported from Asia made use of small intervals, including quarter-tones.[12] The multiplicity of scales made possible by the introduction of small intervals, and the simplicity of construction of the individual oboes etc., may have required the fashioning of different instruments for use in connection with tone series of differing intervallic construction.[13]

It is interesting to note that among the instruments are double-pipes (the Sumerians had them also), and that one of a pair apparently sustained a drone while the other sounded a melody. The resulting harmonic intervals (which should not be understood as having given rise to "harmony" in our sense) would seem not to have been unique. Sachs,[14] through a study of Egyptian and Assyrian reliefs etc., in which individual players are shown striking two strings of a harp at once or in which several players are shown simultaneously

[12] For details, see SachsT, 17, and SachsA, 5. The subject of Egyptian instruments is treated authoritatively in the following also: SachsM, SachsN, SachsGW, SachsD, the last containing many enlightening illustrations.
[13] For further details, see ClosU.   [14] In SachsZ.

striking different strings of similarly constructed harps, has made a good case for the occasional use of fifths, fourths, octaves, and unisons.

With a cultural history of about 4000 years behind it, Egypt saw its music enjoy what proved to be a last flicker of brilliance during the reign of Amasis II (570–526 B.C.). But the influence of Egyptian music did not disappear. Greek music drew upon it about this time, the music of Israel having done so long before.[15] The "orchestras" of the Egyptian temples and of the Temple at Jerusalem had points in common. The Jewish *nevel* (harp) and *kinnor* (kithara) had to be used at every public religious ceremony. In addition, there were the *shofar* (the ram's horn used for signaling purposes, the least musical of the Jewish instruments, but the only one to survive in ritual use), the *hasosra*-trumpet (depicted on the Arch of Titus), the *uggav* (an aerophone of some sort), *halil* (double-pipe), *tof* (little drum), *selsele* (cymbals), and *paamonim* (little bells, attached to the skirts of the high priest). The last-named were doubtless imitations of the bronze bells used on priestly garments in Egypt, and most of the other instruments had their Egyptian proto-types also. I Chron. XXV gives some idea of the choir and orchestra that made music in the First Temple, under King David. The vocal music, destined to outlive the instrumental—which died out after the destruction of the Second Temple (A. D. 70)—invested the psalms with tonal settings that were among the more important forerunners of Christian Chant.

The old vocal melodies of the Jews were not those of most present-day synagogue-song in Europe and America,[16] which is almost all of modern origin (much of it, in fact, dating from the early 19th century) and con-siderably affected by the music of the host-nations. But it would seem that some of the old music does survive, even though the ancient Jews had neither notation nor, so far as we know, treatises on musical theory. During per-formance, Hebrew singers, like the Egyptian (see Plate I), may have given and received reminders in the form of "hand-signs" (cheironomy). We know, at least, from the Talmud, that Hebrew singers used finger-motions early in the Christian Era. About the same time, the Jews adopted cantilla-tion signs similar to, and possibly taken from, the accents of the Greeks.[17] The majority of these written symbols conformed with the curves of the hand-gestures. But the signs, whether digital or graphic, were mere reminders of melodies already known. They showed ascents, descents, etc., and the hand-signs were doubtless an effective means of conducting a non-metrical music. (A cheironomic method is to be found in use today in the conducting of

[15] For an attempt to determine the extent of Israel's indebtedness to Egyptian music, see PulI.

[16] According to Idelsohn. A. M. Friedlander, in Grove II, 594, takes a somewhat different view.

[17] Cantillation signs are still in use, but the systems are not uniform throughout all Jewish communities. Much information concerning the cantillation notation (*ta'amim*) may be obtained from RosoM. See also GasO, 17; JE III, 537ff; Grove II, 596; and StaM, 222 (the last-named containing also much information concerning old Hebrew instruments, as does FineM). For a discussion of cheironomy, see WagE II, 16.

plainsong.) But neither type of signs could show definite pitches or intervals, and therefore neither could by itself convey to a novice any precise idea of a melody. Thus the Jews had to rely almost entirely on oral tradition in transmitting their music (no attempts to write it down precisely seem to have been made until the 16th century, except for a sporadic effort made at the end of the 12th century or in the 13th [18]), and yet this tradition has apparently sufficed to preserve some fundamental elements of the ancient Hebrew Chant down to our times.

These elements are most apparent in the cantillation of the Pentateuch and Prophets as practiced today in synagogues of Northeastern Europe and of isolated communities of the Near East. Idelsohn [19] has shown the existence of substantial agreement among the melodies intoned with particular portions of the Bible by certain widely scattered Jewish communities that had no contact with one another for many centuries. Thus, the Jews of Yemen in South Arabia, who lived in practical seclusion for 1300 years; those of Babylonia, where there remains "the oldest Jewish settlement, dating from the destruction of the First Temple, never ceasing to exist despite changes of conditions"; of Persia, "almost as old as the Babylonian community"; of Syria, North Africa, etc., all have practically the same motives for the intoning of the Pentateuch, and other common motives for other purposes also. Similar motives for the reading of the Pentateuch have been found among the Jews of Germany, Poland, and Russia; indeed it has been suggested [20] that the Northeastern European cantillation of the Bible is the oldest and purest of all.

In addition to the speech-song or intoning of biblical texts, the musical portion of the Hebrew liturgy embraces actual song applied to texts that are only sometimes biblical. The music of this second category employs the extremely elaborate but often expressive coloratura which, sung in most European and American synagogues today, is popularly regarded as characteristic of Hebrew Chant, but apparently originated in, and spread from, Eastern Europe.

Idelsohn's comparative method shows the rhythm of the ancient Chant to have been free rather than metrical. It also shows the use of certain definite

[18] Cf. A. M. Friedlander, *Discovery of an Ancient Hebrew Manuscript Containing Neums,* in *The Musical Times,* LXII (1921), 170.

[19] In IdJ, an important work, from which the above quotations and those on p. 10 are taken. Idelsohn published a 10-volume collection of Hebrew Oriental melodies, IdH, upon which his comparative study was based.

[20] By Joseph Yasser, in *Archaic Elements in Hebrew Music,* an unpublished paper read before the American Palestine Music Association (Mailamm), December 21, 1936. The claim on behalf of the Northeastern European music is based on its prevailing pentatonicism, a trait allegedly characteristic in the main of older music in distinction to the diatonicism of later music. Mr. Yasser has informed us that the results of philological investigations made by a Russian scholar (David Maggid, *On Ancient Hebrew Music and Psalmody,* in *De Musica,* III [1927], published by the State Institute of History of Arts, Leningrad) support his hypothesis.

modes. In this connection, we quote Idelsohn's comprehensive definition of "mode":

A MODE . . . is composed of a number of MOTIVES (i. e. short music figures or groups of tones) within a certain scale. The motives have different functions. There are beginning and concluding motives, and motives of conjunctive and disjunctive character. The composer operates with the material of these traditional folk motives within a certain mode for his creations. His composition is nothing but his arrangement and combination of this limited number of motives. His "freedom" of creation consists further in embellishments and in modulations from one mode to the other.

We shall have several occasions to return to the views expressed in this definition.

The Jews had—and still have—special modal motives not only for the Pentateuch and Prophets, but for the psalms, prayers (different modes being used for prayers of different types), etc. Thus, it is melodic formulas and not fixed melodies that are characteristic of the Hebrew Chant. (We are not, of course, taking modern settings of the liturgical texts into consideration.) This fact is of more than passing interest. Apparently we have illustrated for us here an early stage in the development of the art of composition generally, a stage in which a text is supplied with a stock melody—itself not so definite that it cannot be adapted to texts with varying numbers of syllables—rather than with a fixed melody specially composed for it.

The three ancient forms used for the intonation of the psalms contained a number of features destined to exert an influence upon Gregorian Chant. In one form the leader intoned the first half-verse, which the congregation repeated, the leader singing each succeeding half-line, with "the congregation always repeating the same first half-line which thus became a refrain throughout the entire song." In another, "the leader sang a half-line at a time, and the congregation repeated what he had last sung." The third was responsive, "i. e., the leader would sing the whole first line, whereupon the congregation would respond with the second line of the verse." The refrains used in the first form consisted either of a single word—such as *Amen, Hallelujah,* etc. (but not *Selah,* which was possibly a direction calling for the playing of an instrumental interlude)—or a phrase, such as the recurring half-verse of Psalm CXXXVI (King James numbering), "For His mercy endureth forever." The Hebrews were especially fond of parallelism, of which the second form illustrates the simplest type. The psalms are rich in more intricate, highly poetic uses of it, as in the verse:

Purge me with hyssop, and I shall be clean; wash me, and I shall be whiter than snow.

Chapter 2: GREECE AND ROME

WHILE for information concerning the tonal systems of the ancient musics so far discussed we have had to rely upon instruments and upon melodic material preserved (except for one undecipherable example) by mere oral tradition, when we approach ancient Greek music we have at our disposal actual treatises by trained theorists as well as compositions inscribed on stone and papyrus. But even here the sum of tangible information is exasperatingly insufficient.

Among the Greeks, the preponderant use of what we call music was in conjunction with poetry or dance. "The word music (μουσική, *musica*) had, in the ancient world, two different meanings: one broad, the other narrow. In the broad sense it meant the whole of intellectual or literary culture, as opposed to the culture of the bodily faculties, grouped under the term gymnastic. . . . In the narrow sense, μουσική is approximately synonymous with our word derived from it; but the ancients included under music . . . the dance movements which accompanied singing, and the poetic text itself." [1]

The history of the old Greek music is so interwoven with myths that strands of historical truth can be unraveled only with difficulty. Ascriptions of the art's origin to the gods, tales about Orpheus and Amphion, narratives of Apollo's victories over Linos and Marsyas, the account—once attributed to Plutarch—of the invention of the enharmonic genus (to be discussed presently) by the legendary Olympos, come down to us alongside reports of real events. Our knowledge of this music—fragmentary as it is—spans about nine centuries (*c.* 7th century B.C.—2nd century A.D.), and it is therefore important to bear in mind that its nature must have changed from time to time, and that no cut-and-dried description of any phase of the art is likely to be applicable to the entire period.

The earliest definite figure to emerge from the dim musical past personified by the mythical Olympos is the kithara-player Terpander of Lesbos (*c.* 675 B.C.). We learn that he was summoned to Sparta, by order of the Delphic oracle, to pacify dissension within the state. He is regarded as the founder of Greek classical music and is credited, among other things, with having increased the sections of the kitharodic *nomos* to the hallowed number of seven (*cf.* p. 6, also the seven gates of Thebes, the—at one time—seven Muses, etc.). The nomos (= "law") was a sung strain as distinguished

[1] From ReinD, 2072. (Transl. from MendS.)

from a recitation and appears to have built up a repertoire of "law-giving," fundamental melodic and rhythmic types which might be worked over by musicians into something more or less new. (*Cf.* the Hebrew motives [p. 10], the East Indian Ragas, the melody-types in plainsong [p. 171], etc.) The term was applied to the new productions also. These had no specific musical form common to all, but the division into a definite number of "movements" was essential. That before the time of Plato the Greeks had developed, through the nomoi and other types, a repertoire of melodic formulas considered suitable for specific purposes (as the Hebrews had special motives for the Pentateuch, prayers, etc.) may be implied by the following passage from his *Laws:*

> *Among us, . . . music was divided into various classes and styles; one class of song was that of prayers to the gods, which bore the name of "hymns"; contrasted with this was another class, best called "dirges"; "pæans" formed another; and yet another was the "dithyramb," named, I fancy, after Dionysus. "Nomes" also were so called as being a distinct class of song; and these were further described as "citharœdic nomes." So these and other kinds being classified and fixed, it was forbidden to set one kind of words to a different class of tune . . . ; but later on, with the progress of time, there arose as leaders of unmusical illegality poets who, though by nature poetical, were ignorant of what was just and lawful in music; and they, being frenzied and unduly possessed by a spirit of pleasure, mixed dirges with hymns and pæans with dithyrambs, . . . and blended every kind of music with every other.* (BuryL I, 245. The underscoring is ours.)

Music had its share at the great contests—the Panathenaia, the Olympia, the Pythia, the Karneia. At the Pythian Games at Delphi in 586 B.C., Sakadas of Argos won a celebrated victory with his *Nomos Pythikos* for the aulos, depicting, in five [2] sections, the triumph of Apollo over the Python. Other composers of nomoi for the aulos included Klonas and Polymnestos. That the nomoi furnished examples of program music seems borne out by a passage concerning them in Book XIX, Sec. 15 of the *Problems* attributed to Aristotle, reading: "it was more essential for the music to be imitative than the words." The subjects were apparently a matter of free choice, provided an invocation to Apollo was included.

At the turn of the 5th into the 4th century B.C. the innovations of Phrynis of Mitylene and his pupil, Timotheos of Miletos, introduced a sophistication censured as spoiling the old dignified simplicity. An amusing fragment of a comedy by Pherekrates (an older contemporary of Aristophanes) presents Music as a female character, covered with wounds and complaining that Phrynis,

> *with the fury of a storm*
> *And eddying whirlpool, twisted all my form;*

[2] Observe that we have here the other "significant" number mentioned on p. 6.

And by a mischievous contrivance wrings
Twelve harmonies from my five simple strings.[3]

Bad as Phrynis was, Timotheos, she says, was worse,

And in his twelve strings bound, I nerveless lie.[4]

The last reference is to an increase in the number of kithara strings. The hapless lady's complaint may have concerned dithyrambs rather than nomoi, since the offenders were outstanding exponents of the dithyramb, which usually, to be sure, employed the aulos, but also sometimes the kithara.

The only surviving fragment of the art of the nomos is the text of the *Persians* by Timotheos, which runs rather wild. Perhaps the alleged sophistication of the music helped bring about a decline. At all events, the nomos died out about this time. But it fructified the old Greek hymnody, and it is possible that some of the hymns to be listed later preserve traces of the nomos influence.[5]

The hymns, meant to be chanted in unison by companies of people, could be addressed to any of the gods. From Cretan *hyporchemata* (songs to be accompanied by dancing) were derived such choral dances as the *paian* (originally a magic cure dance), consecrated to Apollo, and the *pyrriche,* or rapid sword dance for young warriors. These choral dances, like the *gymnopaidiai* (ceremonial choral dances performed unclothed by boys and men, the motions being based on those of wrestling), were cultivated particularly at Sparta where they were said to have been instituted by Terpander's contemporary, Thaletas. The *parthenia,* or choral dances for Spartan virgins, are associated with the name of still another contemporary, Alkman. In fact it may be said that the Dorian culture of Sparta, with its strong community life, favored choral music generally, while the Ionian culture of Attica, with its greater stress on individualism, favored music employing soloists.[6]

Archilochos of Paros, still another 7th-century figure, advanced the art of the more intimate song (lyric music—that is, music sung to the lyre) by introducing triple rhythm and quickening the tempo. He may have drawn some of his inspiration from folk-song. The apparently widespread folk-art is mentioned in literary remains which tell us of all manner of work-songs— songs for stamping barley, treading grapes, spinning wool; songs for ropemakers, drawers of water, watchmen, shepherds.[7] Also inspired by the folk-influence, perhaps, were the lyric works of the somewhat later poet-musicians of Lesbos—Sappho, Alkaios, and Anakreon. Still later, the cultural importance of the 6th-century contests, which had already produced the Sakadas

[3] The meaning of this will become clear on p. 34.
[4] For the whole passage, see BromP, 76f or GoodP I, 124.
[5] For a fuller discussion of the nomos, see GriesN or VettM. See also LachmW.
[6] *Cf.* SachsA, 25f.   [7] The subject is comprehensively treated in BüchA.

nomos written in praise of Apollo, was shown at its height by Pindar (522–448 B. C.) with his odes written in praise of victorious athletes.

But it was perhaps in the drama that music received its most extended development. The choruses were sung throughout, and there were monodies for solo voice also. The tragedies of Aeschylus (d. 456), Sophocles (d. 406), and Euripides (d. c. 406) and the comedies of Aristophanes (d. c. 385) were, like *Fidelio* and *Carmen,* musico-dramatic works employing both song and speech. The chorus as such diminished in importance as its members took increasing part in the action and became merged with the *dramatis personæ.* The frequent assertion, founded on Suidas, that the chorus numbered twelve in Aeschylus and was increased by Sophocles to the subsequently standard number of fifteen, has been shown to be wrong. In fact, the *Suppliants* of Aeschylus mentions a chorus of fifty, and it seems likely that the great dramatists of the Periclean Age followed the dictates of artistic judgment rather than those of standardization.[8] In the course of time, the two important forms that had sprung from the cult of Dionysos—the drama and the dithyramb—became vehicles for the display of excessive virtuosity, and fell into decline. Greek music became a very different thing from what it had been in the classical period or in the still earlier Homeric days, when professional singers entertained guests at the feasts of the great with songs recounting the heroic deeds and terrible fates of gods and men.

The instrument considered especially suitable for the cult of Dionysos was the *aulos.* The term *aulos* (Latin *tibia*) has, strictly speaking, a generic rather than specific significance. All *auloi* are aerophones; each consists of a tube in which the performer's breath causes the air-column to vibrate, and the tube is normally of cylindrical bore. But, beyond this, differences arise. While most representations on vases, reliefs, etc., show the player blowing directly into the end of the pipe or pipes which—like an oboe or clarinet—are held pointing downward, literary accounts report a variant, called the *plagiaulos,* that was held horizontally—like the flute. Although single pipes are occasionally depicted and mentioned, art-works, with few exceptions, show double-pipes, such as we have found among the Assyrians and Egyptians. Double auloi with pipes of unequal length were generally used at marriage ceremonies, the smaller representing the bride, the greater the groom. The oboe mouthpiece—with a double-reed—was a characteristic feature. (The frequent translation of "aulos," as a generic term, into "flute" is therefore definitely wrong.) The number of holes, at first three or four, eventually grew to as many as fifteen, and bands that could be turned round on the tube were added to assist the fingers in closing holes not in use. Two writers state that the improvements of Pronomos, the teacher of Alcibiades (5th century B. C.), rendered

---

[8] The whole matter is engagingly and convincingly discussed in HamiG.

Instrumentalists Playing a Vertical Flute, Double Clarinet, and Harp, with Four Singers Indicating the Melody through Hand and Finger Motions, i.e. Cheironomy. From the Tomb of Nencheftkai in Sakkara, c. 2700 B.C.

(*After G. Maspero*, Le Musée égyptien)

A Chorus of Satyrs Rehearsing, One Playing a Double Aulos, while Another Dons his Costume and is about to Put On his Mask. Representation in Mosaics from the Ancient Roman Theatre at Sabratha, Tripolitania

(*After M. Bieber*, Die Denkmäler zum Theaterwesen im Altertum)

PLATE I

Dorian, Phrygian, and Lydian scales all playable on one pair of pipes, whereas previously a separate pair had been used for each. Double-pipes made possible the playing of a melody simultaneously with either a drone (*cf.* the Egyptian double-pipes, p. 7) or simple accompaniment.[9] Aristoxenos states that the full compass of a single pipe or pair of pipes was over three octaves—the total range of the Greek scales as given by Alypios (*cf.* p. 38).

Related to the aulos was the *pan-pipe* or *syrinx,* made of several reeds of different length, each yielding one note whose pitch was determined by the length of the reed and the diameter of its bore. By combining with the principle of the syrinx that of the bagpipe (whose origin is traceable to India), the ancients eventually evolved the *organ.* Although the pneumatic type doubtless came first, our earliest detailed accounts—by Hero of Alexandria and Vitruvius—concern a type of the hydraulic organ called the *hydraulis.* (Our first account, lacking in details, is by Philo of Alexandria, 2nd century B.C.) We have documentary information about water organs also from a writer whose name, in the form of "Muristus," reaches us through the Arabs and who may have been a Greek. The hydraulis was invented, according to Athenaios, by Ktesibios of Alexandria (fl. *c.* 246 B.C.).[10] It was preceded by a less highly developed form of hydraulic organ.[11] The hydraulis became more popular with the Roman than with the Greek world. Nero performed upon it, and it was the favorite instrument at gladiatorial shows since it produced a powerful tone larger than could have been obtained from a small pneumatic organ. Clay models of hydraulic organs, on a reduced scale, have been found at Carthage, one almost perfect; and an actual instrument [12] of the 3rd century A.D., parts of which are well preserved, has been found in the Roman ruins at Aquincum, near Budapest.

In the hydraulis an altar-like receptacle formed the base. This contained some water and an inverted metal funnel which stood on short feet. The water, free to flow back and forth between the feet, was partly within and partly without the funnel. A tube connected the funnel with a windchest above it. On each side of the organ was a pump which, alternating with its fellow, pumped air indirectly into the funnel from above. This air caused the water in the funnel to retreat and, pushed through the room between the feet, to rise in the surrounding space within the receptacle. The weight of the displaced water then subjected the air, both in the funnel and in the wind-

[9] For a detailed study of the aulos, see HowA and its supplement, HowM. See also SachsR, 24. —SchlesA is a book almost entirely devoted to the aulos and its alleged effect upon the development of the modal system, unfortunately received too late to be taken into account in the present work.

[10] GulD II, 291f. From p. 291 to p. 317 there is a good deal of miscellaneous information about instruments.

[11] Further on this subject, see FarmO, 14f.

[12] Described in detail in NagyA. (The body of the book is in Hungarian, but a 30-page summary in German is added.) See also HydeD, BédH, and CellO.

chest above, to the necessary heavy pressure. There were often two or three rows of pipes.[13]

Among the idiophones and membranophones used by the Greeks were castanets, cymbals, and tambourines.

The harp appears among their chordophones.[14] But it was rather the instruments of the lyre-type—which was considered especially suitable for the cult of Apollo—that really held a central position in Greek musical life. The two great representatives of this type, the *lyra* and its close relative, the *kithara,* illustrated different principles of construction. The lyra, like the lute and mandolin, had a soundchest (consisting originally of a tortoise shell covered with stretched leather) made of a vaulted back joined directly to a flat soundboard; the normal kithara, like the guitar and violin, had a shallower soundchest made of two resonating tables joined by sides or ribs of equal width. One of the "Homeric" Hymns describes the invention of the lyra by Hermes, chiefly out of a tortoise shell and sheep-gut strings. Another account credits the Thracians with having used the instrument before the Greeks did, but it is the latter at all events who seem to have developed the classical type.[15] They attributed the creation of the kithara to another of their deities, namely Apollo, but the instrument can be traced back to Asiatic origins, as we have seen in Chapter 1.[16] In both lyra and kithara, two arms protruded from the soundbox; in the former these were originally of horn, but they were later of wood, as in the kithara. The arms were arched, either outward or as in the illustration in Plate II, and were connected near the top by a crossbar. Another bar, affixed to the soundbox, served as a bridge. The strings were oftenest of gut and were stretched from the bridge to the cross-bar in a slightly spreading-fan manner. They were held fast to the cross-bar by strips of fatty oxhide, which could be adjusted to effect the tuning of individual strings.[17] The manner in which they were tuned in relation to each other will be mentioned in connection with our discussion of Greek musical theory. They were vibrated sometimes by the fingers, sometimes by a plectrum. The *barbitos* was a variant of the kithara; variants of the harp were the *pectis* and *magadis,* the last-named—with its twenty strings—making it possible to magadize, i. e. to play in octaves.

The old instruments are remarkable in that their basic principles of construction anticipated so many of those applied to modern instruments, though

[13] For fuller information, see MacIP (which contains a valuable bibliography; the extract from Hero's *Pneumatics* dealing with the hydraulis, in Greek and English; the similar extract from the *Concerning Architecture* of Vitruvius, in Latin and English, etc.); FarmO, Chaps. II and III and Appendix II; WarmH; EB XVI, 891; Grove II, 690. The evolution of the organ from the syrinx and bagpipe is traced in SachsD, 72 (pictorial evidence) f, SchlesR.

[14] For an article on the harp in ancient Greece, see HerG.   [15] *Cf.* GuilS.

[16] For a discussion of the influence of the Near East upon Greek music generally, see VettP, 854.

[17] The claim, frequently met with, that all the strings might be tuned up or down simultaneously by merely turning the cross-bar, is untenable. *Cf.* GomT, 37. For further information about the kithara and lyra, see GomG; ReinL; SachsR, 213, 248.

the principles of the bow, valves, and slides, were among the ones that were missing. If some of those that were present were forgotten and had to be rediscovered, others appear to have been transmitted to medieval Europe, though not necessarily directly.

No account of Greek musical life that failed to stress the importance in it of the lyra, kithara, and aulos, would create a fair impression. The first of these was the instrument of the amateur—student or lover—, the second, the instrument of the professional musician. All three instruments were sometimes played in solo music, for which the aulos was preferred to the lyra or kithara, the stringed instruments finding their chief use in conjunction with the voice, that is, in the *lyrodia* and *kitharodia*,[18] in which they normally accompanied the voice at the unison. There are accounts also of aulos-and-kithara duets. A trained *kitharodos* (singer [19] to the kithara) might be not only his own accompanist, but the composer and the poet as well. His repertoire embraced epic recitations, rhapsodies, odes, and lyric songs. The *aulodia,* since it employed a wind instrument, of course demanded two performers. It was used, among other purposes, for the elegies, or songs of mourning. It was generally less highly regarded than the *kitharodia,* however, since the aulos tended to cover up the voice. (Cicero said singers to the aulos were recruited from among deficient singers to the kithara.) [20] But, inasmuch as the aulos was the special instrument of the Dionysian cult, it was only natural that the drama—an outgrowth of that cult—should have preferred it as the medium for instrumental preludes and interludes (not, however, that the kithara was excluded from the drama), especially since the penetrating quality of the instrument recommended it for use in the amphitheatre.

Our chief sources of historical and theoretical information are the writings of the Greek theorists, philosophers, etc. In fact, we learn more about the actual nature of Greek music from these writings than from the surviving specimens of the music itself, which besides being few in number are often also fragmentary. The more important of our literary sources are: [21]

1) The *Section of the Canon* attributed to Euclid [22] (*c.* 300 B.C.), which

---

[18] The terms for the corresponding instrumental solo music were *lyrike* and *kitharistike*. Solo music for the aulos was called *auletike; music* for voice and aulos, *aulodia.*

[19] A soloist on this instrument was a *kitharistes;* on the lyra, a *lyristes;* on the aulos, an *auletes.* A singer to the lyra was a *lyrodos;* to the aulos, an *aulodos.*

[20] But see also *Problems* XIX, Sec. 43, where it is said the aulos "covers up many of the mistakes of the singer" (ForsP) and where the aulos is therefore *preferred.*

[21] Nos. 4, 7, 9–11, 15, and 16 are printed in Greek with translations and commentary in Latin in MeiA. Nos. 1, 3, 8–11, 15, and 16 are printed in Greek with commentary in Latin in JanM. (The Greek texts of such writings as are included in both MeiA and JanM are more accurately given in the latter.) These are the 2 great collections of Greek musical treatises.

[22] English translation in DavyL II, 269–89; French translation in RuelI. Concerning the authenticity of the tract (*pro* and *con*), see *Revue des études grecques,* XIX, 318.

gives our earliest full statement of the acoustical theory of Pythagoras (6th century B. C.);

2) Passages in the *Laws, Republic, Georgias, Philebos,* and *Timaios,* of Plato [23] (427–347 B. C.) setting forth the ethical value of music, its place in education, etc.;

3) Passages in the *Metaphysics, On the Soul,* etc., of Aristotle [24] (384–22 B. C.), discussing consonance, the use of music, the voice, etc.;

4) The incomplete *Harmonics* of Aristoxenos [25] (born c. 354 B. c.), the chief early source of our knowledge of Greek musical theory, by one of its two greatest exponents, who was a disciple of Aristotle's;

5) Fragments of his lost *Rhythmical Elements;* [26]

6) The *Concerning Music* attributed to Plutarch [27] (A. D. 50–120) but of doubtful authenticity, valuable for both historical and theoretical information;

7) The *Concerning Music* of Aristeides Quintilianos [28] (1st–2nd century A. D.) which despite its date is the sole source purporting to offer information concerning certain aspects of the old music of Plato's time;

8) The *Problems* attributed to Aristotle,[29] but apparently a compilation (c. 1st–2nd century A. D.) by several hands of material partly drawn from him, containing *The Voice* (Book XI) and *Music* (Book XIX) which give, in question and answer form, a quantity of assorted information;

9) The *Manual* of Nicomachos [30] (2nd century A. D.), another work on the Pythagorean theory of music;

10 and 11) The two hand-books, each called *Introduction to Harmonics,* of Kleonides [31] and Gaudentios [32] (both c. 2nd century A. D.), the first transmitting to us helpful information concerning Aristoxenian theory, not preserved in the surviving writings of Aristoxenos himself; the second being partly Aristoxenian, partly Pythagorean, etc.;

[23] All published in Greek and English in the Loeb Classical Library. See also note 78.

[24] Assembled in JanM, with detailed citations making possible the location of the passages in translations. The *Works of Aristotle* have been newly published in English (11 volumes) by the Oxford University Press.

[25] Greek text with English translation and commentary in MacrH. Certain views concerning the modes, expressed in the commentary, are subject to controversy. There are translations in French and German also, by Ruelle and Marquard respectively. An extended study of Aristoxenos, his background, and works, is provided in LalA.

[26] Assembled in MorelA. See also WmsA and WmsR (for discussions in English that are somewhat "popular" in nature), WestA, and WestF. The last includes passages on rhythm (by Aristoxenos and other Greek writers) in Greek, with German translations. See also footnote 96.

[27] Greek text with French translation and commentary in ReinP. Greek text with English translation in BromP; another English translation in GoodP I.

[28] Greek text also in JahnA; German translation with commentary in SchäfA. For a general article on Aristeides, see RuelA. See also MounP.

[29] At present, RuelP (which has a Latin preface) seems to be regarded as the standard Greek text. English translation in ForsP. See also GevP for Greek text, French translation and commentary (partly outdated).

[30] French translation and commentary in RuelN.

[31] Free English translation in DavyL II, 309–411, with the once common misattribution to Euclid. French translation and commentary in RuelI.

[32] French translation and commentary in RuelC.

12) The *Harmonics* of Klaudios Ptolemy [33] of Alexandria (2nd century A. D.), "the most scientific and best arranged treatise on the theory of musical scales that we possess in Greek." [34] This is the same Ptolemy as the famous mathematician who taught the astronomic system that was named after him, and against which Copernicus was to react at the turn of the 16th century;

13) Book XIV of *The Deipnosophists* ("Dinner-Table Philosophers") of Athenaios (2nd–3rd century A. D.), which contains material [35] from the lost *Concerning Music* of Herakleides Pontikos, including information regarding the *harmoniai* (to be discussed later in this chapter) and their ethnological associations;

14) The *Commentary* on Ptolemy's *Harmonics* by Porphyry [36] (3rd century A. D.);

15) The *Introduction to Music* of Alypios [37] (*c.* 360 A. D.), from whose tables of the Greek alphabetical notation (accompanied by descriptions of each letter)—our principal guide in deciphering the intervals in the remains of Greek music—we are able to derive forty-odd scale systems of eighteen notes apiece;

16 and 17) The *Introduction to the Art of Music* of Bakcheios the Elder [38] (4th[?] century A. D.), a partly Aristoxenian hand-book in question and answer form, and a similarly named treatise once attributed to Bakcheios but actually by Dionysios, a contemporary; [39]

18) An anonymous treatise of uncertain date, published by Bellermann and known as the treatise of Bellermann's Anonymus,[39] including information concerning the notation of rhythm.[40]

From this body of material we derive our main knowledge about the acoustical doctrine, scale system, keys, rhythm, and notation of Greek music. In connection with the scale system and keys, in particular, the modern investigator is sometimes left with the difficult task of reading meaning into what the writers say. This task has tormented many excellent minds and has led to extended controversy, and is doubtless what a lecturer before the Musical Association of London had in mind when, in 1932, he introduced a paper ostensibly on Greek music with the words:

[33] Greek text with Latin translation and commentary in WallP. Greek text newly edited in DürH; German translation and commentary in DürP.
[34] MounH, 73.   [35] For Greek and English, see GulD VI, 364 ff.
[36] Greek text with Latin translation and commentary in WallP. Greek text newly edited in DürK; commentary in DürP.
[37] French translation of descriptions, with tables and commentary, in RuelC. See also SamoA.
[38] Greek text, German translation, and commentary, in JanE. French translation and commentary in RuelC.
[39] Greek text and Latin commentary in BellA. French translation and commentary in VincN, which treats No. 18 as 2 tracts.
[40] The treatises printed in DupuT, HillerT, and RuelE might be added also. For a completer list, see AbA, 34ff. In our list, a statement that a tract treats a special subject is not necessarily intended to indicate the absence of other subjects; nor is the mention of a particular subject in connection with a particular treatise an indication that it is not handled elsewhere also.

The only professor of Greek I have ever known who was also a musician always refused on principle to give me any help with a stiff passage from a Greek author on music. His reply was always the same: "Put that stuff away. Nobody has ever made head or tail of Greek music, and nobody ever will. That way madness lies."

There is no use in pretending that all we know, or think we know, about Greek musical theory is easy of comprehension. Within a few pages, in fact, the reader will have occasion to decide whether he wants to be more daring than the professor of Greek or to wish that we had even less information concerning Greek scale and key doctrine than has come down to us.

It is clear that Pythagoras knew that, with strings of equal thickness and tension, the length of the string governed the pitch of the tone. This knowledge he may have obtained from priests in Egypt, where he is known to have travelled. At all events, he handed on to his followers in Greece a principle that has been the basis of acoustical theory ever since.

"Euclid" was aware that, if half a string is allowed to vibrate (i. e. if we have the ratio 1:2), the pitch will be an octave above that of the full string; if two-thirds are allowed to vibrate (ratio 2:3), the pitch will be a perfect fifth above; if three-fourths (ratio 3:4), the pitch will be a perfect fourth above, etc. If eight-ninths vibrate (ratio 8:9), the interval will be the whole tone that is the difference between the fourth and fifth. The ratio for the (dissonant) major third was 64:81. With ratios representing these and other relations the Pythagoreans accounted for all the intervals now used in the Occident plus many others. The single string used by the Pythagoreans for experimental purposes was the ancestor of the medieval monochord.

The intervals subsequently discarded included fractions of a tone that have long been unrecognized in European music. The Greeks apparently sounded with precision many intervals that are strange to the West today.[41] It is understandable that the ear of an ancient Greek, called upon to follow basically one-line music (not requiring a division of attention between melody and harmony), was readier to take an interest in refinements of melodic interval for their own sake than is the ear of a modern Occidental.

Aristeides and Ptolemy report that Aristoxenos and his followers reckoned intervals not by ratios but by fractions. They divided a fourth into sixty equal parts and an interval was said to consist of a certain number of sixtieths. Although the fractions are capable of varied interpretations, they were probably meant to be roughly equivalent to the ratios. But the Aristoxenians, approaching the question as practical musicians, attacked the problem of intonation differently from the Pythagoreans, and controversies resulted. The

---

[41] This statement should not be taken as indicating that the main thesis of TorrG represents actual Greek practice. It is unfortunate that this stimulating article, expounding the personal views of a brilliant writer, should have appeared in such a widely consulted work as OH rather than the equally scholarly but less speculative survey, WinnA. (The present chapter also indulges in speculation, of course, but the reader is not left unwarned.)

former placed more reliance upon the ear; the latter, more upon mathematics. Many modern scholars believe that the diatonic tuning used by the Aristoxenians coincided with our diatonic scale in equal temperament. Ptolemy, on the other hand, like Didymos (b. 63 B. C.) before him, is usually credited with having arrived at just intonation (Ptolemy's "diatonic syntonon").[42]

That music was played and sung before scales were grasped as concepts and arranged in standardized forms by theorists, may be regarded as axiomatic. While such concepts and forms may have existed before the Greeks, we do not know that they did. At any rate, it is from the Greeks [43] that they passed into the music of the Middle Ages, and thence into the music of the Renaissance and Modern Age.

Despite this axiom, however, it will be simplest to begin our discussion of Greek musical theory with the two-octave scale that served as the basis of the Greek tonal fabric at the height of its development, and to explain afterwards how this scale was achieved.

The two-octave scale was called the *Greater Perfect System* and, allowing for differences in intonation, its intervallic structure was the same as that of a two-octave scale extending from $\frac{a}{a}$-A.[44] (The Greeks, at least in the earlier centuries in which they discuss series of tones arranged in order of pitch, regard them as descending rather than ascending, and we shall follow their lead, except where we give warning to the contrary.) This *disdiapason* (i. e. two-octave scale) could be transposed, by means of the Greek scheme of keys. The disdiapason from $\frac{a}{a}$ -A presented the Greater Perfect System in what, in the earlier days, was called the Dorian key. (Regarding the sense in which this pitch level is to be understood, see pp. 27f.) The Greater Perfect System was looked upon as consisting of four tetrachords [45] with an added tone. Each tetrachord had the structure T T S (T meaning tone, S meaning semitone, and the reckoning being downward). The two central tetrachords had no tone in common; one merely lay under the other—that is, they were disjunct. The lower of the two central tetrachords was called the *tetrachordon meson* ("tetrachord of the middle"). The point where this tetrachord reached

---

[42] See TorrG, 4, for a discussion of the Aristoxenians and equal temperament. For a contrast between the Pythagoreans and Aristoxenians, see MacrH, 87 ff. For studies of the Aristoxenian intervals, see WinnI and SchlesN; also *Musical Logarithms* by J. Murray Barbour, to appear shortly in *Scripta Mathematica*. For an account of Ptolemy and intonation, see PhilM (where some conclusions are reached that are rather different from the usual ones). For a general survey of Greek acoustic theories, see EmG, 453ff.

[43] Directly according to SchlesG; indirectly, by way of the Arabs, according to FarmH.

[44] Throughout this book, wherever pitches are designated by letters, we shall use the method ascribed to Odo, which became standard in the Middle Ages from the 10th century on, not only since it would seem most appropriate to the main body of the book, but because it may avoid confusion on the part of the reader turning from this book to actual medieval treatises. Odo's system is explained on pp. 136, 149. Capital letters, however, will also be used for an additional purpose: to indicate an individual degree without confining it to any one octave (for which case Odo makes no provision).

[45] Concerning the derivation of the term, "tetrachord," see SachsI, 290.

its upper limit and the upper tetrachord reached its lower limit was called the *diazeuxis* ("point of disjunction"). The upper tetrachord was called **tetrachordon diezeugmenon** ("tetrachord of the disjunction"). Above this tetrachord there was another tetrachord, its lowest tone being the same as the highest tone of the Tetrachord of the Disjunction. These two tetrachords were therefore conjunct. Another tetrachord was linked conjunctly below the Tetrachord of the Middle. The uppermost of the four tetrachords was called the *tetrachordon hyperbolaion* ("extra tetrachord"); the lowest tetrachord was called the *tetrachordon hypaton* ("highest tetrachord"), owing to its physical position on the instrument rather than to the pitch-level of its sounds: the ancient lyre-player tilted his instrument in such a way that, while he was playing, the high-pitched strings were in a low position and the low-pitched strings in a high one.[46] Below the Highest Tetrachord a *proslambanomenos* ("added tone") rounded out the two octaves. The whole may be presented thus (the reasons for brackets around certain letters will become clear in footnote 51):

$\begin{smallmatrix}a\\a\end{smallmatrix}$ g f [e]	d c [b]	[a] G F [E]	D C [B]	[A]
Tetrachordon Hyperbolaion (Extra Tetrachord)	T. Diezeugmenon (T. of the Disjunction)	T. Meson (T. of the Middle)	T. Hypaton (Highest Tetrachord)	Proslambanomenos (Added tone)

(between columns: Tone of disjunction / diazeuxis)

Each note had its own name. From the repetitions in the conjunct tetrachords, it seems clear that the names were applied first to the central octave and were borrowed for use in the outer tetrachords:

Nete Hyperbolaion	$\begin{smallmatrix}a\\a\end{smallmatrix}$	"Lowest" [47] of the Extra Tetrachord	
Paranete "	g	Next to the "Lowest"	" " " "
Trite "	f	Third	" " " "
Nete Diezeugmenon	e	"Lowest"	" " T. of the Disjunction
Paranete "	d	Next to the "Lowest"	" " " " " "
Trite "	c	Third	" " " " " "
Paramese	b	Next to the middle	
Mese	a	Middle	
Lichanos Meson	G	Index Finger [48] of the T. of the Middle	
Parhypate "	F	Next to the "Highest"	" " " " " "

[46] At least, so it is commonly claimed. But it is possible that the nomenclature with respect to "high" and "low" varied from that used later in the Occident owing merely to a difference in mental perception—to a difference in the attribution of high and low qualities to musical ranges.
[47] The reason for this name, as well as that for several of the others, is the same as that for the name of the Highest Tetrachord.   [48] This term is clearly derived from the practice of lyra and kithara playing. See SachsI, 294, but also GomT, 21.

Hypate Meson	E	"Highest"	of the T. of the Middle
Lichanos Hypaton	D	Index Finger	" " "Highest" T.
Parhypate "	C	Next to the "Highest"	" " " "
Hypate "	B	"Highest"	" " " "
Proslambanomenos	A	Added tone	

There was also a *Lesser Perfect System* which made possible modulation in our sense. In the explanation of Kleonides, this is described as modulation from one system to another, and we can see it actually applied in the surviving Delphic Hymns. The Lesser Perfect System consisted of eleven notes: the octave from proslambanomenos to mese of the Greater Perfect System plus the tetrachord Synemmenon ("hooked") which, as its name implies, was added conjunctly to the mese, thus providing T T S above **a** as follows:

Nete Synemmenon	d	"Lowest" of the Hooked T.
Paranete "	c	Next to the "Lowest" of the " "
Trite "	b-flat	Third " " " "

The tetrachords just discussed belong to the diatonic genus, i. e. they consist of stepwise progressions. But there were two other genera also and several different intonations for each (e. g. with "softenings" and other nuances). At least two varieties of the diatonic were common, three of the chromatic, and one of the enharmonic.[49] But it will suffice for present purposes to comment on only one of each type.

Each genus consisted of a distinctive way of filling in a perfect fourth, the tuning of the fourth itself being invariable. This interval could be filled in by no more than two degrees; and the lowest resulting interval had to equal or be less than the middle one and less than the highest. ("Highest" and "lowest" are here used in the modern sense.) While there was no gap in the diatonic tetrachord, there was one in each of the others, and its size depended upon the closeness of the three degrees at the bottom. These could give rise to two semitones (more or less), with a sesquitone at the top, in which event the tetrachord was chromatic, or they could produce two quarter-tones (more or less),[50] with a ditone at the top, in which event it was enharmonic. The two semitones or quarter-tones were said to constitute a *pyknon,* and the three degrees producing them were, in descending order, named the *oxypyknon,* *mesopyknon,* and *barypyknon.* The three genera, among them, offered, in the

---

[49] These six are explained in MounM, 25. A clear and comprehensive table showing 13 varieties is given in WinnA, 332.

[50] These intervals were called *dieses,* and, while *diesis* is usually translated as "quarter-tone," it is done with the reservation that the expression is not necessarily to be understood as implying an exact division.

forms described, twenty-one pitches to the octave as against the twelve in the octave of the West today. The tones bounding the tetrachords were aptly called *hestotes* ("fixed tones"), the intermediate ones *kinoumenoi* ("movable tones"). The following example [51] presents the three types of tetrachord.

EXAMPLE I.

Except for the mere differences in intonation that we have mentioned, no other tetrachord-shapes than these—one for each genus—are known to have been recognized by Greek musical theory (*cf.* footnote 71).

We learn from Aristeides that the Greeks had a solmisation method. This provided four syllables—tah, tā, toh, teh [52]—for the four tones of the basic type of diatonic tetrachord (ascending). By regarding the Greater Perfect System as consisting entirely of such conjunct and disjunct tetrachords (with proslambanomenos added), the first two syllables could be made to correspond to any two pitches a diatonic semitone apart; the last three to any pitches producing a sequence of two whole tones; the last three plus tah to any pitches producing a sequence of three whole tones; or teh and tah to any two pitches a whole tone apart if immediately followed by a semitone. The rough resemblance of this to the solmisation method of Guido d'Arezzo (see Chapter 6) was noted by Riemann, and it is just possible that the influence of the Greek method was passed on to Western Europe.[53]

If Greek notation and the key aspect of the tonal organization to which it was applied are to be understood, not as semi-abstractions, but as things intimately related to music as it may have been actually practiced, it will be necessary to discuss them in connection with further details of lyre-type structure. It was the keys that, little by little, were instrumental in causing the fully developed Greater Perfect System to evolve. The following account, which draws somewhat on speculation, aims to show how this happened. It follows, in the main, the views advanced by Otto Gombosi, which are, in turn, to some extent consistent with those brought forward in 1894 by D. B. Monro. The latter's book (MonroM) provoked much hostile criticism upon its appearance, but new light shed upon the problems of Greek notation and upon the construction of the lyra and kithara has tended to vindicate his main contentions.

The number of strings on the lyra and kithara varied. While the Homeric Hymn to Hermes states that his lyra was provided with seven strings, it is

[51] In most of our musical examples, the hestotes are distinguished by white notes, the kinoumenoi by black; in some of our tables, the hestotes are bracketed. Quarter-tones, in the examples, are indicated by the sign +.

[52] τα, τη, τω, τε.   [53] See RieL, 658; also RuelS.

elsewhere reported to have had four, and indeed there can be no doubt
that four-stringed instruments, also specimens with three strings as well as
with five (*cf.* p. 13), existed.[54] Terpander is credited with having increased
the number of kithara-strings to seven in the 7th century B. C. As has been
shown by Curt Sachs in a brilliant article (SachsI) providing a most important
clue towards the solution of the mystery of Greek music, the kithara and lyra
were pentatonically tuned. (We have referred by inference to the existence of
pentatonicism in Egyptian music—*cf.* p. 7; it probably was present in Hebrew
music also—*cf.* p. 9, footnote 20.) Thus, if we postulate a six-string lyre with
an e-E compass, we would have strings tuned to e d b a G E, the pitches being
here referred to in the sense in which they will be defined presently. We shall
refer to this tuning hereafter as the *low tuning*. There are good grounds for
believing that instruments were actually so tuned.[54a] The missing tones of the
diatonic series—that is, c and F—could be produced by stopping the b and E
strings. Stoppings would be used also to produce chromatic and enharmonic
tones. When only c and F were stopped, the result—brought about by the fact
that tones produced by stopping without a fingerboard are necessarily less
resonant than those produced without stopping [55]—would have afforded, in
addition to five tones of normal resonance, two that Sachs has likened to the
pièn-tones of Chinese pentatonic music.

Greek notation embraced two systems—the so-called vocal and instrumental. All the surviving fragments of instrumental music are written in the
latter; some of the vocal fragments are in the former, some in the latter. The
grave, acute, and circumflex accents—destined to furnish the basis of the
medieval neumes and hence of our own notation—are absent from both. What
the Greeks have left us is an alphabetical notation.

The instrumental system, which was the older, employed Greek letters
and also some that suggest a Phoenician origin. The source of the notation,
in fact, was probably not Greece but the Near East, the letters very likely being
drawn from one or several alphabets, in use in Asia Minor, that linked the
Phoenician and Greek alphabets. The symbols have been rearranged from the
Alypian tables by Sachs, for the purposes of his investigation, in this order:

[54] See especially DeubL.   [54a] Though not necessarily for believing that the strings yielding
e d b a G E followed one another on the instrument in the order in which the pitches follow each
other in the series. *Cf.* SachsHI, 134f.

[55] The case for the stopping of strings on the early lyra and kithara, despite the lack of a fingerboard, has been presented in SachsI, 292ff. That strings are stopped without fingerboards on the
instruments of some exotic peoples today, is shown in SachsR, 213. In Late Antiquity kitharas were
made with fingerboards—fretted, at that. (A drawing of such an instrument may be seen in
SchlesP, 330.) The arms, cross-bar, and resonating table for each side were all of one piece, and the
opening over which the strings passed was cut through the body of the instrument. The fact that
the cross-bar on this type of kithara might have been used as a fingerboard has been pointed out
by both Schlesinger and Sachs. The latter cites, in support of the pentatonic tuning, not only a
passage from Marcus Fabius Quintilianus, dating from *c.* A. D. 88, but also the passage in Pherekrates's play in which Music states that Phrynis "wrings twelve harmonies from my five simple
strings." On the later type of kithara, the frets made stopping easy enough, and the presence of the
fingerboard made it possible for the stopping to take place without material injury to the tone.

EXAMPLE 2. (After SachsA).

With some exceptions, the three rows present signs which, according to the Greeks themselves, are respectively (1) upright, (2) in horizontal position, and (3) upright and reversed. The characters in Row 1 call for the tones sounded by open strings on the pentatonically tuned instrument; the signs in this row for C and F in the various octaves would come into use only with the alternative tuning to be described presently. (The wide range is necessitated by the possibility of erecting the Greater Perfect System on each of fifteen successive semitones. *Cf.* p. 37.) The characters in Rows 2 and 3 call for stopped tones on the strings indicated by the notes under which they appear. A character in Row 2 calls for a stopped tone one *semitone* above the pitch of the open string, when this pitch *occurs* in the diatonic form of a scale in use at the moment. Thus the ∟ in the second row, under the note E, is the sign for the semitone above the open string—F. A character in Row 3, on the other hand, calls for either a stopped tone one *whole* tone above the pitch of the open string, when this pitch occurs in the diatonic form of the scale in use;[56] or a stopped tone one *semitone* above the pitch of the open string, when this pitch *does not occur* in the diatonic form of the scale in use.[57] The same symbols were used for enharmonic raising as for chromatic raising, but with the addition of a stroke after the oxypyknon in a chromatic tetrachord. This seems to support the belief that the chromatic genus was younger than the enharmonic. The notation was clearly intended to show finger-placement, as in lute tablature during and after the 16th century—and in ukelele notation today.

[56] Thus F-sharp, in the succession a, G, F-sharp, E, would be indicated by the character under F in Row 3, which character, in the absence of an F string, would require performance on the **E string**. This succession would extend from lichanos hypaton to proslambanomenos in the key we would designate by a one-sharp signature. (The reader may determine this fact for himself by first recalling, from the table on pp. 22f, that, counting upward, lichanos hypaton is the fourth degree of the Greater Perfect System and proslambanomenos the first, and by then locating these degrees in the last scale in Ex. 4, where the System is transposed to such a key.) The F-sharp in the chromatic series a, F-sharp, F, E, would be indicated by the same character, notwithstanding the intervening F.

[57] Thus, G-sharp in the succession a, G-sharp, E-sharp, E, would be indicated by the character under G in Row 3, rather than Row 2, since G-natural would not occur in the diatonic form of the key in whose chromatic form the succession would appear. That key is the one we would designate by a four-sharp signature, and the succession would extend from parhypate meson to parhypate hypaton. (The reader may determine this fact for himself by first recalling, from the table on pp. 22f, that, counting upward, parhypate meson is the sixth degree of the Greater Perfect System and parhypate hypaton the third; by then locating these degrees in the second scale in Ex. 4, where the System is transposed to such a key; and by finally lowering F-sharp to E-sharp so that the tetrachord lying between the hestotes G-sharp and D-sharp, in the second scale of Ex. 4, would have the same shape as the chromatic tetrachord illustrated in Ex. 1.)

The so-called vocal notation was perhaps adopted to provide singers and aulos-players with symbols that would indicate tones rather than finger-placement, without, however, departing too far from the style of the older, familiar notation. The symbols, employing Greek letters, may be tabulated as in Example 3, in which there is correspondence to the signs similarly placed in Example 2.

EXAMPLE 3.

It was once thought that in such groups of three as ABΓ, ΔEZ, HΘI, KΛM, etc., the third letters represented "natural" tones, the first the greater semitones above, and the second the smaller semitones. It is true that Greek theory distinguished between diatonic and chromatic semitones, i. e. between the *limma,* which remains after two whole tones are deducted from a perfect fourth, and the larger *apotome,* which when added to the limma yields a whole tone. But Sachs has claimed that, while an extra series of semitone signs is in fact present, it is a concession to the habits of the lyre-player, enabling him to play from this so-called vocal notation, without disturbance to his normal methods.[58]

The account of the notation just given, like that of the Greater Perfect System, obviously pertains to the height of a development, as, necessarily, do the tables of Alypios, upon which that account is indirectly based. Those tables, as they reach us, arrange the notation-symbols, not as we do in Examples 2 and 3 (a fact already implied), but in 30 series representing 15 keys each in the diatonic and chromatic genera plus 12 series (3 of them incomplete) in the enharmonic genus. (It has been assumed that the tables survive in a fragmentary state, because the archetype MS was fragmentary. While this is quite likely so, the MS may have been defective to a smaller extent than is generally supposed, inasmuch as it is possible that only two of the entirely missing scales were ever in it, since, as we shall see, it appears that the third missing scale could never have been played on the lyre.) Each series is set forth in both instrumental and vocal notation and spans the full two octaves of the Greater Perfect System (*cf.* the 7 series in Example 4).

The pitch-equivalents, given above for the Greek notation symbols, follow a convention of modern scholars, to which we shall continue to adhere in this chapter. This translates all the signs a minor third higher than what is thought to have been the pitches they actually called for. The convention has

[58] For a fuller discussion of the vocal notation (and earlier interpretations of it), see SachsG.

the virtue that it makes it possible to present without sharps and flats the key (differently named at different times, as we shall see) that clearly occupied in Greek musical thinking the same position as the key of C occupies in ours.

The keys were known as *tonoi* (*tonos* = "tightening"). The early lyras and kitharas would have been quite incapable of spanning a disdiapason. The hypothetical six-string lyre postulated above would have had the compass of an octave, which was, for that matter, the compass of the actual three- to five-string instruments also.[59] The range e–E (in the special sense just explained; really c-sharp–C-sharp) happens, roughly, to be the most comfortable one for male voices (for which Greek vocal music was primarily planned), being easily available alike to tenors, baritones, and basses. It might, therefore, be called the "central octave" (though we shall presently propose "characteristic octave" as a better name for it). By limiting, for immediate purposes, both a hypothetical singer and instrumentalist within an e–E compass, we may be able to reconstruct the manner in which the evolution of the system of tonoi began.

It is clear that, before men develop an organized system of keys, they will not have an analytical awareness of transposition as such. They will sing their melodies where they find it comfortable to do so—within the octave e–E, let us say—, starting on a tone that will bring the entire melody within that range. Let us assume a descending melodic fragment T S T T S. This, obviously, will not be available within the octave e–E without accidentals. It could be obtained, however, to take one example, by starting on c and flattening the b. Adjustments of this sort might be made by a singer without a full awareness of what he was doing, but they were bound to force themselves upon the attention of a string-player accompanying at the unison, who would be compelled to find the necessary stoppings.

It is possible to obtain seven different diatonic arrangements of tones and semitones within an octave, thus (the brackets measuring off tetrachords or fractions thereof or the diazeuxis):

$$
\begin{array}{l}
\lceil T \rceil T\ T\ S \lceil T\ T\ S \rceil \\
S \lceil T \rceil T\ T\ S \lceil T\ T \\
T\ S \lceil T \rceil T\ T\ S \lceil T \\
\lceil T\ T\ S \lceil T \rceil T\ T\ S \rceil \\
S \lceil T\ T\ S \lceil T \rceil T\ T \\
T\ S \lceil T\ T\ S \lceil T \rceil T \\
\lceil T\ T\ S \lceil T\ T\ S \lceil T \rceil
\end{array}
$$

The fourth of these arrangements, consisting of two disjunct T T S tetrachords, produced what eventually became known as the *Dorian octave*—the nucleus to which the two conjunct tetrachords and the proslambanomenos

[59] For the way in which they were tuned, see GomT, 40ff.

were added to form the Greater Perfect System. The Dorian octave—whose
intervallic series is just the reverse of that of the major scale [60]—was, indeed,
the octave *par excellence* of Greek music. Of the remaining six octaves, as the
above table shows, four have only one T T S tetrachord intact, tetrachord-
fractions being added to it, and the other two, while they each have two such
complete tetrachords, link them conjunctly. These seven species of octave
are recognized in the writings of many of the theorists from Aristoxenos on,
though not in every instance within the e–E octave sooner than within another
octave to be discussed presently. Some modern writers regard the species as
modes, in the full ecclesiastical sense of the term in the West, but there is
nothing in Greek theoretical writing to indicate that each of them possessed a
modality of its own, and they do not receive a set of names before Late Antiquity, although the keys do receive one. It will be best for the moment to
consider only the Dorian octave as having had a modal life. (We shall return
to the question of modality later.) The other octave-species would then have
existed for the purpose of bringing Dorian melodies within an octave range
convenient for the singer, and since this range would be filled with a different
collocation of tones and semitones for each of the seven tonoi, it is best to call it
the *characteristic octave* (spanning e–E or the octave range referred to as remaining for discussion).

Let us illustrate the underlying principle by first drawing, for the sake of
simplicity, upon our familiar key-signatures. The above seven series of
tones and semitones would be obtainable between e and E with the signatures of one flat, four sharps, two sharps, no sharps or flats, five sharps,
three sharps, and one sharp, respectively. Now let us draw also upon our
familiar major mode. The existence of seven different species within the
octave e–E would not mean that a major melody could not be obtained out
of any of the species. Assuming that we had seven major melodies, each
spanning an entire octave, and each octave beginning on a different step of
the major scale, but each of the resulting types of octave being fixed within
the compass e–E, the melody having the leading tone of the major series as
its lowest limit would have one flat in the signature, that having the tonic
as its lowest limit would have four sharps in the signature, that having the
supertonic as its lowest limit would have two sharps in the signature, etc. (The
fact that only the four-sharp signature would produce a tonic at the bottom
of the octave and a dominant on the fifth degree of the octave, would not
prevent each of the melodies from having its normal tonic and dominant
in major; but the tonic and dominant would always occur on different degrees of the available octave—though not of the major scale.)

In the same way, a Greek musician, spanning the e–E compass, would,
if he had a Dorian melody with hypate meson as the lowest limit, choose the

[60] A fact that has been made the subject of a stimulating but speculative discussion in EmH.

key that we would say had no sharps or flats; if he had a Dorian melody
with parhypate meson as its lowest limit, he would choose the key we would
say had five sharps, etc. To a Greek the tonos corresponding to a key without sharps or flats would, in low tuning, have been the one requiring no
stoppings on a lyre except for the missing c and F. The tonos of which
this was true was, as we have stated, called the Dorian in the earlier days and,
obviously, it is the tonos that produced the Dorian series within the characteristic octave. The names of the tonoi producing the six other species may
be found in Example 4, in which the characteristic octave is marked off by a
square bracket above each scale. If for present purposes we place these
seven octaves within transpositions of the Greater Perfect System (even
though our hypothetical instrument could not span a disdiapason), we
obtain the following, it being possible, in a way, to equate the tonoi to our
more familiar keys (but as bearers of the Greater Perfect System—or portions thereof, either before or after its complete evolution—, not as bearers
of the major mode, or even of the minor, in view of its harmonic implications), the Mixolydian corresponding to D, the Lydian to C-sharp, the
Phrygian to B, the Dorian to A, the Hypolydian to G-sharp, the Hypophrygian to F-sharp, and the Hypodorian to E, and the Dorian octave occupying, in each key, a range beginning a fifth above the key-note (a useful point
to remember):

EXAMPLE 4.

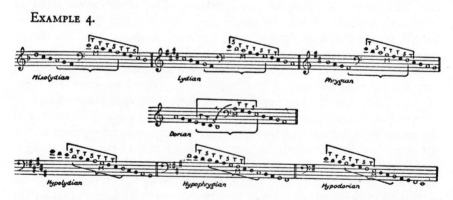

It is possible to think of the content of each characteristic octave not only
(1) as an individual species, but also (2) always as a Dorian octave, redistributed in six instances, with part of the scale above the hypate and part
below it (as we might, if we read modern tendencies into the tones, think
of the second species as a major scale intact and the other six as major scales
with part of the scale above the tonic and part below). In fact, Ptolemy
indicates that he held the second view. In terms of practice rather than theory,
this would mean that, if a player on a lyre limited to an octave was duplicat-

ing a singer's melody at the unison and the singer at times exceeded the compass of the instrument, the player, if he wished to remain as faithful as he could to the vocal line, would have to shift up or down and duplicate at the octave instead. (In Example 4, by comparing what lies within each brace with what lies within the corresponding square bracket, one may see readily how the Dorian octave is redistributed in each non-Dorian species.) [61]

The term *hypo-* means "below," and it will be seen that the Hypo- tonoi are actually lower keys. The choice of nomenclature for these three tonoi shows that, when their names were selected, the Dorian, Phrygian, and Lydian keys were already recognized, and that, with the admission of the Hypo- keys, the development of an organized key system must have been well under way. In fact, the Hypodorian, in the state in which it is presented in Example 4, did not come in until quite late—later than the introduction of the alternative characteristic octave concerning which we have hinted; moreover, it is probably not the only Hypo- tonos of Example 4 to have made its first appearance after that event and to have had its particular collocation of tones and semitones produced within the alternative octave before that collocation was produced between e and E. (In other words, it is not to be thought that the neat system presented in Example 4 was adopted intact, as it appears there in low tuning for purposes of facilitating our explanation, before the other tuning came into existence.)

A complete series, in the chromatic genus, corresponding to the diatonic series given in the table on p. 28, would be as follows. (The reader can conveniently form any of these scales in the chromatic genus by referring to the bracketed octaves in Example 4 and lowering the oxypyknon in each tetrachord by a semitone. The lowest degree in the resulting Phrygian and Hypophrygian series would be unobtainable on the kind of lyre thus far discussed, but obtainable on an instrument with an adequate number of strings, such as we shall describe later.)

⌐T ˈT̂Ŝ S S ˈT̂Ŝ S Sˈ	(produced by the Mixolydian tonos)
Sˈ T ˈT̂Ŝ S S ˈT̂Ŝ S	(" " " Lydian ")
S SˈT ˈT̂Ŝ S S ˈT̂Ŝ	(" " " Phrygian ")
⌐T̂Ŝ S SˈT ˈT̂Ŝ S Sˈ	(" " " Dorian ")
SˈT̂Ŝ S S ˈT ˈT̂Ŝ S	(" " " Hypolydian ")
S SˈT̂Ŝ S S ˈT ˈT̂Ŝ	(" " " Hypophrygian ")
⌐T̂Ŝ S SˈT̂Ŝ S S ˈTˈ	(" " " Hypodorian ")

[61] It will be observed that, if we take the mesai of the seven scales in Example 4 (represented in each disdiapason by the letter M) or, for that matter, all the appearances of any individual degree in the seven scales and regard them as a continuous ascending tonal series, we get a T T S T T S series; in other words, a series that corresponds to a G scale (with the octave not quite rounded out). This point has no immediate significance, but it is useful to call attention to it while we have the seven scales handy, since we shall have to refer to it in Chapter 6.—As will become clear on p. 34, the low tuning took on a slightly modified form to accommodate the first scale in Example 4.

A similar series for the enharmonic genus would be as follows. (The reader can conveniently form these enharmonic scales by again referring to the bracketed octaves in Example 4 and by lowering the oxypyknon in each tetrachord by a whole tone and the mesopyknon by a quarter-tone. Again, not all the series tabulated would be obtainable on the kind of lyre thus far discussed. The subject will receive fuller treatment below.)

T T̄T̄ Q Q T̄T̄ Q Q	(produced by the Mixolydian tonos)
Q T T̄T̄ Q Q T̄T̄ Q	(" " " Lydian ")
Q Q T T̄T̄ Q Q T̄T̄	(" " " Phrygian ")
T̄T̄ Q Q T T̄T̄ Q Q	(" " " Dorian ")
Q T̄T̄ Q Q T T̄T̄ Q	(" " " Hypolydian ")
Q Q T̄T̄ Q Q T T̄T̄	(" " " Hypophrygian ")
T̄T̄ Q Q T̄T̄ Q Q T	(" " " Hypodorian ")

The notation-signs for the chromatic genus and such as reach us for the enharmonic genus show why the alternative tuning, involving the alternative octave (to both of which we have several times referred), was adopted. The signs do this by revealing how the pyknon was performed.

In the Dorian tonos (called Hypolydian by Alypios) the three degrees producing the pyknon were all executed on the same string—open for the barypyknon and stopped at different points for the other two degrees—, a fact that probably explains the name *pyknon,* which means "pressing," "crowding." (The Dorian enharmonic seems to have been an outgrowth of the so-called Spondeion scale, remarkable for having contained an interval of three-quarters of a tone.) [62]

We have mentioned that, in such Alypian tables as are preserved for the enharmonic genus, the symbols agree with those for the chromatic genus (except for a stroke after the oxypyknon in the latter). We may therefore assume that the three incomplete tables and the three missing ones—or, at least, such of them as were given—also corresponded with their chromatic equivalents. (In fact, these six tables have been "restored" by musical scholarship, which has taken for granted both correspondence and the former presence of all the three now absent.) Among the missing tables is that for the Phrygian (called Iastic [= Ionian] in the diatonic and chromatic tables); among the incomplete tables is that for the Lydian (renamed Aeolian). The symbols for the chromatic Phrygian and Lydian, unlike those for the chromatic Dorian, call for an open string on the mesopyknon. The probable reason for this is not hard to find. The chromatically altered Dorian octave in the Phrygian key [63] would be

[62] *Cf.* WinnS.

[63] As we have pointed out, the non-Dorian octaves are merely Dorian octaves redistributed, and it may be simpler for present purposes—especially for the reader who pursues the subject further in GomT, where such a method is followed—to regard the Dorian octave as intact rather than as redistributed; the principles here explained would be equally true in either case.

and the d and G—the mesopykna—would be on open strings. The same octave in the Lydian key would be

and again the mesopykna—e and a—would be on open strings. It is obvious, however, that, in the enharmonic genus, the c-sharp[+] and d-sharp[+] that would respectively replace the Phrygian d and Lydian e of the chromatic genus, and the F-sharp[+] and G-sharp[+] that would replace the corresponding G and a, would not be obtainable by stopping on the d and e or G and a strings, since they would be lower than the pitches of the open strings. However, since the symbols for the chromatic Lydian call for stopping throughout anyway, except for the two mesopykna, it is possible that the enharmonic genus could have been produced by sounding e and a (instead of d-sharp[+] and G-sharp[+]) on open strings and by raising everything else a quarter-tone above the theoretically normal level. But the symbols for the Phrygian call for one open string in addition to the two for the mesopykna, so that there was one string that could not be subjected to stopping in any attempt to raise the key a quarter-tone above the theoretically normal level; the enharmonic Phrygian, therefore, could not be produced in the low tuning.

Even if we grant that a player might just possibly have been able to obtain the enharmonic Lydian on his lyre in the manner described, its execution would obviously have been less convenient than if the three tones of the pyknon were all obtainable from a single string, i. e., than if the barypyknon was played on an open string. But, if a c-string were added—not to the exclusion of the b-string, but as an alternative for it—it would be possible to play the Lydian easily in all three genera, without sacrificing such convenience as the presence of the b-string offered in the playing of certain other tonoi. The Lydian, however, would have to be pitched a semitone higher and would thus be the same tonos as the Mixolydian. The enharmonic genus, then, would take the form:

Since the notation-symbols for this series call for open strings on the barypykna rather than on the mesopykna, it would have been quite easy to perform this enharmonic scale. This series, to be sure, would not require the c-string that we have just mentioned, but in the diatonic genus—producing the same series as that within the brace in the first scale of Example 4—the c (as the notation indicates) would require an open string. We have mentioned that, of the seven keys thus far dealt with, the Dorian, Phrygian, and Lydian tonoi were the oldest and the three Hypo- tonoi the youngest, but we have not given the relative age of the Mixolydian. It is not impossible that this key came in originally as a higher form of the Lydian [64] (it is, indeed, called Lydian by Alypios).

The introduction of an alternative c-string constitutes a transition towards the adoption, alongside the old low tuning, of the alternative high tuning. The strings that are used for the latter are tuned to f, d, c, a, G, F, and the f–F octave is the alternative octave to which we have several times referred in passing. By retaining the b-string in addition to the new c-string, and tuning the outer strings optionally to e–E or f–F, it would be possible to play in either the low or high tuning on the seven-string lyra or kithara. It is, in fact, to its capacity for being played in either tuning that Gombosi has attributed both the introduction of the seven-string kithara by Terpander and its subsequent popularity.[65]

It would seem that the raising of the outer strings to f and F was prompted by the impossibility of obtaining the Phrygian enharmonic in the low tuning. Raised a semitone, the Phrygian enharmonic series would become g, e-flat, ḋ, d, c, a-flat, Ġ, G. Here again, open strings would be called for on the barypykna, and performance would be simple. The notation shows that the c would be played on an open string. It shows also that, in the diatonic genus, the series g, f, e-flat, d, c, b-flat, A-flat, G, would call for an open f-string. If we redistribute this Dorian series within the characteristic octave (which will now, of course, lie between f and F rather than between e and E), we obtain f, e-flat, d, c, b-flat, A-flat, G, F—and, as the notation symbols indicate, open f- and F-strings.[66]

---

[64] *Cf.* GomT, 95; also GomT, 30.

[65] For a special article on Terpander and the 7-stringed instrument, see DeubT.

[66] The reader, recalling that we have mentioned in passing that the Greeks finally developed a system of 15 keys (of which we shall say more within the next few pages), may wonder how the enharmonic genus was achieved in the tonoi other than the 5 just discussed—i. e., the low Dorian, Phrygian, and Lydian, and the high Lydian (= low Mixolydian) and Phrygian. In dealing with these 5, we have found three classes: (1) that in which the barypykna are on open strings (the low Dorian, high Lydian [= low Mixolydian], and high Phrygian); (2) that in which the mesopykna are on open strings and in which the enharmonic species could therefore be performed with all the pitches a quarter-tone higher than the theoretically normal level (the low Lydian); and (3) that in which the mesopykna would not be the only degrees played on open strings and in which the enharmonic would therefore not be obtainable (low Phrygian). To these another class, not yet represented, may be added; i. e. (4) that in which the enharmonic would be obtainable in only one tetrachord, in which tetrachord the barypyknon would be on an open string. Of the 10 tonoi not touched upon in the above discussion of the enharmonic genus, 3 had fingerings that duplicated the fingerings of 3 others, so that only 7 need be considered. Of

Regardless of whether or not the Mixolydian came in as a higher form of the Lydian, it seems (especially since it retained the low tuning for the outer strings, notwithstanding the presence of the c-string) to have been regarded, for a time, as something independent alongside the low Dorian, Phrygian, and Lydian. In fact, although, like the high Lydian, it was a D key and, still like it, had its Dorian octave based on a, its characteristic octave lay between e and E (since that is the range within which the characteristic T T T S T T S series would be obtained with a one-flat signature) while the characteristic octave of the high Lydian lay between f and F (since that is the range within which the characteristic S T T T S T T series would be obtained with that signature). Nevertheless, the similarity of key seems to have been more than the low Mixolydian could combat, and it appears to have merged with the high Lydian. But, c. 475 B.C., the high Mixolydian was discovered by the Athenian Lamprokles, as we are told by pseudo-Plutarch, who points out that Lamprokles realized that a true Mixolydian tonos required the diazeuxis at the top of the characteristic octave. This means that, in high tuning, we would have to have the characteristic octave f, e-flat, d-flat, c-flat, b-flat, a-flat, G-flat, F. And this, in turn, means that, as the notation shows, both the b- and c-strings would have to be used (the b-string being played open to provide an equivalent for c-flat and the c-string being stopped for d-flat). The fact that the employment of both originally alternative strings in a single genus was contrary to custom, would explain the difficulty experienced in finding the high Mixolydian on the lyre and the magnitude of Lamprokles's achievement.[67] In other words, we here arrive at a tonos in which we have not only the high tuning present but each of the alternative strings in use, so that both innovations are exploited together.

We have noted in discussing Example 4 that the tonos bringing the T T S T T S T series within the e–E octave, with the mese at the bottom—i. e. the low Hypodorian—, did not come in until quite late. In fact, each of the seven octave-species seems to have become available within the f–F octave before the low Hypodorian was achieved. The names Dorian, Phrygian, Lydian, and Mixolydian became transferred to the high tuning and the names Hypophrygian, Hypolydian, and Hypodorian became associated with it also—that is, some became transferred to it from the low tuning, while some made their first appearance in it. As a result, the key named Dorian was henceforth not an

---

these 7, 4 belong to class 1; 2 to class 2; and 1 to class 4. To sum up, there were in all (if we disregard the 3 duplications) 7 tonoi belonging to class 1, 3 to class 2, and 1 each to classes 3 and 4. Of the total of 12, in view of the difficulties involved in performing the tonoi belonging to class 2, the enharmonic may possibly have been really practicable in only classes 1 and 4 (in which event it was practicable, among the three early tonoi, only in the Dorian). Of the three enharmonic tonoi added in "restoring" the Alypian tables, one belongs to each of classes 2-4. (The one belonging to class 4, though missing in Alypios, survives in a marginal note in Munich MS 104.) See further GomT, 24ff.

[67] Further on this subject, see GomT, 47.

A key but a B-flat key, and all the other names likewise came to indicate tonoi a half-step higher than those to which we have applied them in Example 4. (It will be easier in most of this portion of the discussion not to confine the keys to either characteristic octave but again to regard them as transpositions of the Greater Perfect System intact.)

When the nomenclature became organized in this sense, obviously, the names became attached to pitch-levels that in two instances were not peculiar to the high tuning. Thus if the low Hypolydian was, as we have said, a G-sharp key and the Dorian an A key, the raising of the Hypolydian would merely have brought it to the pitch-level of the old Dorian. Similarly, if the old Lydian was a C-sharp key and the Mixolydian a D key, the raising of the Lydian would merely have brought it to the pitch-level of the old Mixolydian. We have already had occasion to point out this latter fact and to note that the low Mixolydian became merged in the high Lydian. Similarly the old Dorian became merged in the high Hypolydian. The four remaining tonoi possible in low tuning were not ignored, but eventually received other names than those by which we have hitherto known them. These tonoi, of course, produced exactly the same octave-series as did four of the high tonoi, but between e and E rather than between f and F. All this gave a group of eleven tonoi with key-notes placed on every semitone from F up to e-flat. Aristoxenos continued the series beyond this point by adding tonoi on e and f. The first of these was a low-tuning key and thus brought the T T S T T S T series within the e–E octave; but even so the low Hypodorian did not result, since the mese was at the top rather than at the bottom of the octave. That we are here not dealing altogether with a "distinction without a difference" will become amply clear when, a few pages below, we encounter fuller information concerning the character of the mese. Similar conditions invested the tonos on f with a measure of distinctiveness also, for, while it duplicated the high Hypodorian so far as the interval series between f and F was concerned, the mese was again at the upper rather than at the lower end of the octave. With the addition of these two keys, Aristoxenos rounded out a system of thirteen tonoi, one of them being pitched on every semitone of an octave extending from F up to f.[68]

Before the low Dorian became completely merged in the high Hypolydian, a new name was sought for it. At one time it was called Aeolian, at another Locrian, at another Hypodorian, since it lay "below" the high Dorian. The Hypophrygian and Hypolydian, however, each lay a fourth below the tonos that would be similarly named if the prefix were omitted, and, with the complete merging of the old Dorian into its high equivalent, the

---

[68] The names assigned to the 13 tonoi by the Aristoxenians may be conveniently found in GomT, 6. Which names denote low-tuning keys, and which high, may be determined by comparison with the table in GomT, 26f.

name Hypodorian became attached, as we have seen, to the tonos a fourth below the high Dorian, i. e. to an F key.[69] Nomenclature was so subject to variation that Aristoxenos wrote, concerning the account of the tonoi given by his predecessors, that it "closely resembles the observance of the days according to which, for example, the tenth day of the month at Corinth is the fifth at Athens, and the eighth somewhere else."

The thirteen tonoi receive two upper additions at the hands of Aristeides and Alypios. The latter, in his tables, gives his complete series of fifteen transpositions of the Greater Perfect System (multiplied, as we have seen, to provide for the three genera) in ascending order, since in Late Antiquity, to which he belongs, the earlier tendency to count tone-series downward was replaced by a tendency, similar to our own today, to count them upward. In the new nomenclature of the theorists, all forms of the term "Mixolydian" disappear, while the root-names Ionian and Aeolian are added to Dorian, Phrygian, and Lydian. With the key a fourth below the high Dorian called Hypodorian (F), the key a fourth above (E-flat) is fittingly called Hyperdorian, *hyper* meaning "above"; and each of the five root-names appears without a prefix, with the prefix hypo-, and with the prefix hyper-, in the following trim series:

	MESE		MESE		MESE
Hypodorian	F	Dorian	b-flat	Hyperdorian	e-flat
" ionian	F-sharp	Ionian	b	" ionian	e
" phrygian	G	Phrygian	c	" phrygian	f
" aeolian	G-sharp	Aeolian	c-sharp	" aeolian	f-sharp
" lydian	a	Lydian	d	" lydian	g

C. 400 B. C. the standard number of strings on the kithara had been increased from seven to eleven which, in pentatonic tuning, would be sufficient to span two octaves, thus:

^a_a, g, f or e, d, c or b, a, G, F or E, D, C or B, A

Representations of twelve-string kitharas are found also, and with these it would have been possible to have strings for both degrees in one of the pairs of alternatives. The degrees chosen would doubtless be c and b. The eleven or twelve strings of the large instrument, like the six or seven of the smaller one, were tuned only to the high or low tuning; modifications in pitch were still effected solely by stopping which, however, naturally became applicable to a greater number of strings. The large instrument could give the Greater Perfect System intact or redistributed just as the smaller instrument could yield the Dorian octave both ways, the intact form being produced in either case by the high Hypolydian and redistribution by the remaining tonoi, with

[69] *Cf.* GomT. 86f, 96.

the help of other stopping than the high Hypolydian called for. The providing of symbols for three octaves, in the Alypian tables, was therefore perhaps prompted by the needs of instruments other than those of the lyre-type, e. g. the auloi.

Whether, on the large instrument, the tonos used was the "natural" high Hypolydian or some tonos requiring different stopping, the characteristic octave, if it lay between e and E rather than between f and F, would (as may be seen by consulting the above two-octave series) always have three degrees obtainable above this kernel and four below, the same number as supplement the Dorian octave in the Greater Perfect System. (This point will have relevance in our following discussion of Ptolemy's theory of the tonoi.) The strings making these additional degrees available would increase an accompanist's ability to duplicate what a vocalist sang without suddenly transferring to a higher or lower range.

Ptolemy, instead of augmenting the thirteen Aristoxenian tonoi like Alypios and Aristeides, reduced them to seven. These are all in low tuning and it is thus that the low Hypodorian appears for the first time. The enharmonic species was no longer in use in his day—it was moribund even in the time of Aristoxenos—and the special reason for having a high tuning had therefore disappeared. (Ptolemy does describe enharmonic and chromatic genera, but his account makes it clear that in actual practice the music of his time did not include the enharmonic.) With the exclusion of the high tuning, the names Dorian, Phrygian, Lydian, and Mixolydian were restored to their old meanings, representing tonoi a semitone lower than they did in the high tuning, and the names Hypophrygian and Hypolydian became applicable solely to such tonoi also. Ptolemy points out that only seven tonoi are needed to bring the seven octave-species within uniform compass (i. e. within the characteristic octave); that even an eighth tonos would merely produce the same series of intervals as the first. This is tantamount, as we see it, to saying that, even if the mese of the low Hypodorian was on E and the mese of the twelfth tonos of Aristoxenos on e, the tuning of the lyre would be modified by stopping in exactly the same way for both tonoi; that, in fact, so far as adjustments of an instrument are concerned, there are, in a single genus and kind of tuning—low or high—, only seven (one by the tuning of the strings and six by modifications of that tuning through stopping); and that the question of where a mese is to be placed is one of actual performance and not of instrument-adjustment. In short, he makes it clear that, from his point of view, an eighth tonos is quite unnecessary. Because of his satisfaction with only seven tonoi, producing all the accepted interval-groupings, it is sometimes thought by modern writers that the interest of the Greeks centered for a long while on the key system for its own sake but that it began to veer, about Ptolemy's time, towards distinctions in interval groupings—that is, from the tonoi to the octave-species. It should be remembered, however, that, as long as the presence of the enharmonic genus made the high tuning necessary, there really was some point in a multiplicity of tonoi and that, even after the enharmonic species died out, the old tradition was bound to persist for a while. Beyond twelve tonoi, to be sure, there would be real duplication in instrument-adjustment; the fifteen-tonos system of Aristeides and Alypios seems clearly to have existed for a theoretical purpose, i. e. to produce a ternary grouping (*cf.* the above table). It was Ptolemy's merit that he hewed away the dead wood preserved only by tradition and preferred practical to theoretical requirements.

Ptolemy does not present his seven tonoi in the form of the Greater Perfect System intact in seven different keys; in his arrangement, each group marked by a square bracket in Example 4 serves as a central octave, with three notes added above and four below (*cf.* the last paragraph but one). This arrangement is shown in Example 5, where the square brackets are preserved.

Two nomenclatures—*kata dynamin* ("according to function") and *kata thesin* ("according to position")—are employed by Ptolemy. Example 5 performs service additional to that just mentioned by illustrating the distinction between the two.

Dynamic nomenclature merely names the fifteen degrees of the Greater Perfect System according to their function, i. e. as we have hitherto named them. In the fourth series of our example the fifteen degrees appear in their normal order, but in the other six series they appear redistributed. The reader is helped to find the dynamic nomenclature in each series by the braces, indicating the Dorian octave, and the letters P, M, and N, indicating degrees 1 (proslambanomenos), 8 (mese), and 15 (nete hyperbolaion), respectively. Redistribution of the System in the six tonoi other than the Dorian, of course, does not affect the dynamic names; thus if the System is so redistributed that its upper degrees appear at the bottom of the disdiapason, they still retain their normal dynamic names (so that it is possible for both dynamic proslambanomenos and dynamic nete hyperbolaion to fall on the same pitch).

Thetic nomenclature, on the other hand, *refers to the position of a degree within the fifteen-degree series obtainable on an eleven- or twelve-string kithara in any one tonos and genus.* Degree number 1 would always be thetic proslambanomenos whether it coincided with dynamic proslambanomenos, as in the Dorian tonos, or with some other dynamic degree, as in each of the other tonoi; thetic mese would always be the eighth degree in the series, regardless of what its dynamic significance might be, etc. In Example 5 the thetic nomenclature is given at the top. It will be noted that, as might be expected, this nomenclature matches the dynamic only in the Dorian tonos. Thetic nomenclature comes close to dealing with the position of a degree on the instrument, since, as is shown by reading vertically any of the fifteen columns of notes in Example 5, all the notes in any one column are obtainable on the same string, except for those in columns 2 and 9, since B-flat and b-flat would not be obtainable on the B- and b-strings.

EXAMPLE 5.

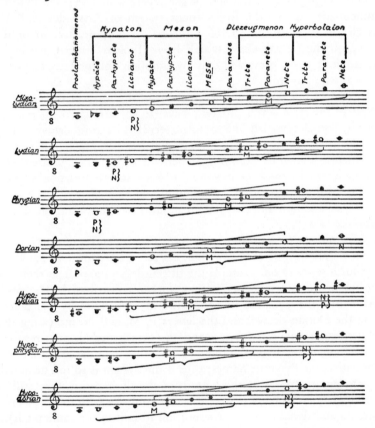

Ptolemy applies the names Dorian, Phrygian, etc., not to the octave-species but to the tonoi. Since, however, he presents the tonoi not, like the Aristoxenians, as transpositions of the Greater Perfect System intact, but as characteristic octaves with additions above and below, his tonoi practically amount to extended octave-species.[70]

[70] Before leaving the subject of Ptolemy it should be added that the account of his system in Grove III, 476, contains several large mistakes. We see no point in presenting the mesai *kata thesin* as parts of "seven modes varying in pitch, but each formed of a section of the Perfect System or white notes of the pianoforte," the whole distinction between dynamic and thetic nomenclature having been occasioned by multiplicity of key. But if the distinguished author wished to do so, he should, with his sequence of tonos names, have shown the mesai in an order exactly the reverse of that in which they appear. His mistake leads him, at the bottom of the page, to give his signatures and tonos-names in conflicting order also.

Any reader observing that the Lydian and Hypolydian mesai *kata dynamin* in Ex. 5 are a semi-

In fact, Bakcheios and Gaudentios do call the octave-species by the names of the tonoi that place them within the characteristic octave. Most modern writers use the names Dorian, Phrygian, etc., for the species also, but as though the names were applied to the species first and to the tonoi afterwards rather than the reverse—that is, as though each of the seven tonoi of Examples 4 and 5 received its name after that of the species it brought within the characteristic octave—an untenable view.[71] It is clear that if the seven octave-species are projected onto an untransposed Greater Perfect System, the names applied to a descending series of tonoi will become applicable to an ascending series of octave-species, since, as Example 4 shows, the lower an octave-species would appear when projected onto the System (cf. Example 6) the higher is the tonos needed to place it within the characteristic octave. The theorists, apparently more for the purpose of analyzing structure than with the aim of describing actual practice, projected the octave-species onto the System in much this way:

EXAMPLE 6.

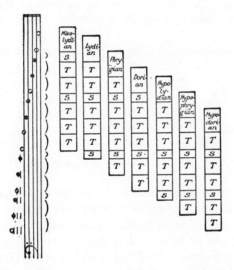

tone higher than those given by Wallis (WallP, 137 of the 1682 edition; 73 of the 1699 edition) should be warned that Wallis is in error, as was pointed out as long ago as 1760 in StilesE, a remarkable paper—considerably more clear-sighted than many a more modern study of Greek theory —which deserves more attention than it has received and reference to which might have eased the tasks of many later writers. Since the nature of Wallis's mistake is very clearly explained by Stiles, there is no need to discuss it here.

Ptolemy's musical insight is illustrated by his having perceived that a modulation from the Greater Perfect System to the Lesser Perfect System, previously regarded as a modulation of system, in fact produced a transitory *modulation of key at the fourth.*

The 15-string instrument used by him for his explanations is to be regarded as a theoretical or experimental one, designed to give each pitch in his disdiapasons its own string to simplify the discussion.

[71] Riemann's neat explanation of octave-scale formation and its relation to the Greater Perfect

In so doing, they implied analyses in terms of tetrachords and fractions thereof, such as we have given earlier in this chapter. These analyses, however, do not represent the only kind that the theorists offered with respect to the species.

Aristoxenos explained that the different species of octave might be divided into different species of fourth and fifth, one of each being linked to one of the other conjunctly. Gaudentios, however, is the theorist who gives us a complete systematization of the octaves as consisting of such components. Belonging to Late Antiquity, he regards tone series in an ascending order, and in discussing these components we shall therefore do likewise. The species of fourth, or *diatessaron,* were (1) S T T (= the familiar tetrachord on which the Greater Perfect System was based), (2) T T S, or (3) T S T The species of fifth, or *diapente,* were (1) S T T T, (2) T T T S, (3) T T S T, or (4) T S T T. (The Greek terms *diatessaron* and *diapente* were adopted by the medieval theorists in their Latin treatises, and the latter is encountered in a work as recent as Bach's *Musical Offering.* The Greek word for octave, *diapason,* survives in modern English.) The combinations may be represented thus:

The Mixolydian octave-species consists of diatessaron 1 plus diapente 1
" Lydian   "   "   "   "   "   2   "   "   2
" Phrygian   "   "   "   "   "   3   "   "   3
" Dorian   "   "   "   " diapente 1   " diatessaron 1
" Hypolydian   "   "   "   "   "   2   "   "   2
" Hypophrygian "   "   "   "   "   3   "   "   3
" Hypodorian   "   "   "   "   "   4   "   "   1
                              or diatessaron 3   " diapente 4

This corresponds with our previous tables for the octave-species.

If we examine Example 5, we see that not only does the pitch of the outer tones of the characteristic octave (*thetic* hypate meson and nete diezeugmenon) remain constant in all seven tonoi, but also that in all except the Mixolydian the *thetic* paramese is always b and that in all except the Hypolydian the *thetic* mese is always a. It would therefore have been possible, besides construing the Mixolydian and Hypolydian as each composed of one diatessaron plus one diapente of the above types, to construe *each* of the remaining five octave-species—not only the Hypodorian—as composed of two possible combinations of diatessaron and diapente—twelve possibilities in all. (Thus, the Dorian

---

System is too neat by far. It is summarized (with references) and proved wrong by WinnM, 16ff, but is perpetuated by RieL etc. Also untenable is the modern naming of the 3 types of diatonic tetrachord as Dorian (T T S), Phrygian (T S T), and Lydian (S T T) on the grounds that the Dorian, Phrygian, and Lydian octave-species are respectively made of 2 of them. The Greeks recognized only the T T S tetrachord and applied no name even to this. *Cf.* WinnM, 12.

might be regarded as consisting not only of diapente 1 plus diatessaron 1, but of diatessaron 1 plus diapente 4.) Why did Gaudentios limit himself to eight?

If we once more consider the *dynamic* relationships of the Greater Perfect System,[72] we find that we can obtain all three species of diatessaron in order by reckoning either hypate hypaton or paramese as the lowest tone of species 1, and the two degrees, next above either, as the lowest tones of species 2 and 3, and that we cannot obtain this result elsewhere. Similarly, by starting on hypate meson—but nowhere else—we can obtain in order the four species of diapente. It is reasonable therefore to believe that, with the relations of the Greater Perfect System deep-rooted in their musical thinking, it was these positions that the Greeks looked upon as normal for the species of diatessaron and diapente as such. Now, if we analyze the structure of the characteristic octave-species for any of the first six tonoi in Example 5, we find that they all consist of a species of diatessaron plus a species of diapente, or vice versa, in normal position. However, to obtain the characteristic octave-species for the Hypodorian tonos diatessaron 1 must be transposed up to nete diezeugmenon to appear above diapente 4, or else diatessaron 3 must be transposed to mese or proslambanomenos and diapente 4 to paranete diezeugmenon or lichanos hypaton. This is unavoidable since the Hypodorian octave cannot be obtained without transposition. The four remaining possible combinations, however, which would all consist of transposed components, would merely duplicate the octaves for the Lydian, Phrygian, Dorian, and Hypophrygian tonoi. They would therefore have served no function but to add a burden to the thinking of the performer. It is for his purposes that the division of the octave into component species of fourth and fifth seems to have been made, for it would facilitate his thinking in terms of basic S T T tetrachords. This becomes clear if we note that, in Gaudentios's eight divisions, the number of each diatessaron degree within its own S T T tetrachord agrees with that of the corresponding diapente degree within its tetrachord. Thus, in the Mixolydian octave, the fourth consists of the dynamic tetrachordon hypaton intact and the fifth of the conjunct tetrachordon meson intact plus degree 1 of the next higher (disjunct) tetrachord. (At the point of conjunction, degree 4 of the lower tetrachord and degree 1 of the upper tetrachord are of course identical, while, at the point of disjunction, 1 represents a really new degree. Thoroughly familiar with the relationships of the Greater Perfect System, the experienced player would make the necessary adjustments at points of conjunction and disjunction automatically.) Or, to take another example, in the Hypolydian octave the fourth (which here lies above the fifth) consists of degrees of the tetrachordon diezeugmenon and of the next higher (conjunct) tetra-

---

[72] Which, for present purposes, may be done most easily by consulting the Dorian tonos in Ex. 5. in which tonos, as we have seen, the dynamic and thetic nomenclature coincide.

chord, the degrees being 2–4 of the former plus 1 (which equals and merges with degree 4 of the tetrachordon diezeugmenon) and 2 of the latter, while the fifth consists of degrees 2–4 of the tetrachordon meson plus degrees 1 and 2 of the next higher (disjunct) tetrachord. Some modern writers have tried to give the division of the Greek octave-species into fourths and fifths an interpretation analogous to that properly applicable to the similar division of the medieval church modes of the West. But there is nothing to indicate that the Greek division was anything but a structure-analyzing aid in performance.[73]

In many of the Greek treatises the word *harmonia* (tonal structure) appears. It seems to be used in more than one sense and modern writers have offered several explanations of its meaning. One explanation is that, before the introduction of high tuning, the term was applied to the various octave-series obtainable in the compass e–E, and that when high tuning came into use and when the eleven- and twelve-string kitharas yielded, as we have seen, a range of two octaves, "harmonia" was employed in at least two senses: as a synonym for tonos and as a name for the individual octave-species as projected upon the Greater Perfect System. It is often difficult to determine which meaning is intended, but it seems fairly certain that such writers as Plato, Aristotle, and Herakleides used it in the sense of tonos.[74] Aristeides presents six gapped scales, varying from a minor sixth to a major eleventh in range and all making some use of the enharmonic genus, as the harmoniai that Plato referred to in his "Republic." [75] While the evidence of Aristeides is certainly not to be disregarded, it must be borne in mind that he was aiming to give information (which unfortunately no other writer corroborates) concerning a period five centuries or more before his time.

Another subject that has caused much difficulty to modern writers, although it is frequently touched upon by Greek writers, is that of *ethos*. The latter ascribe ethical characteristics to the various scales, and while these characteristics vary somewhat with individual writers, there is fairly general agreement on certain fundamental traits. Thus, in the high tuning, with Plato and Aristotle, the Mixolydian is piercing and suitable for lamentations, the Lydian intimate and lascivious, the Phrygian ecstatic, religious, strongly affecting the soul, and the Dorian manly and strong. We are not told in so many words what produced these effects. But it is at least possible to make conjectures. From a pseudo-Aristotelian passage, to which we shall presently

---

[73] And there is therefore no need to "correct" Gaudentios as in AudaM, 94ff (which, however, is in several respects a fine book). *Cf.* ReinM, 42. Further concerning the division of the octaves into fourths and fifths, see GomS I, 152ff, to which the above explanation is greatly indebted.

[74] *Cf.* GomT, 83ff. For a thoroughgoing discussion of the various meanings of "harmonia," see MeyerH.

[75] See MounP; SchäfA, 186ff.

return, we learn that mese is of frequent occurrence in all good music. This would seem to make it a sort of reciting tone and it may be legitimate to call mese and the degrees close to it a tonal nucleus. This nucleus would come high within the characteristic octave in the Mixolydian tonos, in a medium register in the Dorian, and in a low register in the Hypodorian. If we kept the major scale and transpositions of it within the characteristic octave e–E today, the key of E with the tonic at the lowest point of the octave would yield a different ethos from that given by the key of D, producing a redistributed major scale with the tonic next to the top of the octave, while the ethos produced by the key of A, with the tonic at about the middle of the octave, would be different from either. (Thus the theory of ethos does not necessarily have anything to do with a variety of modes.) It is therefore not difficult to see how the Hypodorian, Mixolydian, and Dorian tonoi might have had different ethical effects. What may seem puzzling, however, is that for Plato tonoi with mesai only a degree apart, such as the Dorian and Phrygian, or Phrygian and Lydian, were strongly differentiated from one another. To explain this fact, let us again have recourse to the major mode. In this mode, an octave-species having the tonic two degrees below the highest note would permit the cadence 3-2-1, while the species having the tonic a degree higher would not. Similarly, with the tonic four degrees above the lowest note, the cadence 5-up-to-1 would be possible, while with the tonic a tone lower it would not. Without departing in any way from the major mode, octave-species thus differing in their melodic possibilities would produce dissimilar "ethical" effects even upon us. If the Dorian really had modality—whether or not this had reached as advanced a stage as that of our major—it is not difficult to understand how the Greeks, supposedly possessing a highly developed and subtle melodic sense, would have detected ethical characteristics in the results of the conditioning, produced by the various tonoi, of the approaches to the more important degrees. Ethical character may have been produced by more than intervallic construction and key pure and simple. In lyra or kithara music, the fact that a tone produced by a stopped string would, in the absence of a fingerboard, be more muffled than a tone produced by an open string, may have had an effect on ethos. Symbolical associations [76] not only with scales but with individual tones seem definitely to have had a bearing on the subject. As a result, the relation between ethos and music enters the realm of metaphysics and we should therefore not be surprised to find different philosophers holding different views. Philodemos (1st century B.C.) attacks the writers who distinguish the ethos of melodies and says that theorists who do so can neither sing nor play well and "fall into ecstasies and compare tunes with natural objects." [77] Philodemos would doubtless have approved Reinach's statement that *"Les anciens critiques . . ."*

[76] See HornT.   [77] MounG, 182. See also HarapS, 165.

ont beaucoup raisonné et même déraisonné sur . . . l'ethos des modes." It is easier for us to grasp the attitude of the Greeks when they associate ethos and rhythm. This Aristeides does very clearly. He distinguishes several kinds of rhythm and mentions the effect of tempo.[78]

To what extent the octave-species possessed individual tonalities and to what extent they were merely a Dorian octave and its redistributions are points that have given rise to much difference of opinion. Before entering into a brief discussion of the matter, it is necessary to state that "mode" will be used in the sense of an organized group of tones (or scale) resulting from the use of the motives mentioned in Idelsohn's definition.[79] (Indeed, since he says a mode "is *composed* of a number of motives," he also means the *total* group into which the several motives fit.) Such a mode, through the operation of the motives, tends to give rise to a distinct tonality.[80] If the octave-scales were merely segments of the Greater Perfect System and if they always used as center of the tonal nucleus the predominant tone of the Dorian, they shared among them only one tonality and there was only one true mode; if, however, each had its own predominant tone, then a variety of modes existed, such as we find in plainsong. Did each have its own predominant tone?

The Greeks do not help us out with any formulated theory of tonality. The pseudo-Aristotle *Problems*, XIX, 33, refers to mese as the "leader" and 36 states that all strings are tuned in relation to mese. 33 does not specify in what sense mese is leader, nor can 36 have any modal significance.[81] But 20, reading in part as follows, is more helpful:

[78] SchäfA, 291ff. Further concerning ethos, see GomT, 136ff; AbL, a valuable work in which, however, ethos is ascribed to a variety of modes, rather than to tonoi; WmsA, 102ff, 180. On the special subject of Plato and ethos, see BelliP and RectP; VettA, devoted to Aristotle and music, includes discussion of his attitude regarding ethos.

[79] To which, it is interesting to note, WinnM, 3, comes very close.

[80] Thus a piece is in the major mode not alone because it conforms to the group of intervals T T S T T T S (ascending) but because its motives cluster round the first degree as tonic and the fifth as dominant.

[81] Tuning to mese would be equivalent to a violinist's tuning his highest string a fifth above and his two lower strings in a series of two fifths below his second string. Nobody would claim that a violinist's tuning his other strings to the second string had any modal significance. The lyre-player presumably obtained his pentatonic framework by adopting and adapting the method deriving, with modification, from Pythagoras and described by Aristoxenos as follows: "If . . . a certain note be given, and it be required to find a certain discord below it, such as the ditone (or any other that can be ascertained by the method of concordance), one should take the Fourth above the given note, then descend a Fifth, then ascend a Fourth again, and finally descend another Fifth. Thus, the interval of two tones below the given note will have been ascertained. If it be required to ascertain the discord in the other direction, the concords must be taken in the other direction." (MacrH, 236.) After finding his mese on a, the player probably tuned the other strings in some such way as this to obtain the octave e-E

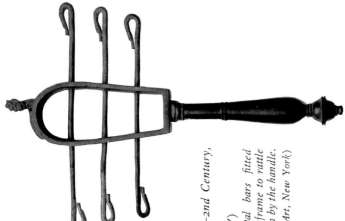

Ancient Agrigentine Vase Showing Alkaios and Sappho with Lyres

The names of the two musician-poets, though not shown on the picture, actually appear on the vase. (Glyptothek und Museum Antiker Kleinkunst, Munich)

Egyptian Sistrum of the 1st–2nd Century, A.D. (Size, 8⅛" x 5½")

In the sistrum the horizontal bars fitted loosely enough into the metal frame to rattle when the instrument was shaken by the handle. (Metropolitan Museum of Art, New York)

Neolithic Bone Flute from the Pile Village of Concise, Vaud, Switzerland

(After G. G. MacCurdy, Human Origins, II)

PLATE II

In all good music mese *occurs frequently, and all good composers have frequent recourse to* mese, *and, if they leave it, they soon return to it, as they do to no other note. Similarly in language, if certain connecting particles are removed . . . the language is no longer Greek; . . .* mese *is as it were a conjunction among sounds, and more so than the other notes, because its sound occurs more often.* (ForsP)

If it occurred frequently, it was very likely something like a dominant [82] or just possibly a tonic. It is clear from other passages in the *Problems* that its compilers referred, in this connection, only to the mese *kata dynamin.* Macran, relying on this passage, put forward the theory that in all the octave-species the same note—mese in the Greater Perfect System—acted as tonic, and that the characteristic effects of these species resulted from the high or low position of that tonic in the octave, a view [83] generally consistent with the one advanced above in connection with the discussion of ethos. In other words, each of the octave-scales would have one requisite of tonality, a distinctive grouping of intervals—but the predominant tone of the Dorian would serve similarly for all of them.[84] Aristeides mentions *petteia,* which "takes the notes of the selected scale and by omissions and repetitions, by use of certain of them as initials and finals, produces the desired effect." [85] (The name *petteia* is that of a game and is here used figuratively.) This method must certainly have produced a modal result while it was in use, but unfortunately we do not know to how many modes it was applied; Aristeides indeed tells us very little about it.

Gevaert, Westphal, Mountford, and others, have all felt that the Greek octave-scales were actually modal and could therefore qualify as forerunners of the medieval modes. But the view that the octave-scales were merely the Dorian octave with its redistributions seems to be the one best supported by the evidence of the theorists. Many writers feel that Ptolemy, restricting the tonoi to the number that will suffice to bring all the octave-species within a uniform compass, showed a strong feeling for modality and some go so far as to say that the mesai *kata thesin* gave each octave-scale its own tonic (or dominant). But we have seen that the restriction to seven tonoi may very well have had nothing to do with modal variety and that the mese *kata thesin* seems to have been merely the tone produced by the middle string of a seven- or eleven-string instrument of the lyre-type. We have seen also that Gaudentios's division of the octave-scales into pentachords and tetrachords

---

[82] Frere in Grove III, 475, prefers dominant. See ClemI, 151, for the suggestion, "predominant."
[83] Which is followed in Grove both in the article "Greek Music" (written by Macran) and in the article "Modes, Ecclesiastical" (by Frere). The latter, like the article "Monochord" (also by Frere) contains some valuable information on Greek music (mingled, as we have seen in footnote 70, with some that is misleading).
[84] See further (and partly *contra*) WinnA, 341.   [85] WinnM, 57; SchäfA, 207.

may likewise be explained without holding that he implies modal variety.

The whole body of evidence for and against modality during the different periods of ancient Greek music has been marshalled by Winnington-Ingram in WinnM, and that author, one of the two best recent English writers on Greek music—the other being Mountford—has deduced from it all the conclusions seeming possible to him, whether reconcilable or not. He feels that the present state of our knowledge does not warrant the selection of any one of his conclusions in preference to the others.

To what extent do the practical examples of Greek music that have come down to us throw light upon the problem of modality?

The repertoire is, as already indicated, pitifully small. This may be in part due to the widespread practice of improvisation among the Greeks.[86] It is not unlikely that the nomoi—stock-melodies, as we have seen—were used as the basis for the improvisations and that compositions definitely reduced to crystallized form, such as those preserved by the surviving examples, represent a fairly late development. The music purporting to be the ancient melody of the beginning of Pindar's first Pythian ode is very likely a 17th-century forgery.[87] Fortunately, however, we have a group of pieces that have reached us preserved on stone and in ancient papyri.[88] Of their authenticity there is no question. These are supplemented by a few other compositions generally accepted as genuine.[89] Most of the pieces have been frequently printed in modern notation and are easily available. The complete list follows: [90]

1) A fragment from the *Orestes* of Euripides, probably the oldest piece of Greek music we have. The bit of papyrus preserving it is mutilated and very small;

2) A fragment, probably from a tragedy, discovered in a Zenon papyrus at the Cairo Museum. The piece is very likely junior only to the *Orestes* fragment among surviving examples of Greek composition. The papyrus

---

[86] *Cf.* SachsA, 19.

[87] The melody is given in modern notation in EmG, 500; SachsA, 12; SachsMu, 79, etc. Its authenticity has been debated for almost 300 years. The question was reopened in 1932 by RomeO (attacking), which was followed by FriedM (vigorously defending). This prompted MaasK (again attacking). The evidence *pro* and *con* is restated and impartially weighed in MounL, the decision, based mainly on philological grounds, being unfavorable, as is that in GomM, based on musical grounds.

[88] All discussed in MounG.   [89] See, however, BarryG.

[90] Nos. 1, 2, 5–8, and 14 are transcribed in MounG; Nos. 1 and 3–14 in ReinM (with French translations of the texts of 1, 3–5, 10, 11, and 14); Nos. 1, 5, 12, 13, and part of 15 in SachsMu; Nos. 1, 5, 10–13, and portions of 14 and 15 in SachsA (which contains facsimiles of 1 and 5 and German translations of the texts of 5 and 10–13); Nos. 1 (imperfectly), 3–5, and 10–13 in EmG. No. 2 is described in MounN, a facsimile is given on Plate V and attempts at transcriptions on p. 99; for more recent transcriptions, see DelN; GomT, 128; MarrouZ. No. 15 is printed in BellA, 94ff. For No. 5, see also p. 115, *infra*. WmsM may be found useful for English translations of the texts of Nos. 3, 5, 10–13, and the "Pindar" fragment. This list of transcriptions is by no means complete.

itself, dating from about 250 B.C., is apparently older than the *Orestes* papyrus, and therefore preserves our earliest specimen of Greek notation;

3 and 4) The two Delphic Hymns to Apollo, discovered in 1893 on marble slabs in the ruins of the Treasury of the Athenians at Delphi. The first, dating from about 138 B.C., is, despite some gaps, the most considerable example of Greek composition known. The second, dating from about 128 B.C. and written by the Athenian Limenios, is also an extended work but is less well preserved;

5) The Epitaph of Seikilos (for his wife Euterpe), discovered in 1883 on a slab at Tralles (Aidin) in Asia Minor. The attractive diatonic melody, dated variously from the 2nd century B.C. to the 1st century A.D., is brief but intact;

6–9) Four fragments in a papyrus at Berlin: (a) a Paian to Apollo; (b) three lines of instrumental notation; (c) a few lines (perhaps for Tecmessa) addressed to the suicide Ajax—possibly from a tragedy; and (d) another three lines of instrumental notation. There is also half a line of a lyric, possibly connected with (c);

10–13) Two brief Hymns to the Muse (sometimes printed as one composition), a Hymn to the Sun, and a Hymn to Nemesis, all preserved in Byzantine manuscripts and first printed in 1581 by Vincenzo Galilei, father of the astronomer. The last piece is almost certainly by Mesomedes of Crete (*c.* A.D. 130) and the Hymn to the Sun is probably his also;

14) A Christian Hymn, of the 3rd century A.D., found at Oxyrhynchos in Egypt, often cited as evidence of the influence of Greek music upon the early Christians (though the fact that the notation employed is Greek does not necessarily mean that the music is Greek);

15) Brief exercises in Bellermann's Anonymus, apparently intended to illustrate certain rhythmical classifications.

The only examples in this list that are both old and complete enough to cast any light on ancient modality are Nos. 3–5 and 10–13. No. 5 seems to show that the Phrygian octave-species may have had an independent life. But the octave-species for whose life the weight of the evidence, such as it is, is decidedly preponderant is the Dorian, and it would seem that hypate meson was a sort of final and mese the tone of most frequent occurrence. The greater number of the examples "are written in series of notes that accord with the theoretical doctrines of Aristoxenos," but some present abnormalities. The *Orestes* fragment can be made to fit the old Phrygian harmonia of Aristeides; the Delphic Hymns use the "hooked" tetrachord as well as the regular tetrachordal structure of the Greater Perfect System; a passage in one of them, as pointed out in GomT, 124ff, requires the use of both alternative strings on the lyre. The Alypian notation, of course, makes it possible to determine the tonos of a piece: thus, the Epitaph of Seikilos is in the Ionian key (and therefore quite properly uses the Phrygian octave-species—*cf*. p. 32).

Most of the examples are too late to give us an idea of musical style at the period in which students of Greek history are most likely to be interested —the Periclean Age. But it seems clear that the Greeks conceived their music as monodic. In performance, however, harmonic intervals were doubtless occasionally sounded, not as a result of any desire for part-writing (which, if it existed, was apparently satisfied by singing in octaves, i. e. "antiphony"), but through the operation of the principle of heterophony. This has been defined as follows:

The principle of heterophony consists in a melody's being employed simultaneously in several voices, but in such a way that the melodic line of the leading voice—which has the "Theme"—is not duplicated in the other voices—which play round the fundamental line freely and vary it, without, however, wandering so far from it that one may say they have melodic independence.

The playing round the fundamental line was probably not very free in Greek music—this definition was written with an advanced type of heterophony in mind—and the accompaniment doubtless duplicated the basic line much of the time. But the description of the Spondeiazon tropos given by "Plutarch" offers some indication of what could be achieved. This would indicate the possibility of sounding, in that tropos,[91] certain tones against other tones, as indicated by the dotted lines in the following example:[92]

EXAMPLE 7.

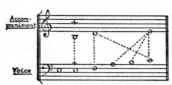

(No accompanying notes are allotted to the first note of the vocal scale.)

It is interesting to note that the *Orestes* fragment contains some symbols that may indicate the use of heterophony.[93] As Example 7 indicates, accompaniments were sounded *above* the vocal line, where, through the use of heterophony, they departed from it.

Musical structure, as illustrated by the examples, was loose. Thematic development and form-producing repetitions, except for cadential formulas that just possibly had some modal purpose, are mostly absent. (A repetition in the Hymn to Nemesis, however, may have formal significance.) While

---

[91] Aristoxenos uses "tropos" to indicate a style, a manner of composition. (*Cf*. the Idelsohn definition of "mode.")

[92] Further concerning the Spondeiazon tropos, see WinnS, 85ff.

[93] We shall return to the subject of heterophony in Chap. 9. The topic is discussed, with respect to Greek music, in BarryG, which deals also with Greek antiphony. See also StumpfG, 18, 47.

the theorists make it clear that they regard *melopoiia* (the art of melody-making) as of the utmost importance, they deal with it only in generalities, and the examples afford but slight evidence of what the governing rules may have been. The vocal pieces most often have only one note to a syllable of text; they contain no extended flourishes. The downward tendency shown by theorists' scales until Late Antiquity is not to be found in the musical fragments. To what extent this is attributable to their lateness, it is not possible to say. Save in the Zenon fragment, there is a noticeable tendency, despite a few exceptions, for the line of the melody to respect the appearance of tonic accents in the text.[94] The Greek speech accents, of course, did not imply stress. The acute indicated a rise in pitch; the grave, a fall; the circumflex, a rise followed by a fall. The language was highly inflected.

The two Delphic Hymns employ quintuple rhythm, which appears to have been much used. The rhythm of vocal music seems to have been dictated, to a considerable extent, by the quantities of the syllables of the text; and the verse meters—often intricate in nature—produced rhythmic patterns that were not only a source of interest in themselves but a means of supplying a principle of coherence to a composition as a whole. In Greek rhythm, the unit of measurement (the *chronos protos*) was multiplied to produce phrases etc. The Greeks did not, like ourselves, adopt as a unit a large value (such as a whole note) and divide it. The degree to which ictus was present is not clear. The Greek writers refer to *thesis* and *arsis*. But the terms refer to the "rise" and "fall" discernible in certain kinds of verse, in which the impetus of a foot is maintained up to a certain point, and then allowed to die down; they do not, therefore, necessarily imply variations in stress (or pitch).[95] While indication of the rhythm was sometimes left to the text-meter, the possibility existed of showing it in notation. The absence of a sign indicated a chronos protos, – indicated the equivalent of two chronoi protoi, ⌐ of three, ⊔ of four, ⊔ of five; a rest was shown by ∧(or ⌒).[96]

The evidence concerning Greek music, afforded by the practical examples and the treatises, is obviously insufficient to give us a comprehensive idea of what it was like. But, annoyingly enough, it is quite sufficient to make us realize how incomplete is our legacy from the Greek stage—consisting, except for a few notes, of mere texts shorn of music—and, necessarily, how partial is our conception of even such shorter works as those of Pindar or Sappho.

The Romans made few important contributions of their own. They adopted Greek theory and practice, though they seem not to have kept the

[94] For a discussion of this point, see MounG, 164ff, but also MounN.

[95] For a discussion of *thesis* and *arsis,* as understood by the Greeks, see SonnW, 9 and Chap. V thereof; also WinnA, 330 (with attention to the end of footnote 13).

[96] For further material on Greek rhythm see WinnA, 328ff, and the works there cited; MounG, 154ff; EmG, 470ff; EmH I, 108ff; ReinM, Chap. II. See also footnote 26.

Greek tradition pure, and Aristeides Quintilianos is still drawn upon for the musical sections of so late a work as the *Satyricon* of Martianus Capella, a Latin writer of the 5th century who lived at Carthage.[97] In the next century, Boethius and Cassiodorus produced writings that were to render them the two great intermediaries between ancient and medieval music. These writings, however, were destined to give rise to considerable misunderstanding on the part of medieval theorists.

That the Romans were musically active, despite their lack of musical originality, is amply attested by passages in the writings of such earlier figures as Cicero, Marcus Fabius Quintilianus, Seneca, and others. From these passages it is clear that, towards the end of the 1st century, music was intensely cultivated throughout the Roman world. Rhythm appears to have received particular attention, and there is evidence for the use of recurring stress at equal divisions of time (such as has been particularly common in Western music for the last three centuries). There is evidence also for the practice of heterophony. Greeks, whether from Europe, Asia Minor, or Alexandria, acted as mimes, singers, and instrumentalists, enjoying the favor of both populace and upper classes, while the Romans themselves, as suited a great military nation, furthered the development of the brasses. The *tuba* was a straight infantry trumpet; the *lituus,* a J-shaped instrument, looking like the Hebrew shofar; the *buccina* or *cornu,* a circular horn.

Music was practiced by the last emperors (except Vespasian) and by their retainers. Nero, as we have seen, had understood the operation of the hydraulis—the favorite instrument of the arena—and had caused coins to be minted depicting him in the guise of a kithara-player. But the moralists considered most of the songs indecent, the dancing immodest, and the melodies effeminate. The religious music, however, sought to maintain the old dignity.[98] The use of music in connection with both vulgar amusements and rites regarded as unhallowed, was bound to cause the early Christians to frown upon the art generally.

Whether or not one rejects, with Spengler, any causal connection between the inner life of ancient culture and that of medieval culture, it is clear that the Middle Ages inherited from the ancients at least the concept of the scale, an acoustical theory, and several principles of instrument-construction. And these ancients were the people who bordered the Mediterranean, chief among them being the Greeks. The North of Europe, to be sure, has yielded us instruments from the Baltic littoral—bronze *lurer,* dating from as far back as 1200 B. C.—but these S-shaped horns, with their hanging plates of metal attached to the smaller end of the tube (probably to heighten, by their rattling, the terrifying effect of the blast) produced a rough, blatant sound. On such

---

[97] Concerning the relationship between Martianus Capella and Aristeides, see DeiS.
[98] For a study of the position of music in the Roman Empire at the period in question, see MaE.

slender evidence, excessive claims should not be advanced—as they have been on occasion—for a powerful influence from the ancient North upon the development of European music.[99] The ancient South, on the other hand, even when its art was misunderstood, exerted a strong influence for more than a millennium and a half—as when certain 16th-century Italians experimented with chromaticism, under the impression that they were reintroducing the Greek chromatic genus, and certain of their later countrymen launched the opera in the mistaken belief that they were restoring to life the vanished glories of the Athenian stage.

[99] For a picture of a lur, see Grove IV, plate opposite 496. See also Galpin's article in Grove III, 251 (from which the above wording has borrowed); Angul Hammerich, *Studien über die altnordischen Luren im Nationalmuseum zu Kopenhagen,* in VfMW, X (1894), 1, and Willy Pastor, *The Music of Primitive Peoples and the Beginnings of European Music,* in *Annual Report of the Smithsonian Institution for 1912,* 679.

Part Two: WESTERN EUROPEAN MONODY TO ABOUT 1300

Chapter 3: THE BEGINNINGS OF CHRISTIAN SACRED CHANT AND THE GROWTH OF SOME OF ITS CHIEF BRANCHES: Syrian, Byzantine, Armenian, Coptic, and Ethiopian

The Beginnings of Christian Sacred Chant

THE vast area over which Christianity spread within the first centuries of its existence, before centralization of ecclesiastical authority had progressed far, furthered the growth of several different bodies of liturgical Chant. Some of these—perhaps all—shared points of resemblance; a common heritage descended to all from the Synagogue, and, in their early stages, the surrounding Greco-Roman world—from Syria to Spain, from North Africa to beyond the Alps—fostered the artistic activity of Late Antiquity, still sufficiently alive to beget life.

Roman Chant, destined to prove by far the most important in the development of Western music and its notation, at first lagged behind the repertoires produced in the Near East. There, before the Mohammedans wrested Syria and Egypt from the Byzantine Empire in the 7th century, the flourishing condition of Christianity bade fair to continue. In fact, early in that century a Nestorian mission, as a tablet in Chinese and Syriac sets forth, carried the Gospel to the Far East, preaching in the Chinese province of Shensi. Earlier, Christian communities had been established, not only in Armenia and Persia, but even in India.[1] Unlike the Christians of the West who, in the practice of their cult, shared one common language—Latin—those of the East used a variety of languages, each people usually employing its own—Greek, for example, or Syriac, or Armenian—, thus increasing the chances for the admission of specifically national elements into both the poetry and music. Such elements—Frankish, Celtic, Visigothic, etc.—crept into the Chant of the West also, but the use of an international tongue presented a counterbalancing element of universality.

---

[1] A colorful passage in the apocryphal *Acts of Thomas* (written before A. D. 230) describes the apostle's supposed landing in India thus: "And they left the ship and entered into the city, and lo, there were noises of auloi and water-organs, and trumpets sounded about them. . . . Now the aulos-girl, holding her aulos in her hand, went about to them all and played, but when she came to the place where the apostle was, she stood over him and played at his head for a long space: now this aulos-girl was by race an Hebrew." (LipA III, 104, 108; transl. from JamesA, 366f, with "aulos" etc.—mentioned in the original–substituted for "flute" etc. Similar substitution will be made elsewhere also.)

Before treating the more important of the several bodies of Chant individually, we shall discuss briefly certain features of the background and some of the traditions that affected all of them, whether directly or indirectly, whether lightly or forcefully.

That such figures as Nicomachos, Gaudentios, Ptolemy, Mesomedes, etc., mentioned in Chapter 2, were active during the early days of the Christian Era—i. e. that the periods of Late Antiquity and Early Christianity overlapped—hardly needs pointing out. Nicomachos, like a faithful neo-Pythagorean, saw an intimate relationship between music and numbers. His drawing upon the number 5 in his calculations concerning the music of the spheres, and his manner of accounting for the significances of other numbers also, belong to the realm of speculation and symbolism. Cassiodorus and Boethius transmitted ideas such as those of Nicomachos to the medieval theorists, thereby contributing an additional element of obscurity to the latter's otherwise often none too lucid writing.[2]

Among the neo-Platonists referring to music were Plotinos (205–70), his pupil Porphyry (233–304), whose commentary on Ptolemy's *Harmonics* has already been mentioned, and Proclos (412–85), all three associated with Alexandria, and the Syrian Iamblichos (d. *c.* 330) who studied with Porphyry at Rome. Plotinos, like Plato and Aristotle, ascribed considerable importance to music as a moral influence but differed from them in regarding its efficacy more from the religious standpoint and less from the political. The Beautiful, according to him, purifies the soul and leads it by degrees to a contemplation of the Good. In his philosophy, music has a magical power capable, in keeping with its nature, of leading one towards either good or evil. In some respects, it resembles prayer.

The tune of an incantation, a significant cry, . . . these too have a . . . power over the soul . . . , drawing it with the force of . . . tragic sounds—for it is the reasonless soul, not the will or wisdom, that is beguiled by music, a form of sorcery which raises no question, whose enchantment, indeed, is welcomed. . . . Similarly with regard to prayers; . . . the powers that answer to incantations do not act by will. . . . The prayer is answered by the mere fact that part and other part [of the All] are wrought to one tone like a musical string which, plucked at one end, vibrates at the other also. Often, too, the sounding of one string awakens what might pass for a perception in another, the result of their being in harmony and tuned to one musical scale; now, if the vibration in a lyre affects another by virtue of the sympathy existing between them, then certainly in the All—even though it is constituted in contraries—there must be one melodic system, for it

---

[2] For extended treatments of the attitude towards music in the early Middle Ages—discussing mathematical and symbolical tendencies, the neo-Pythagoreans, the neo-Platonists, music and magic, ethos, etc.—see AbD and GéroP.

contains its unisons as well; and its entire content, even to those contraries, is a kinship.[3]

Porphyry, though a defender of paganism and a violent opponent of Christianity, came to exercise a definite influence upon the Church Fathers. An ardent advocate of asceticism, he disapproved of the sensuous pleasure afforded by music and placed dramatic spectacles and dances, with their music, in the same class as horse-races. Proclos, while indulging in neo-Pythagorean symbolism, looked upon music much as Plotinos did. Stressing the magical attributes of the art, he sanctioned music that could place men in contact with the divine, and, like Porphyry, disapproved of music emanating from the stage. Iamblichos held somewhat similar views, believing that each of the demons—that is, the spirits serving as intermediaries between the supreme divinity and men—had his own special chant and could be reached through its performance.[4]

Rather suspect are recent deductions made from the appearance in papyri, coming down to us from the Gnostics, of many combinations of the seven Greek vowels, used to strengthen the influence of incantations. Egyptian priests had sung chants on the seven vowels in serving the gods, and Greek-vowel combinations were carried about quite freely as amulets. The Gnostics, having been heretics who sought to combine Christian, Egyptian, and Syrian ideas, and who, in the process, interpreted Christian story in the light of the cosmology and astrology of the ancients, resembled Proclos, for example, in having ties with the world of magic and speculation. Several scholars—taking a clue from Nicomachos, who held that the planets gave out different sounds according to their distances from the center of the sphere—have attempted to decipher these vowels from the standpoint of musical notation. They have correlated the seven vowels with the supposed sounds of the seven planets. Their theory, in the opinion [5] of one modern writer, at least, is unsupported by the sources. Another writer, apparently accepting the transcriptions, believes that the influence on Christian Chant, claimed for the vowel combinations, has been exaggerated.[6] It is true that the Gnostics, neo-Pythagoreans, and neo-Platonists seem to have affected Christianity in the field of music as in other fields, but it is still an open question whether evidence to this effect is offered by the vowel combinations.

In addition to the neo-Pythagoreans and neo-Platonists there was, among the non-Christian sects, the school of Hellenistic Judaism represented by Philo of Alexandria (b. *c.* A.D. 20). Philo's philosophy was a mixture of the Bible

---

[3] MackP, 96.
[4] Works by Porphyry have been translated into English by Thomas Taylor, A. Zimmern, etc. Taylor made translations from Proclos and Iamblichos also.
[5] Expressed in WachsU, 24ff, which is useful also for its full bibliographical references.
[6] GéroP, 52.

and Plato. The degree to which his ideas on the place of music in worship affected the Church Fathers, has been disputed. His writings are rich in references to music [7] which, however, he regarded—together with all art and science—not as an end in itself but as a preparation for philosophy. Of special interest is an account, appearing in a work of once doubted but now accepted authenticity (*On the Contemplative Life*), telling of the Therapeutae—a severely ascetic sect—interesting, since, if correct, the description shows that their musical practice included antiphonal singing, destined to achieve considerable importance among the Christians.—It should be noted that the term "antiphony," when applied to Christian Chant and later music, has a different significance from that attaching to it when applied to ancient Greek music. Greek "antiphony" consisted, as we have seen, in singing in octaves; the later "antiphony," in interchange, i. e. in alternate singing either (1) between two (or more) choral groups, or (2) between a soloist and chorus. Type 2 is distinguished from type 1 in the Roman Church etc. by being called "responsorial singing."—According to Philo the Therapeutae used antiphony in both the Greek sense and the later sense.

They all stand up together, and . . . two choruses are formed . . . , the one of men and the other of women, and for each chorus there is a leader . . . selected, who is the most honourable and most excellent of the band. Then they sing hymns which have been composed in honour of God in many metres and tunes, at one time all singing together, and at another answering one another in a skilful manner. . . . The chorus of male and female worshippers, throughout the singing and the alternation of the melodies, makes . . . a truly musical symphony, the shrill voices of the women mingling with the deep-toned voices of the men.[8]

A brief passage in a rather extended letter sent in the year 115 to the Emperor Trajan by Pliny the Younger, while he was governor of Bithynia, is capable of being interpreted as referring to the practice of antiphonal singing among the Christians themselves.[9]

The history of the primitive Christian Chant has been divided into three periods.[10] The earliest, roughly speaking, embraced the first two centuries. At this stage, little progress was made towards organization, and practices varied in different communities. The Gnostics used music as a means of attracting proselytes; so, quite legitimately, did the orthodox Christians, as well as the Marcionites (whose heresy consisted in composing their own psalms instead of using those in the Bible) and the Manicheans. The second period—

---

[7] Among them are two (*On Drunkenness*, XXX, 116, and *On Dreams*, II, 270) which, if correctly rendered in the Loeb Classical Library translations of Philo's works (now in process, the Greek being given as well as the English), would disturb the views previously held to the effect that (1) the bowing of instruments and (2) singing in parts (conceived as such) did not exist at the period under discussion. The two passages, however, are not clear in the original, and are differently rendered in other translations.

[8] English after YongeP, 19 and WagE I, 19.   [9] See MelP II, 400f or EB XVIII, 79.

[10] See GéroH, 134ff, where there is a fuller discussion.

from the end of the 2nd century to the beginning of the 4th—was one of growth. The conversion of an ever-increasing number of erstwhile pagans confronted Christian leaders with the necessity of combating the transfer, into the important new communities that were taking form in both East and West, of any such musical manifestations from the pagan world as might arouse undesirable associations. This does not mean that, within limits to be discussed later, Greek music failed to have its effect upon Christians living within the sphere of its influence. It is from this period that the Oxyrhynchos Hymn, mentioned in Chapter 2 (p. 49), probably dates, a point showing that, at least in some communities, Christian Chant already included melodies of an artistic nature. The Christians began at this time to count a larger number of erudite men among their writers. The third stage began with the year 313 when Constantine the Great, through the edict of Milan, assured Christianity of toleration throughout the Empire and thus paved the way for its ultimate recognition as the state religion. Spacious churches began to be erected, and a suitable music was required to meet the new conditions.

Vocal execution was early applied in three main directions: (1) In the solemn reading of portions of the Gospels etc., for which cantillation was used in accordance with established formulas; (2) in psalm- and hymn-singing, which ranged from simple cantillation to full-fledged song; and (3) in the ecstatic chanting of the single word *Alleluia* to rich, soaring melismas.

The Church Fathers, from whom we have writings [11] in all three periods, were not uninfluenced by their non-Christian contemporaries in their attitude towards music, as has already been implied. Especially after the first period, they refer to its practice frequently. If, unfortunately, the writings give us no analytical descriptions of the music itself, they, as well as other literary sources we shall mention, do testify to the manner in which the early Christians regarded and utilized music, and occasionally give us a little insight into some possible reasons for the directions taken by Christian Chant in its development.

Clement of Alexandria (*c.* 150, at Athens–*c.* 220) was, as his works show, a cultivated man, interested in music and poetry, and unlikely to have been prejudiced against instruments merely on principle. Yet, while he tolerated the lyra and kithara because King David had allegedly used them, he disapproved of most other instruments, doubtless fearing that they might carry to the ears of Christian listeners echoes of pagan festivities and of the obscene stage:

[11] The great collection of patristic writings is that of Migne, which comprises both a Greek and a Latin series. Its 387 volumes contain a few treatises on music not printed elsewhere. There is an *Index Musicae* to the Latin series in Vol. CCXXI, col. 625ff. Three large collections in English are Ante-Nicene, Nicene Post-N, and PuseyL. AbD, Chap. 2, is devoted specifically to the relations of the Church Fathers to music, as is a portion of Paul Henry Láng's *Music in Western Civilization* and, in its entirety, GéroP.

The one instrument of peace, the Word alone by which we honour God, is what we employ, . . . no longer . . . the ancient psaltery, the trumpet, the timbrel, and aulos, which those expert in war and contemners of the fear of God were wont to make use of also in the choruses at their festive assemblies; that by such strains they might raise their dejected minds.[12]

The oldest known Christian hymn-text ("Hymn of the Saviour") is attributed to Clement but may, in fact, be by an earlier hand.

Tertullian (*c.* 155–*c.* 222), active at Carthage, the scene of his birth, is a witness for the use of responsorial psalmody in the Latin practice.[13] Describing an ideal married couple, he gives us a glimpse of the rôle music might properly play in Christian home life:

Between the two echo psalms and hymns; and they mutually challenge each other which shall better chant to their Lord.[14]

Origen (*c.* 185–*c.* 254), active chiefly at Alexandria, testifies to the wide use of song in worship:

. . . the Greeks use Greek . . . , the Romans Latin . . . , and every one prays and sings praises to God as best he can in his mother tongue.[15]

Origen regards instruments as symbols. The trumpet represents to him the efficacy of the Word of God; [16] the tympanon (a kind of drum), the destruction of lust; cymbals, the eager soul enamored of Christ.[17]

Eusebios (*c.* 260–*c.* 340), bishop of Caesarea in Palestine, author of the *Ecclesiastical History* (the most important church history of ancient times, in which the account of Philo concerning the Therapeutae is quoted), disapproves of the use of instruments, even the kithara:

We sing God's praise with living psaltery. . . . For more pleasant and dear to God than any instrument is the harmony of the whole Christian people. . . . Our cithara is the whole body, by whose movement and action the soul sings a fitting hymn to God, and our ten-stringed psaltery is the veneration of the Holy Ghost by the five senses of the body and the five virtues of the spirit.[18]

Eusebios bears witness that the psalms were not merely recited—"We sing the psalms in melodious tones" [19]—and reports that the singing of psalms and also of hymns was widely practiced.[20]

St. Athanasios (*c.* 298–373), patriarch of Alexandria, exerted himself towards keeping the singing of the psalms from becoming overelaborate. For him, too, instruments have symbolic meanings.[21]

---

[12] MigneG VIII, 443; transl. from Ante-Nicene II, 249.
[13] MigneL I, 1301; Ante-Nicene III, 690.   [14] MigneL I, 1304; Ante-Nicene IV, 48.
[15] MigneG XI, 1574; Ante-Nicene IV, 653.   [16] MigneG XIII, 319.   [17] MigneG XII, 1683.
[18] MigneG XXIII, 1171; WagE I, 12.   [19] MigneG XXIII, 1174; WagE I, 24.
[20] MigneG XXIII, 647, 658.   [21] MigneG XXVII, 42.

4. *Playing a Viol*

(*British Museum. Add.*
35316. Italian, 15th Century)

5. *Playing the Lyre, While Other Musicians Play the*
Horn, Viol, Bell-Chimes and Organ

(*Cividale, Italy, 13th Century*)

3. *Playing the Harp under the Inspira-*
tion of the Holy Ghost, while One At-
tendant Juggles and Others Play the
Rebec, Trumpet (Resting on a Fork)
and Horn

(*British Museum. Cotton MS Tiberius C VI.*
English, 11th Century)

1. *Playing Bell-Chimes*

(*British Museum. Royal MS 2 B II.*
French, 13th Century)

2. *Performing Psalms to the Harp,*
while Three Scribes Commit them to
Writing

(*British Museum. Add. 42131. English,*
c. 1415)

PLATE III

St. Basil (*c.* 330–79), the successor of Eusebios as bishop of Caesarea, wrote the liturgy of St. Basil, still used in the Eastern Church. A letter of his defends the singing of the psalms both antiphonally and responsorially, and states that they are thus sung by "the Egyptians, . . . Libyans, Thebans, Palestinians, Arabians, Phoenicians, Syrians, the dwellers by the Euphrates." [22] He writes that the psalms are provided with melodies to attract children and youths to the end that their souls and minds may be enlightened while, as they think, they are surrendering themselves to the pleasures of music.[23] Here we have an open avowal of the value of music as a help in propagating the faith.

St. Jerome (*c.* 340–420), author of the standard Latin translation of the Bible—the Vulgate—acted as adviser to Pope Damasus, during whose pontificate (366–84) the Roman liturgy reached a high degree of organization. The aversion of this highly cultivated saint to instruments may be attributed to the same cause as Clement's. Advising Laeta on how to rear her daughter, he wrote:

Let her be deaf to the sound of the organ, and not know even the uses of the pipe, the lyre, and the cithara.[24]

It is probably such opposition as this that led to the apparent exclusion of instruments from the conservative rendition of the Roman Chant. At St. Jerome's instance, Pope Damasus added the Alleluia to the Roman Mass. Describing the *jubilus,* the long, often intricate vocal flourish at the end of the Alleluia (it is possible that *jubilus* refers to flourishes in other parts of the Chant also), he wrote:

By the term jubilus *we understand that which neither in words nor syllables nor letters nor speech is it possible to express or comprehend how much man ought to praise God.*[25]

The singing of the Alleluia was doubtless taken over from the liturgy of the Synagogue.[26]

St. Ambrose (*c.* 340–97), bishop of Milan and one of the great Church Fathers, felt that women, although they should be silent in the congregation —as St. Paul adjured—would "do well to sing their psalm." [27] St. Ambrose not only mentions music in his writings but had a definite influence upon the manner of its use in the Western Church. We shall return to him later.

St. Augustine (354–430), in 387 baptized by St. Ambrose, in 396 made bishop of Hippo (near the port Aphrodisium, now Bona, in Algeria), author of the

---

[22] MigneG XXXII, 763; Nicene & Post-N, Ser. 2, VIII, 247.   [23] MigneG XXXI, 1723.
[24] MigneL XXII, 871; Nicene & Post-N, Ser. 2, VI, 193.   [25] MigneL XXVI, 970; WagE I, 33.
[26] For a discussion of this point, see WagE I, 31.   [27] MigneL XIV, 968.

Confessions and the important *De Civitate Dei*, has left us a treatise *De Musica*,[28] but it is devoted largely to meter, versification, eternal and spiritual numbers, etc., rather than to music as we understand it. The last portion, however, is remarkable as an early effort in the psychology of music.[28a] The treatise contains a definition of music frequently quoted by medieval writers: *Musica est scientia bene modulandi* ("Music is the science of modulating well," the context implying that *modulatio* refers to the rhythmical and melodic structure of a composition). St. Augustine's comment [29] concerning the simple manner of chanting the psalms, favored by Athanasios, is interesting as an inference that they were on the whole sung with some degree of elaboration. He affords us some definite information [30] concerning the responsorial singing of certain psalms, naming precisely the verses sung by the congregation as refrains in answer to the chanting of the precentor.[31] He is among those who regarded instruments symbolically:

Nor must we keep back the mystical meaning of the "timbrel and psaltery." On the timbrel leather is stretched, on the psaltery gut is stretched; on either instrument the flesh is crucified.[32]

St. Augustine introduced into the African Church the practice of singing psalms in connection with the offering of gifts, thereby instituting the Offertory (*cf.* p. 181). Like St. Jerome, he describes the *jubilus,* saying:

It is a certain sound of joy without words . . . it is the expression of a mind poured forth in joy. . . . A man rejoicing in his own exultation, after certain words which cannot be . . . understood, bursteth forth into sounds of exultation without words, so that it seemeth that he . . . filled with excessive joy cannot express in words the subject of that joy.[33]

In his *Confessions,* St. Augustine writes of the powerful effect music had on him and of his fear that its charm sometimes caused him to be moved by esthetic pleasure rather than by the sacred words.[34] At other times, however, it led him towards truth:

How greatly did I weep in Thy hymns and canticles, deeply moved by the voices of Thy sweet-speaking church! The voices flowed into mine ears, and the truth was

---

[28] MigneL XXXII, 1081. English translation in TalA. HuréA (a monograph devoted to St. Augustine and music) contains an interpretation in French. PerlA gives a German translation; see also EdelM. Several authors (for example, GéroH, 142) regard the treatise as incomplete. KrepsN, 21, however, considers it a finished work, as does EB II, 683.

[28a] *Cf.* Kathi Meyer, *Bedeutung und Wesen der Musik, Part I* (1932), 34ff.

[29] MigneL XXXII, 800; Nicene & Post-N, Ser. 1, I, 156.   [30] Assembled in WagE I, 72f.

[31] The precentor, or cantor, is the chief singer—and occasionally the instructor also—of the choir. His assistant was formerly called the "succentor." The chief singer of the Schola Cantorum at Rome was called *prior scholae* or *primicerius.* For fuller information, see CE III, 306.

[32] MigneL XXXVII, 1953; Nicene & Post-N, Ser. 1, VIII, 678.

[33] MigneL XXXVII, 1272; Nicene & Post-N, Ser. 1, VIII, 488.

[34] MigneL XXXII, 800; Nicene & Post-N, Ser. 1, I, 156.

poured forth into my heart, whence the agitation of my piety overflowed, and my tears ran over, and blessed was I therein.[35]

The striking diary of the pilgrimage made to the Holy Land by St. Silvia (or Etheria) of Aquitaine, about the year 385, describes the chanting at the Church of the Holy Sepulchre (the Anastasis) built at Jerusalem by Constantine.[36] She mentions psalms, hymns, antiphons, responsories, and names the occasions on which they were used. She mentions also the presence of boy choristers.

St. John Chrysostom ("the golden-mouthed," 345–407), the most famous Greek Father, bishop of Constantinople, bears witness to the popularity of psalm-singing in the East.

If the faithful are keeping vigil in the church, David is first, middle and last. If at dawn any one wishes to sing hymns, David is first, middle and last. At funeral processions and burials, David is first, middle and last. In the holy monasteries, among the ranks of the heavenly warriors, David is first, middle and last. In the convents of virgins, who are imitators of Mary, David is first, middle and last.[37]

He explains why psalms are sung rather than recited, thus:

When God saw that many men were lazy, and gave themselves only with difficulty to spiritual reading, He wished to make it easy for them, and added the melody to the Prophet's words, that all being rejoiced by the charm of the music, should sing hymns to Him with gladness.[38]

In a commentary sometimes attributed to him there is a passage about music in daily life: about nurses who, walking up and down singing, lull to sleep the eyelids of the babes in their arms; about waggoners who, driving their yoked animals at noon and singing to them, ease the hardship of the road with their songs; about peasants who sing while cultivating their vines and gathering and treading the grapes; about sailors who sing while pulling at the oars; about women singing as they weave and separate the tangled threads.[39] Chrysostom shows warm interest in musical activity. Not all music, however, earns his approval. He deplores the tendency of the young to indulge in "songs and dances of Satan, like cooks, and caterers, and [professional] musicians; no one knoweth any psalm, but it seems a thing to be ashamed of even, and a mockery, and a joke." [40] Even Chrysostom felt the need of inveighing against pagan songs for fear they might taint the flock.

Theodoret (*c.* 386–*c.* 457), bishop of Cyrrhus, a small city between Antioch and the Euphrates, mentions a curious form of antiphonal psalm-singing used at a monastery housing both Greeks and Syrians: each group sang in its own

---

[35] MigneL XXXII, 769; Nicene & Post-N, Ser. 1, I, 134.
[36] See HeraS, 28 (Latin) or BernS, 45 (English) or DuchC, 492, 541 (Latin and English).
[37] GerC I, 64; WagE I, 9.   [38] MigneG LV, 156; WagE I, 10.   [39] MigneG LV, 156.
[40] MigneG LXII, 361; Nicene & Post-N, Ser. 1, XIII, 301.

language, every verse being repeated antiphonally.[41] Theodoret has left a report of the accompanying of hymns with the clapping of hands and dance-movements.[42] In the East, religious chanting was often thus accompanied, and also with instruments. The apocryphal *Acts of John,* dating from before A. D. 170, imputes to Jesus and the apostles the accompanying of a hymn with a round-dance, the day before the Passion. The hymn-text, included in the apocryphal account, was in use not only among the Gnostics, with whom these *Acts* originated, but among the Manicheans and, as late as the 4th century, the Priscillianists. The text shows the music sung to it by the heretics to have been responsorial. Here are some of the lines, with the passage that introduces them:

Before I am delivered up . . . let us sing an hymn to the Father . . . He bade us therefore make as it were a ring, holding one another's hands, and himself standing in the midst he said: Answer Amen unto me. He began, then, to sing an hymn and to say:

  Glory be to thee, Father.
And we, going about in a ring, answered him: Amen. . . .
  Grace danceth. I would pipe [with the aulos—αὐλῆσαι ζέλω];
    dance ye all. Amen. . . .
  The whole on high hath part in our dancing. Amen.
  Whoso danceth not, knoweth not what cometh to pass. Amen.[43]

The welcome accorded music by the Christians for purposes of worship, though wide, was by no means universal. Thus, to take one example, the Egyptian abbot Pambo (*c.* 317–67) deplored the use of the art vehemently, but by the same token testified to its popularity:

Woe is upon us, O son, for the days are come in which monks shall relinquish the wholesome food given by the Holy Ghost, and seek after words and tunes. What repentance, what tears proceed from hymns? What repentance can there be in a monk who, whether situated in the church or in his cell, lifts up his voice like a bull? [44]

The various passages quoted and referred to represent activity over a wide area. They make much mention of the singing of psalms, hymns, and canticles, the terms being doubtless often used interchangeably. It has been contended, and not without good show of reason—though folk-song documents are, of course, lacking for comparison—that Christian Chant absorbed folk-song elements (*cf.* p. 57). If so, the scattered Christian communities must have contributed some local features other than those of a specifically Greek or Hebrew character, however widespread Hellenistic culture in particular may have been. Some of these features would have come from the West, some

---

[41] GerC I, 179.   [42] MigneG LXXXIII, 426.   [43] LipA II, 197f; transl. from JamesA, 253.
[44] GerS I, 3.

from the East. One must guard against overemphasizing Greek and Hebrew influences. Nevertheless, they operated in the fields of the liturgy, philosophy, and literary composition, and the history of these subjects would indicate by analogy—as do some of the cited passages directly—that they were not unfelt in the field of music also. In connection with the Roman Chant, at least, there is some actual melodic evidence that tends to support the inference (*cf.* pp. 114f). Whether other branches of Christian Chant can likewise supply such fairly good evidence, perhaps future investigation will show. In the meanwhile, we have at least a little information about these other bodies of Chant, and we shall now discuss them, turning backward occasionally in point of time.

Syrian Chant

SYRIA, a part of the Roman Empire, a neighbor of the Holy Land, and a scene of intense Christian activity, was an ideal center for the development of a Chant combining those basic elements that were to prove characteristic of Christian Chant generally.

The ancient Syrian melodies were not, it seems, usually committed to writing,[1] but transmitted by oral tradition. We therefore lack, in connection with these melodies, equivalents of the remarkable documents from which it has been possible for modern scholars to restore the Gregorian repertoire. But the Syrian Chant, as practiced today, has been a subject for learned investigation. It has not been possible to apply to the material collected the same sort of comparative methods as Idelsohn has applied to the Hebrew melodies, but it has been held "extremely probable" that, despite foreign ingredients, "there exists in the actual Syrian Chant a primitive fund" reaching back to the centuries in which the literary productions used in the liturgy itself were created.[2] This claim rests largely on the strange circumstance that, while the Syrians accepted the general civilization and Arabic language of their conquerors, the Syrian and Arabian musical systems allegedly differ widely. Dom Jeannin, the chief authority on Syrian Chant,[3] has contended that the Syrians would hardly have adopted a *new* system, *dissimilar* to the Arabian, after the invasion, and that the present system must therefore survive from before it. However this may be (the Syrian and Arabian systems do seem analogous in one respect; *cf.* p. 74), striking similarities have been pointed out between passages sung in the Syrian service and melodies from the old Gregorian

---

[1] Concerning an alleged Syrian notation dating from the 14th century, see GasM, 554. JeannO, 283, claims it is a type of Byzantine notation, used in certain Syrian translations of Byzantine liturgical books. See also WelleG, 95f.

[2] BonS, 593.

[3] JeannM contains a collection of melodies from Syria etc. together with extensive commentary. See also JeannC and JeannO.

repertoire;[4] and the influence of Syria upon the West, at least in the field of hymnody, is forcefully attested.

The ancient Syrian Chant drew upon the Palestinian, and in turn influenced not only the Byzantine and Armenian, but bodies of Chant in Italy and Southern France. Syrian custom especially favored antiphony. The ascetics Flavian and Diodoros are credited with having introduced [5] it into the orthodox Christian practice of Antioch in the 4th century when, to combat the Arian heresy, they sought to make the services more attractive by assigning the chanting of the psalm-verses to the congregation. Its members were divided into two semi-choruses, one of men, one of women and children, and the groups alternated with one another in the singing of the psalm-verses and combined in singing an Alleluia or, perhaps, some new refrain. The intercalating of passages of song between psalm-verses became, in the course of time, an organized practice and was destined to be imitated with telling effect in the West. Among the Syrians, the interpolation was called an *enyana*.

Syrian sacred poetry and music flourished particularly from the 3rd to the 7th century, and together gave rise to several forms. These favored the alternation of passages for soloists and chorus, i. e. they favored responsorial singing, itself a species of antiphony. Two forms, the metrical homily, named *madrāshē* (ode), and the *sugyāthā* (hymn), may be singled out to illustrate the uses to which the Syrians put this type of singing: the former consisted of a number of strophes for a soloist with an invariable refrain for chorus, while in the latter the dialogue was carried on by a soloist and two choruses.

The Syrian bent for offering praise in the shape of poetry with an organized rhythmical structure—in these two forms as well as others—led to important results. There was almost certain to be a difference—and one actually existed —between the style of musical settings of prose passages (or, if one will, *unversified* poetry) from the Bible, such as the psalms, and the style of settings in which a system of prosody was followed. The prosody favored by the Syrians was founded not on the ancient metrical law of quantity but on the principle of a line in which a tonically accented syllable alternated with 1 or 2 (rarely 3) unaccented syllables, correspondence between lines being obtained through equality not in the total number of syllables in each but in the number of tonic accents. Thus, if a poem of several stanzas was sung to one musical strophe, adjustments often had to be made in the melody from one stanza to another. If a line had one or more syllables too much or too little for the melody, the necessary number of light beats was added or suppressed, the number of accented beats remaining constant. If an air was well liked, it might serve not only the different stanzas of one poem but any number of different poems, provided the verse-pattern was the same. In other words, it might become a stock-melody. An air, subjected to rhythmical adaptation to

---

[4] See, for example, BesM, 34f; BonS, 597f.   [5] For the circumstances, see GasO, 50.

fit texts similarly versified according to Syrian standards, was known as a *ris-qolo*. Through the application of prosody to expressions of devotion, the word "hymn," formerly applied in a general sense to spiritual songs, eventually came to signify, for the most part, *versified* "poetry intended to be sung in praise of Christian truths or events." [6] The singing of hymns with texts in verse form became highly popular and spread from Syria to Europe.

In their structure, the hymns seem to have been affected by both Semitic and Hellenic traits. The parallelism present in the verses (and reflected in the music by means of repetitions, if Syrian Chant as now practiced bears trustworthy witness) recalls the Hebrew forms described on p. 10). But the rather strict co-ordination of notes and syllables, melismas being generally absent from the hymns, though not necessarily from other Syrian forms, may show a Hellenic influence (*cf.* p. 51).

EXAMPLE 8. Sugyāthā on the Massacre of the Innocents (after JeannM II, 388).

"The children were slain because of Thy Child. O Lord, strike those who have killed our Lord, O Lord of Kings. The tyrant who is scheming to kill the hostages, confound him; conspire to kill him.

"O heavenly hierarchy, receive the hostages who approach to meet you. Blessed be the Lord who crowned them." (Translation and transliteration by Joshua Bloch.)

The chief hymn-writer of Syria was St. Ephraim (d. 373), whose hymn-texts are among the oldest still in liturgical use. Certain early accounts state that the aim of St. Ephraim was to substitute orthodox words for those contained in the popular and liturgical songs of the heretics, while preserving melodies already in existence—that is, while using them as *ris-qolé*. Evidently St. Ephraim was less concerned about the power of music as a contaminator (*cf.* the attitudes of Clement of Alexandria etc.) than about its value as an aid in proselytizing: familiar airs might attract converts and become the carriers of sacred truths (*cf.* the attitude of St. Basil). The originators of the melodies he borrowed, therefore, were probably the Gnostics.[7] The teach-

---

[6] WagE I, 37.

[7] For a full discussion of this point, see JeannM, Chap. 9 (*St. Ephrem a-t-il utilisé les airs de Bardesane ou d'Harmonius?*). See also QuasM. St. Ephraim's activity having followed Constantine's edict of toleration, his reasons for borrowing would presumably not have been those mentioned by Wellesz (*cf.* the quotation on p. 71) as having obtained during the earlier years.

ings of their leader of the previous century, Bardesanes, were among the main targets of Ephraim's attacks. The saint himself wrote, unintentionally complimenting Bardesanes's musical skill:

In the resorts of Bardesanes   *Loved sweet music,*
There are songs and melodies.   *By the harmony of his songs*
For seeing that young persons   *He corrupted their minds.*

(Transl. from JulD, 1110)

Like this alleged corrupter, Mani (b. *c.* 215), familiar with Greek thought, was a poet-musician as well as a spiritual leader. Mani, active in Persia among other countries, is indeed (to paraphrase BesM, 48f) the only great founder of a religion to show a lively personal relationship to art. He expressly demanded that his adherents cultivate poetry, music, and painting, and for centuries they considered him the "inventor of the lute." [8] The teachings of Manicheism were also to be found in a collection of liturgical hymns, while Bardesanes created a book of 150 songs on the model of the psalter. His son, Harmonios, educated in Athens, apparently continued his father's poetical and musical activities. Literary accounts mention a number of other hymn-writers of Greek education, such as the Egyptian Gnostic, Valentinos, and the Alexandrian, Areios, founder of Arianism, and it is fair to assume that Syrian ecclesiastical *poetry* likewise was strongly influenced by Hellenistic traditions, even if the presence of parallelism, already mentioned, shows an Oriental influence also. The outstanding Syriac hymn-writers other than St. Ephraim were Narses, active at Edessa towards the end of the 5th century, and Jacob of Serugh (451–521), called by his contemporaries "the Harp of the believing Church." Of special interest are the nine surviving hymn-texts of the potter, Simeon of Gesir (1st half, 6th century): each of Simeon's poems, according to the 8th- or 9th-century MS that preserves them, is to be sung to a presumably standard melody, which is specifically named. [9]

A preponderance of Hellenic influence upon the *music,* as distinguished from the poetry, has been claimed, [10] mainly on the grounds that (1) melismas are short when they do occur, a syllabic style being more common, and that (2) the periodic structure and the frequent rounding-off of the whole by a repetition of the beginning (as in Example 8) give the impression of a rational form recalling Greek rather than Oriental models. If, for the sake of discussion, we concede the antiquity of the surviving Syrian Chant, we may perhaps grant the first argument (though not necessarily so, in view of the circumstance that the extremely elaborate melismas characteristic of much Synagogue music today are apparently not ancient—*cf.* p. 9). The second

[8] Concerning the use, in connection with certain Manichean hymns, of a primitive notation, consisting of dots and circles placed at differing heights alongside the words, see WelleD, 127, and the writings cited in GéroP, 210.
[9] See EurN.   [10] See BesM, 48f.

argument raises serious doubts. We know no more of well-rounded form, as currently understood, in ancient Greek musical composition than in Hebrew (*cf.* p. 50). In fact, if we search in the literature of the ancients for some hint of organized formal construction in their music, we shall find it in the Oriental parallelism to which we have already referred quite as much as in the strophe and antistrophe schemes of the Greek tragic choruses.

As Wellesz has pointed out: [11]

Christianity started in one of the border provinces of the Roman Empire. . . . This province was administered by a Græco-Roman governing class, the population consisting of a mixture of Aramæans, Cappadocians and Armenians, as well as the Jews. Since Christianity was at first a popular faith in direct opposition to the authorities, it was natural that the art which developed with the new ritual should be to a large extent the product of native artists. The future study of music will have to reckon with this fact. . . .

It is most likely . . . that [many of] the new songs were sung to familiar tunes. . . . A period of real creative musical activity cannot have begun until . . . later, when Christianity had gained strength and Christian ritual had begun to develop. This activity first showed itself in Syria and Armenia.

The activity certainly received some impetus from Hellenistic sources but one should not, as Wellesz indicates, overestimate the influence they exerted upon Syrian Chant, at the expense of that exerted by the Orient. It is true that Hellenism formed a thin upper stratum in Syria, Palestine, and Egypt, that the life along the caravan-trails was Hellenistic well on towards Turkestan and India; but the hinterland and the great masses of tribes and peoples remained untouched.[12] Efforts to determine the relative extent of the Greek and Oriental influences—a point over which there has been some controversy—are in large part futile: our knowledge of the ancient music is too fragmentary.

The consideration of early Christian music becomes still more difficult when viewed from the theoretical aspect. More important to some scholars than such evidence as that provided by the Greek vowel combinations, in attempts at tracing the theory of Christian Chant, are the old reports concerning the Syrian *Oktoechos*. Here we are confronted with something that definitely had a connection with the use of music by the early Christians, but unfortunately they, like their successors, used the term "Oktoechos" [13] in several different senses, and this has offered wishful thinking an opportunity, of which perhaps full advantage has been taken, once again to read into surviving evidence more than its indications warrant.

Etymologically, "Oktoechos" suggests indirectly the idea of eight musical formulas of some sort. However, since the Greeks—at least those of Antiquity —did not use "echos" to designate a scale-species (to them it meant "sound")

[11] WelleB, 6. [12] See WachsU, 90.
[13] Or the Syriac equivalent of this Greek term—"Ikhadias."

there is no reason to assume, as has sometimes been done, that the eight formulas were modal in the scalar sense. A group of eight adaptable melody-types would seem to fill the bill, and we shall find confirmation of such an interpretation in our section on Byzantine Chant. Even if not scalar, a codification of eight echoi, if undertaken for specifically musical reasons, would have testified to the presence of activity in the field of musical theory. It is clear that a codification existed, and the term "Oktoechos" received one of its several meanings by being applied to it, but whether it was at first made for specifically musical reasons is doubtful, as will presently be shown. Other applications of the term were (1) to the oldest collection of songs for liturgical purposes, not taken from the Bible—this was an important use; (2) to the book containing the collection; and (3) to the season of the church year corresponding to the time after Pentecost. The interpretations here given draw upon both Syrian and Byzantine usage.

The earliest known mention of the Oktoechos is a reference to the song collection and is found in the *Plerophoriai,* an important source of church history, written about A. D. 515 by John, bishop of Maiuma (now El Mineh), the port of Gaza. The analogous Byzantine collection, although younger than the Syrian, may suitably be touched upon in this discussion also, since it seems to cast light upon its forerunner.[14]

Syrian evidence tends to show that the melodic formulas, applied to the texts in the song collection, were classified according to their symbolical significance and that it was in relation to this significance that they were assigned their liturgical function. The Syrians, in their efforts to ascribe universal meaning to everything, tried to relate the eight echoi to the four qualities of cold, warmth, dampness, and dryness. Each of the echoi was felt to have one or two of these qualities, and the nature of the qualities determined the choice of the echos for a particular holiday. Information on the subject is preserved in the account [15] of Bar'-Ebhraja (Bar Hebraeus) (1226–86), claiming to report the correspondences perceived by the "inventors of the art of the echoi." The account gives no information concerning the musical structure of the echoi, it does not infer that they differed from one another for specifically musical—that is, technical—reasons, and makes no reference to scale doctrine.

John of Maiuma's mention of the Oktoechos is made in an anecdote about a monk who complains that he is plagued by indifference and sleepiness and that, when he rises at night, he cannot recite a psalm without chanting an echos. In reply, Silvanos—a 4th-century Palestinian abbot who evidently was a kindred soul of Pambo's—tells him that song hardens the heart. The monk

---

[14] For the evidence supporting the priority of the Syrian collection, see WachsU, 99, and the work there cited.

[15] Translated into French in JeannM I, 21: JeannO, 284. Roman Christianity indulged in similar speculations (see AbD).

rejoins, "Since I have been a monk, I sing the Office of the Canon and the Hours and the contents of the Oktoechos." Silvanos has no doubt that the monk's addiction to song is the reason why contrition has fled from him, and condemns in general the singing of echoi etc. The tale [16] is of interest since the monk, by classing the Oktoechos together with the Office of the Canon and the Hours, indicates that it was looked upon as a sort of breviary, while, in almost the same breath, he has referred to an echos as something to which one may sing a text—"echos" being used by him not, so far as appears, as a term with a technical significance, but merely as a term for a melody. In other words, he seems to distinguish between the Oktoechos as a kind of prayer-book and the Oktoechos as a collection of songs arranged from a musical standpoint, and, at the same time, to hint that some relationship existed between the two aspects.

A Byzantine treatise on music, the *Hagiopolites* ("From the Holy City"), [17] attributes the invention of the eight echoi underlying Byzantine Chant—four authentic (*kyrioi,* i. e. lords) and four plagal (i. e. collateral) —to St. John of Damascus (d. 754). That echoi, whether similar or dissimilar to those of the Byzantines, existed before his time, has already been shown. His position as an inventor doubtless rests on legend; but since, as we shall see, he was an active organizer, he may conceivably have been responsible for the division of the echoi into two classes. This, however, would not necessarily imply that he made a division for specifically musical reasons as, apparently, did the theorists of the West (*cf.* p. 153), or that, like such theorists from the 10th century on, he was dealing with scalar modes rather than with formulas. The division may easily have followed some symbolical principle.[18] St. John of Damascus is further credited with having set down in a book called the "Oktoechos," in accordance with the eight echoi, the chants for a cycle of eight Sundays. The account is of interest since it indicates that the arrangement of an eight-week liturgical cycle helped to give the Byzantine collection its typical stamp, and especially since it is not unlikely that the echos selected for each of the eight occasions was chosen for the sake of the suitability with which its supposed significance endowed it.

A final piece of evidence is furnished by a collection of hymns originally written in Greek by Severos of Antioch and others, and freely translated into Syriac (*c.* 619–29) by Paul, bishop of Edessa. Jacob of Edessa revised

---

[16] Fully given in QuasM, 151. See also JeannM, 93; JeannO, 98; or, more particularly (with regard to the implications), WachsU, 82.

[17] Although itself dating from about the 14th century, the treatise is largely a compilation from earlier sources. "Hagiopolites" is applied not only to the treatise but to its anonymous author. There is no complete scholarly edition of it at present. Extracts of the portions dealing with Byzantine music may be found in ThibM, 57ff, GasB, 18ff, 31; etc.; of those dealing with ancient Greek music, in VincN, 259. For further information, see GasI, HöegB, GomS II, 28f.

[18] *Cf.* the passage on p. 86 *infra,* concerning the likelihood that growth towards scalar modes was a rather late development in Byzantine music.

the translation (*c. 675*), inserting literal translations etc. Jacob's text, the oldest that survives, reaches us in two MSS that apparently preserve his own order, and in about forty later MSS in which the contents are disposed in a variety of ways. All these arrangements differ from the one ascribed to Jacob, which falls into three sections and has a liturgical significance. Nothing shows it to have been planned from a musical viewpoint also, but a few pieces bear numbers—apparently later additions—indicating the echoi to which they were to be sung. (There is no actual music.) Nos. 1–4 refer to authentic echoi; nos. 5–8, to plagal echoi. In the later MSS—some from the turn of the 9th century—"hymns are arranged according to the eight Tones [echoi] to which they are set, whence the collection is often known as the Octoechus."[19] The Jacobean version, obviously, does not merit this designation. The later MSS do not ignore liturgical significance; the new feature is that within a group—devoted, for example, to the dead or to the resurrection—the hymns are arranged by echos, each authentic being paired with its plagal so that the usual order is 1, 5; 2, 6; 3, 7; 4, 8.[20] The fact that eight echoi could control the arrangement of the hymns shows that the tonal Oktoechos had at last achieved sufficient independence to be looked upon as a purely musical entity apart from the liturgical function it still continued to serve.

On the basis of all this evidence, modern scholars have arrived at varying conclusions.

Jeannin and Puyade see in the Oktoechos an imitation of the system of Aristoxenos,[21] a classification made by theorists from a definitely musical standpoint, the result to some extent codifying scalar characteristics. This opinion does not prevent these writers from seeing in Syrian music a preponderant Oriental influence: the echoi, they claim, were, during the first centuries of Christianity, *tonalités populaires;* Hebrew and other Oriental music, even if themselves affected by Hellenistic culture, must have retained their distinctive character; it was the idea of classifying according to "modes" that constituted the chief appropriation from Greek sources, though it is also true that a Greek origin may be attributed to some of the music itself.[22] Besseler likewise sees in the Syrian tonal Oktoechos a theoretical system. Although he considers Hellenistic influences to have been stronger than Semitic in shaping Syrian Chant, he observes no trace of Greek scale-doctrine in the Oktoechos, at least as practiced today, finding in it only a group of melodic formulas analogous to the Arabian system of *maqams.* He believes that the original systematization was completed by the year 500 and that it furnished the foundation of church-mode theory, or at least the stimulus leading to its formulation.[23]

The actual literary evidence affords no basis on which to claim that the original Syrian Oktoechos derived its form from Greek or any other scale

[19] BrooksJ, 6. This work contains the hymn-texts and commentary.   [20] See WrightS II, 345ff.
[21] IeannO, 283.   [22] JeannO, 98, 282, 287f, 292.   [23] BesM, 49, 53.

theory or, for that matter, from any purely musical consideration. The melodies were doubtless assigned their places in the Oktoechos according to such symbolical meanings as were attached to them and as ostensibly rendered them suitable for particular liturgical occasions.

As long as the practice of music remains within the sphere of worship it receives order and function therefrom. Cosmic ideas penetrate here as in all artistic and liturgical expressions of the cult. The typical restriction to and canonization of a few motives, as the cult knows them, take possession of it [the practice] and determine its arrangement independently of specifically musical aspects.[24]

In time, the motives become accepted as entities by themselves, as the groupings in the MSS of the hymns of Severos indicate, and acquire a specifically musical status. To the mystical value of the melodic outlines is added an artistic one, but they are not yet necessarily, or even with likelihood, recognized as conforming to particular scales. The old Syrian Oktoechos, therefore, occupies a position in that portion of the history of modes that deals with their early phase, when a repertoire of melody-types or formulas is being organized but scale-doctrine is still something to be deduced. The Syrian echoi—which, roughly speaking, may be regarded as eight specially favored *ris-qolé*—are like ancient Greek nomoi before the heyday of the theorists. Those who feel that the principle of the Oktoechos eventually contributed to the organization of Gregorian modal theory may easily be right. We share this view, and shall return to its discussion in Chapter 6.[25]

Some mention of rhythm in Syrian Chant, apart from that of its poetry, will be made in Chapter 5.

Byzantine Chant

WHEN, in A.D. 328, Constantine the Great founded New Rome—Constantinople—he provided the Empire not only with a bulwark in the East, but with a great metropolis that was to prove a melting pot. Here Hellenic and Oriental forces merged, while the influence of Old Rome did not go unfelt and that of triumphant Christianity helped to mould the diverse elements into a new and brilliant whole. Hence, although the site of the capital of the Roman Empire in the East for more than eleven centuries was that of Byzantium—an ancient Greek town, several times destroyed and rebuilt—and although the old name remained in use alongside the new and the language of the place was Greek, medieval Byzantine culture was in no true sense a continuation of that of ancient Greece. An interest in Antiquity persisted but, in the words of a modern historian,

[24] WachsU, 98. WachsU 78–100 treats the problem of the Oktoechos in considerable detail.
[25] Concerning a Georgian Oktoechos, see JeannM I, 9; concerning a Serbian Oktoechos, WelleO. Further concerning the Syrian Oktoechos, see WelleG, 101f.

"Classical culture . . . at Constantinople . . . was preserved in cold storage." One should therefore guard against assuming too close a connection between Byzantine music and that of ancient Greece, and should, instead, recognize the likelihood of a connection between it and the music of the Near East. For, if Syria was subjected to Hellenistic influences, she in turn affected their source.

The mistaken view that Byzantine civilization was decadent from birth long caused scholars to neglect its music, as well as certain other intellectual manifestations, and it is only recently that a serious effort has been made to explore the riches of its Chant.[1] The fact is that, with the decline of Old Rome, cultural activity, of the type favored by a sophisticated society, found its most hospitable haven in Byzantium, until the West at the time of the Renaissance—itself possibly a result, in part, of Byzantine culture transplanted westward by Byzantine refugees, fleeing before a succession of military onslaughts—was once more qualified to offer it shelter. A real decline did not set in until the 11th century, before which, except in the days of Charlemagne, the Byzantine Empire was the first Power in Europe.

With the exception of some acclamations addressed to the Emperor, the documents do not preserve any secular music. It is possible, however, that Balkan folk-song has saved at least some of it.[2] Moreover, the dividing line between the sacred and the secular in medieval music may not have been very sharp in Byzantium, where theological disputes, often violent, were part and parcel of the average man's activity. The acclamations were addressed to the Emperor on various occasions—upon his returning victorious from war; upon his coming from his chambers into the full assembly at Christmas, when the ceremonies were especially elaborate; upon his entering the Hippodrome, when he was greeted antiphonally by the Greens and Blues. The music of these tributes followed fairly stereotyped patterns. Here is a quite late example (15th century) addressed to one of the family of the Palaiologoi, the monarchs who ruled the Empire from 1260 to its fall in 1453:

---

[1] Most investigation before the 20th century concerned itself not with the genuine Byzantine music but with its modern successor, provided by the Chrysanthine system (see p. 85). While valuable pioneer work has been done by other scholars also, the chief contributions to a study of the medieval art have been made by Fleischer, Gastoué, Gombosi, Tillyard, and Wellesz. The two latter (to whose work, as to that of Gombosi, the present section of this book is especially indebted), together with Höeg, are in the process of editing the MMB which, when completed, will constitute a truly monumental series, presenting original MSS in facsimile, besides transcriptions and commentary as well as publications relating to bodies of music closely linked with that of Byzantium. Facsimiles (of individual pages) may be found also in PetO, TibyB, WelleM, etc.

[2] A perhaps not too far-fetched deduction to make from the fact that certain established formulas of Byzantine Chant are found in examples of the *Colinde* (Roumanian Noëls) etc. See PetO, 31.

EXAMPLE 9. Acclamation to the Emperor John VI Palaiologos (from TillM, 206).

"Many be the years of the sovereigns! Many be the years of John, the most religious king and emperor of the Romans, the Palaeologus, and of Mary, the most religious Empress. Many be the years of Joseph, the most holy Oecumenical Patriarch!"[3] (Transl. from TillB, 59)

Kitharas and auloi continued in use in Byzantium. But organs—at first hydraulic, later pneumatic—are the instruments that apparently figured most prominently. Two small portable organs are carved on the obelisk of Theodosios, as part of a bas-relief[4] showing the Emperor at the Hippodrome, wreath in hand, waiting to crown the victorious charioteer. The Ceremonial Book (*Concerning the Ceremonies of the Byzantine Court*)[4a] of the Emperor Constantine Porphyrogenetes reports that on May 31, 946, Saracen ambassadors were received at the imperial palace to negotiate the exchange of prisoners. To grace the occasion, three portable organs were set in place, a golden organ to accompany the ceremonies of the Empress, and two silver organs intended for the antiphonal performance of the *polychronion*—that is, the acclamation addressed to the Emperor. In two niches, behind curtains, singers from the Church of the Holy Apostles and from St. Sophia ("The Church of the Holy Wisdom") lifted their voices in song.

What the nature of instrumental accompaniment was in Byzantine music, whether it followed the vocal line faithfully or indulged in heterophonic

[3] John VI was the next to the last Eastern Emperor; Mary was his third wife; the Patriarch Joseph II died at Florence in 1439. The figures of John and Joseph are included in Benozzo Gozzoli's famous mural in the Riccardi Palace, Florence. For an article on the acclamation of Emperors, see TillE. (It is likely that Tillyard would revise some of his earlier transcriptions, made to agree with the modal views of Gaisser.)   [4] For a photograph, see WelleM, 82.
[4a] Since this book first appeared, Jacques Handschin has printed his monograph, *Das Zeremonienwerk Kaiser Konstantins und die sangbare Dichtung*, 1942.

embroidery, we do not know. It may easily, at different times, have done both these things and more in a history as long as that of Byzantium. But we do know that the organ was widely used, both as a solo and as an ensemble instrument, at marriages, festivals, and countless other public occasions, though not in the Church where unaccompanied singing of the Chant was obligatory.[5] No instrumental music survives.

It is with the Chant that most of our knowledge of Byzantine music is concerned. The 4th century saw the Greek liturgy improved by St. Basil (*cf.* p. 63), and from this event some writers choose to date the beginnings of Byzantine Chant.

The hymns of the Byzantine Church are Eastern Christianity's most distinctive contribution to music and poetry. Some of them appear to have been translations of Syriac hymns and to have retained their original melodies. As in Syria, intercalations were made between psalm-verses and gained widespread favor. The psalm-verse was called a *stichos* (plural, *stichoi*) and the intercalation—corresponding to the Syrian *enyana*—a *troparion*. In the course of time the *troparia* were greatly lengthened, and, as a result, it became customary to add them to only the last three to six verses rather than to all. The new after-songs were called *stichera* or *epihymnia* and fell into several divisions: such as borrowed their rhythm and melody from a pre-existent work were known as *prosomoia;* such as had their own were called *automela* if they served as models for further pieces, or *idiomela* if they remained unique. It is interesting to note that hymns not sung to a borrowed melody, "with much monotony of text, show the utmost freedom and variety of rhythm, the inference being that the music was felt to be more important than the words."[6] A collection of *stichera* was called a *sticherarion,* the greater part of the contents consisting of *idiomela.* Another important collection was the *hirmologion* containing the music for the kanons (of which more presently). The first strophe of each ode in the kanon set the model for the rhythm, melody, and number of syllables of the others and was named the *hirmos.*[7] It was thus the Byzantine counterpart of the *ris-qolo.* The contents of the *hirmologia* were classified according to the eight echoi and tended, as is perhaps to be expected in view of their eventual choice as melody-types, to be less elaborate than those of the *sticheraria.* Hymns, as a result of the Byzantine enthusiasm for them, prevented psalmody from achieving the same prominence in the

[5] See, however, the point raised in WelleD, 128.
[6] TillB, 11. This is the standard work on Byzantine hymnography. JulD, 456-66, offers helpful information on texts and, incidentally, on liturgy.
[7] Modern scholars long thought that the hymn-texts were written in somewhat stylized prose, until it was shown in PitraH—a pioneer philological work—that they were based not on quantity but on accent etc. The accent, however—unlike that of ancient Greek (or Syriac)—, was one of stress rather than of pitch.

music of the Greek Church as it enjoyed in the Western. Nevertheless, that Hebrew influence was probably present, is testified to, among other things, by the Byzantine legend ascribing the four kyrioi (*cf.* p. 73) to David and the four plagal echoi to Solomon.

Among the early Greek hymn-texts is the famous *Phos hilaron* ("O gladsome light," in Longfellow's translation) which still serves as a Vesper Hymn in the Greek Church. Modern Greek liturgical books attribute it to Sophronios (bishop of Jerusalem, 629), but St. Basil quoted it as early as the 4th century, as of unknown date and authorship. While we no longer have for this poem any setting whose antiquity can be proved, the liturgical melody in most common use bears a resemblance to two old airs whose age can be approximately fixed.[8] A few hymnodists of the time of the Council of Chalcedon (451) are known by name. Somewhat later Romanos, a converted Jew born in Syria and active at Constantinople during the reign (491–518) of Anastasios I, produced hymns, many modelled after St. Ephraim's, that rank him as the greatest Byzantine poet and caused the title *Melodos* ("Maker of Songs") to be applied to him: until the second half of the 9th century, poet and musician (where a new melody was used) were usually one person. According to one version of a legend, the Virgin, appearing to Romanos in a vision, ordered him to eat a scroll, and he, following her command, found himself endowed with the power of writing works of the kind called *kontakia,* his first effort in the form becoming the most famous Christmas hymn of the Eastern Church. The prototype of the *kontakion* is to be found in the Syrian *sugyāthā.* It consists of 18 or 24 strophes that are constructed alike and an introductory strophe or two that are often different in meter from the others. Romanos conveys his name by means of an acrostic consisting of the first letter of each stanza, and at the end of each there is a refrain. The *kontakia,* based mostly on biblical passages and performed at the greater holidays—such as Christmas, Easter, or Pentecost—were virtually poetic sermons, often employing dramatic effects. The form flourished not only in the 6th century, but again in the 9th.[9] Justinian the Great (483–565), besides bringing about the consolidation of the *Corpus juris* and the recovery from the barbarians of Northern Africa, Italy, and a part of Spain, found time to be active as a hymnwright.[10] The *Corpus juris* itself bears witness to Justinian's interest in music, containing as it does a provision for a choir of 25 singers at St. Sophia, a law against the appearance of church singers in the theatres, and other regulations touching

---

[8] See GasZ, 12; PetO vii, 61 (of commentary), 11 (of music).

[9] For fuller information see TillB, 11; WelleM, 29; TibyB, 133ff; etc. Concerning the dramatic effects, see LapB, 174, 180f.

[10] The text of the Hymn of Justinian is conveniently available in Greek and English in JulD, 460. Or see ChristA, 52.

upon the art.[11] Sergios, patriarch of Constantinople in the reign of Heraklios (610–41), wrote a celebrated Akathistos Hymn showing some kinship to the odes of Romanos. (The term "akathistos" simply indicated that the hymn was to be sung standing, in distinction to the *kathismata,* which were sung sitting.) This work was composed as a thanksgiving offering to the Virgin for her defense of Constantinople against Chosroës II, king of Persia. It is still sung today even though Sergios belonged to the Monothelites, who advanced the doctrine—disapproved by the Orthodox Church—that Christ had only one will, as the Monophysites contended he had only one nature. It was under Heraklios that, despite the auspicious beginning of his reign, the Empire lost Syria, Palestine, and Egypt to the Saracens, owing partly to the disaffection of the inhabitants whose support of Monophysitism, and other unorthodox views, expressed not only religious dissent but national sentiment antagonistic to the Greeks and thus advantageous to the Mohammedans. The time of Romanos and Sergios is the Golden Age of Byzantine hymnody. But the Iconoclastic strife arrested the type of artistic activity they represented and caused much of their work to be lost. When the cloud lifted, orthodoxy had triumphed, the ritual had been rearranged, and hymns in a new form had taken the place of the *kontakia.* While the writers of the *kontakia* had been musicians as well as poets, the writers in the new form generally used existing melodies.

The chief exponents of the new form, the *kanon,* are St. Andrew of Crete (*c.* 650–730), St. John of Damascus, and St. Kosmas of Jerusalem (d. *c.* 760). Of these, the second made the most distinguished contributions to hymnography, and is especially important theologically for his *Accurate Exposition of the Orthodox Faith,* an organized system founded on the Church Fathers and the teachings of the Councils from the 4th to the 7th century, the result embodying the theological thought of the early Greek Church. John of Damascus is a saint in both the Greek and Roman Churches, the schism between them not having taken definite shape until 1054, although much strife flared up before then. Theoretically, the *kanon* consisted of nine odes, each embracing several strophes, usually four. All strophes in a single ode followed the same rhythmical plan. The nine odes corresponded to the nine chief canticles of the Old and New Testaments [12]—that is, those regarded as "canonical"—and each ode was expected to refer in some way to the canticle it represented. In actual practice, most *kanones* consisted of eight odes, the second being generally omitted.[13] While philologists prefer the *kontakia,*

---

[11] For more details, see GasM, 544.

[12] 1. The Song of Moses (Ex. XV), 2. Moses's Exhortation (Deut. XXXII), 3–6. The Canticles of Hannah (I Sam. II), Habakkuk (Hab. III), Isaiah (Is. XXVI), and Jonah (Jon. III), 7. the earlier portion of the Prayer of the Three Children, 8. the remainder of this Prayer, and 9. the Magnificat.

[13] See WelleM, 32.

the *kanones,* it is clear from their popularity, more perfectly suited the 8th-century spirit.

Nothing definite is known of the origin of this new form. . . . In any case the kanon exemplifies one principle . . . of . . . importance for the whole of Eastern art—namely the principle of reiteration and variation, whether it be of a thought, of a pictorial representation, or of a musical idea. . . . The European creates a work of art with a view to one single, short, intensely passionate moment of æsthetic appreciation: the Oriental repeats the representation, or provides it with almost unnoticeable variations, so that the appreciation of it becomes a form of meditation. This principle of variation may have worked its way into the Byzantine liturgy and the Kanon poetry under the influence of the new ideas made current by the development of the power of Islam, but the tendency was already there, and was merely accentuated. . . . When the odes of the Kanons took the place of the canticles, they were considered as earthly symbols of the heavenly hymns, in the same way as the singers symbolised the angels. Therefore, . . . they had still to be variations of the old canticles. There was no question of a free, individualistic handling of a theme. . . . The same is true of the music. . . . The composer did not have to compose an entirely different tune for a new kanon: his task was rather that of a modest artisan who wished to add to an admired model something which seemed permissible to him as an intensification, a beautifying, or a small variation. The melodies sung in church were, to the composer and congregation, imitations of the hymns sung in God's praise by inspired saints and martyrs; these hymns in their turns imitating the divine canticles sung unceasingly by the angels in heaven.[14]

Among the more important contemporaries and immediate successors of the *kanon*-writers were St. Germanos (645–745),[15] the gifted nun Kasia (9th century), and the hymnwrights of the school of the Studion (the famous monastery at Constantinople), which included St. Theophanes (759–c. 842)—called *Ho Graptos* because, as an orthodox defender of the Images, he was branded on the forehead by the Iconoclast Emperor Theophilos—and the Emperor Leo VI (reigned 886–917), misnamed "the Wise." [16]

One of Kasia's *stichera* [17] is of special interest because of its structure. It consists of three long phrases, each immediately repeated, and a final unrepeated phrase. In other words, it is in one of the varieties of the sequence form (*cf.* p. 188) which achieved widespread popularity in the West. On the basis of such evidence it has been asserted that the sequence spread to the West from Byzantium, but the claim can hardly be said to have been conclusively proved. In Kasia's *sticheron,* the parallelism in the music corresponds to parallelism in the text.

---

[14] WelleB, 10–13, the theory originating with Wellesz that the Byzantine hymns were sung in supposed imitation of angelic music.

[15] A few *idiomela* of his may be found in PetO. See p. 61, etc.

[16] For a study of Leo's Morning Hymns, including music, see TillL.

[17] For a study and the music of 9 of them, see TillA.

EXAMPLE 10. *Augoustou Monarkhesantos*—Sticheron in Sequence Form
—Kasia (Transcription from MS Koutloumousi 412 ff. 77–77ᵛ,
by Oliver Strunk).

"When Augustus became monarch upon earth,
　The multitude of kingdoms among men was ended.
And when Thou wast incarnate of the Holy One,
　The multitude of divinities among the idols was put down.
Beneath one universal empire have the cities come,
　And in one divine dominion the nations believed.
The folk were enrolled by the decrees of the emperor,
　We, the faithful, have been inscribed in the name of Deity.
　Oh, Thou our incarnate Lord,
　Great is Thy mercy, to Thee be glory."

(TillA, 427)

With the 9th-century division between the functions of musician and
poet, there is a frequent appearance of the direction: "To be sung to the
melody of ——." A poet of this period was no longer called, like Romanos,
a "maker of songs" but a "hymnographer."

The writing of sacred poetry spread to the Greek settlements in Sicily
and Southern Italy, but a check was placed upon it by the codification of
the Greek liturgy in the 11th century. The monastery of Basilians founded
in 1002 at Grottaferrata near Rome, however, remained richly productive
for another century. With the general decline of creativeness in Hellenistic
poetry, there occurred, in the 13th and 14th centuries, a resurgence in the
composition of music. The new melodies were more elaborate than the old
ones and were distinguished by a wealth of melismas, doubtless as a result
of the ever-increasing influence, upon Byzantium, of the Orient. The new
hymnwrights—who were affected by Slavic and Western influences also—
were known as "melurges" or "maistores" and included among their number

John Kukuzeles (fl. *c.* 1300), of whom more presently. Greek musical activity came to an abrupt halt with the fall of Constantinople, but revived in the 17th century. From 1660 to the end of the 18th century many of the old melodies were copied into new MSS, but too often with excessive elaboration—a result of Turkish influence—and other changes. Genuine medieval Byzantine music became buried under layers of accretions until modern scholars, chiefly in the 20th century, undertook the work of restoration.

On the basis of the existing MSS, Wellesz has concluded that some of the surviving Byzantine melodies actually date from the 6th century, that is, from the Golden Age of Byzantine hymnody. The conclusion is based on three main facts which, taken chronologically backwards, are that (1) we have Byzantine MSS in an independently decipherable notation starting with the end of the 11th or the beginning of the 12th century; (2) we have, starting with the 9th century, MSS in a notation which, while undecipherable, makes possible a "comparison of the same poem set to music" in the two notations, a comparison which "shows, by the simplicity of the signs and their grouping, that in each case the melody is [essentially] the same"; (3) the 9th-century *kanon*-writers borrowed their melodies from the 6th-century *kontakia*.[18]

In its long history, Byzantine music gave rise to several different types of notation, and, as may be expected, the periods when they were in use overlapped. While scholars are not wholly of one mind in codifying the types,[19] the following is a grouping that bids fair to be widely accepted:

1) *Ekphonetic notation.* This employed recitation or lection signs that indicated the rise and fall of the voice during the solemn reading of the Gospels and other biblical passages. These signs did not show the size of intervals and were useful only as reminders to executants who already knew the musical inflections hinted at. The signs were adapted from the Greco-Roman grammatical accents, which had been invented by Aristophanes of ancient Byzantium (d. *c.* 257 B.C.). A claim has been made in behalf of the ekphonetic notation as the source of the Latin neumes.[20] Although the oldest MS containing the notation dates from the 9th century, the state of the signs appearing in it is so developed that the notation is believed to be considerably older. It continued in use alongside more precise systems, but became obsolete by the 14th century.[21]

2) *Early Byzantine notation* (*c.* 950–1200). This employed neumes that were

---

[18] For a full discussion of the point, see WelleA. Or see WelleB, 13, or WelleT, 18.
[19] TillH, 17f. gives the differing terminology of several writers and points out the correspondences. Our list gives only a few of the equivalents.
[20] See ThibO.
[21] HöegN is the definitive work on ekphonetic notation. (See the last chapter thereof for a discussion of the possible interrelation between the Byzantine ekphonetic notation and the Hebrew masoretic accents.) ThibM (dealing also with the Hagiopolitan notation) and WelleL are other important works. Discussions of all the types of notation may be found in PetO, 36ff; TibyB, 67ff; TillB 37ff; WelleM, 39ff; etc.; perhaps most conveniently in Grove I, 520ff (by Tillyard).

outgrowths of the ekphonetic signs, which the neumes, in their two earliest stages, resembled in that they too served chiefly a mnemonic purpose; for, although they represented a higher stage of development, they still denoted intervals only approximately. The neumes included an archaic type, now often called Paleobyzantine; an intermediate type; and a more advanced type, called *notation mixte* or *constantinopolitaine*, or, after a famous MS notated in it, the Coislin type. It has been possible, with the help of parallel versions written in the middle notation—the next stage— to transcribe some melodies written in the Coislin System and, in fact, to determine the value of certain of its signs, some being common both to it and to its successor.[22]

3) *Middle or Round Notation* (1100–1450). This is decipherable in all essential respects, thanks largely to the survival of little manuals (belonging to the latter part of this period) for the instruction of church singers. These manuals are known as *Papadikai*.[23] They are much alike, and it is believed that they all go back to one common source, for which Kukuzeles may have been partly responsible. Usually they contain a list of signs with indications showing how the signs denote interval values,[24] together with exercises; and often they conclude with a short song of which the following is the not wholly ingenuous text:

Whoever wishes to learn music well enough to merit praise should be very patient, work many days, honor his teacher, and have plenty of money in his hands; thus he will arrive at perfection.

The signs used in the middle notation—which, in its non-employment of a staff, differs basically from our Western notation—have no pitch value in themselves. Each tone is indicated by means of a sign showing its distance and direction from the tone reached immediately before it, the first tone depending for its identification upon the theoretical starting-note of the echos. To make this note determinable, a signature, called a *martyria*, appears at the beginning and names the echos. Thus, if the echos is the first, in which the usual starting-note is a (*cf*. table on p. 89), and if the first tone of the piece is likewise a, the *martyria* for echos 1 is used and a repetition sign follows. If the first tone is not the usual starting-note, the *martyria* may be followed by whatever sign will show the distance and direction of the tone from that note. Or, since some *martyriai* have by-forms naming the echos but indicating a particular starting-note other than the usual one (thus, the usual starting-note of echos 3 is c but there is a so-called *mesos* showing that the first note is to be a), a by-form may be used instead. Or else an introductory passage or intonation (*cf*. below) may take the *martyria* as its point of departure and lead up melodically to the first tone of the piece proper. The signs for the first 4 of the 8 standard echoi are merely the Greek symbols for the numbers 1–4; the same symbols are used for the last 4 echoi but with the letters πλ—signifying "plagal"—prefixed. The middle system must have been more difficult than staff notation and had the

---

[22] For the most thoroughgoing discussion of the Coislin System, see TillN.

[23] For a Papadike printed in Greek with German translation, see FleiN III, *Teil* 3, 18. For another, dating from 1695, see VilloD, 426.

[24] A table of signs with explanation is conveniently available in Grove I, 521. TillH is the definitive work on the middle notation.

defect that if the singer made one mistake in performance all pitches sung by him subsequently would be wrong, unless, as sometimes happened, signatures were inserted medially as a check. The fact that the last pitch reached had normally to be one of the *finales* of the echos (*cf*. p. 89) acted, in any event, as a final check (a circumstance that is of obvious benefit to the modern transcriber). Interval signs denoting stepwise progressions were fancifully called "bodies" (*somata*) while those denoting leaps were called "spirits" (*pneumata*). (A repetition sign was neither a *soma* nor a *pneuma*.) Shifts from one echos to another were indicated by means of *phthorai,* or "modulants." The middle notation afforded rhythmic and some dynamic indications as well as intervallic signs, but less satisfactorily.[25] At that, rhythm is more clearly represented in the Byzantine MSS, as a body, than in the Gregorian.

4) *The Late Byzantine Notation* (1400–1821). This was merely an expansion of the middle notation, to the interval signs of which it added many subsidiary symbols, including rhythmic indications, abbreviations, etc. These were needed as a result of the elaboration in style mentioned above. The symbols had already been employed by Kukuzeles (after whom the late notation is sometimes called Kukuzelian) but did not come into general use until after his time. The syllables *te-re-rem* were often used in conjunction with meaningless florid passages. The significance of the formula has not been discovered; the practice is known as "teretism."

5) *The Modern or Chrysanthine Notation.* This lies outside the scope of the present book. It might be mentioned, however, that by the 17th century much confusion had arisen in the reading of the old MSS. At the beginning of the 19th century, Chrysanthos, a Greek archimandrite, codified the system that is still used in the Greek Church today. It aimed mainly at simplifying the older notation so that it could be printed, and added a useful solfeggio system.

The alchemist, Zosimos of Panopolis (now Akhmim) in Egypt, who flourished about A. D. 300, has been credited with a brief passage [26] from which several highly reputable modern scholars have made elaborate deductions. They have seen in it a connection with very early Christian music, although the existence of such a connection is not wholly clear; in fact, the attribution to Zosimos of the treatise containing the passage has been attacked by Otto Gombosi,[27] who believes that the work does not date from before the late 8th or early 9th century. The tract is essentially one on alchemy; music is treated only incidentally, being drawn upon to provide parallels

[25] Höeg, Tillyard, and Wellesz have reached a working agreement concerning the meanings of certain dynamic and rhythmic signs, a subject concerning which Wellesz has been particularly active. For their interpretation, see TillL, 115. The reader is cautioned against Riemann's interpretation of Byzantine rhythm and, in fact, against his writings on several other phases of Byzantine music as well. The opening portion of TibyB contains useful comments on the merits of works on Byzantine music.

[26] The original Greek appears in Marcelin Berthelot, *Collection des anciens alchimistes grecs* (in collaboration with Ch. E. Ruelle), Vol. II, 219, 434 (French translation, III, 212, 410). Or see HöegB, 331, or WachsU, 59.

[27] In an unpublished article which we are greatly indebted to him for having allowed us to consult.

for things closer to the basic subject. The system of pseudo-Zosimos is based on six series of four elements (represented by the Greek symbols for the numbers 1-4), producing a total of 24 entities; the formation of all hymns and other religious melodies, he says, is subject to various combinations of these entities.

Gastoué [28] believes that "Zosimos's" system was used in church music and sees in it an expansion from the 4 authentic tones, with their plagals (cf. p. 174) to 24 tones. Auda [29] finds in the system an arrangement of 24 scales distinguished by the changing position of the half-tone within differently constructed groups of fourths and fifths, the fourths and fifths being joined to each other in different ways (cf. p. 156). Höeg [30] finds the roots of Byzantine theory in Egyptian mysticism which, together with the principles of the Pythagoreans and the songs of the Synagogue, go to form the Christian liturgical music.

Gombosi shows a connection between the musical portion of the tract and later Byzantine theory and comes to the conclusion that the tract is itself Byzantine. He interprets the 24 entities as the degrees produced by 6 disjunct tetrachords and the latter as having a T S T structure (since "Zosimos" uses the term *mesokentros*). These tetrachords form 2 series of 3 each; the 2 series are not continuous, one above the other, but seem to occupy the same range. In one series the entities are counted ascending, in the other descending, possibly because melodies beginning on a degree of the ascending series will have a generally ascending movement while those belonging to the descending series will have a correspondingly downward movement. A system consisting of disjunct tetrachords reappears in the *Hagiopolites* [31] (cf. p. 73) and the *Papadikai* (cf. p. 84). We shall meet with such a system again in Western theory. Later Byzantine theory reintroduces us, also, to ascending and descending types, in connection with the kyrioi and plagioi respectively.

   The pseudo-Zosimos treatise offers no information concerning the existence of scalar modes. In fact, even the later medieval writings on Byzantine musical theory do not mention them, although there is evidence in practical music that they were beginning to be deduced. On the other hand, we do encounter the term *echos*—in two senses, moreover: as the name of an individual degree in a tetrachord and as the musical formula for which the degree served as a starting point and to which it thus imparted some degree of modality. Formulas, as might be expected, are important.

I . . . have found that . . . the mode [echos] *is* not *absolutely connected with a certain* finalis, *but with the occurrence of a group of* maqams *which form the melody*

[28] GasL, 130; GasU, 27.   [29] Antoine Auda, *Les Modes et les tons de la musique,* 152.
[30] HöegB, 332. This attempts to connect the 7 Greek vowels (cf. p. 59), as well as the "Zosimos" system, with Byzantine theory.
[31] A point discussed in GomS II, Part 2, not yet published but generously shown us by Dr. Gombosi.

of each mode [echos]. . . . The scales were gradually evolved from the melodies by a process of grouping certain . . . formulae on which all melodies were built.[32]

It is believed that some trace of these formulas is preserved in the *enechemata*, that is, in the intonations mentioned on p. 84. Unfortunately, the earliest MSS do not actually notate them. They are mentioned in Byzantine treatises, however, and appear to be of considerable antiquity. It is likely that certain comments in Latin treatises of the West—one as early as the 9th century—refer to the Byzantine *enechemata*, and that formulas appearing in decipherable notation in a Latin tract of the 10th century actually present them (*cf.* pp. 172f). In the Byzantine MSS, each *enechema* is accompanied by syllables of unknown meaning,[33] and these, except for repetition, are constant for each echos. (The formulas in the Latin tracts are accompanied by syllables also, but those given for any one "mode," while they bear a general resemblance to one another—and in most instances to the Byzantine syllables also—do not remain constant.) The formula for a single echos, however, was not necessarily invariable from the musical standpoint. Here are the syllables with the musical intonations that, according to Tillyard,[34] "are typical of the many varieties found in the MSS":

ECHOS		
	I. Ananes	aGFEDEFGa
	II. Neanes	baGab
	III. Nana *	cc
	or Aneanes	ccbcGaGFEFGabc
	IV. Hagia	GGaGFG
PLAGAL	I. Aneanes †	DFED
	II. Neeanes	GabaGa (Finalis E)
	III. Aanes	FGEF
	IV. Nehagie	GaGG

* The formula Nana is sometimes given to IV Plagal. † Some MSS interchange this with III Plagal.

Although the use of the *enechemata,* in the condition in which they reach us, was merely "to help the singer to find his note," their possession of some modal quality is attested to and their earlier significance perhaps hinted at in a passage in the *Hagiopolites* reading:

[32] WelleB, 21.
[33] For suggested interpretations, see GasI, 353; WelleT, 23. The formula is alternatively known as an *epechema.*
[34] TillH, 31, from which the table is taken, the medieval letter system of the West, however, being substituted, as in the table on p. 89, for the one now generally current (which is the one used by Tillyard). Further examples may be found in PetO, 26–31. See also the discussion in WelleM, 47f.

When we are about to sing or to teach, we must begin with an enechema. *For the* enechema *is the laying-on* (epibole) *of the echos.*[35]

It is interesting to observe that, in the middle Byzantine notation, the signs for the stepwise progressions did not distinguish between whole steps and half-steps. Thus, a singer, in determining whether a second spanned a whole tone or a semitone, had to know the structure of the scale—complete or in a formative stage—into which, in practice, the melody fitted. One is tempted to speculate on the bearing a defective notation, such as that described, might have generally on the deducing of scalar theory. Notation presumably lessens the need for dependence upon melodic formulas as mnemonic devices (*cf.* p. 140). If, however, a system of notation falls short in certain respects, something is needed to supplement it in the singer's mind. If the shortcoming is such a one as that mentioned, consideration of intervallic structure, leading eventually to the deducing of a scalar system, would certainly lend substantial support. Do the evolution of notation and of scalar theory go hand in hand? The absence of an intervallic notation in the West in the early Middle Ages, at a time when treatises discussed scalar theory, would not in itself answer this question negatively, since, as we shall see, the old tradition of scalar theory enjoyed a new lease on life there, even though the old Greek notation had died out. To be sure, documents concerning ancient Greek theory were preserved in the East also. But in the West an attempt was made, however much it may have miscarried (*cf.* pp. 154f), to reconcile old Greek theory and current practice, while in the East ancient theory seems to have been preserved rather as a sort of museum piece, as a subject to be included in works of an encyclopedic nature. That the meaning behind the bare words was understood, seems unlikely. Thus, Nikolas Mesarites, in his account, describes the instruction given at the time to children and youths in the schools surrounding the Church of the Holy Apostles at Constantinople. Here, among other subjects, they learnt something about music, the younger children being taught psalm-singing, the older ones hymns. But their knowledge of theory was conveyed to them in connection with geometry, and Mesarites says that they made use of terms that were neither in common use nor understood, such as "nete, hypate, and parhypate, mese, and paramese." [36] One should guard against assuming too close a connection, then, of Byzantine music with the music of ancient Greece; one should, however, recognize the likelihood of a connection between it and the music of the Near East.

Modern study of Byzantine music was, notwithstanding, long retarded

[35] See TillC, 85; ThibM, 57.
[36] For fuller information, see WelleM, 46; WelleD, 133; WelleT, 22.

by the belief that it was a continuation of the ancient Greek and that it therefore made use of Greek theory. Investigators were misled by treatises, sometimes compilations, "embalming" the ancient information out of historical interest. Attention was focussed too much on such works, dealing with music, as those by Michael Psellos (11th century); [37] George Pachymeres (1242–c. 1310), whose treatise on the four mathematical sciences embraces music; [38] and Manuel Bryennios (14th century), whose commentary [39] on the *Harmonics* of Ptolemy includes old Greek material appropriated also by Pachymeres. Both these men, nevertheless, do treat the echoi to some extent [40] for purposes of explaining points in their discussion of ancient Greek theory. (They apply to the echoi the names of the old Greek tonoi in drawing parallels between the two. The *Hagiopolites* applied them to the echoi also.) But Höeg, Tillyard, and Wellesz have searched elsewhere and have agreed, in connection with their work on the MMB, upon a table of medieval Byzantine echoi. Their scheme [41] "is based on (1) the comparative study of the Byzantine and other Eastern and Western systems of church music; (2) the traces of the mediaeval modal system [i. e. the system of echoi] surviving in the modern or Chrysanthine system of Greek Church music; (3) the practical rules evolved in the course of transcription."

The table follows:

ECHOS		STARTING NOTE OF THE INTERVAL-SIGNS OF THE MELODY	FINALIS
	I.	a (rarely D)	a or D
	II.	b-natural or G	E or b-natural
	III.	c or a	F or c
	IV.	d or G	G or d
PLAGAL	I.	D or G (rarely E)	D (rarely a)
	II.	E or G (rarely a)	E
	III. (Barys)	F or a	F (rarely b-flat)
	IV.	G, a or c	G (rarely c)

There are, in addition, several by-forms to the echoi (as we have indicated in discussing notation), so that this table is not all-embracing, although it includes the principal forms. We are told that in *asma* ("secular music") there were as many as 16 echoi.

Here is an example in Echos I:

[37] Specimens of his writings on music may be found in VincN, 316 (Greek text) among other places; for further information, see RieL II, 1441.
[38] Greek text of the introduction and section on music, French translation of the former, and commentary, in VincN, 362.
[39] Printed in Greek with Latin translation in WallP, 359 (1699 edition).   [40] See GomS II.
[41] In the forming of which Tillyard has been especially active. An article by Oliver Strunk, discussing the echoi in detail, will appear shortly in MQ.

EXAMPLE 11. Ode from the Kanon for the Morning of Easter Sunday—
Poem by John of Damascus (from WelleT, 3).

"Shine, shine, O new Jerusalem, for the Glory of the Lord hath risen upon thee. Now dance and exult, O Sion; but thou, O pure-one, be glad, O Theotokos, in the Resurrection of thine Offspring."
(Transl. from NealeH, 44, the musical section of which work is not authoritative.)

Some scholars have pointed out a strong resemblance between the Byzantine system of echoi and the modal system of the West. Differences exist, to be sure. For example, a comparison between the above table and the exposition of the Western modal system, given in Chapter 6, brings to light immediately the fact that, to make the Eastern system agree with the Western, it is necessary to renumber the Byzantine echoi by inserting a plagal after each kyrios. But a mere difference in numbering is a superficial one. A relationship does exist and will be mentioned again in Chapter 6.

No comprehensive study of the style of Byzantine Chant, comparable with that undertaken in the Gregorian field, is yet possible: not enough of the surviving melodies have thus far appeared in print. But a few remarks may be added to what has already been said on this score. The rhythm of the Chant is free—that is, there is no regular division into equal measures. The music is definitely monodic, and has been held "not definitely choral," although "the choir might join in the melody or some voices might hold a drone on the fundamental note, . . . in essence the music contains nothing that a single cantor could not render." [42] Underscoring of the text, by means of melodic passages illustrating the words, is used to a striking extent: thus, to give only one type of example, "song," "to sing," etc., are regularly accompanied by melismas.[43] It is believed that, although the MSS do not usually give evidence of chromatic mutations, they were added in performance, at least after the ascendancy of Arabic and Turkish taste.[44]

If Byzantine music borrowed from nations brought at one time or another within the Empire, it repaid its debt by affecting them, in turn, and by

[42] TillZ, 271.   [43] Other examples are given in WelleT, 22.
[44] The presence of the special kind of chromaticism that would arise from the use of the disjunct-tetrachord system, mentioned above in connection with the "Zosimos" treatise, will be dealt with in the Strunk article referred to in footnote 41.

spreading its influence to others. This influence, in fact, is still alive in music practically applied, for the Chant of the Greek Orthodox Church—however far it may have wandered from its source—is indebted to it. Especially, it would seem, is this true of the Chant in Serbia and Bulgaria.[45] That the ecclesiastical music of Russia was indebted to it too, will be made clear presently, and we shall have occasion, in our next sections, to refer to its influence in other areas also.

Armenian Chant

ARMENIA, in A. D. 303, became the first country to adopt Christianity as a state religion. Gregory the Illuminator (*c.* 257–*c.* 337) was responsible for the Hellenizing or Catholicizing of Christianity in that country, which had already been converted by Syrian missionaries to the faith later known as Nestorianism, and he became the reputed founder of the Armenian Church. He preached in the native tongue and, through his instrumentality, an attempt was made by the Armenian monarch to destroy all relics of paganism. This action dealt a serious blow to earlier native music.[1] Byzantine and Syrian influences met and mingled at least until the separation of the Armenian Church from the Greek in 536, a somewhat belated result of the condemnation of Monophysite doctrine as heretical by the Council of Chalcedon (451), a doctrine the Armenians favored. The cultural growth of the country took on impetus with the introduction of the Armenian script in the 5th century.

The oldest Armenian notation was of the alphabetical type. It is not known exactly when this was replaced by the neume notation (the invention of which the records place in the 12th century and attribute to Khatchadour of Taron), but it seems that the latter remained uniform for several centuries. Even so the notation is undecipherable, the key to it having been lost during the Turkish occupation and no enlightening tract, apparently, existing. It is thought, however, that the signs indicated (1) duration, (2) punctuation and cadence, and (3) melodic movement.[2] Whether the new notation, introduced early in the 19th century, preserves ancient melodies or merely chants originating shortly before, cannot now be determined. The early music may be irretrievably lost. It appears, however, from the arrangement of the hymn-texts in the *Sharakan* (the great collection of hymns of the Armenian Church) that the Armenians had an Oktoechos system, since these texts are grouped according to the echoi to which they should be sung and there are eight of them (*cf.* p. 73). The echoi now in use are not based on a

---

[45] For a discussion of the survival of the Byzantine influence in the Orthodox Church today, see WelleG, 107. See also SwanM.

[1] See DayanM, 445; MaclerA, 7.

[2] See GasM, 551. A facsimile of a page containing Armenian notation is printed on p. 552.

scalar principle but consist of melodic formulas, a circumstance that may easily point to ancient method. Another possible hint of the nature of the old Chant that may be deduced from the current Chant is offered by the extent to which basic motives are varied.[3] The *Sharakan* is supplemented by the *Janagirkh* (for the Office of the Hours) and other service books.

The most ancient hymn-texts had been in prose. But, during the renaissance in Lesser Armenia under the Rubenian monarchs (who began to reign in 1080, after the collapse of Greater Armenia), versified hymns began to be written. It was during this period that the great Nerses, surnamed Schnorhali ("the Graceful") produced the poems that constitute one-fifth of the 1166 canonized hymns of the Armenian Church.[4]

To what extent comparison of the chants used by scattered Armenian congregations may eventually lead to the reasonably definite identification of some ancient melodies, is most uncertain. The European congregations have been greatly affected by the host nations, past and present. It is believed [5] that national characteristics have been most purely preserved in the homeland—at Echmiadzin, Tiflis, and Erivan. The Armenians of India have a distinctive Chant of their own.[6]

Coptic and Ethiopian Chant

THE early Copts, the native Christians of Egypt, dwelt chiefly in the northern part of the country. Their descendants are regarded, owing to a chain of circumstances, as "racially the purest representatives of the ancient Egyptians." Christianity spread among the natives, as distinguished from the Hellenistic Alexandrians etc., at least as early as the 3rd century. The secession of the Church, after the Council of Chalcedon, did not prevent its service from showing Byzantine traits: the earliest Coptic hymn-texts were translations from the Greek. Native poetry, chiefly religious, flourished with particular vigor about A. D. 1000 and prompted, or was coincident with, much musical activity.

No notated MSS preserving the old Coptic Chant have come down to us, if, indeed, any ever existed. The nearest thing we have to them are a few MSS for the solemn reading, containing a type of ekphonetic script.[1] To what extent the melodies now sung [2] preserve the old ones, cannot be determined. Notation is not used even today, since most of the singers of the Chant are blind, "it being thought that only such people can be expected to

---

[3] Variation in current Chant is discussed, with examples, in WelleMM, 14, an interesting article which, however, should be read in conjunction with WelleG, 83ff (which includes helpful remarks on the value of the works of earlier writers on Armenian Chant), and WelleD, 139f, both written subsequently.

[4] A melody attributed to Nerses by tradition is printed in DayanM, 444.   [5] See WelleD, 140.

[6] A collection of their melodies is provided (with added harmonizations) by ApcarM. See comments in WelleG, 88f.

[1] See WelleD, 138.   [2] For a collection made in 1899, see BadetC.

have the seriousness and other-worldliness necessary for the correct singing of ecclesiastical melodies."[3] The modern Copts use cymbals in accompanying the Chant. They are reported to employ also handbells—beaten, since the instruments are tongueless. This may be a revival of an early custom or even a continuation of it (at least in desert monasteries) despite the prejudice against bells on the part of the Muslim conquerors. They are reported to use triangles also.[4]

A few points about the old Chant may be deduced from the large number of surviving MSS of texts. These make it plain that songs were based on strophic division, the strophes mostly appearing in pairs, thus providing another example of Oriental parallelism. Antiphonal singing appears to have been popular and to have exhibited a dramatic character. Indications designating to which echos out of the eight of the Oktoechos a text was to be sung, doubtless derived from Byzantine practice. As in other Oriental MSS of hymn-texts etc., words sometimes precede the actual texts, naming the melody to be used in performance. The survivals make possible a division of the songs into 3 groups: strictly liturgical chants; songs sung at religious assemblies, but not actually liturgical; and religious folk-songs sung at festivals and other public gatherings.[5]

The Ethiopian tradition that the kings of the country were descended from Menelik, reputed son of Solomon and the Queen of Sheba (herself allegedly an Ethiopian monarch), finds an echo in the claim that Ethiopian psalmody as sung today preserves Hebrew Chant as practiced in the time of Solomon. Psalmody, however, is taught among the Ethiopians exclusively by oral means despite the existence of diacritical signs.[6]

St. Frumentius, a Phoenician, became the first bishop of Ethiopia about A. D. 330, and Christianity took firm root in a culture already or subsequently affected by Egyptian, Syrian, Greek, and Hebrew influences. The bonds between Ethiopia and Egypt were at times exceedingly close; the Abyssinian ritual today generally agrees with that of the Copts. The Ethiopian Chant too, it is claimed, shows relationship to Coptic practice, as well as to Syrian, Armenian, and Hebrew.[7] Sistra resembling those of the ancient Egyptians are used in the church, and tambourines, bells, and cymbals also. Arabian influence seems to be almost entirely absent.[8]

To Abba Yared, in the 6th century, is attributed the organization of the chants of the ecclesiastical year and also the invention of a new manner of singing, this being based on three "modes": *ghe'ez*,[9] *ezel,* and *araray.* Exactly what these were is not known. The names are still used in connection with

[3] WelleB, 6.
[4] Concerning the use of these three types of instruments, see ButlerC I, 327; II, 79–83.
[5] See WelleD, 138, or WelleG, 103ff.   [6] See HerschA, 53.   [7] See DerayE, 135.
[8] *Cf.* HerschA, 52f.   [9] Not to be confused with the Ghe'ez language.

melodic phenomena "corresponding more to our idea of a tone in Gregorian
Chant [an equivalent of an echos], for example, than to our idea of a mode
with a particular rhythmic or melodic character." [10]

No MSS containing Ethiopian notation are known to exist from before the
16th century though there is a tradition that it is 1000 years older. It consists
partly of letters of the alphabet and partly of points, and shows signs of a
possible Byzantine influence.[11] It has not been deciphered.

Descriptions of the rendition of the Chant appear in old church records.
The priests sang in a loud voice till they reached the highest point of ecstasy
and were completely exhausted. A similar practice is followed today. Dancing
accompanies the Chant to the rhythmic incitement of hand-clapping and
drumbeats.[12]

[10] HerschA, 53. See further, concerning the "modes," DerayE, 183; HerschA, 52; WelleK, 80.
[11] On this subject, see WelleK, 101; WelleG, 105.   [12] See WelleD, 139.

Chapter 4: SOME OF THE CHIEF BRANCHES OF CHRISTIAN CHANT: Russian, Ambrosian, Mozarabic, and Gallican

Russian Chant *

PRINCE Vladimir, after his christening at Korsun (Cherson) in the Crimea in 988 and his subsequent marriage to the Princess Anna (sister of the Byzantine Emperor Basil II), brought back to Kiev with him a Bulgarian bishop—Michael—and also many priests, monks, and singers —Greeks and Slavs--who had been sent to him together with Anna by the Emperor and the Greek Patriarch of Constantinople. Vladimir made Michael the first Metropolitan of Russia. Michael moved eventually from Kiev to Rostov where he christened countless numbers of people, erected many churches, appointed a clergy, and organized a choir.

Shortly after these southern Slavs (themselves not untouched by Byzantine influence) and these Greek singers, came the Greek teachers, three arriving, together with their families and assistants, in 1053, during the reign of Yaroslav I.[1] These teachers allegedly inaugurated the "8-mode singing" in Russia ("8-echos singing" would be better; the Russian term for "echoi" is glassy), brought with them examples of church chant books, and became the instructors and directors of choirs in Kiev, Rostov, and thereabouts. Among the most famous of the oldest choirs were those at Kiev, Moscow, Novgorod, Vladimir, Pskov, and the Bogoliubov Monastery.

From reports of such activity, we find that, together with the principles of Christianity, Russia seems to have obtained from Byzantium the religious service, chants, and naturally the notations necessary for the religious service, and that a South Slavic influence was doubtless present also.

Chants at least in part of a truly Russian aspect, however, were not long in appearing, awaiting only a suitable occasion, such as the organization of special services[2] in memory of actually Russian saints. These chants, which were probably given form by native singers, appeared as early as the 11th

---

* By IGOR BUKETOFF.

[1] At least according to the *Stepenaya Kniga,* a not entirely dependable 16th-century document.

[2] Such as those commemorating Theodosius of Petcheri (festival inaugurated in 1095) and Princes Boris and Gleb (1072), and that in memory of the reinterment of the remains of St. Nicholas of Bar-grad (1087)

century and were inscribed in books of the 12th century. Even if their creation consisted merely of the setting of a new text to a given melody, the process was applied with technical skill and a competent knowledge of the contemporary chants and their construction.[3] In time the musical creativeness
of the Russian people—brilliantly displayed in their folk-music—enabled
them to counterbalance the influence from abroad considerably, so far as the
actually melodic phase of the service was concerned, if it did not do so in
certain other respects (cf. pp. 98f).

As is evident from the earliest documents of the 11th century,[4] there did
not at first exist any specifically Russian notation, the method used having
been employed previously at Byzantium, as comparison with Greek MSS has
shown. The Russian documents display an ekphonetic system consisting of
approximately twelve symbols,[5] encountered in one [6] document, to choose
a single example, in connection with 92 of the 160 lines of script. Some of
these signs were admitted by the Russians into the most ancient form of the
notation they soon began to develop for themselves. This was based on
kriuki (= hooks) and was known as *kriuki* or *znamenny* notation (*znamia* =
sign, note).[7] A later (16th-century) variety was known as "demestic."
This resembles the znamenny notation. Demestic Chant appears to have been
considerably older than the notation, having existed alongside the Znamenny
Chant. Its exact nature has not yet been determined by musical scholars.[8]

The introduction of the znamenny notation did not immediately oust
foreign notation. Examples are to be found of the so-called kondakarny notation (*kondak* = short hymn of praise; thus a *kondakarion* is a collection of
such hymns), which consisted in part of a row of small symbols written
above the text and graphically related to those used in the Znamenny Chant.
Above these there was a second row of symbols, much fewer in number
but larger in size, resembling the letters of the Greek alphabet and pointing to Byzantine origin. The key to this system has as yet not been discovered,
but it has been believed that the smaller symbols indicated the melody, the
larger the dynamics. Several details, however, cause one to question this
analysis. On 5 pages of this notation [9] there are 60 different large symbols,

---

[3] See MettR, 44.

[4] The *Ostromirovo Evangelie* ("Ostromirov Gospel") and two parchment sheets of a Gospel,
known as the *Kuprianovskie Listi* ("Cyprian Sheets"), are regarded as the oldest of these.

[5] In the *Ostromirovo Evangelie* only two of these signs are used.

[6] The *Kuprianovskie Listi*. The notation here is much more complete than in the *Ostromirovo
Evangelie* where it occurs only sporadically. See FindR, I, 81ff (there is a facsimile of an extract
from the *Kuprianovskie Listi* on p. 83).

[7] FindR I, 85, prints a table presenting (a) some symbols taken from the MSS mentioned in
footnote 4, (b) kriuki notation in 16th-century Russian MSS, and (c) Greek ekphonetic notation
of the 11th–12th centuries, showing a family relationship among the three groups.

[8] Cf. SwanZ, 235ff.

[9] From the *Nizhegorodski Blagoveschenski Kondakar* ("Kondakarion of the Annunciation
Monastery of Nishni-Novgorod") of the 12th century, considered the best document containing
this form of notation. For facsimile, see FindR, I, 95.

allegedly prescribing dynamics, and but 40 of the smaller type. Is it reasonable to suppose that the upper row, containing a greater variety of symbols than the lower, consists only of marks of expression? Also, the upper row employs symbols used by the lower, and the lower uses combinations of its own symbols. This suggests a faint possibility of two- or even, perhaps, of three-voice singing. It is rash, however, to draw any conclusions about this system of notation, for, even if the key to it is at present lost, the outward resemblances to the znamenny symbols suggest a possibility that a clue to the solution may yet be found.

This double notation, with its large symbols resembling Greek letters, may indicate that music written in it not only was of Byzantine origin, but also was possibly performed in large part by well-schooled Greek singers. It would seem that the same music may eventually have found written expression in the znamenny signs, since so many of the symbols were common to the two systems. Thus it is possible that the same chants, having been renotated in the znamenny symbols, are still being used unsuspectingly by the Raskolniki or "Old Believers" (the sect that produced the heroes of Mussorgsky's *Khovantchina*), and that they survive also in the later five-line square-note system of Kiev (of which we shall read presently).[10]

The znamenny or kriuki notation can be traced as far back as the 11th century. In a document of the 13th century are found over 90 different znamenny signs, of which only part have been deciphered. Some disappeared from practical use in church books before the 15th century, and their musical connotation was lost. Unfortunately no early treatise on the notations of the 11th–14th centuries has been found. The first works on them appeared only in the 15th century [11] and gave the titles of the various signs, not their precise technical or musical meanings. We know, however, that, so far as pitch is concerned, a sign could apply to one of three tones. The notation was based upon a twelve-degree gamut with a theoretical range extending from G to $\frac{d}{d}$ (with b-natural, but $\frac{b}{b}$-flat). This range is obviously too high for male voices, and notation within it was not intended to be taken literally, but merely to

[10] So Findeisen suggests (see FindR I, 94ff). This possibility is inconsistent with the claim of von Riesemann who asserts (RieseR, 141) that, strange as it may seem in view of the almost certain original Byzantine and South Slavic influence, the Znamenny Rospiev—the most ancient Russian Chant deciphered (*Rospiev* = chant)—exhibits no resemblance to the Byzantine, Bulgarian, or Serbian Chants. This claim presupposes a comprehensive knowledge of these Chants, and, notwithstanding von Riesemann's writing on Byzantine music, it is difficult to see how he could have acquired such a knowledge, the corpus of Byzantine MSS not being small and their systematic investigation, apparently, being only now under way. Findeisen makes only a suggestion; von Riesemann, a claim on a possibly insufficient foundation. It would seem that judgment should be suspended on this interesting question until the contents of at least the Byzantine MSS are better known. SwanR, however, points out, in connection with the Byzantine Chant as transcribed by Wellesz and Tillyard and the Znamenny Chant, that, while certain external features are common to the two, their fundamental character and "musical meaning" are strikingly different.

[11] See FindR, I, 99f for facsimiles of pages from treatises on the subject, showing a few samples of the notation.

indicate relative pitch. The gamut was divided into four "realms" (the low, dark, bright, and threefold bright) of three degrees each. In practice, the second and third "realms" were most frequently used. A znamenny sign showed in which "realm" a tone lay, but not its exact level therein. (Concerning a 16th-century improvement, see p. 100.) On the other hand, the notation was well supplied with rhythm signs. It showed also intensity and the place of a note in the melodic motive—that is, whether it belonged to the beginning, middle, or end—and thus indicated phrasing.[12]

The Znamenny Chant proved much more lasting in general use than the Kondakarny and eventually developed into the basis of the "Kriukovoi Znamenny Rospiev." (This name is derived from the system of notation in which the Chant was written and is applied to the whole corpus of Russian Chant since its codification by Mesenetz—see p. 103.) The hooks and signs used were called interchangeably not only *znamiona* or *kriuki* but *stolpi* (signs), and this explains why the Chant is still sometimes called the "Stolpovoi Rospiev." The notation, after about six hundred years of use, surrendered itself in the 17th century (but only partially so, since it is still preserved by the Old Believers) to translation into the five-line system. There were, however, documents containing both systems of notation.[13] Adoption of the five-line system (with its "Kiev signs"), resembling in principle if not in note-shapes that of the West, was prompted by the introduction of polyphony into the church service, the old system having proved inadequate for the demands of the new style. The old system, however, was better suited than its successor to the requirements of the Chant, and the transference of the Chant melodies into the new notation proved harmful to their rendition.[14]

The majority of the earlier MSS were, supposedly, from Novgorod since, during the period of their origin (11th–14th centuries), that city led culturally and since its location removed it from the danger of the Tartar invasions (beginning of the 13th century), which came near to annihilating all the cultural wealth of Southern and Central Russia. We nevertheless possess 26 musical MSS of the pre-Mongol period.[15]

In some documents of the 12th century are found both Greek and Russian texts. This is explained by the supposition that during the 11th–14th centuries the chants were sung in both Russian and Greek, the supposition receiving support from the circumstance that the earliest priests were mostly of

[12] See Cycle I, Introduction, iv; RieseR, 141f. PanóffA prints a table of the kriuki symbols most frequently used, together with their equivalents in modern notation: see his Table II between pp. 16–7, plus Fig. 6, p. 17. See also p. 15.
[13] For a systematic series of facsimiles portraying the development of the Chant in Russia, see either MettR, Appendix, or Cycle I, Introduction. Although the first of these books contains more facsimiles, the second goes into much deeper detail.
[14] See RieseR, 143ff. On pp. 144f there appears a single Chant melody in znamenny, 5-line, and modern Western notation. See also BourR, 2359.
[15] For a list of these MSS, see SwanZ, Part III.

Greek origin and were probably but slightly acquainted with the Russian language. In the middle of the 13th century, at the Church of St. Mary at Great Rostov, there were two choirs, one Greek and one Russian, singing the same melody but in different languages, probably antiphonally. Such a practice helps to explain the presence to this day of Greek passages—not only *Kyrie eleison,* but others—in the text of the Russian service.

It is from the 12th century until well on into the 14th, nevertheless, that the Chant probably became adapted little by little to Russian needs and became a specifically Russian Chant. Late in the 14th century the notation assumed an abbreviated form. Thus far there had apparently been no textbooks on reading the znamenny notation, and it was probably taught solely by oral means. The first known written directions appeared only in the second half of the 15th century in the form of appendices to the chant books. At the end of the 15th century, the success of the changes in notation affected also the actual melody of the Znamenny Chant, which in several cases underwent considerable revision.

In the 16th century, owing to great muddling in the Church Chant, resulting from an abuse of the text,[16] there arose a dire need for schools of singing. This abuse arose partly from the fact that, towards the end of the 14th century, with the development of both the Slavonic language and the Chant, the pronunciation of the semi-vowels, which was difficult in singing (as well as in reading and ordinary speech), became lengthened into that of full vowels. The replacement of the semi-vowels in the Chant texts by *o* and *e,* a practice known as *khomonia,* changed the syllabification and tended to prolong performance. Insertions of another nature—examples of which existed as early as the 12th century—were made also, namely of coloratura passages ornamenting the simple Chant. These additions, sung to the interpolated syllables *a-ne-na* (apparently related somehow to the Byzantine *enechemata*), received the name *anenaiki.*[17] That they further lengthened performance, is obvious. To shorten the service, two or three different prayers were sometimes sung simultaneously. The sacred text received scant respect. To combat the corruption assailing the Chant, a project was drawn up in 1551, at the instance of Ivan the Terrible, for the formation of institutions for the teaching of reading, writing, and singing, the instruction to be given by the clergy. This project met with success in certain directions, although not in that of uprooting the evils. Many schools arose, from which came many masters.[18] The best schools were at Moscow and Novgorod. Numerous choirs were organized, of which those of the Tsar and the Patriarch were

[16] For further information than is given above, see FindR I, 90 ff, with examples on p. 92; also MettR, 46, or BourR, 2358, or RieseR, 142.

[17] For a facsimile of a 12th-century MS containing *anenaiki,* see FindR I, 93. See also note 111 on p. vii of FindR I.

[18] See MettR, 47f.

outstanding. As a result of this activity, the latter part of the 16th century found valuable additions being made to the Znamenny literature as well as revisions and variations of it. Among the best-known masters was Ivan Akimovich Shaidurov who, concerning himself more with the notation than with the melody of the Znamenny Chant, perfected a system of letters called the *Kinovarnija pomieti* ("Cinnabar letters"). Among the several improvements these effected was that of definitely fixing the height of the tones represented in the kriuki notation.[19]

The middle of the 17th century found the following bodies of Chant [20] in Russia: Znamenny (which centered itself in Moscow), Kiev, Greek, Bulgarian, and the Lesser Znamenny.[21] The last, which was used in small daily services, was basically the same as the first, but less ornamental in style. For example: [22]

EXAMPLE 12.

"My help cometh from the Lord, which made heaven and earth."

(Psalm CXXII [in the numbering of the King James version], 2)

The Kiev Chant was so similar to the Znamenny Chant that certain pieces in it could easily be mistaken for their equivalents in the Znamenny repertoire. This fact has led Metallov to suggest [23] that the Kiev Chant may have been a Southwestern edition of the Znamenny, altered to suit local needs, tastes, and traditions.

EXAMPLE 13.

"Arise, O Lord, and help us, and deliver us, for Thy Name's sake."

[19] For fuller information, see MettR, 49f; PanóffA, 17. The statement made in RieseR, 142, that this happened at the end of the 15th century is apparently due to a typographical error.

[20] Not the same music in different notations, but, with the exceptions to be mentioned, actually different bodies of Chant.

[21] There were others also, but these were the most important.

[22] The musical illustrations for this section will be drawn chiefly from *The Notation of the Regular Religious Church Service*, 1909.

[23] MettR, 68.

The Greek Chant [24] is quite different and more nearly resembles the Bulgarian, which is highly melodic and characteristic. The rhythm of these two Chants differs greatly in structure from the unsymmetrical rhythm of the Znamenny Chant (*cf.* Example 16). It is simple, even, and easily grasped by ears accustomed to the standard musical literature of the West. Here are Greek and Bulgarian examples:

EXAMPLE 14.

(a) "All nature, the angelic choir, and all mankind rejoice in thee, Blessed Virgin."

(b) "O only begotten Son and Word of God, Who art immortal and Who didst deign, for our salvation. . . ."

The most richly represented in surviving MSS is the Kiev Chant; the least frequently, the Bulgarian.[25]

All these bodies of Chant were widely diffused first in Southwest and then in Northeast European Russia, during the growth of the Uniate Church [26] in the 17th century. In view of the danger this growth threatened to the Orthodox Church, its Southwestern churches aligned themselves more closely with those of Greater Russia, Greece, and the other Greek Orthodox countries. With respect to church singing the more intimate contact resulted in the borrowing by Russia of all that was best from the other Orthodox countries.

The vast quantity of Russian Church melodies may be divided into two main groups: (1) those governed by the fundamental law of church singing —that of the eight echoi—and (2) those constructed independently of this law.

The law of the eight echoi includes among its requirements melodic patterns, or typical melodic figures. These are called *popievki*. Some are charac-

[24] Consisting of Slavonic translations of the texts of late Byzantine chants, with the Byzantine melodies reputedly retained. A parallel situation obtains with respect to the Bulgarian Chant.

[25] Referring again only to the more important bodies of Chant. For further information see MettR, 67ff.

[26] The church employing the dogmas of the Roman Catholic religion and headed by the pope, but using the Greek Orthodox ritual.

teristic of one echos alone. Some, besides occurring in one echos, are found also in another; and some are common to several echoi. Most often, similar *popievki* are found in echoi 1 and 5; 2 and 6; 3 and 4; 1, 3, and 4; 4 and 8; 2, 6, and 8 (the set of *popievki* for these three is different from that for 2 and 6 alone); etc. There are in addition some that are found in all except one or two of the echoi. There are *popievki* which, although they bear the same name, are formed of different figures in different echoi, and some which, although they bear different names, are formed of very similar figures. Among the *popievki* there are some that are used only at the beginning, others that are used in the beginning and middle, others in the middle only, others at the end and middle, and some only at the end. Of the first and last types there are relatively few—from one to six in each echos—the majority belonging to the other three types. Some are occasionally abbreviated or otherwise varied, the alteration usually occurring in the middle of the actual *popievka,* this depending upon the text. Some never change. There are some which, coupled with another, form a double or compound *popievka.*[27] Occasionally recitative, which is rare in Znamenny Chant, is interpolated between two *popievki* or between a *popievka* and its repetition. As an illustration of the style of the *popievki,* there are printed below three very typical ones from echos 8:

EXAMPLES 15–17.

The last 2 are frequently coupled, the 2nd following the 3rd after a bridge of 2 or 3 notes.

If the idea of eight echoi came to the Russians by way of the Byzantine system, the final result, in details of organization, differed considerably from the source.[28]

Activity became very strong in the 17th century. It was then that the Patriarchate was established, and this necessitated greater pomp in the service and singing, so that variations were welcomed in the treatment of chants that required repetitions.

But this spurt was accompanied also by a deterioration. The evils fought against in the previous century flourished anew. Whether this was caused

[27] See MettZ, 7.
[28] As the reader may see by comparing the descriptive table of the Russian echoi printed in PanóffA, 14, with the table printed on p. 89 *supra.*

by the teachers' offering liturgically unsound instruction or by the younger men's refusing to forego the opportunities the insertions gave them of vying with one another in inventiveness, the fact remains that the methods followed in the singing and reading of the church books caused the service to grow ever longer. To shorten its rendition and still have it complete, the practice was indulged in, in the early part of the 17th century, of singing and reading in two, three, four, five, or even six voices, a few passages of text being sung or spoken at once.[29] (We have already encountered a rather similar practice in an earlier period.)

It naturally followed that the contents of the chant books became disorganized and inaccurate, so much so that, in 1655, Tsar Alexis Michailovitch appointed a commission of fourteen to revise the texts. A plague assailing Moscow at the time, however, cut short their efforts. In 1668 a second commission of six was appointed, headed by the monk Alexander Mesenetz. With material of the previous four hundred years at their disposal, they corrected and organized the church literature, Mesenetz himself writing an excellent treatise [30] on the translation of the kriuki. It was not long after this that the five-line square-note symbols were introduced from Kiev and spread all over Russia. The reforms of the commission led to a schism within the church, the "Old Believers" rejecting them as well as the new notation.

Shortly after, and especially during the reign of Peter the Great, Russian music fell strongly under Western European influence, notably that of Italy (Galuppi and Sarti were long active at St. Petersburg) and Poland. Even though Bortniansky, Lvov, and others, did make attempts to use the old liturgical chants in their compositions, the European influence under which they had fallen led them to modify the melodies to suit Western tastes and to harmonize them according to Western rules of harmony and counterpoint.

Departures from the methods of these composers are represented by the settings of Turchaninov and Potulov. The latter, leaving the melodies absolutely intact, limited his choice of chords to only fundamental triads and their first inversions, thereby achieving a very strict and solemn result. In his system practically every note is treated as an independent chord tone.

With the appointment of Balakirev as the director of the Imperial Chapel in St. Petersburg, church music generally began to take on a more national style. Rimsky-Korsakov and Lvovsky continued somewhat in this style, as did also Tchaikovsky.

The greatest step towards harmonizing the chants in a strict, national Russian style (assuming they should be harmonized at all) was taken by Kastalsky (1856–1926). To him, perhaps, is due most of the credit for the tremendous advance made by the later composers—Gretchaninov, Tchesno-

[29] MettR, 56ff.   [30] Printed in SmolA.

kov, Nikolsky, Rachmaninov, Shvedov—in their attempts towards rejuvenating the Chant.

Ambrosian Chant

AMBROSIAN Chant, which is used in Milan, derives its name from the attribution of its origin to St. Ambrose. How the doughty bishop, while engaged in a fierce struggle with the Empress Justina and her followers of the heretical Arian sect, introduced the Syrian custom of singing hymns at Milan, in order to buoy up the spirits of his Catholic adherents, is told by his younger contemporary, St. Augustine:

> For it was about a year, or not much more, since Justina, the mother of the boy-Emperor Valentinian, persecuted Thy servant Ambrose in the interest of her heresy, to which she had been seduced by the Arians. The pious people kept guard in the church, prepared to die with their bishop, Thy servant. There my mother, Thy handmaid, bearing a chief part of those cares and watchings, lived in prayer. We, still unmelted by the heat of Thy Spirit, were yet moved by the astonished and disturbed city. At this time it was instituted that, after the manner of the Eastern Church, hymns and psalms should be sung, lest the people should pine away in the tediousness of sorrow; which custom, retained from then till now, is imitated by many, yea, by almost all of Thy congregations throughout the rest of the world.[1]

St. Ambrose defines the nature of the hymn thus: "Song with praise of the Lord. If you praise the Lord and do not sing, you do not utter a hymn. If you sing and do not praise the Lord, you do not utter a hymn. If you praise anything that does not pertain to the praise of the Lord, and if you praise in song, you do not utter a hymn. A hymn, therefore, has these three things: song and praise and the Lord."[2] Of the many hymn-texts whose authorship has been ascribed to the saint, only four are now generally accepted as authentic. They are *Aeterne rerum Conditor; Deus Creator omnium; Iam surgit hora tertia;* and *Veni Redemptor gentium.*[3] The first of these having been adopted by the Romans is still in the Roman Breviary. The texts of all four hymns are written in iambic dimeters (each iamb consisting of two feet) and each hymn consists of eight four-line stanzas. Later hymns written in this verse-form were sometimes called *hymni Ambrosiani.*

Nothing definite is known of the melodies that were originally applied to the hymns of St. Ambrose. They may have been composed by him or adapted from earlier music. Since the hymns were intended for the use of the congregation, it seems logical to assume that their melodies were simple and syllabic. We learn from St. Augustine's definition of the iambic foot

[1] *Confessions,* Book IX, Chap. 7. MigneL XXXII, 770; Nicene and Post-N, Ser. 1, I, 134.
[2] Quoted in GerC I, 74.
[3] Some writers attribute 14 other hymn-texts to St. Ambrose. See DrevesA; also JulD, 56.

that it was "a short and a long, of three beats," [4] and most modern transcriptions of the hymns are based on the assumption that the rhythm of the melody followed the meter of the text.[5] Ambrosian meter was governed by the laws of quantity, although the gradual change from quantity to accent had already begun in St. Ambrose's time.

EXAMPLE 18. *Aeterne rerum Conditor*—Hymn—Ambrosian (after DrevesA, 111).

Ae : ter - ne re - rum Con - di - tor   Noc - tem di - em - que qui   re - gis   Et   tem - po -

rum   das   tem - po - ra,   Ut   al - le - res   fa - sti - di - um.

        Framer of the earth and sky,
          Ruler of the day and night,
        With a glad variety,
          Tempering all, and making light;
              Etc.

(From John Cardinal Newman, *Verses on Various Occasions*, 200.)

Ambrosian hymns spread throughout Europe. During the Middle Ages ecclesiastical writers of various regions yielded to the fashion of embroidering the simple hymn melodies with small melismas. Attempts have been made by shearing off such excrescences to uncover the melodies presumably used by St. Ambrose.[6]

A hymn written not to a metrical but to a prose-text is the *Te Deum*. Its structure, like that of the psalms, is governed by the principle of parallelism. According to legend, it was improvised jointly by St. Ambrose and St. Augustine while the former was baptizing the latter. In the Middle Ages it was sometimes called *Hymnus Ambrosianus*. The *Te Deum* is now believed, however, to have been written probably by Niceta of Remesiana (*c.* 335–414). It seems to have been well known and widespread as early as the 6th century and it eventually found its way into the Roman liturgy. The music of this hymn, as it has come down to us, seems to be a composite creation; the first part of the melody is thought to be of pre-Gregorian and possibly Milanese origin, while the latter part is Gregorian in character.[7]

[4] *De Musica*, Book II, Chap. VIII, in MigneL, XXXII, 1108.
[5] Further concerning the rhythm of the Ambrosian hymns, see Handschin in Acta, X (1938), 17f.
[6] See, for examples, DrevesA, 110ff.
[7] For evidence in favor of Niceta's authorship, see MorinN. The *Te Deum* as now used in the Ambrosian rite may be found in Antiphonale (Ambrosian), 636. For details concerning its structure, see WagE III, 225ff, the discussion being based on the Roman version.

Another Eastern custom introduced by St. Ambrose to the West is the practice of antiphonal singing—that is, the chanting of the verses of a psalm in alternation between two choirs. Antiphonal singing [8] is implied by St. Augustine when he speaks of "psalms" sung "after the manner of the Eastern Church." This practice spread from Milan to Rome, where it was officially adopted during the papacy of Celestine I (422–32).

In the course of time all the music of the Milanese liturgy came to be known as Ambrosian Chant, although none of it can be traced definitely back to the saint himself. Ambrosian Chant, while remaining a separate entity, influenced the Gregorian and was in turn influenced by it. Sometimes, it would seem, Gregorian Chant borrowed a melody intact from the Ambrosian liturgy. Thus, it is possible that the music for the famous Gregorian hymn *Veni Creator Spiritus* is older than its text and previously served as the melody for the Ambrosian hymn *Hic est dies versus Dei*.[9] Occasionally melodies in both repertoires are much alike, but the Ambrosian, when ornate, are usually more ornate than the Gregorian. There is some indication that at least a few Ambrosian melodies were borrowed by the Roman Church and then pruned in the Gregorian codification of the Roman Chant. Compare, for example, the following Ambrosian version of the *Jubilate Deo* with the Gregorian version (p. 166 *infra*, where a translation is given).[10]

EXAMPLE 19. *Jubilate Domino*—Offertory—Ambrosian (after Antiphonale [Ambrosian], 97).

[8] Not the singing of antiphons, as some writers have it. See DrevesA, 96. Antiphons eventually, however, did become popular at Milan as elsewhere.
[9] See DrevesA, 136; CE I, 392.
[10] The Gregorian version contains 67 syllables and 300 notes (not counting the *Alleluia*, which

The simple Ambrosian melodies, however, are even simpler than those of
the Gregorian repertoire. This may be seen in a comparison of the Ambrosian
psalm-tones with the Gregorian. A psalm-tone is a recitative-like formula to
which the verses of a psalm may be chanted. The simple Ambrosian tones,
which are reputedly earlier than the Gregorian, consist only of a reciting-note
with a simple cadence at the end of the verse. The Gregorian psalm-tones, on
the other hand, contain three main divisions: intonation, reciting-note, and
cadence, the last two of which undergo certain modifications made necessary by the text of the psalms. In addition to the simple formulas, the Ambrosian repertoire contains some more elaborate psalm-tones for festive
occasions.[11]

Despite the antiquity of the Ambrosian liturgy, the earliest collection of
Ambrosian chants that has survived is the 12th-century Codex Add. 34209
in the British Museum.[12] A melodic trait of some interest is found in certain of the chants of this MS—namely, musical rhyme. Musical rhyme is

is lacking in the Ambrosian version), while the above Ambrosian *Jubilate Deo* contains 380 notes
although it has only 6 more syllables.

[11] For a discussion of the Gregorian psalm-tones see *infra*, p. 172ff. The Ambrosian psalm-tones
are printed in PothM, 270ff; OrtD, 119ff; etc. See also BasM.

[12] A facsimile of the MS is printed in PM V and transcriptions into modern plainsong notation
in PM VI.

the recurrence of a melodic formula at the end of some or all of the phrases of a melody. This may be clearly seen in the Confractorium,[13] *Dicet Domino:*

EXAMPLE 20. *Dicet Domino*—Confractorium—Ambrosian (after PM VI, 172).

where each of the four phrases ends with the formula:[14]

We shall have further occasion to refer to musical rhyme.

Ambrosian Chant remained popular for a long time in various regions of Northern Italy. The monastery of Monte Cassino employed it exclusively until the monks were directed by Pope Stephen IX (1057-58) to substitute the Gregorian. As late as the 14th century some churches employed it together with Gregorian Chant. But Ambrosian Chant never achieved the wide dissemination and intensive development of Gregorian Chant. Perhaps those

[13] While the Ambrosian liturgy corresponds in its essential components to the Gregorian, it contains several parts that are peculiar to Milan. The Confractorium is such a part; it is sung in the Ambrosian Mass at the breaking of the Host and its text usually has some reference to the Gospel of the day.

[14] The text is the second verse of Psalm XC in the Roman Breviary, Psalm XCI in the Protestant Bible. "He shall say to the Lord: Thou art my protector, and my refuge: my God, in him will I trust." In this book we shall sometimes give the English of the King James version, but, where that is not in reasonable agreement with the Vulgate, we shall, as here, follow the Douai (Catholic) version.

The psalms in the Roman Breviary and the Protestant Bible correspond up to and including Psalm VIII. Psalm IX in the Breviary is divided into Psalms IX and X in the Protestant Bible, and thereafter the Catholic version is always one number behind the Protestant up to Psalm CXLVI (CXLVII). This psalm, however, No. CXLVII in the Protestant Bible, appears as two separate psalms—Nos. CXLVI and CXLVII—in the Breviary; consequently, the numbers of the last three psalms correspond in both versions. In the rest of this book the psalm number of the Roman Breviary will be given first, and then the Protestant number in parenthesis.

scholars who point out that at least some of its melodies are rather formless and overgrown, are at the same time pointing out the cause of its comparative unpopularity. But, although most authorities agree that Ambrosian Chant represents a loosely constructed, unpolished, and primitive precursor of the Roman Chant, at least one scholar finds the Ambrosian melodies esthetically more satisfying than the Gregorian.[15]

Mozarabic and Gallican Chant

EARLY Spain, excluding the North, developed the Visigothic liturgy, eventually called Mozarabic, in a manner investigation has not yet revealed. This liturgy shows divergences from the Roman, together with similarities, and relationship to the Byzantine and especially the Ambrosian and Gallican rites.

The last of these—one of the four great Western liturgies, the others being the Roman, Ambrosian, and Mozarabic—flourished among the Franks until Charlemagne ordered the substitution of the Roman rite (*cf.* p. 122f). Unfortunately for the survival of Gallican Chant, it was outlawed at a time when even neume notation was not widely used. The old Chant continued alive for a while, however, at points not easily controlled by the court, and a MS dating from 877 (63 years after Charlemagne's death), from the Abbey of Fleury, includes among its contents a Credo apparently of native origin. It could not have come from Rome, since the Roman liturgy did not adopt the Credo until 1024. Nor does the fact that the text in this MS is in Greek imply that the music came from Byzantium or elsewhere in the Orient, as the Credo was never sung there, but only recited.[1] In practical use, however, Gallican Chant eventually died out, except for such portions as the Roman Chant incorporated. Among these are three that became part of the Good Friday service: the powerfully moving *Improperia* (Reproaches), the *Crux fidelis,* and the hymn *Pange lingua . . . certaminis.*[2] Some examples of Gallican Chant survive in an Antiphonary written in the 11th century for the Cathedral of Albi and in the Gradual of St. Yrieix.[3] The suppression of the Gallican liturgy did not, as we shall see in Chapters 5 and 6, result in the cessation of creative activity on the part of Frankish church musicians, who continued to produce within the framework of the Roman rite.

The Spanish liturgy was destined to survive longer. It is not clear when

---

[15] See HuréA, 133, footnote.

[1] For a fuller discussion, see UrG, 203f.

[2] Not to be confused with the *Pange lingua . . . corporis.* The above chants, as they serve today, may be found in Liber 704, 709.

[3] Both of these MSS (the latter is reproduced in PM XIII) are in the Bibl. Nat. in Paris. For a list of published transcriptions of melodies claimed as Gallican, from these and other sources, see GasCG (1937), 133. See also, concerning portions of the Gallican repertoire added to the Roman, GasG, 55f; GasD, 264; concerning the adoption by the Roman rite of the Gallican (and Mozarabic) method of chanting the responsories, WagK, 132, or WagE I, 120. Information about the Gallican liturgy may be found in DuchC.

it became equipped with an extensive musical repertoire. The hymns of Prudentius (4th century) may have had some effect, through the rhythms employed in their texts, upon hymns later admitted into the Chant.[4] In 589 it became necessary for the Council of Toledo to object to the custom of dancing during the divine service. The earliest reasonably definite information about musical activity—and this is scant enough—dates from the end of the 6th century and the beginning of the 7th. There is evidence showing that contributions were made then at three great centers—Seville, Toledo, and Saragossa.

St. Leander, archbishop of Seville (d. 599), is mentioned [5] as having "composed many pieces to sweet sound." He had been sent, while archdeacon, as ambassador to Constantinople, where he and St. Gregory lived at the house of St. Eulogios. Both the Spaniard and the Roman apparently had opportunity to witness the musical splendor instituted earlier by Justinian, and to each is attributed the rôle of organizer of a body of Chant.[6] St. Isidore (d. 636), Leander's brother and successor as archbishop, did not ignore music in his encyclopedic writings, which have been characterized as "a literary Noah's ark." His *Etymologies* contain (in Bk. III, Chapters 14–22) [7] a summary of musical theory as propounded by Cassiodorus (*cf.* p. 125), thus showing more effectively the author's knowledge of the past than his interest in the musical Spain of his time. Such an interest is exhibited, however, in his *De Ecclesiasticis Officiis,* in which he gives some information [8] concerning the use of hymns, antiphons, *laudes* (= Alleluias), etc.

At Toledo, St. Eugenius (d. 657), St. Ildefonsus (d. 667), and St. Julian (d. 690) are all reported as having contributed [9] in some way to the Chant, as did Conantius (d. 639), bishop of Palencia, which came under the influence of Toledan musical culture.

At Saragossa, compositions were written for the church by Johannes (d. 631), its bishop.

In 711, Tariq landed at Tarifa and thus began the Moorish invasion. As a result, information is slight concerning the Chant in the 8th century, during which the Christians of Southern Spain found it necessary to adjust themselves to new conditions. The conquerors proved reasonably tolerant, and the Christians, who received the name of Mozarabes,[10] were allowed to continue

---

[4] See GéroH, 150.   [5] By St. Isidore. See MigneL LXXXIII, 1104.
[6] See further GasG, 21, or WagK, 111f.
[7] See LindE or MigneL LXXXII, or, for extracts, GerS I, 19.
[8] MigneL LXXXIII, 743f.
[9] Further concerning the little information we have about these contributions, see WagK, 112f, where citations of the sources are given. Or see RojoC, Chap. I, or the opening portion of Higini Anglès, *Hispanic Musical Culture from the 6th to the 14th Century,* to be published in MQ.
[10] Probably from *musta rab,* meaning an Arab by naturalization or a Christian who has adopted Arabism. (The name, however, was applied generally to Christians living under the Moorish yoke.) See DAC XII, 391.

the practice of their religion. Strangely enough, Cordova became a Christian liturgical-music center.

Our earliest Mozarabic Chant MSS date from the end of the 9th century and from the 10th and 11th. The completest and best preserved, the Antiph- onary of León, dates from 1066. Of special importance, as we shall see, is another 11th-century MS written for the monastery of St. Millán de la Cogolla.

The use of the Mozarabic liturgy and Chant continued not only in the land held by the Moors but in adjacent territory also until the latter part of the 11th century. Complaints had been made to Rome from time to time about non-conformance, but the popes had either refused to condemn or had required only slight changes. In 1071, however, the so-called "superstition of Toledo" was suppressed in the part of Spain held by the Christians, and the Roman rite was substituted. No change was needed in the North, in Cata- lonia, where the Roman liturgy had been in force and where the Chant was actively cultivated at Ripoll. The Catalonians developed a distinctive nota- tion of their own.[11] After the recapture of Toledo (1085) King Alfonso VI made the Roman rite obligatory there, in spite of much opposition from the people. Roderigo of Toledo relates that the Gregorian and Toledan liturgical books were subjected to a trial by fire, as a result of sedition, that the Gregorian book was consumed by the flames while the Toledan book remained intact, but that the king nevertheless ordered adoption of the Roman rite.[12] Reten- tion of the Mozarabic liturgy, however, was permitted in six Toledo churches, and it survived for a while in territory not reconquered from the Moors. On the whole, however, it eventually died out, so that no reliable tradition has come down to us with respect to the performance of the Chant.

This is especially serious in view of the fact that the old MSS were originally written in a neume notation that does not show intervals.[13] As a result, while we have a heritage of Mozarabic chant books, they are almost entirely un- decipherable. One of them, however, the MS from the monastery of St. Millán de la Cogolla already mentioned, contains several pages on which a 12th-century hand has written in Aquitanian notation (cf. p. 138) sixteen melodies originally inscribed in Mozarabic neumes. These pieces, all from the Office of the Dead, are, with five others, the only authentic Mozarabic melodies thus far deciphered.[14]

There is a less ancient source, however, that may preserve some more of

[11] Early Chant in Catalonia is treated in AngR.
[12] For a French translation of Roderigo's account (with reference to the original Latin), see GasG, 53f.
[13] Full discussions of this notation will be found in RojoC, Chap. III and SuñP, Chap. XIII. For a discussion in English, see PradoM, 219ff.
[14] The 21 pieces are printed in RojoC, 73–81.

the old music, probably in garbled form. Cardinal Francisco Ximenez de Cisneros, towards the end of the 15th century, sought to revive the old rite and in 1500 had his version of it printed. At about this time three *Cantorales,* or chant books, were inscribed, possibly at the order of Cisneros. They were written in mensural notation, but purported to contain Mozarabic melodies and were, in fact, "probably inspired in part at least by some Mozarabic *Cantoral* which may have survived in one of the Mozarabic parishes of Toledo." [15] An attempt has been made, by abandoning the measured rhythm of the notation and by eliminating extraneous material, to restore certain of these to the form in which they were sung before the 16th century (not necessarily, however, as far back as the Visigothic or even the Mozarabic period).[16] Whatever the date of the *Gaudete populi* [17] for Easter, one of the restored melodies, it is a strikingly beautiful piece. The *Cantorales,* however, contain many Gregorian pieces, not to be found in the Mozarabic MSS and therefore not common to the two bodies of Chant. Since the *Cantorales* have been drawn on for musical examples in writings on Mozarabic Chant, the reader should, without deafening his ear to possible beauties, bear this fact in mind for historical reasons.[18]

Some of the Mozarabic melodies show a resemblance to chants in the Ambrosian repertoire, paralleling, in a way, the resemblances in the liturgies.[19]

The surviving melodies for the *Preces* (literally, "prayers") are quite simple, as was desirable, since the congregation had to take part in their rendition, singing the respond. These Spanish supplications consisted of short strophes, the respond serving as a refrain (*cf.* p. 169, footnote 14). They were sung on certain days of penitence, after the psalm. Philologists once thought they were derived from the proses and sequences of France etc. (discussed on p. 187ff), but the Antiphonary of León attributes two Preces to Julian of Toledo (a 7th-century figure, as we have seen) and thus indicates that they existed before the proses and sequences.[20] Here is an example.

EXAMPLE 21. Preces from the Office of the Dead—To Be Sung at the Door of the Church—Mozarabic (after RojoC, 74).

[15] PradoM, 223.   [16] See RojoC, 117–40.   [17] Printed in PradoM, 233, and RojoC, 139.
[18] He should also guard against modern plainsong settings of Mozarabic texts, such as those in Dom Pothier's *Variae preces.* Useful warnings concerning printed versions of purportedly Mozarabic melodies will be found in WagK, 141. PradoM, 226f mentions some of the melodies in the *Cantorales* that are probably ancient.
[19] See RojoC, Chap. XIII.
[20] For further information concerning the Preces, see RojoC, 63.

℣. Ad te clamantes exaudi Christe,   ℣. Benigne Deus aurem appone,
    Flentium voces audi maerentes.   Rugitum nostrum pius intende.
          ℟. *Deus miserere.*   ℟. *Deus miserere.*
                                                    Etc.

℣. "Lord have mercy, Lord have mercy, O good Jesus, have compassion for him. ℟. *Lord have mercy.* ℣. Hear, O Christ, those crying to thee, listen to the mourning voices of the weeping. ℟. *Lord have mercy.* Bless, O Lord, turn thine ear, tenderly bend towards our groaning. ℟. *Lord have mercy.*" Etc.

The following, eloquent psalm setting, though brief, presents a more developed specimen of the Chant:

EXAMPLE 22. Antiphon from the Office of the Dead—To Be Sung at the Burial—Mozarabic (after RojoC, 78).

"If I ascend up into heaven, Thou art there: if I make my bed in hell, behold, Thou art there (*Psalm CXXXVIII* [*CXXXIX*], 8). Reach out thine hand, O Lord, deliver me from lower hell."

All the genuine Mozarabic examples can be made to fit into the Gregorian modal system (treated in Chapter 6), only modes I, II, III, and probably VIII, however, being represented. The fact that the Ambrosian and likewise the supposedly Gallican melodies can also be classified according to this system and the further fact that the Gregorian, Ambrosian, and Mozarabic neumes all bear a family resemblance, seem to lend weight to the theory that the Gregorian, Ambrosian, Mozarabic, and Gallican Chants— the four great Chants of the West—represent four musical dialects of one originally common language.[21] This cannot be true in the sense that one fully perfected language was once shared by all and was later modified in different ways by each. On the contrary, it took time for centralization to develop. The theory may be true, however, in the sense that to local folk-elements, already in existence, were added elements from the Greco-Roman world and the Orient, these preserving their essential character whenever and wherever they joined the local elements but, by contact with the latter, having that character eventually modified in different ways.

[21] This theory is brilliantly stated in PM I, 33f.

Chapter 5: GREGORIAN CHANT: Its History and Notation

The History

THAT the influence of Greco-Roman and Hebrew music came to bear directly on Gregorian Chant is attested, as we have noted in passing (*cf.* p. 67), by some actual musical evidence. This is to be found in melodies, of the old, pre-Christian order and of the new, which show striking similarities. It would be too much to claim in comparing these melodies that a particular chant is derived from a particular ancient piece, but it may reasonably be inferred that both probably drew on a common fund of idioms, passed on by the ancient cultures to the Christian.

The influence of Hebrew music has been acknowledged by most modern writers, among them Wagner, Gastoué, Ursprung.[1] It has been dealt with in detail by Idelsohn, from whom we borrow the following example, illustrating one only out of several parallels that have been discovered.

EXAMPLE 23. (After ldG, 517).
(A) Kyrie in Mode III (from Processionarium, Rome, 1894, p. 36).

(B) Babylonian Jewish Pentateuch Melody.

A. "Lord, have mercy. Lord, have mercy."
B. "Then Moses called for all the elders of Israel, and said unto them," etc. (*Exodus XII, 21.*)

Circumstantial evidence of a connection is afforded by the derivation of the post of the Christian precentor or cantor or *psaltes* or *psalmistes* (*cf.* p. 64, footnote 31) from the analogous position in the Synagogue, and by the admission into the liturgy of portions of the Synagogue service, such as the Alleluia [2] (*cf.*

---

[1] WagE I, 31 *et passim;* GasO, 3–24; UrK, 2 *et passim.*
[2] St. Isidore writes: *Laudes, hoc est alleluia canere, canticum est Hebraeorum* ("*Laudes*—that is, to sing Alleluia—is a song of the Hebrews"). MigneL, LXXXIII, 750.

p. 63) and the "Holy, Holy, Holy," the latter having been adopted, as is indicated by a letter of Clement I, about the end of the 1st century.

A parallel similar to that shown in Example 23 is offered by the Greek Epitaph of Seikilos (*cf.* p. 49) and one of the Gregorian antiphons for Palm Sunday.

EXAMPLE 24. Epitaph of Seikilos—Greek (Late Antiquity) and *Hosanna filio David*—Antiphon—Gregorian (after VivD, 46).

"A mortal's span dost thou live, vex not thyself with vain cares: thy life doth endure but a short while: its ending will Time soon demand of thee."

(Transl. C. F. Abdy Williams, *The Music of the Ancient Greeks,* 4.)

"Hosanna to the son of David: Blessed is he that cometh in the name of the Lord. O King of Israel: Hosanna in the highest" (*Matthew XXI, 9*).

Notes belonging to the Greek song, whether peculiar to it or common to it and the Roman chant, are in black; those peculiar to the Roman chant are in white.

The famous Oxyrhynchos hymn likewise has been held to show traits linking Christian Chant with the music of Greek paganism, both through its stylistic features [3] and through the Greek notation in which it survives (but *cf.* p. 49 *supra*).

The rarity of ancient melodies makes it impossible to determine whether the Hebrew influence or the Greco-Roman was the stronger, but such parallels as those given above support the long-held belief, based on cultural grounds, that both influences were at work.[4]

Obviously the value of such parallels would be slight if the authenticity of the church melodies could not be upheld. But the preservation of the ancient Gregorian tradition is, in fact, well attested. Keeping the Chant intact was long regarded as a religious duty, the respect for which seems not to have diminished notably until after the advent of polyphony. Remarkable evidence of the persistence of the tradition is furnished in the *Paléographie Musicale,* a sumptuous and invaluable series of facsimiles, in Volumes II and III of

---

[3] *Cf.* ReinU, 19.
[4] For an article claiming that the Greco-Roman influence was the stronger see MaN. For further details concerning the influences, see GéroP, Chap. I; GasJ; GasOH.

which the melody *Justus ut palma* is printed as it appears, with an extraordinary degree of uniformity, in 219 MSS dating from the 9th to the 11th century. "The fidelity with which the traditional Chant has been handed on from singer to singer is attested by the very large measure of unanimity which the earliest MSS show, in spite of the wide diffusion and the independence of the existing musical centres." [5] Such of the music as is claimed to come down from the 7th century or earlier is probably recoverable in substantially the form it had in that century, when the Chant, it seems, was codified (*cf.* p. 120); if, as eventually happened, the musical text became corrupt, it is possible for modern scholarship to weed out, with reasonable certainty, at least such corruptions as are more recent than the first half of the 11th century, when staff-notation was perfected. What was intended in the 17th century as an attempt at a restoration sadly miscarried, and the garbled Medicean edition of the Gradual resulted. A real restoration had to await the brilliant efforts of the monks of Solesmes, three pioneer generations of whom contributed mightily: Dom Prosper Guéranger (1805-75) by providing, through his liturgical studies, the impetus for a new edition of the Gregorian melodies; Dom Joseph Pothier (1835-1923, a pupil of Guéranger's) chiefly by restoring the melodic outlines; Dom André Mocquereau (1849-1930, a pupil of Pothier's) chiefly by attempting to restore the rhythm and by making available to scholars the *Paléographie Musicale*.[6]

While the early MSS just mentioned show a continuance of tradition beginning with the 9th century, there is evidence, of another sort, upon which the claim is based that the tradition is at least two centuries older:

> *The version of Scripture from which are taken the portions to which the music [of certain chants] is set . . . is the old Latin one known as 'Itala.' Now even at the time of St. Gregory it had not entirely given place to the Vulgate, yet from this time onwards the latter prevailed. . . . It is natural to seek the explanation of preserving an obsolete text of the words in the respect felt for the melodies to which they were set. It is therefore reasonable to conclude that these melodies existed for the most part before the definite abandonment of the Itala at Rome, that is to say before the middle of the 7th century.*[7]

What music is claimed to have come down from that century—the so-called Golden Age, the period of the Gregorian reform? Gastoué has listed as among examples of it the music for certain portions of the Mass. In order to appreciate the position of this music in the liturgy it is well to digress for a moment to bring the following information to mind:

The great bulk of the liturgy is divided into the Mass and the Daily Hours

---

[5] FrereP, 158.
[6] All the volumes of this series are listed in the bibliography under PM. Another valuable series instituted by Mocquereau is MG, containing various studies relating to the Chant (see bibliography).
[7] WyattG, 26. See also WagE I, 184.

of Divine Service. The texts for the former may be found in the Missal, those for the latter in the Breviary. The music for the Mass is contained in the Gradual, that for the Hour Service in the Antiphonary.[8] The Mass itself is divided into the Ordinary and the Proper. The former consists of those portions which, when present, do not change their texts; its musical parts are the Kyrie, Gloria, Credo, Sanctus (including the Benedictus), and Agnus Dei. The Proper consists of those portions whose texts change according to the season or saint being commemorated: the Proper of the Season, the Proper of the Saints, and the Common of the Saints, this last group differing from the second in that its contents are not reserved to a special occasion but used for a whole group of saints (Apostles, Evangelists, Martyrs, etc.). The *Kyriale* is a collection containing the music of the Ordinary (this music is included also in the Gradual); the *Vesperale* contains the music for vespers (also to be found in the Antiphonary). The *Officium Maioris Hebdomadae* contains the full service for Holy Week. The *Liber Usualis,* the most comprehensive modern Chant collection, contains music for both the Mass and the Hour Service.[9]

The music, then, which Gastoué lists [10] as dating back to the turn of the 7th century or earlier, is that for the following portions of the Mass:

a) All the Proper of the Season [11]
b) All the Common of the Saints [12]
c) The Requiem Mass [13]
d) From the Ordinary: Kyrie and Gloria XV, Mass XVIII, Credo I [14]
e) From the Proper of the Saints: almost all the chant sections of 47 different feasts.

The cultural background against which the Gregorian melodies were codified and flourished was one which, if we may judge by literary documents, differed considerably from that of later generations in its attitude towards music, although these documents include also writings that have their parallels today. The literature falls into two main classes: practical and theoretical. The first, in turn, falls into two divisions: works for the training of pupils (e. g.

---

[8] The term *Graduale* designates also the respond sung at Mass between the Epistle and the Gospel (*cf.* p. 178). The term *Antiphonale* did not originally have its present restricted meaning. See Grove I, 100.

[9] This may be had in (1) plainsong notation with Latin rubrics, (2) plainsong notation with English rubrics, (3) modern notation with Latin rubrics. The *Compendium* is an abbreviation of (3). Despite the comprehensive nature of the *Liber* we sometimes give one of the other chant-books as the source of a piece which the *Liber* contains, lest the *Liber* tend to overshadow unduly, in the student's mind, these important books. For details concerning the liturgy, see FortC. RobI, 110ff provides a useful bibliography including some further liturgical books.

[10] GasG, 121f; GasD. See also GasO, 201ff; FrereG, ixff.

[11] Except the Feast of the Holy Trinity and the Feast of Corpus Christi. The music for the Proper of the Season may be found in Liber 317ff. The services for the following feasts have been added since Gastoué made his list: the Feasts of the Holy Name, the Holy Family, and the Sacred Heart.

[12] Liber 1111ff.   [13] Except the Kyrie, *Dies irae, Libera.* The Mass is printed in Liber 1806ff.

[14] Liber 56ff, 62f, 64ff.

the *Musica Disciplina* of Aurelian of Réomé, middle of the 9th century) and
works for professional musicians (which become more plentiful beginning
with the 14th century). The second class likewise falls into two divisions:
works wholly devoted to music (e. g. the *De Institutione Musica* of Boethius)
and general works including sections on music. The latter, in turn, fall into
two subdivisions: philosophical (e. g. the *De Musica* of Cassiodorus) and
encyclopedic (e. g. the *Etymologies* of Isidore of Seville).

In the Middle Ages music was looked upon as a branch of mathematics—
a view that has never been and probably never will be altogether discarded,
since there is much truth in it—and was accordingly taught among the seven
liberal arts, not in the *trivium* (Grammar, Rhetoric, Logic), but in the *quadrivium* (Arithmetic, Geometry, Astronomy, Music).

The tradition of Greek theory was passed on to medieval writers by Boethius and Cassiodorus (*cf.* p. 52), as the Greek texts themselves were not
much read in the West until about the time of the Renaissance. The general
tendency of medieval culture was not so much to set up new systems as to
understand and develop those transmitted by *auctoritas* (authority) with the
aid of medieval *ratio* (intellectual studies). Thus the medieval theorists constantly refer,[15] for a variety of purposes, to the *Septem discrimina vocum* of
Vergil (*Aeneid* VI, 646), whose prestige soared so high in the Middle Ages,
owing to the "Messianic prophecy" in the Fourth Eclogue, that he qualified,
in the early 14th century, to serve as Dante's guide in the *Divine Comedy*.

Boethius divided music into (1) *musica mundana* (harmony in the macro-
cosmos), (2) *musica humana* (harmony in the microcosmos, i. e. man), and
(3) *musica instrumentis constituta* (practical music, an imitation of 1 and 2).
Several modern authors have thought that (3) consisted of instrumental music
only,[16] but it seems, in fact, to have included vocal music as well,[17] the word
instrumentis here representing all natural and artificial means whereby man
may wilfully produce music. Cassiodorus divided music into (1) *scientia
harmonica* (dealing with the structure of melody), (2) *scientia rhythmica*
(dealing with the correspondence between melody and text), and (3) *scientia
metrica* (dealing with metrical analysis). Like St. Augustine (*cf.* p. 64), he
defined music as the art *"bene modulandi."* Just as Cassiodorus here borrowed
from St. Augustine, so later writers borrowed heavily from him and Boethius, whose classifications etc. served as models. An eminent writer with a
different classification, however, was the Arab Alfarabi (d. 950) whose ideas
reached Christendom partly by way of borrowings made by the 12th-century
Spaniard Domenicus Gundissalinus (Domingo Gundisalvo) in his *De Divisione Philosophiae*.[18] The division there made between *musica speculativa*
(theoretical) and *musica activa* (practical) really repeats a Greco-Roman

[15] See, for example, GerS I, 23, 96 (PiperS, 853).   [16] E. g. AbD, 165.   [17] See PietzschK, 43ff.
[18] Printed in BaurG. See also FarmW, 16ff.

classification distinguishing between *musica theoretica* and *musica practica*.[19] Regino of Prüm (d. 915) divided music into *musica naturalis* and *musica artificialis,* the former corresponding to Boethius's *musica mundana* and *humana* combined, the latter to his *musica instrumentis constituta.* Later writers furnished other classifications. Much work remains to be done towards clarifying the relations between music and general culture in the Middle Ages. Medieval reports on the classification of music seem, however, actually to reflect contemporary attitudes and should not be regarded as merely mystic speculations filling a gap between the "saner" writings of Antiquity and those of a more modern age.[20]

Obscurity veils much of the history of specifically Roman Chant before Gregory the Great. Some facts, however, are known, beyond those mentioned in our section on the background of all Christian Chants.

It is very probable that Rome had an ecclesiastical singing school in the second half of the 4th century. Celestine I (422–32) is said to have introduced antiphonal chanting, previously used in the Hour Service, into the Mass, in which it was applied to the Introit. Such chanting presupposes a body of trained singers. Under Leo the Great (440–67), the monastery of St. John and St. Paul was built near St. Peter's, and its members performed liturgical prayers and chants. About the end of the 6th century, to escape the Lombard invaders, the Benedictine monks left Monte Cassino for Rome, where Pope Pelagius II (578–90) settled them near the Lateran Church. It was chiefly Benedictine monks who thereupon performed the Office at Rome; after their return to Monte Cassino during the reign of Gregory III (731–41), their duties at Rome were continued by other monks. Besides the foregoing popes, certain others are mentioned, by an anonymous Frankish monk whose Latin account [21] is of somewhat doubtful value, as having contributed to the growth of the liturgical Chant. The enumeration begins with Damasus I (366–84) who introduced the liturgical Order of Jerusalem into the Roman Church and ends with Boniface (530–2) who is said to have arranged a course of Chant for the whole year.

Three MSS have been preserved [22] which supposedly contain rather late copies of Roman Chant as sung before the time of Gregory I. Their contents are said to constitute "Old Vatican Music." Only a few examples [23] have thus far been published, and further investigation would doubtless prove valuable. The

[19] The extent of the influence of the Arabic musical system on Western Europe is a subject of controversy. It has a strong advocate in H. G. Farmer. See especially FarH; for further bibliographical information on Alfarabi, see MosL, 14.

[20] Further on classification, see PietzschK. On early medieval education, see PietzschM.

[21] MigneL CXXXVII, 1347.

[22] Gradual MS 5319 of the Vatican Library and Gradual F 22 and Antiphonary B 79 of the Archives of St. Peter's.

[23] See UrK, 20; FrereP, 147, 153ff; PM II, 6ff.

little printed creates the impression that this music, tending, as it does, to make excessive use of lengthy melismas, lacks the balance and moderation of the Chant now known as Gregorian.

To what extent Roman Chant was subjected to the influence of Byzantium is a matter of controversy.[24] Peter Wagner warmly supports the case for a strong Byzantine influence, because of two facts: "first, until the end of the 3rd century the liturgical language in Rome was Greek. . . . Secondly, the first and most complete development of the liturgical chant took place, as we know, in the countries of the East . . ." [25] Ursprung, on the other hand, vigorously opposes this view, believing such an influence discernible only in the texts, not in the music. Most of the popes between c. 650 and c. 750, however, were Byzantines or Orientals, a fact supporting Wagner's point of view with, at least, circumstantial evidence and there is considerably more, as we shall see.

At the turn of the 7th century Roman Chant appears to have undergone some sort of reform resulting in the codification of a repertoire which, with only a few additions, still constitutes the corpus of Roman plainsong. In view of the tendency, to which we shall repeatedly refer, of medieval musical expression to progress from a stage of fluidity to one of stability, it may be that this reform consisted to some extent in definitely associating particular melodic outlines with particular texts. We have found melodic formulas, not fixed melodies, characteristic of Synagogue Chant (cf. p. 10). The Church may have followed the practice of the Synagogue. And it is possible, analogous examples being furnished by other developments, that formulas, previously applied inconsistently and elastically to the various portions of the liturgy, were linked finally with those portions by the reform and that the method of the linking was settled. The fact that among the Greeks a similar evolution seems to have reached its culmination long before the 7th century, their nomoi having been replaced by melodies definitely reduced to form, furnishes no valid objection to this possibility. The Greeks had perfected a notation also, likewise a drama. But the West had to develop a notation and a drama over again from simple rudiments, and a fresh growth in the method of musical composition would not have been unparalleled.

The tradition ascribing the reform, whatever its precise nature, to Gregory I was apparently not questioned during the Middle Ages. Pierre Gussanville in 1675 and Georg von Eckhart in 1729, however, queried it, and at the end of the last century Gevaert [26] attacked it anew and forcefully. In defense of the tradition new evidence was brought to light, which tended only to reaffirm it, and most modern writers hesitate to disregard, in the absence of

[24] See UrK, 24ff; WagE I, 44ff. For a view (based only, however, on general cultural grounds) that Gregorian Chant did not derive so much from Greek and Hebrew as from Byzantine sources, see RobI, 104ff (including quotations from Cecil Gray).
[25] WagE I, 44.   [26] GevO; GevM, ixff.

conclusive evidence, a tradition so old and deeply rooted. One of the chief documents supporting it is John the Deacon's life of Gregory the Great, dating from *c.* 870, unfortunately almost three centuries after the Saint's death. There are, however, passages in earlier writings also [27] which, even if they are incidental, seem to mention or bear indirectly on the part that Gregory reputedly played. According to John's narrative, Gregory founded or—what is likelier—reorganized the Schola Cantorum and, more important, compiled the Roman Antiphonary. Circumstantial evidence for the tradition is Gregory's visit to Byzantium where, with St. Leander, he had the opportunity of observing the practice of Byzantine Chant at St. Sophia (*cf.* p. 79). Even the legends that Gregory added four plagal tones to the four authentic tones, supposedly introduced by St. Ambrose, and that he received his melodies by inspiration from the Holy Ghost—there are numerous medieval pictorial representations of the Saint with the dove singing into his ear—confirm, by their persistence, the strong impression obtaining in the Middle Ages themselves, that Gregory had performed an important musical rôle. It was he who, apparently, extended the occasions for singing the Alleluia from Easter to all Sundays and holidays (except during times of fasting and penitence) and it may have been he who curtailed the Alleluias' former apparently excessive melismas. Nevertheless, the exact nature of Gregory's rôle is uncertain.[28]

Because of this, the propriety of the term "Gregorian" Chant has been questioned and the substitution of "Roman" Chant urged. But this is in the nature of quibbling: that St. Ambrose had much to do with "Ambrosian" Chant as it survives is exceedingly doubtful, yet we are not aware that the substitution of "Milanese" for "Ambrosian" Chant has been seriously recommended. Further with respect to terminology: it is not quite sure when the term *cantus planus* was first used, though it was probably by Odo of Cluny in the 10th century.[29] It seems then to have been applied to melodies in the plagal modes, i. e. to such as were lower in pitch than those in the authentic modes, and therefore "plane" or "lying flat." The suggestion has even been made that it referred to the fact that it was Chant melodies that *lay* beneath added melodies in early polyphony.[30] Some of the synonyms occurring in the old Latin texts are: *cantilena, cantus ecclesiasticus, carmen gregorianum,* etc. Not until the 13th century did *musica plana* etc. come to connote music in free rhythm as distinguished from measured music, as do the English words "plainsong" and "plainchant."

Gregorian Chant gradually became the norm for all Western churches. During Gregory's lifetime St. Augustine of Kent, the first Archbishop of

---

[27] Conveniently assembled in JohnG, 182ff; WagE I, 168ff; GasG, Chap. I.
[28] The whole question is studied afresh in *Music in Western Civilization* by Paul Henry Láng.
[29] See GerS I, 259. *Cf.* also Aribo Scholasticus in GerS II, 201.
[30] See WagE II, 371f; WagD, 99.

Canterbury, brought the Roman liturgy to England; he was later assisted by Paulinus, first Archbishop of York. The Venerable Bede, in writing of Putta, who became Bishop of Rochester *c.* 669, states that he derived from "the pupils of Blessed Pope Gregory . . . his knowledge of the Roman Chant." [31] About 680, John, Archicantor of the Papal Chapel, was sent to England by Pope Agatho to improve the practice, and through his instruction the monastery at Wearmouth became a renowned and authoritative center of plainchant activity. England gave as well as received. From that country came St. Boniface (680–754; real name Wynfrith; born in Devonshire), who was the principal figure in the spread of Roman Chant in Germany. From England also came Charlemagne's adviser Alcuin, who influenced the practice of the liturgy in Gaul.

On the Continent, Gregorian Chant was disseminated in the North and in Switzerland by oral tradition. The old German tradition, which had developed at the important liturgical center of Mainz, died out as a result of the activity of St. Boniface, whose successor as bishop of that place, Hrabanus Maurus (also a pupil of Alcuin's), continued in his path. The chief work of cultivating the Roman tradition in the German-speaking countries was carried on at the monasteries of Reichenau and St. Gall.[32] The importance of the latter, however, was overstressed by its chronicler Ekkehard IV, upon whom, until recently, some modern historians [33] have placed too much reliance. To proclaim abroad the authenticity of the Chant as practiced at his monastery, Ekkehard records as fact the legend of Petrus and Romanus, stating that they came direct from Rome, the former implanting Gregorian Chant at Metz, the latter at St. Gall.[34] In time Gregorian Chant prevailed throughout Germany, but slightly modified. The outstanding feature of the so-called German chant-dialect consisted in the frequent substitution of the interval of a third for that of a second.[35]

By the 11th century, Roman Chant prevailed practically throughout Spain (*cf.* p. 111).

In Gaul, Charlemagne's father Pepin had organized the liturgy according to the Roman model, and it was in furtherance of his wishes that Remigius, bishop of Rouen, and Chrodegang, bishop of Metz, had Roman Chant cultivated within the spheres of their influence. Pepin's purpose was further to unite his subjects through the bonds of one liturgy. Thus it was a political

[31] MigneL XCV, 175.
[32] Concerning Reichenau, see BramR. Concerning St. Gall, see SchubG, but in the light of DorenE.
[33] E. g. SchubG.
[34] Concerning the fictitious nature of this account, see WagE I, 219, and DorenE (which quotes Ekkehard's Latin text), 128.
[35] *Cf.* BesM, 83, and UrK, 49ff, where further bibliographical references may be found. The Introduction to WagT, Vol. 2, mainly devoted to the German dialect, contains many musical illustrations comparing melodic figures as they appear in the Vatican Edition and in Italian, English, French, and German versions.

aim that caused Gallican Chant to begin losing ground in its native land to the Roman. But, although Pepin and his brothers favored Roman practice, the Gallican liturgy lingered. Three generations of Frankish monarchs were sent model chant books from Rome: Pepin by Paul I; Charlemagne, who was most zealous in promoting the adoption of the Roman rite and Chant, by Hadrian I; and Louis the Pious by Gregory IV.[36] About the first quarter of the 9th century, the liturgy for the Frankish Empire was in its essentials settled by Amalarius through a combination of Roman and Gallican elements, concerning which he gives details in his *De Ordine Antiphonarii*.

To what extent the organ, kithara, and other instruments were used during the earlier centuries in the performance of church music is a point on which no conclusive answer can be reached. Pepin in 757 received an organ as a gift from the Byzantine Emperor, Constantine Copronymos VI. Bishop Aldhelm (d. 709) mentions *organa* in his writings, but he is not using the term with reference to instruments (*cf.* p. 252).[37] The oft-repeated tale that a pneumatic organ was adopted to improve congregational singing in Rome by Pope Vitalian, *c.* 666, is not authentic. Other claims on behalf of a prior appearance of the organ in the West are likewise incapable of substantiation. As for the organ that Harun-al-Rashid is supposed to have presented to Charlemagne some 50 or 60 years later—the legend was appropriated in all seriousness by musical histories from *Les Chevaliers du Cygne*, a romance by Mme. de Genlis.[38] Germany made considerable progress in constructing organs in the latter part of the 9th century. We actually have a little treatise from the late 9th or early 10th century, containing information concerning the measurement of organ-pipes.[39] St. Dunstan (925–88) furthered the installation of several organs in England. He seems to have been a most musical person, performing on the organ, psaltery, harp, and chime-bells, among other instruments, and gaining, to quote Canon Galpin, "the unenviable name of a sorcerer by constructing an Aeolian Harp which played when placed against a crevice in a wall." A remarkable organ was erected at Winchester about 950. It is described by a monk, Wulstan (d. 963), as having had 26 bellows and 400 pipes.[40] The hydraulis, for the first time since *c.* 483, reappears in the West *c.* 826, when such an instrument was constructed for Louis the Pious by a certain Georgius Veneticus. He may quite possibly have learned from Arabic sources how to build it, for the work of Muristus, mentioned in Chapter 2, was known to the Arabs perhaps as early as the 8th century (certainly in

[36] For details, see WagE I, 206–12.
[37] *Cf.* Handschin in Acta, VII (1935), 160.   [38] FarmO, 139ff; BittH.
[39] Printed in PiperS, 857; GerS I, 101. For a discussion, see SchmidtgO.
[40] Further concerning the medieval organ, see p. 329, *et passim*. For an introduction to the early history of the organ in the Middle Ages, see BittO, which is corrected in a few details in *Speculum* V, 217ff, but remains on the whole a useful contribution.

the 10th). We continue to hear of the hydraulis occasionally during the Middle Ages from both European and Arabic writers.[41]

The tradition of playing the kithara did not die with the Roman Empire. We learn that Theodoric, king of the Ostrogoths, sent a kithara-player to the Court of Clovis. The instrument is found in Western Europe far into the Middle Ages. (By the 9th or 10th century, however, the term *citharisare* meant "to play any stringed instrument.") Venantius Fortunatus, bishop of Poitiers in the 6th century, in some verses mentions the *lyra* among other instruments:

> *Romanusque lyra plaudat tibi, Barbarus harpa,*
> *Graecus achilliaca, chrotta Britanna canat.*[42]

The *chrotta* or *rotta* (rote) was a lyre-shaped instrument which usually had five to eight strings. If some lyras and kitharas in old Western miniatures are merely copies of ancient representations, this is by no means true of all.[43]

Another instrument of ancient origin—the *musa* (bagpipe)—is again mentioned. The writer commonly referred to as John Cotton (*cf.* p. 127) declared it, *c.* 1100, superior to all other instruments, because it simultaneously employed the human breath like the *tibia,* the hand like the viol, and bellows like the organ.[44]

The whole subject of the use of instruments in church music is beclouded by the symbolical references to instruments, common in medieval writings (*cf.* p. 64). Some authors—whether for symbolic, poetic, or encyclopedic reasons—mention instruments no longer actually in use or else fundamentally changed. Cassiodorus is by no means alone in using the psaltery as an allegorical symbol of Christ, but it is not always possible, as it is here, to know whether an instrument is being mentioned as a mystic symbol or as a source of musical sound. On the other hand, there are so many miniatures and larger representations suggesting the practical use of instruments, sometimes even illustrating different stages in their history, as, for example, the Utrecht Psalter does with the kithara, that it seems not unreasonable, in doubtful passages, slightly to favor a musical rather than a mystical interpretation.[45]

IF the music of the Golden Age is anonymous, probably for the good reason that it consisted in sizable measure of an adaptation of formulas that were common property (Gregory's rôle, after all, was at most that of "editor"),

[41] Further on this subject, see FarmO, 146ff.

[42] MigneL LXXXVIII, 244. "The Roman praises thee with the lyra, the Barbarian sings to thee with the harp, the Greek with the kithara and the Briton with the rote."

[43] SachsH, 158.   [44] GerS II, 233.

[45] *Cf.* GéroP, 175f, 180ff, 190. For a facsimile edition of the Utrecht Psalter, see UP; for an article on it, SchlesU. For a study of symbolism as applied to the 11th- or 12th-century sculptural representation of the 8 Tones (*cf.* p. 172ff) in the pillar-capitals of the abbey-church of Cluny—a study involving instruments—see SchraD.

we know the names of the authors of a fairly large number of medieval treatises and also of some composers of the Silver Age, the renaissance of plainsong activity that ended in the 12th century.

The following list gives thumbnail sketches of certain outstanding medieval writers on music up to *c.* 1100, to all of whom further reference will be made.[46]

1. Boethius (*c.* 480–524) was mainly a philosopher and mathematician.[47] He served as counsellor to Theodoric, but was executed by him on charges of treason.

2. Cassiodorus (*c.* 485–*c.* 580) also served Theodoric and later Athalaric. He retired upon the entry of Belisarius into Ravenna and founded two monasteries.

3. Isidore of Seville (*c.* 570–636): see p. 110.

The musical writings of Boethius, Cassiodorus, and Isidore constituted the material for musical studies within the *quadrivium* until the beginning of the 9th century. The first perpetuated the influence of Ptolemy into the Middle Ages; the second, that of Aristoxenos.

4. Alcuin (753–804): see p. 122. The fragment printed under his name by Gerbert contains the first mention of the Occidental equivalents of the eight echoi. We shall say more about this in Chapter 6.

5. Hrabanus Maurus (d. 856): see p. 122. His work is chiefly a compilation of Cassiodorus and Isidore, intended for the training at the abbey of Fulda, where he taught before his removal to Mainz.

6. Aurelian of Réomé (middle of the 9th century), a monk, is the first Western writer to give details about the structure of melodic formulas having modal significance and about the correspondence between the rhythms of text and melody.

7. Rémy, a monk of Auxerre (fl. towards the end of the 9th century). He has left us a commentary on the musical portion of the *Satyricon* of Martianus Capella.

8. Hucbald, a monk of St. Amand, near Valenciennes (*c.* 840–930). The *De Harmonica Institutione* is the only surviving work on music that scholars generally admit to be his. Several other treatises, including the

---

[46] Musical writings by these men are printed in the original languages as follows: by No. 1 in FriedlB and MigneL LXIII; by No. 5 in MigneL CXI; by Nos. 2–4 and 6–16 in GerS; duplications, in better editions, by No. 2 in MynorsC, by No. 11 in PiperS, by No. 12 in AmelM, and by No. 14 in EllinM; other works by Nos. 9, 10, and 12 in CouS. Where a writing appears in both GerS and MigneL, no reference is made here to the latter. Throughout this book, references will be made to treatises not only in the most modern editions, but also in the GerS and CouS editions, if the treatises appear there, since these 2 works are likely to be generally available. For other thumbnail sketches of the theorists, see GasM II, 558ff and HughT and, for a study of their treatises, RieG, an important and comprehensive work, certain details of which have been corrected by later writings.

[47] A German translation of his musical treatise is provided by PaulB which, however, has been subjected to some criticism.

famous *Musica Enchiriadis,* were formerly assigned to him, but their authenticity was forcefully attacked by Hans Müller.[48] Hucbald's undis-
putedly genuine tract is not of great interest. We have seen that in the
Middle Ages many theoretical works, out of respect for *auctoritas,* duplicated what had been written before. Such works, Hucbald's included, are
of interest to us chiefly as showing that some special technical device or
system was still used, or at least inventoried, at a particular time. The
medieval respect for *auctoritas* should not be mistaken for a too easy con-
science with respect to plagiarism. Borrowings such as Hucbald's are
common in musical treatises throughout the Middle Ages. Hucbald, whatever his merit, enjoyed a considerable reputation in his own day. A curious
Latin Elegy of his on the death of Charles the Bald is still extant. Every
word in it begins with *c* for *calvus* (bald), which, according to one writer,
"explains how it was that he had no time to write the *Musica Enchiriadis."*
This work,[49] whoever its author may have been, affords valuable information concerning notation, organum, etc. It dates from not later than the
9th century and may be earlier.[50]

9. Regino (d. 915), who became abbot of the Benedictine monastery of Prüm
   in 892, opens the long series of *tonalia* or *tonaria* (systematic arrangements
   of antiphons, responses, etc. according to the mode; *cf.* the *Oktoechos*).
   Regino borrows heavily from his predecessors, among them Cicero, Boethius, Cassiodorus, Isidore, and Aurelian.

10. Odo (d. 942), from 927 abbot of Cluny, is the putative author of certain
    theoretical writings, of which, for simplicity, he will be regarded in this
    book as the actual author. Their authenticity has been attacked by some
    scholars; others claim that at least the important *Dialogus* and one other
    tract, if not in fact composed by him, were written under his authority.
    The *Dialogus* contains the first comprehensive example of the use of
    letters for pitches in the meaning that was to become standard for the
    Middle Ages and still prevails except for changes in capitalization etc.[51]
    (See further, p. 136.)

[48] In MülH. The authorship of the *Musica Enchiriadis* has been variously assigned to the abbot
Otger of St. Pons (d. 940), the abbot Hoger or Noger of Werden (d. 905), etc. For a bibliography
on the subject of authorship, see Handschin in the *Deutsche Vierteljahrsschrift für Literaturwissenschaft und Geistesgeschichte,* V (1927), 339.

[49] Printed in GerS I, 152 (see also CouS II, 74), where it is followed, on p. 173, by the *Scholia
Enchiriadis,* a dialogue consisting of a pupil's questions and a master's replies, both based on the
Musica Enchiriadis. A German translation of the manual may be found in SchlecM. SpittaM in-
cludes some corrections of Gerbert's text. An article on certain variations in the MS texts of the
manual is furnished by SowaT. A partial summary, in English, may be found in FoxT. See also
GrutH.

[50] There is some disagreement over the date of the treatise. The above statement follows the
opinion of Handschin in the *Revue du Chant grégorien,* XL (1936), 181.

[51] For a German translation of the *Dialogus,* see BohnO. Extensive passages of it are translated
into French and the rest summarized in LambiE, 123ff. The *Musicae artis disciplina,* attributed
to Odo, is similarly treated in LambiE, 146ff. A book of readings in the history of music, now in
preparation by Oliver Strunk, will contain an English translation of the *Dialogus.*

11. Notker Labeo (d. 1022), like Notker Balbulus, who lived about a century earlier and with whom he is not to be confused, was an instructor at St. Gall. He is the author of the first-known writings in German that deal with music, these including the little treatise on the measurement of organ-pipes, mentioned a few pages back.[52]

12. Guido d'Arezzo (c. 995–1050), a Benedictine monk, perfected staff-notation, so far as plainsong is concerned, and re-established solmisation, as is shown by his letter to the monk Michael (cf. p. 150). He is an important source of our knowledge of organum (cf. p. 259). The Micrologus is the most extensive of his valuable writings.[53]

13. Berno (d. 1048), from 1008 abbot of Reichenau, gives us another tonale and supplies information concerning monochord experiments.[54]

14. Hermannus Contractus (1013–54): [55] see below.

15. Wilhelm (d. 1091), abbot of the Monastery of Hirsau in the Black Forest. His De Musica et Tonis [56] is one of several medieval musical treatises written in the form of a dialogue between master and pupil. The obsequiousness of Wilhelm's pupil and the smugness of the master are sometimes amusing.

16. The theorist (c. 1100) whom historians usually call John Cotton and regard as an Englishman, but whom it may well be more correct to name Joannes of Liége (without the surname "Cotton").[56a] His treatise [57] includes information concerning progress made in the development of organum (see p. 261).

Some of these theorists, then, were statesmen; more were abbots or humbler inhabitants of monasteries; several were poets as well as musicians.[58]

The monasteries of Reichenau and St. Gall were each able to boast at least one man to whom distinguished original contributions are accredited, and these institutions were therefore partly responsible for the plainsong renaissance to which we have referred.

At Reichenau, while Berno was abbot, Hermannus Contractus (Hermann the Cripple) proved not only a clear-thinking theorist, but also, through his Salve Regina and Alma Redemptoris Mater, a composer of marked ability. Many medieval melodies have individual histories spanning centuries—

[52] There are, in all, 5 German tracts by Notker. 2 have been translated into modern German by P. H. Piper in his Die älteste deutsche Litteratur bis um das Jahr 1050, 1884.

[53] Mikros = Greek for "short, small"; logos = Greek for "account, word," etc. For a German translation, see HermM or SchlecG. Extensive passages are translated into French and the rest summarized in LambiE, 182ff. For a study of the work and its sources, see WolkG. A German translation of the letter to the monk Michael is included in HermE; LambiE, on p. 163ff, treats the letter as it does the Micrologus and, on p. 172ff, translates still other passages from Guido. The Strunk book mentioned in footnote 51 will contain an English translation of the letter.

[54] See WantM.　[55] EllinM contains not only the definitive text of the original of Hermannus's Musica, but a translation into English.

[56] German translation in MülW.　[56a] Cf. WaesM, 336ff.　[57] German translation in KornT.

[58] Examples of the poetry of Boethius, Alcuin, and Hrabanus Maurus are included (with English versions) in Helen Waddell, Mediaeval Latin Lyrics (4th ed., 1933).

that is, they are used over and over again for different purposes, often as part of the texture of polyphonic compositions. We shall occasionally mention the use of the *Alma Redemptoris Mater* in different connections, thus giving some slight suggestion of the kind of history a medieval melody might have and a partial idea of the length of time during which it could remain a fertile source of inspiration for essentially new compositions. The medieval popularity of the *Alma Redemptoris Mater* is attested by Chaucer's mention of it in the Prioress's Tale:

> *This litel childe his litel book lerning,*
> *As he sate in the scole at his primere,*
> *He Alma Redemptoris herde sing,*
> *As children lerned hir antiphonere:*
> *And as he dorst, he drow him nere and nere,*
> *And herkened ay the wordes and the note,*
> *Til he the firste vers coulde al by rote.*

EXAMPLE 25. *Alma Redemptoris Mater*—Antiphon—Hermannus Contractus (after LiberM, 239).

Mother of Christ! hear thou thy people's cry,
Star of the deep, and Portal of the sky!
Mother of Him who thee from nothing made,
Sinking we strive, and call to thee for aid:
Oh, by that joy which Gabriel brought to thee,
Thou Virgin first and last, let us thy mercy see.

(**Transl.** Edward Caswell, *Lyra Catholica, containing all the Breviary and Missal hymns* [1849], 38)

"In the powerful creations [of Hermannus] Occidental music achieved its own distinctive ring in a free and convincing way for the first time. It is the very beginning of its history." [59]

At St. Gall, Notker Balbulus ("the Stammerer," d. 912) made important contributions which, however, were probably all literary (cf. pp. 187f). To him is wrongly attributed the justly famous *Media Vita*—another medieval melody with a long history, which possibly came into the body of Roman Chant from the Gallican repertoire.[60] This melody achieved the rank of an ecclesiastical folk-song. "Miraculous powers were ascribed to it. . . . When in the year 1263 the Archbishop of Treves appointed a certain William to be Abbot of the monastery of S. Matthias against the will of the monks, they prostrated themselves on the ground and said the *Media vita* and other prayers, and thus hoped to get protection from the Abbot who was being forced upon them. . . . The Council of Cologne in 1316 forbade the *Media vita* to be sung against anyone without the bishop's permission." [61]

Liége seems to have been an active musical center *c.* 900–*c.* 1125. Rodulphe, of the monastery of St. Trond, is known to have composed plainsong melodies and may also have been a theorist.[62]

Among chant composers of the Silver Age, other than Hermannus, were King Robert the Pious of France (995–1031), the famous Abelard (1079–1142), and the nun, St. Hildegard of Bingen (d. 1179). Abelard worked at a hymn-book intended for the use of his monks and for the nuns presided over by Heloïse. It is possible that his lost love-poems addressed to Heloïse were among the important sources that served as an impetus to the troubadour art. The songs of Hildegard of Bingen mix liturgical and folk-elements,[63] and have therefore been held to act as a link in the chain leading from the antiphons of Hermannus Contractus to the *Minnelieder* of Walther von der Vogelweide. Further important musical figures of this period will be mentioned towards the end of Chapter 6.

The productions of the Silver Age constitute, with only a few exceptions, the last important contributions to the plainsong repertoire. With the increasing vogue of polyphony the decline of plainsong set in—but not its eclipse, as its restoration by the monks of Solesmes shows.

So far as the present state of scholarly investigation makes it possible to judge, Gregorian Chant represents the greatest body of monomelody in

---

[59] BesM, 87. There is a 12th-century MS (taken into account in EllinM) containing Hermannus's *De Musica* in the possession of the Eastman School of the University of Rochester. This MS contains also the *Musica* of Berno of Reichenau, the *Musica* of Wilhelm of Hirsau, etc.
[60] *Cf.* WagM, 18. The piece is printed in Vesperale, 154*.   [61] WagE I, 233.
[62] For a discussion of music in medieval Liége, see the opening portion of WaesM (in which an attempt is made to assign Aribo Scholasticus to Liége instead of to Freising, where he is usually believed to have held forth), and AudaE. See also StegQ and AudaO.
[63] *Cf.* UrK, 63f, where further bibliographical references are given, UrH, and BronH. For facsimiles of a MS containing Hildegarde's musical works, see GmelchK.

existence and therefore the chief product of a whole large branch of music, worthy of extended study. We shall give its stylistic features more attention than we have given those of other bodies of Chant. And this, not only because the subject has already been more closely investigated, owing to the greater quantity of MSS and dependable transcriptions, but also because the music provides the material for a study of the essentials of one-line music, a material "classic" in the way Bach's fugues or Beethoven's sonatas are classic, the standard examples of their types, upon which any study of the nature of the forms would normally be based.

Like sculpture, as Frere points out,[64] monody reached its highest degree of perfection at an earlier period, while harmony, like painting, achieved its climax much later. As a result, to the average man of today, sculpture and monody have a less immediate appeal than painting or harmony. But there is no justification for regarding "either the masterpieces of Greek sculpture or the masterpieces of Latin plainsong as being anything less than unsurpassed. . . . Plainsong is archaic only in the sense in which Greek sculpture is archaic."

Notation

I. THE NOTATION OF INTERVALS

IT will be simplest to describe first the definitive form of Gregorian notation and then the development through which that form was reached.

The neumes employed in modern editions of Gregorian Chant may be classed in four groups: simple, compound, "strophici," and liquescent. Here are some of the principal neumes of each group:

I. SIMPLE NEUMES [1]

Virga	¶	▪	♪
Punctum	●	▪	♪
Podatus or Pes	▮	▪	♫
Clivis	▶	▪	♫
Torculus	♨	▪	♫♫
Porrectus	Ν	▪	♫♫
Scandicus	♬	▪	♫♫
Salicus	♩	▪	♪♫
Climacus	¶••	▪	♫♫

It will be noticed that, at least as transcribed in the last column, all the elements of each neume have the same value regardless of the shapes of the notes. The virga and the punctum are the same; the virga originally indicated

[64] In Grove IV, 196.
[1] Strictly speaking, only a neume containing a single note is a "simple neume," and the term is sometimes restricted to a symbol of this type. Our classification follows SuñP, 3ff.

a relatively higher tone and the punctum a lower one. (It is obvious that some such distinction would have been helpful before adoption of the staff.) The scandicus and salicus differ in that the second note of the latter receives an "ictus" in performance (*cf*. p. 142), while in the former, as in all the other neumes consisting of two or more notes (except the pressus—see below), it is the first note that receives the ictus.

2. COMPOUND NEUMES

Torculus Resupinus	♪	•	♫♩
Porrectus Flexus	♪	•	♫♩
Scandicus Flexus	♪	•	♫♩
Pes Subpunctis	♪	•	♫♩
Climacus Resupinus Flexus	♪	•	♫♫	etc.

3. *"Strophici"*

Apostropha	˛
Distropha or Bistropha	˛ ˛
Tristropha	˛ ˛ ˛
Oriscus	˒
Pressus	▬♪▬ or ▬♪♪▬ or ▬♪▬ etc.

The apostropha, distropha, tristropha, and oriscus are all often printed today as simple puncta but their function is not quite the same. The apostropha is thought originally to have indicated a kind of vocal nuance imparted to the neume to which the symbol was added.[2] Today no nuance is applied to the apostropha—although the distropha and tristropha are still supposed to be sung with a gentle vibrato and a diminuendo. The oriscus is always joined to the end of a neume and is sung more lightly than the notes of that neume. In the pressus the two notes of equal pitch are sung as one sustained tone, upon which the ictus falls.

4. LIQUESCENT NEUMES

Epiphonus	♪
Cephalicus	♫
Torculus Liquescens	♫
Porrectus Liquescens	♫
Climacus Liquescens	♫
Quilisma	♫

Liquescent neumes usually occur where there are two or three consonants together, or on a diphthong, or sometimes on *g* or *m* between two vowels, and are designed to render smooth the passage from one syllable to the other. They are sung legato, with a very slight *ritardando,* and the undersized note

[2] For more information see SufiP, 489.

is sung softer though not necessarily shorter (*cf.* Ex. 35). The diamond-shaped notes in the climacus liquescens are smaller than the corresponding notes in the simple climacus. The quilisma is used between two notes that almost always form a minor third, sometimes a major third, and occasionally a fourth. When it occurs within an interval of a fourth it is usually adjacent to the upper note of the interval. As befits its transitional character, the quilisma is sung lightly, *portamento,* the preceding note being retarded (*cf.* p. 160).

Modern plainsong notation employs a four-line staff and two clefs: the C clef, which occurs only on the 3 upper lines and the F clef, which occurs usually on the 3rd . There are four kinds of bars The bar through the fourth line indicates the end of an incise, the smallest melodic division; the bar through the second and third lines, the end of a member of a phrase; the bar through all four lines, the end of a phrase; and the double bar, the end of a piece or a change of choirs. The custos: is a small note placed at the end of a line to prepare the singer for the first note of the next line.

The modern neumes, as we shall see, are outgrowths of the symbols found in medieval manuscripts. Medieval notation had nothing in common with Greek notation which, indeed, was already partly forgotten or misunderstood by the 5th century. How, then, did neumes originate? In the absence of reliable documentary evidence, the subject is a matter of conjecture. Several hypotheses have been advanced regarding the source of Latin neumes. According to one theory Latin notation was drawn directly from the Byzantine ekphonetic signs (*cf.* p. 83), [3] according to another, from the Hebrew cantillation signs.[4] But the most plausible hypothesis, buttressed with the most convincing evidence, is that which finds the immediate origin of Latin neumes, as well as of the ekphonetic notation, in grammatical accent-signs. According to this theory it was the grammatical accents of Greek and Latin which were the models for the primitive neumes (as for their Eastern counterpart). Thus the "tonic" or acute accent ∕ , indicating an elevation of the voice, became the virga ∕ ; and the "grave" accent ∖, indicating a lowering of the voice, became the punctum − . The acute and grave accents illustrated graphically the movements made by the hands of ancient orators and choirleaders to indicate corresponding inflections of the voice. Hence early Latin musical notation employing neumes is sometimes called oratorical, or cheironomic, notation (*cf.* p. 8).

The circumflex ⌃ (acute + grave) became the clivis ∧ ;
the anticircumflex ⋎ (grave + acute) "   " podatus ⋁ .

[3] *Cf.* ThibO. [4] *Cf.* GasC, 15.

Accents were combined   ⤢ (acute + grave + acute) became the porrectus 𝘕 ;
                        𝘏 (grave + acute + grave)   "   "   torculus ⋏ ;
                        𝘑𝘓 (grave + grave + acute)   "   "   scandicus ⸗ ;
                        𝘛 (acute + grave + grave)   "   "   climacus /. ;

and so on. The liquescent neumes owe their existence to purely textual causes, and may therefore also be said to come from grammar, although their graphic form has no model in written symbols such as the accents. It is only the quilisma for which a grammatical origin cannot be found.[5]

When did Latin neumes first come into general use? The earliest complete MSS that contain neumes date from the 9th century, but fragments are extant that were written in the 8th century.[6] A significant fact about the neumes in these early MSS is that they are already developed well beyond the stage of accent-signs. This fact points to a still earlier and more primitive stage of neume notation. Indeed the history of Gregorian Chant would seem to support the assumption that neumes existed as early as the 6th century. For it is difficult to conceive how the complex task of codifying plainsong melodies could have been undertaken during the time of Gregory the Great without the aid of some system of notation. And it is extremely unlikely that the emissaries of the Schola Cantorum could have transmitted the musical repertory of the Church as faithfully and disseminated it as widely as they apparently did entirely by word of mouth. Evidence of a system of notation is clearly implied in the following quotation from the text of the Council of Clovesho (Glasgow) in 747: "[The Festivals of our Lord] . . . in the Office of Baptism, the celebration of Masses, *in the method of chanting,* shall be celebrated in one and the same way, namely, in accordance with the *sample* that we have received *in writing* from the Roman Church." [7] But no MSS with neumes have come down to us from the Gregorian Era.[8] Many MSS exist, however, that date from the 9th century on. The most imposing collection of facsimiles is the *Paléographie Musicale,* already mentioned.[9]

Oratorical or cheironomic notation, while it indicated exactly the number and grouping of tones, gave no hint about the nature of the *intervals* between them. The neumes were written above the text and are spoken of as being *in campo aperto,* "in an open field"—that is, there are no staff-lines to show the precise intervals desired. How, then, did the early singers read this nota-

[5] This mysterious neume has been made the subject of special study. See VivQ; also YasQ, 182ff, 343ff.

[6] For example, there are neumes applied to part of the Introit *Ad te levavi* in the 8th-century Brussels Codex 10127–10144, reproduced in SuñP, 33.

[7] The Latin quotation is in SuñP, 34, from Mansi, *Amplissima Coll. Conc.,* XII (1901), 399.

[8] Dom Alban Dold, Director of the Palimpsest Institute of Beuron, possesses a secret process which has enabled him to discern, in photographs of the 6th-century palimpsest MS, Codex 912 of St. Gall, traces of symbols which he believes belong to an even earlier period. These symbols have the appearance of true neumes. See SuñP, 480f.

[9] Other important volumes containing facsimiles are BannM, FrereA, FrereG, FrereB (13 plates), FrerePA, NichE, WagT, EbelA, WackG. Interesting plates also in FerM.

tion? It must have been necessary for them first to memorize the whole liturgical repertory; then the notation became a guide, recalling the contours of this
or that known melody. Since the intervals of Gregorian melodies did not often
exceed a fifth, the singer had usually only to determine which of the intervals
from minor second to perfect fifth was represented by a particular neume in
a particular place. The singers "knew the neumatic language; they knew the
melodic repertory by heart, and consequently usage, context, the liturgical
text, then certain contours of the neumes, their particular combination, the
place they occupied, and the melodic pattern they formed, themselves suggested at once the determined interval." [10]

Oratorical neumes survived alongside intervallic notation in Italy up to
the 11th century; in France, England, and Spain, to the 12th; and in Germany
and Switzerland to the 13th and 14th centuries. But the inadequacy of this
system of notation was strongly felt and we find theorists like Hucbald [11] and
the so-called John Cotton [12] complaining that the neumes did not show the
difference in intervals. Attempts were made to represent the relative pitch of
tones. One of the most interesting of these experiments involved the combination of neumes with letters.

What may be the earliest adaptation of Latin letters as a musical notation
appears in MSS of the *De Institutione Musica* of Boethius.[13] This author, in
part of his treatise, shows how the tones of the diatonic, chromatic, and enharmonic genera may be derived from divisions of the monochord (although
at least the enharmonic genus was without vitality in his time) and applies
Latin letters to the tones of each genus. The application to the diatonic genus
may (if we omit overlapping tetrachords) be illustrated thus (the letters representing relative intervallic positions rather than absolute pitches, as they will
do also throughout the following paragraph):

EXAMPLE 26.

This system of notation was employed, with slight changes, by later theorists
like Hucbald [14] and Bernelinus.[15] Boethius uses,[16] in a different part of the

---

[10] SuñP, 45.   [11] See GerS I, 118.   [12] See GerS II, 257.

[13] This adaptation has been called "Boethian Notation" or, by those who claim that the letters
are later insertions (none of the several surviving MSS antedates the 9th century), "so-called
Boethian Notation." Whether the notation may properly be attributed to Boethius is a minor
point. But the question is mentioned here since it persistently recurs in histories, books on notation,
etc. For details of the controversy, see Meibom, *Antiquae Musicae Auctores Septem*, preface to
Alypii Introductio Musica, 7; Charles Burney, *General History of Music* II (ed. of 1782), 29f;
I (ed. of 1935), 429; WolfH I, 39; RieL I, 244; CelM, 515f.

[14] See GerS I, 122, and the table facing it.

[15] See GerS I, 326 (but also WolfH I, 38, footnote 2).

[16] See MigneL LXIII, 1284; FriedlB, 347; PaulB, 146.

treatise, the letters A–P (omitting J, which, in the Latin alphabet, merges with I) to represent a series in a way that has given rise to several interpretations.[17] We find these same letters employed [18] to represent the tone-series in the above example, not only in an anonymous treatise,[19] but also, combined with neumes, in the 11th-century MS H.159 of the School of Medicine of Montpellier.[20] The letters A to G, used to represent a series beginning on the

[17] The letters are usually interpreted as standing for A – $\overset{a}{}$ (see, for example, WolfH I, 39). They are, however, accompanied by a diagram in FriedlB, 347, distinguishing, through differences in spacing, whole tones from semitones. These are distributed in such a way as to yield a major disdiapason. Nothing in the context, however, indicates that Boethius had such a disdiapason in mind. The diagram, as given in the late 11th- or early 12th-century MS at the Newberry Library, Chicago (the only Boethius MS we have consulted), does not distinguish between whole tones and semitones nor does the Venetian print of 1492 nor that of Basle, dated 1570 (nor, for that matter, the modern editions of Migne or Paul). The FriedlB form of the diagram, whether originating with some medieval scribe or Friedlein, would seem to be the result of an error. GomS I suggests that it may be legitimate to interpret the diagram as indicating intervallic relations similar to those of a 2-octave series extending upward to g, since, almost immediately before the diagram, Boethius discusses the distances from one another of the mesai in what he calls *modi* (i. e. of the middle degrees of his 2-octave tonoi or "keys"—not "modes"; *cf.* p. 153). The resulting interval-relationship is, indeed, T T S T T S T—the same as that of a G scale without sharps or flats—(this, in fact, is what would result if, like Boethius, we added one key above the 7 presented in Ex. 4 and took the mesai in ascending instead of descending order). Against this interpretation, however, there are the following possible objections: Boethius has been talking before the diagram about 2-octave units, but speaks after it of 1-octave units; before it he uses the names Dorian, Phrygian, etc., but after it switches to numbers; before it he definitely uses the term *modus*, while immediately after it he uses the term *species diapason*. Boethius says that the letters A-H represent the first species, B-I the second, etc., up to G-O, which represent the seventh. He then adds an eighth (represented by the letters H-P) and states that this is Ptolemy's eighth modus (*cf.* p. 153f). While Boethius certainly uses *modus* to equal *tonos*, he may very easily mean here that this is the octave-species produced by Ptolemy's (alleged) eighth tonos. Since this tonos would appear above the 7 tonoi in Ex. 4, it would produce an octave-species which, in Ex. 6, would be still lower than the Mixolydian. It would duplicate the Hypodorian an octave below. Now Gaudentios *et al.* numbered the octave-species beginning with the Mixolydian as the first and proceeding upward to the Hypodorian as the seventh (*cf.* p. 41); but if an octave-species is to make its appearance below the Mixolydian the latter can no longer be No. 1. In fact, Boethius seems to indicate that his No. 1 is at the top rather than at the bottom, since otherwise the species produced by Ptolemy's supposed eighth tonos could not appear at the bottom. We suggest that Boethius's A-P series represents a Greater Perfect System *descending*. (The interpretation that it is a GPS *ascending* is untenable. For [1] if the first species is regarded as the Mixolydian, the diagram would have to represent a B disdiapason; while [2] if the first species is regarded as an A octave, "1" is being assigned to the octave to which Boethius definitely assigns "8." On the other hand, if we regard No. 1 as an A octave, we find ourselves at the top and are compelled to descend, which is what we suggest doing.) If Boethius starts at the top, he starts with the species produced by the modus which, in his discussion of the modi, he named first (the Hypodorian) and ends with the species produced by the modus he discussed last ("Ptolemy's eighth") so that our suggestion is not without some support in Boethius's organization of his material. If we regard A-P as a descending GPS, and start with the Hypodorian species as No. 1, every species will fall perfectly into its proper position. (To be sure, in FriedlB, 341, Boethius has an A-O series definitely ascending and definitely representing a 14-degree series beginning on B. If P is merely an addition to this same series, then A-P would be a B disdiapason and the Mixolydian would retain its traditional position as first species. But then we must charge Boethius with having made a mistake in calling the species produced by "Ptolemy's eighth tonos" the eighth species, for it would be a b octave, whereas Boethius's preceding discussion of the modi shows clearly that it would have to be an A octave.) Since the foregoing was typeset, my attention has been called to the study of Boethius's diagram made in KunzT, in which conclusions are drawn that in several respects agree with ours. (Kunz examined all but one of the MSS upon which the text of FriedlB is based.)

[18] Probably as a result of a misunderstanding of Boethius.   [19] See GerS I, 342.

[20] Printed in PM VIII. One page of this codex is reproduced in SuñP, 395 and another, with its transcription into modern plainsong notation, in WagE II, 252f.

modern C, appear in other medieval sources, e. g. the *Scholia Enchiriadis*.[21] The employment of these letters to indicate what we would call a major diatonic scale seems to have been especially connected with music for stringed instruments and organ: the result has, in fact, been dubbed "organ notation." Both systems—A to P in the sense of the modern C to c', and A to P in the sense of the modern A to a'—survived side by side until about the 12th century. From the 10th century, they survived side by side also with a double series of seven letters (A–G and a–g) plus a⁄a, the whole used in the sense of the modern A–a'. This is part of the notation ascribed to Odo (concerning his one remaining degree, see p. 149), which, so far as letter notation is concerned, became, with additions, standard for the Middle Ages.

In the Montpellier MS mentioned above, each of the tones of the disdiapason on A (including both b-flat and b-natural) was given a letter:

EXAMPLE 27.

It will be noticed that b-natural was indicated by an undotted i written vertically, and b-flat by the same letter slanted. The signs for the notes marked with asterisks are believed by some authorities to have referred to intervals that were roughly quarter-tones.[22] The letters and signs are written between text and neumes, and there is consequently no doubt as to the identity of the scale-degrees indicated by the neumes.

Another system of notation was employed by the author of the 9th-century treatise *Musica Enchiriadis*. The system is known as daseian notation, after the Greek *daseia* or "rough breathing," [23] which was used as a symbol. The daseia was combined, in certain instances, either with the letter S or C or C reversed,[23a] and the three compound symbols that resulted were presented in normal position, reversed, inverted, and reversed-and-inverted, each symbol representing a different pitch. Two of the symbols were used in slanting position also. To the three compound symbols were added four without S or C, each used once. The total of eighteen symbols was sufficient to provide a sign for each of the eighteen tones in the author's gamut, and it was possible to notate a melody accurately (except for its rhythm) by using these signs without additional indications. The author, however, unnecessarily added a staff of five or more lines, only the spaces of which were used to represent pitches.

[21] GerS I, 209.

[22] *Cf.* p. 161. A strong case for this view is presented in GmelchV. For a recent article on Montpellier H. 159, with references to the earlier literature on it, see SidM.

[23] The Greek alphabet has no separate letter equivalent to our *h*. But many Greek words begin with an aspirated sound, which is indicated by a "rough breathing" over the initial vowel or over initial ρ(r).   [23a] None of these, however, in upright position.

Syllables of the text, not notes, were written in the spaces. At the beginning of the staff, a daseian symbol appeared in each space to denote the pitch at which any syllable appearing in the space was to be sung. Sometimes the author preceded the symbols by the letters T and S (indicating Tone and Semitone) to show the distances between adjacent scale-degrees.[24]

EXAMPLE 28.

Staff-notation was on the way.

Hermannus Contractus is responsible for still another medieval experiment in the notation of intervals. His system made use of letters to indicate intervals in melodic progressions, as follows: e = equisonus (unison—use of the letter implied a repetition); s = semitonium; τ = tonus; τ^s or $\overset{s}{\tau}$ = tonus cum semitonio (minor third); $\underset{\tau}{\tau}$ = tonus cum tono, i. e. ditonus (major third); D = diatessaron (fourth); Δ or δ = diapente (fifth), $\overset{s}{\Delta}$ = diapente cum semitonio (minor sixth); $\overset{\tau}{\Delta}$ = diapente cum tono (major sixth). A descent from the pitch represented by one symbol to that represented by the next was indicated by a dot placed under the second symbol; absence of a dot indicated ascent. The symbols were placed above the syllables of text. No staves were needed or used. The system denoted pitch accurately, but had the disadvantage that, in any one piece, a single error in performance would render all subsequent translation into sound wrong.[25]

None of these systems caught on. It was another line of investigation—the experiments that produced the staff—that was destined to develop modern notation.

[24] See GerS I, 174ff. A full description of the system, in English, is given in GrutH, 509f, 704ff
[25] See GerS II, 149; EllinM, 9; or WolfH 1, 143.

Italian and English scribes were among the first to start this new development. Assuming an imaginary horizontal line, they grouped the neumes above this line in such fashion that the relative positions of the neumes corresponded with the size of the interval desired. Neumes arranged thus are sometimes called "heighted" neumes. This scheme, clearly discernible in MSS of the 10th century, spread rapidly, and by the end of that century actual lines were employed in some MSS while in others the line, real or imaginary, that served to guide the horizontal alignment of the text also served to guide the vertical disposition of the neumes.[25a]

Another phase in the development of diastematic notation (*diastema* is Greek for "interval") was that in which the elements of a neume were detached from each other and, in the shape of dots or points, so placed in the MS as roughly to indicate the size of the intervals between them. This type of notation is especially characteristic of Aquitanian MSS.

From about the beginning of the 11th century the practice of using a line colored red to indicate F was gradually adopted. Later a second line, generally yellow but sometimes green, was added and represented c. From this stage the passage to three and four lines was easy. The invention of the staff has often been attributed to Guido d'Arezzo, but we have just seen that the idea of one or more lines to fix the pitch of certain notes antedated him by some years. What Guido did was to improve an imperfect system already in use. He also employed in his Antiphonary (c. 1027) the letters F and G as clefs.

The adoption of the four-line staff, perfected by Guido and bringing to a climax the development of diastematic notation, proceeded slowly. By the 12th century it had spread to many Italian, French, Spanish, and English cloisters, but some German monasteries did not employ it until the 15th century.

The early neumes varied considerably in appearance according to locale—scholars consequently divide neume-notations into those of St. Gall, Metz, Chartres, Nonantola, Aquitania, Catalonia, etc.[26]—and the idiosyncracies of individual scribes, but, by the 12th or 13th century, neumes had crystallized in most of Southern and Western Europe into the square or quadratic form characteristic of modern neumes.[27] The neumes in Germanic MSS, however, took another form. The note-heads became diamond-shaped, the stems thick and pointed, and their resemblance to hobnails earned for this type of notation the designation *Hufnagelschrift*. It is also called Gothic notation.

The influence of a perfected diastematic notation on the development of music was enormous. Not only were the ecclesiastical singers freed from the necessity of laboriously committing to memory the whole liturgical repertoire, but the existence of a dependable notation made possible the rapid spread of

---

[25a] WagB and WagD, 95f, advance the unorthodox theory that the Latin neumes were "heighted" from their inception and that horizontal neumes represent a decline. The theory is skilfully developed, but necessarily rests on circumstantial evidence and is not very convincing.

[26] For thoroughgoing analyses of various types, see SuñP; WagE II.   [27] This form penetrated without much delay even to Iceland. See the 13th-century example in WolfH I, 119.

CHART Illustrating the Development of Plainsong Notation
(after Pm I, 121)

new and original compositions such as tropes and sequences. The teaching of music henceforth became a comparatively simple matter. And composition could proceed more freely, since the heavy reliance upon melodic formulas in the older music was probably due in no small degree to the practical reason that the absence of an accurate notation placed on the singer's memory a considerable burden which the use of standardized formulas tended somewhat to ease. With the invention of an accurate notation, the composer was at greater liberty to let his fancy roam.

2. NOTATION OF RHYTHM

WE come now to the notation of *rhythm*. In MSS of certain regions are found, in addition to neumes, a number of special signs that have a rhythmical significance. These signs are of two main types: short lines added to the neumes, and letters written above the neumes.

The line attached to a neume is called an *episema*. Lines are found in the notations of St. Gall, Metz, Chartres, Nonantola, Benevento, and Aquitaine, and are believed to have indicated a lengthening of the value of the neume.

In St. Gall MSS we find also the so-called Romanian letters, which are said to have been first used by Romanus, the legendary Roman singer who is supposed, *c.* the end of the 8th century, to have introduced Gregorian Chant at St. Gall. Some of these letters refer to rhythm, others to melody. The most important of the rhythmic letters are t (*trahere* "to drag," or *tenere* "to hold"), x (*expectare* "to retard"), m (*mediocriter* "moderately"), and c (*celeriter* "quickly"). Sometimes these letters are combined with a b (*bene* "well"), v (*valde* "very, extremely"), or m (*mediocriter*), which qualify the rhythmic indication. Other letters sometimes found are p (*pressio*), f (*cum fragore*) and k (*clange*), which are thought to call for intensity or energetic emphasis. As a rule, the letter affects only the neume—according to some, only the part of the neume—that it accompanies, but occasionally c or t is followed by a line that extends over a whole group or series of groups, which are then governed by that letter.

Rhythmic letters are also found, but to a lesser degree, in MSS originating at Metz and Chartres. In the Metz MSS in addition to t and c, we have a (*augete* "broaden, augment") and n (*naturaliter,* indicating that the normal value is to be restored or not to be departed from).[1]

The whole problem of the rhythmical interpretation of plainsong in the Middle Ages (and consequently the exact significance of the rhythmic signs and letters) has been a subject of intense controversy, a controversy that still rages today. There have been three main schools of thought.

I. *The Accentualists.* The members of this school, of which Dom Pothier

---

[1] For a theory that the rhythmic signs called for a type of performance that conformed, not to the traditions of the Golden Age, but to a transitory fashion, see DavidS.

was the head, point out that around the 5th century, when Gregorian Chant was in process of formation, a change took place in the pronunciation of Greek and Latin. While, up to that time, syllables had been measured according to quantity and divided into longs and shorts, thenceforth they became equal in time-value, and the accent or *stress* given to a particular syllable became the rhythmic element.[2] The accentualists believe that the Chant adopted the equal time-values of the syllables, and they consider the accent the principal—according to some, the only—rhythmical determinant of its melodies. The stressing of the verbal accents in the performance of the music, according to this school, results in a free rhythm that faithfully reflects the oratorical nature of the Chant. In passages where long melismas occur on a single syllable, the function of the word-accent is taken over by the first note of each neumatic group.[3]

II. *The Solesmes School.* The monks of Solesmes, under the leadership of Dom Mocquereau, retained Dom Pothier's theory that all the notes of the neumes are basically equal in duration and that plainsong rhythm is free, as opposed to measured, but they discarded his theory that the verbal accent is the predominating rhythmical element. Dom Mocquereau has stated: "Nothing in the nature of rhythm requires that a special place be reserved for intensity";[4] the tonic accent, accordingly, is not necessarily stressed in performance. It is thrown into relief in other ways: by melodic elevation; by shortness (it is often limited to one note, even in chants that are mainly melismatic).

In his *Le Nombre musical grégorien*—the Bible of all adherents of Solesmes —Dom Mocquereau works out in great detail a system of rhythmical interpretation of the Chant, based on intensive study of the old MSS. The system is constructed upon the theory that plainsong rhythm is free, a theory that has been approved by the Sacred Congregation of Rites. In this system a single indivisible pulse is the time unit. In the Solesmes editions in square notation this is represented by a punctum or virga; in the Solesmes editions in modern notation[5] it is represented by an eighth-note. The pulses are gathered up by twos and threes into binary and ternary time-groups—the smallest rhythmic combinations—and these groups, freely mixed, are combined into the larger

<hr/>

[2] Concerning the change that came over Latin accentuation in the Middle Ages, see F. J. E. Raby, *A History of Christian-Latin Poetry* (1927), especially pp. 13–22.

[3] Aubry attempts to bolster his claim that the accent-theory was applied to Gregorian Chant, by pointing out that it was actually used in the related medieval liturgical music of various Christian communities in the East (see AuD). The accuracy of his conclusions, however, has been questioned. For a detailed exposition of the accentualist theory, see PothM 179ff; DavidM, Chap. IV–V; DavidR.

[4] MocqL, I, 59; MocqN, 71. Jeannin (JeannE, 150) concluded from the occasional employment of the word *tabula* in medieval writings on plainsong that castanets were used to accompany the singing of the Chant. This view—which, if correct, would provide evidence tending to weigh against Dom Mocquereau's claim, so far as it concerns Gregorian Chant—is based on a misinterpretation by Du Cange of the word *tabula,* which refers simply to the cover (often of ivory etc.) of chant books. See WaesC.

[5] E. g. the Compendium.

rhythmic divisions—incises, members, phrases, and periods (*cf.* p. 169). The rhythmic flow is characterized by alternations of arsis, "upbeat," *élan,* and thesis, "downbeat," *repos.*[6] Thus a binary group will contain one note for the arsis and one for the thesis; a ternary group may contain one arsic note and two thetic notes or two arsic notes and one thetic note.[7]

The first note of each group of two or three notes bears an ictus, which is of great importance since without it the group would not exist as such: the ictus divides into sections what would otherwise be a formless sequence of beats. The ictus may be arsic or thetic according to the nature of the group. Exactly what the Solesmes scholars mean by an ictus is somewhat difficult to grasp. Here is a typical definition:

> *The rhythmical ictus is simply a "dip" of the voice, an alighting place sought by the rhythm at intervals of every two or three notes in order to renew or sustain its flight until it reaches its final resting place. The ictus must be divorced from any idea of force or lengthening out. It is a common fault to assimilate it to the accent of the words and give it their value. In itself it may be strong or weak; it only gains its dynamic or quantitative value from the note which happens to correspond to it. If the ictus chances to be strong by its position, it does not appropriate the intensity thus bestowed upon it; its stress extends to the whole of the compound time which it commands, and it keeps only the function of an alighting or resting place. It can be readily understood that this must be so in order to safeguard the unity of the compound beat.*[8]

To modern perception, the idea of grouping rhythmic units without a stress, as this definition indicates, is likely to be puzzling. For this reason we offer a second explanation, which is somewhat different from, but nevertheless consistent with, the other: The ictus is a mental division by the performer of beats of equal force into groups of two and/or three. Since, however, the ictus, while allegedly neither a stress, a shortening, nor a prolongation, is definitely perceptible, it is perhaps up to the physio-psychologist to settle the problem of determining what communicable form it takes.[9]

It remains to be added that the ictus is as independent of the Latin tonic accent as it is of any stress accent: it may coincide with the tonic accent and it may not.

With regard to the rhythmic signs and letters in medieval MSS, the Solesmes school maintains that the *episema* and the Romanian t, x, and m, all

---

[6] In Solesmes teaching editions cheironomic signs (wavy lines graphically reproducing the gestures made by the conductor in performance; *cf.* p. 8) accompany the notes.

[7] For Dom Mocquereau, as for Hugo Riemann, the normal order, the "primordial and natural rhythm" (MocqL I, 45; MocqN, 57), is arsis, thesis, and not thesis, arsis, as many modern musicians believe.

[8] SuñG, 73.

[9] Perhaps, despite statements to the contrary, the Solesmes ictus does take a communicable form by means of prolongation. *Cf.* MurG, 56.

indicate a prolongation whose duration is not fixed but varies considerably according to the place of the neume in the musical phrase or member. Similarly with the acceleration indicated by the letter c.[10] More or less fixed prolongations are prescribed by the Solesmes authorities for the final tone of some incises and of members (where these authorities double the note) and of phrases and compositions (where the note may be tripled).[11] As to the other Romanian letters, although the Solesmes scholars are insistent that the Chant should be sung smoothly and without stress, they agree (see PM IV, 13f; SuñP, 134) that the letters p, f, and k indicated intensity. Yet, inconsistently with this interpretation but in line with their main tenet, their modern editions contain no intensity sign. If it is the Solesmes view that intensity exists in the Chant only as gradual *crescendi* and *diminuendi* (MocqL I, 62; MocqN, 74), then it might be pointed out that p, f, and k stand over individual neumes in the MSS and that the Solesmes scholars themselves subscribe to the view that these signs affected only the notes which they accompanied.[12]

The monks of Solesmes have evolved four rhythmical signs. These signs are a short horizontal line (‾), which retards the note or group it affects; the dot (·), which doubles, or sometimes triples, the value of the note it follows; the vertical line (I), which marks the ictus; and the comma ('), which guides breathing.

The Solesmes rhythmical theories, adopted in the official editions of the Chant, are very intricate. We have indicated, very briefly, only the main principles.[13]

III. *The Mensuralists.* Under this head are loosely grouped a number of scholars who agree in their opposition to Solesmes and in certain general principles which they believe should govern the rhythmical interpretation of the Chant. Perhaps the most important of these principles is that the notes in the early medieval MSS do not represent tones of equal duration but are definitely longs and shorts, the longs being always twice as long as the shorts. (Although some of the earlier mensuralists—Dechevrens,[14] Gietmann,[15] and Bonvin [16] —thought that there were at least three different durations, the members of this school are now inclined to accept Dom Jeannin's claim [17] that only two durations seem to have been used.) These notes of different, proportional

[10] MocqL I, 162; SuñP, 460ff.

[11] Most writers feel that it is the prolongation of the final tone of a rhythmic division that Guido d'Arezzo referred to when he used the term, *mora ultimae vocis* (GerS II, 14; AmelM, 35). See, however, DAC XII (1935), 2.

[12] MocqL I, 168; PM IV, 17.

[13] Besides MocqN, the reader will find, in English, fuller information than is here given in SuñG Chap. III, and WardG, *passim*.

[14] Dechevrens—whose chief work is DechV—, one of the pioneers among the mensuralists, is honored but not wholly followed by later members of this school.

[15] For his theories on Gregorian rhythm, see GietC.

[16] His English writings on Gregorian rhythm are BonG, BonL, and BonM, all helpful expositions of the mensuralist views.   [17] JeannE, 47.

duration are arranged in groups of two to eight beats, such groups constituting *measures*.[18]

The mensuralists maintain that Gregorian Chant was sung from its beginnings up to the 12th century in measures *irregularly* grouped,[19] the first note of each measure receiving a stress, and that during this time, therefore, the rhythm of the Chant followed the same principles as the rhythm of Eastern music, from which the Chant derived. Syrian Chant as now practiced, for example, employs measures of unequal length, the stress at the opening of each measure being purely musical (i. e. not necessarily the result of accents in the text). But, about the 12th century, so it is claimed, the exigencies of organum—in which one or more parts were added to a liturgical melody (*cf.* p. 253)—ironed out the longs and shorts of the Chant into notes of equal value. While today singers of different parts find no great difficulty in singing a variety of time-values, it is apparently believed that the alleged novelty of organum presented such difficulties to the singers that it was necessary to ease their problems by having them sing notes of uniform time-value. As we have seen, it was in the 12th century that staff-notation became widespread. The monks of Solesmes, in their restoration of plainsong, were forced to depend upon the MSS of this period and later (the intervals of the earlier, staffless neumes could not be decisively determined except by comparison with the later versions on staves); they concluded that the prevalent equality in the value of notes, indicated by 13th- and 14th-century writers,[20] must have been characteristic of Gregorian rhythm from the beginning. The mensuralists claim, however, that this was not so, and adduce a great deal of evidence for their view from treatises written in the 4th to the 12th centuries.

From this evidence, too, the mensuralists conclude that the *episema* and Romanian letters were, not indications of rhythmic nuances that varied according to context, but precise directions: *episema* and t, x, and a, requiring a doubling of the note-value, and c and m reminding the singer of the exact observance of the short or long.[21]

As regards the tonic accent, the mensuralists are among those who point out that its character had changed to that of a stress accent early in the development of Gregorian Chant. "In Gregorian music the first beat of the

---

[18] A mensuralist who advocates groups of 3 beats (♩ ♩ or ♩ ♩) but who dispenses with barlines is Sowa (see SowaQ, 161ff).

[19] In some controversial literature their opponents seem to imply that the mensuralists believe that plainsong originally had "measure" in the sense of a recurring rhythmic division of constant length. This is not true. Plainsong rhythm, according to the mensuralists as well as the Solesmes school and the accentualists, was in a sense "free": that is to say, it was, in the mensuralist view, rhythm formed not by a *regularly* recurring stress but by freely mixed groups not necessarily of equal length.

[20] And implied by the fact, pointed out by Dom Mocquereau, that in early organum the virga and punctum were employed simultaneously, note against note, the former in the "tenor" part and the latter in the "bass" part. See MocqP; PM I, 151f.

[21] JeannE, 211f, footnote.

measure was comparatively really strong. This quality of the first beat follows from the fact that the Latin word-accent (as primary or secondary accent) selects with preference, that is, in the majority of cases, the musical thesis, the first beat of the measure. . . . The Latin word-accent was intensive from . . . the very first beginnings of the Gregorian Chant." [22] Thus the really fundamental distinction between the accentualists and the mensuralists is one connected not with stress but with time-values: the former agree with the Solesmes view concerning the equality of time-values, while the latter, as we have seen, contend that there were at least two different and proportional time-values.

If the mensuralists agree among themselves in fundamental principles, they disagree in important particulars. For example, Peter Wagner and others believe that the virga signified a long note and the punctum a short one, and that medieval neumes containing two or more notes consequently represented metrical feet—the scandicus (♪), for example, representing an anapest (∪∪—), the climacus (∧) a dactyl (—∪∪), and so on.[23] Dom Jeannin, on the other hand, holds that the punctum and virga were equal in duration, the episema and other rhythmic signs accounting for the strictly proportional differences in time-values of the notes.[24]

One medieval theorist, Jerome of Moravia, the author of a treatise written in the second half of the 13th century, gives fairly definite rules for the rhythmic performance of the Chant. But he is of too late date for his writings to be regarded as evidence of ancient practice. Moreover, he wrote at a time when the measuring of part-music was one of the chief problems occupying musicians (see Chapter 10). As a result, the kind of performance he describes was very likely affected by the great stride that was being made in the field of polyphony. While we know conclusively neither the antiquity of the method he mentions nor the extent of the area over which it was used, it is of interest for its definiteness, and we shall give a few samples of the rules since the method represents a medieval practice, however temporary.

All notes, says Jerome, are of equal value, with certain exceptions. Among these are the first note which, if it represents the final of the mode (but not otherwise), has twice the normal value; the second of several notes over one syllable of text, which likewise has a double value unless it is immediately preceded or followed by a note itself doubled as the result of some other exception to the rule; the last note before a pause, which, like the pause itself, varies in length according to the portion of the piece it concludes, the note always being longer than the pause to the extent of one normal time-value. If from four to seven notes (or even more) are connected with one another musically (regardless of textual considerations),

[22] BonM, 27.   [23] See WagE II, 396ff.
[24] JeannE, 36ff. Worth noting among the mensuralists, besides those already mentioned, are Fleischer (see FleiN, II, 103ff), Fleury (see FleuryG), Houdard (see HoudR), and Jammers (see JamG).

they consume nine time-values—these being disposed in groups of three—and the manner in which the available time is divided among the notes is clearly specified, some of the notes having three times the normal value, some (if there are more than four) less than the normal value. It will be seen, even from these selected examples, that, although Jerome enunciates the general principle that all notes are equal, his rules furnish so many exceptions that his Chant-rhythm is a far cry from that of the monks of Solesmes.[25]

For practical purposes, the versions of the Solesmes scholars have at least the advantage of agreeing with one another in method, which the transcriptions of the mensuralists do not. It is hard to keep from admitting, however, that the mensuralists as against the Solesmes school and the accentualists—assuming that any of the three are really on the right path—seem to have an impressive amount of historical evidence on their side, so far as the vague and sometimes contradictory medieval treatises may be relied upon with respect to rhythm.[26] There is no need, in the present state of our knowledge, to reject any of the three views as wholly wrong. The Chant came originally from unnumbered directions—not merely from the Hebrews and Greeks (*cf.* pp. 66f). It is just possible that the modern theorists are referring to practices actually used at different times and places and are therefore all of them right, but with respect to melodies of different provenance.

Thus the accentualists seem to derive some support from Cassiodorus,[27] who wrote: *Rithmica est, quae requirit in concursionem verborum, utrum bene sonus an male cohaereat* ("The rhythmic [part of music] is that which investigates into the meeting of words [with the melody to see] whether the sound fits well or ill"), and from Isidore of Seville [28] and Aurelian of Réomé, who

[25] For a fuller discussion of Jerome's rules, see CserbaM, LX–LXV. Jerome's treatise is printed in CserbaM and also, but less accurately, in CouS I. The discussion of rhythm occurs in Chapter 25.
[26] The occasional ambiguousness of the Latin of the medieval theorists treating the subject may be illustrated by the fact that two serious investigators have found it possible to give the meaning of a single passage in the *Commemoratio brevis* in ways as different as these:
A. "This evenness of the Chant is called rhythm in Greek, and *numerus* in Latin: because without any doubt all melody should be measured with care after the manner of metre. This evenness, the master of the Scholae ought diligently to instil into their pupils, and mould the children from the first, by this very discipline of evenness or rhythm, *indicating this numerus, during the singing, by gestures of the hand or foot, or in some other way* . . ." (Aileen Tone, after Dom Mocquereau, in MocqN, 29. Dom Mocquereau adds: "The rest of the passage is defective; its general sense is however not necessary to our argument, and the first part is so very clear, so precise, that no further explanation is necessary.")
B. "This regularity in singing is called in Greek *rhythmos;* in Latin *numerus; since every melody must be carefully measured off like a metrical text.* The teachers should impress this rhythmical regularity on the youths very early, and for this purpose they should beat time with the foot, the hand or in any other way; so that by the observance of *equal and unequal* notes from the start the youths show themselves to be versed in the art of praising God." (SchmidtG, 7. Schmidt's useful pamphlet gives, in parallel columns of Latin original and English translation, passages on rhythm by medieval theorists of the West.)
The italics in the first translation are retained from Mocquereau and Tone; those in the second, from Schmidt.
[27] GerS I, 16; MynorsC, 144.
[28] *Etymologiarum*, Lib. III, cap. XVIII, in LindE I and MigneL LXXXII. Also in GerS I, 21, where, however, the important verb *requirit* is omitted.

are among others to repeat the definition. Among these others is the compiler of an 11th-century *Vocabularium musicum* (Joannes Presbyter?), the earliest known attempt at a dictionary of music, earlier by four centuries than the famous work by Tinctoris that usually receives the credit for priority.[29] Aurelian adds to the definition: *In rhythmica autem provisio manet, ut cum verbis modulatio apte concurrat ne scilicet contra rationem verborum cantilenae vox inepte formetur* [30] ("For in rhythm the responsibility rests that the melody run suitably with the words lest, obviously, the articulation of the cantilena be unfittingly formed against the sense of the words").

As we have seen, there are medieval writers who support the mensuralists, and, as Dom Mocquereau has amply shown, there are others—though to be sure of comparatively late date—who support the Solesmes views.

If, in fact, the three modern points of view all have some historical justification, it may follow that early Gregorian rhythm was not definitively systematized at all for universal application. Still, if the Chant was to be sung by choral groups, some means had to be devised of keeping the singers together, and possibly each monastery, or group of monasteries, evolved a method of its own, more perhaps as a result of purely practical considerations arising from the needs of performance than from any theoretical considerations or clear and conscious recognition of rhythm as a musical element as fully deserving of standardization as melodic outline. The Romanian signs may have represented a local usage that in time gained fairly wide application, and they may provide an indication of a transition in Western music generally towards rhythmic systematization, achieved, only after long groping, in the 13th century.

So far as melodies with metrical texts are concerned—such as those for hymns and the later type of sequences (*cf.* p. 189)—it may well be that, even if the old laws of quantity no longer prevailed, recurring rhythmic divisions of constant length were applied rather than the free rhythm that all three main schools of thought believe applicable to the Chant as a whole (*cf.* footnote 19). It would seem wholly likely that metrical texts would have an effect on a musical setting different from that of prose texts (*cf.* p. 68 and Ex. 30).

Whatever may be true of the original plainsong rhythm, it seems reasonably fair to believe that at some remote time before the Solesmes scholars themselves appeared on the scene, at a time when perhaps organum flourished and the transition was well under way, Gregorian Chant really was sung with basically equal time-values. Even if the mensuralists are right in placing this time as recently as the 12th century and in assuming that the "authentic" Gregorian rhythm declined from then on, the decline did not necessarily lead to something less valid, if judged solely from the artistic point of view, than what had preceded. And perhaps the views of the Solesmes school, even

[29] The *Vocabularium* is printed in LafE, 404ff. [30] GerS I, 33.

if they should ultimately be shown to be historically unfounded, will, because of the beauty of their results, prove the investigation and misunderstanding of early medieval rhythm as profitable as the investigation and misunderstanding of the music of the ancient Greeks have been. Nevertheless, while admiring the beauty of the Solesmes interpretations, one should not overlook the fact that they are historically suspect and should ponder the statement of a distinguished scholar to the effect that the Solesmes method "probably stands in the same relation to its medieval counterpart as a Romanesque church of 1880 to its 11th-century model." [31]

EXAMPLE 29. Three Different Rhythmical Interpretations of the Antiphon, *Videntibus illis.*

(a) From JeannM I, 170

(b) From DechV, Pt. 2, 31

(c) From Compendium, 656

[31] BesM, 15.

Chapter 6: GREGORIAN CHANT: Its Modal System and Forms

The Modes and Related Subjects

THE gamut with which the plainsong theorists began was apparently the Greater Perfect System of the ancient Greeks, including the *synemmenon*. We have seen (p. 136) that an early medieval letter notation assigned Latin letters (A–P) to each of the fifteen degrees in a two-octave diatonic series and that for some musicians this was an A–$\frac{a}{a}$ series. The author of the *Musica Enchiriadis*, by the way in which he uses Latin letters in addition to daseian symbols in certain examples,[1] implies, in place of A–P, a double series, A–G plus a–g. He does not, however, present the series completely. Moreover, he adopts a gamut differing from the one regarded as structurally normal in the West (*cf.* p. 254). Odo of Cluny seems to have been the first to apply the complete double series to a gamut of normal construction and to add $\frac{a}{a}$ at the top and extend the series downward by adding Γ.[2] (The *Musica Enchiriadis*, however, had had an equivalent for Γ in daseian notation.)

Solmisation, which, as we have seen, was known to the ancient Greeks, was rediscovered in Europe in the 11th century, and as a result the tones in this series all eventually received an additional set of names.[3] This rediscovery has been attributed to Guido d'Arezzo. Although there is some indication that the utility of the six syllables employed in the nomenclature was recognized before Guido adopted them, he is apparently the first to have established their application in a really practical way. The six vocables were derived from the first syllable in each of the first six hemistichs of the text of a hymn to St. John the Baptist. The music setting the first of these hemistichs began on c, and that for each of the others began a scale-degree higher than its predecessor. The syllables are: *ut re mi fa sol la,* which are still used in France and, with

---

[1] GerS I, 157f, where a few obvious errors occur. Concerning translations of the *Musica Enchiriadis* and certain other treatises to be mentioned in this Chap., see the series of footnotes in Chap. 5 that begins with No. 47.

[2] Thus Odo's complete gamut is:

Γ	A	B	C	D	E	F	G	a	(I) ♭ (II) ♮	c	d	e	f	g	$\frac{a}{a}$
I	II	III	IV	V	VI	VII	VIII	IX	IX	X	XI	XII	XIII	XIV	XV

See GerS I, 253. Further concerning Odo's gamut, see BalT, 46–54.

[3] Solmisation systems similar to the Western one exist, or have existed, among the East Indians, Persians, and Arabs. It has been claimed that the Western system was derived from the Oriental. While this is possible, there is no conclusive evidence showing that the Western system may not have been independently developed. For further information, see FarmH, 72–82; LangeZ, 549–52.

one exception, in Italy to designate the degrees of the diatonic scale of C major, with the addition of *si* for the seventh degree. This name is derived from the first letters of the two words constituting the fourth line of the hymn. It was not adopted until the early 17th century, during which *ut* was replaced by *do* in Italy. Six syllables sufficed for Guido, since his system was based on a six-note group (i. e. hexachord; he, however, did not use this term himself) rather than on an eight-note group (octave). The hexachordal system had, in itself, no modal significance; it had meaning only for purposes of solmisation. The first stanza of the hymn follows:

EXAMPLE 30. *Ut queant laxis*—Hymn—Poem by Paul the Deacon, *c.* 770 (after the rhythmical interpretation in HaasA, 87).

"That with enfranchised voices thy servants may be able to proclaim the wonders of thy deeds, remove the sin of [their] polluted lips, O holy John."

Guido in a letter to his friend, the monk Michael, reports [4] that the association of one of the syllables with each of six successive degrees has enabled his choirboys to learn in a few days what it formerly required them many weeks to master. As may be deduced from the foregoing, the interval sequence formed by this group of six degrees was invariable: T T S T T.

By the 13th century the gamut [5] was extended four degrees beyond Odo's $_\mathrm{a}^\mathrm{a}$, to $_\mathrm{e}^\mathrm{e}$.[6] Guido's method achieved such widespread popularity that, by then, each of the seven possible T T S T T sequences within the gamut was recognized as a hexachord. These, inevitably, overlapped. Thus c might be *sol* in one hexachord, *fa* in another, and *ut* in still another. This is shown by the following diagram, which illustrates the hexachord system *in its final form*. The full name of each degree in the complete gamut came to consist of what might be called its denominational name (i. e. its letter) plus its particular name (consisting of all its possible hexachord designations). Thus the full name of the c we have just mentioned was c *sol fa ut*. (The name of every degree can be deduced from the diagram by reading upward from the line that gives the

---

[4] See GerS II, 45.

[5] The term "gamut" is a compound of *gamma,* the name of the lowest recognized pitch of the time, and *ut,* the name of the lowest tone in the Guidonian hexachord.

[6] See, for example, Jerome of Moravia in CouS I, 21. The gamuts of Guido, "Cotton," etc., did not go beyond $_\mathrm{d}^\mathrm{d}$. Guido divided all the degrees except T into 3 groups: the *graves:* (A–G), *acutae* (a–g), and *superacutae* $_\mathrm{a}^\mathrm{a}{-}_\mathrm{d}^\mathrm{d}$. The 3-group distinction is found in later theorists also, $_\mathrm{e}^\mathrm{e}$ being added to the *superacutae* in due season. See, for example, GerS III, 120.

denominational names.) The hexachords, even though the combination of tones and semitones was the same in all of them, were divided into three groups: a hexachord was *durum* (hard) if it contained b-natural, *molle* (soft) if it contained b-flat, *naturale* if it contained neither:

Durum		ut re .. mi fa sol la
Molle		ut re mi fa .. sol la
Naturale		ut re mi fa sol la
Durum	ut re .. mi fa sol la	
Molle	ut re mi fa .. sol la	
Naturale	ut re mi fa sol la	
Durum	ut re mi fa sol la	

Γ A B C D E F G a b b c d e f g a b b c d e
                        a b b c d e

♮   ♭ ← *for hex. mol.* → ♭

                        ♮ ←*for hex. dur.*→ ♮

The process of shifting from one hexachord to another was known as muta-tion. This, in a way, was the medieval equivalent of our modulation.[7] (A closer equivalent, however, was the shift from one mode to another.) In pass-ing from one hexachord to another, the singer at some convenient point changed the particular names of the syllables to conform to the new hexa-chord. The point chosen for this change was generally determined by the desire to retain the *mi-fa* designation for the half-step in the new hexachord. Thus, for example, in the progression Γ–G the transition would be made at D, which became D *re* instead of D *sol*.

A mnemonic device intended as an aid in solmisation is the so-called Gui-donian hand, which is not treated in Guido's surviving works but may be found drawn or mentioned in various other old documents.[8] This assigned the degrees of the gamut to different portions of the left hand. The assignment is not made the same way in all the old MSS. The usual one is as here given:[9]

EXAMPLE 31.

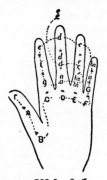

[7] For an explanation of this system, see OH I, 283ff.
[8] See, for example, the drawings printed in VivF, 99; CouS I, 21; IV, 3, 222; HawkH I, 233; HaasA, 89. See also MigneL CLX, 579.
[9] A less usual one may be found in Grove II, 478.

Although the medieval theorists of the West retained the Greater Perfect System (plus Γ), the octave-species, as understood by the Greeks, had, in the West as in the East, ceased to have any meaning. The tonal material offered by the gamut, however, was eventually grouped into a series of eight octave-scales having modal significance. These are the early *church modes*. We shall, for simplicity, first describe what they were in their definitive scalar form and then trace briefly their prior history.

The tetrachord from D to G comprises four tones on each of which a diatonic scale is built with the compass of one octave. The four resulting series constitute the scales of the authentic modes. As the following diagram shows, these scales, with the exception of the Phrygian, are divided into a pentachord and a tetrachord by the tenor or tuba (that is, the "reciting" tone, often called the "dominant" by modern writers, though not by the old theorists; the harmonic connotations of the term make it an unfortunate choice). The corresponding Hypo- or plagal modes are formed by retaining the pentachord and adding a tetrachord below. The finals [10] are here indicated in bold type, the tenors [11] in italics:

Dorian				**D** E F *G* a b c d
Hypodorian	A B C **D** E *F* G a
Phrygian				**E** F G a b *c* d e
Hypophrygian	B C D **E** F G *a* b
Lydian				**F** G a b *c* d e f
Hypolydian	C D E **F** G *a* b c
Mixolydian				**G** a b c *d* e f g
Hypomixolydian	D E F **G** a b *c* d

The fifth above the final (i. e. the tenor in all authentic modes except the Phrygian) may serve as *confinalis* (or *affinalis* or *socialis*). This means (1) that the fifth may serve as the degree on which a melody ends, in place of the normal final, if the melody has been moving in the higher range [12] or (2) that it is the note that becomes the final of a melody or portion thereof when transposed a fifth above the normal pitch level of the mode.[13] The terms *confinalis* and *socialis* are applied also to the upper fourth, a transposition on the flat side being then presumably implied.[14]

Degrees other than the final and tenor may play a part in helping to give

[10] Some *modern* writers distinguish between "tonic" and "final," the first term being applied to the lowest tone of the scale, the second to the tone upon which a piece in the mode normally ends. In the 4 authentic modes, the two coincide; in the plagal modes, the tonic is a fourth below the final.

[11] An easy means of remembering the tenors is that, except where the note would be b, the tenor of an authentic mode is always its fifth, while the tenor of a plagal is always a third below that of the corresponding authentic. Where the tenor would be b, c is substituted. This, however, had not always been so; cf. p. 160. Hermannus Contractus gives a particularly detailed table; see EllinM, 42ff.

[12] VivC, 31.   [13] GerS II, 76.   [14] GerS II, 75; GlarD, 31 or BohnG, 24.

a mode its special character. Thus, the way in which a melody might start in a particular mode already began to be limited before we hear of medieval octave-species. To be sure, a melody in an authentic mode might generally start anywhere between the subfinal and the upper fifth (but there are exceptions) and a melody in a plagal mode might start as far down as the fourth below the final.[15] It is not so much the initial tones as initial *figures*, however, that are accredited with modal significance. While some of these figures actually had the modal character (judged from the standpoint of scale) attributed to them, owing to their possessing a structure possible only within one collocation of tones and semitones, others, having a structure possible within more than one, seem to have suggested chiefly through association the mode to which they were assigned. Figures of the first type provided modal differentiation through interval relation; those of the second type, through idiom. Initial figures are given by many of the theorists, of whom Aurelian (discussing formula-modes) is the earliest.[16]

Scales with the same final plainly form a pair. Consequently the eight-fold classification of modes often becomes, with the medieval theorists, a four-fold system of so-called *maneriae:* the *protus,* comprising modes 1 and 2; *deuterus,* 3 and 4; *tritus,* 5 and 6; *tetrardus,* 7 and 8. A difference between the Byzantine and Roman classifications of scalar modes lies in the fact that in the former the authentic modes constitute modes 1–4 and the plagal modes a second series (*cf.* p. 89), while in the latter the authentics and plagals alternate, each authentic being followed by its plagal. Another difference between the Eastern and Western systems may be found by comparing the finals of the modes in the above diagram and in the chart on p. 89: in Byzantine Mode I, for example, a occurs as final more frequently than D which, in Roman Mode I, is the normal final. Foreshadowings of the twelve-fold classification of modes, finally adopted in the 16th century, occur in the writings of Aurelian, who reports that Charlemagne added four psalm-tones to the eight regular ones; Berno; etc.[17]

If we trace back the history of the church modes, we find that, after Boethius, no kinds of octave-species are unequivocally mentioned as such before the 10th century. Boethius's terminology embraces *species* of *diapason* but the octaves are ascribed no modal significance. His terminology embraces also the word *modi* but, when he uses it, as happens in a discussion of the tonoi, he is merely translating the Greek term *tonos* by the Latin word *modus.* His tonoi are those of Ptolemy except that he attributes to Ptolemy an 8th modus

---

[15] Examples of discussions of initial tones may be found in GerS I, 257; GerS II, 173, 357; CouS II, 325, 437; IV, 26.

[16] The subject of the initial figures is enlighteningly discussed in AndrM, an unpublished work to which we take pleasure in acknowledging our indebtedness in connection with this point as well as some others.

[17] GerS I, 41, 149; II, 73; additional forerunners of this system are mentioned in WagD, 119.

(= tonos), the Hypermixolydian. Ptolemy did, in fact, mention an 8th tonos but without approval.[18] This modus, if added to Example 5 in Chapter 2, would appear at the top and would correspond in all respects to the Hypodorian except that the mese *kata dynamin* would be an octave higher and the other dynamic relationships would have to be adjusted accordingly.

Cassiodorus and Isidore of Seville discuss neither octave-scales nor melodic formulas, their accounts being concerned only with tonoi, which they do not, like Boethius, call *modi,* but, respectively, *toni* and *partes musicae.* Nomenclature becomes highly confused in the course of the Middle Ages.[19] Alcuin and Aurelian deal with melodic formulas (the latter with *tonoi* also) but do not in any way connect them with the compass of an octave.[20] The idea of these formulas may very well have been taken over from the Byzantine echoi.[21]

The turning point in the history of medieval modal theory is reached in the 10th-century treatise, *Alia Musica.* This has been shown to be a composite work. Passages, perhaps by four different authors, discuss formulas in one way or another; a possible fifth author believes himself to be discussing Ptolemy's tonoi. His attempt is based on Boethius's interpretation, but he does not understand Boethius aright. According to Boethius's explanation, the Mixolydian—if we disregard the Hypermixolydian—is the highest modus and the Hypodorian the lowest,[22] which is correct (*cf.* Chapter 2, Example 4). The 10th-century theorist misinterpreted this statement as applying to octave-species. Thus, when he came to assign the old Greek names to his own scales, he called the highest the Mixolydian and the lowest the Hypodorian, this order conforming to that of Ptolemy's tonoi. The order was necessarily the reverse of that of the Greek octave-species, when they received names in Late Antiquity, since these octaves were necessarily named in an order the reverse of that of the tonoi, as we have seen in Chapter 2. The mistake of the medieval

[18] DürH, 60ff; DürP, 75; *cf.* footnote 17 on p. 135.
[19] It is possible to find *tropus, modus,* and *tonus,* or two of them, used interchangeably by medieval writers. Some of them such as Aurelian (GerS I, 39), use *tonus* quite freely in the formula sense of "mode." Others, such as Notker Labeo (GerS I, 96, 98; PiperS, 853, 855), sometimes use *tonus* in this sense, but, like Boethius, apply the term *modus* to the Greek transposition-scales. Hucbald (GerS I, 119) uses *modus, tonus,* and *tropus* without distinction, and "John Cotton" (GerS II, 241) actually states that they are synonymous. Hermannus Contractus, on the other hand, reserves *tropus* for the consecutive arrangement of the tones of an octave-species (EllinM, 31; GerS II, 132), and applies *modus* to the melodic patterns by which such an octave-species is characterized (EllinM, 57, 59; GerS II, 145). Equating *tonus* and *modus* is condemned by most theorists who discuss the matter. Guido (who is among those to equate *tropus* and *modus*) disapproves unequivocally (GerS II, 10 [AmelM, 28], 48, 51, 56), and the practice is condemned also by both earlier and later writers (GerS I, 180, 335; II, 68; CouS IV, 229), some of whom specifically reserve *tonus* as the term for the interval of a major second (CouS I, 260; GlarD, 22, or, in German transl., BohnG, 17). Rémy of Auxerre (GerS I, 64) reports that *tonus* was also employed for *sonus* ("sound"), but he objects to this use. Gombosi adds a modern, admittedly arbitrary distinction among terms. See GomS I, 149.
[20] They designate these *protus,* authentic and plagal; *deuterus,* authentic and plagal, etc. (i. e. as *maneriae*) rather than Dorian, Phrygian, etc.
[21] GomS II.   [22] FriedlB, 345ff; PaulB, 145ff.

theorists was not that they were "unaware of the fact that in the written Greek scale the lowest note is at the top and the highest at the bottom" and that "in applying the Greek names therefore to their own scales, in which the lowest note is at the bottom, they reversed the whole system of nomenclature [of the Greek octave-species]." [23] The error was simply one of mistaking the tonoi for modes.

Still relying on Boethius, the 10th-century writer mentions the Hypermixolydian, but can find no 8th species. His contribution, however bungling, towards efforts to revive Greek theory, broadened the way for attempts to superimpose a scalar modal system upon a body of music already in existence independently of it.

A special modal function was no more ascribed by this 10th-century writer to the different degrees of the new octave-scales than it had been four centuries earlier by Boethius to the degrees of the octave-scales dutifully taken over from the Greeks. One of the other putative authors of the *Alia Musica*, however, in commenting upon the passage ostensibly on the modi attributed to Ptolemy, merges the formulas and the scales and thus, for the first time, ascribes modal functions to degrees within octave-scales. This is the beginning, in the medieval tracts, of the theory of the church modes as we ordinarily think of it today.[24] Here music history furnishes us with another example, to couple with that of the Florentines who created opera when they meant to revive Greek drama, of the occasional fruitfulness of human error.

This theory reached its complete fulfilment (except for the 16th-century additions) at the hands of the brilliant Hermannus Contractus when he recognized the existence of a mode which he called the Hypomixolydian, thus finally solving the problem of supplying musical doctrine with a substitute for the Hypermixolydian. This did not lie between a and $\frac{a}{a}$, as might be expected of such a substitute, but between D and d like the Dorian, from which, however, it differed in several respects, as the table on p. 152 helps to show.[25] Since the Hypomixolydian lay a fourth below the Mixolydian, just as each of the other Hypo- modes lay a fourth below its authentic, the admission of this plagal mode to theoretic rank completed the symmetry of the medieval system.

[23] There are still other explanations aiming to show in what the misunderstanding of the medieval theorists consisted. The one offered in AudaC is especially interesting, but is subject to criticism. Further concerning the fundamental difference between the modes of Boethius and the church modes, see BalT, 144–77.

[24] The *Alia Musica* is printed in GerS I, 125, where it is attributed to Hucbald. His authorship, however, is disproved in MühlA, which shows the composite nature of the work and, on p. 50ff, gives a German translation, the various sections appearing, not in the order in which they are printed in GerS I, but chronologically according to the apparent succession of the five authors Mühlmann believes were involved. The significance of the treatise in the development of modal theory is discussed in much greater detail than above in GomS I, 162ff.

[25] For Hermannus's criticism of the Hypermixolydian, see EllinM, 35f.

This symmetry consisted of more than merely supplying a mode that started a fourth below the Mixolydian: the Dorian already did that. The system of the octave-species, as discussed in the *Alia Musica,* soon yielded ground in the analytical writings, being replaced in large part by consideration of what might be called the *modal nucleus,* consisting of the notes immediately about the final, and of the various species of pentachords and tetrachords.[26] The admissible pentachords were T S T T, S T T T, T T T S, and T T S T; the admissible tetrachords were T S T, S T T, and T T S; the diminished fifth and augmented fourth were inadmissible species. By recognizing the Hypomixolydian, Hermannus, as reference to the table on p. 152 will show, raised the number of combinations of pentachords and tetrachords in the plagal series to four, the number already present in the authentic series. It is interesting to find an equivalent for the Hypomixolydian, perhaps taken over from the West, appearing in Byzantine theory, as is shown by a passage in the *Hagiopolites.*[27]

It is from the pentachords and tetrachords that Aribo [28] derives 80 possible melodic figures, 28 of which, however, he rejects, leaving only 52 useful ones. Aribo's discussion is of considerable interest in several respects: (1) he judges the melodies by their relation to the species of the fourth and fifth rather than of the octave; (2) he mentions national differences in melodic structure—the Lombards prefer stepwise progression, the Germans progression by leaps (*cf.* p. 122); (3) his melodic figures furnish additional evidence of the importance of formulas in the modal concept. That the scale intervals in themselves are an insufficient criterion of mode is forcefully illustrated by the identity, already alluded to, of the intervallic structures of the Dorian and Hypomixolydian scales and the diversity of their finals, tenors, etc. The history of the psalm-tones, however sketchy its reconstruction may be, likewise shows the outstanding significance of formulas. Here, in fact, the structural aspect of the melodic patterns is so important that the study of these tones straddles the subjects of Mode and Form; indeed we shall in this book treat the psalm-tones in our section on the Gregorian forms.

The classified species of the Middle Ages are bounded solely by medieval consonances—the fourth, fifth, and octave. To obtain a full complement of early medieval consonances one need add to these only the unison and such octave-compounds as the twelfth. The compass of the authentic modes is often extended downward by one degree (the fifth mode excepted, since there was a prejudice, in striking contrast to later preferences, against reach-

---

[26] As we have seen in Chap. 2, an attempt has been made (in AudaM, 94ff) to connect the medieval analyses of pentachords and tetrachords with ancient Greek theory, by "correcting" a passage in Gaudentios so as to make it seem that the Greek octave-scales divided the octave into pentachords and tetrachords in the same sense as did the church modes. Not only is the "correction" unwarranted (as shown in Chap. 2), but no connection can be traced. (See GomS I, 150ff.)

[27] See GomS II, 134. [28] GerS II, 212.

ing the final from a semitone below), but these modes, nevertheless, continued to be classified according to the species, not of their ninths, but, like the others, of their octaves. The added sub-final was one of the extensions (to octaves, fifths, fourths) to which the term *emmeles* was applied.[29] The sixths also, dissonances in the early Middle Ages, are among the intervals that never bound classified species: the hexachord, though used for purposes of classification, was not applied to the distinguishing of species. It could not have been, in its Guidonian form, since its T T S T T structure never varied.

While Aribo in the above-mentioned passage treats the tetrachord-species C–F in cavalier fashion, a 14th-century writer like Marchettus of Padua already finds it necessary to defend the retention of the tetrachord, pentachord, and octave on D as the first species against claims being urged in behalf of those on C.[30] This suggests the slow growth of the conception of the major scale, which was not "officially" acknowledged before the 16th century. This scale appears, however, in the writings of Notker Labeo (in the so-called "organ notation"; *cf*. p. 136). The major mode appears also when, in the tritus tonality, b-flat is used instead of b-natural, the availability of both giving this *maneria* a major as well as a true Lydian aspect.

The frequent appearance of b-flat (b *rotundum*) in addition to b-natural (b *quadrum* or *quadratum*)—the two, however, do not occur in immediate succession in plainsong—constitutes the element most disturbing to the symmetry and stability which the early medieval theorists apparently sought to establish in their modal system. The avoidance of the tritone is frequently given by later theorists as a reason for introducing b-flat.[31] But there are two other factors that may explain more cogently this sole example of notated chromaticism [32] in medieval theory: transposition and an underlying pentatonic structure.

While, as we have seen, the Greek transposition scales achieve mention by the theorists, the comprehensive Greek concept of transposition finds no expression in medieval practice.[33] Transposition does occur to some extent, but, as used in actual music, it is only sketchily dealt with in the medieval treatises. Nevertheless, by studying their hints, and by comparing copies of individual Gregorian melodies as they existed at different stages, Gustav

[29] See GerS I, 129; MühlA, 14f; BommW, 186f.

[30] GerS III, 96.

[31] As we shall see in Chap. 9, the tritone was forbidden as a harmonic interval as early as the 9th century. It is thereafter frowned upon as a melodic interval (see, for example, VivC, 28 [11th century]; *cf*. also Hermannus Contractus in EllinM, 28; GerS II, 130). But, despite the opportunity to "edit" tritones out of Gregorian Chant during the centuries of its existence, instances of the indirect (i. e. filled-in) tritone are even now not infrequent. (See, for example, the music to the last syllable of *potaverunt* in Liber, 600.) See further MG IX, 17f.

[32] "Chromaticism," in this section, does not refer to chromatic progressions, such as bb–b♮, but simply to alterations of the natural gamut (b-flat, for present purposes, being included, although it was an integral part of Odo's gamut).

[33] *Cf*. AudaM, Chap. II.

Jacobsthal [34] was able to marshal evidence showing that the medieval musicians employed transpositions to conceal in notation what in performance were actually F-sharp and E-flat (and possibly other chromatic alterations as well). Transposition was applied for another purpose also. If, through modulating from one mode to another, too many phrases ended on tones other than the final of the mode in which the piece was intended to lie, transposition of portions of the melody could cause the whole of it to have the semblance of adhering principally to one mode. The limited range of most phrases in Gregorian Chant facilitated transposing without its becoming obvious through chromatic alteration, since the degree that might have to be altered in a literal transposition might not occur. Often the transposition was not literal, emendations being made in the melodic structure, these frequently consisting of adjustments at the linking passages. [35]

That chromaticism was fully recognized may be gathered from the writings of Aurelian, Regino, and the author of the *Musica Enchiriadis*. (The form of scale used by the latter—*cf.* p. 254—and given by him in daseian notation, clearly implies f-sharp and c̲-sharp; he calls a chromatic alteration *absonia*.) At a later stage the alteration is regarded as something to be emended. Apparently emendation is nothing unusual in the period of Odo of Cluny, for he complains of its employment by unskilled musicians. In the course of time, alteration is avoided through transposition to the upper fourth or fifth. Berno discusses both; "John Cotton" only the transposition of the fifth. The following diagram illustrates the elimination of F-sharp and E-flat through transposing so as to make use of the help of b-flat and b-natural: [36]

D E♭ E♮ F G a b♭ c d transposition to the upper fifth	⎫ a b♭ b♮ c d e f g ♮
E F F♯ G a b c d e " " " " fourth	⎬
F G a b♭ c d e♭ e♮ f " " " " fifth	⎫ a b♭ b♮ c
G a b c d e f f♯ g " " " " fourth	⎬ c d e f g a b♭ b♮ c

Transpositions to avoid inadmissable alterations could be made to the adjacent scale-degree as well as to the upper fourth and fifth. Thus passages containing E-flat or F-sharp could, respectively, be transposed up or down a whole tone. The adjacent scale-degree is important also in modulation, since the most frequent shift from one mode to another in Gregorian Chant is that in which the finals of the modes lie a whole tone apart. [37]

A melody sometimes appears in different modes in different MSS, possibly as a result of inexact transposition. Or its mode may be inconsistently identi-

[34] In JacC. The subject is dealt with also in BommW and MG IX.

[35] *Cf.* BommW 24, 43, 83ff, 91f, 187f, etc.

[36] Since the diagram merely presents material that could be available within the compass of an octave, it does not imply that e♭–e♮, f–f♯, etc., would occur in direct succession in a melody. For the possible connection between transposition and the coming in of staff-notation, see JacC, 368ff.

[37] See FrereK, 132.

Guido d'Arezzo and Bishop Theobald of Arezzo with Monochord
(Vienna, Nat. Bib. 51. South German, 12th Century. After GéroH.)

Cymbals, Instrument of the Zither Family, Psaltery, and Plucked Viol, as Depicted in the De Musica section of the De Universo of Hrabanus Maurus
(Monte Cassino, 11th Century)

Page from Guido d'Arezzo's Micrologus as it appears in the 12th-Century Admont MS
(Cf. GerS II, 23a and p. 259 infra)
(Eastman School, Rochester)

PLATE IV

fied in different treatises. Here again transposition, exact or inexact, may have been at work. For example, it is possible that a Dorian melody has been transposed to G with flattened b and has been ascribed to the tetrardus tonality, simply because the final is G.[38] But not every melody is necessarily restricted to one mode: in fact, in the *Musica Enchiriadis* and other early treatises [39] certain melodies are led through several modes (*cf.* Example 28 in Chapter 5). We have here an interesting anticipation of Ockeghem's 15th-century *Catholica*.

The medieval theorists seem to have felt obligated to attribute ethos to their modes, since the Greeks had perceived ethos in what the medieval theorists believed to have been equivalents. Guido, Hermannus Contractus, and "John Cotton" are among those professing to note an ethical character in the modes.[40]

The climax of the development we have traced from Odo in the 10th century, through a further stage represented by Berno and "Cotton" in the 11th, seems to be reached in the Cistercian reform of the first half of the 12th century. Besides calling for other changes, this restricted the compass of each mode to ten notes, through a misunderstanding of a passage in Psalm CXLIII (CXLIV); "Upon a psaltery . . . of ten strings will I sing praises unto Thee." *Ambitus* (range) had been one of the features considered by Odo [41] and other writers in discussing modal characteristics, but they did not entirely agree about the limits. The Cistercian reform brought about a multitude of transpositions, whether to avoid inadmissible chromatic alterations or an excess of phrase-closes on degrees other than the final of the supposedly prevailing mode or to bring within the permitted range passages that roamed too far.[42]

Knowledge of chromaticism dwindled as a consequence, and had to await the development of polyphony to regain its former rôle in Western music.

Our account of the growth of emendation does not affect the contention that, in the main, the tradition of the old Chant continued through the centuries with remarkable persistence (*cf.* p. 115). The emendations might be described as chiefly examples of "editing" applied to a corpus of melody that in essence remained intact.

As has been indicated (p. 157), the use of both b-flat and b-natural has been accounted for not only by transposition, but also by the pentatonic structure of at least some Gregorian melodies. Whether or not virtually the entire ancient repertoire was based on a pentatonic groundwork, as has

---

[38] *Cf.* VivC, 25; etc.   [39] See GerS I, 156, 165, 179; II, 47.
[40] For a table showing the ethical qualities attributed to the modes by 5 theorists, see WolfC, 409.
[41] GerS I, 259.
[42] BommW is especially useful in showing how far the Cistercian re-edition of the Chant was carried out from the modal point of view. See also WagE II, 449ff.

been claimed,[43] the fact remains that a considerable number of Gregorian melodies are clearly pentatonic. The following melody is purely so, E and b being omitted throughout.

EXAMPLE 32. *In splendoribus*—Communion—Gregorian (from Liber, 395).

Jn splendó·ri·bus sanctó·rum, ex ú·te·ro   an·te lucí·ferum   gé·nu·i·te.

"In the brightness of the saints, from the womb before the day star, I begot Thee." (*Psalm CIX [CX], 3*)

It has been asserted that in old melodies actually containing half-steps the groundwork is still pentatonic and that the tones filling in the minor thirds are ornamental—being *pièn*-tones, in fact, like those used in Chinese music. The *pièn*-tone theory does not reject the traditional eight-mode classification, but merely implies that in each mode two tones were subordinate in nature to the other five. Ponderable circumstantial evidence for this theory is provided by statistical data on the occurrence of the quilisma: of some 1600 Gregorian melodies about 900 contain quilismas "of which 81.5% are placed within minor thirds . . . about 330 items have the quilisma exclusively on b, about 170 on E." [44] It is claimed that the quilisma represented a *pièn*-tone. Aribo does in fact seem to imply that the quilisma in notation called for an ornament in performance, since he states that it is to be rendered *tremolando*.[45]

Obviously there are two ways of filling in a minor third: a–c, for example, may be filled in by either b or b-flat. Thus b-flat as well as b could be a *pièn*-tone. The E-flat, which could replace E as the *pièn*-tone between D and F, was, it seems, eliminated in notation by means of transposition.[46] B, moreover, was not always a *pièn*-tone: a melody, for example, might lie in a pentatonic scale that omitted not E and b, but F and c. But frequent service as a *pièn*-tone may have rendered b undesirable as a tenor under any conditions and may have been responsible for the shift of the Phrygian tenor from b to c in the 10th–11th century.[47] Uneasiness with respect to the tenor in the Phrygian may possibly account for the fact that this mode is the one that is least used in Roman Chant.

The *pièn*-tone theory, when its implications are fully worked out, shows that b-flat is not merely a faintly undesirable substitute for b-natural, as the

[43] *Cf.* YasQ, to which our discussion of pentatonicism is greatly indebted; earlier writers on the subject, among whom Riemann is most important, will be found listed in that article. [44] YasQ II, 344f. [45] GerS II, 215. [46] See YasQ II. [47] YasQ II, 355.

theorists too often imply, but its peer; and the melodies themselves, with their frequent use of b-flat, bear out the theory.[48]

The medieval writers mention the chromatic and enharmonic genera of the ancient Greeks, but there is nothing to show that these genera as such were used in Gregorian Chant. The modal significance, if any, of the approximate quarter-tones, appearing in the Montpellier MS H 159 (*cf.* p. 136) and referred to in treatises,[49] has not been established.[50] In this MS, the quarter-tones occur most frequently, as might be expected, between b and c and between e and f, and they appear most often in melodies in the deuterus tonality.[51] Ancient theory, however, was apparently kept alive with respect to intonation. Boethius had explained the differences between the Pythagorean, Aristoxenian, and Ptolemaic tuning systems and had favored the first. His authority sufficed to make the system of Pythagoras the choice of the medieval writers.[52]

That the substitution of b-flat for b-natural changed the character of a mode —in fact, changed it into another mode—was not widely recognized until the 16th century. Thus, in the Middle Ages the fifth mode with b-flat was regarded as a form of the tritus tonality, not as major, and the first mode with b-flat as a form of the protus tonality, not as natural minor. But the struggle between b-flat and b-natural, on the one hand, and the theorists' bugbear, the tritone, on the other, was bound in the course of time to direct attention to the transformation that b-flat effected in the basic scale structure and thus to cause the position of the octave as the unit by which modality was judged to outrank definitively that of the smaller units (*cf.* p. 156).

The portion of a melody that was looked upon as determining the mode to which the whole was to be assigned was not always the same. Aurelian and Regino who, let us remember, were apparently not concerned with scalar modes, regarded the beginning rather than the ending of an antiphon as decisive for its modal classification.[53] In the scalar modes, it was the final that ultimately prevailed as the modal criterion. Its choice may have been due to

---

[48] YasQ urges that, whether or not the Chant was accompanied in the Middle Ages, an accompaniment worked out according to the "quartal" system (outlined in the article)—a system based on fourths and fifths—is desirable as an aid to the modern listener, for whom the pentatonic structure will thereby become clarified. If accompaniment is desirable at all (historical considerations disregarded), the "quartal" system certainly furnishes a better basis for it in connection with the many melodies showing unmistakable pentatonic traits than does what YasQ calls the "tertian" system—the familiar system based on the triad—which is the outgrowth of diatonic structure, i. e., of a structure in which all the tones of a 7-degree scale are integral (and may be ornamented by 5 chromatic tones).

[49] See GmelchV, 69ff.

[50] For explanations accounting for them in the light of a non-modal consideration, see YasQ I, 193. See also UrK, 84.

[51] GmelchV, 57, 75.   [52] *Cf.* BarbP, 288.

[53] GerS I, 42ff, 231. Concerning the applicability of the opening to the classification of Offertories and Responds, see BommW, 183.

a practical reason: the psalm-tones mentioned on p. 156 were recitation-formulas: they were used for the chanting of psalm-texts between the singing of a free melody—i. e. an antiphon—and its repetition. (Thus the antiphon was the equivalent of the Syrian *enyana* and Byzantine *troparion*.) The tone on which most of the reciting was done was the tenor. When the relation between the modes and psalm-tones was regulated—which is equivalent to saying: when an attempt was made to reduce to a system a method of determining what psalm-tone should be used between two performances of an antiphon—the final of the antiphon obviously took on uppermost importance. For it was to the conclusion of the antiphon that the psalm had to be fitted, and the mode of this conclusion was therefore more important to the singer than the mode of any previous portion of the melody.

The fact that an entire melody, even if it wandered, was assigned to one mode, sometimes according to how it began, more often according to the degree upon which it ended, does not mean that medieval musicians completely disregarded the structure of a melody as a whole, whether they judged according to the criterion of a scalar mode or according to earlier standards. Regino [54] paid attention to this structure when he noted that some antiphons and Introits began and ended in different modes, and, as we have seen, one of the ideals of the Cistercian reform was homogeneous modality. This ideal, however, did not achieve universal adoption: the Gregorian repertoire is rich in melodies whose gentle flow calmly glides beyond the boundaries such an ideal would have imposed. Something like the condition of the Gregorian melodies before the Cistercian reform may perhaps be seen in the Ambrosian repertoire, where there are Chants which appear substantially the same in various MSS except for the important difference that the finals are not alike. Thus the mode of a piece may fluctuate. In fact, the Ambrosian MSS do not even state the modes of pieces.[55] The number of Gregorian melodies that have in the course of centuries been touched up here and there to conform with the systematized theory of the modes is doubtless considerable.

Enough has been said about mode, in connection with Hebrew, Greek, Syrian, Byzantine, and Gregorian music, to show how misleading it is to regard awareness of a scale system as present in the early stages of modal development. We have even seen, in connection with Gregorian Chant, how reluctantly a mode consents to being restricted within the strait jacket of a single scale: thus, the assigning of a melody to the Dorian mode, regardless of whether the b is natural or flattened, tends to show, among other things, that melodic idioms or formulas are more conclusive in fixing the character of a mode than is scale structure by itself. To be sure, melodic formulas, if they are to be strikingly distinctive from one another in character, are likely to

[54] GerS I, 231.   [55] Cf. Antiphonale (Ambrosian), xi; *Enciclopedia italiana* VIII, 794.

have different scales underlying them, especially if they cannot avail themselves of a variety of time-values. The deducing of what these scales are, however, necessarily belongs to a higher stage of modal development. And, while
a difference in the scales underlying the formula complexes that constitute
different modes may be postulated as generally existing, it cannot be claimed
as present without exception, as is shown by those initial figures, the structure
of which, judged from the scalar point of view, would qualify them for assignment to more than one mode, but which are, in fact, assigned to only one
(*cf.* p. 153).

Perhaps it is possible to map out the development of systematized modality,
which is likely to be reduced to rule in sacred music earlier than in secular, in some such way as this: 1. Melody types are classified, but are assigned
their rank for symbolical or other non-musical reasons believed to render them
suitable for special purposes (*cf.* pp. 12, 72f). 2. The melodies are recognized as entities aside from their symbolical significance and are assigned a
specifically musical status—that is, they come to constitute a repertoire of
which the constituents are classified not *qua* symbols but *qua* music (*cf.* p.
75). 3. An attempt is made to analyze the melodies. The degree on which a
melody is to begin obviously takes on importance for the singer (the degree
on which it may end may also assume importance for practical reasons; *cf.*
p. 162). But how is this first degree to be located except through its intervallic relation to other degrees? In the process of determining this relation,
some light is inevitably thrown on differences in underlying scale structure,
it being unlikely that any reasonably large repertoire of purely melodic
formulas, designed to differ in character, should all accord with one scale.
4. The various interval combinations that can produce different scales are
investigated and codified, at least in theory. It is not unlikely that investigation of such combinations in the Middle Ages led the theorists to turn for
guidance to the ancients, with all the attraction of their *auctoritas,* and that
it was such a search that led to the codification begun in the *Alia Musica.*
Whether, in the very earliest stages of codification generally, each scale at
once stands for a living mode not represented by another scale (two or more
scales perhaps merely representing different but overlapping segments of a
larger ground-scale) will be a matter of pure chance, depending upon what
modes have been in practical use before the codification. (Thus the octave-
scales of the Greeks—who would seem to be likely candidates for the rôle of
analysts, their theoretical results reaching the medieval writers after a fashion
and the latter trying without much understanding to establish agreement
between those results and the music of the Church—need not all have had
distinctive modal significance.) In the course of time, if the music remains
purely melodic and the general culture is on a high level, a well-rounded
modal system, taking variations in underlying scale structure into considera-

tion, is evolved. 5. With the relation between modal character and scale structure even partially determined, musicians find it possible to preserve modal character without adhering slavishly to formulas only. They may continue to use the established, familiar formulas, but the retention of the old will go hand in hand with liberty in creating the new, gained through the knowledge that the modal color will not be destroyed if the scale structure together with the significance of the degrees in their capacity as final, tenor, etc., are preserved.

The Forms of Gregorian Chant and of Some Outgrowths

THE FORMS OF THE CLASSIC CHANT

The medieval theorists made no adequate attempt to codify the Gregorian melodies from the standpoint of form. Such occasional ventures in classification as those of Aurelian of Réomé [1] and the anonymous author of the *Commemoratio brevis* [2] are narrow in scope. The intensive study of Gregorian form is definitely a modern contribution. We are fortunate today in having available the results of years of painstaking investigation, undertaken in the spirit of modern scientific research, by scholars like Paolo Ferretti and Peter Wagner, and it is upon their findings that the following exposition is largely based.[3]

The early Gregorian composers, like their fellows in the Near East, were interested not so much in composing new melodies as in adapting old and traditional phrases to new liturgical purposes. Yet in spite of the fact that a limited number of melodic types frequently recur in the ecclesiastical music of the early Middle Ages, they were cast in an amazingly abundant variety of forms.

In using these forms, musicians did not neglect esthetic principles. Many medieval treatises exhort composers and singers to observe the relationships between text and music and to shape their melodies so as to make them euphonious and symmetrical.[4] The formal laws that actually governed the individual categories of plainsong will be discussed presently. Let us first glance at characteristics common to the Gregorian melodies as a whole.[5]

From the point of view of melodic formation, the Gregorian compositions fall into three categories. In the first, or *syllabic* style, the melodies are quite simple: each syllable of the text is set to one note; sometimes a syllable has a neume of two or at most three notes. In the second, or *neumatic* style, while some syllables have one note, most have two or even three groups of notes.

[1] GerS I, 53.   [2] GerS I, 213.
[3] Their works on the subject—which are standards in their field—are FerE and WagE III.
[4] *Cf.* Odo (GerS I, 275f); Aribo Scholasticus (GerS II, 213). See also AbT.
[5] Since the melodies to be mentioned are easily accessible in one or more of the four large chant books—the Liber usualis, Graduale, Antiphonale, and Vesperale—citations will not always be given for them.

In the third, the *florid* (or *melismatic*) style, a single syllable is sung to many groups of notes.

The choice of style was determined by several factors. One was the place of the melody in the liturgy. Melodies of the Office, for example, were generally short and were simpler than those of the Mass. Another determinant was the degree of liturgical solemnity. The distinction made by the Church between ordinary (ferial) days and holy days is reflected especially in the Chants of the Office; the antiphons for Sundays or saints' days are more ornate than those of the Ferial Office. Similarly, the melodies for the culminating points of the two principal hours of the liturgical day—Lauds and Vespers—are richer than those for the other hours. Finally, the style of the Chant was chosen to conform to the ability of the performers. Thus the Chants entrusted to the ministers who surrounded the bishop and to the people were necessarily simple, therefore syllabic. The trained singers of the Schola, or choir, were given more elaborate Chants, in neumatic style, as, for example, the Introit and Communion of the Mass. The leaders of the choir, however—the first cantor and his assistants—were *virtuosi* and they sang melodies in florid style, like those of the Gradual, Alleluia, and Offertory. It is possible, indeed, that some melismas of the Gradual and Alleluia owe their origin, at least partly, to the desire of the performers to display their skill.

The ecclesiastical composers were careful to observe the melodic style required in the setting of a particular text for a particular place in the liturgy. If the same text was assigned to more than one liturgical position, it was set to a different style of melody each time. The following example presents a single text set to two versions of the same melody, a florid version for the Gradual of the Mass, and a syllabic one for the Antiphon of the Ferial Office:

EXAMPLE 33. *Ecce quam bonum*—Elaborate and Simple Versions—
Gregorian.

Grad. (from Liber, 1071).

Ant. (from Vesperale, 46).

"Behold how good and how pleasant" etc. (*Psalm CXXXII* [*CXXXIII*], *1*)

Such use of a single root melody for different liturgical functions had its limits. The melody of an Introit, for example, would not ordinarily be used for a Communion, but could be applied to other Introit texts. The virtual non-transferability of a root melody from one section of the Mass or Office to another is of some importance from the standpoint of form (in the broader sense). Graduals and Introits, for example, differ from one another not only in their ground-plan, as we shall see, but in the types of melody upon which they may draw.

Gregorian melody is built on the grammatical accents of the liturgical text. Melodic peaks generally coincide with the tonic accents [6] of the words. The accented syllable of each word is normally higher than the one that precedes it. Here is a fine illustration of this principle in a florid chant, the *Jubilate Deo* (see p. 181 for further analysis; see Example 19 for the Ambrosian version):

EXAMPLE 34. *Jubilate Deo*—Offertory—Gregorian (after FerE, 18).

† Secondary accent

"Make a joyful noise unto God, all ye lands: Sing forth the honour of His name: Come and hear, all ye that fear God, and I will declare what He hath done for my soul. Alleluia" (*Psalm LXV [LXVI], 1, 2, 16*)

Thus we see that at least in regard to tonic accent Gregorian melody is definitely oratorical melody; and from its oratorical nature result two characteristics. Firstly, the intervals, whether ascending or descending, very seldom exceed a fifth. Leaps of a sixth are extremely rare and occur usually after a pause,

[6] *Cf. p. 51.*

while the octave is found only in sequences and proses, which are of relatively late origin (*cf.* pp. 187ff), as well as in some Credos, also of late date. Secondly, the accent in the chants is indifferent to quantity; some accented syllables are adorned with many notes, often they receive but one (*cf.* p. 141). Moreover, the feeling of finality at the end of a chant is frequently emphasized by a melodic extension of the final syllable.

The law of accent is one of the fundamental laws of Gregorian Chant. Yet there are occasions when it must yield to superior esthetic laws based on the exigencies of musical phrasing, style, tonality, rhythm, and the particular form to which the melody belongs. Even so, according to Ferretti,[7] it finds application eight out of ten times.

Here, by way of samples, are some sources of the exceptions to the law of accent:[8]

1. The psalms in the Hours of the Office and the recitations of Mass and Office are simple and syllabic. They are chanted to formulas (*cf.* p. 172) in the main section of which—the tenor, or reciting tone—inflections vary the reiterated tone at given points. The prescribed reiteration makes observance of the tonic accent impossible.

2. Just as there is a privileged syllable in every word, so there is in every phrase a word that dominates the others. The emphasis on this word is called the phraseological accent. Gregorian composers placed this word at the height of the musical phrase, often without detriment to the tonic accent of single words. But sometimes in an ascending progression in a melodic phrase the final syllable of a given word, as a result of the superior esthetic law that governs musical phraseology, is higher than the earlier accented syllable.[9]

3. The origin of defective accentuation in some Gregorian melodies may be found in the revision to which they were eventually subjected, a revision due to new tastes and prejudices brought about by the spread of polyphony. As we have seen (p. 160) in the 10th–11th century b (as tenor) yielded to c. Likewise E (which held no rank as a tenor) often yielded its place in a melody to F. Consequently the major thirds G–b and C–E gave way to the perfect fourths G–c and C–F; and the major seconds a–b and D–E to the minor thirds a–c and D–F. These changes resulted in incorrect accentuations. Thus, for example, where we have different versions of a melody in the 3rd mode and the *podatus* of accent b–c follows the tenor b in the earlier version, faulty accentuation will arise in the later version through the appearance of the same *podatus* after c instead. The fact that the new versions were not adopted everywhere accounts for the variations in the MSS.[10]

4. In some unskilful adaptations of old melodies to new texts the resulting accentuations are incorrect.

5. Since the melody of the first stanza of a hymn was applied to all the other

[7] FerE, 24.   [8] The reader will find a completer list of exceptions in FerE, 24ff.
[9] *Cf.* antiphons *Fulcite me floribus, Beatam me dicent omnes, In illa die.*
[10] The Vatican Edition restores not a few examples of b and E, but sometimes retains the corrupt version, as in the verses of several Tracts in the 8th Mode, and in the Introits *Reminiscere* and *Domine, ne longe.*

stanzas, verse by verse, foot by foot, syllable by syllable, tonic accents could not be observed (except in the first stanza), unless by accident. A somewhat analogous situation obtains with respect to the sequence (*cf.* p. 188).

There is very little deliberate word painting in the melodies of Gregorian Chant. Sometimes words like *ascendit* and *descendit* are coupled with rising and falling melodic progressions. The following Communion contains a rare example of word painting in the charming imitation, through the use of liquescent neumes, of the cooing of the turtle-dove. (The Vulgate refers to a *turtur* where the King James Version mentions a "swallow.")

EXAMPLE 35. *Passer invenit*—Communion—Gregorian (from Liber, 556).

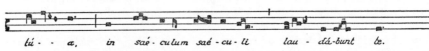

"Yea, the sparrow hath found an house, and the swallow a nest for herself, where she may lay her young, even Thine altars, O Lord of hosts, my King, and my God. Blessed are they that dwell in Thy house: they will be still praising Thee." (*Psalm LXXXIII [LXXXIV], 3, 4*)

The musical period of Gregorian Chant is normally constructed like an arch. There is a rise, a resting on the height attained (phraseological accent), and a fall. The tonal range spanned by the arch may be as much as an octave. One variation of this normal type of period results from suppressing the initial, ascending part in order to fit the melody to a brief text. In this variation the melody begins usually on the fourth or fifth of the mode and descends gradually to the final. Authentic modes especially lend themselves to this variation because the center of the melodic range is the fifth.[11] In another variation the melody starts high, descends to a point of rest below the final, and rises to finish on the final.[12] A third and less common variation may be

---

[11] Examples of this type occur in the antiphons *Sit nomen Domini benedictum, Veniet Dominus,* and the Communion *Vox in Rama.*

[12] Some examples: antiphons *Ite et vos, Liberavit, Cogitaverunt impii.*

called circular; here the melody winds about a central note, usually the final.[13] Quite often, where rise, resting, and fall are all present, the rise is short and unobtrusive, while the more extended descent is very gradual and calm.

Ferretti defines the Gregorian *period* merely as a melodic unit of rather large proportions. He divides the period into *phrases* and the phrases into *half-phrases* or "members." The half-phrase contains two or three *incises.* If two, the incises can, of course, be related to each other only as *a a* or *a b*.[14] If three, the possibilities naturally increase: the grouping may be *a a a, a b c, a a b* (a favorite pattern in Gregorian compositions), *a b b,* or *a b a.* The types *a b* and *a b c* are most common, while *a a a,* doubtless because of its monotony, is avoided. Often the incise or half-phrase is expanded by a short prolongation or coda which helps to define the segments. All these groupings are found also in phrases, periods, and double periods.

There are certain short formulas (as distinguished from extended melodies which may themselves be formulas—*cf.* p. 171) that recur in chants and represent the most traditional part of Gregorian art. Ferretti classifies these formulas under three general headings: (1) according to style, tonality, and melodic type; (2) according to the position they occupy—there are formulas for the intonation, for the middle section, and for the cadence of a melody; and (3) according to their internal structure. In all of these categories the formulas frequently submit to modifications demanded by the exigencies of the text. These modifications take the form of suppression of one or more elements, of addition, contraction, division, or permutation. The recurrence of the formulas throughout the old Gregorian repertoire made them, in the absence of accurate notation, valuable mnemonic aids in the mastering of the liturgical melodies. Moreover, the Gregorian composer's skill could be displayed by his use of these figures, just as a harmonist's skill may be displayed by his use of chord groups, which in themselves amount, practically, to formulas also.

Gregorian Chants may be grouped in four main classes:

I. To the *strophic* compositions belong hymns and sequences, which are characterized by the literal and immediate repetition of melodic sections of some length. Hymns have already been briefly described (see pp. 69, 104f); sequences will be treated later. In the typical hymn each stanza, as we have seen, is composed of a group of lines each containing a prescribed number of feet. While not all the lines necessarily have the same number of feet in a single stanza, the first line of one stanza will have the same number as the

---

[13] Some examples: antiphons *Tu Domine, In illa die, Exiit sermo.*

[14] The symbols used for formal musical divisions in this book are Latin letters printed in italics. Ordinarily lower-case letters are used, but where there is repetition of a musical member with repetition of the text—i. e., a refrain—capitals are used. Students pursuing further the study of form in medieval music will find that some writers, in indicating form, use Latin letters with reference to texts and Greek letters with reference to music.

first line of the other stanzas, and so on throughout. Since the melody of the first strophe is invariably repeated for all the other strophes, the hymn may be termed a monostrophic composition. In the sequence, however, two lines have the same literary and musical form, but the melody normally changes for every group of two lines. The sequence, consequently, is a polystrophic composition. In strophic chants, especially in hymns, the melody takes absolute preference over the text, on which it imposes its own musical accentuations.

II. Strophic form was known to the Greeks. It was used, for example, in the strophes and antistrophes of the choruses in the dramas. *Psalmodic* composition, on the other hand, was unknown to the Greeks; it is peculiar to the Synagogue and the Christian Church. The psalm-text is composed of a number of non-metrical verses, each of which is divided into two members that balance each other as antecedent and consequent. (*Cf.* p. 10.) [15] Since the musical formula is repeated for each verse, there is a certain analogy between the form of a strophic piece and that of a psalm, but, in the latter, the formula is subject to the modifications described on p. 174. Moreover, the styles of strophic and psalmodic chant differ from one another radically. The style of the latter compares with that of the former somewhat as the highly inflected speech of recitative compares with the sustained melody of folk-song.

III. Almost all the chants of the Mass and Office that do not have strophic or psalmodic structure are *commatic* compositions. In these there are no strophes or verses properly so called, but sections of free composition. While in strophic and psalmodic chants different texts may have the same melody, in commatic chants every incise, every half-phrase, every phrase may have its special melodic design. Hence the musical inflections of commatic chant are dependent upon the tonic accentuation of the single words.

Commatic chants came into being by three different processes:

In the *first* of these, melodies were composed directly to the texts. There are a great many of these original melodies in the music for both the Mass and the Office; and, in most instances, the text for which each melody was composed has for centuries remained bound to its music. The different units in a chant of the commatic type are linked together by devices such as counterbalancing, ascending and descending melodic progressions, rhyme (*cf.* p. 107f), identical and reversed curves, thematic reminiscences, melodic sequences,[16] and so on.[17]

[15] The two parts of a verse are separated by an asterisk in modern plainsong editions.

[16] It is unfortunate that the word "sequence" must serve a double function in music: to denote not only the form to which we have already referred and to which closer attention will be given on p. 187, but also the melodic device whereby a tonal pattern is repeated on other scale degrees than the original. To avoid confusion with the *form*, we are referring to the *device* as a "melodic sequence."

[17] It is interesting to note that Guido d'Arezzo is the only one of all the medieval theorists to refer to these artifices. See GerS II, 16; AmelM, 35. (*Cf.* FerE, 107.)

The *second* process involves the adaptation by Gregorian artists of traditional and somewhat extended melodies to new texts. These favorite airs constitute melodic types and may be compared with the *nomoi* of the Greeks, the *hirmoi* of the Byzantines, and the *ris-qolé* of the Syrians. Not only with these, but with the melodic types that occur in folk-song. As Samuel P. Bayard has put it,[18] dealing with current British-American folk-tunes:

In the British Isles and in this country there exists a repertory of distinct melodies, limited in number, and set for the most part to texts in English. . . . These airs are clearly perceptible in numerous versions of varying lengths. . . . This repertory constitutes the life-blood of the folk-melodic organism in English-speaking tradition; and the airs included in it (about forty in number) . . . are universally diffused, and in their various forms they account for by far the greater part of the musical settings to our traditional songs in English, as well as for the music to a fair number of songs in Gaelic, Welsh and Manx.

Thus, the Gregorian melodic types illustrate—with the loftiest distinction—a musical law of universal application. They are found in some Graduals and Alleluias of the Mass and are particularly numerous in the antiphons of the Office. In the Antiphonary of Hartker (Codex of St. Gall),[19] for example, there are more than thirty antiphons composed according to the melodic type of the antiphon *Omnes de Saba venient.*[20]

The *third* process was that of centonization. The word *cento* originally denoted a patchwork quilt or dress; the name was applied to a literary composition made up of fragments taken here and there from the works of an author or of different authors and pieced together in the form of a literary mosaic. The texts of many chants are themselves real centos. The Gregorian artist often selected a few significant bits from the verses of a psalm and produced a short, concise text that corresponded better to his special purpose than any of these bits with its original context. The Gregorian melodists followed the example of the liturgical writers.[21]

IV. The fourth type consists of chants that have the character of *monologues and dialogues.* The monologues are sung by the celebrant (either a bishop or a priest), or by the other ministers (deacon, subdeacon, or lector); the dialogues occur between the celebrant and the congregation or choir.

[18] In the paper, *Aspects of Melodic Kinship and Variation in British-American Folk Tunes,* read Sept. 13, 1939, before the International Congress of the American Musicological Society (to be published).

[19] PM, Ser. 2, I.

[20] Modern scholars, in illustrating the application of a melody type to different texts, follow a fairly uniform procedure. A table is made with, at the top, a melody line containing *all* the notes used by the pieces allegedly based on the type. The texts of all the pieces are written below the melody, one under the other, each syllable vertically aligned with the note or group to which it is sung, notes omitted in a particular application of the type, therefore, having no syllables below them in the line giving the text of that application. The notes present in all or most of the applications are regarded as belonging to the basic type; notes rarely present, as accessory. (See, for example, FerE, table facing p. 112, or the several tables in FrereA.)

[21] It is believed that in the earliest times the Gregorian composer and writer were ordinarily the same person.

As we shall see, many ecclesiastical forms strongly influenced secular music—such as that of the troubadours, trouvères, and Minnesinger; and even polyphony appropriated such forms as those of the sequence and hymn, besides borrowing from the Gregorian repertory the actual melodies on which at first all part-pieces were built.

The great majority of the chants of the Mass and Office are cast in the form of psalmody. Their texts are furnished largely by the 150 Psalms and the Canticles [22] of the Old and New Testaments. There are three different ways of chanting a psalm. In *responsorial psalmody* the soloist sings the verses of the psalm and the Schola answers him with a short chant like a refrain, i. e. the response. This refrain is composed of a verse or sentence that the soloist has already sung. In *direct psalmody* no refrain is interpolated between the verses.[23] Less ancient than these two systems (*cf.* p. 68) is *antiphonal psalmody,* in which, in Roman Chant, the choir always divides into two groups which sing the verses in alternation, one group echoing the other. Here too, there is a refrain (the antiphon), sung to comparatively free melody. In earlier times this was sung before the psalm and repeated after each verse. In the 9th or 10th century, however, it became the custom not to repeat the antiphon until after the psalm plus Gloria Patri (*cf.* p. 176). In current practice even one of the two remaining appearances of the antiphon—the first of them—is curtailed on some occasions (see Example 36).

Since antiphonal psalmody of the Office was sung by monks, while that of the Mass was chanted in churches by trained singers, the psalmody of the Office is the simplest and will therefore be discussed here before the other, and older, psalmodic forms. We shall first describe the manner in which the psalm-verses etc. are treated, and thereafter the nature of the antiphons.

The Tones (i. e. formulas) [24] of the psalmody of the Office varied greatly in the early Middle Ages, and the theorists of that period seem to have felt no need of clearing up the resulting confusion. These formulas, used for the recitation of the psalm-verse itself between renditions of the fairly free melody or antiphon, have something of the character of speech-song. *Tonaria* (tonaries) existed which gave, often in neumes, the formulas assigned to each mode or occurring most frequently in it, and which listed the texts according to their place in the liturgy and the Tone to which they were sung. The *Commemoratio brevis de Tonis et Psalmis modulandis,* a 10th-century tonary, is

---

[22] Among the canticles in the Roman liturgy are the *Nunc Dimittis* ("Song of Simeon," *cf.* Luke II, 29); the *Benedicite omnia opera* ("Song of the Three Children," *cf.* v.35 thereof in the Apocrypha, or Daniel III, 57, in the Vulgate); the *Magnificat* (Mary's Song of Thanksgiving after the Annunciation, *cf.* Luke I, 46); and the *Benedictus Dominus Deus Israel* (Canticle of Zacharias, *cf.* Luke I, 68).

[23] Wagner's statement (WagE I, 23) that direct psalmody is not of very ancient origin is refuted by Ferretti (FerE 138) who finds evidence of its use in the 4th century. *Cf.* the above description of direct and responsorial psalmody with the description of Hebrew forms on p. 10.

[24] We shall capitalize "tones" when it is used to indicate a formula, if no qualifying word before it makes the meaning unequivocal.

of especial importance since it records a series of melodies[25] exactly, by means of daseia signs (*cf.* p. 136). The melodies are there set to the syllables *Noanoeane Noeagi* (the system represented is frequently referred to as the *Noeane* system), which bear an obvious resemblance to the syllables associated with the Byzantine *enechemata* (*cf.* p. 87). Similar syllabic combinations are mentioned in the earlier treatise of Aurelian of Réomé, in which he refers, as we have already stated, to the supposed invention by Charlemagne of four Tones, and in which he gives syllabic combinations as indicative of their form. He states that contemporary Greek singers had such combinations also and reports that he asked a Greek musician to explain the meanings of the designations, but that the Greek said they had no meanings and were merely cries of joy. On the basis of this passage,[26] several scholars [27] have concluded that the Westerners derived their musical formulas, with the syllables, from the Byzantines. This is not at all unlikely.[28] Other Western theorists besides Aurelian mention the syllables—Regino,[29] Berno,[30] *et al.*

The Western *Noeane* tropes were gradually, beginning with the first half of the 10th century, displaced by similar sets with Latin texts, in each of which the first word corresponded to the number of the mode. Thus, the text for the first formula began *Primum quaerite regnum Dei;* for the second, *Secundum autem simile est huic,* etc. In the music, the initial figure for each mode was one widely used to open chants in that mode, and the conduct of the rest of the formula resembled that of the melody representing the mode in the old *Noeane* system.[31]

Although the tonaries failed truly to crystallize the various formulas, since they did not completely agree with one another melodically, they doubtless served as excellent mnemonic devices for cantors until the general acceptance of staff-notation removed their reason for existence. Even so, they lingered on in some regions into the 15th century. A uniform practice was gradually worked out so that, by the 12th or 13th century, the details of the psalmodic

[25] Printed in GerS I, 229, also in AudaM, 171ff, where they are accompanied by transcriptions into square notation.

[26] GerS I, 41f (German translation of portion in KunzU, 11).

[27] E. g. Fleischer (see FleiN III, Teil 3, 43) and Gombosi (GomS II).

[28] There are other scholars who feel that both the Eastern and Western series were adaptations of some ancient formulas linked to 8 standard modes. *Cf.* AndM, 150. See also GaiS, 68; RieH I, 210ff. But Riemann was apparently wrong, as is claimed in KunzU, 15, in associating the combinations with the ancient Greek solmisation syllables tah, ta, toh, teh (*cf.* p. 24). Kunz believes the Western *Noeane* system was an independent growth, and gives a clever but perhaps not wholly convincing explanation of the meanings of the syllables. The interested reader might do well to refer to Kunz's article, on pp. 6–8 of which there is given a comparative table showing the different sets of syllabic combinations appearing in the Byzantine and Latin sources.

[29] GerS I, 247.   [30] GerS II, 77.

[31] Guido d'Arezzo's *Primum quaerite* set may be seen in CouS II, 81f, 88, 91, 94, 97, 99, 102, 107. GerS and CouS contain other sets also. For a comparative table after 5 sources, for Modes 1 and 2, see AudaM, 176f. MathS, 49ff prints a *Primum quaerite* series that is especially useful since the *Noeane* set of "Cotton" is printed on pp. 48f, and correspondences possible between the two systems (if one omits the initial figures of the former) can therefore easily be determined.

formulas were fairly definitely fixed within the old framework of eight Tones. (If, as we have suggested, Gregorian rhythm may not have been a definite, systematized thing in the early centuries, we have here yet another example of a transition from a fluid practice to a fixed one. In fact, such a development with respect to the Tones would lend color to our suggestion. Perhaps too much effort has been spent in recent years in attempts to rediscover widespread systems that never existed.) All that can with reasonable certainty be claimed as ancient are the reciting tones and many terminations. The formulas for the intonation and mediation (concerning which more presently), with the chief rules for adapting them to the text, are of different periods.[32] Even after the systematization, some of the old formulas it discarded continued for a while, owing to their popularity, to be sung—but without texts—after certain antiphons on holidays.[33]

There are nine systematized psalm-tones grouped together in the Vatican Edition of the chant books—eight regular and normal, of which one is associated with each of the modes, and one "irregular" called the *Tonus peregrinus* ("strange, foreign") which has two reciting tones.[34] Texts are fitted to the Tones according to definite rules,[35] so that it is not necessary for the books to print out the music for each psalm.[36] The second, fifth, and sixth Tones have a single final cadence, but the others have more than one. These optional cadences are called *differentiae*.[37] They arose from the necessity of ending the verse with some note that would be in harmony with the first notes of the different antiphons (upon their repetition), which do not all begin on the final: an antiphon may start with any note in the pentachord and, in plagal modes, with any in the lower tetrachord also (*cf.* pp. 153, 162). The *Tonus peregrinus* seems to have been introduced in the 8th or 9th century. It is the only one to survive of many "irregular" tones that flourished in the Middle Ages. It is considered by some to be of Byzantine origin and by others of Hebraic. It may be repeated here that the Byzantines themselves seem to have considered their echoi to be of Hebrew origin (*cf.* p. 79). The reciting note in each Tone is the degree that ranks as tenor of the mode to which the Tone is assigned. In fact, the psalm-tones are evidently not the least important of the formulas that helped to stamp the scalar modes with their ultimate characteristics.

[32] A table aiming to fix the time of their origin appears in GasH, 274.

[33] For further details, see MathS, 52f, a book in which a large amount of information concerning the tonaries is conveniently assembled.

[34] The Tones are printed in Liber, 113-7. Antiphonale, 3*-27*, and Vesperale, 3*-30*.

[35] These may be found in SuñG, 51ff, BenP, 64, and JohnG, 68ff (Chap. VII of JohnG is quite helpful about psalm-tones in general).

[36] The Tone to be used in each case is the one whose number corresponds with the mode number printed before the antiphon linked to the psalm. If the *Tonus peregrinus* is to be used "*tonus pereg.*" appears under the mode number of the antiphon.

[37] Concerning the history of the *differentiae*, see WagE III, 130ff.

In addition to the Tones of simple psalmody of the Office, we have formulas, also called Tones, for some of the recitations (*cf.* p. 182)—the Collect, Prophecies, Epistles, Gospel, and Preface—and for Canticles and other parts of the liturgy. It must be remembered, however, that all these Tones originated outside the scalar modal system. In the recitation-Tones, especially, the cadences are so meager that it is impossible to establish a relationship with a particular final. It was after both the formulas and the new octave-species were well known that *the desire arose to reduce the former to a place within the scalar modes,* largely for the purpose of linking up psalm-verses chanted to Tones with antiphons that fitted into definite scales. (In terms of the hypothetical account of the development of modes, given on p. 163, we might perhaps say that here we find, in the course of adjustment to one another, two different stages of such a development; stages that happen to exist simultaneously in two different fields in which a modal system is being cultivated.)

Here is an example of an antiphon of the Office as it is sung today:

EXAMPLE 36. *Miserere* and *Ecce nunc*—Antiphon with Psalm—Gregorian (after Antiphonale, 47).

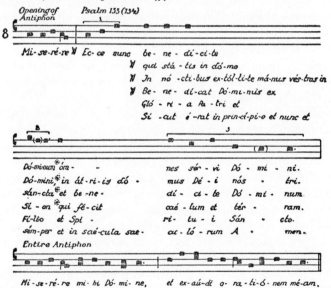

"Behold, bless ye the Lord, all ye servants of the Lord, which by night stand in the house of the Lord. Lift up your hands in the sanctuary, and bless the Lord. The Lord that made heaven and earth bless thee out of Zion" (*Psalm CXXXIII* [*CXXXIV*]). "Glory be to the Father," etc. (See footnote 38.) "Have mercy on me, O Lord, and give ear to my prayer."

The first word of this antiphon is chanted; then, because the antiphon is in the eighth mode, the four verses of the psalm are sung to the tone assigned to that mode; the *Gloria Patri* follows and finally the entire antiphon.

The *Gloria Patri*,[38] the so-called "lesser doxology" (the "greater doxology" is the *Gloria in excelsis* in the Ordinary of the Mass), was directed by St. Benedict (*c*. 530) to be used after each psalm. The letters *e u o u a e,* under the *differentiae* in chant books, represent the vowels of the last two words of the *Gloria Patri*—i. e. *saeculorum. Amen*—and are used as an abbreviation.

The psalm-tone in this example contains three main elements: an intonation (or *initium*), a tenor (the equivalent of which is called *tuba* in the recitation-Tones), and a cadence. The intonation (see 1 in example) is designed to render the passage from the end of the antiphon to the tenor—which is the reciting tone—smooth and pleasing. There are two cadences: the mediation or mediant cadence, i. e. the melodic fragment that ends the first part of the verse (see 2 in example), and the final cadence (see 3 in example). The point of division between the two parts of the verse is known as the *caesura*. In settings of long texts the tenor of the first half of the verse may be interrupted by a downward inflection called the *flexa,* which is also a type of cadence. If the tenor is sub-tonal (that is, if the scale degree immediately below it is a whole tone away), the inflection descends a whole tone; if it is sub-semitonal (that is, if the scale-degree immediately below is a semitone away), the inflection descends a minor third.[39]

The antiphonal psalmody of the Mass is among the divisions of psalmodic chant that are more elaborate than the simple antiphonal psalmody of the Office, just described. The musical formulas of the more developed psalmodic chants retain the same structural frame but fill it more elaborately. Thus, in direct psalmody, where there is no antiphon, the intonation has the character of a more or less solemn introduction. The tenor, in all these chants, becomes the note round which the melody moves. Tenors other than those in the psalm-tones may be simple or ornate. In some pieces a single tenor is employed, in others two (*cf.* the *Tonus peregrinus* in the psalmody of the Office) and in still others three. Most cadences are called tonic because they are based on one or two accents, but in some ornate and solemn psalmodic melodies we find final cadences that are cursive, i. e. that employ the *cursus*. This is either a *metrical* or a *rhythmical* arrangement of the last syllables of a sentence or part of a sentence, the metrical *cursus* being based on the long and short quantity of syllables, the rhythmical *cursus* on their number and accent. The former type was much used in the 4th and 5th centuries. The three main forms of the latter are the *cursus planus,* with five syllables; *cursus tardus,* with six; and

---

[38] English version: "Glory be to the Father, and to the Son: and to the Holy Ghost; as it was in the beginning, is now, and ever shall be: world without end. Amen."

[39] An additional bit of evidence for the pentatonic nature of at least some of the Chant.

cursus velox, with seven. In these, also, there is a caesura, and it occurs after the second syllable from the beginning in each form. In the following example of the commonest form, the *cursus planus,* the *cursus* starts with the word *meam* and the caesura falls immediately after it:

EXAMPLE 37. Illustration of the *cursus planus* (from JohnG, 236).

"I have lifted up my soul."

In the formation of such cadences, the verbal accent obviously becomes of primary importance. Five syllables are counted back from the last one, each is set to a neume, and the cadence is conceived as a single rhythmical unit.[40]

Antiphonal psalmody of the Mass is represented by the *Introit* and the *Communion.* The Introit serves as a prelude to the Mass; it establishes a liturgical theme that will be analyzed and developed in the other parts of the Mass. Ferretti, referring to the text, calls it the *leit-motiv* of the sacred drama.[41] The Introit is generally livelier in style and much more developed than the Communion. Both are neumatic and were intended to frame the psalm itself with melodies that are in the main original (i. e. that do not employ centonization or melodic types). The eight Tones for the psalms of the Introits, unlike the Tones for simple psalmody of the Office, have remained undisturbed by local vicissitudes. In these Tones the tenor is the same for both parts of the psalm-verse, except in the sixth Tone, in which we have two tenors. The psalm of the Communion, however, has been suppressed, leaving only the antiphon, except in the Communion of the Mass for the Dead, which retains a versicle, *Requiem aeternam,* with the antiphon *Lux aeterna.*

While there are 403 surviving antiphons of the Mass, the number for the Office is enormous, varying in old MSS from 1200 to over 1900.[42] Some of these are original melodies, others may be reduced to relatively few melodic types,[43] and still others are centonized melodies. Most of them are syllabic in style. Neumatic, however, and at some points moderately florid, are the four Marian antiphons with which the Office is concluded: *Alma Redemptoris Mater* (cf. p. 128), *Ave Regina Coelorum, Regina Coeli,* and *Salve Regina.*

[40] For treatment of the *cursus* see PM IV; JohnG, 235; BenP, 84ff; or, especially, FerC.
[41] FerE, 293.
[42] The Antiphonary of Lucca (PM IX) contains 1550; that of Worcester (PM XII), 1910; that of Compiègne, 1783. There are 1235 in the *tonarius* of Regino of Prüm (CouS II, 1–54). See FerE, 318.
[43] Gevaert (GevM, 125), pioneering in this field, found that all the antiphons in the tonary of Regino of Prüm could be reduced to 47 themes. Ferretti (FerE, 363, footnote) questions the soundness of Gevaert's methods and suggests that a revision of his catalogue is in order, but does not imply that the number of melodic types would be greatly increased.

The artists of the classic Gregorian Age saw no objection to having several antiphons, written in the same mode and linked to the same psalm-tone, follow each other. Monotony was avoided by the employment of different melodic types in the antiphons and varied *differentiae* in the Tones. But with ecclesiastical composers of the late Middle Ages it became a rule that successive antiphons should be each in a different mode and should follow each other according to the progressive numerical order of the modes. The taste of these later writers ran to floridity, and their antiphons consequently lack the simplicity and sobriety of the earlier examples.

The only division of the Chant that represents direct psalmody in the Mass is the *Tract*. Since this was originally a chant for a soloist, the melody is ornate and florid. A characteristic of the Tract that is not found in any other Gregorian type is the great variation to which the melody of the first verse submits when set to the other verses. Moreover the numerous melismas do not underscore the text, as do those of the Offertory, for example, but seem rather to have a structural, purely musical, significance. Thus, a melisma that serves as final cadence is never used as a mediant cadence, and *vice versa*. There are only two melodic types, one in Mode 8 and one in Mode 2. The former is gay and energetic in character and simpler in construction than the latter. Both types have two tenors. Ferretti adduces a great deal of evidence to prove that in the primitive organization of the ecclesiastical Chant the Tract had only one melodic type, the one in Mode 8, and that the melody in Mode 2 was originally intended for some Gradual responsories, but was later converted into a Tract.[44]

The responsorial chant originally consisted of several verses, and had the following structure: *A Ab Ac A*, etc. That is, *A*—refrain (or respond) sung by soloist; *A*—refrain by Schola; *b*—first verse by soloist; *A*—refrain by Schola; *c*—second verse by soloist; *A*—refrain by Schola, etc. It has been claimed that the rondo of modern music is indirectly derived from this form of Gregorian Chant. In the course of time responsories were shortened. They now have only one verse, and, save in exceptional cases, have the pattern: *AAbA*. The responds furnish clear-cut examples of the use of melody types.[45] They differ in style from the antiphons in that they have more of the character of recitative, the antiphons being distinctly melodic.

The *Gradual* of the Mass was at one time called *Responsorium*. It seems to have been customary, as early as the 4th century, for the solo cantor to sing from the steps (*gradus*) of the ambo, or altar. The contrast between the read-

[44] The few examples of direct psalmody in the Office include the Canticle *Nunc Dimittis*; Psalm LXIX (LXX) *Deus in adjutorium meum intende*; Psalm CXLV (CXLVI) *Lauda, anima mea*; and Psalm CXXIX (CXXX) *De profundis*, in the Office of the Dead.

[45] A thoroughgoing study of the subject may be found in FrereA. See especially pp. 8–58. The same author incorporates a greatly shortened study of the subject in his article on *Psalmody* in Grove IV.

ing by the minister at the altar-railing and the singing from the steps may have led to the designation "Gradual" for the piece sung after the reading of the Epistle.[46] The Gradual is a florid chant with one verse. Many centuries ago its primitive responsorial form became modified. Today, most often, the soloist chants the opening of the Gradual-respond, the choir enters and together with the soloist sings the rest of it, the soloist then sings the verse, and is joined near the end of the verse, at the point marked by an asterisk in the modern chant books, by the full choir. This, then, leaves the form, not *AAbA*, but *ab*. On some occasions, however, the form *AAb* is used. It is thought that the introduction in the 9th century of sequences and tropes (*cf.* p. 185) made the ecclesiastical function too long, and resulted in the mutilation of the Gradual.

While we have Graduals in all eight Gregorian modes, those in the tritus tonality predominate in several codices. Here the frequent recurrence of the members of the major triad F–a–c lends the chants a lively and joyous character and makes them sound closely akin to modern melodies in major.[47] The Graduals as a group contain some of the most expressive melodies in the whole Gregorian repertory. The melody of the following Gradual, from the Mass for Easter Sunday, must have greatly pleased the old composers, since we find it adapted to Graduals of other holidays. It is a real melody type, one of the oldest in this division of the Chant.[48]

EXAMPLE 38. *Haec dies*—Gradual—Gregorian (after Liber, 778).

---

[46] This is the opinion of many authorities. Sachs, however, writes (SachsS III & IV, 19) ". . . fifteen Psalms, Nos. 120–134, were called even in the original Hebrew *shire hama'alot,* or—literally—'songs of the steps.' However there was no pulpit with steps in the temple, and nothing indicates this very special sense. . . . It seems more likely that the obscure term designates a musical form, just as in the Syrian language the same word is used to designate a ladder and a certain type of melody." Gastoué, on the other hand, recalls that the adjective *gradalis* meant "well ordered, composed with care" and believes that the Gradual derived its name from the application of this adjective to the *responsorium* (GasG, 174).

[47] Wagner believed the Graduals in the tritus tonality to be the most recent ones. Ferretti leaned towards the opposite conclusion. See FerE, 173.

[48] Ferretti questions the authenticity of the flat before the b on *Haec.*

nur: quó-ni-am in saé   culum   mise-ricór-dia é-jus.

"This is the day which the Lord hath made; we will rejoice and be glad in it. O give thanks unto the Lord; for He is good: because His mercy endureth for ever." (*Psalm CXVII [CXVIII], 24, 1*)

We find especially common in Graduals not only *melody* types but also certain types of *melisma* which recur so frequently in the florid forms of the Chant that they have been called "migratory melismas." [49]

The *Alleluia* was sung during Easter in Rome before the time of St. Gregory, but that pontiff allotted it to all Sundays except those of Lent. Of the ancient Alleluias in the Vatican Gradual, those in the protus and tetrardus tonalities predominate. As in the other responsorial chants, we must distinguish here between the verse and the refrain. The melody of the latter is a solemn acclamation and consists of two parts: a moderately neumatic passage on the word *Alleluia,* and a melisma added on the last vowel. This melisma is the *jubilus* of which St. Augustine speaks (*cf.* p. 64). The melody of the verse consists of several members; it is rather moderate in style but contains occasional melismas that emphasize a significant word. An interesting feature of the settings of the verse is thematic repetition: melodic fragments of the refrain often recur in the verse, interwoven with new material. A lovely example of this is the verse of the following Alleluia:

EXAMPLE 39. *Alleluia Justus germinabit*—Gregorian (from Liber, 1192).

"*Alleluia:* The just man shall spring as the lily: and shall flourish for ever before the Lord." (*Hosea XIV, 6*)

[49] WagE III, 374.

As a general rule the verse ends with a repetition of part or, as in the example, of all of the melody of the refrain, this producing rhyme. Sometimes the verse has a special, contrasting ending. Most of the Alleluias of the Mass are original melodies, with no trace of centonization. "Alleluiatic" melodies continued to be composed throughout the Middle Ages.[50]

The custom of performing a chant during the ceremony of offering bread and wine seems to have been introduced before the time of Gregory, but not earlier than the 4th century. Originally the *Offertory,* like the Introit and Communion—indeed, like all chants that accompany an action—must have been simple and antiphonal in form. But at some undetermined time the verses of the psalm were greatly reduced, and the melody of the refrain was greatly enriched. As a result, the Offertory became a chant especially appropriate for a soloist, but the participation of the Schola was retained, its function becoming responsorial. The refrain was still called an *antiphona.* Most of the Offertories in the old MSS contain two verses; some have three and a few have one. Today the verses are omitted, except in the Offertory of the Requiem Mass, which retains one, and what we call the Offertory is only the *antiphona* that in ancient times was sung before and after each verse. The suppression of the verses was probably due, at least in part, to the discontinuance of the offering of gifts by the congregation.

In the Offertory, "the composer gives free rein to his own fantasy; under the impetus of a healthy and sacred lyricism he sings and comments on the text, pausing from time to time on this or that word to underline its mystical significance with long melismas." [51] A characteristic peculiar to Offertories is the repetition of words and phrases of the text. This repetition occurs not only in Gregorian Offertories but also in those of the Ambrosian repertoire. Ferretti surmises that the practice of repeating words began when it was found that the singing would be over before the rite of the offering was completed, and believes that this occurred at a time when the number of verses was already fixed so that the only choice left the cantor was to repeat a word or phrase. The *Jubilate Deo* on page 166 contains a repetition of the first phrase of the text. But this beautiful melody is interesting also because it illustrates the principle of *thematic* repetition, applied with the utmost delicacy and expressiveness. In the long melismatic passage on the second *jubilate* the phrase that includes the highest note is a repetition, a fifth above, of the first descending theme of that passage. The fragment on *te* is an echo of the phrase immediately preceding. Moreover, the incise accompanying the second *Deo* is an exact repetition of that on the first *Deo.* This is a true melodic rhyme. A study of this chant will disclose other thematic correspondences.

---

[50] For a list specifying those believed to be early (late 6th century-2nd half of the 8th century), see GasO, 274. Further concerning the Alleluia, see footnote 60 on p. 264 *infra.*
[51] FerE, 214.

Note the delicate designs formed by the repetitions of the porrectus that appears for the first time on the syllable *la* of the second *jubilate,* and of the torculus that is first heard on the first *Deo.*

Perhaps the finest of the responsorial chants of the Office, from the point of view of correct accentuation of words and flow and naturalness of musical phraseology, is Psalm XCIV (XCV) *Venite, exsultemus Domino.* It is joined by an antiphon called an *invitatorium,* which constitutes a refrain that is sung first by the soloist, then by the choir, and is repeated wholly or in part after every verse of the psalm. Each verse contains three musical periods, each of which has an intonation, tenor, and cadence. The cadences of the first two periods are mediant and tonic, and that of the last is cursive. Unfortunately this psalm is rarely sung today.

A responsory is performed after each lesson at Matins. The pattern is *AbA,* in which *A* is the Responsory and *b* the verse sung by a soloist. In the authentic Tones the reciting tone is first the fourth, then the fifth of the mode. In the plagal Tones, however, the recitation is done first on the third, then on the final of the mode.

It will be noticed that the number of times the response occurs varies in different forms. The essential difference between responsorial and antiphonal psalmody is definitely that the former involves alternation between choir and soloist while the latter involves alternation between two choirs.

Not employing psalm-texts, but similar to the psalm-tones in structure (though simpler) are the liturgical *recitations,* already mentioned in passing —Lessons, Epistles, Gospels, Collects, etc. They are wholly syllabic, with an intonation of one or two notes at most and often no intonation at all, a *tuba* with few inflections, and a brief fall or rise as cadence. The inflections are indicated in old MSS by punctuation signs (*positurae*) called: *punctus versus* (·), *punctus elevatus* (⸴), *punctus circumflexus* (⸝) , and *punctus interrogativus* (⸮) . The formulas for these inflections—especially the one for the *versus*—vary slightly in MSS of different localities and also according to the position of the recitation in the liturgy.[52] The most interesting of the recitations are two of the Orations: the Pater Noster and the Preface. Their special character is shown by the fact that their melodies are not merely indicated in the MSS by *positurae,* but are written out in notes. In form they differ from the other recitations in that they are divided into two parts, with a mediant cadence for the first part and a final cadence for the second. Some MSS contain Pater Nosters and Prefaces with two tenors. As a general rule the second tenor is lower than the first.

One of the oldest of the recitation forms is the Litany. Borrowed from pagan rites, it comprised, in the earliest centuries of Christianity, a series of invocations by the priest, each of which was answered by the people with the

---

[52] For further information, see WagE III, 37ff.

cry of *"Kyrie eleison"* ("Lord have mercy"). The invocations resembled each other in structure. This has remained the pattern of the Litany down to the present day; it is now omitted in the Roman liturgy, however, except on certain saints' days.[53]

Of later origin than the psalmodic melodies and recitations are the chants that form the *Ordinary of the Mass.* Originally sung by the congregation, the earliest Kyries, Glorias, etc. were melodically simple, but in the 9th century the Schola Cantorum adopted and elaborated them and there began a new development that reached its highest point centuries later in the polyphonic Mass. The older pieces, originally designed to be sung by the congregation, do not usually exceed the range of a sixth, but the less ancient ones, intended for the choir, have a range of about an octave. The five sections of the Ordinary—*Kyrie, Gloria, Credo, Sanctus,* and *Agnus Dei*—were taken into the liturgy at different periods; at first they led a separate existence: MSS of the late Middle Ages grouped the Kyries together, the Glorias together, etc. It was only later that the arrangement as we know it today was established and the designation "Ordinary of the Mass" applied. Even today the chant books still group the Credos separately.

The *Kyrie* was at first a rather monotonous, recitative-like chant, but it developed and finally acquired rich and formally interesting melodies. The Kyries of the Vatican Gradual divide into three types which represent various stages of development. The simplest is cast in the form *AbA* or *Kyrie AAA Christe BBB Kyrie AAA.*[54] In the second form: *Kyrie AAA Christe BBB Kyrie CCC* an attempt at coherence is made by the repetition in the ninth invocation of a melodic fragment from the first part. The third form is undoubtedly also the latest: *Kyrie AbA Christe CdC Kyrie EfE.* Here figures or even whole melodies out of the earlier invocations reappear in the later ones, and melodic repetition in the ninth invocation is always observed. The style of most of the Kyries now in common use is neumatic or moderately florid.

The melodies of the *Agnus Dei* are either syllabic or moderately neumatic and usually have the form *aba,* although there are some examples of *AAa.*

The oldest Roman *Gloria* melody (in Mass XV), now assigned to ferial days, is a simple psalmodic recitation, with intonation, tenor, and cadence in the first verse. The other verses use the melodic material of the first in this way: short verses employ the melody of the cadence, longer verses the intonation plus cadence, still longer ones the whole formula, and finally, if

[53] For a discussion of still other recitations (*Te Deum, Praeconium paschale,* Lamentations of Jeremiah, the Passions, Genealogies, the Gospel of the Visitation, and the All Saints Litany), see WagE III, 224ff.

[54] Having, in footnote 14, adopted joint textual and musical repetition as the sole criterion of a refrain, we retain the distinction between capital and small letters, in connection with the *Kyrie* and *Agnus Dei,* for the sake of consistency, even though some of the forms may seem to consist entirely of refrains.

necessary, one or two parts are repeated. The later Glorias, however, are more or less free compositions. These lively melodies are as a rule syllabic in style. While the verses are essentially independent of each other, there are frequent melodic correspondences among them.

The text of the *Sanctus,* which in the Chant forms one larger unit together with the *Benedictus,* falls into three periods: the second beginning with *Pleni* and the third with *Benedictus.* The melodic material of the third period is usually based on that of the second. The style of the piece as a whole is either syllabic or moderately neumatic but the first of the three utterances of the word *Sanctus* is often treated melismatically.

Although the *Credo* was employed in the Syrian liturgy at the end of the 5th century, in the Mozarabic at the end of the 6th, and in the Gallican at the beginning of the 9th, it was not definitely established in the Roman Mass until 1014. The oldest Credo melody in the Vatican Gradual (No. I) dates from the 11th century, but a Credo melody survives in northern MSS of the 10th century.[55] The typical Credo is a syllabic Chant with a two-part formula; the *tuba* of the first part is G and of the second, a. Occasionally one or two notes are prefaced to the normal intonation, and a transitional member is added to lead from the low register of the first part to the intonation of the second. Sometimes a second cadence is introduced which recites on G so that we have the *tuba* succession G–a–G and "thereby a beautiful framing of a higher *tuba* by a lower one, a phenomenon that occurs nowhere else in liturgical recitative." [56]

The chanting of *hymns* during ecclesiastical rites is, as we have seen, as old as Christianity but, like the completed Ordinary of the Mass, hymns were taken into the Roman liturgy long after the psalmodic chants—probably in the second half of the 9th century. While the Ambrosian hymn-melodies, which incorporated material borrowed from folk-melody, were wholly syllabic in style and based on the meter of the text (*cf.* p. 105), rhythmic verse based on word-accent was later substituted for syllable-measured quantity (*cf.* p. 141).[57] As a consequence the melodies were elaborated and embellished so that even short, unaccented syllables were set to groups of notes. Finally, hymns appeared in which the accentuation of the melodic line was almost completely divorced from that of the text, while at the same time others were sung with strict observance of the tonic accents of the first stanza (*cf.* p. 167f).

Hymns, like the other chants, vary according to their place in the liturgy from simple airs for week-days to extended melodies for Sundays and feast days. The strophes form patterns ranging from bipartite structures like *ab ab* (as in *Lucis creator optime*) to longer ones like *ab cd cd* (as in *Lustra sex*

[55] WagE III, 458. [56] WagE III, 459.
[57] The definitive work on the texts of medieval Latin hymns is *Analecta Hymnica.* Much valuable information may be found also in JulD and Ancient & Modern. Neither of these two, of course, is restricted to medieval hymnody. See also Gustav Milchsack, *Hymni et Sequentiae.* 1886

qui iam peractis). Some hymns contain motive-like repetitions of a melodic figure in another register (melodic sequences), sameness of cadences (rhyme), and other devices by which an attempt at inner coherence is indicated. Certain hymns differ from the ordinary hymns of the Office in that they were sung at processions. Their melodies are distinguished by a refrain, which was sung by the people at the beginning and after every stanza of the hymn. Here is a beautiful example, which Wagner believed one of the oldest of the procession-hymns:

EXAMPLE 40. *Rex sanctorum*—Procession Hymn—Gregorian (from WagE III, 481).

"*King of the holy angels, help the whole world.*" The chorus repeats the same after every verse. "First pray thou for us, Virgin mother of the bud, And high ministers of the Father, Angelic hosts."

Tropes and Sequences

THE most outstanding development in the evolution of the Chant from the 9th to the 12th centuries is represented by tropes. The origin of tropes as a class is shrouded in darkness. Their invention has been ascribed to Tuotilo, or Tutilo (d. 915), a monk of St. Gall in Switzerland, but, while he did write tropes, his reputation as an innovator is based on legend.[1] Apparently the custom arose, in the 8th or 9th century, of adding florid melodies to those parts of the liturgy that, it was felt, invited such treatment—as, for instance, the Alleluia and other melismatic chants of the Mass and Office. The additions were joined to the beginning or end of a liturgical melody or were sometimes interpolated between its parts.

Singers had found the old melismas hard to remember, and they encountered an added difficulty trying to memorize the new ones. Eventually they discovered that if text was applied to melismas, whether old or new, a syllable to each note, memorization would be simplified. The practice of thus applying text spread rapidly, especially in the monasteries, and eventually many parts of the established liturgy were interlarded with new melodies set to new words which enlarged upon the sentiments expressed in the passages

---

[1] For evidence of the existence of at least one kind of pre-Tuotilo trope, see Notker's story, *infra*, p. 187.

embellished. These additions to the regular portions of the liturgy (1) of text
that dissolved old melismas into syllabic melody and (2) of both text and
music that extended older chants, as well as (3) of combinations of (1) and
(2), were called tropes. In types (2) and (3) the trope melody is often a paraphrase of the Chant melody. While, as has been indicated, the first group was
syllabic in style, the second assumed the style of the antiphonal or responsorial
chant which it extended. Here is an example of the first—and more numerous—group:

EXAMPLE 41. *Cunctipotens dominator*—Kyrie trope (from WagE III,
504).

"All powerful Ruler of the heavens and angels, of the earth, of the sea and the
dead, *Kyrie eleison,* who from the mire formed Adam, the first man, and set up
Paradise, *Kyrie eleison,* Ever to mankind, longing for the grace of the High King
with a whole heart, *Kyrie eleison,*" etc. (*For the full text, see Analecta XLVII, 146.
The melody is used, in the Vatican edition, for the Kyrie of Mass XIV.*)

It must be remembered that tropes never formed part of the *official* liturgy,
though they were attached to it, but occupied a secondary position outside
the fundamental body of Gregorian plainsong.

*Tropes have not come down to us as an independent product, but as "adapted art."
The canonical "Gregorian" repertory could not be* supplanted *by another one; thus
it was amplified, added to, interpolated. Every trope is in principle intended to
combine with a given Gregorian song, as an introduction to it, or as an appendix,
or as an interpolation breaking up the Gregorian chant. This union was unavoidable; to creep into the liturgy was for the new art the only chance to live, because
the church was the foremost concert hall of the epoch.*[2]

Another kind of composition that made its way into the church—the *conductus*—will be treated in later chapters, since its connection with the liturgy
was apparently still less intimate than that of the trope.

[2] HandW, 35.

The kind of trope that most nearly crystallized into a definite form is the *sequence*. ("Trope" is rather generally used by scholars to designate a trope that is not a sequence, and it is in this sense that we shall employ the term henceforth.) The origin of the sequence may be sketched as follows: Long melodies were added to the *jubilus* on the final vowel of the Alleluia and were broken up into melodic strophes to enable the singers to breathe. Then, in performance, each strophe was repeated. Later, words were fitted to some of the strophes, naturally producing pairs of lines of parallel or approximately parallel structure whenever the words were added to both a strophe and its repetition. As a result of this development a collection of melodies without words or with words under only parts of the melody came into existence.[3] These pieces were called *sequentiæ* or *sequelæ*,[4] from *sequor*, "to follow." The terms had served as alternatives for *jubilus* in designating the passage that "followed" the Alleluia proper, and they were not unfittingly appropriated to specify the new pieces generically. Individually the pieces were identified by titles that sometimes came from the first words of the source-Alleluia, but at other times had an independent and even a secular origin. Eventually the custom found favor of applying text to all the strophes.

Some writers have wrongly attributed the invention of the sequence to Notker Balbulus, the monk of St. Gall. In a preface [5] to a collection of his sequences, Notker tells how, as a young man, he was much troubled by the task of learning by heart the *longissimæ melodiæ* (i. e. the *jubili*). One day (*c.* 860) a monk, fleeing from the abbey of Jumièges (near Rouen), which had been sacked by the Normans, arrived at St. Gall, carrying with him his antiphonary. This book contained some verses set to the *jubili* (or *sequentiæ*). Notker, inspired by the example before him, set to work to supply suitable texts for the melismas in use at St. Gall. He showed his first attempts to his master, Yson, who suggested that he remodel them on the principle of one note to a syllable, thus making the melodies easier to remember. It is interesting to observe that the syllabic style was destined to be retained in new sequences, as part and parcel of the form, by writers unconcerned with its originally mnemonic function.

This story shows that Notker did not invent the sequence form but merely

---

[3] Several suggestions have been made concerning the origin of these added melodies. One suggestion (GennF, 117ff) is that melodic material from the *verses* of Alleluias was borrowed. This would tend to explain the practice of melodic repetition (*cf.* p. 180). As we have seen in Chap. 3, the sequence has been accounted for also as a Western imitation of Byzantine models. Still another theory suggests (see HandU) that it may have had its origin in secular art. (See also WagE III, 483, footnote.)

[4] Pieces of this type, with text, have also been called *versus ad sequentias* and *sequentia cum prosa*, the latter term being preferable from the standpoint of medieval precedent (*cf.* HandW, 159). Some modern writers, e. g. Dom Anselm Hughes, use the term *sequela* for the melody alone, and *sequence* for the text or text and music combined.

[5] The full text of Notker's preface is printed in MigneL CXXXI, 1003. This is the same Notker whose poems "had been Mr. Porteous's . . . passion" in Aldous Huxley's "Antic Hay."

adopted it. He was probably not a composer at all, but simply a writer of words to melodies already in existence.[6] The sequence seems to have originated in Northern France, as the reference to Jumièges in Notker's own account indicates.[7] Its original name in France was *sequentia cum prosa* (*jubilus* with prose), but Notker called his sequences hymns. Later, pieces in the form were termed proses in France and sequences in Germany.

Two schools of sequence-composition arose, one Anglo-French, centering round the monastery of St. Martial, the other German, with its focal point at St. Gall. While, in the early productions of both these schools, one characteristic of the sequence form—syllabic style—is pervasive, a second characteristic destined to remain—the immediate repetition of each melodic strophe to different words—while normal, is as yet less consistently present. In some pieces there is no repetition at all (that is, they are sequences only by virtue of their position as extensions of the Alleluia); in others the repetition is not exact; and in many—following a favorite form—some strophes, especially the first and last, are not repeated. The more general practice may be represented by the pattern: *x* (unpaired introduction), *aa, bb, cc,* etc., *y* (unpaired postlude)—*x* or *y* or both being optional.

In the performance of these early sequences the Anglo-French singers first chanted the word *Alleluia* to the liturgical melody. Then came the sequence proper, with two choirs alternating in the singing, each choir performing one verse in each pair, both choirs, perhaps, singing the unpaired verses, if any, at the beginning and end. A French MS of the 11th century lists under the heading *Incipiunt sequentiæ* about 60 Alleluia melodies with their *sequentiæ.* In the margin next to each of these melodies is a word—such as *Precamur, Salus, Veniet,* etc.—which is the first word of the sequence text to be sung to the melody.[8] Many French and English MSS of the 12th and 13th centuries still preface each sequence with its source-Alleluia. The German singers, however, apparently began at once with the new text to the original Alleluia melody, while it seems to have been characteristic of the Italian sequences (some of which are closely related to the German) to insert the original Alleluia melody between the two verses of the first double versicle.[9]

As the original name *prosa* indicates, the earliest texts were unmetrical; moreover, the two lines of a pair were frequently, as implied on p. 187, uneven in length; and in a single sequence some pairs were long while others were short. But the idea of repeated melodic fragments took root for its own sake, and soon a new stage was reached: fresh melodies were composed to fresh words; the text-writer, no longer bound to a fixed melody, was free to devote his skill to the production of metrical verses. A peculiarity of the

[6] See DorenE, Chap. 9. There is an example of a sequence with text by Notker, and with music sometimes ascribed to him, easily available in ScherG, 3.
[7] See FrereW, xii; HughA, 8f; and Blume's preface to Analecta LIII. [8] BluV.
[9] Further concerning the sequence in Italy, see WolfMR, 274ff.

French proses of this transitional stage is that the verses generally end on the vowel *a*, a last reminiscence of the origin of the sequence melody.[10]

From the musical point of view a new feature of the early and transitional sequences was that "half-way through the melody in many cases a change takes place which is very analogous to a modern modulation into the dominant."[11] Such a change may be seen in the 11th-century sequence *Victimæ paschali* (*cf.* Example 42).

An interesting formal variant of the sequence is the sequence with doubled *cursus*.[12] In this variant a group of melodies, each of which is set to its pair of verses, is repeated *as a group,* so that the musical pattern of such a sequence may, for example, appear as *aa bb, cc dd ee ff, cc dd ee ff, gg hh.* This variant seems to have been known in France as early as the end of the 9th century.[13]

Sequences became extraordinarily popular and spread all over Western Europe—including even Denmark,[14] Sweden,[15] and Finland.[16] Some well-known melodies were set to new texts. The melodies were identified in the MSS by tags consisting of the first word or two of the original text. A tag of this sort is called in French *timbre* and in Latin *incipit*.[17] Some of the new verses to favorite melodies were written in the vernacular. The 11th-century sequence *Lætabundus* became the model for over a hundred imitations (*cf.* pp. 218, 422).[18] An unusual feature in this sequence is a refrain, which appears at the end of most of the double versicles. Numerous parodies of certain sequences were invented. The *Victimæ paschali laudes,* for example, became the basis for many parodies[19] in honor of the Virgin, which began with the words *Virgini Mariæ laudes.*

The sequence was carried to the highest point of its formal development by Adam (d. 1192) who, about 1130, became a monk in the Abbey of St. Victor, which was then outside Paris, but later, through the growth of the city, became included within its walls. His texts are both metrical and rhythmic, the verse-pairs rhyme, and the structure is simpler and more even. In fact, so regular is the structure that Adam's works in the form are indistinguishable from hymns poetically; musically, however, they remain sequences

---

[10] For examples, see VilleO, *versiculus* on p. 136; *Ynni* on pp. 143, 146, 149, etc.
[11] FrereW, xxxvii.   [12] The doubled *cursus* must not be confused with the metrical and rhythmical cursus discussed on p. 176.
[13] GennF, 142. An example of the sequence with doubled *cursus, Planctus Mariæ Virginis,* by Godefrid of Breteuil, sub-prior of Saint Victor (d. 1196), is printed in GennF, 143ff.
[14] See HammM.
[15] See MobergU. A review of this book, by Handschin, in ZfMW XVII (1935), 242, contains much information on the sequence and is well worth reading for its own sake.   [16] See HaapZ.
[17] These foreign terms are in general use. They are not always employed in quite as limited a sense as they are here, however. In fact, we have already encountered *timbres* on p. 188 (even though they were not so designated) in the words *Precamur, Salus,* etc., where they referred to texts to be set to melodies, while the timbres mentioned above refer to melodies to be set to texts.
[18] *Lætabundus* and some of its imitations are printed in GennI.
[19] "Parody" here has no frivolous connotation. It means simply a new work using as a model the music—sometimes, as here, the text also—of an older one. At the height of the polyphonic period, one encounters "parody-masses."

because the melody is changed for each pair of verses. In determining the form of a medieval composition one must quite often regard text and music as inseparable; this fact will become increasingly clear when we approach the music of the troubadours and trouvères. Eventually the sequence approached the hymn form musically also (cf. p. 191).

Sequences became so exceedingly popular that they tended to threaten the uniformity and purity of the liturgy. By the 15th century some had actually made their way into the Mass, but the Council of Trent (1545-63) banned all of them but four: *Victimæ paschali laudes, Veni sancte Spiritus, Lauda Sion Salvatorem,* and *Dies iræ, dies illa.* The *Stabat Mater,* despite the age of its text (cf. p. 192), was not added to the Roman liturgy until 1727.[20]

The authorship of the Easter sequence *Victimæ paschali* has been attributed to Wipo of Burgundy (d. c. 1048). It is somewhat retouched and shortened in the modern Roman Gradual.[21] This sequence represents the transitional stage in the development of the form: the text does not rhyme, the verses are uneven, and the first line is unpaired. In the revision (given below) the last lines are unpaired also.

EXAMPLE 42. *Victimae paschali*—Sequence—Attributed to Wipo (after Graduale, 222).

* The 1st time, this should be sung as a cephalicus.

[20] Current practice, if not confined to the Roman Catholic, employs five additional sequences: The English Hymnal preserves, besides four that are in the Roman liturgy, five that are not, and, of course, gives each an English rather than a Latin text. The five pieces are *Salus aeterna* (earlier than the 11th century); *Lætabundus; Jerusalem et Sion filiæ* (ascribed to Adam de St. Victor); *Jesu, dulcis memoria* (16th century); and *Sponsa Christi* (17th century). The reader may find some sequences no longer in liturgical use in HughA, SchubS, and ClémentC (with accompaniments, based on the triad, by Clément), among other places, and the texts of a great number in Analecta. For a comprehensive *catalogue raisonné* including sequences, see ChevR.

[21] It is also printed in ScherG, 4, where its rhythms are not treated according to Solesmes principles (cf. p. 141ff); Schering uses a variety of time-values. Concerning the retouching in the current version, see WagE I, 235.

"1. Forth to the Paschal Victim, Christians, bring your sacrifice of praise: 2. The Lamb redeems the sheep; And Christ the sinless One Hath to the Father sinners reconciled. 3. Together, death and life In a strange conflict strove: The Prince of Life, Who died, Now lives and reigns. 4. What thou sawest, Mary, say, As thou wentest on the way. 5. I saw the tomb wherein the living One had lain; I saw His glory as He rose again; 6. Napkin and linen clothes, and Angels twain: 7. Yea, Christ is risen, my hope, and He will go before you into Galilee. 8. We know that Christ indeed has risen from the grave: Hail, Thou King of Victory, Have mercy, Lord, and save. Amen. Alleluia." (*Trans. from Dom Gaspar Lefebvre, Daily Missal, 1927.*)

Parts of the melody were later transformed into the German chorale *Christ ist erstanden.*[22]

Its syllabic style rendered the sequence form the most folk-like of all the divisions of the Chant, and thus made it especially suitable ground for the religious folk-song in the vernacular to draw sustenance from.

In the sequence for Whit Sunday *Veni sancte Spiritus,* sometimes attributed to King Robert the Pious (d. 1031), sometimes to Innocent III (d. 1216), sometimes to Stephen Langton, who became Archbishop of Canterbury (d. 1228), and in the Corpus Christi sequence *Lauda Sion,* written by St. Thomas Aquinas (d. 1274), with a melody that had been used to several texts by Adam de St. Victor, we find the regularity of construction, the rhyming of both text and music, and the strict observance of the rule of polystrophic formation (*cf.* p. 170) characteristic of the proses of Adam. Indeed, the melody in the form in which it is used in Adam's *Laudes crucis attollamus* is so much like that of the *Lauda Sion* that the former work may well have served as the musical source directly drawn upon for the latter.[23]

The approach to the hymn form is represented by the sequence of the Mass for the Dead, *Dies iræ,* attributed to Thomas of Celano (d. *c.* 1250). This famous sequence—the melody of which was to be used centuries later by Berlioz and Liszt, among others—grew out of a rhymed trope added to the responsory *Libera me, Domine.* The melodic pattern is: *aa bb cc aa bb cc aa bb cc de* (*d* being derived from *b*). The group *aa bb cc,* appearing three times in succession, as a unit performs the function of a hymn melody; it is by virtue of the internal structure of the unit and because of the postlude that the piece ranks as a sequence.

[22] The text has also continued productive. In so recent a work as Anatole France's "Thaïs" the slave Ahmes sings to Thaïs:
"Tell us, Mary, what thou hast seen, where thou hast been?
I saw the shroud and the linen cloths, and the angels seated on the tomb. And I saw the glory of the Risen One."
This is an adaptation of the 4th, 5th, and 6th lines of our sequence, but the order of the last two lines is reversed and a few words are omitted.
[23] For Adam's proses and a discussion of them, see MissetP (but in the light of Analecta LIV, viiiff). We shall have more to say about Adam in the discussion following Ex. 72 in Chap. 10.

The authorship of the *Stabat Mater* has been variously ascribed to Jacopone da Todi (d. 1306), Innocent III, St. Bonaventura (d. 1274), *et al.* It is found in European missals of the 15th century. In form it is still more regular and song-like than the *Dies iræ;* fragments of the melodic members frequently recur. The date of the melody now in use is uncertain, but it is apparently subsequent to that of the text.

As we have indicated, certain parts of the Mass other than the Alleluia were also troped. A troped Kyrie was called a Kyrie *cum farsura,* or *farsa* (from *farsæ,* "fillings"); other parts of the Ordinary and troped Lessons were also said to be "farsed." In some MSS the intercalations in the Gloria, Sanctus, and Agnus were called *Laudes.* The only parts of the liturgy that seem to have remained immune to interpolation were the Gradual proper (as distinguished from its verse) and the Tract, the latter by reason of its employment exclusively during Lent. Tropes to the *Credo* are exceedingly rare.[24]

The *Benedicamus Domino,* which is sung at the end of Mass in Lent and Advent, was frequently troped. Tropes were even added to other tropes. In some troped Epistles a text was given in the vernacular to render the meaning intelligible to those who did not understand Latin. Sometimes this text was simply a translation of the Latin and was set to the same melody, as in this example from a 12th-century French MS:

EXAMPLE 43. *Lectio libri Apocalypsis*—Epistle trope (from WagE III, 514).

"Lesson from the book of the Apocalypse of the blessed Apostle John. O."

Other MSS contain long French texts which serve as introductions to and commentaries on the Epistle and are set to new melodies:

EXAMPLE 44. *Or escoutés*—Epistle trope (from AuN, 34).

24 For two examples, see VilleO, 140, 172.

"Now hear, great and small, draw yourselves here towards this Scripture, then heed what I have read, this lesson and this (uttered) chant. I preach (?) to all that each one pray the good Lord that He dwell in us and in our hearts make his bed and not hold our end in disdain. Lesson from the Book of the Apocalypse of the blessed Apostle John. Hearken to the meaning and the sense of the vision of St. John," etc.

German tropes survive also, and there are numerous troped Epistles extant in Catalan, though none so far as is known in Castilian.[25]

The popularity of tropes other than sequences reached its highest point in the 10th and 11th centuries and then declined. During the next two centuries (that is, when the sequence was at its height) they gradually disappeared from the variable chants of the Mass, although they lingered on in the Kyries of the Ordinary and in parts of the Office.[26] Finally, the Council of Trent, besides reducing the number of admissible sequences, banished tropes from the service altogether, thus almost excluding from the liturgy examples of the distinctive contributions of the Silver Age. Some small trace of the tropes, however, has survived. The Gregorian chant books in use today contain a body of Kyries labelled after trope-texts that once were added to them. Thus, the Kyrie *Cunctipotens Genitor Deus* was at one time troped by the text, *Cunctipotens Genitor Deus,* attributed to Tuotilo.

The Liturgical Drama

The liturgical drama is a *direct* outgrowth of troping. It is thus not part and parcel of the liturgy and might therefore better be called "ecclesiastical drama." Since, however, the term "liturgical drama" is standard, we retain it. The germ of the earliest dramas is apparent especially in tropes to Introits for Christmas and Easter. The trope *Hodie cantandus* (*c.* 900) is arranged in dialogue form and leads directly into the Introit of the Mass for Christmas.[1] It has been

[25] See AngL, 306.

[26] For the texts of many tropes, see GautT, which is a comprehensive study of trope-texts. Concerning tropes to parts of the Office see WagE III, 508f.

[1] This trope, which is often attributed to Tuotilo, is printed in ScherG, 2.

pointed out that, of two elements required by the liturgical drama, one—dramatic action—was latent in the ceremonies of certain ecclesiastical rites (e. g. the Offertory) and the other—dialogued speech—in the practice of antiphonal singing.[2] Thus, such rites and such a kind of singing were *indirect* sources of the liturgical drama. In fact, it has even been suggested [3] that the first impulse leading to its development is to be found in the antiphonal chanting of dialogued scenes in the Gospels, by the early Syrians. The freedom with which medieval artists added both text and music to the established liturgy developed naturally to the point where tropes with dramatic content were actually dramatized.

The trope *Quem quæritis* (it appears first in two 10th-century MSS, one of St. Gall and the other of St. Martial), which was prefixed to the Introit of the Mass for Easter, may be considered one of the earliest, if not *the* earliest, of the liturgical dramas. The text (based on Matthew XXVIII, 1–7 and Mark XVI, 1–7) relates, in dialogue form, how the three Marys came to the tomb of Jesus and what the angel told them there. We are fortunate in having an unusually detailed account of the way it was performed in the 10th century. This account occurs in the *Concordia Regularis,* drawn up between 965–75 by Ethelwold, bishop of Winchester, and describes the *Quem quæritis* performance at Winchester as part of the 3rd nocturn at Matins on Easter morning.

While the third lesson is being chanted, let four brethren vest themselves. Let one of these, vested in an alb, enter as though to take part in the service, and let him approach the sepulchre without attracting attention and sit there quietly with a palm in his hand. While the third respond is chanted, let the remaining three follow, and let them all, vested in copes, bearing in their hands thuribles with incense, and stepping delicately as those who seek something, approach the sepulchre. These things are done in imitation of the angel sitting in the monument and the women with spices coming to anoint the body of Jesus. When therefore he who sits there beholds the three approach him like folk lost and seeking something, let him begin in a dulcet voice of medium pitch to sing Quem quæritis. *And when he has sung it to the end, let the three reply in unison* Ihesu Nazarenum. *So he,* Non est hic, surrexit sicut prædixerat. Ite, nuntiate quia surrexit a mortuis. *At the word of this bidding let those three turn to the choir and say* Alleluia! resurrexit Dominus! *This said, let the one still sitting there and as if recalling them, say the antiphon* Venite et videte locum. *And saying this, let him rise, and lift the veil, and show them the place bare of the cross, but only the cloths laid there in which the cross was wrapped. And when they have seen this, let them set down the thuribles which they bare in that same sepulchre, and take the cloth, and hold it up in the face of the clergy, and as if to demonstrate that the Lord has risen and is no longer wrapped therein, let them sing the antiphon* Surrexit Dominus de sepulchro, *and lay the cloth upon the altar. When the antiphon is done, let the prior,*

---

[2] ChamM II, 6.   [3] WelleD, 137.

*sharing in their gladness at the triumph of our King, in that, having vanquished
death, He rose again, begin the hymn* Te Deum laudamus. *And this begun, all the
bells chime out together.*[4]

This manner of performing the *Quem quæritis* did not originate—at least,
wholly—at Winchester: the *Concordia* contains a statement to the effect that
its rules are based in part upon the customs of Fleury-sur-Loire and Ghent.

In the course of time the text of the play—one might perhaps say that originally it was a play with incidental music consisting of selections from the
Chant—was extended, scenes were added, and additional music applied to the
new text.[5] By the 13th century several versions of the *Quem quæritis* trope
included the sequence *Victimæ paschali* (*cf.* p. 190), the last six lines of
which fall naturally into dialogue. *Quem quæritis* became the model for many
similar tropes for Christmas and Ascension.

Plays came into being that were performed at other festivals of the ecclesiastical year; their subjects were derived from incidents described in the New
and Old Testaments and from miracles of the saints. "The three or four
thousand statues and figures which peopled the portals and windows of the
cathedral of Chartres must have descended from their niches and panes . . . ,
at least once a year, to play their drama in the nave and the choir of the
vast edifice. In other words, the same events . . . as were sculptured in statues
and painted on glass were played, at different festivals of the year, by living
people in the cathedral itself." [6]

The story of the three Marys and various other subjects were popular in
Spain also. A favorite subject there, the music for which may have had a
Mozarabic origin,[7] is the famous Song of the Sibyl, to which we shall return
in Chapter 7. This was not, strictly speaking, a play. The Sibyl appears as a
character in many different versions of the play *Ordo Prophetarum,* found
in MSS from various parts of Western Europe. In these versions she sings a
rather long prophecy. It is this prophecy that seems to have been sung and
performed in Spain as an independent little scene.[8] The origin of the
famous "Mystery of Elche" (Elche is near Alicante) may date back to the
13th century. So much of its music, however, in the state in which the mystery
reaches us, is of much later date, that a discussion of it lies outside the
scope of this book.

The music of the liturgical plays was drawn from various sources. Antiphons, sequences, hymns, secular music—both religious and profane—and,

---

[4] Translation from ChamM II, 14f. We use "antiphon"—*antiphona* occurs in the original—
instead of Chambers's "anthem."

[5] A version dating from *c.* 1100 is printed in ScherG, 5.

[6] Quoted from Adolphe Didron in CouD, ix. This work contains the text and music of 22
plays from MSS dating from the 11th to the 14th centuries.

[7] See AngR, 134.

[8] The reader will find full information about the liturgical drama in Catalonia in AngL, 267ff.

no doubt, original compositions, were pressed into service. For example, the 14th-century Provençal play of St. Agnes [9] contains, among melodies of uncertain origin, two based on the hymn *Veni Creator Spiritus,* one borrowed from the alba ("dawn *chanson*") *Reis glorios,* by Guiraut de Bornelh (*cf.* p. 215) and several taken from other *chansons.* Most of the dramas end with an ecclesiastical Chant—an antiphon, responsory, sequence, hymn, *Te Deum,* etc., according to the liturgical occasion celebrated.

Melodic formulas borrowed from the Chant are rather frequently incorporated in the music of a play. Thus, the following antiphon-phrase [10] appears in one form or another in three plays in a 14th-century MS from Cividale (near Caporetto, in Italy):

EXAMPLE 45.

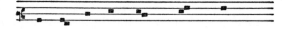

In some of the dramas the composer or adapter seems to have exerted little effort on the musical underscoring of the dialogue. For example, in two plays found in a 12th-century MS at Fleury-sur-Loire, dealing with miracles of St. Nicholas (*Tres Filiæ* and *Tres Clerici*), there is little musical variety: the *Tres Filiæ* employs only two different musical strophes while the *Tres Clerici* is sung throughout to one musical strophe.[11] In other dramas, however, such as the *Daniel* play, from Beauvais,[12] the music is fairly developed. One of the settings of the story of the Massacre of the Innocents (inspired by Matthew II, 18) contains the following expressive lamentation of Rachel, a character intended to represent Jewish motherhood:

EXAMPLE 46. Lamentation of Rachel—From a Liturgical Drama on the Massacre of the Innocents (from CouD, 170).[13]

Heu! Heu! Heu! quomodo gaudebo, dum mortua membra videbo; dum sic commota fuero per viscera tota? Me facient vere pu-e-ri sine fine do-le-re.

[9] For text and music see JeanJ.
[10] This is one of the 47 basic formulas tabulated by Gevaert. See GevM, 239. *Cf.* antiphons *Ecce nomen Domini, Jesus autem transiens, Ecce puer natus,* and *Dominus veniet,* in Liber.
[11] *Cf.* Gennrich's "litany type," discussed on pp. 203, 219ff. Concerning these plays, see AlbrF.
[12] Printed in CouD.
[13] For an attempt at a rhythmical interpretation in modern notation, see GéroM, 62.

O *dolor!* O *patrum muta-ta-que gau - di-a ma-trum!*

Ad lugubres luctus lacry-ma-rum fundite fluctus Jude-e florem, patrie lacrymando dolo - rem.

"Alas, alas, alas! How shall I rejoice, when I see the dead limbs, when I shall have been so stirred through all my heart? Verily, the children will make me mourn without end. O sorrow! O changed joy of fathers and mothers! To mournful lamentations; pour streams of tears in weeping for [our] sorrow, [in weeping for] the flower of the Judean fatherland."

From the point of view of form, the music of the liturgical dramas—whether borrowed or freshly contrived—ranges from loosely constructed recitative to closed forms similar to that of the hymn (here, however, there is sometimes a refrain at the end of each of the several strophes). A particularly interesting form is displayed by the 12th-century play *Sponsus* ("The Bridegroom"), based on the Parable of the Wise and Foolish Virgins (Matthew XXV, 1–13). Here the melodies accompanying the lines given to the virgins and oil merchants are paired and then repeated as a group, the melodies thus by themselves applying the principle of the sequence with doubled *cursus* (*cf.* p. 189), while the whole drama, with the music of the introduction recurring in the epilogue, presents the pattern of the reinforced *lai* (*cf.* p. 226). Another interesting point about this play is the fact that some of the text is in French.[14]

While the liturgical drama is of consequence in the history of music, since it drew upon that art, it is still more important in the history of the drama.[15] Modern European drama grew out of it by way of the Mystery plays, which were direct outgrowths of the liturgical drama, and not out of classic Greek drama, which, for practical purposes, was awakened from its long slumber only in the 16th century. Thus the church was not only the "foremost concert hall" of the Middle Ages: it was also its principal theatre—indeed, its opera house.

[14] The music of the *Sponsus* is printed, and the form analyzed in detail, in GennF, 148ff; LudG, 170; LiuV; and UrSS. See also the philological studies by Lucien-Paul Thomas in *Romania* for 1927 and 1929. [15] For the chief study of its place in that history, see YoungD.

Chapter 7: SECULAR MONODY: The Latin Songs (Including the Conductus and the Songs of the Goliards), the Jongleurs, Troubadours, and Trouvères

THE secular music of the early Middle Ages does not survive in as fair a state of preservation—imperfect, doubtless, but not beyond restoration of the melodic lines—as does the sacred music. (Under "secular music" we include all non-liturgical music except that of the various kinds of tropes, even if the subject may sometimes be religious.) The songs of the laity apparently had no custodians resembling the choirs at Rome, Rouen, Metz, St. Gall, Salisbury, and indeed throughout all Christian Europe, whose duty it was to preserve a musical literature and hand it on to a succeeding generation. In transmitting songs from mouth to mouth, lay singers doubtless felt free to change melodies, even taking pride perhaps in skilfully elaborating them. Because of the absence of a precise system of notation and of a feeling that it was sacrilegious to recast a melody—a feeling apparently widespread with regard to Gregorian Chant before the advent of part-writing, though destined to lose much of its force later—it is impossible to restore the oldest secular melodies with anything approaching accuracy. A number of MSS, some dating as far back as about the 9th–11th centuries, survive with melodies notated in staffless neumes;[1] but since the singing of most of these non-liturgical melodies was not required year in and year out, as was that of the liturgical melodies, the neumes in these MSS were probably for the greater part as near to being dead letters when staff-notation and the later measuring of time-values became general as they are now. At all events, so far as we know, their contents in all save two instances (unless we include an ode of Horace's set to the music of *Ut queant laxis,* notated diastematically about two lines), do not survive rewritten in staff-notation. Attempts at transcriptions[2] into modern notation, made by Coussemaker and others, necessarily rest largely on conjecture.

One 9th- or 10th-century MS,[3] at Madrid, contains, in Visigothic neumes, laments on the deaths of the Visigothic monarchs, King Chindasvinthus (reigned 641–52) and Queen Reciberga (*c.* 657). These *planctus,* with Latin texts, are believed actually to date from the 7th century and to be composi-

---

[1] Several examples may be found in facsimile in CouH.

[2] For one piece in three transcriptions, see CouH, iiiff (in back); F. J. Fétis, *Histoire générale de la musique,* IV (1874), 477; Emil Naumann, *History of Music,* English edition of Praeger and Ouseley, I (1880), 199.

[3] B.N. (Madrid) 10029. For more details, see AngE I, 25.

tions, perhaps, of St. Eugenius. Another MS of about the same period, at Paris, contains a body of songs also with Latin texts and also dealing with historical events, some of considerable interest. These pieces include laments on the death of Charlemagne (814) and his son Hugo of St. Quentin (844), a song on the battle of Fontenoy (841), etc.[4] Elsewhere there survive settings of several odes by Horace, of lines from Juvenal and the *Aeneid,* of poems by Boethius, and of other Latin verses.[5]

One non-liturgical Latin song of the early Middle Ages about whose melodic outline we have some definite knowledge is the Song of the Sibyl, remarkable in that, although not a part of the Chant, it endured essentially unchanged for many centuries. What is probably the earliest known version of the music—in staffless neumes of the detached-point type (*cf.* p. 138)—appears in a Spanish MS dating from about the middle of the 10th century.[6] It reads, as transcribed by Anglès:

EXAMPLE 47. Cordovan Version of the *Song of the Sibyl* (from AngL, table opposite p. 294).

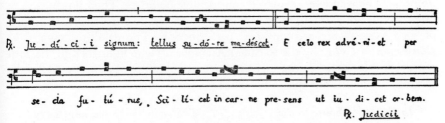

R̥. Ju - di - ci - i signum: tellus su - dó - re ma - désçet. E celo rex advé - ni - et per

se - cla fu - tú - rus, Sci - li - cet in car - ne pre - sens ut iu - di - cet or - bem.

R̥. Judicii

> "Judgment shall moisten the earth with the sweat of its standard,
> Ever enduring, behold the King shall come through the ages,
> Sent to be here in the flesh, and judge at the last of the world."
> (From Nicene and Post-Nicene Fathers, Ser. 1, II, 372)

Many other versions, in French, Italian, and Spanish MSS of the 11th–16th centuries, are extant.[7] The text of the Song of the Sibyl—originally Greek and at least as old as the 5th century—is to be found incorporated in Book XVIII, Chapter 23 of St. Augustine's *De Civitate Dei.* It is a twenty-seven-line acrostic on the Greek words meaning "Jesus Christ, Son of God, Savior."[8] As we have noted (p. 195), the Song of the Sibyl was performed as a brief dramatic scene.

---

[4] The MS is Bib. Nat. lat. 1154. (The lament on the death of Charlemagne is the piece mentioned in footnote 2. The facsimiles referred to in footnote 1 as being in CouH include 5 plates of reproductions from this MS, the piece in question appearing on one of them. Further about this MS, see HandU, 122.)

[5] For more details see LudG, 160f; CouH, 83ff; GéroM, 75ff.

[6] The page containing the Song of the Sibyl is reproduced in AngL, 290.

[7] Anglès prints 23 with Latin texts in plainsong notation (AngL, table opp. p. 294); 10 with vernacular texts in modern notation (*ibid.,* table opp. p. 294); and 6 polyphonic versions (*ibid.,* table opp. p. 298).

[8] Printed in the Latin version given by St. Augustine, in MigneL XLI, 579; etc.

Latin songs loom large in the history of medieval verse. Recent literary historians claim that the songs had a direct bearing upon the vernacular poetry of the troubadours, trouvères, and Minnesinger, who, among their apparent borrowings, included several forms found in Middle-Latin verse.

Carolingian court poetry was succeeded by the songs of the *goliards,* also written in Latin. The goliards were students and young men in minor ecclesiastical orders who roamed at large over Western Europe and appear to have been particularly active in England and France, and more especially in Germany. They considered their name to be derived from that of a perhaps mythical "Bishop Golias," whom they regarded as a sort of patron. The first period of these *vagantes* or wanderers coincided with the reigns of the Ottos (last half of the 10th century and early years of the 11th). They reached their height in the 12th century (during the time of Frederick Barbarossa) and in the early 13th.

Their songs cover a wide range of subjects: They include drinking songs, spring songs, rehashings of ancient classic poems, love-songs, songs moral and immoral. The wanderers achieved considerable notoriety. Their writings were often frothy, sometimes obscene; their conduct was in accordance. But some of their verses were accomplished performances. The drinking song, *The Confession of Golias* by the so-called Archipoeta (who flourished in the 12th century), "the most spirited [poetic] composition of the whole Goliardic species," [9] contains this sprightly stanza:

> *In the public-house to die*   *That will make the angels cry,*
> *Is my resolution:*   *With glad elocution,*
> *Let wine to my lips be nigh*   *"Grant this toper, God on high,*
> *At life's dissolution:*   *Grace and absolution!"*

The disreputable conduct of the goliards and their satires against the Church led to their finally being denied the "privileges of clergy." Their influence waned about 1225 as that of the great medieval universities grew and wandering students were replaced by resident ones.

The major goliard-collections include an 11th-century MS at Cambridge; [10] a set at the British Museum, ascribed to the same Walter Map (or Mapes), who is supposed by some to have helped shape the Arthurian legends; a 13th-century MS (now at Munich) from the monastery at Benediktbeuern, the verses of which were published in 1847 under the title *Carmina burana* [11] (there is only a little music and that, like most surviving goliard music, in

[9] According to J. A. Symonds, *Wine, Women, and Song: Mediaeval Latin Students' Songs,* 1907, from which the translation is taken. A selection of felicitous translations may be found also in Helen Waddell, *Mediaeval Latin Lyrics,* 4th ed., 1933.

[10] Concerning this, see StreckC or BreulC.

[11] For a description of the poetic and musical forms used in the songs in this collection, see SpaC. HilkaC, if completed, will furnish a definitive edition of the *Carmina burana.*

staffless neumes); MSS at Berne, Florence, Rome, and elsewhere. The Cambridge MS includes the lascivious *O admirabile Veneris ydolum* with a melody notated in staffless neumes. This melody is preserved also in a MS at Monte Cassino in an alphabetical notation on lines that is decipherable as to pitch. It is one of the earliest melodies, associated with a medieval secular text, that we can reconstruct, and is therefore of special interest. But, incongruously enough, in the Monte Cassino MS it is joined to the verses of a pilgrims' song in praise of Rome, *O Roma nobilis*.[12] The line between sacred and secular music was to remain a hazy one for centuries.[13]

Medieval writers of the 13th century and later applied the name *conductus* (or *conductum*),[14] with some degree of looseness, to certain Latin songs of the 11th to 13th centuries.[15] Two traits became characteristic of the *conductus:* (1) The texts are normally metrical. Modern students of medieval Latin meter have found in the texts of some early *conducti* the primitive prototypes of the metrical forms of the *rondeau, ballade,* and *virelai* (all to be described presently); some other texts have the form of the *lai* (the secular equivalent of the sequence). (2) The music does not seem to have been drawn, as a rule, from the Gregorian repertoire—as was that, for example, of such tropes and sequences as paraphrased the chants to which they were affixed —or, for that matter, from pre-existent pieces in the popular repertoire.

Little is known of the original distinctive character of the one-line *conductus,* if indeed it had any.[16] It is assumed that at first a *conductus* was probably a trope sung during processions (when the officiating priest was "conducted" from one part of the church to another) and other pauses in the performance of the liturgy. On the basis of this assumption Spanke considers those pieces, called *Versus,* which are associated with some *Benedicamus*-tropes in MSS of the 10th century or even earlier, to be an early form of *conductus*.[17]

The rubric *conductus* first appears in two MSS that date from about 1140. One of these is the French MS, originating at Beauvais, that contains the litur-

---

[12] Printed in LudG, 161, among other places; facsimile in FerM, plate II; another goliard song, *Aurea personet*, appears in LudG, 162. Further concerning the goliards, see BrinE and DentS, 200. A summary of available information concerning the identities of "Golias" and the Archipoeta appears in FarJ, 263ff. See also JarV.

[13] For a melody that served both for a *Veni, sancte spiritus* (not the sequence-poem) and a love-song *En ma dame ai mis mon cuer,* see LudG, 184; GennR I, 85. It is interesting to note that the Latin poem, as well as the French one, is in *rondeau* form. (*Cf.* pp. 202, 222.)

[14] The purest Latin would treat *conductus* as a 4th declension noun, with the plural form *conductūs,* but the medieval writers, while sometimes placing the word in this declension (and sometimes, as a neuter noun, in the 2nd declension), most frequently placed it in the 2nd declension as a masculine noun. We shall follow their usual custom.

[15] Anglès designates as *conducti* still earlier songs, such as the 9th-century lament on the death of Charlemagne mentioned above. See AngE I, 25, text and footnote.

[16] There is a summary of the views of different scholars concerning the origin of the *conductus* in AngE I, 307ff.

[17] See SpaM, 285. According to the same scholar (SpaS, 116) the oldest *conductus* of which the approximate date can be established is the *Sacrata libri dogmata* of Hartmannus, abbot of St. Gall (d. 925). The text is published in Analecta L, 250.

gical drama dealing with the story of Daniel (*cf.* p. 196). The passages sung at the coming and going of personages in this play are called *conducti*. The other MS is the Codex Calixtinus of Santiago of Compostela, which contains four procession songs called *"conducta sancti Jacobi."* [18] Rhymed Latin instructions which appear at the end of the texts show clearly that three of these songs were employed as chants that introduced the reading in the Office of St. James.

By the end of the 12th century, however, the name *conductus* seems to have lost its supposed original significance. Many *conducti* are extant in MSS dating from the late 12th and 13th centuries.[19] Neither the texts nor the music throw much light on the nature of the *conductus* as an independent musical form, for the texts may be religious or secular, grave or gay, and the music includes forms that range from the simplest hymn-strophes to elaborate patterns based on the sequence.

The largest collection of monodic *conducti* is found in a 13th-century French MS now in Florence (*cf.* p. 297). Most of them are religious, non-liturgical songs (some, however, intended for use in connection with the service), and still others are secular, these being of a serious nature. The texts of many of the *conducti* in this MS are thought to be by the Parisian chancellor Philippe [19a] (d. 1236). Perotin (*cf.* pp. 296, 299ff) is believed to have composed many one-line *conducti,* although only one is definitely attributable to him.[20]

In the last fascicle of the same MS are found a group of 60 short compositions with Latin texts, called *rondelli* or *rotundelli*. They are strophic songs, each stanza, in the simplest type, consisting of four lines of which the second and fourth are refrains. The melodic pattern is *aAbB*. About half of the *rondelli* in this collection are rather more elaborate and have the musical form of the French *rondeau* (*aAabAB, cf.* p. 222). An interesting point about the texts is that some of the refrains are taken from antiphons of the Office and Graduals of the Mass. Since the originals are in prose, the *rondellus*-authors altered the texts slightly to adjust them to the meter of the poems.[21]

Wayfarers like the goliards, but not usually possessing their education, were the *jongleurs* in France and their counterparts, the *Gaukler* (or *fahrende Sänger*) in Germany. They began to appear about the 9th century and may have been descendants of the Latin mimes. Jongleurs and Gaukler were seldom composers. These men—and women—were often poor vagabonds who

[18] Santiago = Sanctus Jacobus = St. James. For the texts of these *conducti* see Analecta XVII, 197ff, or WagJ, 39ff. The music of the first song, for two voices, is printed on p. 226, and of the second and third, for one voice, on p. 227 of Analecta XVII; the music for all four is printed in WagJ, 94ff.

[19] E. g. the MS containing the Office of Pierre de Corbeil. See VilleO.

[19a] Not Philippe de Grève, as often stated. See RoksM IV, 227.

[20] It is printed in LudG, 187; for a facsimile after MS Wolfenbüttel 1206, see VerC, 518. Transcriptions of 15 one-line *conducti* are printed in AngE III, 380–90.

[21] These *rondelli,* as well as a few in other MSS, are described in detail in SpaL. The music of four of the *rondelli* in the Florentine MS is given in Analecta XXI, 212f; Aubry has published others in AuI, IX, 41f; AuN, 46; AuO, 355f; AuS, 216, and there is another in BesM, 117.

sang songs that others wrote, did tricks with trained bears or such other collaborators, animal or human, as might be at hand, found themselves especially in demand to enliven less elegant wedding festivities, behaved scandalously, and were in general the despair of the clergy. But there were also among them men who approached their work seriously, and were sufficiently talented and cultured to perform in good society. If one of these was fortunate enough, he gave up his wandering for a position in a feudal household; [22] if not, he travelled from court to court, rendering selections from his repertoire. This he replenished from time to time at "schools" of minstrelsy, which convened at Lent, when the services of the jongleurs were not in demand. A *confrérie* of jongleurs existed in Fécamp as early as the end of the 10th or the beginning of the 11th century. These "schools" were not conservatories but gatherings of jongleurs sent by their employers or by their own initiative to centers chosen as meeting places. The repertoires consisted of pieces, not in Latin but in the vernacular of the country, eventually embracing not only *chansons de geste* but also troubadour and trouvère compositions. As written comments and pictorial evidence show, the jongleur's accomplishments usually included the ability to play some instrument—a bowed instrument, perhaps, such as the *vièle,* or else a harp, guitar, lute, psaltery, or small organ (portative). Sometimes the jongleurs assisted troubadours or trouvères, who often sang their own compositions to hired support.[23]

What share instruments had in the performance of vocal music (as distinguished from instrumental dances) we do not know; surviving MSS confront us with one-line compositions only. It has been contended that the instruments were restricted to playing brief—perhaps improvised—introductions, interludes, and postludes, and that they did not, as a rule, actually accompany the voice.[24]

A *chanson de geste* was an epic chronicle of the deeds of such heroes as Charlemagne, Roland, or Huon de Bordeaux (the hero of Weber's *Oberon*). The music appears to have consisted of a brief snatch of melody, which usually had one note to a syllable, and which was repeated over and over like the phrases of a litany.

It was easy to fit the lines to the music since they were of equal length throughout. They did not fall into recurrent stanza-forms or strophes, but followed one another without a break until the end of a "thought" had been reached. The unequal paragraphs-in-verse that resulted were known as *laisses*

[22] "Originally these household entertainers seem to have been classed with servants, and to have borne the title of *ministri* from whose diminutive *ministrelli,* was derived the French word *ménestrel"* (AuT, 130) and the English word *minstrel.*

[23] Further concerning the *jongleurs,* see AuT, 129; BeckT, 12; FarJ; GéroM, 214, 368; DentS, 202.

[24] Further concerning the use of instruments in performances of the troubadour and trouvère songs, see NefG, HandU, 6, and FerandM, 294f.

or *tirades*. The melodic formula, to lend itself the better to repetitions, seems to
have been ended with a melodic half-close which, at the termination of a *laisse,*
gave way to a full close. It seems also that, after the *laisse,* the formula with
full cadence was repeated complete, or shortened, on an instrument while
the singer paused. Or else the full cadence was sounded only in the instrumental extension, or *cauda,* the singer confining himself to literal repetitions
even at the *laisse*-close.

   Only one authentic *chanson de geste* melody survives, incorporated in Adam
de la Halle's pastoral play *Le Jeu de Robin et Marion* (concerning which
see p. 213), where it is quoted by one of the characters. The melody consists
of two motives.

EXAMPLE 48. *Audigier, dit Raimberge* (from GennF, 41).

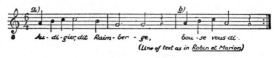

(Line of text as in Robin et Marion)

The first six lines of the text (which survives apparently intact elsewhere)
form a complete "thought." If allowance is made for an instrumental postlude,
the form of the first *laisse* is

$$ab \; ab \; ab \; ab \; ab \; ab \; c.$$

A "restoration" of the whole rather ribald piece may be found in GennF, 41.
Whether or not certain other snatches preserved in MS are *chanson de geste*
themes is uncertain. An abbreviation appearing in a 12th-century MS of the
Chanson de Roland at Oxford (MS Digby 23) may designate the formula
to be used in performing the epic, and one of the surviving snatches may
be the prescribed melody.

   The scarcity of the material that remains is not surprising. Probably very
little was ever written down. Notated copies could seldom have been needed
as reminders: the short tunes, constantly repeated, would scarcely have taxed
the memories of professional performers or of listeners wishing to reproduce
what they heard. We are aided in reconstructing the method of execution
by a description in the *Theoria* of Johannes de Grocheo,[25] a treatise that is
of special importance since it contains the most considerable information
we have concerning medieval secular music prior to 1300.[26]

   The *chante-fable,* part prose and part verse, differed in form from the
chanson de geste. But the charming poetic portions of the well-known

---

[25] Printed in WolfM (some corrections in MüG). For a study of the treatise, see RohG.
[26] Further concerning the *chanson de geste,* see GennF, 40; GennV; GéroM, 79; OH II, 258;
DentS, 202.

Aucassin et Nicolette,[27] which is a *chante-fable,* constitute *laisses* of the *chanson de geste* type. The music is preserved.

It contains not only the formula for the body of the *laisses* but the *cauda* as well. This *cauda,* as might be expected, supplies a full-close, but one that is more than a mere adaptation of the latter part of the formula. The melodic interest of the little tune, as in other survivals of the type, is rather slight.

Of more moment, in comparison, are the lyrical compositions of the troubadours and trouvères, who were musicians as well as poets: their lines were intended to be sung, not spoken. "A verse without music is a mill without water," wrote Folquet of Marseilles (d. 1231), a troubadour who, in rhyme at least, was to be admitted into Paradise by Dante. The troubadours hailed from Provence, which much later (in 1487) was to become the southeastern part of the kingdom of France. Their tongue was the *langue d'oc,* comprised of the dialects of the Midi. The trouvères were their Northern French imitators (sometimes spoken of as constituting an *école provençalisante*), whose tongue, the *langue d'oil,* was to grow into modern French. The simplest and most plausible derivation of the French verb *trouver* and noun *trouvère,* as of the Provençal *trobar* and *trobador,* connects their origin with that of the Latin *tropus* (trope).[28]

The troubadours and trouvères were not wanderers like the jongleurs, but especially in the earlier years, persons of rank—noblemen, princes, occasionally ladies of high position. They flourished for some two hundred years, from the end of the 11th century to the end of the 13th, the best part of the Age of Chivalry. Their songs in many instances reflect conditions and events in the social and political world of the time. A number of them deal with the Crusades,[29] the first of which was proclaimed by Pope Urban II in 1095. Then there are two melodies extant by the troubadour Bertran de Born, who sowed discord between Henry II and his sons (the Plantagenet line was founded by Henry in England in 1154) and who, for having "parted persons

[27] For an authentic edition of the text, see that of Mario Roques (2 *me édition, nouveau tirage* . . . , 1936); there is a discussion of the music by Th. Gérold on p. xxiff. English version by Andrew Lang, 1887. Facsimile published by F. W. Bourdillon, 1896. For an adaptation of the formula and *cauda* to the opening song, see OH II, 26of; for an adaptation to Aucassin's song to the evening star, see GennF, 43. Why the transcribers should differ on rhythmical matters is explained on pp. 206ff *infra.*
[28] Gaston Paris, in *Romania,* VII (1878), 418f; A. Thomas and Gaston Paris, in *Romania,* XXXI (1902), 6ff and 625ff. Certain German scholars, however, have accepted the suggestion first made by Friedrich Dietz in his *Etymologisches Wörterbuch der romanischen Sprachen* (1853) that *trouver* comes from the Latin *turbare* ("to throw into confusion," hence "to ransack," "search for," hence "to find"). Neither morphologically nor semantically is this German view as easy to accept as the French one, but it has been persistently defended by H. Schuchardt in the *Sitzungsberichte der kaiserlichen Akademie der Wissenschaften (Philosophisch-historische Classe),* CXLI (1899), III Abhandlung, and in the *Zeitschrift für romanische Philologie,* XXVI (1902), 385ff; XXVII (1903), 97ff, 101ff; and XXVIII (1904), 36ff. Other derivations have been suggested: Old French *treu,* from Latin *tributum* (Du Cange's suggestion); Gothic *drupan,* which is modern German *treffen* (Grimm's suggestion); Latin *reperire;* Latin *recuperare;* etc.
[29] AuC constitutes a collection of such songs.

so united," is represented in Dante's *Inferno* as carrying his head in his hands, so that his brain was "parted . . . from its beginning, . . . [his] trunk." Richard the Lion-Hearted, himself a trouvère, died in 1199, and his passing was mourned in a noble lament [30] by a Provençal confrère, Gaucelm Faidit, who died *c.* 1216. The Crusade against the Albigenses in 1208 was naturally a severe blow to the troubadours, one of whom, Peire Cardenal, utters in a satirical song [31] heretical protests such as might easily have helped to prompt the Crusade.

The music of these singers is preserved in manuscript collections or *chansonniers*, of which about twenty at Paris, Arras, London, Milan, Rome, and Siena, are of major importance.[32] Many are handsomely illuminated, doubtless made for the libraries of princely and noble patrons or practitioners of the art. The more modest ones may have once occupied the wallets of less affluent jongleurs. The music, when given, appears at the beginning of a song, with the text of the first stanza written below the notes, subsequent stanzas, sung to the same melody, following without music. The *chansonniers* we possess all date from the 13th and 14th centuries, although their contents are often older.

There are only 264 troubadour melodies extant, whereas the words of some 2600 have come down to us. The Northern French survivals reach us in much richer quantity: Johannes Wolf gives the figures as almost 1400 melodies and roughly 4000 poems.

Most of the MSS employ the symbols of plainsong notation on staves. They therefore present no difficulty to the transcriber seeking to determine relative pitches. Less than a third of the songs are written in a notation measuring time-values, such as is employed in a 13th-century *chansonnier* at Paris.[33]

The task of determining the rhythms has given rise to the display of much ingenuity—and to controversy. That many melodies were sung in ordered rhythms, i.e. that they constituted a type of measured music in performance whatever they may have been in MS, seems fairly certain, since a good number of them are dancing-songs: these, it stands to reason, had to be performed with definite beats definitely grouped. Some melodies survive in MSS that contain similarly notated motets. It has been claimed that where motets (part-compositions by no means limited to point-against-point style and therefore requiring the measuring of time-values in some way if the parts were to be held together in performance) are written in a notation that affords no direct indication of the rhythm, it is likely that any one-line songs, contained in the same MS, apparently in the same scribe's hand, and

[30] Printed in BeckT, 92; GéroL, 2778. Richard's *Ja nus hons pris* is printed in GennA, 20; etc.
[31] Printed in BeckT, 88.
[32] Facsimile editions have been issued of 5 *chansonniers*. See AuA; BeckC (Ser. 1, I and Ser. 2, I); JeanC; RayC. For a special study of Egerton 274 at the British Museum, see GennH.
[33] Bib. Nat. fr. 846, the *chansonnier* that is reproduced in BeckC, Ser. 1, I.

in the same sort of symbols, should also be regarded as measured.[34] This argument, while clever, is not conclusive.

A system of notating measured music is discussed in several treatises, dating from 1230-40 onward, and is represented by specimens—almost all polyphonic. This system, however, was preceded by another method which imposed upon notation not in itself mensural a rhythmic interpretation according to what is called the modal system, and this last gives us clues to the rhythms that may have been applied to some (certain scholars would say all) of the troubadour and trouvère songs. (Both systems are discussed in further detail in Chapter 10; here we shall give only such information concerning the modal method as is needed to make possible a discussion of the supposed rhythm of troubadour and trouvère music.) J. B. Beck and later Pierre Aubry—also, with most influential results, Friedrich Ludwig—in the early years of the present century acted on these clues. Through recourse to certain rhythmic patterns described by the theorists, they devised the only scheme available to us for transcribing into modern notation, in accordance with a reasonably methodical system, the melodies not measured in the MSS.

The patterns, or moods, or rhythmic modes [35] employed by the modal system are, as codified by the medieval theorists, all ternary. (The alleged use of some binary patterns in the earlier stage of the development of measured music will be discussed in Chapter 10.) These rhythmic modes derive, ostensibly at least, though not always faithfully, from the meters of classical prosody.[36] Their number varies in the several treatises, according to the special preferences of their authors, from four to nine. The most significant rhythmic modes are, to follow the more usual numbering, the first ♪ ♩ (trochaic — ◡); the second ♪ ♩ (iambic ◡ —) and the third ♩· ♪♩ (dactylic —◡◡). In the dactylic mode a secondary accent falls at the beginning of the second half of the figure. (Thus our example should be read as in $\frac{6}{4}$ meter, not as in $\frac{3}{2}$ meter.) The fourth mode ♪♩ ♩· (anapaestic ◡ ◡ —), supposedly unused in troubadour and trouvère music, consists of the same two half-measure elements as the third, but in reverse order.[37]

Old Provençal and old French had accentuations such as modern French almost completely lacks, and advocates of the modal theory claim that the music must have been stressed in accordance with the stresses in the words,

---

[34] For a fuller discussion of this point, see AuT, 153.

[35] Not to be confused with the ecclesiastical modes. The term *maneries*, also, here used as a synonym for "rhythmic mode," should not be confused with the term used on p. 153 to designate a pair of ecclesiastical modes consisting of an authentic mode and its plagal.

[36] The lack of correspondence between the rhythmical modes and the meters of classical prosody is discussed in EmH I, 254.

[37] Our indications are given in modern notation, with the original time-values divided by 8. The reasons for the division are made clear on p. 275f.

and that the absence of time-value indications in the notation did not greatly matter since a singer would know by observing the distribution of accents in a line of text what rhythmic mode to use. Thus the line

Póur confórter má pesánce fáis un són = ♪ ♪♪ ♪♪ ♪♪ ♪♪ ♪♪ ♪

and therefore calls for the first rhythmic mode.

To find the rhythmic mode suitable to a line like *Robért veéz de Perrón* is more difficult. The accents fall as indicated on *bert, ez, on,* the last being a masculine rhyming syllable, like the *son* in the foregoing example of the first mode. It is claimed that the rhyming syllable is always set to a heavy beat. (Where the rhyme is feminine, the rhythmic treatment of this syllable and of the uncounted syllable after it varies according to the number of syllables in the line: sometimes the rhyming syllable fills an entire measure in transcription and the uncounted syllable, plus a rest, fills another measure; sometimes it is possible for the normal figure to persist unaltered.) [38] If, because of the accents on *bert* and *ez,* we try to apply the first rhythmic mode, starting with the up-beat, we get ♪|♩ ♩♪ ♩ ♪ ♪ , in which the rhyming syllable fails to fall on an accent. (It could be made to do so only by altering the pattern slightly and assigning a dotted half-note—which would be the longest note in the phrase—to the unaccented *Per.*) If, while retaining the first mode, we instead work backwards, thus assuring the rhyming syllable of an accent, we get ♩ ♩♪ ♩♪ ♩♪ , which is just as unsatisfactory, since the two other accented syllables fall not only on off-beats but on shorter time-values than the preceding unaccented syllables. If now, however, discarding the first mode but keeping the final accent for our rhyming syllable, we interpret the other text-accents musically by means of length of time-values rather than stress, we get

which is entirely satisfactory. The rhythmic mode needed, then, proves to be the second.

Because of the importance of the rhyming syllable in ascertaining the rhythmic mode, it has been suggested that, in transcribing into modern notation, one should immediately place a bar to the left of the note corresponding to this syllable, and scan backwards. If accents divide the syllables into groups of twos, the mode will be the first or second; if into groups of threes, probably

---

[38] It may not be amiss to remind the reader that French scansion is by syllables instead of feet, and that a "mute" *e* or *es,* producing a feminine rhyme at the end of a verse, goes uncounted, though it is normally fully sounded in music and may be lightly sounded in poetry.

[39] Where two or more notes indicated by ligatures in the MSS accompany one syllable of text, it is claimed that they share the allotted time-value.

the third. It is claimed that a trouvère reading a colleague's composition for the first time would be able to tell readily what rhythmic mode to employ. (However, one medieval theorist, in praising the notation definitely measuring time-values, states that before its invention much time was often lost in determining the rhythm of a notated piece.[40]) He would simply apply retrograde analysis to the first line, a line purposely constructed by its author with sufficient care in the distribution of accents to give the needed clue clearly. (*Cf.* the *ris-qolo* and *hirmos*.) A less rigorous agreement between verbal stress and musical stress in the succeeding lines would not matter.

Where ten syllables form a line, they are very likely to fall, if viewed backwards, into a rhyming syllable plus three groups of three, thus:

Mólt m'entremís de chantár voluntérs,
10   9 8 7   6   5 4   3 2 1

in which event the third rhythmic mode is used:

(Under certain circumstances, however, ten-syllable lines may call for the first or second mode.)

The foregoing exposition gives the essentials of the method applied by Beck (in his earlier writings) and Aubry.[41] Their works contain also discussions of details for which there is no room here, e. g. how to know when to start with an up-beat; how to divide, among two or more notes, the time-value to which a single syllable is entitled if the syllable is set by more than one note; etc.

In 1927, Beck, still faithful to the modal theory in principle, revised his application of it.[42] The fifth mode, mentioned sometimes as related to the spondee in verse and sometimes as related to the molossus, consisted, like these, entirely of longs ♩· ♩· ♩. The sixth mode was related to the tribrach and, like it, consisted entirely of shorts ♪ ♪ ♪ ♪. Beck claims to have found proof in Grocheo's *Theoria* and elsewhere that "annuls the hypotheses previously pronounced, in accordance with which the songs of the Middle Ages were all ternary and admitted only the trochaic, iambic, and dactyllic modes." He states that the fifth mode was binary and that this mode and the sixth,

[40] See CouS I, 344.

[41] Detailed expositions of the system, by Aubry and Beck, may be found in AuR; AuT; BeckM; BeckR; BeckT; etc. See also LudZ. Riemann's theory, calling for transcriptions fitting the songs into certain structural molds and making free use of binary rhythm, has been severely attacked. It may be found in RieB; RieH I, 224; RieD. Gastoué, in GasT, attacks, in varying degrees, Beck, Aubry, and Riemann, but advances no very definite theory of his own. He is not, however, necessarily altogether on the wrong road, as will presently appear.

[42] In BeckC, Ser. 1, II.

embodying, between them, simple binary and ternary rhythms, represent the fundamental types of the primitive rhythms of the Middle Ages. Besides, he regularly transcribes the third mode as ♩ ♪♪ instead of ♩. ♪♩ (♩ ♩♩) . Some of the transcriptions in Beck C—in Ser. 1, Vol. II of which the new theories were enunciated and applied—have given rise to controversy.[43]

Friedrich Gennrich, the outstanding authority, to whom frequent reference will be made in the course of this chapter, applies the modal theory along the general lines laid down by Ludwig, Beck in his earlier days, and Aubry.

Higini Anglès asserts that both binary and ternary rhythm have been well known in all periods and to all peoples. He believes that most troubadour melodies are best transcribed according to the ternary modal rhythms, but points out that where strict application of rhythmic modes results in insipid and senseless melodies, there may be a gain if binary rhythm is used instead. He also advocates frequent use, for the most pleasing results, of what he calls the mixed mode (first plus second, or second plus first),[44] to which we shall return in Chapter 10.

Jacques Handschin, aiming to define the limits within which he believes the modal theory might properly be applied to troubadour and trouvère music, asks whether our seeking for fixed rhythmic values throughout medieval monody may not be the result of the fact that part-music, necessarily measured, is a portion of our modern background and has influenced our point of approach. Were definite time-values necessarily assigned to *all* medieval secular monody? (*Cf.* what we have said on p. 147 with respect to Gregorian rhythm.) Handschin favors a negative answer. Dance-songs lend themselves to measurement easily, as might be expected, and may well be modal. Other songs sometimes lend themselves easily to modal treatment, sometimes not. All the troubadour and trouvère examples used in this chapter are modally transcribed and produce thus a natural, unforced result, though *Reis glorios* (Example 50) might sound just as well, if not better, treated more freely. Handschin recommends discretion in the application of modal rhythms to troubadour and trouvère music, not their abandonment. He cites a brief passage in the *Theoria* of Johannes de Grocheo as possibly indicating that *cantus publicus* (or *vulgaris*—that is, the music of the people) was "not precisely measured."

Many questions concerning rhythmical interpretation are still open to discussion. Handschin's position [45] is certainly on the side of what a modern

---

[43] In, for example, Georg Kuhlmann, *Die zweistimmigen französischen Motetten des Kodex Montpellier . . . H 196, I* (1938), 128ff. Kuhlmann, following Gennrich, gives a fuller summary of the way in which the modal theory may be applied to troubadour and trouvère melodies than there has been room for here.

[44] See AngL, 352, 361.

[45] Stated in HandV. Unfortunately the passage from Johannes de Grocheo does not furnish conclusive evidence. Nor is such evidence found in a circumstance to which Handschin attaches importance. He points out that while, as we shall see, a secular song sometimes served as one of

ear is likely to regard as artistic results. Where the transcriber wishes to assign time-values to the notes, transcription in accordance with the rhythmic modes, whatever discrepancies there may be in their interpretation and application, seems to furnish the best-founded method, historically and theoretically, that is available. Where a melody gives evidence of having never fitted into a modal strait-jacket, transcription of the notes without the assigning of time-values to them will not render the melody unperformable by an intelligent and sensitive singer with the necessary linguistic background—a rare creature, to be sure. Even where a melody lends itself to modal transcription, it is probable that the old executants did not observe the pattern of the mode too rigorously, monody by its very nature lending itself to greater rhythmic freedom than polyphony. If some of the melodies were, in fact, sung in free rhythm, that might explain why the *chansonnier* scribes mostly avoided the new mensural notation: it provided a means of showing the rhythms of only part of the repertoire, and they perhaps on the whole preferred a uniform notation for all the contents of a single collection.

The troubadours and trouvères are usually grouped into three periods: (1) from the end of the 11th century to the middle of the 12th; (2) from the middle of the 12th century to the middle of the 13th; (3) from the middle of the 13th to its end. The troubadours were in the ascendant in the earlier years, the trouvères in the later. The earliest troubadour of whose work we still possess some examples is Guilhem IX, seventh count of Poitiers and ninth duke of Aquitaine, who wrote from 1087 to 1127. Several of his poems and part of the melody for one of them have come down. Other important troubadours whose poems survive with melodies, are Marcabru of Gascony (d. *c.* 1147) who, incongruously enough, was both troubadour and woman-hater;[46] Jaufré Rudel (fl. 1130–41), the hero of Rostand's *La Princesse lointaine* (which is based on a probably apocryphal story); Bernart de Ventadorn (or Ventadour, d. 1195),[47] apparently the son of a kitchen-scullion, the finest poet of all the troubadours, and an outstanding melodist, if the melodies that

the voices of a part-composition, such a song, so far as the remaining MSS show, was always a rondeau or other dance-piece with a refrain (*cf.* p. 222ff)—that is, a piece likely to be definitely measured and therefore likely to lend itself to the application of modal rhythm. It might be pointed out *contra* that Gregorian melodies, with modal rhythms arbitrarily imposed upon them, were also made to serve as voices in part-compositions. If secular melodies intended for purposes other than the dance were really not appropriated (that is, if their absence from part-compositions is not due merely to the incompleteness of our legacy), this must have been for some cause other than unbending reluctance to impose modal rhythms upon melodies not originally divided into measures of equal length. Handschin's main conclusion, however, has so much to recommend it that the weakness of a link in the chain of argument does not invalidate it. It is only fair to mention that this conclusion was anticipated by Gastoué in GasT.

[46] According to his own declaration in *Dirai vos senes doptansa*, printed in AuQ, 108, GennA, 15, and LudG, 189. Marcabru's 4 surviving songs are printed, with transcriptions into modern notation, in AuQ. Facsimiles of 2 are printed on p. 143 of the commentary section of RibC.

[47] The 18 surviving melodies attributed to Bernart de Ventadorn appear, without time-values, in AppS (reviewed in HandV). 5 appear with time-values in MosZ.

accompany his verses are his own; Guiraut de Bornelh (d. *c.* 1220), called "Master of the Troubadours" by his contemporaries; and Guiraut Riquier (d. 1292), the last and one of the best of the band. Guiraut Riquier lived after the Albigensian Crusade, when the genial and cultured society of Provence was sinking into barbarism: the wars, waged against the southerners by Pope Innocent III and the Northern French to stamp out the Albigensian heresy, destroyed the native poetic and musical growth also. Guiraut himself wrote: "Song should express joy, but sorrow oppresses me, and I have come into the world too late." [48]

The art of the troubadours is said to have been introduced into Northern France when Eleanor of Aquitaine, granddaughter of Guilhem IX, married the French prince who was destined, a month after the nuptials, to mount the throne as Louis VII. She probably had some influence, but it seems likely that other forces—such as the Latin songs and the Crusades, in which northerners and southerners mingled—had more. Eleanor had patronized the troubadours in Aquitaine—Bernart de Ventadorn, whom she took north with her, had addressed to her many of his best songs—and she encouraged the northern poets to emulate their southern colleagues.

Among the most prominent trouvères were Gace Brulé (d. *c.* 1220), one of whose songs, wrongly attributed to Thibaut of Navarre, is praised by Dante in his *De vulgari eloquentia;* Conon de Béthune (*c.* 1150–1224), politician, statesman, and soldier, who figured prominently at Constantinople in the Crusade of 1204, and among whose surviving songs there are two *chansons de Croisade;* Blondel de Nesle, celebrated for having carolled across Europe a strain known to the missing Richard and himself, until he heard his master sing it in reply from a dungeon whence the faithful minstrel rescued the monarch—a pretty but fictitious story; the Châtelain de Coucy, castellan, apparently between 1186 and 1203, of the famous feudal fortress, the Château de Coucy, whose ruins were bombarded and destroyed in 1917-18; Colin Muset (early 13th century) who, though socially assignable to the jongleurs, wrote and composed, and thus rose to the distinction of a genuine trouvère; [49] Thibaut IV, count of Champagne and king of Navarre (1201-53), who did not hesitate to betray his allies or disregard his feudal obligations to the French kings, but had few rivals among the troubadours as a writer of love-songs in the Provençal style, and none among the trouvères; Moniot d'Arras, one of a group of burghers who, after the trouvère development had almost run its course among the nobles, brought the movement to a brilliant close at Arras, upon which a 13th-century *puy* (academy) [50] shed

[48] Guiraut Riquier's 48 surviving melodies are all printed in modern notation in AngM.
[49] For the works of Colin, see BeckL.
[50] The troubadours founded the earliest society of the kind in the 12th cent. at Puy Notre Dame.

luster a century before the city became famous for its tapestries; and Adam de la Halle (*c.* 1230–*c.* 1288) the composer of part-music as well as of trouvère melodies, and of the dramatic pastoral, *Li Gieus [Le Jeu] de Robin et Marion,* sometimes described as the first *opéra comique.* This piece, whose text Adam wrote for the French court at Naples, was first performed in 1275 or 1285. Its incidental songs are claimed to be folk-songs etc., introduced into the play by Adam, rather than works of his own composition.[51] The notated music preserves melodies only. It is probable that the airs were performed with the help of instruments: a country-bumpkin among the *dramatis personæ* specifically mentions the presence of a *chevrette,* a kind of bagpipe. We shall return to Adam as a composer of part-music in Chapter 11.[52]

The following list shows the number of poems by some of the men we have mentioned, that survive with melodies:

Thibaut de Navarre	68	Folquet de Marseille	13
Guiraut Riquier	48	Conon de Béthune	9
Bernart de Ventadorn	18	Colin Muset	8
The Châtelain de Coucy	15	Marcabru, Jaufré Rudel, Guiraut de Bornelh	4 each

Whether each melody is by the man who supplied the words is not certain. It has even been suggested that the knightly poets were unable to write down their verses or to notate—or compose—music, and that the jongleurs reduced the poems to writing and adapted them to current or new melodies. In some instances, we have more than one melody for a single poem: there are two for the *Merci clamant* of the Châtelain de Coucy, and three for the *Adan, vaurriés vous manoir,*[53] the text of which is at least partly by Adam de la Halle. In other instances, the same melody sometimes survives in several sources with variants.

The love-songs were once considered expressions of genuine chivalrous devotion, but are now more generally looked upon as having been, for the greater part, flights of the imagination, contributions to the pleasures of a refined society, and a means of winning recognition therein. The musical and poetic thoughts were at times trivial. In admiring the variety of form displayed, we need not exaggerate the value of the content. But that genuine

[51] TierS. For a general article, see KirbyT. For a practical acting version, with added harmonizations, see BeckP.

[52] Adam's complete works are printed in AdO. Better transcriptions of many pieces may be found in GennR.

[53] This piece is a *jeu parti,* a form that requires 2 participants and may have more. The 3 surviving melodies for *Adan, vaurriés vous manoir* (requiring 2, not 3, participants) are printed, one below the other, in LudG, 199. It is possible that each of the 2 participants had 1 of the 3 melodies, but just as likely that one air replaced another in the course of time.

emotion sometimes pervaded both poem and music may be deduced from an examination of such songs by Bernart de Ventadorn as *Can vei la lauzeta mover*,[54] or *Pois preyatz me senhor*. Here is the last-named:

EXAMPLE 49. *Pois preyatz me senhor*—Bernart de Ventadorn (from GennS, 91; GennZ, 220).

1. Pois preyatz me— sen- hor,2. qu'en chan eu chan- ta- rai; 5. Greu vei- retz chan · ta-
3. cant cu it chan-tar, eu plor,4. a to- ra c'o es- sai. 7. Vai me doncs mal— d'a-
don, 6. be chan, si mal li vai. 9. E doncs, per que m'es mai!—
mor? 8. Ans me ths que no fetz mai!

"Since you ask me to sing, my lords, I will sing, but when I think to sing I weep whenever I try. You will scarcely find a singer who sings well when he is sorrowful; but I fare much better with love-sickness than ever I did, so wherefore am I dismayed?"

(From Barbara Smythe, *Trobador Poets* [1911], 37; for complete text, see AppS, 29.)

There was a rule that no song should be like an earlier one, but very slight changes were sometimes considered sufficient to avoid a breach. The melodies of many love-songs were adapted to religious or political texts.

Besides the love-song or *canso*, the chief types of lyric poems found in both North and South include the *joc partit* (*jeu parti*) or *partimen*, a poetic discussion in dialogue, usually on a question of love, like Adam de la Halle's *Adan, vaurriés* mentioned on p. 213; the *tenso*, devoted to matters of a more general order but also a debate, which, however, could be feigned as well as actual and could involve only one singer arguing against an unstated but clear "proposition," like Example 58; dance-songs like *A l'entrada del tems clar*, mentioned on p. 224; and dramatic or character songs. Among the last of these are the *pastourelle* (pastoral), in which a knight—the poet —woos a shepherdess more or less discreetly, with virtue often but not always emerging triumphant; the *chansons de toile* (spinning-songs), in which the principal character is invariably a woman—an ill-mated wife, or a girl who either pines for an absent lover or complains because her relatives object to the man of her choice; and the *alba* (dawn-song), an interesting form, in which the singer is a vigilant friend of two lovers in whose behalf he stands watch and announces the break of day (e. g. *Gaite de la tor*, mentioned on p. 470). The following *alba* of Guiraut de Bornelh is remarkable for the beauty of its musical setting, which shows ecclesiastical influence not only in its use of the Dorian mode but in the style and general contour of the melody. (The small notes are examples of the *plica*, concerning which see p. 283.)

[54] Printed in AppS, 6; BesM, 106; GennF, 237; GennS, 68; GéroM, 163; MosZ, 150; AngL, 409.

EXAMPLE 50. *Reis glorios*—Guiraut de Bornelh (Paris Bib. Nat. MS Fr. 22543, f. 8).

B Reis glo-ri-os, ve-rais lums e clar-tatz,
Deus po-de-ros, se-nher, si a vos plats, Al meu com-panh si-as fi-zels a-iu-da,

Qu'eu non lo vi pos la noitz for ven-gu-da, Et a-des se-ra l'al-ba.

I

"Glorious King Who Heaven and earth did make,
Almighty God, Lord for sweet pity's sake,
Protect my friend, I pray, who is not deeming
That sunlight soon will o'er the earth be streaming,
And soon will come the morning."

III

"Bel companho, en chantan vos apel;
Non dormatz plus, qu'eu auch chantar l'auzel
Que vai queren lo jorn per lo boschatge,
Et ai paor quel gilos vos assatge,
Et ades sera l' alba!"

(For complete text, see Adolf Kolsen, *Sämtliche Lieder des Trobadors Giraut de Bornelh*, I [1907], 342ff; the last stanza [which does not fit the music] is spurious [cf. Kolsen, *op. cit.*, II, 96].)

"Dear comrade, sleep no more, the bird I hear,
Who seeks day in the woods, in accents clear
Singing his song, and singing now I hail you,
Wake, lest your jealous rival should assail you;
And soon will come the morning."
(From Barbara Smythe, *Trobador Poets* [1911], 142.)

Several transcriptions of this piece, varying considerably in rhythmical interpretation, have already been published. Aubry (in AuT, 71) applies the third mode, as we do, but differently (also, he inserts notes not in the MS); Gérold has two transcriptions, both in the first mode, but dissimilar in their use of it (in JeanJ, 61, and GéroH, 302 [this is the later version]); Besseler (in BesM, 107) employs the second mode; and Anglès (in AngL, 395), his *modus mixtus*. (There are also early, non-modal transcriptions by Restori and Bohn.) Some of these interpretations proceed without regard for the accentuation of the text. *Reis glorios* may be looked upon as a good example of the type that Handschin feels might well be treated freely.

The chief poetic types of troubadour-trouvère song include in addition the *sirventes,* with certain related forms, and the religious songs. The subject of the *sirventes* ("song of service," originally a troubadour poem written by a retainer of a great lord) was political or moral (the protest of Peire Cardenal mentioned on p. 206 is an example). It was intended to be sung to a melody already known. Related to the *sirventes* were the *planh* or song of mourning (e. g. the lament on the death of Richard the Lion-Hearted, mentioned on p. 206) and the *enueg* or satire, in which the poet gave account of the things that particularly displeased him in the world. An *enueg* of special interest is an energetic diatribe by Conon de Béthune against the haughty barons who profited from funds intended for the Crusades.[55] The melody possesses originality and distinguishes the song from most *chansons de Croisade,* many of which are crude and lacking in elegance, though still attractive by virtue of a fitting, uncouth simplicity. The religious songs belong to the end of the period. They figure chiefly in the output of Guiraut Riquier and of the *moine-trouvère,* as he has been called, the Benedictine Gautier de Coinci (d. 1236) whose large collection, *Les Miracles de Notre Dame,* contains some 30 songs with their melodies. It is interesting to note that the opening phrase of the Perotin conductus, mentioned on p. 202, appears in Gautier's work, as it does in a *canso* by Bernart de Ventadorn. We probably have here evidence of the employment of melodic formulas in secular monody. From the standpoint of versification, Gautier's *Les Miracles* is noteworthy as an early example of the use of the Alexandrine, which first appears, in surviving MSS, about 1115, in the *Pèlerinage de Charlemagne à Jérusalem.*[56]

So much for the poetic types.

The melodies themselves normally remain within the compass of an octave: a range of a sixth is not unusual; that of an eleventh is rare.

Many melodies lie within one or another of the ecclesiastical modes: the Dorian and Mixolydian appear to have been particularly favored. A large number, also, are in major and minor. Johannes de Grocheo declared explicitly that secular music, in contrast to liturgical, was not restricted to requirements of the church modes. The extent to which the rules of *musica falsa* (cf. pp. 380ff) were applied is unclear. It is customary in modern transcriptions and performances, to avoid the tritone by flattening B or sharpening F where the two appear successively, and to flatten B where it is flanked by A. The frequent flattening of B often has the result that a melody appearing to be Lydian turns out to be major. The seventh step of the scale, when it is the penultimate note in a cadence, is often raised to form a leading tone if it is not already a semitone below the final. Here we see a tendency, perhaps new, contrasting strikingly with the aversion to the subsemitonal cadence, shown so strongly in the Chant of an earlier period by its not tolerating a subsemitonal *emmeles* (cf. p. 157; also p. 176).

Phrases usually consist of four measures, and periods of eight. Three-measure phrases and six-measure periods appear also, as well as other com-

[55] Printed in AuC.   [56] For a study of Gautier's work, with facsimiles, see VerC.

binations. (That is, this is what appears to be true if we apply the rhythmic modes.)

The musical forms are of astonishing variety. They have sometimes been disposed of as being built for the most part after the pattern *aab*—that is, after the *Bar* form (the term is German). As Hans Sachs puts it in *Die Meistersinger,* when he speaks of the form of a mastersong, a derivative of the Minnelied, itself, as we shall see, a derivative of the art of the troubadours:

> *Das war ein Stollen: nun achtet wohl,*
> *Dass ein ganz gleicher ihm folgen soll.*
>
> .   .   .
>
> *Nun stellt mir einen Abgesang.*

The first *a* sometimes ends with a half-close, and the second with a full-close. When this happens, the first is said to be *vert* (*ouvert*) and the second *clos*. It is true that the pattern *aab* is often, though by no means always, applicable, if consideration is given only to the larger sections of a melody. But in the structure of the individual sections, the greatest variety of imagination is shown. The genius of the 12th and 13th centuries, which constructed architectural marvels in stone, achieved delicately balanced and infinitely varied forms in tone also, both in one-line music and in the newly flowering polyphony. And, as with the cathedrals, if the ground-plans are often much alike so far as they concern the whole, they allow for the greatest diversity in details. Far from being primitive, the forms of the troubadour and trouvère melodies anticipate practically all later song-forms.

The songs, as we have seen, were created by and for an upper class. Where did its poet-musicians find their models? Ribera has claimed [57] the songs were derived from Spanish prototypes imitated by Provençal travelers, and that the Spanish examples themselves had Moorish forbears. But his claim rests on circumstantial evidence, and has not met with general acceptance. Beck [58] is one of several who have suggested a connection between some troubadour songs on the one hand and proses and sequences on the other. Gennrich has developed this idea brilliantly as part of a broader theory to be discussed presently. Spanke has pointed to the *conducti,* as practiced at the monastery of St. Martial (at Limoges) and to the poetic contributions of Abelard, as among the sources of the new art.[59] Aubry and others have cited at least one example (the *Kalenda maya* of the troubadour Reimbautz de Vaquieras, *fl.* 1180–1207) in which the melody, according to a pretty story,[60] appears to have been an adaptation of a pre-existent *estampida*.

[57] See note 4 on p. 245.   [58] E. g. BeckT, 16.   [59] In SpaM.
[60] For a biography of Reimbautz, in Provençal, that includes this story, see p. 293 of ChabB. which contains biographies of the troubadours in Provençal, Catalan, Italian, or Latin. The story of *Kalenda maya* may be found in English in AuT, 41.

(*Estampidas* or, in French, *estampies,* among the earliest known examples of medieval instrumental music properly so called, were tunes meant—at least eventually—to be played by the jongleurs on their *vièles* to the tripping— or stamping?—of the dancers.) As we have seen, the melodies introduced into *Le Jeu de Robin et Marion* are claimed to have been folk-tunes. It seems reasonable, therefore, to assign the derivation of some troubadour and trouvère pieces to instrumental and folk-music. But where did these instru- mental and folk-pieces find their archetype? Very probably in the Church too, like such troubadour and trouvère melodies as Gennrich and others have accredited to its direct influence. It may be claimed that the church music itself was affected by folk-elements, and this, in the nature of things, is probably so, as we have already pointed out. But the Church, with its cultural advantages, was able to systematize, and make widely influential, art-expressions which, among laymen, sprang up more or less at random. The music of the Church was doubtless enriched by the music of the people; but it was very likely more influential than influenced.

For the troubadour to model his songs directly on ecclesiastical melodies was both natural and easy. He heard music in the churches, and he attended the churches frequently—who did not in those days? As we have noted (p. 201), there was no sharp line of demarcation between sacred and secular music; to adapt a love-poem to a liturgical melody was not considered in- congruous. A piece resulting from the adaptation to a melody of a text other than its original one comes under the head of a *contrafactum*. Some melodies were particularly favored by poets, and served in the making of *contrafacta* in many countries and through several centuries. Thus, the melody of the sequence *Lætabundus* [61] served not only for two trouvère pieces—a drinking song, and a Christmas song by Gautier de Coinci—but for a German piece contained in a 15th-century MS and for a 16th-century Huguenot song. *Contrafacta* were made not only by adapting vernacular poems to melodies of Latin pieces; Latin verses were set to the music of French songs etc. as well, the originals being sometimes specifically named,[62] and, furthermore, one poem in the vernacular might be substituted for another.

Gennrich, in his *Grundriss einer Formenlehre des mittelalterlichen Liedes* and elsewhere, makes out a strong case for the influence of church music. The troubadours, it seems, preferred hymns as models and the trouvères sequences. But preferences apparently did not prevent both forms—and others as well—from exerting influence in all lands developing the medieval lyric. These lands, as we shall see, included Germany, Spain, England, and Italy, but none produced a monodic song-literature as significant and varied as that of Provence and Northern France.

---

[61] As Gennrich has shown (in GennI).   [62] See GennL.

In penetrating to the essence of the troubadour and trouvère songs, it is necessary, as Gennrich has shown, for musicology and philology to make a joint approach. Music and text are here one entity, and a full understanding of either's form is impossible without a comprehension of the other's. To take one single example: a piece may consist of two musical sections, each immediately repeated, and be either a *rotrouenge* or a *lai*-segment. One cannot tell which it is without recourse to the texts. That this is not a distinction without a difference we hope presently to make clear.

In the following discussion, based on Gennrich's *Formenlehre,* we shall not speak of "two-" and "three-part" song-forms. As Gennrich points out, these tags hint only at superficial characteristics; they give no clue to those differences in the structure of individual "parts" that constitute the real basic distinction between one type and another. Moreover, the tags are to a certain extent misleading: a troubadour or trouvère strophe of the finest type (like many a hymn melody, for example) seems conceived as a whole: this whole, to be sure, may be analyzed and dissected, but it is not a mere assemblage of separately conceived sections. The designations here given are sometimes those used by the troubadours and trouvères; where no name has come down from them, Gennrich has supplied what he believes to be a suitable one, and the nomenclature employed is his. It should be stressed that the names used for the poetic types give no clue to the structure of the music, e. g. *"pastourelle"* refers only to the subject-matter of the text, never to the musical form.

The Forms

A CLASSIFICATION is possible under four main types: those deriving from the *litany,* the *rondel,* the *sequence,* and the *hymn.* During the 12th and 13th centuries, the lands nurturing the development of these types no longer supported a secular half-culture likely to find satisfaction in an unembellished application of the litany-principle (see p. 203). But, applied in the *chanson de geste,* the principle must at one time have met with a wide enough acceptance to prevent its survival, with modifications, from being surprising. That psalmody gave birth to no secular type is to be expected: recitation on a tenor or *tuba* is not fitted to the requirements of secular song. The antiphon might have been qualified by its musical characteristics to function as the pattern for a song-type—if its text had not been in prose. The hymn possessed many of the same characteristics, but in addition had a text in verse and was therefore admirably fitted to serve as the model of a song-type. That the sequence was qualified to stimulate the imaginations of medieval musicians, we have already observed in seeing it act as one of the outlets through which musical creativeness chiefly flowed during the Silver Age.

I

To the litany-type belong the *chanson de geste,* the strophic *laisse,* the *rotrouenge,* and the *chanson avec des refrains.*

A. The epic *chanson de geste,* with its constant repetition of a melodic formula relieved only by an occasional *cauda* at the end of a *laisse,* has been discussed (pp. 203f).

B. It is obvious that a method practically calling for unequal *laisses,* such as appeared in the *chansons de geste,* could not be applied in lyric forms, which had stanzas of parallel structure. But song-forms could and did grow from the epic. A single *laisse*-pattern, i. e.

  a a a a etc. . . . b or *ab ab ab ab etc. . . . c (cf.* p. 204)

could be used for all stanzas, and when it was so used may be said to have constituted a strophic *laisse.* The form was well adapted to the lengthy *chansons de toile.* It was possible for the phrase following the body of the *laisse* to be a refrain, i. e. its text as well as its tune could be the same for all stanzas. As we shall see, it is at times a matter of much importance in determining the form of a song to know whether or not a refrain was made possible by its text.

C. Refrains appear to have been intended for execution by an audience, the body of a strophe for execution by a soloist. Obviously it helped the audience if the body had a conclusion presenting them with the very melody they would need for the refrain. Where this happened, and the strophic-*laisse* form was in other respects retained, the result was a *rotrouenge.* The following graph shows the structure of a typical rotrouenge, a structure subject, however, to variation:

BODY OF STROPHE	CLOSE OF STROPHE	REFRAIN
a (a number of times)	*b*	*B*

The anonymous *pastourelle* here quoted may be taken as an example.[63]

EXAMPLE 51. *A la fontenele*—Anon. (from GennA, 60).

IV

"Dites moi, Marote, seroiz vos m'amie?
A bele cotele ne faudroiz vos mie.
Et chainse et ride et peliçon avrez, se je ai vostre amor."
Merci, merci, douce Marote, n'ociez pas vostre ami doux.

[63] This piece is printed in modern notation in SpaA also, together with 42 other anonymous pieces.

V

"Sire chevalier, ce ne di ge mie
C'onques a nul jor, fusse vostre amie;
Ainz ai a tel doné m'amor dont mi parent avront anor."
Merci, merci, douce Marote, n'ociez pas vostre ami doux.

(For complete text, see GennA.)

"Beside the little fountain, which gushes forth under the bower, I found a pretty shepherdess. And there she was lamenting because of love: 'Lord, when will my sweet friend come?' *Pity, pity, sweet Marote, slay not your dear friend.*

" 'Tell me, Marote, will you be my love? You shall have a beautiful robe and a skirt and money and a furred cloak, if I have your love.' *Pity, pity, sweet Marote, slay not your dear friend.*

" 'Sir Knight, I do not say that I never would have been your sweetheart. But I have given my love to a man whom my parent will hold in honor.' *Pity, pity, sweet Marote, slay not your dear friend."*

(Translation by Pauline Taylor.)

D. The *chanson avec des refrains* (song with several refrains) doubt-less furnished the occasion for as much fun-making in its day as the *quodli-bet* did at a later period that extended right into the life of Bach. And the earlier form further resembled the quodlibet in making use of an assortment of material already widely popular, though it differed in not stringing one tune after another in the manner of a *potpourri*. The popular material consisted of the refrains of well-known songs. Each strophe ended with a different one, the selection depending upon textual appropriateness to the preceding stanza-body. In other words, refrains were such by origin, not through their fulfilling, within an individual *chanson avec des refrains,* the requirements described in paragraph B above. The body of the strophe, though it applied the litany-principle to some extent, was not restricted to any one pattern. But the strophe did have one special feature: at the end there was a verse that prepared the way for the refrain. This verse rhymed with the line or lines of the refrain but did not necessarily contain the same number of syllables and therefore did not always have the same melody, though it could. If desired, the refrain-melody could be presaged only in part, and it was not necessary that the portion chosen be the beginning.

II

Somewhat like the *rotrouenge* and *chanson avec des refrains* are three forms belonging to the rondel-type: the *rondeau, virelai,* and *ballade.*[64] These were widely applied to dance-songs whose words and music, to judge by surviving examples, were often of singular charm and grace. A soloist,

[64] GennR provides a collection of pieces in these forms from the late 12th, 13th, and early 14th centuries.

probably the leader of the dance, sang phrases called *additamenta,* and the chorus answered with the refrain.

A. Musically, a *rondeau* consisted of two units, which were not necessarily single phrases. These units supplied the melodic material for both the refrain and the *additamenta,* all according to a fixed design. In the simplest kind of *rondeau,* which had a six-line text, the design was

SOLOIST	CHORUS	SOLOIST	CHORUS
a	*A*	*ab*	*AB.*

If the text had eight or more lines, the refrain appeared complete at the beginning as well as at the end.

It may easily be seen that, if the complete text of a true *rondeau* survives, the whole piece may be reconstructed, even if the music is preserved in connection with the refrain text alone. The *rondeau* continued in high favor for several centuries: a polyphonic eight-line example, written by Guillaume de Machaut in the 14th century (when the *rondeau,* become an "art-form," was no longer danced or performed with the aid of a chorus), may be found on pp. 351f. Here is an anonymous trouvère example, a charming expression of *amour courtois.*

EXAMPLE 52. *Amereis mi vous, cuers dous?*—Anon. (from GennR I, 26).

> Gentle heart, could you love true,
> Heart to whom my love I've tendered?
> Night and day I think of you.
> Gentle heart, could you love true?
> Live I cannot without you,
> To your beauty I've surrendered.
> Gentle heart, could you love true,
> Heart to whom my love I've tendered?

(Translated by G. R.)

Grocheo, in his *Theoria,* said,[65] "In the west, in Normandy, for example, this kind of *cantilena* is sung by maidens and youths at their celebrations and important feasts to embellish them thereby." Under the term *cantilena,* he includes dance-songs with refrains, the *rondeau* being one type.

The influence of the *rondeau* may be detected in some comparatively free pieces, such as the lovely *Robins m'aime* sung by Marion at the opening of *Le Jeu de Robin et Marion.*

[65] WolfM, 92f.

*Frauenlob with a Group of Musicians
(Drum, Flute, Shawm, Viols, Psaltery,
and Bagpipe)*
(*Heidelberg, the* Manessische Handschrift. *After
BesM.*)

Musicians with Rebec and Lute
(*Miniature from the Escorial MS j b 2
of the* Cantigas. *After RibC.*)

*Facsimile of the Music of Guiraut de
Bornelh's Reis glorios*
(*Paris, Bib. Nat. fr. 22543. Cf. Example 50*)

*Adam de la Halle (Adam le Bossu) as
Depicted by a Miniature in the Chanson-
nier d'Arras*
(*After JeanC*)

Bagpipe Player
(*Miniature from the Escorial MS j b 2 of the*
Cantigas. *After RibC.*)

PLATE V

EXAMPLE 53. *Robins m'aime*—Attributed to Adam de la Halle (from GennR I, 71).

Robin loves me, Robin mine;
  Robin would have me wed him,
    He'll be mine.
Robin bought me with his money,
Scarlet kirtle, fine and bonny,

Gown and girdle, gay as any,
  Fa la la la.
Robin loves me, Robin mine!
  Robin would have me wed him,
    He'll be mine.

(Translation by J. Murray Gibbon. From BeckP.)

The form is *AB aab AB*. The first line of the refrain fails to do duty in the central portion; the *a*'s and *b* of that portion do not repeat the music of *A* and *B* with complete faithfulness; and no chorus is employed. But the *rondeau* style is there: the varied possibilities of the unpretentious but interesting little form were making themselves felt.

B. If the two-unit refrain is kept at the beginning and end, but the central portion opens with a third unit, repeated and followed by the music of the refrain (linked to new words and therefore sung by the leader), a *virelai* results, the standard structure of which is

AB cc ab AB

We shall encounter the *virelai* again not only in 14th-century France (see pp. 349f.) but, under a different name, in 13th- and 14th-century Italy (see pp. 237, 366). The French designation is thought to spring from the word *virer* ("to turn round" or "veer") combined with *lai*, the name of the secular equivalent of the sequence form, to be discussed presently. The combination would thus indicate a *lai* "with the melody bent back into a refrain." [66]

C. If the music of the refrain is dropped from the middle section of the *virelai* and a fourth unit is substituted, we have one kind of *ballade*. Another kind results from retaining the refrain melody in the central portion, but inserting a fourth unit before it. Still another is obtained by dropping the introductory refrain from the first variety, in keeping with a later tendency to subordinate refrains. The forms may be represented thus:

I. *AB cd cd ef AB*   II. *AB cd cd e ab AB*   III. *ab ab cd E*

A Spanish example related to the first two varieties will be found on pp. 247f. Musical rhyme occurs in it between the close of the melody of the refrain

[66] Manfred Bukofzer in M&L, XIX (1938), 130.

and the close of the body of the strophe, a feature that recurs in some other *ballades* not strictly of the second variety (*cf.* those printed in GennR I, 102, 165, 213, 259). Here is an example of the third variety—which, with its seven lines, is more typical than the other two—by Thibaut of Navarre. Stanza IV incorporates the Crusaders' curse, *Mort Mahom!*) This is the piece whose first line we used to illustrate rhythmic mode 1 on p. 208.)

EXAMPLE 54. *Por conforter ma pesance*—Thibaut de Navarre (from AuA, 4 of Transcriptions).

"To ease my grief I sing a song. It will be good if it advances me [in her favor], for Jason, he who acquired the Golden Fleece, ne'er had such bitter punishment. *E, e, el*"

IV

"Mieuz aing de li l'acointance
Et le douz non
Que le rëaume de France,
Mort Mahom!
Qui d'amer quiert achoison
Por esmai ne por doutance?
E, e, el"

"I would rather have her love and her sweet name than the realm of France—cursed be Mahomet! Who seeks a pretext for love because of fear or hesitation? *E, e, el*"

(Translation by Pauline Taylor.)

(For complete text, see BeckC, Ser. 1, II, 222.)

It is possible that where only repeated vowels or syllables appear under the music of the refrain, as happens here, they may indicate that the refrain is intended for instruments instead of choral groups.[69] The plan of *Reis glorios,* printed on p. 215, is similar to that of *Por conforter ma pesance.* The frequently printed *A l'entrada del tems clar* [70] has brief refrain-interjections and only one unrepeated phrase in the course of the strophe, and a comparatively long final refrain after it, but in other respects it belongs to the same variety. The plan is

aB aB aB ac D D D E E F G (the 3 *D*'s representing melodic sequences).

[67] In transcriptions into modern notation, ligatures are sometimes indicated by slurs, sometimes by brackets, according to the preference of the transcriber.

[68] In scholarly transcriptions into modern notation, accidentals present in the source appear in normal position, while accidentals that the transcriber feels may have been employed through the application of the rules of *musica falsa* (*cf.* Chap. 13) usually appear above the notes affected.

[69] See GéroM, 83.   [70] A list of transcriptions is given in the Record List for this Chapter.

We should like to suggest that responsorial chanting (*cf.* p. 178) and the use of the antiphon as a refrain (*cf.* p. 172) may have prompted such forms, characterized by the refrain, as the *rondeau, virelai,* and *ballade,* or that, alternatively, some ancient folk-practice, which made use of the refrain and of which the *rondeau, virelai,* and *ballade* are comparatively modern examples, may have inspired liturgical practice, whether among the Syrians, the Byzantines, or the Western Christians.

III

The sequence-type embraces the *lai,* reinforced *lai, estampie, notula,* strophic *lai,* reduced strophic *lai,* and *lai*-segments.

A. "Lai" was the name given to a secular piece constructed on the plan of the ecclesiastical sequence, a plan already discussed in Chapter 6. The chief musical characteristic, therefore, of the *lai* and of all other forms described in this section, is the appearance of successive melodic units each immediately repeated to new words (i. e. of double versicles. See p. 188). As in the sequence, an unrepeated unit could, at will, be used as an introduction or as a postlude. There were three ways in which a *lai* might deviate from the standard sequence. (1) It could have repetitions inside each unit. These repetitions could be literal, or they could employ *vert* ("open") and *clos* ("closed") endings, or they could be on different steps of the scale, i. e. they could constitute melodic sequences. (2) It could employ variations in the repetitions, i. e. variations in the course of a melodic unit, not mere substitutions of a *vert* for a *clos,* or rhythmical alterations such as may have been used in (3) the *descort* (the name implies "discordance"). Inability to trace the "discordance" has long prevented scholars from determining the distinguishing feature of the form. Gennrich believes he has found it. His theory takes it for granted that the rhythmic modes are applicable to the *descort,* and, in fact, would be incapable of formulation without them. The theory might be simply explained thus: Assume a series of notes that is to be repeated, and assume that it is to be sung once to a six-syllable masculine line of text and once to a feminine line with five counted syllables (plus one uncounted final light syllable). Graphically: suppose that

$$\smile - \mid \smile - \mid \smile - \mid \text{ (masculine line)}$$
$$\text{or} \quad - \smile \mid - \smile \mid - (\smile) \mid \text{ (feminine line)}$$

are each to be fitted to the same series of notes. Obviously, under the modal theory, the time values of the notes and the accents, produced by association with one line, would not be in "accord" with those produced by association with the other. A *descort* would result. (The lack of "accord" would not necessarily obtain throughout a piece.) The explanation is ingenious, but it should be borne in mind that it is a hypothesis built on still another hypothesis.[71] If it is correct, the 19th century, for all its efforts, produced no form in which the interdependence of music and poetry was greater.

B. The reinforced *lai* differed from the ordinary *lai* in applying the sequence-with-doubled-*cursus* device (described on p. 189). The form, like its model, was especially suitable for long works. The *Lai de l'ancien et du nouveau Testament* by Ernoul le Vieux (printed in neumes in AuL, 113) illustrates the type.

C. The instrumental *estampida* (Provençal) or *estampie* (French) mentioned on p. 218, resembled the sequence in consisting of double versicles—here called *puncta* ("points")—but differed in having the first statement normally end with a *vert* and the second with a *clos*. Usually the same *vert* and *clos* served in all sections, reminding one somewhat of musical rhyme in ecclesiastical Chant. The endings do not serve quite thus in the well-known and frequently printed *Kalenda maya,* which has three *puncta,* though the *clos* endings, at least, are much alike; moreover, the piece is bound together by other means: almost all the melodic material is derived from the first unit.[72] There are no examples of the *estampie* extant with more than five *puncta,* but they tend to run to great length. The following graph illustrates an *estampie* with four *puncta*:

$$ab_1 \quad ab_2 \quad cb_1 \quad cb_2 \quad db_1 \quad db_2 \quad eb_1 \quad eb_2 \text{ [73]}$$

Despite the similarity in name, the *estampie,* as a dance, may not be the same as the *stantipes;* [74] the point, however, is subject to debate.[74a]

D. The two examples that reach us with the designation *notula* (= *note*) resemble each other in containing many double versicles (as well as some unpaired ones) and in having recurrent terminations that link the form to the *estampie.* These, however, are not of the alternating kind as in the *estampie,* and in one example the terminal group takes the form, not of a cadence within the unit, but of an appendage (to the last appearance of a versicle only, this often having new, unrepeated material added to itself before the terminal appendage appears). This example—*La Note Martinet*—is like a

[71] Gennrich's full discussion may be found in GennF, 138ff. His view that the *lai* and its variants are based on the sequence is derived from WolU, a pioneer work upon which he has brilliantly elaborated. It should be pointed out, however, that WolU was attacked by Aubry, who concluded: "As the origin of a lai we find a lai and not a sequence." (See AuL, xx, 162, etc. The interested reader would do well to consult this work if only for the music it contains.)

[72] Analysis in GennF, 164. Several transcriptions into modern notation, displaying interesting differences in rhythmical interpretation, are referred to in the Record List for this Chapter.

[73] In graphs such as this, *vert* and *clos* endings are often distinguished by the figures 1 and 2, depressed at the right of the letter symbols.

[74] See SachsW 292f. In MosS, Moser, regarding *stantipes* as the Latin of *estampie,* contends that *estampies* were not intended to accompany dancing, but were pieces which the player performed on "standing foot" before a courtly audience. The view seems not to be tenable. For a collection including instrumental *estampies* of the end of the 13th century, see AuE. For further information see HandU (which dates the pieces 14th century; but see Handschin in *Acta* X [1938], 29) and WolfT. [74a] See Lloyd Hibberd, *Estampie and Stantipes,* in *Speculum,* XIX (1944), 222, an article published since this book first appeared.

sequence with doubled *cursus* except that, in the group repetition, some units are omitted. The other example—incorporated in the *Ludus super Anti-claudianum* of Adam de la Bassée (d. 1286)—is much like a *lai*. Grocheo gives a description of the *notula*, but it is at variance with the examples and reflects upon his complete reliability as an authority.[75]

E. The strophic *lai* occupies the same position among forms of the sequence-type as the strophic *laisse* occupies among those of the litany-type.

It may employ the doubled *cursus,* but is nevertheless intended for briefer pieces: the repeated set of pairs, if used at all, is short. Length would be out of place since the same strophic design is applied to each stanza, and a long strophic design might therefore make for an interminable piece. A typical pattern (without doubled *cursus*) would be

$$a \quad bb \quad cc \quad d$$

Variations, melodic sequences, and such other deviations from the normal liturgical sequence-form as are found in the *lai* are admissible in the strophic *lai* also.

Attempts to create shortened strophe-patterns seem to have taken three main courses. The first consisted in retaining the typical sequence- or lai-form, but with only a few double versicles, and with these short in themselves (a not especially popular method); the second, in retaining the strophic-*lai* pattern, but with only one double versicle in the middle; and the third, in omitting the unrepeated introduction, retaining two double versicles, and having at the end an unrepeated postlude consisting of a single restatement of the first versicle.

F. If the last-named course was altered so that the middle section consisted of a single unrepeated unit, i. e. if the pattern were *aa b a,* the form represented the reduced strophic-*lai*—an exact forecast, in miniature, of the *aria da capo*. An example of the reduced strophic-*lai* will be found in the Minnelied printed as our Example 59. The form was subject to variation.

G. Pieces showing certain other attempts to find shortened strophe-patterns may be marshalled into three main groups, collectively classified by Gennrich as *lai*-segments. The first group consists of unrepeated introduction and one double versicle, or simply of one double versicle (i. e. of the initial constituents of the sequence- or *lai*-pattern); the second, of two or more double versicles (i. e. of the middle constituents); the third, of one or two double versicles and an unrepeated postlude containing fresh material (i. e. of the last constituents).[76] The second type is illustrated by the exquisite

---

[75] *La Note Martinet* is printed in GennF, 169; a somewhat different transcription appears in HandU II, 127. The other example is printed in GennF, 168. For information concerning Adam de la Bassée, see LudQ, 214f.

[76] While it is easy to see that the 3 types in question fit neatly into Gennrich's classification, it should be borne in mind that they are so simple that they might easily have been employed without being derived from the sequence or *lai*.

spring-song, *Ce fut en mai,* by Moniot d'Arras, printed below; the third, by the song of Bernart de Ventadorn, printed on p. 214.

EXAMPLE 55. *Ce fut en mai*—Moniot d'Arras (from GennF, 208).

I

It was in May, sweet time and gay,
When all is fresh and gleaming,
I rose to play and took my way
To where a fount was streaming.

Where blossoms bright hedged fruit-
    trees white
I heard a *vièle* entrancing.
Before my sight a gallant knight
And noble maid were dancing.

II

Cors orent gent et avenant,
et molt tres bien dancoient,
en acolant et en baisant
molt bel se deduisoient.
En un destour au chief du tor
doi et doi s'en aloient,
de sor la flor le gieu damor
a lor plaisir faisoient.

(For complete text, see K. Bartsch, *Altfranzösische Romanzen und Pastourellen* [1870],
78f.)

They spoke a while with beck and smile,
Right oft they trod a measure,
With sportive kiss and light caress
They stored the time with treasure.
A-down a path, the tow'r beneath,
Hands claspt, they walked at leisure.
The flowers above, the game of love
They gently played at pleasure.

(Translation by G. R.)

It will be seen that, if, for example, the stanzas consisted of three lines of body plus one line of refrain, rather than of four lines of body, the song would be classifiable as a *rotrouenge* rather than as a *lai*-segment (second type), even if the hypothetical melody, consisting of two phrases each immediately repeated once, remained the same, since it would be a piece for soloist and chorus.

IV

Derived from the hymn were the *vers, chanson* (without refrain), and rounded *chanson.*

A. The music of the hymn and *vers* shared the same outstanding structural features: the melody of each strophe was through-composed within itself. Examples of the *vers* are furnished by the plaint on the death of Richard the

Lion-Hearted, referred to on p. 206, and Bernart de Ventadorn's *Can vei la lauzeta,* referred to on p. 214. Here is an actual example.

EXAMPLE 56. *Haut honor d'un commandement*—Li Tresoriers de Lille (= Pieros li Borgnes) (Chansonnier de l'Arsénal, f. 232, after Aubry facsimile).

I

High Honor's charge o'er me doth reign
When Spring comes over hill and plain
And birds pour forth their glad refrain
And flowers and leaves come back again;
   Then I my joy would tell,
   For he again fares well
Whom Love as vassal doth retain.

III

Ja la dolor que mes cuers sent
Ne sentira nul faus amant,
Car la douçor est si plesant,
Dont la haute merci descent,
   Qu'en faussement amer,
   Ne puet nus savorer
Les biens ne les maus qu'amors rent.

(For complete text, see A. Scheler, *Trouvères belges, nouvelle série* [1879], 137f.)

This sorrow that my heart now rends
To lover false its pain ne'er lends;
Yet in this grief, what sweetness blends
Whose mercy on my soul descends!
   False lover cannot share
   Nor know the taste so rare
Of joy or woe that true Love sends.

(Translation by Marian Judell.)

B. The *chanson* somewhat resembled such pieces of the third *lai*-segment group as had only one double versicle. In both, a repeated passage made up the opening and an unrepeated one made up the rest. But there was this difference: in the songs of the *lai*-type, the repeated passage (i.e. the sequence-like passage) was of greater length than the unrepeated one; in the *chanson,* the unrepeated, through-composed section (i.e. the section resembling the hymn) was longer than the repeated one. *Reis glorios* and *Por conforter ma pesance* would be examples of the *chanson* if the final lines of their texts were not refrains.

C. The rounded *chanson* is like the *chanson,* except that part of the opening repeated section is once more heard at the end. It is like the reduced strophic-*lai* also, except that in the pieces of the *lai*-type the entire opening section is repeated. The plan may be represented thus:

$$ab \quad ab \quad cdb$$

The form is illustrated by *Nu alerst lebe ich mir werde* (Example 57).

What guided a troubadour or trouvère in selecting a form for a particular piece, the state of our information does not permit us to say. But it does permit us to admire the wealth of structural devices employed by the French and Provençal poet-musicians of the 12th and 13th centuries.

Chapter 8: SECULAR MONODY (*continued*): The Early Minnesinger, the Laude and Geisslerlieder, English Monody, Spanish Monody

The Early Minnesinger

ON JUNE 9, 1156, Frederick Barbarossa, famous alike in history and legend, the first Hohenstaufen to be emperor of the Holy Roman Empire, married Beatrix of Burgundy. Guiot de Provins, the trouvère, was attached to her retinue, and she and he have been jointly credited with making French and Provençal song a living influence in Germany. A song of Guiot's with text and music (*Ma joie premeraine*) and a German poetic imitation of it (*Ich denke underwîlen*) by Friedrich von Hûsen (d. 1190) both survive.[1] The imitation lacks music, but fits the western melody perfectly. There are other German poems that similarly fit Provençal or French melodies, among these poems being another by Friedrich von Hûsen, *Deich von der guoten schiet,* the verses of which closely resemble those of Bernart de Ventadorn's *Pois preyatz me senhor.*[2] But the Germans already had a flourishing native development when, largely through von Hûsen, the French influence was allowed to permeate. This native development, like that in France, had yielded Latin songs (including goliard songs), and the productions in the vernacular, in Germany as in France, were an outgrowth of Latin sources. The native art was to accept foreign influence, but without losing its own identity.[3] One of the two oldest non-liturgical German songs known, the *Galluslied,* composed in the 10th century, survives with a Latin text; the other, the *Petruslied,* from a MS of the 9th–10th centuries, is in German.[4]

The 12th- and 13th-century German poet-musicians were called *Minnesinger* (*Minne* = chivalrous love, *amour courtois*). They came mostly from the South, many from Austria. Their musical legacy is left principally in MSS of dates later than their own period: the 14th-century Jena Song-MS,

[1] The music with both texts appears in BesM, 108; GennF, 197.

[2] The music with both texts appears in GennS, 91f. (With the Provençal text only, it appears as our Example 49.)

[3] The thesis of a derivation from Middle-Latin epistles and verse (including goliard songs) is developed, from the literary standpoint, in BrinE; the indebtedness of the Minnesinger to the troubadours and trouvères has been discussed at length by both philologists and musicologists. Readers of this book may find GennD, GennS, and GennZ of special interest.

[4] For transcriptions of both these songs, see MülleF.

231

which contains 91 melodies, and the 15th-century Colmar MS, preserving a collection made from the point of approach of the Meistersinger; its copies of *Minnelieder* incorporate revisions made by them. It contains *Meisterlieder* also. 107 melodies are preserved in it. Among other survivals, a MS at Heidelberg containing 2 songs by "Kaiser Heinrich" (Henry VI, 1165–97, the son of Frederick Barbarossa), a fragment at Münster containing 1 complete and 4 incomplete melodies by Walther von der Vogelweide, a MS at Vienna containing pieces by Frauenlob and others, and 2 MSS containing songs by Neidhart von Reuenthal, are of special interest.[5]

The *Minnelieder,* like their Romanic equivalents, have presented problems in rhythmical interpretation, which are discussed at length in articles by Moser and others. The fundamental differences in prosody between Romanic and German verse of the period—the former measuring by syllables, and the latter by the number of heavy accents (the number of syllables off the accent not necessarily being constant)—are held, even by adherents of the modal theory, to show a sufficient basic difference between troubadour-trouvère and Minnesinger rhythm to rule out any assumption that the rhythmic modes can be consistently applied to the Minnelieder, although modal interpretations are often quite suitable. The Minnelieder are transcribed in either binary or ternary rhythms in accordance with the nature of the texts.[6]

The early Minnesinger fall into three main groups. The first belongs to the period, 1150–90, when the movement was gathering momentum and before the French influence became strong. The second and best belongs to the end of the 12th century and early part of the 13th, and, besides Friedrich von Hûsen, includes Reinmar der Alte, master of Walther von der Vogelweide; Hartmann von der Aue, who wrote the famous narrative poem *Der arme Heinrich;* and the celebrated Walther von der Vogelweide himself. The third early group belongs to a period of work on a less lofty plane that extended to about 1318, the year of the death of Heinrich von Meissen,

---

[5] HagM, a monumental collection of Minnesinger poems, contains, in Vol. IV (besides biographies), the music of the Jena MS in the old notation, and melodies from other sources also. MüllP is a facsimile edition of the Jena MS. SarJ contains the music of the MS in the old notation, modern transcriptions thereof, and essays on the rhythm by Saran and on the melody by Bernoulli. SarJ contains also some excerpts from the Colmar MS. The contents of this MS are published complete together with the contents of the Donaueschingen MS in RunS, which includes also comments partly devoted to rhythmic questions. (Frauenlob is generously represented; nos. 16 and 116 are of special interest through their connection with Tannhäuser.) Any reader consulting these comments or those by Saran should bear in mind that they antedate the publication of the earliest literature on the applicability of the rhythmic modes to 12th- and 13th-century monody. For a description of the Münster fragment, with facsimiles, see MolL; see also WustW. DTO XX, 2 *Teil,* contains facsimiles of the Vienna *Minnesängerfragment* 2701 with transcriptions and commentary. (The pieces are by Frauenlob, Reimar von Zweter, and Alexander.) The *Lieder* of Neidhart von Reuenthal are published in DTO XXXVII, *I Teil;* for a study, see SchmiedN. The sumptuous Manessische Handschrift, which contains the texts of many songs and a few illustrations showing musical instruments, is reproduced in MH.

[6] For a concise explanation of the situation, see LudG, 204, where our Ex. 57 is transcribed in ternary rhythm as well as in the binary version given here. Possibly "free" rhythm would be better than either (*cf.* p. 210).

called "Frauenlob" supposedly because, in a *Liederstreit* with Regenbogen, a rival Minnesinger, he championed the use of *Frau* (i.e. *frouwe*, "lady") instead of *Weib* (*wip*, "woman"). Sometimes this period is regarded as one of transition to the Meistersinger and Frauenlob as the first of their number, though to see matters thus is to rush history. Neidhart von Reuenthal (*c.* 1180–*c.* 1240, a younger contemporary of Walther's) whose songs of summer and winter seem to possess a folk-quality, is an early member of this group. Tannhäuser and Wolfram von Eschenbach, also contemporary with Walther, both actually participated in a *Sängerkrieg* held at the Wartburg by the Landgrave Hermann of Thuringia in 1207, as shown by Wagner in his music-drama. One of Wolfram's epics, *Parzival,* was destined to serve Wagner as a source for his last work. Minnelieder attributed to both "Der Tanuser" and "Her Wolveram" are included in the Jena MS, but are not among its more attractive pieces. *Lieder* attributed to Wolfram survive elsewhere also.[7]

The poetic forms used by the Minnesinger included the *Lied* (= Provençal *canso*), the *Tagelied* (= Provençal *alba*), the *Leich* (= lai), and *Spruch* (literally, "proverb"). In the *Lied,* the treatment of love was generally more "idealistic" than in the Provençal and French songs: the singers were more apt to express devotion to the ideals of chivalrous love than to love for a particular lady or to sing about nature or a religious subject. Wagner had recourse to the tradition of the *Tagelied* (or *Wächterlied*) when he wrote Brangäne's warning-call in *Tristan*. The story of Tristan, incidentally, was a favorite theme with both the trouvères and, apparently in emulation of them, the Germans. The *Sprüche* were often cast in the form of a fable and sometimes dealt with political or social questions.

In the music, all the modes are employed, the Mixolydian being least favored.[8] Many melodies have a pentatonic character, which is apparent less in the use of a pure pentatonic scale than in the frequent employment of minor thirds, with the intervening tone, if present, of such a character that it may fairly be interpreted as a *pièn*-tone.[9]

The general structure of two *Stollen* and an *Abgesang*—that is, the *Bar* form—is favored, but not to the exclusion of others. When applied to 13th-century monody, this structure, as we have seen, admitted of considerable variety in the handling of important details.

One method is illustrated in the following beautiful song by Walther von der Vogelweide, a piece apparently associated with the Crusade of 1228. Walther, though a member of the lower nobility, spent several years em-

---

[7] The several melodies attributed to Wolfram are discussed in MosG I, 163.

[8] Moser feels that 12 of the melodies in the Jena MS display traits characteristic of the major mode. See MosD, 277ff. Exception to Moser's opinion is taken, on not very convincing grounds, in JamU, 296f.

[9] See JamU, 287.

ployed as a minstrel. The expressive Dorian melody illustrates the rounded-*chanson* form; that is, a portion of the *Stollen* melody is repeated at the end (but not as a refrain) and thus "rounds off" the song (*cf.* p. 230).

EXAMPLE 57. *Palästinalied*—Walther von der Vogelweide (after LudG, 204).

Life's true worth at last beginneth,
Now my sinful eyes behold
The holy land, the earth that winneth
Fame for glories manifold.
I have won my lifelong prayer:
I am in the country where
God in human shape did fare.

(From Frank C. Nicholson, *Old German Love Songs* [1907], 71; for complete German text, see F. Pfeiffer and K. Bartsch, *Walther von der Vogelweide* [7th ed., 1924], No. 79.)

The return of part of the melodic material of the *Stollen* or of all of it, sung once, in the course of the *Abgesang* is present in many Minnelieder. Another application of the principle is shown in a *Streitgedicht* (= Provençal tenso) [10] by "Der Unvürzaghete" ("The Dauntless One") in the Jena MS. In this piece, the two-phrase *Stollen* melody is incorporated almost bodily (except for the first half of the first phrase) in the second and third phrases of the four-phrase *Abgesang*. "*Der Kuninc Rodolp*" is Rudolph I, the first Hapsburg Emperor, whose virtues, judging by the text, did not include generosity to musicians. The melody is squarely in the major mode and has a strangely modern ring.

EXAMPLE 58. *Der kuninc Rodolp mynnet got*—"Der Unvürzaghete" (after SarJ II, 26).

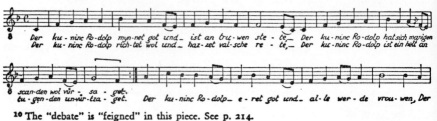

[10] The "debate" is "feigned" in this piece. See p. 214.

"King Rudolph loves God and is steadfast in his loyalties. King Rudolph has right well eschewed many temptations to shame. King Rudolph judges righteously and hates false speech. King Rudolph is a hero, dauntless in his virtues. King Rudolph honors God and all worthy ladies. King Rudolph oft displays himself in honorable acts. I wish he may achieve reward in measure with his bounty. The masters' singing, fiddling, discourse, to this he harkens gladly—and for it gives them nothing!"

(For complete text, see SarJ I, 71f.)

Another song [11] by the same Minnesänger (also in the Jena MS), urging a "young man of twenty years" not to waste his youth, but to lead an honorable life and to respect the ladies, is among the examples of the reduced strophic-*lai* form; that is, the *Abgesang* has a single recurrence of all the melodic material of the *Stollen* at the end (*cf.* p. 227). This is a form for which Witzlav von Rügen showed a preference and which he used with much charm in the well-known song [12] in which he says he has thought all night of the sorrow a maid has inflicted upon him, but that he would gladly suffer the pain of a little kiss from her mouth. It is used felicitously also by Neidhart von Reuenthal in two of his songs welcoming the return of Maytime.[13] In the following example of this form, Meyster Rumelant treats delicately of the mystic *Minne* of the Almighty for the Blessed Virgin:

EXAMPLE 59. *Daz Gedeones wollenvlius*—Meyster Rumelant (Jena Song MS, f. 51^r & v, after Müller facsimile).

11 Transcribed in GennF, 192. 12 Transcribed in MosG I, 170.
13 See, for one, DTO XXXVII [1] 31 (facsimiles on pp. 3, 21) and, for the other, BesM, 176, or DTO XXXVII,[1] 32 (facsimile on p. 6).

I

On Gideon's woolen fleece, as dew appearing,
  Fell heaven-fruit, the offspring bright
    That God's own love had bidden.
In wonder Moses saw, as he was nearing,
  The bush in which God took delight,
    For in it He was hidden.
The heav'nly fire did not consume,
It wasted not the house, the verdant bower.
We hail thee, heaven's Queen, thy rule revering!
  Thy rod, O Aaron, fresh may bloom,
    For fruits ungendered flower.

II

Das vlius in hymeltouwe lac begozzen,
  Eyn busch unbran, eyn trocken gart
    Trûch blûmen unde mandel:
Der hymele gheist quam in ir lib gevlozzen,
  Der sûzen maget die mûter wart
    Des kyndes ane wandel.
Sie grûner busch in viure klar,
Sie blûende gart, sie mûter maget an ende,
Ir vlius daz trûch den hymeltou beslozzen:
  Maria maget ein kynt gebar,
    Got gab sich an ir hende.

(For complete text, see SarJ I, 89f.)

The fleece was drenched with dew when dawn was breaking,
  A bush burned not, a rod though dried
    Bore almonds, bud, and blossom:
The Holy Ghost her body holy making,
  The Virgin stainless did abide,
    Though Babe lay in her bosom.
She is the bush green 'mid the flame,
Rod budding, mother though no man did woo her,
The spotless fleece, of heav'nly dew partaking.
  A Child from maiden Mary came,
    God gave Himself unto her.

(English version by G. R.[14])

In the late 14th and early 15th centuries, a revival of the art of the Minnesinger went hand-in-hand with the practice of polyphony. We shall deal with this recrudescence in Chapter 13.

The Laude and Geisslerlieder

THAT the influence of the troubadours extended into Italy is amply attested.[1] Sordello, the hero of Browning's poem, was an actual Italian troubadour (d. after 1269) some of whose poetry survives. Reimbautz de Vaquieras, Peire Vidal (d. c. 1215), and Gaucelm Faidit are among the Provençal troubadours who, at one time or another, sojourned in the peninsula. Dante admired the poet-musicians of Provence and did not hesitate to copy from

---

[14] With help, gratefully acknowledged, from W. W.
[1] Accounts of the activities of the troubadours in Italy may be found in BertT and ChayT.

them: he borrowed the form of the *sestina,* for example, from Arnaut Daniel (d. 1199, i. e. sixty-six years before Dante's birth). But, so far as research has revealed, the immediate influence of the troubadours in Italy was chiefly poetic rather than musical. We may say that secular music, if we here interpret "secular" as meaning "worldly," did not take on the proportions of an artistic movement in Italy until the 14th century.

If, however, we continue to interpret "secular" as meaning "non-liturgical," we may speak here of religious songs in Italian, as we have already spoken of religious songs in Provençal and French. Such songs apparently existed in Italy at the time of St. Francis of Assisi (1182–1226). A MS at Assisi contains not only the words of his famous Canticle of the Sun but space for the melody with which it apparently was once provided, space which, exasperatingly, has come down to us blank.[2] The songs that survive found their origin in a strange source. About 1259, fraternities of penitents spread over most of Northern Italy. The brotherhoods practiced flagellation, and, as they journeyed in procession, were joined in large numbers by laymen who followed their example, frightened by devastating wars and plagues into seeking atonement for the sins of the age. As they journeyed forward, the bands of flagellants sang songs of praise known as *laude spirituali.* About 100 pieces appear in two 14th-century *lauda-MSS* at Florence, 46 in a 13th-century MS at Cortona, and a few in a MS at Cambridge. (Besides the forms *lauda,* singular, *laude,* plural, there are the alternative forms *laude,* singular, *laudi,* plural.)

The literary form of the *lauda* was closely related to that of the purely secular *ballata* (the Italian equivalent of the French *virelai*). However, the form was not invariable; in fact, one might say that the *lauda* represented a general type rather than a form. The outer feature of this type was a division into three parts: a *ripresa* (refrain), a middle section (*stanza*) consisting of two *piedi* and a *volta,* and a repetition of the *ripresa.* Often the *volta* was melodically the same as the *ripresa,* and Liuzzi believes that in *laude* of many stanzas the refrain was repeated not after each of them but only at the end.[3] Within this three-part framework there was a great variation in the number and disposition of the melodic members. Sometimes the two *piedi* were the same or similar, so that they resembled the German *Stollen,* with the *volta* forming the *Abgesang.* Where this happened and the *volta* resembled the *ripresa* (i. e. where we find *ripresa* AB, *piedi* cc, *volta* ab), the musical form of the *lauda,* as well as the poetic form, agreed with that of the *virelai.* Thirteen of the *laude* in the Cortona MS are cast after this pattern.[4]

[2] See LudG, 207.
[3] LiuM, 534. But see HandUL, 29f. The terms *piedi* and *volta* were derived from round-dance figures (see *Enciclopedia italiana* V, 982). In music and literature they represent only outer musical and poetic divisions (even where the original terpsichorean significance of the terms no longer obtains), and do not refer to the structure of those divisions.
[4] Liuzzi disputes what he calls Ludwig's derivation of the *lauda ballata* pattern from the *virelai.* The correspondence of the *lauda* with the *virelai* is only occasional But see HandUL, 15, 19n.

The tonality tended towards the major and minor modes, and it is thought that the rhythm was usually binary.[5]

In the Florence MS Magl. II I 122 there are some *laude* having the music written out not only for the first strophe but also for the beginning of the second, which presents a somewhat varied version of the first. This is interesting since we have here documentary evidence that the basic melody, in medieval strophic pieces, could be varied upon repetition.

The melodies in the Cortona MS tend towards simplicity, while those in the Florentine MSS are on the whole more elaborate. Here is a *lauda* from the former. The pattern is

RIPRESA	PIEDE I	PIEDE II	VOLTA	RIPRESA
AB	*c*	*d*	*ab*	*AB*
			(modified)	

EXAMPLE 60. *Venite a laudare* (from LiuM, 538).

"Come to praise, for love to sing the loving Virgin Mary. Mary glorious, blessed, ever be greatly praisèd: I pray that thou shouldst be my advocate with thy Son, O compassionate Virgin." [6]

(For complete text, see LiuL I, 257 [where the above transcription recurs] ff.)

The penitential mania spread across the Alps into Northern Europe and was especially rampant in Germany in 1349 during the plague of the Black

---

[5] On the basis of evidence offered by a report in a contemporary chronicle, by the text of certain *laude,* and by miniatures, Liuzzi concludes that horns or trumpets were not infrequently used to announce or sustain the singing. LiuB, 9f.

[6] Further concerning the early *lauda,* see LiuL (which, with its facsimiles, transcriptions, and commentary, is the chief work on the subject) or LiuB, LiuP (which contains 6 melodies), LudG, 207ff, OH II, 303ff, HandUL (particularly with respect to rhythm), WolfMR, 284ff. The reader's attention is directed especially to the exquisite *Laude novella sia cantata* ("Sing a new song of praise to the exalted crownèd lady. Fresh Virgin, damozel, first flower, new-blown rose, all the world calls unto thee; in a blest hour wast thou born," etc.) in LiuL I, 261, and to the powerful *O Cristo 'nipotente* ("O Christ omnipotent, where hast thou been who so meekly didst wander as a pilgrim? I took a bride; having given her my heart, I adorned her with gems to gain honor. She left me in dishonor; let me go in penance," etc.) in LiuL II, 98. The *Alta Trinita beata* has been printed several times since Burney published it, not altogether correctly, in his *History;* and the Christmas *lauda, Gloria in cielo,* has also become well known since its appearance in LudG.

Death. A body of German *Geisslerlieder* survives in several MSS.

The chief MS—containing both texts and melodies—is the "Chronikon" of Hugo Spechtshart von Reutlingen (*c.* 1285–*c.* 1360), now in a library at Leningrad.[7] Hugo describes the ceremony attendant upon the arrival of the *Geissler* (flagellants) in a town, the penitential rites, and the farewell procession. Each of these activities was accompanied by a group of *Lieder* in the vernacular. The basic formal unit of these songs was a four-line stanza. In some of the stanzas the first three lines rhymed, a pattern indicating that the German verse forms were borrowed from or influenced by the verse forms of the Italian *laude*.[8] As to the music, the *Geisslerlieder* were "religious folk-songs."[9] A few tunes, some of them taken from older pilgrim songs,[10] served for the whole ceremony; and their arrangement, on the fundamental melodic pattern *a a b b*, is primitive in comparison to the richly varied forms of the *lauda*. The longer strophes of the entrance procession contain musical repetitions such as *a b c b c b* (the second and third appearances of *b* being somewhat varied), a pattern that may show the influence of the litany.

In melodic outline and form the *Geisslerlieder* anticipate to some degree the Lutheran chorale. One of the *Lieder* reappears in 1666 as a procession-song at Ascension.[11] The following is perhaps the most famous *Geisslerlied*:[12]

EXAMPLE 61. *Maria, muoter reinû mait* (after RunL, 9).

a) *Bb for Repetition only*

Oh Mary mother, Virgin mild,	Our refuge here alone art thou;
Forget not Christendom thy child;	From sudden death defend us now.
Have pity on our misery,	We have no help but him and thee,
We have no help but only thee.	Thy Son who reigns eternally;
Oh Mary mother, full of grace,	Oh Mary, hear thy children's cry;
Why hast thou turned away thy face?	Have mercy on us, or we die.

(Freely translated by E. L. Voynich; for complete German text, see RunL, 31f or HübG, 187.)

In time the penitential mania died out—sooner in Italy than in the North, possibly because the disapproval of the papacy could more easily be made effective in the peninsula—but the singing of spiritual songs continued. Cer-

---

[7] Hugo's narrative, in Latin verse with a German translation, and the *Geisslerlieder* are reproduced in RunL. Hugo was the author also of a treatise, *Flores Musicae Omnis Cantus Gregoriani*, first published in 1488 and reprinted in a modern edition with a German translation by Carl Beck in 1868 (concerning which see MfMG II, 57, 110).

[8] For further details, see HübG, 130.   [9] HübG, 64.   [10] MülleG, 8.   [11] MosT, 186.

[12] Further concerning the *Geisslerlieder*, see MosG I, 231ff; RunL; RunM; etc.

tain brotherhoods survived as such in Italy, but shorn of their early practices, so that the *Laudisti* (or *Laudesi*) had radically amended their ways by the time the 16th century arrived, a century during which they not only exerted an influence upon Palestrina, but played a rôle in preparing for the creation of the oratorio.

English Monody *

SOME attempt was made to introduce troubadour song into England. In 1152 the marriage of Louis VII of France to Eleanor of Aquitaine was annulled, and she became the wife of Henry of Anjou, founder of the Angevin line of English kings. In England she no doubt encouraged troubadour composition as she had already done in Aquitaine and in Northern France. From one of the poems of Bernart de Ventadorn it appears that he crossed the Channel and was for a time in England.[1]

The efforts to transplant the fine flower of troubadour art in England, however, were not successful. A few songs in Anglo-French which may be of troubadour origin are extant, reproduced in the two miscellaneous collections of facsimiles of early English music, StaE I and EEH I; but certainly no schools of troubadour music sprang up in England comparable to those in France. Practically none of the existing early monodic songs in the English language shows the troubadour or trouvère stamp. Possibly the only exception is the "Prisoner's Prayer," a 13th-century song with French and English words bound in with a book of laws at the Guildhall, London. As the French text stands above in the MS and is carefully aligned with the notes, it has usually been assumed [2] to be the original one. While this may be correct, it is worth noting that the English has rhymes falling on similar musical figures at certain points (indicated in the example below by braces) where, in the French, rhymes are not present, and also that the English text seems to be mirrored by the melody at one point where the French is not. If merely a translation, the English text is much closer to the music than one, on first looking at the MS, would suppose it to be.

EXAMPLE 62. Excerpts from *The Prisoner's Song* (from GennI, 347).

Among the native English, apparently, the older traditions in art-music continued. In Anglo-Saxon times, music had been widely practiced among warriors and churchmen, but particularly it had been the province of the

* By WILLIS WAGER.
[1] An account of Bernart de Ventadorn in England, and of the influence of the troubadours there, may be found in ChayE.   [2] As by EllisO, 432, and GennI, 346.

scops and gleemen. The classical distinction between these two is that the *scops* were resident in the hall of an atheling (or petty king), while the *gleemen* travelled about. That the two categories often merged, however, is shown by the fictional autobiography of an idealized scop, *Widsith* ("The Far-Traveller"), which is the oldest poem extant in English. How far the scops and gleemen are to be considered primarily as musicians, and how far they belong rather under the category of poets and historians, we cannot determine, since no authentic examples of their music exist. After the Norman Conquest, gleeman and scop gave place to minstrels (the name changing more than the function), both resident in the court of the feudal lord and travelling on the highways. They continued to recite long narrative poems to the accompaniment of the harp: there is even evidence that so late and extensive a poem as Chaucer's "Troilus" was sung rather than recited.[3]

Liturgical music seems to have had a greater direct influence upon native English musical composition than did the art—indebted to the same source—of the troubadours. The earliest extant lyrics in England after the Norman Conquest are those of St. Godric (d. 1170), an uneducated Saxon hermit, who lived in a cave in the wilds of Northern England,[4] and to whom, we are told, these songs were dictated through angelic visions. The following song, for example, was supposedly sung to him by the soul of his dead sister, attended by angels, in answer to his persistent entreaties of God to know how she had fared in the other world.

EXAMPLE 63. *Crist and Sainte Marie*—Godric (Brit. Mus. MS Reg. **v.** F. vii, f. 85—Transcription by G. R.)

"Christ and St. Mary so led me on a footstool that I did not tread on this earth with my bare foot."

Upon analysis the melody of the English song appears simply to be an elaboration of the *Kyrie eleison* formula that precedes and follows it. On the basis of the text it has been argued that the song preserves for us some of the

---

[3] Further concerning the scops etc., see PadelE, which has the further virtue of containing a glossary of early English musical terms.

[4] The Godric songs are given in facsimile as the frontispiece to SainH, Vol. I. They are discussed in SainH, and also in TreE; and the Latin life of Godric in which the songs are preserved has been published in RegL.

features of the earlier, unrecorded Anglo-Saxon popular song;[5] but from a musical standpoint it appears rather to be a vernacular outgrowth of the liturgy, an English farse.[6] The other Godric songs may also have had some liturgical source: one is a prayer to the Virgin to "help thine Godric," another a prayer to St. Nicholas.

From the church service there developed also a topical song with music, *In Rama sonat gemitus,* which appears in the Scottish MS, Wolfenbüttel 677, also known as Helmstedt 628 (*cf.* p. 297). It refers to Thomas à Becket as being alive and in exile. It was therefore composed probably between 1164 and 1170 (although the MS itself probably dates from the 14th century); for Thomas escaped from England in 1164, setting out at night in an open boat to cross the Channel, and remained in France until the year of his martyrdom, 1170. The text is derived from Matthew II, 18, which is used in the church services for the Holy Innocents and the Flight into Egypt. The life of Thomas à Becket, incidentally, inspired many monodic antiphons in England. Before his canonization three years after his death, an antiphon in English had allegedly been dictated by a group of angels to a Norfolk priest in a manner that recalls the inspiration of Godric's songs.[7] MS Edinburgh Univ. 123, of the 13th century, has several pages of Latin antiphons to St. Thomas. Musically they are quite various; but most of them seem to be elaborations of the *Gloria* melodies that follow each of them in the MS.

Turning from these semi-liturgical songs, we find a fragment, "Mirie it is while sumer ilast," with purely secular text, dated about 1225.[8] The general tone of this lyric is close to that of Anglo-Saxon poetry, sad and foreboding; and the descending melody of each line is expressive of that mood. Another solitary song of the 13th or early 14th century, beginning "Bryd one brere," an attractive love lyric with descending melody and coloration of the word *rewe* ("have pity") in the text, has been discovered written on the back of a 12th-century papal bull.[9]

The tone of foreboding appears also in a few extant religious and moralizing songs of the period: "Worldes blis ne last," with its music, is extant in two slightly differing versions.[10] Another 13th-century song, of a rather grisly character, is "Man mei longe him lives wene":[11]

---

[5] See RankH, but also the criticism of this theory in the *Year's Work in English Studies,* IV (1923), 45.

[6] That St. Godric was familiar with the method of farsing is shown by RegL, 288f, where he is credited with composing—again by divine inspiration—a Latin farse that actually appears in a 12th-century missal which has been published by the Surtees Society (LIX [1872], I, vii).

[7] BrownE, 67, 196ff. The music of the English antiphon to St. Thomas is not extant, but the account of its inspiration specifically mentions its being sung three times to the sleeping priest.

[8] Facsimile in StaE, plate 3. [9] Facsimile, transcription, and commentary in SaltT.

[10] Facsimiles in EEH I, plates 23 and 24, reproduced from MS Rawlinson G 18 and MS Arundel 248. The words occur without music in MS Digby 86.

[11] Professor Carleton Brown has printed the text of it under the title "Death's Wither-Clench" in BrownE, 15, to which any reader is referred who wishes to see the other four stanzas appear-

EXAMPLE 64. *Man mei longe him lives wene* (Maidstone MS A 13—
Transcription by Manfred Bukofzer).

Man mei lon-ge him li - ves we - - ne,— ac of - te him— li - yet þe wreinch; þar - vo - re,
fair we-der of-te him went to re - - ne,— an fer - li - che— ma - ket is blench.

man, þu þe bi - þench,— al sel va - lu - i þe gre - ne, wel - a - wey! nis king ne Que - ne þat

ne sel drin-ke of deth-is drench. Man, er þu fal - le of þi benoh,— þu sin - ne a - quench.

"Long may man ween his life to be, but oft for him there waits a trick; fair weather often turns to rain, and sunshine is wondrously made. Therefore, man, bethink thyself,—all thy green youth shall fade. Well-a-day! there is neither king nor queen who shall not drink the draught of death. Man, ere thou fallest off thy bench, quench thy sin."

There are gay, strongly rhythmical pieces in the remains of 13th-century English music, as well as sad ones. In fact, Kenneth Sisam, who is perhaps as familiar with English culture of the late Middle Ages as any scholar to-day, characterizes the mood of the century as that of "Sumer is icumen in." [11a] The instrumental dance in MS Douce 139 is of exactly that character—clear, fresh, "major" throughout. The piece has been reproduced and transcribed several times, and carefully analyzed in more than one study of the early dance.[12] Its musical significance is partly appreciated when we realize that there are only three other extant dances of a clearly instrumental nature that are older. Structurally this English dance is highly significant because— monodic throughout the first part and rising to a climax of gaiety—it suddenly bursts towards the end into three-voiced harmony. Apparently this polyphonization of the dance-form was an English development, for the other three instrumental dances just mentioned are also English, and are polyphonic throughout.[13] But the dance in Douce 139 is more striking than these other three English dances because its composer has been able to use both monody and polyphony and to good effect.

In general, the 13th century in England was one of great cultural com-

---

ing in Maidstone MS A 13 and also the complete poem as it appears, without music, in another manuscript. [11a] About the date of that piece, however, see p. 396, including footnote 49[a].

[12] Facsimiles, EEH I, plate 24, and StaE, plate 7; transcriptions, WolfH I, 231; WolfT, 22; HandU, 13; EEH II, 40; and StaE II, 11. Analyzed WolfT, 13; HandU, 8; and SchraI, 55. SchraI, 74n, questions the time-values of the transcription in WolfH; and HandU, 8, recognizes that his own interpretation of the rhythm of the piece is perhaps not final. This transcription, however, and the one in WolfT are probably the best ones.

[13] There will be a return to these dances in Chap. 14.

plexity.[14] Nothing will impress that fact upon the student of early music more clearly than a glance at the five pages of MS Arundel 248, reproduced in EEH I.[15] Here one finds side by side Latin, French, and English songs, one-, two-, and three-voiced compositions. *Angelus ad Virginem* (*cf.* pp. 390, 404f) appears as a one-voiced song with an English translation beneath it.[16] More than one of the pieces are *contrafacta,* with varied antecedents.

The other most important English musical manuscript of this century is Harley 978. In addition to some interesting polyphonic material ("Sumer is icumen in" and the three polyphonic dances), it contains an interesting monodic composition, *Samson dux fortissime* [17]—a Latin *planctus* of dramatic character. There are solo parts for Samson and Delilah. The opening and closing portions are apparently sung by a commentator or chorus. The *planctus* appears also in two MSS now in German libraries,[18] in versions not so complete as that in Harley 978: in one there is no music, in the other there is apparently only the chorus and one soloist, Samson. But the presence in England of such a work, perhaps with a part for quasi-Greek chorus, on the Samson theme, is hard to fit into our preconceptions of the subjects that could be treated of in medieval drama. Could Milton, who is supposed to have written *Samson Agonistes* in the full flush of renaissance enthusiasm for the rediscovered Greek drama, have been looking at the medieval MS Harley 978?

The 13th century in the music of England has thus left us fragmentary remains [19]—not only monodic but, as we shall see in Chapter 14, polyphonic —which, in flashes of brilliance, show us that the musical impulse was strong there. In the century of unrest that followed, secular music gave place to literary, moralistic, and theological interests. Little advance was made until the country had achieved some measure of political, social, religious, and economic unity. Only with the 15th century did England again fully show her musical abilities.

Spanish Monody: *The* Cantigas

LITTLE is known of the secular music of the Spanish peninsula prior to the 13th century. We have already mentioned a Visigothic lament (pp. 198f) and

---

[14] In view of the unsettled state of 13th-century English music, it is interesting to read a 13th-century English complaint against the difficulty of learning music. The complaint is printed in WrR, 291f.

[15] Plates 32–36.

[16] Transcriptions, GennF, 179, and TreE, 113. GennF contains a transcription of another of these Arundel 248 songs on p. 205.

[17] Facsimile, EEH, plates 12–17.

[18] MS St. Georgen 38 at the Badische Landesbibliothek, Karlsruhe, and MS I Ascet. 95, at the Landesbibliothek, Stuttgart.

[19] From time to time, English songs from the 12th–14th centuries are discovered, and reference is usually made to them in the annual supplements of WellsM, which lists all the extant pieces of Middle English literature.

the Song of the Sibyl (p. 199). 12th-century chronicles report that music was sung at royal festivals, in the castles of the nobility, and at popular celebrations, but none of this music has survived.

The earliest known decipherable examples of peninsular secular monody in the vernacular are the Galician songs, *Siete canciones de amor,* attributed to Martim Codax, a *jongleur* or troubadour. Of the seven songs, six survive with music.[1] The melodies consist of three elements, one belonging to the refrain. A resemblance between the material in the Codax pieces and certain traits in available melodies of Mozarabic *Preces* has led to the belief that the latter "represent a portion of the rich musical sources whence these secular songs derived." (PopeM, 25.)

By far the most considerable legacy of Spanish songs of the Middle Ages is the great collection, with texts in Galician-Portuguese, assembled by Alfonso X, *el Sabio* ("the Wise"), king of Castile and León (1252–84). This collection, known as the *Cantigas de Santa Maria* and comprising over 400 songs, has been called "one of the greatest monuments of mediæval music." *"Cantigas"* itself is a generic term that was applied to the religious and secular poems of the Galician-Portuguese literature.

Alfonso, though in many ways an unsatisfactory monarch, founded Spanish historiography in the vernacular and is sometimes called the father of Castilian prose.[2] He was fond of music, the patron of many troubadours, and established a course in music at the University of Salamanca. Guiraut Riquier, the last of the troubadours, is known to have spent some time at Alfonso's court. He was, however, by no means the first Provençal poet-musician to have been active in Spain. The Monk of Montaudon (fl. *c.* 1200) and Guiraut de Bornelh are among troubadours who had been active there in earlier times.[3] The rulers of Provence and the Iberian kingdoms frequently exchanged visits, and troubadours and *jongleurs* belonging to their entourage no doubt assisted in what might be called the cross-fertilization of the indigenous verse and music. It is not surprising, therefore, that we find a style similar to that of the troubadours in the *Cantigas de Santa Maria.*

Ribera would have us believe that the *Cantigas* (dating from quite late in the troubadour and trouvère period) were the product of an Arabic influence that had long before flowed from Spain to Provence, not from Provence to Spain.[4] The Arabic *zajal,* a poetic form characterized by the appearance of a refrain before and

---

[1] Facsimiles of the Codax songs, with comments and transcripts in original notation, appear in VindS. Transcriptions of 6 into modern notation appear in PopeM, 18–20, 22–24, and TreM, 213–5; and one of them appears also in OH II, 295. PopeM gives a full account of the pieces and contains further bibliographical references.

[2] For an entertaining essay on Alfonso and his part in the *Cantigas,* see TreA.

[3] More information concerning Riquier at Alfonso's court is available in MitM, p. 1938. See also AngM. An account, in English, of Provençal troubadours in Spain may be found in Chay'T.

[4] Ribera's views are expounded in RibA; RibC; RibM; and RibT.

after the stanza proper, had, after a period of development, been raised to a high literary rank in the first half of the 12th century. The pattern of many of the *Cantigas* is that of the *zajal*, i. e. a strophe (*estrofa*) is preceded and followed by a refrain (*estribillo*), and Trend [5] and Westrup,[6] who oppose Ribera's main contentions, agree that it was probably from the *zajal* that the *Cantigas* derived their form. The *zajal* clearly resembles the *virelai* and *ballade* (the absence of an internal refrain differentiates it from the *rondeau*),[7] and Ribera's theory is that the Arabic form produced early Spanish imitations, of which, however, no specimens survive, and that the influence of the Spanish poems spread to Provence and to the rest of Western and Central Europe. In support of his contention of a Moorish influence, Ribera points out that the MSS of the *Cantigas* are handsomely illuminated with miniatures, some showing musicians in Arab dress, performing on instruments known to be of Arab origin. The influence of Arabic instruments upon Europe is widely accepted: the very name of the lute, in English, French, German, Italian, Spanish, etc., is derived from the Arabic name *al'ūd,* and it is generally agreed that the instrument, of oriental origin as we have seen, became known throughout the West in the time of the Crusades. The questions naturally arise: If the poems apparently derive their form from a Moorish model, and if the miniatures adorning the *Cantigas* show Arab musicians and instruments, may not the melodies have been associated with the Moors also? And if songs from north of the Pyrenees resembled the Spanish ones, may not they also have been derived from Arabic influence—but indirectly, by way of Spain? The answer of Gennrich and others is that, in the complete absence of Arabic musical MSS, any assumption of an Arabic influence upon European secular monody must be regarded as speculative. Such an assumption is held to be less reliable than one accepting derivation from the litany, sequence, and hymn, i. e. a belief based on comparisons with actually available material which, as Gennrich has shown, displays striking parallels with whole groups of secular forms. As regards the *virelai* pattern of many of the *Cantigas,* Anglès has discovered Latin *conducti* with the musical form of the *virelai* in the Catalonian monastery of Ripoll; these *conducti* antedate the *Cantigas* by about a century and could easily have served as their prototypes. Since, as we have seen, the Church offered ample material (quite aside from these *conducti*) from which the conception of the *virelai* and *ballade* might have been derived, there is no reason why the source of their form—or, for that matter, that of the *Cantigas*—should have to be sought in the *zajal*. Many writers try to trace a Moorish influence on Christian art. It certainly existed. But may not the situation have been reversed with respect to the *zajal*—that is, may it not have been suggested by Christian art? Or, since the *zajal-virelai-ballade* idea is simple enough and could easily have originated independently in several places, why must we look for an influence either way? The evidence adduced by Ribera must, in the absence of fresh discoveries, remain purely circumstantial.

Ribera claims also that European secular monody derived from the Arabs its rhythms and its tendency towards the major mode. The questions he raises are

[5] Trend's views are given in his article, *Alfonso el Sabio,* in Grove; and in TreM, 63.
[6] Westrup's views are given in OH II, 298.
[7] The *rondeau* type, however, is not totally absent from the *Cantigas*. *Cf.* No. 122 in RibC.

too involved and controversial to be more than touched upon here. An excellent introduction to them is furnished by Ursprung in UrA, in which the author presents both sides of the various questions in more detail than is possible here.

The *Cantigas* survive in four MSS,[8] only three of which contain notation. The fourth has staves, but they have come down to us blank. Transcriptions by Aubry and others apply the rhythmic modes. Anglès employs both ternary and binary rhythms but considers the mixed mode (*cf.* p. 210) characteristic of the *Cantigas*. Ribera has gone his own way, and his transcriptions, with their drawing-room accompaniments, are quite fantastic.[9]

The poems as well as the music were probably drawn from many sources, of which Alfonso himself was quite possibly one.[10] Most of the canticles narrate miracles of the Virgin, every tenth piece, however, being a song of praise. The legend of the Virgin taking the place of a nun who had fled from her convent—a story that has served playwrights of our own day—makes its appearance, as well as a canticle belonging to the history of the bull-fight.[11]

Of the several forms which, like the *zajal,* have refrains at the beginning and end, the *virelai* design appears most often. The following charming example, with the pattern

AB   ccdb   AB

is related to the first two of the three *ballade*-types described on p. 223, where attention has already been called to the use the piece makes of melodic rhyme. The notation has certain mensural features that make it possible to recognize deviations from the prevailing third rhythmic mode.[12]

EXAMPLE 65. *Rosa das rosas*—From the Cantigas of Alfonso the Wise (Transcribed by Higini Anglès).

8 Ro - sa das ro - -sas___ E fror das fro-res,   Do - na das do - nas, Sen - nor das Sen-no-res.

8 Ro   sa de bel dad'e de pa-re - cen.   E fror d'a - le - gri-a   e de pra - zer,

8 A facsimile of the Madrid MS (B.N. 10069) is contained in RibC. Facsimiles of pages from Escorial MS jb2 appear in ColC; Marqués de Valmar, *Las Cántigas de Santa Maria . . .* (1889); and on pp. 109–18 of section 2 of RibC. Bibliographical notes appear in RiaC.

9 Transcriptions made along scholarly lines appear in AngC; see also OH II, 297ff. The transcriptions in AuI (IX), 32 and TreM are less good.

10 One of the *Cantigas* employs the melody of the Song of the Sibyl (*cf.* p. 199). It is printed in AngC, 20.

11 Some of the legends used in the *Cantigas* were drawn from a collection made by a Franciscan monk, Gil de Zamora, tutor to Alfonso's son, Sancho.

12 The author has had the opportunity to read an unpublished paper by Dr. Anglès analyzing the notation. In AngL (1935) Anglès announced that he was preparing, with the assistance of Hans Spanke, a complete edition of the *Cantigas*.

8 Do - na en mui pi-a - do sa se er,   Sen - nor en tol - ler coi - tas e do - o - res.

I

Rose of all roses, fairest of flowers!
Queen of all women, endowed with all powers!
Rose of rare beauty and symbol of truth,
Flow'r shedding joyousness, flow'r of all youth!
Lady who reigns on high piety's throne,
Liege! So long bearing the world's moan despairing!

IV

Esta Dona que tenno por Sennor
et de que quero seer trobador,
se en per ren poss' auer seu amor,
dou ao demo os outros amores.
Rosa das rosas et fror das frores,
Dona das donas, sennor das sennores.

(For complete text, see Marqués de Valmar,
   Las Cántigas de Santa María . . . , I
   [1889], xf.)

Such then is she who as Liege governs
   me;
She whose dear troubadour I fain would
   be.
If I may win her sweet love for mine
   own,
Then let all devils claim love's earthly
   revels!
Rose of all roses, fairest of flowers!
Queen of all women, endowed with all
   powers!

(Translated by Lorraine Noel Finley.)

Part Three: POLYPHONY BASED ON THE PER-
FECT CONSONANCES AND ITS
DISPLACEMENT BY POLYPHONY
BASED ON THE THIRD.

Chapter 9: THE EARLIER STAGES OF ORGANUM

In writing on the folk-music of Georgia (U.S.S.R.), Victor Belaiev has said:

> It is generally understood that polyphony . . . was invented in Europe, on the basis of certain theoretical forerunners which drew a sharp line between the "natural" unisonal folk-music and the "cultural" polyphonic species. This opinion is radically wrong and should now give place to the very obvious proposition that polyphony came into existence far earlier than the date assigned to it on theoretical grounds by European musicologists, and that Europe did not invent it but acquired it elsewhere in a ready-made form. . . .
>
> There can be no doubt that further study of the Georgian polyphony (which . . . dates back to ancient times) will reveal . . . methods characteristic of the various periods of the early European polyphony, and appearing in the European literature . . . under the names of organum, diaphony, descant, fauxbourdon, etc. A comparison of the facts to be ascertained from an investigation of . . . early folk-polyphonies with the theoretical data of relatively early forms of the so-called art-polyphony of Europe will certainly lead us to conclude that the latter was evolved from the traditional folk-polyphony.[1]

Many comparative musicologists would doubtless agree with Belaiev's conclusion, at least in part. But while a study of musical developments outside Europe lends color to the theory that "the so-called art-polyphony of Europe was evolved from the traditional folk-polyphony," there is no need to believe that Europe "acquired" its polyphony "elsewhere in a ready-made form." Part-music may have grown spontaneously among Europeans as well as among others. This view is consistent with the deductions of Marius Schneider, which will be dealt with later in this chapter.

Belaiev uses "polyphony" to denote any music that is not unisonal. Obviously, however, the generic term covers many types. We have already encountered the border-line case of heterophony. Wooldridge distinguishes between "symphonious" and "polyphonic" music, the former consisting for him of music in which only the fourth, fifth, octave, and certain compounds thereof (e. g. an eleventh, consisting of a fourth plus an octave, etc.) are regarded as consonances.[2] "Symphonious" is derived from συμφωνία (symphonia), a term which, in its long history, has had many and varied mean-

---

[1] BelF, 425, 433. A remarkable collection of folk-polyphony (Russian) is provided by LinR.
[2] For the symphoniae, as defined in the 9th-century Musica Enchiriadis, see GerS I, 160ff.

ings:[3] at one time a full ensemble, at another a kind of drum, at another a kind of keyboard instrument. Today "symphony" means something still different. The original meaning of *symphonia* was "a concord of sounds," and the fourth, fifth, and octave were, in fact, consonances for both the Greeks and the medieval "symphonists"—but from different points of view. Basically, the intervals constituting the consonances were melodic (i.e. successively sounded) with the Greeks, harmonic (i.e. simultaneously sounded) with the "symphonists." Such modern writers as draw a line between the two distinguish polyphonic from symphonious music chiefly by its admission of the third and sixth as consonances. There are other differences also, but this difference in the conception of consonance is fundamental.

Why should fourths and fifths be the first intervals to appear in those documents that provide us with evidence concerning the growth of European part-music? Speculation has offered several answers.

The first interval in the series of overtones is the octave. The second is the fifth, the third is the fourth, the fourth is the third, etc. It has been claimed that the intervals appearing in the series of overtones are accepted by the ear as harmonic consonances in the order in which they occur in the series. Thus, the octave was employed in magadizing (see Chapter 2); the admission of the fifth and fourth as harmonic consonances was due next, and took place in organum; polyphony and pre-modern harmony admitted the third.

Another explanation is offered by the natural ranges of the four main classes of human voices, which, roughly speaking, lie at pitch levels a fifth away from one another, in consecutive order from bass to soprano. The congregations that sang responses at services did not consist of trained singers, but sang within ranges they found comfortable. Machabey,[4] on the basis of this, writes: "The division of men's voices into two parallel lines, and of the high-pitched [women's and boys'] voices into two other lines paralleling the first, must have followed as a matter of course, without the executants' noticing it." In 1908, in France, he heard an untrained congregation singing in organum without, apparently, intending to. The men and women each broke into two groups singing a fourth or a fifth from one another, according to the texture of the melody. Soprano, alto, tenor, and bass lines were produced simply because the worshippers sang where convenient.

Organum has been regarded also as a product of the semitoneless pentatonic scale. Let us recall that the five degrees of this scale have two auxiliary tones, as the seven degrees of our diatonic scale have five chromatic tones to which ornamental rôles may be assigned. Yasser, as we have seen, believes that the modal scales used in plainsong were basically pentatonic, i.e. that two of the seven degrees in each modal scale were merely auxiliary. He further believes that organum went hand in hand with the use of the eccle-

[3] For a discussion of these, see GalpS, 67; AppelT, 23, 31–3, 89; SachsHI, 84f.
[4] See MaH, 52.

siastical scales just as a body of part-music, in which unisons, octaves, fourths, and fifths are the basic intervals, has co-existed with the employment of the pentatonic scale in China. Organum, according to this point of view, bears the same relation to the pentatonic scale that polyphony, with its heavy reliance on the third and sixth, bears to the diatonic.[5]

A fourth view, expressed by Gastoué,[6] sees in the two primitive parts of vocal organum an imitation of two-part music played on the organ—hydraulic or pneumatic—and believes organum to have been named after the instrument. Now it is obvious that choral singing antedated the organ, and that organum—apparently an inevitable though not necessarily recognized concomitant of such singing (cf. p. 250)—must have preceded the instrument also. It has been contended, therefore,[7] that the rudimentary part-music performed on the organ—or other instruments—was conceived as a copy of primitive vocal part-music, and that it is from this copy that stylized vocal "polyphony" derived its name. A connection between the name and instruments other than the organ is quite possible, the Latin word organum, besides meaning "organ," being a generic term for a musical instrument of any kind. While choral singing doubtless did antedate the organ, the particular kind of part-singing represented by organum may in fact be the result of practice on an instrument of some sort, though this cannot be proved. The pros and cons have been succinctly presented by Hornbostel.[8]

A fifth theory has been advanced by Dom Anselm Hughes:[9]

In Gregorian chant . . . a normal range of baritone is predicated for the chorus, while the soloist . . . is expected to be able to extend his range upwards for a fourth or a fifth. Now in the sequelae [see Chap. 6] this . . . range is needed by the chorus as well. . . . The division into tenor and bass voices thus seems as if it came into being before the birth of polyphony in its formal styles; and in the primitive organum . . . we can more easily discern an answer to a need than a gratuitous and arbitrary experiment. . . .

One of the new features of the sequela-composition is the repetition of a melody at the fifth above; . . . another feature is that the phrases are repeated twice each, by alternative sides of the choir presumably, or at least by cantors and chorus. And from the repetition of a melody at the fifth above by a different set of voices, to the simultaneous performance of that melody by the two sets of voices, at the interval of a fifth, is a very short step. Yet we may perhaps see in that step the actual birth of harmony.

Jubilemus omnes [10] is one of several sequela melodies furnishing particularly apt illustrations.

We shall return to some of these theories, in which speculation plays a

[5] YasT, Chap. VIII; YasQ. [6] GasM, 572. [7] MaH, 69. [8] In HornI, 311f.
[9] HughA, 13f. The same theory is put forward as a "guess" in HughH. [10] HughA, 99.

prominent part, but all of which are of interest.[11] But let us first consider our actual documentary evidence, which deals with organum as an existing thing and not with its genesis, and which consists of music itself, passages in the treatises of the musical theorists, and passages in writings not primarily on music but in which music receives incidental mention.

There are some early medieval passages that may refer to simultaneous singing of different sounds but that are obscure. St. Augustine and Boethius appear to have grasped the concept of harmonic consonance, Cassiodorus and Martianus Capella are less definite, Isidore of Seville is unclear, but all these writers have left passages that may possibly refer to part-music.[12] A tract, *Musica Theoretica*,[13] attributed to the Venerable Bede (*c.* 672–735) but of disputed authenticity, contains passages explaining how to obtain simultaneous consonances on the monochord. Bishop Aldhelm (640–709), whose writings included Anglo-Saxon poems set to his own music—works still popular in the time of King Alfred, but not now extant—is the earliest medieval writer known distinctly to refer to part-song.[14] An account attributed to the Monk of Angoulême relates that the *cantores* brought from Rome by Charlemagne in 787 instructed their Frankish colleagues in *arte organandi,* but the tale seems to be a late insertion.[15] Johannes Scotus (Erigena) (*c.* 815–*c.* 877), the Irish philosopher and theologian, a retainer of Charlemagne's grandson Charles the Bald, in his chief work, *De Divisione Naturae*,[16] draws analogies between musical and cosmic harmony, referring in the process to music in parts but not giving a technical description of it.

Ambiguous passages that may refer to either melodic or harmonic intervals occur in the *Musica Disciplina* of Aurelian of Réome [17] and in the *Musica* of Rémy of Auxerre,[18] both dating from the 9th century. Regino of Prüm, in his *De Harmonica Institutione,* is perhaps the first to use the term organum, for more-than-one-line music.[19] He defines consonance as "fall-

---

[11] We wonder whether any adherents of the Schenker doctrine would be inclined to regard "symphonious" music as an *Auskomponierung* of the dyad, as they regard polyphony an *Auskomponierung* of the triad. (We are aware that Salzer does not do so.)

[12] See discussion in HandZ, 326. See also MaH, 53f (but bearing HandZ, 327, in mind with respect to St. Isidore) and LudG, 159. P. Wagner believed that, in a passage in the first *Ordo Romanus* (7th century, the oldest surviving Book of Ceremonies for the papal services), mentioning singers called *paraphonistae,* he had found an early reference to part-music (WagP, WagU). This view was forcefully attacked in GasPP and is not generally accepted.

[13] The tract is printed in MigneL CX. See especially cols. 911–20. (This is not part of the material printed by Migne under the name of the Venerable Bede, but actually by pseudo-Aristotle [= Lambert], a theorist to whom we shall return in Chap. 10.) For discussion, see SchlesG, 198.

[14] See HandZ, 322–4; HandE (1932), 513; Handschin in Acta, VII (1935), 160.

[15] See HandL, 180.

[16] Printed in MigneL, CXXII, 638. (There is no inconsistency between "Scotus" and "Erigena," since Ireland was known as *Scotia major.*) The references to music are fully discussed in HandM. They include material on the Music of the Spheres, discussed by other medieval writers also and referred to *supra* on p. 58f. See on the subject, HandB. For an interpretation claiming that Erigena was not referring to part-music in the passages usually thought to touch upon it, see FarmH, 348.

[17] GerS I, 35.   [18] GerS I, 64.   [19] See GerS I, 234.

ing upon the ear pleasantly and uniformly" and dissonance as "coming harshly to the ear." [20] Hucbald, in his *De Harmonica Institutione,* is a little more definite: [21]

Consonance is the judicious and harmonious mixture of two tones, which exists only if two tones, produced from different sources, meet in one joint sound, as happens when a boy's voice and a man's voice sing the same thing, or in that which they commonly call Organum.

The *Musica Enchiriadis* [22] affords us the first account we have that is sufficiently detailed to give us an idea of what organum was. More than one type of organum is described in it.

Let us imagine a group of voices (or instruments, or both) rendering a Gregorian melody, not in the beautifully flowing manner we believe within the correct tradition of plainsong style, but slowly and deliberately, as though the executants wished to make sure that another group, not performing in unison with them, would be prevented from going astray. (The author of the *Musica Enchiriadis* specifically recommends a slow tempo as suitable for organum.) Let us imagine the second group duplicating the church melody a fifth below throughout. The result would be the strict type of simple organum at the fifth or *diapente.*[23] The group performing the plainsong would have the *vox principalis;* the other group, the *vox organalis.* If, in addition, the *vox principalis* were doubled at the octave below and the *vox organalis* at the octave above, we would have strict composite organum at the fifth. The strict type of simple and composite organum at the fourth or *diatessaron* would result from substituting the interval of the fourth for that of the fifth. In each kind of composite organum there would be four lines, but they would hardly be able to qualify as genuine "parts": melodic independence would be rendered impossible by the paralleling of the plainsong.

EXAMPLE 66. Composite Organum at the Fifth—*Musica Enchiriadis.*

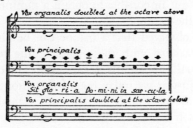

"May the glory of the Lord endure for ever." (*Psalm CIII [CIV], 31*)

[20] GerS I, 237.   [21] GerS I, 107.
[22] See Chap. 5, Sec. 1, footnote 49 for information concerning a translation, variants, etc.
[23] "Strict" because unvaryingly parallel; "simple" because employing only one parallel line.

EXAMPLE 67. Simple Organum at the Fourth—*Musica Enchiriadis.*

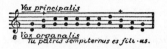

"Thou art the everlasting Son of the Father." (From the *Te Deum.*)

In Example 67, at each place marked +, an augmented fourth, or tritone, occurs as a harmonic interval. The author of the *Musica Enchiriadis* says of this example that "the voices will be perceived as sounding agreeably together." But he is inconsistent: later, he describes the symphony of diatessaron as often quite unsuitable for diaphony (= organum; the terms are interchangeable) without alteration, because of possible occurrences of the tritone. He makes no mention of diminished fifths, which are also dissonant: his gamut was so constructed that such fifths could not occur in strict organum. This gamut consisted *entirely*—and, for the West, abnormally— of disjunct tetrachords, each tetrachord consisting of TST, thus:

EXAMPLE 68.

The structure of this gamut evoked the criticism of Hermannus Contractus [24] and Wilhelm of Hirsau,[25] who regarded the author of the *Musica Enchiriadis* as in error. Their view is shared by some modern writers.[26] It is entirely possible, however, to believe with Otto Gombosi that the gamut was taken over from Byzantium (*cf.* p. 86); it may have been borrowed with the deliberate purpose of facilitating the author's exposition of organum.[27] It will be observed that the three augmented octaves, B-flat to b, F to f-sharp, and c to č-sharp, make it impossible to obtain a diminished fifth by combining any two tones in the gamut.[28]

But it will also be observed that a tritone can be obtained by combining the third of one tetrachord with the second of the tetrachord above. The author of the "Manual" apparently regarded the tritone as arising out of such a combination, just as we today regard the tritone as arising, in major, from a conjunction of the fourth and seventh scale-degrees. He therefore gives this as the reason why, in organum at the fourth, the *vox organalis* should never pass below the fourth sound of the lower tetrachord. When the *vox principalis* begins in such a way that the *vox organalis* cannot ac-

[24] EllinM, 56f.   [25] GerS II, 168f; or, with German translation, MülW, 43ff.
[26] E. g. Sowa in SowaT.   [27] *Cf.* JacC, 319ff.   [28] *Cf.* FoxT, 187.

company at the fourth without passing below the fourth degree of the lower tetrachord, the *vox organalis* has to begin in unison with the *vox principalis* and, unless the interval of a fourth is immediately thereafter reached, remain stationary until it is possible to parallel the *vox principalis* at that interval. Similarly, the *vox organalis* has to close in unison with the *vox principalis* if the ending does not admit of a duplication at the fourth. Thus we find that intervals other than the "symphonies" were occasionally sanctioned by theorists (although these intervals were not recognized as consonances) and that the author of the "Manual" supplemented parallel motion, for the sake of avoiding the tritone, by oblique motion; very occasionally, in quitting a unison at the beginning or approaching one at the end (or just before the end, in which event there are consecutive unisons), he used contrary motion also, for the same purpose. A free organum, pregnant with great possibilities, resulted; or perhaps we should say that a free organum—even freer than this—was probably already in existence and was thus, with a little twisting and turning, accounted for in theoretical writing (*cf.* p. 259).

EXAMPLE 69. Free Organum—*Musica Enchiriadis.*

"King of heaven, Lord of the wave-sounding sea."

(From a sequence, printed complete in HandU I, 19f, with the *Musica Enchiriadis* organal part.)

Irrespective of the pronouncement in the "Manual," it should not necessarily be inferred that, chronologically, strict organum, as a recognized and systematized phenomenon, actually came first and free organum later: in fact, we shall presently find it likely that, as given *conscious* application, the concept organum was linked primarily with the departing from and returning to a unison rather than with a mere bald progression of fifths or fourths.[29] Nor, to return to the point made by Belaiev, should it be inferred, because the examples just given have sacred texts, that organum must have begun in the Church. The author of the *Musica Enchiriadis,* in fact, seems to apologize slightly for its presence there when, at the end of his treatise, he says he has just discussed "a kind of surface (*superficies*) of musical science intended for the decoration of the ecclesiastical chants." [30] To quote Handschin: [31]

One might say that he wished to appease the scruples of those who found that organum was not suitable for the church (and why did they find the thing un-

[29] On this important subject, see RieG, 22.   [30] GerS I, 171.
[31] HandL, 181. See also HornI, 311.

suitable: perhaps because it reminded them of the secular music in which organum had surely long been practised?).

"Free" organum was itself most probably nothing but a crystallization of the same kind of procedure as had produced ancient heterophony. It may even have been a continuation of this heterophony.[32] Monody and polyphony had very likely developed side by side in popular practice, and, whatever the date of the *Musica Enchiriadis,* the "symphonious" music it treats may have existed long before the tract was written.

Marius Schneider[33] believes, indeed, that organum, far from being an embryonic stage of "symphonious" music, is in reality a culminating point in its development. This belief is based on a study of the music of primitive peoples in Africa, Oceania, Asia, and South America. On the basis of phonograph recordings Schneider divides primitive vocal music into four spheres of culture (the division is perhaps debatable), according to the musical idiosyncrasies of the various races and the complexity of their polyphony, ranging from the most primitive sphere comprising music of southern Asiatic and South American tribes to the comparatively highly developed sphere represented by the music of certain African tribes. He finds that the fourth sphere contains "symphonious" forms very similar to those of the early Middle Ages. There is no question here of African music influencing medieval composers; it is rather that the development of polyphony seems spontaneously to have followed very similar paths in all parts of the world. When, in the most primitive culture, two singers chant the same melody, each voices it as he conceives it and variations in the melodic line often result. Consequently, when the melody is sung by two singers simultaneously vertical intervals arise where the two versions differ—that is, we have heterophony. These intervals are accidental, and in this culture their intonation is vague. In primitive music of the next stage of development, however, such intervals become deliberately achieved and clearly defined, and the two melodic lines acquire a definite relationship to each other: one becomes the principal voice and the other an accompaniment.

What is the nature of the intervals? They are determined by the melodic structure peculiar to the tribe or race or culture. Broadly speaking, all the primitive music based on a definite tonality-system displays as its most important structure-determining interval either the fourth or the fifth. Since the pentatonic scale, which we may indicate by the symbols C D F G a c (there are, of course, other forms also, and Schneider discusses them), is fundamental in all such music, the interval C–F (or its equivalent) governs

[32] *Cf.* HandR, 9.   [33] In SchneiderG.

the melodic structure in some cultures (generally the more primitive) and the interval F–c (or its equivalent) is predominant in others. And when a melody is sung simultaneously by two performers in a more primitive culture, the variation-technique that governs the subordinate voice tends to supplant important tones of the main melody with others a fourth above, while in a more advanced culture important tones of the subordinate voice will be a fifth above corresponding tones of the principal voice. The third as a structure-determining interval appears only in highly developed primitive music.

All this, says Schneider, is analogous to what occurs in medieval European music. He believes that different spheres of culture may be discerned in Western Europe; and, like Yasser, he considers the pentatonic series basic in them. The melodies, and consequently the symphonious music, of the Franco-Italian sphere are, says Schneider, characterized by the predominance of the fourth, the music of the early English and Northern French sphere by the predominance of the fifth and third, and the peculiarities of both spheres are taken over and further developed by the St. Martial school in the 12th century (cf. p. 266). That the harmonic principles governing early medieval music must have been derived, not from Gregorian Chant but from the tonal structure of the indigenous folk-melody (cf. Belaiev's theory), concerning which we can only speculate, is shown, says Schneider, by the fact that early theorists found it necessary to distinguish between liturgical melodies that could fittingly be used as the basis of a polyphonic setting and those that could not. (Cf., for example, Guido d'Arezzo in GerS II, 21; AmelM, 43. This assertion, which implies that the liturgical melodies regarded as unsuitable were diatonic, would, if well founded, limit the validity of Yasser's theory concerning the pentatonic nature of the Chant.) Schneider claims that the structural principles outlined above are valid not only in what is *commonly* meant by organum (parallel movement of two voices at the fourth or fifth), of which actually very little appears in the MSS that have come down to us, but also in the other polyphonic forms and materials, such as canon, drone, discant, and contrary motion. In connection with parallel organum, it is of some interest to observe that in Volume I, p. 33, Schneider accounts for an example of it among a primitive people in much the same way as Machabey accounts for it among Europeans (cf. p. 250).[34]

The impulse towards polyphony seems to come from *at least* two sources: the desire on the part of people with different ranges to sing at

---

[34] In Vol. I, p. 22, Schneider makes a statement that lends some support to the Hughes theory. It should be added that Guido Adler, in several contributions, by many years anticipated some of the more important theories later developed in different ways by younger men.

comfortable pitch-levels, and the varying of a melodic line by people intending to sing it simultaneously (heterophony). May we not, then, be wrong in regarding parallel and free organum as two phases of the same thing? It is altogether likely that parallel organum was an outgrowth of the first source just mentioned and free organum of the second. If so, there is certainly nothing far-fetched in the belief that early medieval organum, as a *consciously* applied device, was viewed essentially as the departing from and returning to a unison rather than as a mere bald progression of fifths or fourths (*cf.* p. 255): such a type of polyphony—bearing obvious signs of a heterophonic origin—would, with its occasional dissonances and departures from the main melody, be almost certain to force itself upon the attention of singers unconsciously applying it, before they would become aware of singing in more or less unrelievedly parallel progressions. The very incorporation of such progressions, deliberately used, in the free examples in the *Musica Enchiriadis* would tend to support the view that the treatise itself deals with a practice perfected after a long period of evolution. For it would seem that only thus could there have been time to recognize, besides heterophony, the unconscious singing in more or less parallel intervals; to systematize the method; to combine it with the other; and to develop a well-planned doctrine—a doctrine which in some respects (especially in connection with the tritone, as the inconsistency mentioned on p. 254 would tend to indicate) may very well represent theorists' rationalizations of existing phenomena rather than a historical account of their evolution.[35]

An instrument sometimes referred to as especially fitted for playing in strict organum was evolved from the monochord. It was called the *organistrum,* and is the subject of a brief tract, *Quomodo organistrum construatur* ("How to make an Organistrum"),[36] attributed by Gerbert to Odo of Cluny. The instrument had three strings. These could be set in simultaneous vibration by a revolving wheel placed beneath them and operated by a crank. It has been suggested, without adequate foundation, that the outer strings were tuned in octaves and the middle string a fifth or fourth below the higher string. With the introduction of the small portative organ, the organistrum lost its former vogue in the churches and monasteries, and, in a degenerated state, became popular with wandering minstrels and country folk. Thus debased, it was, in function as well as form, the ancestor of the hurdy-gurdy.[37]

[35] *Cf.* Riemann's statement that the *Musica Enchiriadis* "can be regarded as merely the final results of his [the author's] attempts to fit into a theoretic system the species of polyphonic music common to the time."

[36] GerS I, 303.

[37] In its early stages, the organistrum was large and was placed over both knees. It required one executant to turn the handle and another to manipulate small rods which appeared outside the case containing the strings. Bridges, which stopped the strings, were attached to these rods. See GalpO, 102; HayesM II, 228; SachsH, 162; SachsR, 119 (especially concerning the tuning of the strings).

In the next [38] important account we have of organum after the *Musica Enchiriadis*—an account contained in the *Micrologus* [39] of Guido d'Arezzo—the strict forms are apparently still esteemed but the free forms seem greatly preferred. Organum at the fourth is described; organum at the fifth is no longer allowed. The tetrachords implied are properly joined. The lower limit of the *organalis* in each tetrachord is now the third sound instead of the fourth. Avoidance of a tritone is no longer alleged as the reason for the lower limit fixed. The interval would, in fact, no longer exist at three of the points at which it occurred in the gamut of the *Musica Enchiriadis*. The continued appearance of a limit in spite of this is rather striking and subjects the explanation in the *Musica Enchiriadis* to suspicion. [40] No example employs more than three voices: a *principalis,* an *organalis* below it, and a doubling of the *organalis* an octave higher; but further doublings at the octave are possible. No interval larger than a fourth is permitted between the *principalis* and *organalis;* the minor second is prohibited in free organum. The *Micrologus* indicates that, whereas the *Musica Enchiriadis* and *Scholia* advocated the free style as a means of avoiding the tritone etc., Guido preferred it for its own sake. Although, on the whole, no great progress is shown, it is clear that the intervals used are no longer theoretically regarded as mere results of an almost mechanical application of a principle concerned with the combining of voices; they are treated as entities by themselves and their merits and demerits subjected to study.

The outstanding feature of Guido's section on organum is the considerable attention paid to the *occursus,* i. e. the "coming together" of the two voices in the cadence group, ending with a unison, in free simple-organum. The unison, as we have seen, appeared at the close in certain illustrations in the *Musica Enchiriadis* also. Contrary motion appeared in certain illustrations there too. But, while Guido does not especially recommend contrary motion, his preoccupation with the *occursus* perhaps indicates that the characteristics of contrary motion were being more clearly recognized than be-

[38] Unless we except a short work in the Cathedral Library of Cologne, which Hans Müller (in MülH, 79) believed earlier than the *Musica Enchiriadis,* but perhaps only because he did not place the latter as early as does HandL, 181.

[39] Printed, as previously stated, in GerS II, 2 and AmelM. Concerning translations etc., see Chap. 5, Sec. 1, footnote 53. For a summary, in English, of the section on organum, see OH I, 2. The musical examples as printed in AmelM are preferable to those in GerS II, which are not wholly correct. The 12th-c. Admont MS, now at the Eastman School in Rochester, reveals still other readings (*cf.* L. Ellinwood in *Bulletin of the American Musicological Society,* II [1937], 20 and the illustration in Plate IV of this book). The Library of Congress also has a MS including the *Micrologus;* for description, see the Librarian's *Report* for 1933, p. 93f.

[40] Could the limitation really have arisen as a rationalization of singers' starting in unison (since that would be easier than starting in fifths) and maintaining oblique motion until reaching a fifth? (*Cf.* HornI, 306.) Guido's tetrachord system and lower limits are discussed in further detail, with references, in OH I, 23ff. Wooldridge's statement that "the tetrachords implied in Guido's Diaphony . . . are conjunct" is probably subject to the qualification that there was a *diazeuxis* between G and a (rather than between a and b, as with the Greeks); *cf.* GerS II, 61.

fore.[41] It is of some interest to note that, where a unison was reached by contrary motion from a third, the third had to be major, not minor. Where it was reached by oblique motion from a second, the second likewise had to be a major interval and not the forbidden semitone. Also of interest are examples of the *occursus,* in which the *organalis* reaches and sustains its last note while the *principalis* sings a concluding group, i. e. we have instances in which one note of counter-melody is sung against more than one note of a chief melody. Another feature, new at least in theoretical writing: some of Guido's illustrations employ crossing of parts. These illustrations seem clearly to embody what had been found agreeable in actual practice.

The *Micrologus* treats of organum only briefly. How widespread and how popular it was in the Church in the first half of the 11th century, is a matter of question. The method is not described in the treatises of Guido's contemporaries, Berno of Reichenau and Hermannus Contractus. But it does receive attention from the famous Arabian philosopher and physician, Ibn Sīnā (= Avicenna, d. 1037).[42] In the same century, we are told by Vergilius Cordubensis, two teachers gave instruction at the University of Cordova in *musica (de ista arte quae dicitur organum)*, and he may be using the word *organum* in the sense in which we employ it here.[43] If so, it is at Cordova that we first hear of organum, as a consciously applied art, being taught publicly, our other early accounts of it apparently dealing only with instruction within the monastery.

Evidence of the planned and recurrent use of contrary motion in actual practice—surviving practical examples of organum seem not to antedate Guido (but *cf.* footnote 55)—is obviously important, since it indicates the development of a feeling leading away from mere heterophony and towards real polyphony. An English MS of the first half of the 11th century, one of the Winchester Tropers, contains more than 150 two-part organa, these being intended chiefly for responsorial chants of both the Mass and Office, for chants of the Ordinary, and for tropes and sequences. Winchester had been the scene of unusual musical activity as far back as about 950 (*cf.* p. 123). It can be observed in the Troper that contrary motion, though rare, appears in passages other than the *occursus.* The writing is essentially point against point. The MS is unfortunately in staffless neumes without clefs, but the

---

[41] OH I, 31, is misleading on this point when it implies that contrary motion is foreign to systems earlier than that described by Guido. Doubtless the intention is to indicate that, if contrary motion occurred, it was incidental, i. e. not an integral part of any organizing system, for there are instances of contrary motion in examples from the *Musica Enchiriadis* and *Scholia* printed in OH I itself. See pp. 14–6, 18–9. It is clear, however, that these instances are incidental, and that the contrary motion is not adopted for its own sake.

[42] A work that may have been written by Al-Kindi (d. 874) contains passages about organum also. Farmer has suggested a possible Arabian origin for the device (FarmH, 102, 327). But see SchlesG, 197 *contra.*

[43] FarmH, 106. There is some possibility, however, that the "Vergilius Cordubensis" document is a forgery.

neumes are "heighted." [44] It may also be observed—and this is important since, as we shall see, adoption of the principle was destined to have a vital effect upon the development of polyphonic structure—that the *vox organalis* is *above* the *principalis*. [45] Winchester later—perhaps before the end of the 12th century—became the place of origin of another organum repertoire, of which there is evidence in the form of a table of contents, preserved at the British Museum, in which a certain W. de Win[cestre] is named as a composer. The lost MS, itself apparently dating from *c.* 1300, contained also motets and conducti. [46]

The changes that were taking place in the treatment of organum were paving the way for a transition to measured music. How the transition was effected we do not fully know. But treatises and actual music of the period— the *Musica* of the so-called John Cotton (*cf.* p. 127) and the Winchester Troper among them—help us to follow some steps in the process.

The older organum as described by the theorists, even the free variety, used only one consonant interval for its parallel passages, e. g. it did not organize part of the time in fourths and part of the time in fifths. The organum described by "Cotton" [47] differs in that it mixes carefully, for the sake of variety, *all* the traditional consonances—the unison, octave, fourth and fifth. And—most important—the value of contrary motion becomes increasingly apparent in the process, although parallel motion is not forbidden. "Cotton" writes:

Diaphony . . . is practised in many ways; but the most easily comprehensible manner is when contrary motion be especially considered—in which the organizing part descends while the Cantus Firmus ascends, and vice-versa. If the Cantus closes in a deep position, the organizing voice should be above it and rise to the octave; but if the Cantus ends in a higher position, the organizing part must seek the octave below; and when the Cantus concludes in a middle position, the two parts should close in unison. A well-considered conduct of the Organum will therefore be the result of pains taken that the closes in the unison be alternated with those in octaves—the former having the preference. (GerS II, 264, as translated in PulE [1933], 893.)

In the organum described by "Cotton," crossing of parts is not only allowed, as in the *Micrologus,* but is considered desirable. Two or even three notes in the *vox organalis* are permitted against one note of plainsong. (Guido, as we have seen, sanctioned the reverse, i. e. more than one note

---

[44] See the facsimiles in back of FrereW and the explanation on p. xxxviii thereof. HandW is likewise an important study of this MS (and of another).

[45] It is not implied, of course, that adoption of the principle was made for the first time in the Winchester pieces. They doubtless represent a style current at the time of their composition.

[46] See LudK, 107; LudR, 267; also p. 94f of the study described on p. 396 *infra,* footnote 49[a].

[47] GerS II, 263f. The theorist's example, missing in GerS, is printed, in different forms after different MSS, in HandO, 57 (Ex. 2) and KornT, 21. (See discussion in HandO, 53.)

in the *principalis* against one note in the *organalis*.) A means of measuring time-values, so that the parts may be kept together, becomes more and more needed.

"Cotton" devotes only one of his twenty-three chapters to organum and concludes that chapter as though he were glad to be through with it. If, as it seems, he and Guido preferred plainsong, their judgment was probably not bad: even in its more advanced state, the new-fangled method of the "moderns" still lacked the grace and refinement of the ecclesiastical Chant. But that method was pregnant with great possibilities. Important musical developments are not necessarily made through but towards beauty.

If "Cotton" was indifferent to organum, the anonymous author of *Ad Organum Faciendum*,[48] apparently a Frenchman, is full of enthusiasm. His entire treatise is devoted to the subject. In his examples—which are historically interesting—the *vox principalis* is, as in the Winchester pieces, *below* the *vox organalis*. The author expounds five modes—not melodic or rhythmic modes, but organum modes. These deal with methods of combining two parts under circumstances that seem somewhat arbitrarily selected. But the treatise sets forth two points that are of considerable interest. The first, as we shall see, is important in the history of the theory of harmony: b is flattened in the musical examples to avoid the augmented fourth as a harmonic interval; the author abandons the old method of avoiding the interval by keeping the lower voice stationary. The second point is significant in the history of the theory of counterpoint: several musical examples employ the *same* melody in each *principalis* but have a different melody in each *organalis*—a result that is made possible by the interchange of the consonances.

A passage in a little 12th-century tract at Montpellier [49] is capable of being interpreted as indicating that the *vox organalis* may be added either above or below the *vox principalis,* but does not entirely clinch the matter.

That the gains that had been made in deliberate practice were held beyond the first half of the 12th century is indicated not only by some actual compositions but by at least one more treatise, attributed to Guy, abbot of Charlieu.[50] This gives twenty-one clear rules for the leading of the organal voice in almost any circumstances likely to arise at the time. For example, if the two parts were at the octave and the lower one rose a fourth, the organal voice could descend a fifth or an octave, etc. etc. Another writing, the anonymous *Quiconques veut deschanter*,[51] the earliest known musical tract in

---

[48] Printed in CouH, 229, with French translation. For a commentary, see OH I, 37. See also SteinZ, 224, 231.

[49] Printed in HandO.

[50] Not of Châlis. See HandZ, 331. The treatise is printed, with a French translation, in CouH, 225. For summary, see OH I, 47.

[51] Printed in CouH, 245 (with a translation into modern French), RieG, 98 (with a German translation); and GéroM, 424. For a summary see OH I, 46.

French, although preserved in a 13th-century MS may also record 12th-century doctrine.[52] Here the fourth is omitted from the list of available concords, and definite rules are given for the treatment of the *organalis,* which is referred to as the discant.

But, as "John Cotton" had said, *"Diverse diversi utuntur":* musicians, it would seem, did not bind themselves too strictly to an observance of the rules. The surviving French examples of actual composition—much less numerous than those from Winchester, but apparently in a similar style—bear out this supposition. Perhaps the rules were more strictly observed in improvising from the book *(cantus supra librum)*—that is, in improvising counter-melodies against a plainsong melody notated in a large choir-book placed within sight of the singers—than they were in the compositions actually written down.[53]

There are two codices of the 9th or 10th century at Chartres, one containing five [54] and the other eight two-part Alleluias, all added to the MSS in the 11th century.[55] Of these, only five, from the second MS, are in staff-notation. Ludwig prints one of them (in LudG, 175). On the whole it carries out the ideals of the theorists concerning contrary motion and the choice of consonances (including the fourth), but it also contains a liberal sprinkling of freely used dissonances (including the third and sixth): a systematized use of dissonance was, as we shall find in other examples, still to be achieved.

A MS originating from Fleury, but now at the Vatican, contains, in incomplete state, nine two-part responds on St. Peter—but they are in staffless neumes. Another MS at the Vatican, from either Fleury or Tours, contains three more pieces.[56] The MS containing *Ad Organum Faciendum* (now at Milan, but deriving from Laon) preserves, besides the examples in the treatise itself, three additional *organa.*[57] The second of these pieces supplies its chief melody with apparently alternative organal parts, there being as many as three for more than half the piece. A 10th-century Cornish MS, now at Oxford, contains a two-part organum added to the MS in the 12th century; we shall return to this piece on p. 392. A two-part trope of the *Benedicamus Domino (cf.* p. 192) exists in a MS at Lucca, where the MS probably originated in the first half of the 12th century. The small repertoire of early organa includes also a few other items, for a description of which the reader is referred to HandL and LudK.

[52] *Cf.* CouH, 244 (followed in RieG and OH I).

[53] For a full discussion of the use of organum in improvisation, see FerandM, Chap. IV.

[54] Facsimiles of three are printed in PM I, pl. xxiii; comments appear on p. 151.

[55] It is possible that a little antiphon contained in a MS at Einsiedeln (reproduced in PM IV, 416) is still earlier, constituting a 10th-century example of the application of organum. (See LudG, 164, 166.) If so, it would be the oldest example surviving from a practical source (that is, from a source not a theorist's treatise). But it is by no means certain that the 2 melodies are not independent. (See HandL, 182.)

[56] See BannM, nos. 228, 230.

[57] Transcribed into modern notation in CouH, 226ff; one in OH I, 45.

Most of the early examples of organum, then, come from France and England. There is but little such material from Italy, which nevertheless can still boast of having been the native land of Guido (unless Dom Morin's claim that he was French should some day prove correct). While no early examples survive from Germany, there are indications that organum was applied there also. In a Latin fable, *Ysengrimus,* written in the 12th century by a German poet, the wild sow, Salavra, describes to the wolf, Ysengrimus, how she and other sows and boars sing in parallel organum.[58] The scarcity of documents, regardless of country, may well be due to the simplicity of organum, which obviously lent itself to improvisation against a given melody, whether secular or ecclesiastical.

In the Church, as the author of the *Musica Enchiriadis* stated, it was designed to decorate the Chant. Its function, therefore, was much like that of troping.

We can easily realize the connexion which exists between the art of tropes and early polyphony, the latter having been cultivated generally at the same centres as the former: this is because polyphony, or at least liturgical polyphony, was considered, like tropes, as an embellishment of the Gregorian repertory; polyphony did by superposition what the tropes did by interposition; and in the case of a polyphonic trope superposition was added to interposition.[59]

There are, in fact, several examples extant of organum applied to sequences, a kind of trope, as we have seen. Example 69, as indicated, is from one of them. Sequences, with their syllabic style, plainly supplied melodies of a type against which it was easier to set another voice, point against point or only slightly embellished, than against any other kind. The application of organum, however, was by no means restricted to the sequence. Among the several kinds of chant to which it was joined is the Alleluia. Here the documents show three different methods of adding it. In one of the Chartres MSS it is applied only to the sections customarily assigned to soloists and not to those reserved to the choir—that is, it is not added to the *cauda* and the end of the verse.[60] These were apparently sung by the choir as unadorned plainsong while the other sections were sung by soloists as part-music. In the other Chartres MS the *cauda* is decorated by an organal part but the end of the verse is not. Possibly the MS is associated with an older practice in which all the music to the word "Alleluia," *including* the *cauda,* was first sung

---

[58] For a synopsis of the passage in question, and further concerning early organum among the Germans, see HandR, 10–19.   [59] HandW, 36.

[60] The "classic" manner of performance is as follows: The soloist sings the word *Alleluia* up to the melisma (or *cauda* or *jubilus*) added to the last syllable. (The point at which the *cauda* begins is marked by an asterisk in modern chant books.) The choir repeats what the soloist has sung and adds the melisma. The soloist sings the verse up to the point marked by an asterisk in modern chant books, and the choir continues it from there on. After its conclusion the soloist sings the portion of the *Alleluia* he had sung at the beginning and the choir, without repeating this as at first, continues with the melisma, with which the performance ends.

through by the soloists and then repeated by the choir in unison. In the Alleluias in the Winchester Troper, organum is applied without distinction to all sections of the Chant. Perhaps this refers back to a still older practice. The general plan of the first of the three methods described was destined to survive (*cf.* p. 301). Alternation in responsorial chant, between a choir and soloists, the latter singing in composite organum at the fifth, is specifically mentioned in a 12th-century poem.[61]

The small repertoire we have mentioned represents attempts possibly not yet carried to a high enough degree of perfection at any one center to exert a widespread influence such as was exercised later by the organa of the Parisian Notre Dame school (Chapter 11). The repertoire consists of pieces which, in the main, do not depart from a point-against-point technique. The earliest known actual example in which more than two notes in an added part are juxtaposed against one note in the main melody occurs in an 11th-century MS [62] (*cf.* p. 261). Although the author of the *Musica Enchiriadis* had recommended a slow tempo for organum, it was possible, if desired, to preserve fairly intact the original general pace of whatever Gregorian melody was used as a *cantus firmus*. When crossing of parts occurred, however, that may have modified the rhythm (as distinguished from mere tempo): when the highest and lowest points of a melodic line lost their original status as extreme points, they may have lost with it the rhythmic influence they were capable of exerting when uncrossed. But otherwise it was at any rate possible to retain most of the original flow—until the practice of writing more than one note in one part against one note in another became an object of special attention. We have observed the cropping up of this practice in the *Micrologus*. In the 12th century, or perhaps earlier, the French—destined to be pioneers throughout the Middle Ages in evolving new musical structures—became strongly attracted by the possibilities of creating counter-melodies richer in their tonal content than the borrowed melodies, and, as a consequence, more individual rhythmically. A very important result was that the borrowed melodies became more and more long-drawn-out as the counter-melodies became increasingly elaborate. One of the most significant structural devices in all medieval music was in process of formation: the *tenor,* every note of which, if need be, could in organum support above it a whole group of notes in a second part, or *duplum.* In other words, each note of borrowed melody could be made to function as a sort of organ-point. It is from the characteristic "holding" of its notes that the *tenor* received its name (Latin *tenere* = to hold).[63] We may perhaps see here the eventual transfer, to "artistic" uses, of the drone, common in folk-music.

The earliest known applications in goodly number of what may be called

---

[61] For further details, see HandL, 14f, 17ff; HandR, 16ff.   [62] See HandL, 15.
[63] The term *tenor*, of course, did not yet mean "high male voice."

the sustained-tone style are contained in four early 12th-century MSS originating from the monastery of St. Martial in Limoges. These MSS contain works of a simpler type also. Thus, two main types may be said to be represented: that bequeathed by the more "primitive" period, in which the writing was chiefly note-against-note, and that in which the sustained-tone style appeared. The latter may be subdivided, since this style was applied in some examples at the cadence only while in others it was admitted in the course of the piece. The first type is illustrated by the fairly well-known *Mira lege, miro modo.*[64] This has as its subject a metrical song rather than an ecclesiastical melody, and falls rhythmically into well-defined strains. The piece shows ten instances of two notes against one, but nothing more elaborate. Though the composition is therefore fairly conservative in form and not characteristic of the St. Martial school, it is worthy of observation,[64a] as Wooldridge has pointed out, that it contains as many as 17 thirds as against 22 fifths and only 9 fourths (besides a few seconds and sixths). The really distinctive contents of the MSS are the remarkable organa in sustained-tone style described by Ludwig [65] (among other writers), who prints three examples. Here is one, the opening of a troped *Benedicamus Domino:*

EXAMPLE 70. *Benedicamus Domino*—Trope with Organum—St. Martial
School (from LudG, 179).

Since the original is not in mensural notation, Ludwig has interpreted the rhythm as "free," the upper part resembling plainsong. When the word *Domino* follows in the tenor, the duplum sings to the trope-text, *Humane prolis,* i. e. the piece has two simultaneously sung texts, and thus possesses the chief feature of the early motet (see p. 311). Only one other piece in the MSS can qualify as a motet by this standard. But the melismatic style displayed

---

[64] Facsimile in CouH, pl. 23. Transcriptions into modern notation in CouH, xxi (in back); OH I, 53.   [64a] That is, if the transcription is correct; owing to the uncertain nature of the original notation, it is in part necessarily hypothetical.   [65] LudG, 177.

in the upper voice is the outstanding feature of the dupla of the contents as a whole, as is the necessarily concurrent drawing out of the tenor.

One example printed by Ludwig shows marked artistic judgment in the contrasting of styles. The first two verses of its text are set to a repeated musical section, the opening of which is characterized by several notes of duplum against one of tenor, while the latter portion consists mostly of elaborate simultaneous melismas in both voices; the third verse and most of the fourth are in point-against-point style, the conclusion again consisting of melismas in both voices. This close is characterized by much contrary motion and contains a one-part cadenza that has the compass of a ninth and was apparently designed to display vocal virtuosity.[66]

Although, with these pieces as with those of the 11th century, definite evidence of a wide diffusion of influence is lacking, it seems altogether likely that there was a connection between the St. Martial organa and the famous Parisian contrapuntal works of the latter part of the 12th century. In the St. Martial pieces, theorists' rules were not allowed to interfere with the free flow of the melodic lines, a flow often attended by sharp clashes. These were apparently accepted without scruple: they were doubtless regarded as passing and as preparations for the consonances at the cadences. A preference is shown for such forms as allow for the responsorial activity of soloists and chorus (forms that we have already seen among those preferred in 11th-century organa), and the dupla, which may have been for soloists, show a strong artistic feeling for the requirements of solo singing. The flow of the melismas that embellish these dupla is far removed from the angularity that seems sometimes unavoidable in note-against-note writing. The model for the style of the melismas must have been found in the solo melodies of Gregorian Chant.[67]

The northwest corner of Spain is the only part of the country that never fell to the Moors. It was there that the reconquest for Christendom was launched; Christian fervor there was intense. A legend had arisen claiming that St. James the Apostle, after martyrdom in Palestine, had been brought to Compostela for burial, and, when bones reputed to be his were discovered, the place—as Santiago de Compostela—became an object of pilgrimage comparable to Canterbury. After the marriage of the heroic Alfonso VI of Castile (1065-1109) to Constance of Burgundy, French pilgrims became especially numerous. The *Cantigas* of Alfonso X include a piece describing German pilgrims on the road to the shrine. The remarkable Codex Calixtinus of Santiago, already mentioned on p. 202, dating from about 1140, shows

---

[66] For another St. Martial organum, printed complete, see GasG, 157, and for still another, printed as it appears in two different MSS, see HandUU, which contains much information concerning the St. Martial music.

[67] This paragraph is a summary of a paragraph in LudG, 180.

strong evidence of French origin: among other things, French names appear in it as those of composers, some names belonging to princes of the Church to whom pieces were ascribed probably without foundation. The contents are mostly monodic, but include twenty organa, one of them apparently the oldest three-part composition known.[68] This is ascribed, interestingly enough in view of the importance of the musicians of Notre Dame de Paris shortly thereafter, to a certain Magister Albertus, a Parisian. The piece is a *Benedicamus Domino* trope, *Congaudeant catholici,* in which the two lower voices sing in organum of the kind described by "John Cotton" while the top pàrt sings a flowing melody in the melismatic style characteristic of the St. Martial school. The notation is non-mensural: the time-values in the following are "restorations" by Ludwig.[69]

EXAMPLE 71. *Congaudeant catholici*—A 3-part *Benedicamus Domino*
Trope—From Santiago de Compostela (from LudG, 182).

"Let Catholics be glad together, the heavenly citizens rejoice this day."
(For complete text, see *Analecta hymnica*, XVII, 208, or WagJ.)

The St. Martial MSS show that the need, already mentioned, for a means of measuring time-values was becoming increasingly pressing.

Eventually the name "discant" came to be associated with measured music as distinguished from unmeasured. But it is clear that the name was not coined especially to designate work written under the new system.[70] *Discantus* is merely Latin for διαφωνία (diaphony = organum),[71] and it seems that the earliest use of the new term and the actual adoption of measured music were independent of one another. But chronologically the new term does appear during the period of transition: as we have seen, it is employed in the *Qui-*

---

[68] That is, if one disregards two-part organa as potentially three-part pieces through the use of doubling at the octave in the manner described by the theorists. Transcriptions of all 20 pieces may be found in WagJ, 112–25. WagJ, 166, departs from the usual view that this is a three-part piece, holding that the two upper parts are intended as alternatives.

[69] A transcription by Handschin may be found in HandZ, 336, and a facsimile in H. Anglès, *El Còdex musical de Las Huelgas* I, 65.   [70] See HandZ, 333ff.   [71] See OH I, 46; SteinZ.

conques veut deschanter, which may belong to this period. It is used in a pre-mensural sense also in the anonymous 12th-century *Tractatus de Musica,* printed by La Fage.[72] Here "discant" indicates note-against-note writing, while "organum" designates a rhythmically decorated counterpoint. This distinction was to take on considerable importance, but it is by no means to be assumed that it was at once generally made. The *Tractatus* gives detailed information concerning the sustained-tone style, and internal evidence points to the possibility that it was written by a member of the St. Martial group. (A portion of another treatise, looking upon the upper part as richer in organum than in discant, and preferring individual fourths to parallel progressions of them, as does the St. Martial style, is printed in SchneiderG II, 106. Part of still another treatise belonging to the same stage of development is printed in FiO.)

To recapitulate: in the earliest tracts on "part"-music, "organum" stood for note-against-note writing; "Cotton" used it for the same thing, but also for part-writing containing rhythmical embellishments; the *Tractatus de Musica* used "discant" for the simpler style and "organum" for the more elaborate. It would seem that, as long as the added part pitted a single note, or only a little more, against each note of the borrowed melody, the old nomenclature sufficed for what were potentially two different styles. But, as the added part became increasingly elaborate, a need was felt for a distinguishing terminology. This need, however, was not immediately met by a nomenclature receiving general acceptance. It is important, therefore, not to have too definitely preconceived an idea of the meaning of *"discantus"* when approaching a 12th-century treatise.[73]

The period of transition, lacking as it was in symbols denoting time-values, called upon the intelligence to determine—with the aid of certain indications less satisfactory than such symbols would have been—which notes were to be regarded as long and which as short, and how counter-melodies were to be fitted to one another. Thus, writing parts out in score, one above the other, helped, through vertical alignment, to show how the voices were meant to combine. The possibility of forming consonances at particular points also helped to show this. Long and short values were indicated by the word-accents; possible exceptions were apparently regulated by oral instructions from the master. A valuable 13th-century theorist who was probably an Englishman (usually referred to as either the Anonymus of the British Museum, because Dr. Pepusch's transcript of the original treatise—damaged by fire—lies there together with a half-burnt fragment of the original, or as Anonymus IV, because his treatise is the fourth anonymous one in CouS I) observed, looking backward while writing about the mensural theory of his own time:

[72] LafE, 355.　　[73] The whole question of terminology is treated in much detail in HandZ.

The notes they had in the old books were excessively ambiguous, because the simple materials were all equal, and they were occupied solely with the intellect saying: I understand this as a long note, I understand this as a short one. (CouS I, 344.)

Among pieces belonging to the period of transition are several already mentioned (e. g. the St. Martial organa). Yet another is the fairly well-known *Verbum bonum et suave,* beginning:

EXAMPLE 72. *Verbum bonum et suave*—A 2-part Sequence (from GennF, 128).

"We sound forth the good and sweet word, that *Ave.*" [74]

This early 12th-century piece is of interest on several counts. There are three strophes of music and six stanzas of text, each strophe serving for two successive stanzas, so that the *Verbum bonum* is yet another sequence in the form of part-music. The melody sung by the lower voice is to be found associated with two sequence texts of the contemporary Adam de St. Victor.[75] Its beginning is the same as that of another melody used by Adam for several additional sequences, including the *Laudes crucis attollamus* which, as we have noted in Chapter 6, was probably drawn upon for the melodic material of the *Lauda Sion.* This popular beginning appears in connection with still a few other of Adam's sequences.

In the 13th century, the developed organum style achieved great heights. (It will be discussed in Chapter 11.) Meanwhile, the parallel organum style did not die out, as is attested by the 13th-century French theorist, Elias Salomon.[76] In Germany, there is evidence of its survival as late as from the 14th to the 16th centuries.[77] Striking use of it has been found among the Icelanders in our own times,[78] as is shown by this *Tvisöngur* ("two-part song") [79] of modern student-life:

[74] The above transcription follows a MS at Limoges. A simpler version exists at Douai and is transcribed in OH I, 80 and CouH, xxii (at back). CouH gives a facsimile of the Douai original on plates xxiv, xxv.

[75] MissetP, 243, 294.

[76] GerS III, 59. See the discussion of the passage in question in FerandH.

[77] For a selection of 14th–15th-century examples from three MSS, see WolfQ. See FeldQ for a 16th-century example.

[78] See HammS, HornI, and ThorI.

[79] *Tvisöngvar,* plural.

EXAMPLE 73. Icelandic *Tvisöngur* (from ThorI, 790).

"My mother has said that I should buy ships and fair oars, and journey about with Vikings."

(Translated by Margaret Schlauch.)

It would be interesting to know whether the *Tvisöngur* represents a tradition continuous from the early Middle Ages (there is evidence possibly pointing to the singing of such music in 14th-century Iceland [80]) or is, as the 16th-century Italian *villanella* may have been, a recrudescence of an old practice.

Organizing in parallel intervals is not restricted, in European music history, to fourths and fifths. We shall later treat of organizing in thirds, and also in thirds and sixths simultaneously. There is even mention, by Gafori in the 15th century, of the use at Milan, at funeral services and on certain other mournful occasions, of organizing in seconds.[81]

[80] See HammS, 351.
[81] Such organizing is not described by Elias Salomon, however, as is claimed in RieG, 348, and elsewhere. See FerandH and BukE, 103.

Chapter 10: THE RISE OF MEASURED MUSIC AND THE DEVELOPMENT OF ITS NOTATION TO FRANCO OF COLOGNE

WE have seen that the part-compositions dealt with in Chapter 9 were notated in the same kinds of neumes as the ecclesiastical melodies, these neumes varying according to locality. The belief that where the text happened to be metrical it gave the rhythm (cf. p. 269), receives a measure of support from certain preponderantly syllabic compositions that have reached us not only in the old notation but also, apparently as a result of their popularity, in later copies (complete or partial) using a notation showing time-values, these values being just the ones that the meter of the text would call for.[1] That is, they are such as the meter would require if its musical equivalent were determined in the light of the rhythmic modes, mentioned in Chapter 7, to which we must now return. Thus, a trochaic text would have required the pattern ♩ ♪|♩ ♪ etc., which came to be the first rhythmic mode; an iambic text, the pattern ♪♩ |♪♩ etc.—the second mode; a dactylic text, the pattern ♩. ♪♩ |♩. ♪♩ etc.—the third mode. In their accounts of the modal system the theorists almost always include three more modes, even though the fourth mode— ♪♩ ♩. |♪♩ ♩. etc., the alleged equivalent of the anapest—hardly existed in practical music, and application of the fifth—all long values: ♩. | ♩. etc. supposedly representing the spondee—was usually restricted to the tenor of motets.[2] The sixth mode—all short values: ♪♪♪|♪♪♪ etc. equivalent to the tribrach—is the remaining one belonging to what may be called the nucleus of the modal system. Other modes, described by only an occasional theorist, need not concern us here.

It is interesting even if not surprising to observe, as the above-mentioned pieces with metrical texts would indicate, that at least part of the modal system was applied in practical use before there was any way of representing it in notation. As Aubry has said:[3] "The doctrine of mensuration took form little by little. It began to appear in the works of composers before it was codified by the theorists." A graphic means of measuring time-values, to be sure, prepared the way for forms whose development would have been im-

[1] For three examples illustrating this point, see WolfH I, 215–19. [2] Cf. MichalT, 14.
[3] AuM III, 115.

272

possible without it; but at first it presented merely a method of notation called into being by problems already existing among practical musicians. How was the rhythmical mode to be indicated in a part having *no* text? How was it to be indicated if the composer did not wish to set the text one note (or little more) to a syllable, but preferred to use, whether occasionally or frequently, flourishes like the melismas in plainsong?

The first answer offered, unfortunately, was not the simplest that might have been made. Musicians did not immediately evolve a set of note-symbols, each with a fixed—or, rather, a proportional—time-value, such as we have today. Instead they indicated the modes by certain *hints,* to which we shall return presently. The result is that, roughly speaking, the notation of part-music passed through three stages—"roughly speaking," since there were intermediate stages also. First, that in which the symbols did not indicate time-values at all; second, that in which the time-values were hinted at indirectly but not represented by corresponding symbols directly; third, that in which the time-values *were* indicated by corresponding symbols. Only the last stage may properly be said to have supplied a mensural notation. The second did produce mensuration in performance but not in writing, so that, in the discussion of this stage, the terms "long" and "breve" (short) will refer to sound-durations, not to the note-symbols called "long" and "breve" in the third stage.

The fact that the classic Greek and Latin meters, which the modal system professed to imitate, were based on quantity rather than stress, has already been referred to. A long syllable was theoretically equal to two shorts. Thus there was a *measuring* of extent in time (hence the term "meter") and the unit of measurement was the foot. Long before musicians contrived the modal system, Latin medieval poetry had—as has also been mentioned—veered from the quantitative system to the accentual. But it was obviously convenient for musicians to adopt, or at least profess to adopt, the classic method. What liberties they were prepared to take with this method, however, may be observed by examining the ostensible equivalents they furnished for the poetic dactyl and anapest. These poetic meters were binary, but the third and fourth rhythmic modes were perverted by the modal system and rendered ternary.

Why the systematized modes should ever have all been triple, has been a matter for occasional discussion. A retrospective passage [4] in Walter Odington's *De Speculatione Musicae* (*c.* 1300) has been cited as evidence that binary rhythm was recognized in the early days of their evolution. But the basis this passage affords for such an interpretation is by no means unequivocal. What Odington says is that *apud priores organistas* ("among the

[4] CouS I, 235.

earlier singers [or composers] of organa"—*cf.* p. 296) the long had two *tempora* ("times" or beats). Now, it has been claimed, with a good show of reason, that the conscious development of a system differentiating time-values would naturally begin with an alternation of longs and shorts. Thus the first mode in the modal system would be a good candidate for the rôle of chronologically first mode. (This does not imply that the numbers of the other modes, as given above, necessarily represent their chronological sequence.) The second mode, as has been observed, likewise alternates longs and shorts. In these modes we find the long occupying two beats against the one of the breve. And apparently all Odington was doing was to stress that among the old *organistae* the long always had two beats, since, as will presently appear, in his day—indeed, as soon as modes 3 to 5 came into being—it sometimes had three.[5] Odington was, of course, dealing with practice among "learned" ecclesiastical musicians; there is, as we have seen, some indication (*cf.* pp. 232, 247) that binary rhythm was used in the 13th century in circles less concerned with theory, and it is well to recall Anglès's claim (p. 210) that (lack of recognition on the part of theorists notwithstanding) both binary and ternary rhythms have been well known in all periods.

Whether the various steps necessary for the development of the system of rhythmic modes were first taken by Europeans or by Arabs is a question of some interest. Ribera has made a claim on behalf of the latter that perhaps deserves more respect than some of his other contributions, since he has offered evidence that the Arabs actually had a system strikingly similar to that of the Europeans and that it is of greater antiquity.[6]

Medieval writers, with their love of mysticism, explained that the triple rhythms were adopted in honor of the Holy Trinity—but the explanation seems to have been made after the event. A strictly musical explanation offered by some modern writers is that the measure was "actually a sixfold unit in practice." A group of 4 beats would be divisible by 2 only; a group of 6 beats by either 2 or 3. A measure of 6 beats in one voice would, therefore, "give an opportunity to the other voice of singing in 3 groups of 2, or 2 groups of 3, at choice. It is this feeling after duple rhythm in one voice with triple rhythm in another, and still more the desire (brought in from the plainsong world) of varying the rhythm frequently, that lies at the back of all the old dominance of the triple unit . . . in the medieval systems of notation and composition."[7] It would be pleasant to believe that medieval musicians had an attitude specifically artistic enough towards their calling to be possessed of such a feeling, and it is by no means impossible. But extraneous

---

[5] Further *contra* the view that Odington's testimony in itself weakens the case for the erstwhile privileged position of ternary rhythm, see KuhlM I, 133ff.

[6] See RibM, 79f; Chap. XVI. See also H. G. Farmer in the *Journal of the Royal Asiatic Society of Great Britain and Ireland* for 1925, p. 61ff.

[7] HughW, 14. Compare with this Wooldridge in OH I, 61ff.

considerations, such as affected medieval music in other connections, may very well have exerted their influence here too. Medieval speculation regarded the number 3 as a symbol of perfection long before the development of the modal system. Its imputed quality was recognized by the theorists also. In fact, when binary rhythm finally received their sanction alongside ternary, it was termed imperfect, the latter, as we shall see, being termed perfect. It is not impossible that a widespread notion, not specifically musical in origin, may have affected early attempts to measure music, though, of course, definitely musical forces would be bound to supersede it eventually.[8]

A few definitions: A note-group consisting of a single appearance of a modal pattern or of repetitions of one, if separated from other rhythmically similar groups by a rest, constituted an *ordo*. If, between the last complete repetition of the pattern within the *ordo* and the rest, there was a note having the initial time-value, the mode was considered perfect. If the initial value did not so recur, the mode was imperfect. If an *ordo* displayed a complete modal pattern once only, it represented the first *ordo* of the mode—"perfect" if the initial value returned between the end of the pattern and the symbol of rest, "imperfect" if it did not. (Thus the "perfection" and "imperfection" of *ordines* depended, like those of the modes, upon the nature of the termination.) If the modal pattern occurred twice, the *ordo* was the second; if it occurred three times, the *ordo* was the third, etc. The isorhythmic principle illustrated by reiterations of *ordines* was destined in time to produce structures of considerable complexity.

By the 12th or 13th century, as was pointed out in Chapter 5, neumes had crystallized in most of Southern and Western Europe into the square or quadratic form characteristic of modern neumes. It was from such plainsong symbols that musicians derived those they used in both the second and third stages of the notation of part-music mentioned above. Thus the virga, used for special purposes in the second stage (*cf.* pp. 279f), was taken over in the third stage to represent the long, and a sign which, whatever its origin, resembled the punctum, to represent the breve.[9] As already pointed out, the terms "long" and "breve" will be used in our discussion of the second stage (even if the eventually corresponding note-symbols were not yet endowed with the meaning they were to receive), since the *values* existed. The virga-like and punctum-like signs will likewise occasionally be referred to in the discussion of the second stage, but the reader must guard against thinking that they necessarily represent the values of a long and breve respectively, except through coincidence.

Today the symbol of the normal unit of time is the crotchet or semiminim (quarter-note). But the normal time-unit has been represented at different

[8] *Cf.* AbD, 179f.
[9] Despite its appearance, the breve was not necessarily derived from the punctum. See MichalM, 277–9.

periods by different symbols: in the 16th century, by the minim (half-note), in early mensural notation, and in the stage that led up to it, by the value of a breve. This, of course, does not necessarily mean that *tempi* were slower in the Middle Ages and Renaissance than they are now. For us, the breve, on the rare occasions when we see it, has twice the value of a semibreve (whole note) and is therefore long; but in the 13th century the value of a breve was regarded as short, as its name implies. With the passage of time, once mensural notation came in, note-values were, for various reasons, divided and redivided. As the "shorter" values became commoner, the "longer" ones became rarer. Thus, the symbols for the long and double long (or large or maxima) are today obsolete. Transcribers into modern notation, in order that a piece may give a present-day reader the impression of *tempo* its notation was likely to have aroused in the mind of a contemporary, are apt to use the quarter-note for the normal time-unit. Thus, the note-values originally used in a 16th-century piece are, in a modern "practical" edition, most often halved. And the note-values of early mensural pieces are often divided by 8. The division by 16, however, is by no means uncommon, the choice sometimes depending upon the character of the piece, sometimes upon the mere preference of the transcriber.

With the invention of "shorter" note-values, obviously, the duration of the "longer" ones actually increased. Attempts have been made to ascertain the fluctuations in time-value of individual note-symbols. We shall return to the subject in Chapter 12.

If it is important from the historical standpoint to remember, when reading most modern versions of medieval or renaissance pieces, that the time-values of the originals have been divided, it is important to bear in mind from both the historical and practical standpoints that bar-lines are the additions of modern editors. A vertical line, such as that appearing in plainsong notation to show the termination of distinctions, was not used to rule off measures (i. e. as a bar, though it was used for another purpose) in copies of mensural music intended for practical use until the second half of the 15th century, and even then its employment was restricted. The conception of "measure" has changed through the ages. In the music most frequently performed today, i. e. that of the 18th and 19th centuries, a measure consists of a pattern of beats, of which the first is accented, and the pattern recurs over and over. In 20th-century music the feature of recurrence is no longer essential: a composer like Stravinsky may sometimes change his time-signature in almost every measure. Fifteenth- and 16th-century polyphony, on the other hand, is an example of music in which the initial accent is the unessential feature: the stress may occur at the beginning of a measure but it does not have to. Therefore, in reading a modern edition of a 15th- or 16th-century work, the editor's bar-line should not by itself be interpreted as implying a stress, for, if an accent occurs at the beginning of a measure, it does so as the result of special causes, such as the influence, under certain conditions, of accents in metrical texts, etc. Throughout the period in which modal patterns were used, however, accents were probably called for, since, without them, the first and second modes would, after the first few notes, have been indistinguishable from one another; likewise the third and fourth.[10] (The use of the heavy beat in connection with the rhythmic modes has already received some attention in Chapter 7.)

In modern notation, as we have seen, it is possible to write the patterns of all the rhythmic modes, using ♩ and ♪ as the only basic note-shapes. If the old musicians implied many more values, they nevertheless regarded the *underlying musical values* as only two: longs and breves. But these were not always of the same quality. Thus, the longs in modes 1 and 2 (represented by half-notes in our illustrations for those modes on p. 272) were *longae rectae* ("normal longs"); those in modes 3–5 (represented by dotted half-notes in our illustrations) were regarded as *ultra mensuram* ("beyond measurement"). These terms are interesting in the light of what has been said on p. 274 concerning the order in which the modes came into existence. If the alternation of 2-time longs and 1-time shorts came first, then 3-time longs, when subsequently admitted, would at first have seemed to be "beyond measurement," while the 2-time longs would have stood out as "normal." There are other names for these two types of long, and there is a name for the 3-beat unit filled either by a *longa recta* plus a breve or by a 3-beat long. The order in which these other terms were adopted may possibly be as follows: (1) If the steps towards the development of a system of rhythmic modes began with an alternation of longs and shorts, probably without any particular cerebration about whether the rhythm was binary, or ternary, or anything else, the day must inevitably have come when the nature of the rhythm was actually grasped; it would have been found ternary; the shortest 3-beat unit would have been regarded as a standard unit of measurement and would eventually have received a name. The medieval theorists called such a unit a "perfection." [11] (2) Once the 3-beat unit was so named, it would have been a short step to calling the 3-beat long a *longa perfecta* and the 2-beat long a *longa imperfecta,* names actually adopted. The breves were also regarded as of two kinds, one of which, the 1-time

---

[10] Concerning accents in the modal system, see also OH I, 73. For a forceful argument to the effect that the second mode was not merely the first mode with an upbeat, see MichalT, 26.

[11] Its adoption as a unit of measurement does not mean that it is justifiable to regard the perfection as the equivalent of one measure, as is often done. Each of the modal patterns quite properly fills a measure in modern transcriptions, but the patterns of modes 3 and 4 each cover *two* perfections. (*Cf.* MichalT, 36.)

breve, known as the *brevis recta,* we have already encountered. The undotted half-notes appearing in the patterns for modes 3 and 4 on p. 272
were regarded not as longs but as breves; that is, each of these modes was
looked upon as alternating a long and a pair of breves. The 2-time breve was
called *brevis altera.* It will be simpler to discuss presently, rather than here, the
possibility of regarding values smaller than the 1-time breve as constituting
jointly a long or breve.

Modes 1, 2, and 6 (those using only "normal" values) were grouped as
modi recti, the others at first as *modi ultra mensuram* and later as *modi
obliqui.*[12]

It was the peculiarity of the method of notation constituting what we have
called the second stage—a method sometimes called "modal notation"—that,
while it occasionally used some single note-symbols for special purposes, it
was based essentially on compound figures derived from those plainsong
symbols that represented more than one tone. These figures have, since
Jerome of Moravia, been called ligatures (Latin *ligare* = to bind). A ligature
was said to be ascending or descending according to whether its second note
was higher or lower than the first.

When, like the first note of an ascending figure comprising more than one
note in plainsong notation (*cf.* pp. 130f), the first note of an ascending ligature
had no tail, the ligature was said to be *cum proprietate* ("with propriety").
A descending ligature was *cum proprietate* if, as in a descending figure comprising more than one note in plainsong, the first note had a tail going downward at the left. If a tail was omitted from a first note where it would have
been present in plainsong, or if it was added, descending, where it would
have been absent, the ligature was said to be *sine proprietate* ("without
propriety").

If the ligature, whether ascending or descending, had a tail ascending from
the left, it was said to be *cum opposita proprietate* ("with opposite propriety").

Ligatures were spoken of also as *cum perfectione* or *sine perfectione.* Just
as the form of the first note governed the "propriety" of a ligature, the form
of the last note governed its "perfection" (which was unrelated to the "perfection" of a mode or *ordo* or to the "perfection" as a unit of measurement)
If the last note was placed at the lower right of the penultimate, or per-
pendicularly above it, the ligature was "perfect"; if the last note was represented by the lower end of a transverse bar (in which event the note had no
head of its own) or if it was placed at the upper right of the penultimate,
the ligature was "imperfect." A transverse bar represented two notes only—
those on which it began and ended.

---

[12] *Cf.* SchmiD, 31 (with citations); MichalT, 21ff.

EXAMPLE 74.

That the time-values of the notes in ligature varied according to the rhythmic mode of the music for which they were used, is strikingly illustrated by the fact that a three-note ligature with propriety and perfection could imply long-breve-long in the first mode, breve-breve-long in the third and fourth modes, long-long-long in the fifth mode, or breve-breve-breve in the sixth. The important thing for the performer to do was to "spot" the mode. And the theorists tell us how the selection of ligature shapes furnished the clue, as shown below. (The reason why the applicability of the rhythmic modes to the secular monody of the troubadours etc. cannot be actually proved from the bulk of the MSS is that the preponderantly syllabic style of the music precluded the frequent use of ligatures that "modal notation" called for, so that ordinary plainsong notation was used.) As long as the modes were strictly adhered to, the rests mentioned in the description did not usually have to vary in shape according to their length, since the value of a rest was normally that of the second note before it.[13] A simple vertical stroke then sufficed for most purposes.

Perfect Modes

FIRST. A single three-note ligature followed by a group of two-note ligatures, all with propriety and perfection. (But where the trochaic rhythm is expressed solely in the first perfect *ordo,* only three-note ligatures are used, these likewise being with propriety and perfection, and being separated from one another by rests.)

SECOND. A group of two-note ligatures with propriety and perfection followed by a single three-note ligature without propriety but with perfection. Some theorists substitute for the three-note ligature a two-note ligature plus a single note, in appearance like the breve of mensural notation. (But where the iambic rhythm is expressed solely in the first perfect *ordo,* only three-note ligatures are used, these likewise being without propriety and with perfection, and being separated from one another by longer rests.)

THIRD. A single note, in appearance like the virga of plainsong or long of mensural notation, followed by a group of three-note ligatures with propriety and perfection. (In the course of the 13th century, the long became merged with the first three-note ligature into a four-note ligature.)

FOURTH. A group of three-note ligatures with propriety and perfection followed by a single two-note ligature with propriety but without perfection.

[13] Johannes de Garlandia says (CouS I, 98) *quanta est penultima, tanta est pausatio* ("so long as the penultimate, thus long is the pause"). (See also CouS I, 378f.) The applicability of the rule to all modes except the third and fourth is clear. In these modes the rest normally equalled a perfect long.

FIFTH. Three-note ligatures with propriety and perfection, separated from one another by rests longer graphically (and musically) than those used in the first mode when only the first perfect *ordo* was expressed. (But ligatures were rarely used to indicate this mode.)

SIXTH. (1) A single four-note ligature followed by a group of three-note ligatures, all with propriety and perfection; or (2) a single four-note ligature followed by a group of three-note ligatures without propriety but with perfection; or (3) a single four-note ligature followed by a group of two-note ligatures, all with propriety but with terminal notes having stems added at the right and pointing either up or down; or (4) a succession of two-note ligatures with propriety and perfection.

Imperfect Modes

FIRST. (1) A single three-note ligature followed by a group of two-note ligatures, all with propriety and perfection, the group being succeeded by a single, concluding note, in appearance like a breve; or (2) a succession of two-note ligatures without propriety but with perfection; or (3) a succession of three-note ligatures with perfection and alternately with and without propriety.

SECOND. A succession of two-note ligatures with propriety and perfection. (*Cf.* the fourth method given above for the Sixth Perfect Mode. Which of the two modes is called for in a particular piece can be ascertained by trying to fit the part notated in such ligatures against the other parts.)

THIRD. A single "long" followed by a group of three-note ligatures, the group being succeeded by a single two-note ligature and all the ligatures being with propriety and perfection.

FOURTH. A succession of three-note ligatures with propriety and perfection.

FIFTH. This mode does not appear in ligature.

SIXTH. (1) A single four-note ligature followed by a group of two-note ligatures, all with propriety and perfection, and with a stem on the terminal note, or (2) a succession of two-note ligatures with propriety and perfection, and likewise with a stem on the terminal note.[14]

In the MSS preserving practical music inscribed in modal notation or in a notation approximating it, it is the ligatures with propriety and perfection that exhibit real life; the other ligatures mentioned by the theorists in their expositions of modal notation do not take on true vitality in the practical monuments until we reach those in mensural notation. The imperfect modes, though accounted for in theory, take on no life in the monuments at all.

The theorists do not always continue the rows of ligatures, described above, without variation. To be sure, the modal system greatly restricted rhythmic freedom, but even so the first mode perfect, to take one example, was not always represented by an unremitting series of two-note ligatures introduced by a three-note ligature, a series to be broken only by a rest or the end.

[14] WolfH I, 223ff, and LudR, 42ff, give in greater detail the methods of indicating modes through the use of ligatures. WolfH is the finest comprehensive manual on notation. (Unfortunately, *The Story of Notation* by C. F. Abdy Williams is very uneven; a new manual by Willi Apel is scheduled for publication in the near future.)

Anonymus IV, in expounding the *minutio et fractio modorum* ("the diminishing and breaking up of the modes"),[15] states that each two-time long may be split into from 3 to 6 notes, each three-time long into from 3 to 8, each breve into 2 or 3. One way of notating the division was to represent the insertions by ordinary square notes and to admit them within the ligature. The result would be that a ligature, having, let us say, a total of five notes, would represent a total time-value no greater than the ligature without the insertions. Another method consisted in adding the ornamental notes, in the shape of lozenges (*currentes,* "running notes"), after a single note, in form like a virga. Thus, in the first mode perfect, the opening three-note ligature could be broken up so that the initial note, normally having the value of a long, would be separated from the other two notes and would have lozenges appended to it. Notes which together equalled a time-value subjected to division were known as *aequipollentiae* ("equivalents").

If the value of a *breve* was to be broken up within a ligature into two or three values, a ligature with opposite propriety was used, in which case the last note was a long and the preceding ones were shorts (in the "equivalent" sense, i. e. the total value was still that of a breve, but the last note was long, and the previous ones short, in relation to each other).[16]

Repeated notes, Johannes de Garlandia tells us,[17] were not to be used in ligature. If a note was to be repeated, the repetition had to start a new ligature or stand by itself. In the former event, the ligature consisted only of the left-over notes—more than one, of course, would be necessary—of what would, without the repetition, have been the original ligature. In the latter event, the note had a stem descending at the right (i. e. it looked like a virga) if it would have concluded the ligature, had this not been broken; otherwise it had no stem. In other words, whether the note had a stem or not had nothing to do with its long or breve value, but only with its position within the group that, without the repetition, would have constituted a normal ligature.[18]

Unfortunately for the modern transcriber, the MSS preserving the music belonging to the second stage by no means always furnish the clues in the systematic manner the theorists might lead us to hope for. On the contrary, they abound in passages capable of interpretation in more than one way. Still, the information of the theorists enables us to be certain concerning the rhythm of such systematically notated pieces as, for example, the two-part *Regnat* preserved in MS Pluteus 29.1 at Florence [19] and helps us even where the notation is not quite so regular.

---

[15] CouS I, 336ff. See also AuM III, 120f; MichalT, 25ff.
[16] See CouS I, 100, 342. Or WolfG I, 4.   [17] CouS I, 103.
[18] *Cf.* CouS I, 101, col. 1, ex. 3 and 5.
[19] For a facsimile of the page on which it appears, see WolfH I, opposite p. 228. (There is a transcription on p. 229ff.) This important MS will be further discussed in Chap. 11.

We have just noted that, where there is a repetition, a single note is detached from its ligature and stands by itself, and may appear in form like a virga or punctum (though not necessarily derived from the punctum genetically). It has been suggested [20] that the separation of a repeated note from its ligature may be regarded as the first step towards the third—the mensural —stage. It has been pointed out also that, in the third mode (both perfect and imperfect), a single note, in appearance like a virga, ushers in the series of three-note ligatures. It so happens that the time-value the context gives this single note is a long one. That this coincidence may likewise have some connection with the development of mensural notation is not impossible. (Similarly, the single "breves" used in the first methods we have given for notating modes 2 perfect and 1 imperfect actually receive a breve value.) However this may be, the earliest treatise dealing with mensural notation, the anonymous *Discantus Positio Vulgaris* (*c.* 1230–40) [21] presents •, the breve, and ۹, the long. With their introduction, the perfection of a mensural system is by no means achieved, but a great step forward is taken. Ligatures continue in use, but the single note begins to assume fundamental importance. With an alternation of breves and longs it is possible to notate mensurally, without ligatures, the first and second modes; the breve by itself suffices for the sixth. Two basic rules make possible the mensural notation, with only these two symbols, of the remaining modes:

(1) If two breves appear between two longs (or between a long and a rest), the second has normally twice the value of the first—i. e. the first is a *brevis recta,* the second a *brevis altera*—and each of the enclosing longs has three times unless a single breve precedes or follows.

(2) A long before a long has three beats.

The first rule makes it possible to notate the pattern of the third mode thus: ۹••۹; [22] the second rule, to notate the fifth mode with a series of longs.

The mensural system was doubtless called for by a desire to break away from the rigidity of the modal system. A fully developed mensural system would make possible the notation of any rhythmic pattern. We have, nevertheless, drawn on the rhythmic modes in introducing our discussion of the mensural system, feeling that this would make for simplicity, in view of the fact that the patterns have just been dealt with at some length. The old familiar patterns, moreover, were by no means wholly abandoned (*cf.* p. 292). In much of the newer music, however, they could not have been precisely notated according to the modal system since, as we shall see in Chapter 11, the style—

[20] LudR, 47; MichalM, 269; MichalT, 40, 108.

[21] Not before 1150, as was once thought. See LudQ, 287ff. The treatise is printed (with French transl.) in CouH, 217, and (in Latin only) in CouS I, 94.

[22] As stated on p. 272, mode 4 had hardly any existence in practical polyphony. Passages employing it do occur, however, e. g. in the course of the motet transcribed in RoksM III, 115. Comparison with the facsimile in RoksM I will show the pattern to be represented by 2 breves and a long, the group being preceded by a long or ligature.

at least for the upper voices—was syllabic and therefore unsuitable for nota-tion in ligatures, useful essentially for melismatic or instrumental music.

A definition in the *Discantus Positio Vulgaris* characterizes as *ultra men-suram* not only the 3-time long but all notes worth more than two times or less than one.[23] The latter bring us to the semibreve, represented by a lozenge. It does not appear singly, but only in conjunction with a long or breve or other semibreves, whence the compound figures embracing it are called *conjuncturae* (*cf.* the virga with appended lozenges used in the modal nota-tion for the *minutio et fractio modorum*). Here are examples:

EXAMPLE 75.

Johannes Wolf has shown [24] that, in notation, shorter time-values are apt to begin life as decorations of longer ones, and only gradually to achieve independence. We see the point illustrated here, for, strange as it may at first seem to the modern musician, the note that is here so short as to be *ultra mensuram,* i. e. the semibreve, is our whole note.

Another type of ornament was notated by the *plica*. This was attached to either single notes (except semibreves) or ligatures. It could be either *ascendens* or *descendens*. When it was the former, it corresponded to the epiphonus in plainsong; when it was the latter, to the cephalicus. When it was applied to single notes, usually two parallel strokes of unequal length were added to the note-head. These strokes, enfolding the head, gave the *plica* its name (*plica* = "fold"). In some instances one stroke could suffice. Where there were two, the shorter stroke, in longs, was at the left; in breves, at the right. In ligatures, the *plica* was indicated by a stroke attached to the right of the last note, the only one that could be *plicata*.

EXAMPLE 76.

The earliest mensural theorists to describe the *plica* in detail seem to have been Garlandia and Dietricus.[25] A comparative study of MSS and of the statements of later theorists shows the special feature of the *plica* to have consisted in its providing what, to our way of thinking, was an ornament sounded *after* the tone it decorated. Franco of Cologne wrote: "The *plica* is a note in which the same sound is divided into low and high," [26] and he thereby shows that the device was not recognized in his day as consist-ing of two notes, but, impossible as it may seem according to modern con-ceptions, of one note proceeding up or down. The early theorists assign no time-value to what we perceive as the ornament. Its pitch was governed by

[23] See CouS I, 94. [24] WolfG I, 3. [25] CouS I, 99; MülA. [26] CouS I, 123.

the note following the plicated one. Thus, if this succeeding note indicated the same pitch as its decorated predecessor, the ornament, sounding between the two, was executed a second above or below, depending upon the direction of the stroke (or strokes).[27]

The description of the ligatures used as indications of the modes, given above, shows that, except in the sixth mode (both perfect and imperfect), two-note ligatures with propriety and perfection happen always to call for a breve followed by a long. The three-note ligatures in modes 3 and 4 likewise have a constant value, the successive notes again increasing in value within the ligature. The intermediate phase, between the period represented by the *Discantus Positio Vulgaris* and the full development of the Franconian mensural notation, provided, little by little, the further fixing of time-values of ligatures until at long last a ligature with a particular shape called for only one particular group of time-values in performance. The intermediate phase will here be treated very sketchily.[28]

The *Discantus Positio Vulgaris* itself fixes [29] the values of certain ligatures but, not unnaturally, under the influence of modal indications. Where MSS of practical music use longs and breves but mingle ligatures with them in the notation of modal patterns, it is obviously possible to deduce the values of the ligatures, and such MSS are thus a valuable aid in tracing the growth of the mensural system. The famous Montpellier MS H 196, with its eight fascicles representing several different types of notation, takes on an importance quite aside from the considerable musical value of its contents (to which we shall return in Chapter 11).[30]

Dietricus is apparently the earliest theorist known to define the value of a semibreve, though not the first to name it. He says that two semibreves are needed to equal a breve. His modal doctrine resembles that of other writers, but he refers to the fourth mode as not in current use. His interpretation of the value of notes in ligature still shows the influence of modal indication.

Theorists from the British Isles contribute to our knowledge of the second and third stages, and also of the transition from one to the other, as they do to our knowledge of other aspects of medieval theory. We have already mentioned, in this chapter, Garlandia, Anonymus IV, and Walter Odington. We shall refer to these men again as well as to other Britishers.

One of them is Alfred, the prologue to whose tract, probably written in Genoa, describes him as an English priest serving under Cardinal Octoboni de' Fieschi in 1271. Alfred mentions the *plica* as having the value of a semibreve—the ornament is taking on value. Of special interest are his state-

---

[27] For fuller information concerning the plica, see WolfH I, 238f; WolfG I, 4ff, 48ff; BohnP, 47ff.

[28] For more information see WolfH, WolfG, JacM, NieL. [29] CouS I, 94f.

[30] Facsimile of the MS with transcriptions and commentary in RoksM. Concerning the notation, see RoksM IV, 25ff.

ments that two breves or four semibreves can equal one long, and that a semibreve can equal one-half a breve.[31]

Anonymus VII [32] is among theorists to mention the duplex longa, a single note having twice the value of the long. Like Anonymus IV he gives information concerning the *minutio et fractio modorum*. Of special interest are his comments concerning the tendency of certain modes to merge, a tendency about which we shall soon say more.

Dietricus gives rests with fixed time-values, thus:

EXAMPLE 77.

Johannes de Garlandia describes rests along somewhat similar lines, but provides for more types.[33] Some other symbols classed as pauses by the theorists, though having no time-values, were the *finis punctorum* ("end of the clauses"), which was drawn through the whole staff and corresponded to our double-bar, and the *suspiratio* ("sigh"), described as an "apparent and non-existent pause . . . shorter than a *recta brevis*." This was indicated by a stroke shorter than that for the one-time breve. Garlandia says that the *divisio modi* was indicated in the same way, but this customarily appears as a dot.

The *divisio modi* was a most useful device. Odington,[34] in discussing the modes, lists not only the usual ones but also what he calls *modi secundarii*. The first of these is written as we have notated the pattern for the third mode on p. 282, with the important difference that a *divisio modi* appears between the two breves. This has the effect of preventing the second breve from being a *brevis altera*. Instead, the succession becomes: two-time long, one-time breve, one-time breve, two-time long. In other words, we have a mixture of modes 1 and 2.

With his use of the actual symbols for the long and breve and of the *divisio modi,* Odington is drawing upon symbols having a definite mensural significance. Some actual polyphonic works mixing the modes are preserved for us in unmistakable mensural notation. But whether or not the modes could be mixed in the *second* stage, has been a subject for controversy among modern scholars. Anglès has proved that the *modus mixtus* made its appearance in some examples of 13th-century secular monody, but the evidence [35] consists of pieces preserved in mensural notation. To argue backwards from this that other secular monody, preserved in plainsong notation, mixed the

[31] Concerning Alfred, see KromP, where, however, he is called Amerus. With regard to the correct form of the name, see LudQ, 198.
[32] CouS I, 378.   [33] CouS I, 104, 181f.   [34] CouS I, 238.
[35] See, for an example of it, the facsimile in AngL, 354.

modes also (cf. p. 210), is tempting but risky, and the theory has been attacked.[36]

The practical monuments show that a change of mode was entirely possible in the course of a single composition, even before the advent of mensural notation, the changes occurring at the beginnings of new sections. Each section, however, adheres to one mode, so that what we have is not exactly a *modus mixtus*. The changes are shown by merely starting a series of mode-indicating ligatures different from the preceding one. Several such changes may be conveniently noted in the fascimile of a page from the Florence MS Pluteus 29.1, printed in OH I, opposite p. 128. This reproduces a portion of a three-part piece, in which the changes occur in the two upper parts. In these, the first two systems give the ligature series for mode 1; after the first ligature in system 3 there is a shift to mode 3; slightly after the middle of that system there is a change to mode 2 and near the end of it a change back to mode 3; while, after the second ligature in the fourth system, we again have the ligature series for mode 1.[37]

Combination of modes is illustrated by Garlandia vertically also—that is, he gives an explanation of the manner in which the modes could be pitted against one another in different parts. In the process, he still uses modal notation, but we may nevertheless see, in the interweaving of the modal patterns, additional evidence of a tendency towards greater elasticity. (In his discussions of modal notation he calls virga-like notes longs and punctum-like notes breves. This is because he belongs to the transitional period—he describes the true long and breve symbols as well as modal notation—and is therefore presumably accustomed to calling the notes so shaped by such names. Even so, however, it should not be assumed that these notes necessarily have long and breve values—cf. pp. 275, 281.) Here are two of his examples of combination: [38]

EXAMPLE 78.

---

[36] In behalf of the theory, see AngL, 352ff; against it, KuhlM I, 156ff, 170f; also MichalT, 115ff.

[37] The transcription accompanying the facsimile in OH shows the changes of mode correctly. OH, however, is wrong on p. 75f in its attempt to transcribe certain one-line examples in CouS I, 102, as showing real mixture of mode.

[38] Original notation in CouS I, 112, col. 1, ex. 1; 108, col. 1, ex. 2.

[39] "The dissonance of a second upon the [relatively] strong beat" occurs not only here but in several of Garlandia's examples. It is "inserted deliberately for the sake of ornament . . . and always takes this form of a kind of *appoggiatura* proceeding to the note itself with which it is discordant." (OH I, 100, where the debatable implication is made that this kind of ornament is included by Garlandia under the designation *color*. Cf. pp. 305f, *infra*.)

EXAMPLE 79.

Johannes de Garlandia—the supposed, and for our purposes the actual, author of the *De Musica Mensurabili Positio*,[41] upon which this chapter has drawn considerably—was born *c.* 1195. He wrote in his *De Triumphis Ecclesiae:* "Although my mother was England, France was my nurse, and I prefer my nurse to my mother." He has been confused with an 11th-century mathematician who did not write on music. The 13th-century Garlandia—sometimes referred to by modern writers as Johannes de Garlandia the Elder in distinction to a possible Johannes de Garlandia the Younger [42]—attended Oxford (mentioned as a *studium generale* as far back as the 1160's), went to Paris, took part in the Crusade against the Albigenses, taught at Toulouse University, 1229–32, and returned later to Paris. He wrote on mathematics, theology, and alchemy. He was probably still alive in 1272.

A somewhat confused tract,[43] dating from about 1240, by an apparently younger English contemporary of Garlandia's, shows markedly the transition towards the Franconian system of notation—the system that is in un-

[40] In OH I, 102, the last three "measures" of this example and the conclusion of the one there printed after it appear in each other's places by mistake. (The old edition was correct.)

[41] Printed in CouS I, 97, in the form in which Jerome of Moravia incorporated it in his *Tractatus de Musica,* and in CouS I, 175, in abbreviated form, after a MS at the Vatican. The authenticity of this treatise and of the others on music attributed to the Johannes de Garlandia here described has been questioned, though not actually attacked, by Louis J. Paetow in *The Life and Works of John of Garland,* in Memoirs of the University of California, Vol. 4, No. 2 (1927), 142.

[42] A younger Garlandia was suggested in CouS I, ixf, as the author of a brief tract, which seems to be a 14th-century production, printed in CouS III, 12. This exists in a MS at Einsiedeln and, according to CouS I, ixf, in one at Pisa. While CouS I, ix, indicates that the Einsiedeln MS bears the name of Johannes de Galandia (*sic*), it apparently does not (see M. Bukofzer, *Geschichte des englischen Diskants* . . . , 111); in the Pisa MS a work is preserved, claiming to be *secundum* ("according to") *Magistrum Johannem de Guerlandia* (*sic*), but the description in A. de La Fage, *Essais de diphthérographie musicale,* 388, hardly warrants an identification of the treatise as the same as that in CouS III, 12. The name "Guerlandia" may be invoked merely for the sake of *auctoritas,* and, in any event, is not given as that of the actual author. (The MS, moreover, is no earlier than the 16th century.) The idea of a younger Garlandia was further developed in RieG, 174f, 244f; on p. 535 (footnote) RieG connects with him, on not very strong grounds, a second work which is said to be *secundum Magistrum de Gallandia* (*sic*) in a MS from St. Dié (the MS followed by CouS I, 157), but which bears no indication of an author in MSS at Seville and Barcelona (see G. Pietzsch, *Die Klassifikation* . . . , 29); a 15th-century MS at the Library of Congress—including a completer version of the treatise than the one printed in CouS—contains the entry: *Explicit ars cantus plani magistri Johannis de Galadia.* At the beginning of the *De Musica Mensurabili,* Garlandia "the Elder" says he has already written a work on plainsong. It is possible that the 4 MSS mentioned preserve this work in one form or another. From RieG, reference books have taken over the attribution of both this work and the one mentioned above to a younger Garlandia. Hanboys (CouS I, 424) names Johannes de Garlandia as the inventor of the *minima,* etc., introduced only in the early 14th century. If the attribution is not made merely for the sake of *auctoritas,* there really was a younger Garlandia; but he is certainly a shadowy creature.

[43] Printed in CouS I, 251.

derlying principle the basis of the notation we still use today. The author of
this tract, "pseudo-Aristotle," has been identified [44]—through a tract on
mensural notation by an Anonymus of St. Emmeram (near Regensburg),
which attacks passages traceable to the pseudo-Aristotle treatise, the author of
which is stated to be Lambert—as the Magister Lambert named by Johannes
de Grocheo.[45]

This "Aristotle" provides certain definite measurements for notes in ligature—a step towards the Franconian system. He classifies the semibreve
as either minor (= ⅓ of a *brevis recta*) or major (= ⅔), the *brevis* as
either *recta* (= 1 time) or *altera* (= 2 times), and the *longa* as either *imperfecta* (= 2 times) or *perfecta* (= 3 times). Lambert describes no fewer than
nine modes, but this is not surprising when we learn from Anonymus IV
that, in England, a whole series of irregular modes was in use. This
Anonymus supplies a rest for the semibreve: the vertical line extends half
a space and has the value of one-third of a breve.[46]

With the isolation of the long and breve, it became possible, even during
the transitional period, to notate patterns, intended to function isorhythmically
—i. e. like *ordines*—without adhering strictly to modal designs. Thus:

EXAMPLE 80.

Obviously a method—or, rather, a series of methods, several often in
simultaneous use—with the complexity we have only hinted at, needed
sooner or later to undergo simplification. With the decline of rigidity in
the application of the rhythmic modes it became increasingly desirable that
notes within a ligature have the same values in all contexts. It was the great
contribution of the *Franconian system* that it furnished the much-needed
stabilization. Unfortunately, the abandonment of ligatures altogether and
the invention of the slur seem not to have occurred to the medieval mind.

Anonymus IV reports that there were two Francos:

*Master Franco the First and the second Master Franco of Cologne, who began
in their books to use a somewhat different notation, and for that reason handed
down different rules suited to their own books.*[47]

This indicates that the Anonymus was as late as, if not later than, the
Francos, even though he gives information concerning notation older than
the Franconian. Franco of Paris (the earlier Franco) is a shadowy figure

---

[44] SowaA, xvii.   [45] WolfM, 102.
[46] It seems that this important Anonymus went to Paris, his arrival there being variously placed
at c. 1260 and c. 1272 (see WolfMM, 60; SowaZ, 422), about the time of Garlandia's death.
[47] CouS I, 342, as translated in Grove II, 305.

and not to be regarded as the author of the highly important *Ars Cantus Mensurabilis,* generally accepted as the work of Franco of Cologne, although he may have been the author of a treatise upon which the 14th-century English theorist Robert de Handlo wrote a commentary [48] and which is summarized in the *Abbreviatio Magistri Franconis a Johanne dicto Balloce* [49] and in the tracts of Anonymi II and III.[50] All four tracts begin with the encouraging words, probably contained in the original, *Gaudent brevitate moderni* ("The moderns rejoice in brevity").

Franco of Cologne, who flourished *c.* 1250–after 1280,[51] was a practical musician as well as a theorist: a 14th-century writer mentions having heard a three-part work of his in Paris.[52] Two MS copies of the treatise describe him as chaplain to the Pope [53] and preceptor of the Hospital of St. John of Jerusalem at Cologne. While the *Ars Cantus Mensurabilis* [54] (dating apparently from shortly after 1280) offers little that is new, that little is important. The tract furnished a codification of rules that was to be regarded as standard for years, and it made it possible to put an end to the arbitrariness and ambiguity that prevailed before. Franco's system survived with most of its essential features intact, but with important accretions, into the 16th century, and, however far we may have travelled from it in details in almost seven centuries, still provides the fundamental principles upon which our own notation is based.

The following familiar figures constitute Franco's supply of single notes:

EXAMPLE 81.

With the exception of the *duplex longa,* all the note-values are regarded as normally ternary. The unit of measurement, as in the past, is the *brevis recta,* having the value of 1 *tempus.* The long is "perfect" ($= 3$ *tempora,* i.e. a "perfection") or "imperfect" ($= 2$ *tempora*); the *brevis* is recta ($= 1$ *tempus*) or altera ($= 2$ *tempora*); the semibreve is "minor" ($= \frac{1}{3}$ *tempus*) or "major" ($= \frac{2}{3}$ *tempus*).

The corresponding rests, with their Latin names, are:

---

[48] CouS I, 383.   [49] CouS I, 292.   [50] CouS I, 303, 319.

[51] The assignment (possibly in emulation of Fétis) of Franco of Cologne to the 11th century(!), adopted by certain English writers—for example, S. T. Warner (Grove II, 305), whose contributions to Grove III, 646, and OH Int, 66, contain much of value—would quite upset the theory of a gradual growth of the mensural system towards standardization. It is wholly at variance with the views of Besseler, Wolf, etc., and is, in fact, untenable. For fuller information concerning Franco, see BesS II, 157; KuhlM I, 84, 160.

[52] See CouS II, 402.

[53] See CouA, 22. (The reader, however, must guard against attaching too much weight to the ascriptions, made in CouA, of compositions in the Montpellier MS to Franco of Cologne and other theorists.)

[54] Printed in GerS III, I (where it is attributed to Franco of Paris), after a MS at the Biblioteca Ambrosiana (Milan), and in CouS I, 117, in the form in which Jerome of Moravia incorporated it in his *Tractatus de Musica.* An English translation will be included in Oliver Strunk's forthcoming book of readings in the history of music.

EXAMPLE 82.

The following rules regulate the values of the notes.

1. "If a long follows a long, the first will be . . . a perfect long, whether the second is a note or a rest."[55]

2. A single breve before or after a long makes the long twofold (imperfect). If a breve is flanked by longs, either of which it is capable of making twofold, its effect on the note that precedes has preference over its possible effect on the one that follows. If it is desired to have a long perfect even though it is followed by a breve, a *divisio modi* or *signum perfectionis* ("sign of perfection") may be written after the long. The two terms imply no graphic difference. Indeed, Franco says the "division" and the "sign" are the same thing. While, in the situation just described, this sign *happens* to have the same effect as a dot after a note today, its basic function is not the same but is, as we have seen (*cf.* p. 285), to keep the two notes it separates from belonging to the same perfection.

3. If two breves stand between two longs (or the corresponding rests), the first *brevis* is *recta* and the second *altera*. The *divisio modi* may be used to prevent the operation of this rule.

4. If three breves follow a long, the breves together equal a perfection and they make the long threefold. If there are more than three breves, the first makes the long twofold, and each group of three succeeding the first equals a perfection. If two breves are left over, the last will be *altera;* if one breve remains, it renders the succeeding long imperfect. But changes in values can be effected through the *divisio modi.*

5. The values of rests are definitely shown by their forms: they cannot be rendered imperfect or *altera,* etc.[56]

6. Where groups of 2 or 3 semibreves appear, either group equals a *brevis recta.* Where there are 2, the first is minor, the second major; where there are 3, all are minor. Where there are more than 3, Franco of Paris[57] says that they are to be grouped by twos and that the first has half the value of the second ($\frac{1}{3}$ $\frac{2}{3}$); if 3 are left over, they are equal ($\frac{1}{3}$ $\frac{1}{3}$ $\frac{1}{3}$). The *divisio modi* can alter the mensuration. Franco of Cologne writes "concerning semibreves, the rules are the same as for breves." He says[58] that not

---

[55] GerS III, 4; CouS I, 119.   [56] CouS I, 126ff. See also WolfH I, 253.
[57] CouS I, 387; WolfH I, 253f.
[58] In the version of the *Ars Cantus Mensurabilis* printed in CouS I (see pp. 122f). But the version printed in GerS III says, on p. 5, that not less than 3 or more than 9 (!) semibreves can be contained in a *brevis recta.* Possibly the scribe of the MS printed in GerS blundered, or perhaps Gerbert did. (WolfH I, 254, follows GerS and, apparently not having taken CouS into

more than 3 semibreves can be contained in a *brevis recta;* not less than 4 or more than 6 in a *brevis altera.* The possible effects of the *divisio modi* are recognized by him also.

The *Ars Cantus Mensurabilis* breaks no new ground in dealing with the *plica.* But in its treatment of ligatures the attempt to make the interpretation of values independent of the modal system achieves complete success. Franco specifically states [59] that the form of ligatures *cum proprietate* is derived from that of the plainsong figures representing more than one note, and he defines "propriety," "perfection," the lack of them, and "opposite propriety," in ways consistent with the descriptions on p. 278. In ligatures *cum proprietate et cum perfectione,* the first note is now always a breve and the last a long; lack of "propriety" (whether or not "perfection" is retained) makes the first note a long; lack of "perfection" (whether or not "propriety" is retained) makes the last note a breve; this second lack does not affect the breve-value of the first note if propriety is retained. If the ligature is *cum opposita proprietate,* the first two notes (but not more) are semibreves. Middle-notes (except the second in a ligature *cum opposita proprietate*) are breves. "Concerning the value of . . . conjunctures," says Franco, "no other rules can be given than those given above for simplenotes and ligatures." [60]

Franco's tabulation of the modes is closer to the usual one than Lambert's. He limits their number to five, however. He observes that all the modes may be reduced to the one consisting entirely of perfect longs [61] and he therefore calls this mode the first instead of the fifth. Old mode 1 becomes a mere subdivision of Franco's mode 1; old modes 2, 3, and 4 retain their old numerical order, and old mode 6 becomes mode 5. Just why Franco's modes 2–5 are not subdivisions of his mode 1 also, is not explained.[62]

During the last quarter of the 13th century a tendency towards merging the modes, for one reason or another, becomes evident. The Anonymus of St. Emmeram states,[63] in the year 1279, that modes 3–5 were discarded in favor of modes 1, 2, and 6, and Anonymus IV mentions [64] that "certain Parisians" had for some time been substituting, in actual practice, mode 2 for mode 5 by reducing the tenor from the latter mode to the former and

account, finds it strange that it should have been possible for a *brevis recta* to contain more semibreves than a *brevis altera.*)

[59] GerS III, 7; CouS I, 124.

[60] GerS III, 8; CouS I, 126. A fuller discussion (in English) of Franco's system is included in StainN (but read the notes as black and the semibreve as a lozenge).

[61] GerS III, 9; CouS I, 127. *Cf.* Garlandia in CouS I, 98. Franco's observation—made, doubtless, as the result of a series of experiments (including older ones than his own) in combining different rhythmic patterns contrapuntally (*cf.* Examples 78 and 79)—lends some support to the belief, mentioned on p. 274f, that medieval "learned" musicians may have preferred ternary rhythms for really musical reasons.

[62] For the enumeration, see GerS III, 3; CouS I, 118. See also BesS II, 156f.

[63] See SowaA, xix, 103ff.   [64] CouS I, 350.

then making the upper part or parts agree.[65] Singers, dissatisfied with the limping rhythm of modes 3 and 4 and regarding mode 5 as tedious, were inclined to reduce modes 3 and 4 to mode 6 and change mode 5 into mode 2. The process of substitution is called modal transmutation. It was possible to improvise the rhythmic alteration from the MSS if necessary, however they were notated, and it was therefore not necessary to rewrite compositions with the rhythms altered. But some documentary evidence of the process, aside from theorists' statements, may nevertheless be studied in the form of certain "twin settings" preserved in mensural notation.[66] Once achieved, this kind of notation, of course, could be and was used in writing modal as well as other patterns,[67] the modes having by no means entirely died out with the arrival of a method of notating other rhythmic figures. In fact, the modal system was dealt with in every important treatise from the *Discantus Positio Vulgaris* (c. 1230–40) to Odington's *De Speculatione Musicae* (early 14th century).

In delving into the intricacies of the early mensural system, we should not lose our perspective. The notation was brought into being by actual music, not *vice versa*. And this music was measured rather than free because the development of part-music made it necessary to keep all the voices together. And the part-music reached a degree of complexity requiring measurement because organum had been found full of possibilities, which the musicians were cultivating. From early organum straight through to the growth of a mensural system we really have part of but one development. And this development was primarily rhythmical—even when it dealt with unmeasured organum (itself merely a stage in the evolution towards a measured discant)—for it dealt with a new way of weaving designs in time, designs different in nature from those contemporaneously applied to plainsong. The development was harmonic also. But, for all its value, the harmonic aspect was secondary in importance to the change that took place in the conception of rhythm. For rhythm (or form—the two are basically phases of the same thing since they both deal with laying out

[65] Concerning the renotation of certain pieces, showing a discrepancy in mode even where modal rather than mensural notation was used, see LudR, 24. The MSS involved belong to different periods and probably reflect contemporary modal preferences.

[66] Further concerning transmutation, see SowaZ, especially p. 426f.

[67] A circumstance that accounts for the use of single breve and long *symbols* by Franco, for example (GerS III, 3), in his exposition of the modal *patterns* (as Garlandia used the *words* "long" and "breve" for the virga-like and punctum-like notes in his exposition of modal *notation; cf.* p. 286), although these patterns, during the modal-notation stage, were not represented by such symbols. Many modern works (OH, for example) unfortunately follow suit without giving warning, the result being that the unprepared reader is almost certain to receive a false impression concerning the nature of the modal-notation stage. The importance of the notations of this second stage, and of the transition following it, is attested by the large number of surviving MSS in which they are used (consult LudR or WolfH I, 258–63). And that they have importance even for those without access to the libraries containing the MSS is shown by the occasional appearance of a facsimile edition unaccompanied by transcriptions into modern notation (such as BaxO).

designs in time) is the underlying framework of music. The creation of a mensural system, therefore, constituted a revolutionary step in music history, a step more difficult of achievement and hardly less important than the creation of the staff. Even though this is not essentially a book on notation and the subject is only occasionally treated here as other than incidental, this step is far too important to be dealt with any more sketchily than it has been. Our discussion of notation will perhaps have made it clear that, although on some subjects (e. g. the distinctions between consonance and dissonance) we need feel under no compulsion to accord the theorists more deference than was apparently given them by contemporary practical musicians,[68] we must acknowledge a tremendous debt to them for the light they shed not only on modal but on mensural notation. Without this light we would possibly be unable to solve many of the rhythmical problems presented by the MSS, which contain a valuable and fairly large repertory of compositions displaying Western polyphony based on the perfect consonances at the greatest height it has so far achieved. This polyphony, slightly antedating and contemporary with the treatises, will form the subject of our next chapter.

[68] Concerning reservations which it is well to bear in mind generally when consulting some of the theorists, see HughT, 126.

Chapter 11: THE CULMINATION OF CONTINEN-
TAL ORGANUM AND DISCANT IN
THE 12TH AND 13TH CENTURIES: The
Organa, Conductus, Early Motet, Cantilena;
Methods of Performance; Instruments

THE Gothic period is best represented in music by the polyphonic works in the performance and notation of which the mensural system was worked out, just as it is in architecture by the Cathedral at Chartres, Notre Dame de Paris, and the other mounting prayers in stone and glass that from about 1180 to 1250 were offered by the religious fervor of Germany, England, Spain, and—first and foremost—France. The French excelled not only in Gothic architecture, but in Gothic music; and Notre Dame de Paris was the greatest music center of the time. If it was from folk-polyphony that the Church at first adopted organum (*cf.* p. 255), in the art-music of the Gothic period it was the Church that cultivated polyphony more intensively than did the contemporary secular music of the troubadours and trouvères.

The polyphony of the period falls into four chief classes [1]: *organum, conductus, motet,* and *cantilena.* If they are called "forms," it must be with reservation. For it is not so much distinctive formal structure as distinctive style that draws the line between them. While, as we shall see, the last of these classes proved especially alive with possibilities for the 14th century, it is the first three that furnished the main channels through which musical thought expressed itself most characteristically at various times during the period of the culmination of Continental organum and discant.

In all these classes, the harmonic basis is more or less the same. The consonances are still, in the main, the unison, fifth, and octave,[2] the fourth having—*cf.* p. 263—already lost ground. Johannes de Garlandia [3] is among the theorists admitting both the major and minor thirds as consonances, but he qualifies them (as we still rather automatically do today) as imperfect. In the early 12th-century piece printed as Example 71, thirds occur

---

[1] Judged mainly from the musical standpoint. The classification in OH I, 106, according to whether (1) all parts have the same words, (2) each part has its own words, or (3) not all parts have them, is apparently based on a misinterpretation of CouS I, 130, so far as the last category is concerned. See p. 307.
[2] *Cf.* CouS I, 95.   [3] CouS I, 104f.

many times; but in almost every instance they appear between a unison and a fifth, and are the result of what we would today call passing-notes. The feeling that thirds needed resolution to perfect consonances is illustrated by Anonymus XIII (late 13th century ?), who states,[4] in his treatise in French, that the major third should be followed by a fifth and the minor third by a unison. This theorist admits the sixths as imperfect consonances also (although sixths were generally considered inferior to thirds), but he states that the major sixth should progress to the octave and the minor sixth to the fifth. Practical music in the 13th century, however, gave greater liberty to the third in particular. Franco of Cologne propounded the important and, with one qualification, long valid rule—resulting from the inevitable bearing of the recent rhythmic developments upon harmony—that there should be a consonance at the beginning of every perfection [5] (cf. p. 277). Anonymus XIII states [6] that a good discant should begin and end with the unison, fifth, or octave: during the early polyphonic period consonances were especially desired at the beginning and end of a piece. But there are 13th-century compositions not only having thirds at the beginnings of measures, but actually opening with major and minor thirds and even with major and minor triads. While, even where these things happen, octaves and fifths predominate in the course of the pieces, the increasing recognition accorded the third foreshadows the eventual downfall of a harmonic system based on unisons, octaves, fifths, and (originally) fourths—a system, that is, betokening a pentatonic feeling for melody (cf. pp. 250, 256f)—and the approach of a harmonic system based on the triad. It may be queried whether music based on the former system ever realized its fullest potentialities in the West and whether the acceptance of the third—as a result, possibly, of English influence (cf. pp. 388ff)—may not have been premature. The downfall, however, was still far off during the period of early Gothic music, and the triad had by no means as yet ousted the supremacy of octave and fifth.

Anonymus XIII prohibits [7] consecutive fifths and octaves against the tenor, but consecutives, permitted by earlier theorists under certain conditions, continue common enough in 13th-century polyphony.[8] While this polyphony is characteristically in three parts, two-part writing continues and real four-part writing begins.

It was about the second third of the 12th century that the school of Notre Dame de Paris assumed the leadership in musical development—or perhaps one should say "the so-called school of Notre Dame," since it includes Leonin

---

[4] CouS III, 496.

[5] GerS III, 13; CouS I, 132. Franco gives his classification of intervals in his Chap. XI (German transl. in BellerF), in which the rule occurs.

[6] CouS III, 497.   [7] CouS III, 497.

[8] Further concerning the varying fortunes of the intervals at the hands of the theorists of the period, see OH I, 87ff, 94ff; RieG, Chap. 6.

who, as we shall see, flourished possibly before the laying of the Notre Dame corner-stone by Pope Alexander III in 1163 and almost certainly before the completion of its choir twenty years later, and whose activity may therefore have run its course at the earlier cathedral at Paris. This school kept its leadership and continued to affect the main stream of polyphonic composition throughout the 13th century, so that the whole period might be called that of the Notre Dame school or, to give it the name of its greatest representative, the period of Perotin. The MSS of the time unfortunately omit the names of individual composers, but Anonymus IV provides some welcome information. He states [9] that Leonin—whom he calls *"optimus organista"*—composed the *Magnus Liber Organi de Gradali et Antiphonario pro servitio divino multiplicando,* a cycle of two-part compositions for the services of the whole year, and that afterwards Perotin—*"optimus discantor"*—shortened many of the pieces and inserted or composed as substitutes many new and better *"clausulae sive puncta"* (*cf.* p. 299).

Some scholars have thought that the term *organista* might mean merely "an organist" in the modern sense; but the word appears at Chartres before 1150 with the meaning of *clericus cantor* (singing cleric), and here, therefore, doubtless means "singer [or composer] of organa." [10] An organist was apparently called *organator.* [11] The name *discantor,* applied to Perotin, points out that he was considered remarkable chiefly as a composer of discant pieces. "Discant" is now applied to part-pieces with modal rhythm in all the voices.

The *organa,* on the other hand, are pieces in which the music is partly unmeasured.[12] Thus, discant and unmeasured music may alternate in a piece of organum, or, in the Perotin period, one voice may be measured and another not. While the term, *organum purum,* mentioned by several theorists, is applied solely to music in two parts, its exact meaning is in certain details differently explained in different tracts.[13] But it would seem reasonable, and it accords with Odington's definition, to assume that it was intended to designate the wholly unmeasured sections (which, as we shall see, Notre Dame polyphony offered only in two parts), included together with measured sections in the larger compositions called simply organa. Where (1) all parts are unmeasured or (2) only one is unmeasured, the way in which these parts are to be fitted together is indicated by their

---

[9] CouS I, 342.

[10] The term appears still earlier—in the 11th century—and the meaning, while not made clear, is probably the same. See Handschin in Acta, VII (1935), 159.

[11] See HandND, 13.

[12] *Cf.* Franco in CouS I, 118. By "measured," in this discussion, we do not necessarily imply that the music is mensurally notated; it may be—and, in fact, usually is—written down in one of the phases of modal notation; all that we imply is that modal rhythm, and therefore time-values, are to be deduced.

[13] *Cf.* CouS I, 96, 118, 245.

vertical alignment in the MSS, which give the organa (including the discant passages) in score. Where (2) obtains, the "unmeasured" part is, of course, actually measured in one sense: though there is nothing in the notation of the part by itself to indicate time-values, the duration of each note is determined by the length of the notes to be performed against it. The tenors of the organa continue to be drawn from the plainsong repertoire, for which reason some modern authorities, notably Handschin, refer to the compositions simply as *Choralbearbeitungen.* Apparently, in such pieces, all the parts sang the same text simultaneously, when they sang text at all (*cf.* p. 307).

There are four main MSS whose contents include, in differing versions, music from the *Magnus Liber,* which has not itself reached us. The oldest version, and therefore probably the one best preserving Leonin's style, is that in MS Wolfenbüttel 677, written in the 14th century, very likely at St. Andrews, Scotland.[14] The other three MSS are Pluteus 29.1 at the Biblioteca Medicea-Laurenziana in Florence, a sumptuous codex written towards the end of the 13th century in France; Wolfenbüttel 1206, probably written in France in the 13th or 14th century; and Madrid Bibl. Nac. 20486 (formerly Hh 167), sometimes referred to as the Toledo Codex, a younger MS than Wolfenbüttel 677, emanating from Spain.[15] Other MSS important as repositories of polyphony of this period are the *discantuum volumen* (which includes also *Quiconques veut deschanter* and another treatise, printed in CouH, 262), of unknown provenance, bound together with other MS material in Paris Bib. Nat. f. lat. 15139 (formerly St. Victor 813, because it is among the MSS once in the library of Adam's old Abbey of St. Victor); the copious musical MS inscribed at and still retained by the nunnery of Las Huelgas at Burgos; and some others at Munich and London.

Leonin's technique—if, as may fairly be assumed, it can be at least partly identified in the MSS—would place him in the second third or third quarter of the 12th century—midway, that is, between the St. Martial school and Perotin. This technique was guided by that of St. Martial. Here, too, we find the more or less note-against-note style and the sustained-tone style (*cf.* pp. 265f), the two being juxtaposed in individual pieces.[16] The former type

---

[14] Reproduced in facsimile in BaxO. Although this MS (sometimes referred to in scholarly writing under its former mark, Helmstedt 628, and often simply as W 1) is the next to the youngest of the 4 in question, its versions of the Notre Dame pieces are in the oldest style. See LudR, 7ff, the masterly *catalogue raisonné* of the organa of this period and of the oldest motets, giving exhaustive information on all relevant MSS of the period, known at the time it was written.
[15] The Florence MS is often referred to merely as F, Wolfenbüttel 1206 (of which there is a photostat at the Library of Congress) as W 2 (or sometimes under its former mark, Helmstedt 1099) and the Madrid MS as Ma. Concerning the provenance of all 4 MSS, see especially LudU; with special reference to that of the Madrid MS, see HandE, 511. Concerning the respective ages of the style of their contents, see (in addition to LudR) HusM, 174ff, in connection with the Madrid MS, and HusO, 47ff, in connection with the others.
[16] SchmiM, 134, attributes the juxtaposition to Perotin's recasting of the *Magnus Liber* and ascribes only the melismatic style to Leonin. But, since both styles had already existed in the St. Martial music, there would seem to be no reason to assign the more restrained one to a "modern" like Perotin (*cf.* HandNDS, 548f).

is named *diaphonia organica* in the *Summa Musicae* and the latter, *diaphonia basilica*.[17] Leonin alters the less florid style only by allowing the organal voice to have short melismas over every syllable, thus producing greater differentiation between the two voices. These short melismas are to be performed according to rhythmic mode 1, 2, or 3, and the tenor according to rhythmic mode 1, 2, or 5. Discant results. The very extended melismas—which, together with the long-held, unmeasured tenor-notes, characterize the second style—are to be sung freely. Thus, in this style, neither part is measured. The combining of the two styles in single pieces illustrates one of the uses of contrast made by the Notre Dame school. The places where the juxtaposition is to occur are generally determined on the principle that, where the plainsong melody serving as tenor is syllabic or only slightly melismatic, the sustained-tone style should be used, and, where it is richly melismatic, the less florid style should be used. In the latter style, the tenor melody may be repeated several times, producing a sort of *ostinato*. The larger sections into which the alternation of these styles divides a composition are called the *clausulae* or *puncta*.[18]

Contrast in rhythm was obtained not only by the juxtaposition of the two polyphonic styles but also by the continued use of alternation between passages of plainsong sung by the choir and passages of organum normally sung by soloists (*cf.* p. 264), which produced a contrast in *timbre* as well. Two-part settings were provided for the intonations of the first section and of the verse of the Graduals etc. of the Mass (and likewise for the responds of the Office); the rest of the first section and verse were sung in plainsong (*cf.* Example 84).

Leonin's melodies contain no broken triads and only rarely a melodic leap larger than a third. But they often contain *glissando*-like passages running through a whole octave or even more. These may be the result of Arabic influence,[19] a hypothesis strengthened by the fact that Anonymus IV states [20] the terms "elmuahym" and "elmuarifa" to be synonymous with *currentes* (*cf.* p. 281). Leonin's melodic curve is much broader than Perotin's, which tends towards squarer rhythms and short motives. With Leonin (as with his successor) the melody frequently consists of sequences, some of which become fixed formulas. The following sequence-group, for example, has been found reappearing thirteen times in various places, always above the same tenor notes, F–E, and even oftener in slightly altered form.

[17] GerS III, 239f.
[18] The term *clausula* is used by several modern writers, notably Ludwig (e. g. in LudR, 15), for the discant sections only. It is applied in UrK, 122, however, to sections of both types. The passage from Anonymus IV in CouS I, 342, does not exclude either interpretation.
[19] See SchmiM, 129f; also Handschin in ZfMW, XIV (1932), 321f.
[20] CouS I, 339f. See also FarmC, 76.

EXAMPLE 83. (After SchmiM [where further sequence-formulas are given], 130).

Perotin was active at Notre Dame beginning, apparently, *c.* 1183. Since the name Perotin is a diminutive of Pierre, the Petrus Succentor mentioned eight times in documents referring to the years 1208–38 may be identical with the *optimus discantor*.[21]

Perotin's chief contributions consisted in the new *clausulae sive puncta* in discant style that he substituted for other *clausulae* in this style and for sections in free organum contained in the *Magnus Liber*. While not all the substitute *clausulae* are attributable to him, their important new characteristics doubtless derive from him. The tenor melody is habitually disposed in reiterated rhythmic patterns, the pattern being occasionally changed in the course of a piece. Sometimes where, in addition to the pattern, the tenor melody is repeated too, the ending of its first presentation does not coincide with the ending of one of the appearances of the pattern, so that, in the second presentation (beginning immediately after the first and therefore not with the initial time-value of the pattern), its rhythmic shape is altered. This interesting feature is illustrated in Example 86, in which, after an introduction, there are seven appearances of a four-measure pattern and, spread through these seven appearances, four presentations of a nine-note melody (each entry of which is marked *).[22] The melody does not quite fill the first two appearances of the pattern, falling short by one note. As a result, the melody, when accorded its second presentation, starts on the last note of the second appearance of the pattern and therefore has a rhythmic shape different from the one it had previously, the rhythmic shape, indeed, necessarily continuing to change with each of the remaining two presentations. (Leonin sometimes repeats the tenor in altered rhythmic guise also, but his examples are fewer and less developed.[23]) Constant rhythmic patterns (*ordines* or expansions thereof) may be said, in the absence of melodic repetition, to have produced a rhythmic ground-bass (if we disregard, for present purposes, the fact that an upper part might cross below a tenor). Where the end of each melodic repetition coincided with the end of a pattern, a real ground-bass resulted. Where melodic repetition and rhythmic pattern overlapped, as in Example 86, the result was a kind of ground-bass for which modern music has no labelled equivalent. A comparison of Examples 84 and 86, showing the rhythmically amorphous character of

[21] For further information, see FiS, 25f; GasP, 18f; HandND, 10ff.

[22] The melisma occupying all but the last measure of the first line constitutes the introduction. The first appearance of the four-measure pattern opens, as transcribed, with a dotted half-note plus a rest of the same duration, whereas the subsequent appearances begin with a dotted whole note.   [23] *Cf.* LudR, 24.

the tenor of a typical Leonin discant *clausula* and the rhythmically organized character of the tenor of a typical Perotin *clausula,* illustrates how, with Perotin, both voices of a two-part piece may move in sharply defined independent rhythms. The new two-part *clausulae* add an important element—organized rhythmic independence of parts—to the technique of polyphony.

A wealth of substitute *clausulae* survives in the MSS, several such *clausulae* often being interchangeable as substitutes for a single original, all of these, of course, being then based on the same liturgical tenor. In its present state, the Florence MS alone, despite its inclusion of only 90 organa, has no less than 308 substitute *clausulae* in discant style and 154 substitutes—some of them merely abbreviations—still in organum style, all gathered into a fascicle of their own, which forms a sort of appendix. While a substitute *clausula* in organum style is often a shortened version of the original, a *clausula* in discant style, replacing one in organum style, is not necessarily brief. In the Florence MS and also in Wolfenbüttel 1206, the Leonin *clausulae* are very often replaced by new ones in the organa themselves and are relegated to the appendix or are even omitted.[24] The following examples show the styles of Leonin and Perotin in comparison.[25] In No. 84, Perotin retains Leonin's music almost intact, making only a few melodic changes after the plainsong passage.

EXAMPLES 84–86. *Alleluia Pascha nostrum*—Organum—Extracts from Settings in Leonin and Perotin Styles (after LudB, 448ff).

EXAMPLE 84.

[24] *Cf.* LudL, 207f. [25] For another such example, see BesM, 99.

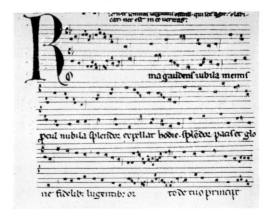

Figure of Music, with Bell-Chimes,
Viol, and Psaltery
From the Portail Royal of the Cathedral of
Chartres, 12th Century

Facsimile of the Conductus Roma gau-
dens iubila *as it appears in Bibl. Medicea-*
Laurenziana, Pluteus 29.1
(Cf. *the facsimile after Wolfenbüttel 677 in*
BaxO, and Example 89)

Group of Monks Singing before the Lectern
(*Italian, 15th Century*)

PLATE VI

Leonin continues in the same style over the word *nostrum,* while Perotin, naturally retaining Leonin's tenor-notes, substitutes a *clausula* in discant style. His abandoning the sustained-tone style and substituting crisper rhythm, however, makes it necessary for him to repeat the tenor once to give the section proper length. Both composers then continue with the same short section of organum over the first two syllables of the word *immolatus.* Leonin writes a discant *clausula* over syllable 3, as follows, and free organum over syllable 4.

EXAMPLE 85.

Perotin writes one discant *clausula* over both syllables 3 and 4. Thereafter, in both versions, comes a passage of plainsong. Then Leonin repeats the whole Alleluia as given in Ex. 84, all 6 incises of the plainsong included. Perotin substitutes the following discant *clausula,* using (as does Leonin) the first incise as his tenor, but he assigns to the choir only the remaining 5 incises.[26]

EXAMPLE 86.

[26] The tenor derives from the plainsong printed in the *Liber Usualis,* 770.

Perotin wrote organa not only in two parts but also in three and four, these being called *tripla* and *quadrupla*. Only three quadrupla are known—the *Viderunt*,[27] *Sederunt*,[28] and *Mors*—which occur in several MSS. Anonymus IV definitely states the *Viderunt* and *Sederunt* (and likewise the tripla, *Alleluia Posui adjutorium* and *Alleluia Nativitas* [29]) to be by Perotin. It is possible that an order of the Bishop Odo de Sully, dated 1198, referring to music for New Year's Day, relates to the *Sederunt,* which is liturgically assignable to that season.[30] The three-part organa seem to have remained in favor longest, since they are the only ones known to have been taken over into mensural notation, to which they are transferred without important changes.

The Notre Dame tripla and quadrupla differ from the earlier organa partly in that the importance of the melodic quality of the added parts is on the whole secondary. Sometimes melodic material is appropriated from two-part pieces, and the influence of folk- and dance-pieces seems to be present also. The upper parts have short phrases in modal rhythm, mode 1 appearing much more often than the others. In a piece like the *Sederunt*—a work of grand proportions—the protracted maintenance of a single mode in all the voices in discant passages and in the upper voices in organum passages, producing throbbing columns of tone, is overpowering in its relentlessness and,

[27] A portion is transcribed in OH I, 132ff, after the Florence MS. Transcriptions from this MS appeared in print for the first time in the first edition of OH. The rhythmical interpretations, however, no longer represented up-to-date musicological knowledge when the second edition appeared, as may be seen by comparing the *Viderunt* transcription with the fragment in LudG, 229. (Compare also OH I, 121f, with FiG, 490, or HandZB, 15ff; or see LudR, 54.) Another portion is transcribed in SchneiderZ. Our Exx. 87 and 88 are excerpts from the LudG and SchneiderZ transcriptions.

[28] Printed in FiS in both a "critical" transcription and a transcription for practical use.

[29] Transcriptions of the first in RoksM II, 31, and, for practical use, by Ficker in *Neue Musik-Zeitung,* XLIX (1928), supplement to article beginning on p. 48; transcription of the second in RoksM II, 16.

[30] *Cf.* HandND, 6f.

in the organum sections, contrasts strikingly with the "unmeasured" sustaining of the tones in the tenor. Both Perotin and Leonin, as has been indicated, used an organum as well as a discant style, but with Perotin the former style approaches the condition of the latter through the modal rhythms in the upper voices, the rhythmic distinction between the two styles being dependent upon the measured or unmeasured nature of the tenor. The upper voices do not, as a rule, constitute soprano, alto, etc., lines in the modern manner, but are of more or less equal pitch-level and often cross one another, this being true of 13th-century polyphony generally.

Perotin's melodic phrases are in many instances broken triads, thus differing markedly from Leonin's (cf. p. 298). While full triads sounded chordally are not characteristic of the Notre Dame music, the effect of triads is nevertheless pronounced, owing to the frequent sounding of root, fifth, and octave simultaneously and of a broken triad melodically, and more especially through the fact that one triad so treated is likely to remain the back-bone of an extended passage, being embellished by what we would today call passing-notes etc.[31] Thus, the character of a composition is established more by chord color and the nature of the rhythm than by the quality of the melody. Frequent departure from and return to a single chord would seem to bear some relation to the practices of folk-heterophony (cf. pp. 255f). The upper voices, in weaving about the tones of the triad, often supplement them by the second and sixth, thus producing a strong pentatonic effect. But the forcefulness with which the triad makes itself felt also and, in addition, the increasing appearance of the third show that the pentatonic and diatonic systems are poised in the balance. There are many progressions of parallel fifths and fourths [32] (frequent fourths, of course, do not re-establish the interval as a consonance as long as they are confined to upper voices), so that, if it is true that the early parallel organum and free heterophonic organum represented two different lines of development (cf. p. 258), those two lines would seem to have become closely intertwined by the time of the Notre Dame organa.[33] Where a tenor-note group reappears in different pieces, all the upper-part lines that go with it in one piece are sometimes to be found with it again in another (cf. p. 298).

An additional feature of the Notre Dame compositions—a most striking one for their date—is the appearance of canon. This device may possibly, in art-music at least, be an outgrowth of interchange of melodies between two or more voices—*Stimmtausch,* as the German writers call it—illustrated in this example from the *Viderunt:*

[31] For examples illustrating these points, see SchmiD, 11, 14ff. They are illustrated also to some extent in our Ex. 88.
[32] See, for instance, AngE III, 300, or SchmiD, 22.
[33] Further concerning the possible relationship between the early parallel organa and the Notre Dame pieces, see SchmiD, 7f.

EXAMPLE 87. Extract 1 from *Viderunt*—Perotin (after LudG, 229).

We shall have occasion to return to this device several times. If one voice delays its entry, *Stimmtausch* produces imitation with respect to one of the interchanged melodies, and canon technique has emerged. (For example, if we delay the entrance of the lower voice for one measure in Example 87 and, for the sake of illustration, regard the resulting intervals as acceptable, a two-measure snatch of imitation, based on the lower-voice melody, will result.) Another possible source of canon in art-music may have been overlapping in antiphonal singing, overlapping such as might conceivably have occurred in the performance of a liturgical sequence if the responding group of singers did not wait for the first group to finish its portion of a double versicle. Still another possible source might consist in sheer accident in folk-singing, one singer or group lagging behind another unintentionally, the result being observed and later used deliberately.[34] Sometimes, in these organa, the imitation assumes lengthy proportions, as in Example 88 (beginning with the syllable *um*).[35]

Ornamentation plays a prominent rôle in the Notre Dame pieces. Odington states that the sustained tones of the tenor should be sung *tremolando,* but apparently this was a matter of choice.[36] Anonymus IV [37] mentions the use of a duplex long (in all parts) at the opening, the resulting combination being consonant and being called the "beginning before the beginning." This, it would seem, may also have been sung *tremolando.*[38] As written, the organa do not always abide by the rule that the opening be consonant, there being present what might be called an *appoggiatura,* which forms a dissonance with the tenor. But Anonymus IV points out that a dissonance at the outset is to be avoided in performance by delaying the entry of the tenor: in the MSS the first tenor-note is, in fact, frequently shifted a bit from left to right.[39] Apparently the ornamenting of the tenor was sometimes left

[34] Further concerning earlier canon technique, see MülleGF, 5ff; GennF, 80; SchneiderZ; ChomT, 116ff; FeinK, 1ff; BukP, 34f. Concerning canon among primitive peoples, see SchneiderG I, 22.

[35] The tenor derives from the plainsong printed in the *Liber Usualis,* 409.

[36] See HandE, 699. Odington's statement is in CouS I, 246.   [37] CouS I, 363.

[38] It is thus that SchmiD, 10, suggests Anon. IV's application of the term *florata* to this duplex long might be interpreted.

[39] See HandE, 699. Anon, IV's statement follows immediately after the passage cited in footnote 37.

EXAMPLE 88. Extract 2 from *Viderunt*—Perotin (after SchneiderZ, 406).

to the performer, since Franco writes[40] that in organum the tenor must avoid a dissonance with the upper parts (at the beginnings of their measures only?) and that it might do this by inserting a new tone; it might also do this by pausing. The *currentes,* characteristic of the Leonin style (*cf.* p. 298), provide still another type of ornamentation. Apparently *Stimmtausch* was regarded as a sort of vertical ornament since it is the last of several devices designated as *color* by Garlandia,[41] and the others are definitely ornamental. One consists in filling in a fifth or octave with its intervening tones, these

[40] GerS III, 15; CouS I, 135.   [41] CouS I, 115f.

being repeated according to some pattern. Thus, within a fifth there might be (1) a return to the first tone of the interval after the sounding of each intervening tone, or (2) repetition, within the framework of some sequence pattern, of the intervening tones, as in the melodic succession: aGaF, GFGE, FEFD. Another device, the *florificatio vocis,* consists in the immediate repetition of tones or short motives, themselves containing repetitions. Thus *color,* whatever its exact nature, involves repetition, this affecting melodic as distinguished from rhythmic material. At points where important changes take place in the organa, as for instance at the division between a discant section and an organum section, rhythmically free transitional passages, called *copulae,* are inserted that have something like the effect of a modern *cadenza.* These can be long or short, the longest occurring at the very end in the manner of a modern coda.[42]

While Paris as chief cultural center of France developed new technical styles, the French provinces preserved a more conservative organum technique, resembling that simultaneously current in Britain, where it may have originated (*cf.* pp. 393ff). In what may be called the peripheral style, to which this technique belongs, the tenor flows along quietly, without sustained tones, whether the borrowed plainsong is syllabic or melismatic. There is thus less rhythmic difference between the upper voices and the' tenor. The compositions in general avoid the highly melismatic style of Notre Dame, and are either not melismatic at all or only slightly so. The absence of the sustained-tone style makes it possible to embellish whole Chant-melodies, rather than mere segments, with organum.[43]

That Spain followed up the early cultivation of polyphony, evidenced by the Codex Calixtinus, is shown not only by MS Madrid Bibl. Nac. 20486, which is of Spanish origin (*cf.* footnote 15), but by the MS of Las Huelgas.[44] Both show the influence of the Notre Dame style and actually contain Notre Dame pieces, including organa. Although the Las Huelgas MS dates from the 14th century, it is clearly an anthology, some of whose contents were already of considerable antiquity when it was written. Thus the early 12th-century *Verbum bonum* (*cf.* p. 270) reappears in it, and such a two-part organum setting as that of the *Victimae paschali*[45] is an interesting example of the application of fairly early organum technique. The *lauda* MSS of Cortona and Florence (*cf.* p. 237) contain a few examples of polyphony, and here too a

---

[42] For further information concerning the *copula,* see SchmiD, 37ff; OH I, 119f.

[43] For further information concerning this style, see HandS and HandH.

[44] Published in facsimile with transcriptions and commentary in AngE. Citations directing the reader to Las Huelgas pieces will here be given to transcriptions only (also, later, in connection with pieces in the Montpellier and Bamberg MSS), references in the captions of the transcriptions making it easy to locate the corresponding pages of facsimile (as is true also in the scholarly editions of the Montpellier and Bamberg MSS, to be mentioned presently). For a list of other Spanish MSS containing 13th-cent. music, see AngF, 160f. For transcriptions of 3 two-part examples from one of them—MS 1 of the Orfeó Català, Barcelona—, see AngL, 227, 229, 243. (For some facsimiles from this MS, see AngE I, 77, 79, and E. Lopez-Chavarri, *Historia de la Música,* I [3rd ed., 1929]. 63.) [45] AngE III, 92.

few compositions come down to us in which this technique is represented.[46]

At Paris, the increasing use of discant passages within the organa caused the pure organum style to decline during the second half of the 13th century. But the singing of organa did not entirely die out. And, as we shall see when we discuss the motet, they carried the seed of a new life within themselves.[47]

In the Notre Dame polyphonic *conductus,* the tenor is never in sustained-tone style. All parts, which may be as many as four, move in a more or less uniform rhythm. Thus, on the whole, the music of the conductus tends to progress more in block chords than does that of the organa or motets. The text is normally metrical (*cf.* the monodic conductus, pp. 201f). It is in Latin and is shared by all the voices. Franco gives the conductus and organum as the types *cum littera et sine* ("with text and without") and this has been interpreted [48] as meaning that not all the parts had words. Such an interpretation, and also the claim that the upper parts were played on instruments, would, at first glance, seem to receive some support from the fact that in the MSS the conducti have words only under the lowest part. But, since the pieces are notated in score and all the parts proceed in fairly uniform rhythm, there would have been no need to write out the words more than once. It was characteristic of one class of conductus, however, that at points of structural importance, such as the beginnings and ends of lines or stanzas or over the penultimate syllable, all the parts, still maintaining fairly uniform rhythm, simultaneously broke out into melismas of their own. Apparently what Franco meant to imply is that portions of the conductus—i. e. the melismas—were performed without words and portions of it with them.[49] In short, all the parts sang the same text in the passages in which it was to be sung at all. The *Discantus Positio Vulgaris* says [50] that the conductus was a polyphonic piece *super unum metrum.* The word *metrum* differentiates the conducti from the organa, based on Gradual (i. e. prose) texts etc., and the word *unum* differentiates them from the motets, in which not all the parts had the same text.

The class of conductus with melismas at points of structural importance (i.e. the conductus with *caudae*) stands in striking contrast to the class in which a more or less syllabic style is maintained throughout. In one passage in which Anonymus IV mentions three-part conducti, Coussemaker's edition, through punctuation, makes him seem to apply the adjective *simplex* to them, and this has caused some modern writers to believe he intended the term to designate pieces that do not have *caudae.* But a change in Coussemaker's doubtless faulty punctuation removes the cause for this belief (though

---

[46] *Cf.* WolfMG, 292, where there is a transcription (appearing also in WolfH I, 267). Not all the polyphonic examples in these MSS are of the primitive type, however (*cf.* the description of the Latin pieces contained in the 2 Florence MSS, given in LudQ, 299f, where some motets are listed).   [47] For some organum transcriptions see, besides those already referred to, HandC, 161; SchmiB; AngE III, *passim;* RoksM II, 9, 24, 38; LudG, 217.—Since this book first appeared, HusD has become available, containing transcriptions of 29 organa and 17 *clausulae.*
[48] E. g. in OH I, 106.   [49] See HandNDS, 551; HandN, 209; RoksC, 8.   [50] CouS I, 96.

it substitutes another difficulty). Moreover, in another part of his treatise, the Anonymus uses the term unmistakably to distinguish monodic from polyphonic conducti.[51] (Grocheo twice uses the words *ex pluribus concordantii, compositus ad modum simplicis conductus,* but is referring to melodic, not harmonic, concordance—i. e. to monody.)

The forerunners of the polyphonic conductus are such early organa as were based on melodies with metrical texts, frequently sequences—*cf.* pp. 264, 270. (In such an organum to a metrical text as the St. Martial *Mira lege*—*cf.* p. 266—one can already find melismas in both voices at a point of structural importance.) Thus, in these transitional pieces, the tenor melodies, not being from the Gregorian repertoire, are of much later date than those of the organa. At Notre Dame, even recent pre-existent tenors seem to have been passed by in favor of entirely new ones. Franco states [52] that whoever wishes to write a conductus should first compose his own tenor, "as beautiful as he can," and then add the *discantus* (i. e. the duplum); if a third voice is wanted, care should be taken always to have it in concordance with either the tenor or the *discantus*. This passage is interesting not only as evidence of the frequent originality of conductus tenors but also as indicating that, even in the absence of a pre-existent tenor, the parts were written one at a time rather than simultaneously. In the absence of a Gregorian tenor lies one of the main differences between the conductus on the one hand and the organa and motets on the other. The conductus is thus the first polyphonic type in which the composer was able to give entirely free rein to his imagination.[53]

By stating that the tenor should be written first, Franco implies that it is the main voice. But in practice it on rare occasions yields up its prerogative.[54]

Leonin apparently did not write conducti. Perotin did, however; and to him Anonymus IV specifically attributes the three-part *Salvatoris hodie*, the two-part *Dum sigillum*, and the monodic *Beata viscera*,[54a] the latter with text by Chancellor Philippe (*cf.* p. 202). In the polyphonic pieces he used the fairly chordal style described above, with melismas at stanza or verse ends, etc. He sometimes used melismas also in the body of the periods—for example, to stress important syllables or produce a descriptive effect.

Conductus texts, in polyphonic as in monodic settings, varied considerably in character. They could be religious and in some way related to the liturgy or they could be definitely secular. Texts of the latter type are of a serious nature, containing moral reflections or comments on important state events that show them to be occasional pieces.

[51] The two passages are in CouS I, 354, 350.   [52] CouS I, 132.

[53] It should be added, however, that some non-Gregorian melodies are to be found not only as voices in polyphonic *conducti*, but singly. Most of these may have existed first in the part-pieces and have been liked well enough to be sung singly; but the practical certainty that at least one of them was pre-existent is not to be overlooked. The point will be dealt with in an article on the conductus, by Leonard Ellinwood, to appear shortly in MQ.

[54] *Cf.* LudG, 277; also Chap. 14, footnote 69 *infra*.

[54a] But not a monodic *Iustitia,* as indicated in CouS I, 342; *cf.* LudQ, 187, note 2.

Eleven Notre Dame conducti reappear in mensural notation in the Las Huelgas MS. The great bulk of such conducti, however, does not survive in this kind of notation. Moreover, since the music is in large part syllabic, it naturally often fails to lend itself to real modal notation, the very nature of this being, as we have seen, to indicate rhythm through selection of ligature shapes. The transcriber is thus frequently faced with knotty problems. Where melismas do occur, however, they provide the occasion for notation in ligature and permit of modal interpretation, though sometimes only with considerable difficulty. Whether or not the Las Huelgas versions can cast much light on the rhythm of 13th-century conducti is open to question, since these versions perhaps show the influence of the 14th century, when the MS was inscribed (*cf.* p. 373; see also p. 313). It would seem that, in the syllabic music, the patterns of modes 5 and 2 predominated.[55] Where the former did so, the underlying rhythm was much more likely to have a binary than a ternary feeling if the meter of the text was trochaic [56] or iambic. But on the whole the ternary rhythm characteristic of 13th-century music still obtains.

The following illustrates the characteristics of a Notre Dame conductus.

EXAMPLE 89. *Roma gaudens iubila*—Conductus for Christmas (Florence, Pluteus 29. 1, ff. 318–318ᵛ; Wolfenbüttel 677, ff. 116–116ᵛ, after Baxter facsimile).

[55] The Las Huelgas versions, however, do not lend support to the mode 2 interpretation. Handschin believes that, in the earlier conducti, each syllable (in the absence of melismas) has the value of 1 perfect long. If there are 2 notes to a syllable, 1 must be an imperfect long and 1 a brevis recta—that is, they must divide the value of the perfect long, and the mode will be 2 (or 1). Where there are more than 2 notes to a syllable, they must be treated as *aequipollentiae*. Not until the middle of the 13th century were conducti written in which each syllable could be set by notes having the value of an imperfect long or of a brevis recta. (HandNDS, 553.)

[56] For a transcription of Handschin's emphasizing this fact by using binary measure with occasional triplets rather than ternary measure with a multiplicity of dotted half-notes, see EinSH 260.

ad - est do - mi - nus, Ut _____ tu - o fi - at ter - mi - nus Ex - i -

li - o cum _____ gau - di - o, Jam _____ re - gem re - gum su - sci -

pe.

Rome, exult with joy this day,
Let thy woe be far away,
Let light drive out the clouds of sin
With peace on earth, good will to men
  Of true belief
  Or lost in grief,
A light that from thy Prince now springs.

Zion, for your daughter fair,
Come, put off your deep despair,
For now the Lord of Peace is come
To give you all at last a home;
  From exile free,
  Make jubilee,
Receive ye now your King of Kings.

(Translated by Willis Wager).

The conductus being like organum merely a type (cf. p. 294), it can take on a variety of forms, these being largely influenced by the text. Its music became the subject for interesting experiments. Thus, in the St. Victor MS, there are 10 two-part conducti [57] (dating from c. 1244 to c. 1248) in several of which the melismas or *caudae* (or, as Yvonne Rokseth neatly calls them, the *caudae sine littera*) are made to serve somewhat as refrains after the main periods. They are not always repeated literally, however, but are subjected to interesting variation. In one conductus (*Transfretasse*), in which the melisma recurs, the two parts, while interchanged upon repetition, do not produce ordinary *Stimmtausch*: the upper voice is transposed down a fifth and the lower voice up an octave—a real example of double counterpoint, the earliest one known.[58] Some of these conducti are of considerable historical interest. The text of the first is in praise of St. Louis, and the last eight refer to the Crusade that was to be undertaken in 1249 and that led St. Louis into Egypt.

The Las Huelgas MS contains, besides the 11 Notre Dame polyphonic conducti mentioned above, 6 not known elsewhere.[59] The last of these is attributed to Johannes Roderici (Rodriguez), who appears as the composer of several other pieces also. Another apparent conductus in this group has

[57] Made the subject of a special study in RoksC, which contains more general information on the conductus than its title would seem to indicate. A transcription of a three-part conductus from the same MS is printed in CouH, xxii (in back); OH I, 85 (with the unwarranted statement—at least for date of 2nd ed. of OH—that the piece contains earliest attempt "at present known" of imitation). [58] For the music, see RoksC, 10. (CouH incorrectly uses the term "double counterpoint" for simple *Stimmtausch*.)   [59] AngE III, 156, 268, 306, 328, 331, 373.

been pointed out as remarkable in that it has two simultaneously sung texts and yet lacks the kind of tenor we shall find normal in the early motet (but *cf.* p. 314). Further concerning the Las Huelgas conducti, see p. 373.

About 1250, the vogue of the motet was such as to put an end to the writing of conducti, but Johannes de Grocheo mentions them as still current, a fact that shows they were being performed until at least *c.* 1300. Later in the 14th century their neglect is deplored (*cf.* p. 331). But the dying out of the conductus is more apparent than real. Its technique actually became merged in that of the motet (*cf.* pp. 416f) and it became, as we shall see, one of the main sources of Italian *trecento* music.[60]

The *motet* was the most productive of the 13th-century polyphonic types. Its chief traits were (1) multiplicity of text—a feature we have more than once had occasion to mention in passing—and (2) a tenor with a pre-existent melody, disposed in reiterated rhythmic patterns—a feature we have already encountered in connection with the discant *clausula* of Perotin (*cf.* p. 299). Thus the 13th-century motet was a very different thing from the type of composition similarly named in the times of Palestrina and Bach.

It will be recalled (*cf.* p. 266) that the St. Martial organa included 2 pieces in which the tenor and organal voice had independent texts, and there are other such old pieces also. Obviously, in pure organum style, the performer of the upper part had many more notes to remember than the performer of the tenor. It is probable that this fact caused the old process, whereby the Alleluia of Gregorian Chant gave birth to the sequence form, to lead to the adoption of a separate text for the upper voice, the text of the plainsong being clearly insufficient to provide each note or small group of notes in this voice with a syllable of its own. The situation would obviously be much the same even where discant style rather than the sustained-tone style was in use, in any instance in which the tenor had a melody that was itself a plainsong melisma. Apparently the solution offered by polytextuality was not immediately adopted at Notre Dame, possibly owing to objections having at first existed (such as were raised later) to the obscuring of the liturgical text by the singing of other words against it. However this may be, polytextuality does appear in Notre Dame *clausulae* of the time of Perotin. There are *clausulae* existing in some MSS as melismas that reappear in others as motets, i. e. with upper parts in syllabic style as a result of the addition of texts. Pluteus 29.1 contains some music in both states. The Parisian motet, then, began its career as a kind of substitute *clausula*. And, since it came into being in Perotin's day, the *clausula* was, understandably enough, normally of the discant type.

[60] For a guide to conducti published up to 1931 (transcriptions, facsimiles), see AngE I, 323ff, 374f. For a listing of polyphonic Notre Dame conducti that includes references to transcriptions published up to 1939, see GrönR, 64ff (a listing that should be supplemented by references to AngL 261, 262; a piece apparently not a Notre Dame conductus is printed on p. 257). The article mentioned in footnote 53 will provide several additional transcriptions.

Trait 1 is the real criterion of the motet in its early history. Trait 2, although soon adopted and characteristic in a general way, was constantly present neither at the beginning of the century nor, as we shall see, during its second half. Since both traits could appear in discant *clausulae* in the style of Perotin, he has been called, by some, the initiator of the motet.[61] Organum, a musical trope of plainsong (*cf.* p. 264)—or more generally its outgrowth, discant, with a reiterated rhythmic pattern in the tenor—, was itself troped literally, and the motet was born.[62]

The tenors of motets were apparently often performed on instruments. Thus motets in two, three, and four parts (these being the numbers of parts to which motets were restricted in the 13th century) may be said respectively to have given rise to the vocal solo, duet, and trio with composed accompaniment. When the tenor of a two-part motet was played on an instrument, polytextuality, of course, disappeared in performance; but as the tenor was normally derived from a primarily vocal source it may still have carried the hint of a second text.

In the motet the part above the tenor, the duplum of organum, acquired the name of *motetus,* derived from the French *mot* ("word")—for obvious reasons—and this name it gave to the entire species. A third part was called the *triplum* and a fourth part the *quadruplum.* A three-part motet with two added texts is called a double motet; a four-part motet with three added texts, a triple motet. It is customary to entitle a medieval motet by the first words of each part—that is, by each *incipit* or (to use the French term instead of the Latin) each *timbre.* It is understandable why, with texts rendering the upper parts syllabic, a 14th-century writer should have found occasion to say that ligatures were no longer often used except in the tenors.[63]

Example 90, on the next page, illustrates the chief characteristics of a 13th-century motet.

The early motet is represented in the four great Notre Dame MSS as well as in the others specifically named on p. 297. Wolfenbüttel 677 contains the first *clausulae* troped with extra Latin texts, from which fact the beginnings of the Notre Dame motet are placed *c.* 1200. While, in this MS and the Madrid MS, the organa and conducti are in fascicles separate from one another, the motets are merely distributed among them, not yet, apparently, being regarded as a distinctive species. Other important collections of motets are contained in the famous Montpellier MS H 196. Its first six fascicles contain more motets of all kinds belonging to the first half of the 13th century than any other MS. The last of these fascicles is devoted entirely to the two-

---

[61] 2 Perotin *clausulae* for the composition from which Exx. 84–86 give excerpts, furnished the basis for motets. See LudB, 450f, 453ff. Further concerning organum *clausulae* serving as motet sources, see particularly LudR, 88ff.

[62] For an article especially on the origin of the motet, see HandUU. [63] CouS II, 405.

EXAMPLE 90. *In seculum Artifex—In seculum, supra mulieres—In seculum* (after AngE III, 223).

Triplum—"For all eternity, the Maker of eternity was born for a little time, for the sake of the people's life. The Father of the flock, the Creator of the law took on the shape of a little lamb, learned the rule of a disciple, took the shape of a little slave and a tiny child." Motetus—"For all eternity, above all women, Blessed Virgin, [above all] women, hailed by a messenger from heaven, oh! for the salvation of the faithful now beseech and pray to thine own Son." (Transl. S.L.E.)

part motet, a type greatly in favor during the first half-century.[64] Fascicles 7 and 8 represent stages of the motet style as it was in the latter part of the 13th century, fascicle 8 containing pieces in the "peripheral" style (*cf.* pp. 319f). A dividing line in style appears, accommodatingly enough, *c.* 1250. Motets of the later period appear also in Bamberg Ed. N. 6[65] (which, not-withstanding, includes music from the old Notre Dame repertoire, as does the Montpellier MS also), and in MSS at Darmstadt, Turin, etc.[66] At first the motets were written down in a partially modal notation, some existing even in Gothic neumes and letter notation. The mode indicated for a piece in one MS is not necessarily the same as that indicated for it in another, possibly owing to a difference in tradition. (This is true of discant *clausulae* also.) Partially modal notation continued in use even in the later period, mensural notation being generally reserved for the more complicated pieces. This clearer notation made it unnecessary for motets always to be notated in score, and advantage was taken of this possibility. Thus it became usual for the

[64] KuhlM is devoted almost entirely to a study of this fascicle. The whole MS is sumptuously published in facsimile with transcriptions and commentary in RoksM. (A copy of the commentary became available to me only on the day the final proofs of this book had to be handed in. I have therefore been unable, except on p. 284, to take that very impressive contribution into account in this volume.)

[65] Published in facsimile with transcriptions and commentary in AuM.

[66] LudQ supplements LudR in furnishing a *catalogue raisonné* of motets of the earlier period. The motets in AngE constitute a further addition to the repertoire. See also RosM.

upper parts of three- and four-part motets in mensural notation to be written down in columns, one beside the other, the bottom of the page, however, being reserved for the tenor, which extended from margin to margin. In less advanced circles, however (e. g. Germany), score notation continued. Occasionally a MS, notably Madrid Bibl. Nac. 20486, fails to give the tenor. Where this happens, the notated music may look like a conductus, especially if all the parts that remain have the same text (*cf.* below), and the true character of the music as portion of a motet becomes apparent only when the piece is found in another MS with the tenor present. (It is not likely that a tenor would have been *added* to a conductus, since the method of composition was to write *from* a tenor. It is more likely that in such a case a tenor was dropped from the motet and the upper parts sung as a conductus, or else that the melody and also its connection with the piece as tenor were too well known to make its notation necessary.)

The practice, so far as three- and four-part *clausulae* are concerned, of adding a single text to all the upper parts came first but did not last long. The new texts were soon replaced in the tripla and quadrupla by still newer ones, in such a way that each part had its own text, the double and triple motets mentioned above thus resulting. Perotin's contemporaries, and perhaps he himself, represent both of these practices in their motets. They add only Latin texts, some being attributable to Chancellor Philippe. A little later, but still before 1250, we find French texts, which occur, for example, in the St. Victor MS and in Munich mus. 4775. In fascicles 3–5 of the Montpellier MS, the main bodies of which were intended to contain only three-part pieces, 3 is devoted to motets combining French tripla with Latin moteti; 4 to motets wholly in Latin; 5 (with a few exceptions) to motets with upper parts wholly in French. The tenors are practically all in Latin. French tenors begin to appear in the first half of the century, but are more characteristic of the third quarter, when the use of French words was especially popular. Many French texts are *contrafacta* of earlier Latin ones. In the last quarter, Latin texts were again generally favored, and many *contrafacta* are to be found of texts originally French.[67]

In the earlier period, the texts sung by the upper voices are generally paraphrases of the one assigned to the tenor—that is, they are true tropes. With the advent of French texts, the upper voices lose connection with the tenor, especially in the third quarter of the century, as the new texts are often secular, many being taken from trouvère songs. These French texts are most varied in character, some illustrating the life of the different social classes in Paris (*Gesellschaftsmotetten*). They include love-poems and verses in praise of drink, among the latter being a piece addressed to lovers of English *goudale* ("good ale").[68] Remarkable discrepancies sometimes arise between

---

[67] For more details, see LudM, 523ff, or LudG, 238f.   [68] Transcribed, in part, in BesM, 122.

the texts in Latin-French double motets, the motetus being, perhaps, a Latin hymn to the Virgin Mary and the triplum a French love-song. While some modern investigators have regarded such a mixture as blasphemous, one has ingeniously suggested that it illustrates the naïve simplicity with which the men of the Middle Ages associated the Virgin Mary with all the phases of their lives.[69] With the return to the all-Latin motet, a closer connection was re-established between the senses of the texts used in the different voices.

The 13th-century motet was a secular as well as a sacred class of composition—an important point, since the motet and the cantilena furnish us with our first examples of secular art-polyphony. Thus, the motets dealing wholly with secular life were not intended for performance in church, and it is likely that those with too unseemly mixtures of text were not sung in church either and that secular musicians merely appropriated, when piecing these compositions together, motet elements already in the current repertoire.[70]

Examining the musical style of the earlier part of the century, we find that in Notre Dame motets the tenor, as might be expected in view of the derivation of the pieces, may be repeated several times (cf. Example 86). It is normally disposed in reiterated rhythmic patterns, and continues throughout the half-century to be derived from the Notre Dame organa. The patterns, however, are most of the time chosen in such a way as not to do violence to the borrowed melody, rigid application of patterns regardless of melodic qualities appearing often, however, in St. Victor pieces, which thus foreshadow later developments.[71] Certain tenors are favorites and reappear in many motets. Among these tenors are *In seculum* (consisting of the notes over the words *in seculum* in the *Haec dies . . . Confitemini—cf.* Example 90), *Latus* (cf. Example 85), etc. These two melodies are melismas in their original plainsong contexts (with which they could remain associated if the motet served as a substitute *clausula* or from which they could be severed if the motet was an independent piece), and *"In seculum"* and *"Latus"* are the complete texts that belong to them. The derivation from melismas, here illustrated, is characteristic of the tenors of motets, and serves as a lively reminder of the origin of such pieces. Sometimes, however, a tenor presents all the music of a piece, but the text is not given in full, only the *incipit* appearing. The upper voices (as in the organa tripla and quadrupla) are written almost entirely note against note, and their phrase-lengths coincide. It is not characteristic of these lengths, however, to agree with those in the tenor, which, in following its rhythmic pattern, ordinarily produces phrase-lengths different from those shared by the upper voices.[72] There is no attempt to connect the

---

[69] BesS II, 162.   [70] Cf. GasP, 47f.   [71] Cf. KuhlM I, 14–42.
[72] For an interesting example in which the 2 upper parts are disposed in 3-measure phrases, while the tenor is disposed in 2-measure phrases, all, however, being in the 3rd mode, see FiG, 495. Concerning the frequency with which the phrase-lengths of the superstructure and tenor fail to coincide, cf. LudR, 109.

parts thematically, the canon technique (which, to be sure, is rare enough in the organa) not reappearing in the early motet. Some of the features characteristic of the second half of the century already occur in the first half, but less prominently.

As we have remarked, a new style appears about 1250. This is named after Franco of Cologne.[73] Its outstanding feature is that the triplum becomes the predominant part, gaining in speed and rhythmic independence. The short time-values in this part may be derived from using the 6th mode, for example, against modes employing the long (*cf.* Example 79) and they may be further shortened by means of the *fractio modorum*, already applied before Franco, but more sparingly. The following illustration is taken from a motet that was apparently quite popular in the latter part of the 13th century, pseudo-Aristotle being one of the theorists to quote from it. (For information concerning the theorists' motet citations, see LudQ, 289ff.)

EXAMPLE 91. Opening of *O Maria, virgo davidica—O Maria, maris stella —Veritatem* (after BesM, 115).

Triplum—"O Mary, Virgin of [the house of] David, flower of virgins, sole hope of life, path of forgiveness . . ." Motetus—"O Mary, star of the sea, full of grace, at the same time mother (and maiden) . . ."

At about this time the tenor sources increase. Some are liturgical, like the old ones, but draw on additional parts of the service, such as the Kyrie. Tropes are favored choices, e. g. the *Rex virginem* and *Spiritus et alme*. Instrumental dance tunes are selected too, e. g. the *Chose Tassin* and *Chose Loyset*, tenors named after their probable composers. (Tassin is mentioned by Grocheo and is traceable as a *ministerallus* in the service of Philippe le Bel in 1288.) The instrumental origin of these *Choses* renders the three-part pieces they serve incontrovertible duets with accompaniment. Still other tenors are trouvère melodies, and in one Montpellier MS piece even a Paris street-cry appears as tenor. Towards the end of the century the MSS often merely indicate the tenor as such, without giving any words to connect it with a pre-existent piece. In the next century, words were to be added to the tenor again, but frequently these gave only the general sense of the upper parts and

---

[73] For a special study, see BesS II. Although Franco's famous tract dates, as stated in Chap. 10, from after 1280, he appears to have been active as a composer before that (*cf.* LudG, 261).

had no connection with Gregorian Chant. Tenor repetition continues after 1250. In one Bamberg MS piece the tenor is repeated 10½ times. In a Montpellier MS piece, the *ostinato* effect is still more remarkable, the short three-note tenor being repeated 32 times.[74] But the tenor, though it retains modal rhythm, does not always move in constant rhythmic patterns, being often disposed in unequal groups, which frequently consist entirely of perfect longs, thus foreshadowing 14th-century technique. Even where equal groups are retained, the pattern is not necessarily constant, and where it is so it is likely not to use a strict *ordo,* but some sort of *ordo*-expansion. With rhythmic patterns not always constant in the tenor, a new reason for lack of agreement between its phrase-lengths and those of the upper parts sometimes comes into play. It would seem that the tenor's phrase-lengths are occasionally determined by what may have been the original rhythmic shape of a borrowed trouvère or dance melody, quite independently of the nature of the upper parts. The Montpellier MS piece just mentioned as having a Paris street-cry as its tenor provides a charming example of a three-part motet in which all the parts go their own way so far as the timing of the phrase-ends is concerned. Another is provided by a gaily babbling piece with a tenor (whose arrangement in *ordines* seems to be merely coincident with the melody's original shape) consisting of *Hé! resvelle toi Robin* from Adam's *Le Jeu de Robin et Marion.*[75] One Montpellier MS piece implies binary rather than ternary rhythm.[76]

As the rhythmic interrelationship of the parts became freer, the thematic relationship became closer. *Stimmtausch* appears, and even canon, as in a motet in the Bamberg MS.[77] But there are motets that piece together pre-existent melodies by assigning them simultaneously to different parts and thus disregard thematic relationship completely. The street-cry composition is such a motet, as is a piece [78] in which the motetus part sings the delightful *Robins m'aime* (*cf.* p. 223). Such compositions, as might be expected, on the whole tend to be rather stiff.

Well-known refrains—made of material taken from Notre Dame pieces as well as from secular sources—become woven into the motet in various ways. Some pieces consist almost entirely of them and, like the *chanson avec des refrains* (*cf.* p. 221), foreshadow the *quodlibet* of later times.

Although, as already pointed out, the 13th-century motet is a style and not a form, definite forms on rare occasions become superimposed upon it: songs with refrains are among the trouvère melodies sometimes to be found constituting an upper part (as we have already found them constituting tenors) and bringing their peculiar forms into the motet. Thus, in some two-part motets

[74] For the Bamberg motet, see AuM II, 46; for the other, RoksM III, 238. Concerning the *ostinato* device in the 13th century, see NowakO, 20ff.
[75] The pieces are printed in RoksM III, 221 and 116.   [76] See LudC, 209; RoksM III, 136.
[77] See AuM II, 180.   [78] Printed in RoksM III, 108; AuM II, 182.

the tenors are fitted into the *rondeau* form of the trouvère melodies employed as moteti.[79]

There is a variety of motet that has the appearance of having a melody "grafted" (*enté*) upon the motetus part in such a way that normally its first half comes at the beginning of the piece and the second half at the end. Occasionally the division is in three parts and one of them is inserted in the course of the composition, as in *He! ha! que ferai—Pro patribus* in the Montpellier MS.[80] The words and melody grafted onto this motet survive elsewhere as the refrain of a *ballade*.[81] Material apparently grafted, however, cannot always be thus traced to a source proving that the divided elements belong to each other; yet the relationship shown by them—through the sense of the text, for example, or through the rhyme scheme—is sometimes so close that there can be little doubt that a *motet enté* is present. They are said to form a refrain, though, in the strict sense of the term, there is no opportunity for a refrain to function as such in a motet. What we have is another type which, like the *chanson avec des refrains,* may introduce familiar material (melodic and poetic)—which, as in the piece just cited, may be a real refrain in the independent piece to which it belongs—with results entertaining to the singer and listener. There would be opportunity for cleverness to be shown not only in fitting the grafted material to the rest of the motetus but in making it fit against the tenor. It is possible that in some motets with related elements at the beginning and end of the motetus the material may, if untraceable to an independent piece, be new in the motet but be intentionally constructed so as to form a sort of frame. There is even evidence that some real refrains were appropriated from motets.[82]

It is clear that by the end of the century the main current of development had split into several channels. New styles are being sought, new techniques are being tried out. Pierre de la Croix, on the whole a representative of the Franconian style, stands out as an innovator, but his contribution is so closely connected with developments in the 14th century that discussion of it will be reserved for our next chapter. The following example gives the opening of a motet that appears repeatedly in MSS of the period and was evidently a well-known piece. Over a tenor consisting of the music for the first three words of the *Alma Redemptoris Mater* (this music being performed twice), the motetus (which is especially powerful) and triplum 1 were added, each with text from the "Song of Solomon." In the Bamberg MS, triplum 1 (which appears in the Montpellier MS) is replaced by triplum 2; [83] still another MS substitutes

---

[79] For a discussion of these motets and for examples of trouvère songs employed in motets, see GennT.

[80] KuhlM II, 118; RoksM III, 52.   [81] Printed in GennR I, 148.

[82] Further concerning the *motet enté,* see KuhlM I, especially 57f, 77ff, 90, and the examples therein referred to and appearing in KuhlM II. See also LudQ, 190; LudG, 241ff.

[83] For a complete transcription of the Bamberg version, see AuM II, 51; for one of the Montpellier version, see RoksM III, 148.

triplum 3, which is in Franconian style. The example illustrates several features of the second period.

EXAMPLE 92. The Motetus *Descendi in ortum* and Tenor *Alma Redemptoris Mater* with 3 Different Tripla (after LudG, 257).

(Alma Redemptoris Mater)

Tenor—"Gentle Mother of the Redeemer . . ." Motetus—"I went down into the garden of nuts . . ." Triplum 1—"My soul failed [when he spake] . . ." Triplum 2—"Rejoice above all, Mother Church . . ." Triplum 3—"Thou ornament of virgins and special defense of the clergy, law of chastity, Virgin Mary, holy Mother . . ."

Alongside the main current, the course of which was apparently directed by Paris, smaller streams are to be found, which, while they cannot be said to be wholly unrelated to Paris, nevertheless reveal certain features of their own, melodic paraphrase being especially notable. The early organa based on melodies with metrical texts, mentioned on p. 308 as forerunners of the conducti, were developed in provincial centers in a way that related them also to the motet. The peripheral style in continuing to give polyphonic treatment to melodies with metrical texts growing out of the liturgy—tropes, including sequences—often handled the upper parts not in the more or less note-against-note, chordal manner of the conductus but in the rhythmically freer polyphonic manner that became characteristic of the motet. While all the parts had the same text, they did not necessarily sing it at the same time, one part occasionally entering after the other, sometimes in imitation, sometimes not.[84] And the paraphrase technique applied in deriving a trope melody from the Chant melody to which it was affixed (*cf.* p. 186)) was carried even further in these polyphonic tropes. Sometimes not only the tenor but the upper parts likewise paraphrased the plainsong, different portions of the melody being paraphrased in different voices at the same time. Occasionally

[84] For examples, see HandZP, 553f.

one voice started the paraphrase and another took it up. The paraphrase technique found its way not only into tropes having the rhythmic fluidity of the motet but also into tropes in conductus style and into the motet itself. Fascicle 8 in the Montpellier MS contains pieces in peripheral style, among them a three-part motet *Alle psallite cum luya—Alleluya,* in which the upper parts quaintly trope the single word *Alleluya,* by inserting *psallite cum* between *alle* and *luya.* These parts share their text, but in alternation, one part singing a melisma while the other sings words, the two parts using *Stimmtausch.* Paraphrase is illustrated in the tenor, which repeats its melody several times in altered forms.[85] The text of the upper parts tropes that of the tenor, and the tenor and triplum texts begin simultaneously with *Alle.* Occasionally, in peripheral style, such syllabic agreement is replaced by assonance. Another motet with an embellished tenor is the *Ave gloriosa mater,*[86] an especially interesting example. Here the tenor melody is at first grouped in three-note *ordines* and then, on repetition, in five-note *ordines.* Upon its first appearance, the borrowed melody is already somewhat decorated; upon its repetition it is more so.[87] These two motets, which may just possibly be of British origin, will be mentioned again in Chapter 14.

The style of motet influenced by the polyphonic trope flourishes until about 1300 and survives even later in England and Avignon, although it no longer represents a living technique. Some features, however, such as the assonant beginning, persist.

There are 21 motets that appear for the first time in the Las Huelgas MS, which would indicate that the Spaniards in their cultivation of the motet probably went beyond merely performing French examples and composed some of their own. But no 13th-century motets are known with Catalan or Castilian texts. Portuguese texts are absent also.

Walloon dialect is present in Turin Reale Bibl. Vari 42. There are some rare examples using Provençal.[88] The only instance of German in an old motet is in Darmstadt MS 3317, in which the predominantly Latin tenor sings *"Brumas e mors . . . Brumas ist tôd, O wê der nôt";*[89] the tenor survives elsewhere in Latin, but the piece is probably of German origin.[90]

A class of composition apparently not very important for its own sake, but the technique of which was sometimes used to ornament motets (and also conducti)—whether sacred or secular—is the *hoquetus* ("hocket"). The Madrid MS contains an *In seculum* applying this technique throughout, a

---

[85] For a transcription, see RoksM III, 256.

[86] Transcribed in AuM II, 1; RoksM II, 125. (A somewhat different version is preserved in the Las Huelgas MS; see AngE III, 182; see also p. 394f.)

[87] *Cf.* HandZP, 516f.   [88] E. g. AuM III, 27.

[89] Partly printed in BesM, 123; complete in FiD, 517.

[90] For a catalogue of motets (from *c.* 1250–1400) printed up to 1926, see BesS II, 230. The most considerable additions published since then are in RoksM and AngE. 6 from the Madrid MS, not printed elsewhere, are transcribed in HusM, 181ff.

piece concerning which we shall say more presently. Odington states that in the hocket "A truncation is made over the tenor . . . in such a way that one voice is always silent while another sings." [91] The part above the tenor was known as the *hoquetus* and gave its name to the whole type, just as the *motetus*, also lying above the tenor, gave its name to its type. Four kinds of hocket are described: duplex, in which two voices alternate with one another; triplex, in which a pair of voices alternates with a third; quadruplex, in which four voices sing in turn; and contraduplex, in which two pairs of voices alternate. Notwithstanding the implication of Odington's description, it seems that the hocket technique was sometimes used when no borrowed tenor was present. There are three degrees of complexity in this technique. In the simplest, each melody-note is repeated, though not necessarily to the same time-value, this depending upon the rhythmic mode, and each voice sings it once (see Example 93a). In another type, the melody-notes are sung alternately without repetition (see Example 93b). In a third type, the truncation occurs between groups rather than individual notes and there may be rhythmic overlapping of parts (see Example 93c).

EXAMPLE 93. Hocket Patterns (after SchneiderH, 392).

There is some doubt about the origin of the name *hoquetus* (*hoketus*, *ochetus*). According to Farmer,[92] it is derived from the Arabic *iqâ' ât*, meaning "rhythms." Popularly known as "oket," the technique is called by some theorists *cantus abscisus*. "Oket," still meaning "rhythms," merges by popular etymology with "hoquet," meaning "hiccough," which vividly describes the technique. Several theorists mention two types of hoquetus, *hoquetus vulgaris*, in which notes of every available time-value are used, and *musica resecata*, which used only the long and breve.

As might be expected, there were churchmen who objected to finding portions of the sacred Chant reduced to the position of a tenor to upper voices which, moreover, obscured it, and hocketing was hardly likely to recommend itself to them. Here is a derisive passage about it from Ailred, a 12th-century English writer:

Sometimes thou mayst see a man with an open mouth, not to sing, but as it were to breathe out his last gasp, by shutting in his breath, and by a certain ridicu-

---

[91] CouS I, 248.   [92] FarmC, 75.

lous interception of his voice to threaten silence, and now again to imitate the agonies of a dying man, or the ecstasies of such as suffer.[93]

The earliest surviving examples of hocketing in European art-music date from the 13th century. But hocketing occurs in primitive music and may be connected with primitive instruments such as drums, panpipes, and xylophones.[94]

The polyphonic *cantilenae* correspond with the monodic—that is, they include dance-songs with refrains: *rondeaux, virelais, ballades.* It is natural that, as may be indicated by the *rondeau*-motet, the more venturesome trouvères should have tried to combine the forms of their monodic songs with the technique developed by the learned ecclesiastics. The combination contributed much of value to secular art-polyphony, which was destined to flourish brilliantly, especially in the 14th century. Most of the polyphonic cantilenae are anonymous, but two of the *virelais* and four of the *rondeaux* are by Adam de la Halle. One of the *virelais* is the charming *Fines amourettes,* mistakenly called a *rondeau* in several modern printings.[95] Adam de la Halle appears also as a composer of motets, but his examples are uneven in style, being either old-fashioned for the time of their composition or unskilful in their use of the new technique.[96]

The polyphonic *rondeaux, virelais,* and *ballades* [97] are apparently settings of monodic pieces. The borrowed melody is not always assigned to any one part, such as the lowest. The melody is either (1) in the lowest voice and of a simple, folk-like character, the middle voice being then comparatively elaborate, these two voices not crossing, or (2) in the middle part and less folk-like, the lowest part then functioning as a support and the voices crossing frequently.[98] All the voices had the same text in cantilenae. In such *rondeaux* as assimilated the technique of the conductus, there was mainly, of course, but one note to a syllable, whence resulted a slightly embellished note-against-note counterpoint, as in the following:

EXAMPLE 94. *Amours et ma dame aussi*—Rondeau (after GennR I, 63).

[93] For some other 12th–14th century attacks on music in the church, see OH I, 290.

[94] For fuller information on the hocket, see SchneiderH.

[95] E. g. CouH, xxxv (in back); OH I, 176. See GennR I, 57; II, 77.

[96] For transcriptions, see AdO, 242, 251, 261, 268, 272; RoksM III, 92, 103, 138; for further discussion, see LudC, 211; BesS II, 154.

[97] Printed in GennR, *passim.*   [98] See HandUV, 30.

"Love and my lady too, with clasped hands I beseech your pity! It was to my misfortune that I beheld your very great beauty, *Love and my lady too.* If you do not take pity on me, then it was to my misfortune that I beheld your very great merit. *Love and my lady too, with clasped hands I beseech your pity!"* (Transl. S.L.E.)

As with the monodic *rondeau,* it is possible to reconstruct a polyphonic *rondeau* where a MS preserves a complete text even if music is written out only for the words of the refrain (*cf.* p. 222). The texts of the cantilenae, as might be expected, usually deal with love, but occasionally treat other subjects also, as in the charming Noël, *Dieus soit en cheste maison.*[99]

Concerning the manner in which all this music was performed, we have some information, but it is unfortunately scanty.

The organa were normally sung by soloists, but with the tenor doubled if the volume was not sufficient. On festive occasions additional men might join in the performance. It is possible that less complex compositions, such as the simpler St. Victor pieces, may have been sung by the choir, since they would not require skilled soloists. Jerome of Moravia makes it clear [100] that conductors were not unknown to the 13th century, but he stops short of defining their technique. It has been possible to establish, through two Brussels MSS laying down the order of processions and containing some of the music, that 14 or 15 pieces in the Florence MS were intended for processions at Notre Dame.[101] We have items of information about ritual dancing there and about eating between renditions of two chants.[102]

The Las Huelgas MS contains a two-part exercise in *solfeggio,* the text of which shows that the piece was intended for the nuns of the convent. Yet the customary clefs are used. From this fact it may be deduced that neither the choice of clefs nor the apparent tessitura indicates that works in 13th- (or 14th-)century MSS were intended for the exclusive use of men's voices. The clefs were chosen with a view to placing all the notes on the staff, and it is wholly likely that motets, conducti, etc., were sometimes sung by women—whether as nuns in convents or as trained or amateur singers in secular life.[103]

We have seen in Chapter 7 that in the monodic *rondeaux* the refrain was sung by a chorus while the *additamenta* were sung by a soloist. While it is possible that the polyphonic *rondeaux* were rendered with a similar apportioning of the sections, only the refrain being then sung polyphonically, it is

[99] Printed in GennR I, 69.
[100] CserbaM, 188; CouS I, 93.
[101] See HusO, 48f. For a list of organa and selected motets from 3 of the 4 great Notre Dame MSS, arranged in accordance with the liturgical calendar etc., see UrK, 129f.
[102] See HandND, 51.
[103] See RoksF, 479. Concerning women musicians in the Middle Ages, see also Kathi Meyer, *Der chorische Gesang der Frauen* . . . , 1917.

just as likely (if we may judge from the interpolation of organum by soloists into choral renditions of plainsong) that the apportioning was between a group of soloists and a chorus, the *additamenta* being sung in parts by the former and the refrain monodically by the latter. It is also possible, of course, that the pieces were rendered polyphonically throughout.[104]

It has been suggested that the *caudae* of the conducti may have been performed on instruments. While this cannot definitely be proved, there is a little circumstantial evidence that may perhaps support the suggestion. In some conducti, although, to be sure, the opening melismas have the first syllable under their first note, the second syllable does not appear until the second note of the verse proper is reached—that is, the first note of the verse seems reserved for the first syllable. Indeed, the first syllable may even be written in again under this note.[105] A similar situation obtains with respect to some Italian *trecento* and German 14th- and 15th-century music. In other respects, the vocal character of the conducti seems clear. In the course of the 13th century they became more and more a form of social expression, and their already loose contact with the liturgy tended to become still looser. They were primarily sung by solo voices, but were doubtless performed chorally also.

Which of the instruments known to have been used during the Gothic period reinforced the singers at Notre Dame, can only be conjectured.[106] (We first hear of an organ there towards the end of the 14th century.[107]) There seems to be nothing in the style of the surviving polyphonic works of this period to show that any of them were composed, in whole or in part, with the character of specific instruments in mind. The conductus melismas just referred to do not differ in style from definitely vocal music. Notwithstanding the existence of the instrumental polyphonic dances of 13th-century England, mentioned in Chapter 8, the conclusion to be drawn from the body of material at hand is that instruments were in the main used as substitutes for voices or to aid the singers. It would appear that laymen sometimes drew upon the discant *clausulae* for material to perform on instruments outside the Church. This view receives support from two sets of discant pieces, one of which—in the St. Victor MS—lacks text intended for singing,[108] and the other of which—in the Bamberg MS—lacks text altogether, but neither of which otherwise displays traits that would stamp the pieces in them as having been especially conceived for instruments. One of the compositions in the set in the St. Victor MS, in fact, appears as a vocal substitute-*clausula* in the older MS Pluteus 29.1.

---

[104] *Cf.* BukP, 40.   [105] *Cf.* RoksC, 8f, 12f.

[106] Ficker inclines to think they were considerable in number. See FiS, 30; FiG, 494.

[107] RauO, 80. Thus modern writers referring to Leonin and Perotin as "organists" (in the conventional sense) do so entirely without firm grounds.

[108] *Cf.* HandR, 40.

The Bamberg set consists of 7 three-part compositions, 5 of which are based on the *In seculum* tenor. Verbal indications in 13th-century musical MSS do not give us much help when we attempt to ascertain whether any of the few probably instrumental examples of the time were intended for particular instruments. It is possible, however, that one of the Bamberg group is intended for viols, since it is entitled *In seculum viellatoris* ("*In seculum* of the viol-player"). But the evidence afforded by this title is not unequivocal.[109] We have already met with the viol in Chapter 7 and shall encounter it again presently. Anonymus IV reports [110] that a Spaniard, whose name he does not give, wrote a hocket *In seculum*. This is the piece concerning which he states (as we have noted in Chapter 10) that certain Parisians were substituting mode 2 for mode 5. Two of the five *In seculum* settings (other than the *In seculum viellatoris*) answer perfectly to his account. In fact, the one using mode 5 is the hocket mentioned a few pages back as being in the Madrid MS and is doubtless the piece referred to by the Anonymus; it appears also in the Montpellier MS.[111]

However chary of information the MSS may be, literary references and artistic representations give numerous hints concerning the instruments upon which a musician might draw. They furnish better data about medieval music-making than would a mere list of modern instruments about contemporary practice, since it is wholly likely that in the Middle Ages a part assigned to an instrument was usually played on any kind on which it was performable and which happened to be at hand. Yet some thought seems to have been given, where more than one instrument participated, to the obtaining of contrasting sonorities, though of course the orchestra as such was quite unknown. To be sure, a poet, to display his learning, might refer to some instrument of antiquity, and a painter who was not himself a musician might misrepresent the details of an instrument or the manipulations of a performer; so that the evidence must be regarded with caution. But where there is substantial agreement among several sources, especially when they include writings of theorists, they enable us with reasonable safety to restore the medieval instrumental apparatus, at least in our imagination.

The references to instruments are particularly plentiful in 12th- and 13th-century French poetry.[112] In his *La Bataille des VII Ars*, the 13th-century trouvère, Henri d'Andeli, describes Music and her retinue as follows:

---

[109] The piece is printed in AuM II, 226; ScherG, 13. Further concerning the possible significance of the title (and its failure to be conclusive), see Handschin in Acta X (1938), 29 (footnote).
[110] CouS I, 350.
[111] *Cf.* SowaZ, 426f. For a facsimile of the piece as it appears in the Madrid MS, see AngE I, 73; for transcriptions after the Bamberg and Montpellier MSS, see AuM II, 224, and RoksM II, 160, respectively.
[112] For numerous attractive and sometimes helpful extracts, see Chapters XX of GéroH and GéroM, where much information is conveniently assembled. See also TrederM.

Ma dame Musique aus clochetes | Madame Music, she of the little bells
Et si clerc plain de chanconnetes | And her clerks full of songs
Portoient gigues et vieles, | Carried rebecs and viols,
Salterious et fleüteles; . . . | Psalteries and small flutes; . . .
Par mi l'ost aloient chantant, | Through the army they went singing,
Par lor chant les vont enchantant. | They go enchanting them with song.

(From L. J. Paetow, *The Battle of the Seven Arts*. . . . , in *Memoirs of the University of California*, IV, No. 1 [1914], 49—with slight change in transl.)

There is evidence that, among the plucked chordophones, the harp was used in varying sizes, but diatonically tuned. Harps with a string for each semitone—i. e. chromatic harps—did not come into use until the end of the 16th century. Harps were particularly important in the medieval music of the British Isles (*cf.* pp. 391, 408). The term *cithara,* recurring in medieval documents, came to apply to several varieties of harp and rote.

We have found the psaltery mentioned by the Church Fathers, and the medieval poets furnish evidence of its continued use. Various types of psalteries are represented in illuminations and other iconographic records, which indicate that ten strings and a shape resembling an inverted Δ were general. The psaltery was sometimes referred to as the *rotta* [113] (but *cf.* p. 124). A variant in rectangular form, introduced into Spain by the Moors, derived its European names from the Arabic *qânûn.* Thus, it was called *canon* in French, *canale* in Latin, *kanon* in German, *caño* in Spanish; a smaller type was known as *micanon* or *medium canale* (which became *medicinale*) or *metzkanon* or *medio caño.*

The introduction of the lute into Europe by the Moors has already been mentioned (*cf.* p. 246). An ivory dating from 968, which originated at Cordova and is now at the Louvre, is perhaps the oldest piece of evidence enabling us to establish the presence of the lute in Europe. Of this instrument with its vaulted back and bent-back peg-box, there existed several varieties. The mandore or mandola was a small lute, with a shorter neck, usually having four double strings. It is one of the ten instruments Guiraut de Calanson, in his *Conseils aux Jongler,* written in 1210, said an accomplished *jongleur* had to play.

Among the many instruments illustrated in the Escorial MS of the *Cantigas* [114] is the guitar, of which two kinds are shown: the *guitarra morisca* and the *guitarra latina.* The former seems to have had a vaulted back, the fingerboard was large, several holes pierced the soundboard, the tail ended in a crescent. The back of the latter was flat, as in the modern guitar, and was attached to the soundboard by ribs, there was one soundhole and the strings passed over it.

[113] SachsH, 161.
[114] For reproductions of 40 miniatures showing instruments, see RibC, after p. 152 of commentary.

The citole, mentioned by the poets, was a pear-shaped instrument with four wire strings and ribs.

Guiraut de Calanson mentions a rote (*cf.* p. 124) with seventeen strings. The lyre-shaped type was favored in Germany and England (*cf.* p. 407), a somewhat triangular type in Spain (*cf.* Lydgate's poem, p. 385).

Of the chordophones played with a bow [115] the viol, already encountered in Chapter 7 (French *vièle;* German *fiedel*, etc.),[116] was by all odds the most important. Its incurved sides were a prominent feature. Johannes de Grocheo wrote [117] of it:

Among all the stringed instruments seen by us the viol appears deserving of first place. For as the soul having understanding virtually includes within itself all other forms of ability, and as the tetragon the triangle, and as the larger number the smaller, thus does the viol virtually include within itself all other instruments. It may be that some move the minds of men more with an earnest sound, as do the drum and trumpet in feasts, jousts, and tourneys, but on the viol all musical forms are more precisely distinguished . . . . A good artist plays on the viol every cantus *and* cantilena *and every musical form in general.*

Jerome of Moravia gives [118] three tunings for the open strings thus, the first letter in each series giving the pitch of the bourdon: D Γ G d d or Γ D G d g or Γ Γ D c c.

The rebec was a lute-shaped instrument played with a bow.[119] Its type appears to be older than that of the viol. It is referred to as a *lyra* as early as the 8th century. Three and five were the standard numbers of strings. The tone was shrill. Among other names for the rebec were *gigue* in France and *geige* in Germany. The rubebe was a larger but related instrument with an oval or oblong body and a separate neck; Jerome of Moravia reports that it had two strings, tuned a fifth apart: C, G.

The organistrum (*cf.* p. 258) was known by other names also—*armonia, symphonia*. From the latter the French word *chifonie* was formed. The poets use other variants also.

The monochord, long employed in teaching, appears in miniatures of the 11th century and is mentioned as early as 1155 in a poem containing a list of instruments performed upon for practical purposes. How it was used, however, is not stated. Possibly bowing it, traceable to the 14th century (*cf.* p. 384), was already customary.

Among the idiophones, cymbals receive attention from both artists and

[115] Concerning the earliest evidence of the bow, see SachsHI, 275.

[116] See GalpE, 139, or GalpO, 84f, where "viol" is preferred to "fiddle" as the English term.

[117] WolfM, 96.

[118] In his Chap. 23, printed in CserbaM, 288. See also CserbaM, lxxivff; GalpO, 88. Concerning some other references to the viol, made by 13th-century theorists, see HandR, 38.

[119] For comment concerning the suitability of plucking, but not bowing, an instrument so constructed, see Schles I, 86.

writers, the latter, however, occasionally using *cymbala* to mean bell-chimes.

The *Cantigas* supply only one of several sources of evidence for the use of castanets. Medieval music knew also the use of the triangle (= French *trepie*).

Single bells, large and small, and sets of small ones (bell-chimes) appear again and again in literature under a variety of names. Among the sculptural representations is one of the wonderful figures adorning the façade of the Cathedral at Chartres, Music striking her little bells with a hammer.

Membranophones included the tambourine. Drums existed in several forms and were known under a variety of names. These instruments included the naker (French *nacaire*), an old form of kettledrum copied from the Saracens. Nakers are frequently pictured as a pair of small kettledrums worn by the player on a belt around the waist and played by sticks, one held in each hand. The small tabor, on the other hand, was hung from the neck by a strap and struck with a stick by the right hand while the left hand played a pipe.

The aerophones included flutes and reed instruments as well as horns and trumpets and, of course, the organ.

Colin Muset in a charming poem mentions the *flajolet,* or flageolet. This was a small flute—not transverse—with a mouthpiece in the form of a large whistle. It was rather shrill, like other small whistle-flutes referred to under the names of pipes, *flaüstes,* and *flaüsteles*—the last being mentioned as played on by the shepherds in *Aucassin et Nicolette.* The long flute—the *flûte douce* in France, recorder in England, *blockflöte* in Germany—was a whistle-flute with a softer tone and usually with six holes. The transverse flute is illustrated in one of the miniatures in the Escorial MS of the *Cántigas.* It had reached the West probably in the 12th century and possibly by way of Byzantium.

The panpipes, usually with seven pipes, survived in France under the name *frestel.* It is possible that the name *ele* refers to this instrument also.

There were several types of reed instruments. The shawm (French *chalumeau,* from *calamellus,* the Latin word for reed), the ancestor of the oboe, had six to nine holes. It belonged to the group of *instruments hauts* (i. e. loud instruments—cf. p. 385), but was to be heard in pastoral as well as military scenes.

The bagpipe (*muse* or *cornemuse* [120] in French), the chanter of which was also known as the *chalumeau,* was equipped with one or two drones besides the *chalumeau,* which had eight or nine holes. Other names for bagpipes were *chorus* and *choron.* The *pipe à forel* (German *platerspiel*) was a smaller variant with a bag made of a bladder.

---

[120] *Cornemuse* is a compound of *corner* ("to blow") and *muse,* obviously derived from *musa* (*cf.* p. 124).

The early horns were intended not for musical but for signalling purposes. If sometimes made of metal, they seem more often to have been made of horn or wood. The famous horn blown by the hero of the *Chanson de Roland* was apparently an olifant, a type made of ivory and introduced from Byzantium in the 10th or 11th century.[121] The *Chanson de Roland* mentions also *graisles,* instruments of smaller dimensions, with a high and clear tone. Often early horns were capable of producing only one tone; sometimes the octave and 12th of the fundamental were obtainable also. In Germany a very large instrument, the *herhorn,* almost attained the size of a man. Eventually horns were pierced with several holes to render a greater number of tones obtainable. The new type was known as the *cornet* (*zink*). It came in a variety of sizes and was sometimes straight, sometimes bent. It is mentioned in *Aucassin et Nicolette.*

The trumpets include the *buisines,* which in the *Chanson de Roland* are blown by the pagans. It is possible that the term *cors sarrasinois,* appearing in some poems, is intended to apply to a *buisine.* In Germany the term *buisine* by a gradual metamorphosis became *posaune.*

The *trompes* were larger and deeper sounding than the *buisines.* The *trompette* appears in the 13th century; it was a long instrument sometimes bent into the form of an S, sometimes bent back upon itself, to facilitate its use.

The greatest advance in instrument construction made during the 13th century, the discovery of the keyboard, revolutionized the organ. Previously, wooden sliders were withdrawn and reinserted to admit or prevent the entrance of air into the pipes. Obviously the performance of rapid passages was impossible on an instrument so constructed. Improved, it became very popular. Small organs that could be carried about—called "positives" if they had to be set down, in distinction to the "portatives," which were so small that they could be played while held—abound in pictures. French representations are particularly numerous in the 13th century, and there is evidence of the use of the instrument in England, Germany, Italy, and Spain also. King David, the favorite instrumental executant of medieval artists, being variously shown as playing the harp, rote, viol, and other instruments, is apparently the monarch depicted in the 13th-century Belvoir Psalter,[122] performing on a positive.

The 13th century is one of the greatest in music history, being comparable with the 16th, 18th, and 19th. Such a volume as this, besides devoting four

[121] The suggestion is made in E. Wiedemann and F. Hauser, *Byzantinische und arabische akustische Instrumente,* in *Archiv für die Geschichte der Naturwissenschaften und der Technik,* VIII (1918), 155, that Roland's horn may have been a hydraulis. This becomes less far-fetched than it may at first seem when it is borne in mind that the name "horn of Alexander the Great" was applied to the instrument.

[122] See Plate XLIV in GalpO. For a monograph on the portative, see HickP. For further information on early instruments, see GalpE, SachsH, SachsR, SachsHI, BuhleB, and PanS.

chapters almost entirely to it, must frequently refer to it even in other sections. The leading musical nation of the period was clearly France. England, as we shall see, was at the same time doing some path-breaking of her own, destined later to open up bright new vistas. But on the whole France was leaned upon so heavily by her sister nations that a modern writer has, not without justification, referred to their contributions collectively, despite the indisputable distinctive value of some of them, as *l'art musical français en dehors de France.*

Chapter 12: THE 14TH CENTURY: French Music—
French and Italian Notation

THE organa of the time of Leonin and Perotin did not lack performance at Notre Dame in the 14th century.[1] The old music continued here and there to have its champions, such as Jacques de Liége, the author of the voluminous *Speculum Musicae*,[2] formerly attributed to Jean de Muris. But in praising the old music this conservative author bemoans its generally falling into neglect: organum and the conductus are being abandoned, contemporary musicians write only motets and cantilenae.[3] Certain of his contemporaries were, in fact, much occupied with innovation, and *Ars nova*, the name of Philippe de Vitri's famous 14th-century treatise, has often been used—not, however, with full justification [4]—to characterize the whole period. If certain new technical features were to find more expert use in the 15th century, the 14th century nevertheless produced works that were of distinct value in themselves—like the compositions of Guillaume de Machaut —as well as harbingers of things to come.

The urge towards change had already been made evident during the Franconian period by Pierre de la Croix (*cf*. p. 318), whose activity can be traced as late as 1298. He is noteworthy on at least two counts: (1) He was the first, according to the *Speculum Musicae*, to divide the perfect breve into 4 semibreves.[5] The treatise gives examples of his having later divided it into from 5 to as many as 9. He used points of division to mark off the extent of semibreve groups equalling a breve. Though the form and name of the semibreve were retained, the way was clearly being prepared for the adoption of the minim. Pierre de la Croix applied the new divisions to the triplum, and thereby (2)

[1] See HandND, 5ff, 49ff.
[2] See BesS I, 181. The treatise consists of 7 books, divided into 518 chapters. GrossS publishes Chapters I–XIX of Book 1. Books 6 and 7 are printed in CouS II.
[3] CouS II, 428.
[4] *Cf*. BesM, 136. The term *Ars antiqua* has likewise been misused by modern writers. The "advanced" musicians of the 14th century intended it to apply to late 13th-century motet writing, not to the music of the time of Leonin and Perotin; *cf*. BesS II, 187.
[5] CouS II, 401. His innovation is mentioned also in the *Regulae* of Robert Handlo (1326)— see CouS I, 388—and in the *Summa* of John Hanboys (15th cent.)—see CouS I, 424—but not in his own surviving treatise, printed in CouS I. The perfect breve = the *brevis recta* of Chapter 10.

he contributed substantially towards freeing the triplum from the shackles of modal rhythm. One effect of this was to give the voices more scope within which to become individualized. Another was to cause melodic style to become more flowing. The frequent sounding of many notes by the triplum against the slower-moving tenor and motetus produced, clearly, a less full-blooded effect than that resulting from the older Gothic polyphony (though this could on occasion, by combining modes 5 and 6, for instance—*cf.* Example 91—thin out the texture somewhat also). The new music clearly had qualities that could develop in the listener a more delicate ear than polyphony had hitherto called for.

EXAMPLE 95. *Aucun ont trouvé—Lonctans me sui—Annuntiantes—* Pierre de la Croix (after RoksM III, 81).

"Others have sung because of fashion, but with me love, which cheers my thoughts, gives the occasion . . ."—Motetus: "Long time withheld I myself from singing . . ."—Tenor from the Gradual, *Omnes de Saba venient* . . . *annuntiantes*. ("All they from Sheba shall come: they shall bring gold and incense; and they shall shew forth the praises of the Lord." Isaiah LX, 6.)

Modal rhythms loosened their hold on the motetus only slowly and on the tenor still more slowly. Insertion of "shorter" values in the triplum actually slackened the pace of the lower voices. Evidence of this is furnished by theoretical writing which tells us,[6] without following chronology, that the basic time units were to be taken slowly (*more longo*) in works containing divisions of the breve into many semibreves, i. e. works in the Pierre de la Croix style; moderately (*more mediocri*) in works in Franconian style (*cf.* p. 316); quickly (*more lascivo*) in hockets. Changes in style had a not surprising effect, over the centuries, on changes in tempo. Besseler has investigated the subject[7] and has found justification for the following table[8] (which makes use of metronomic indications):

[6] See CouS I, 388. See also comment in BesS II, 159.
[7] See BesS II, especially pp. 212ff.
[8] Transcriptions of the 8 compositions listed in it may be found (the references being given in the same order as the pieces are named in the table) in LudB, 450; RoksM III, 88, 81; WolfG III, 191; BesS I, 249, 245; MachM III, 82 (186); StaD, 187. The authenticity of *Douce playsence—Garison—Neuma* is well established, that of the other pieces attributed to de Vitri, less conclusively. *Cf.* p. 337. Further concerning tempo, see WolfG I, 69.

c. 1200, Time of Perotin: *Gaudeat devocio*	♩ = 80	
	Thereafter the tempo of the basic time units slackens:	
c. 1250, Time of Franco: *Je me cuidoie*	♩ = 44 / 𝅗𝅥 = 132	almost twofold
c. 1280, Pierre de la Croix: *Lonc tans me sui*	𝅗𝅥. = 54 / ♩ = 162	more than twice again
c. 1315, Philippe de Vitri: *Tribum—Quoniam*	𝅗𝅥. = 40 / 𝅗𝅥 = 60 / ♩ = 120	threefold since Franco
" Douce playsence—Garison etc.		
c. 1325, Philippe de Vitri: *Tuba—In arboris*	𝅗𝅥 = 42 / ♩. = 84	about a third more
c. 1350, Guillaume de Machaut: *Felix virgo-Inviolata*	𝅗𝅥 = 40 / ♩. = 80	only slightly more
c. 1400, Jean Tapissier: *Eya dulcis—Vale placens*	𝅗𝅥. = 50 / 𝅗𝅥 = 150	almost twofold again

MS. f. fr. 146 at the Bib. Nat. in Paris contains two works which, while still adhering fairly closely to the past, also indicate the imminence of change. These are a collection of 31 *rondeaux, virelais,* and *ballades* by Jehannot de l'Escurel (who was executed at Paris in 1303) and a series of musical pieces interpolated in the *Roman de Fauvel*. The Jehannot de l'Escurel compositions are alphabetically arranged, but leave off at the letter G; perhaps there once were others. All but one of the surviving pieces are monodic, the exception being a three-part *rondeau* in conductus style, containing a noteworthy number of thirds and complete triads.[9]

EXAMPLE 96. End of the *Rondeau: A vous, douce debonnaire* (Jehannot de l'Escurel) (after GennR I, 307).

The interpolations in the *Roman de Fauvel* were inserted in 1316 by Chaillou de Pesstain and constitute an anthology of pieces in favor at the time, some existing in several other MSS also. Among these other MSS are two in the unusual roll (*rotulus*) format, the height in these specimens being almost 8 times the width (*cf.* illustration in Plate VIII). Part I of the poem had been written in 1310, Part II in 1314. The author, Gervais de Bus, launches a vigorous attack against the disorders and abuses wasting the Church and hampering

[9] The l'Escurel pieces are all printed in GennR I, 307–72. (The 3-part *rondeau* may be found transcribed also in WolfG III, 26; original notation in WolfG II, 15.) For a facsimile of the page containing the 3-part piece, 4 monodic pieces and a part of a fifth, see AuP, plate 20. See also the commentary in GennR II, 246–54.

it in the performance of its mission. The name of Fauvel—a symbolical animal (ass or horse)—is derived, so the text tells us, from the first letters of *Flaterie, Avarice, Vilanie, Variété, Envie, Lascheté*. The poem, which survives in several MSS, reveals men of all walks and conditions trying to cleanse Fauvel. The interpolations comprise 23 motets in three parts, 10 in two parts, 32 proses and *lais,* 14 *rondeaux, ballades,* and refrains, and 52 Alleluias, antiphons, responds, hymns, and verses. All but 2 of the two-part motets are in the old style, but as many as 17 of the three-part motets contain instances of the new semi-breve movement, and some display also certain other features we shall find typical of the 14th-century music.[10] Chancellor Philippe is represented by the texts of 14 interpolations. One of the motets is an adaptation of an old Notre Dame *clausula* that had had a checkered career.[11] The *Roman,* in MS f. fr. 146, is richly decorated with miniatures. In some of the interpolations the presence of thirds and full triads is again noteworthy. For example:

EXAMPLE 97. End of the Motet *Desolata mater ecclesia—Quae nutritos filios—Filios enutrivi,* against the Templars, from the *Roman de Fauvel* (Bib. Nat. Paris, MS. f. fr. 146, f. 8ᵛ, after Aubry facsimile. The preceding measures are transcribed in BesM, 127).

Transl. of the entire motet: Triplum—"Forsaken mother church seeing herself despised by her sons weeps above all because the Father sees the open crime of these, the works of the priests, the heinous crimes of the brothers of the Temple, [and] the other sins in the clerics. He who has courage says the same. Mother (?), speak to me, Christ, speak to me, if there be any sorrow like this sorrow." Motetus —"She who raised on high the children she had nourished, now, scorned, finds by proof that they are impious, whereat she groans bitterly, displaying the wickedness of these, namely that she is scorned by all. None the less, she opens her bosom to him

---

[10] See BesS I, 177. AuF is a facsimile edition of the *Roman* after Ms. f. fr.146. The *rondeaux, ballades,* and refrains, are transcribed in GennR I, 290–306; there is commentary, including other transcriptions (motets), in GennR II, 230–45. Other motet transcriptions are available in WolfG III, 5–26, 191 (10 nos.—original notation in WolfG II, 2–14, 144); WolfH I, 282 (incomplete—preceded by original notation); WolfO, 19; DTO XL, 1–3; BesM, 127 (incomplete). The whole poem, without the texts of the interpolations, may be found in LangfR.

[11] See LudL, 212.

who returns." (Transl. S.L.E.) Tenor—"I have nourished and brought up children, and they have rebelled against me." (Isaiah I, 2)

In a way, the new sonority, when it occasionally appeared, acted as a substitute for the gradually discarded modal rhythms, by providing a means of unification in polyphonic music. Not that a system of harmonic progression had been developed. Only at the ends of phrases did what was much later perceived as harmonic method begin to take form, and this was caused by the new lyric style in melodic writing, which prompted the raising of the leading tone—or, as in measure 2 in Example 97, of even two different leading tones simultaneously in different parts. The sharpening was often not indicated in 14th-century (and even later) notation but was called for by the rules of *musica falsa,* discussed on pp. 380ff. (The same holds true with regard to flattening.) It was merely through the sounding of fuller sonorities on the heavy beats—especially noticeable in the l'Escurel *rondeau*—that unification was aided.

To the early part of the century belong also some of the works in an important MS [12] at the Chapter Library at Ivrea, near Turin (itself dating from after 1350 and therefore to be discussed again in a later part of this Chapter), containing 81 compositions,[13] including 37 double motets, 25 Mass fragments, 11 French secular works in small forms, and 4 pieces in canon. These last are of special historical significance since they too are French and, together with still another French canon in another MS, indicate, contrary to the view held before their discovery, that the *caccia* type (*cf.* pp. 365f) originated not in Italy but in France.[14] Here is an excerpt from one of the French *chaces*,[15] an extended composition which describes a hunting scene and thus uses canon (as well as hocket for ejaculations) with complete appropriateness. While the hunt is encountered elsewhere as the subject of such pieces, it does not exclude other themes.

EXAMPLE 98. Extract from *Chace* of the First Half of the 14th Century (from BesS I, 252).

"He's off on a different scent, Heaven be praised. Hau, halau, etc. He is dead. Let us feed our falcons, etc."

12 Described in BesS I, 185ff; BorgP. The plans for VanM provide for several fascicles to be devoted to selections from this MS.   13 Listed in BesS I, 188ff.   14 *Cf.* BesH, 52; NovatiC.
15 Printed complete in BesS I, 251. Further concerning this piece and the French *chace* generally, see FeinK, 7ff.

Another French canon in the Ivrea MS, recurring slightly amended in MS XI E. 9 at Prague, displays, at this early period, a remarkable degree of technical ingenuity. In the Prague MS the antecedent of the canon supplies a strict illustration of the musical equivalent of palindrome in literature (e. g. "Madam, I'm Adam" or "Able was I ere I saw Elba," to quote examples from James Joyce's *Ulysses*), in which it is possible to read a passage the same backwards as forwards (and, therefore, the same from the end backwards to the middle as from the beginning forwards to the middle). The consequent (which lacks the last fourteen notes of the melody) may therefore be looked upon not only as proceeding in ordinary canonic imitation, but, just as easily, as starting with the last note of the antecedent and progressing backwards to the fifteenth note from the beginning; so that it is possible to consider the piece an example of *canon cancrizans* (crab canon). We see the 14th century early in its career preparing the way for the tests of skill that were to become especially popular with composers in the century following.

EXAMPLE 99. *Talent mes prus* (after KamP, 137).

"The wish has taken hold of me to sing like the cuckoo."

In the Ivrea MS is represented the elder of the two chief French musicians of the 14th century, Philippe de Vitri (b. October 31, 1291 at one of the six towns in Champagne now known as Vitry; d. June 9, 1361 at Meaux, of which he had become Bishop in 1351), composer, theorist, poet, diplomat.[16] Two letters survive from Petrarch to Philippe. The Italian poet praises the Frenchman as a musician, as a poet, and as the possessor of an inquiring spirit. Theodoric

[16] For full biographical information, see CovA.

of Campo (middle of the 15th century) calls him the "flower and gem of singers"; [17] Simon Tunstede (d. 1369 at Oxford), "the flower of all the world of musicians." [18]

Very few of his compositions survive, but they do not belie his reputation. The Ivrea MS contains, without ascriptions, 3 motets cited as his by theorists and one ascribed to him in another MS, formerly at Strasbourg but destroyed in the war of 1870. It survives also in a later MS at Apt.[19] The authenticity of these works may be regarded as reasonably established. The Ivrea MS contains also 3 more motets (2 [20] being likewise in the Apt MS, to which we shall return), and the *Roman de Fauvel* still another 4 that may be his, but these 7 cannot at present be so well authenticated as the first 4. Two of the *Fauvel* pieces (*Tribum—Quoniam secta* and *Firmissime—Adesto sancta— Alleluia Benedictus*) exist also, transcribed for organ, in Brit. Mus. Add. 28550 (*cf.* pp. 406f).[21]

These works are characterized by emancipation of the melody from modal rhythms—by the new lyricism. Hocketing is used for expressive purposes. There is enough full harmony on the accents in a motet like *Hugo princeps-Cum structura* (DTO XL, 4), to take only one example, to be distinctly noticeable. It should be stressed, however, that, as in the pieces already mentioned in connection with fuller harmony, there is no organized method of using such material. And it does not predominate. With respect to chord structure, the 14th century is definitely transitional. Fuller harmony is sometimes to be found, but notwithstanding this the polyphony that was evolved from organum, i. e. polyphony based on the perfect consonances, continued to run its course into this century, when it rounded out its existence as a living style.

The unifying device characteristic of the authentic de Vitri motets and those ascribed to him is *isorhythmic structure,* elaborated far beyond the stages represented by the old tenor *ordines* and such patterns, also for tenor, as the one given in Example 80. The 14th-century isorhythmic design is occasionally quite long and is free of modal restrictions. It receives the name *talea* ("cutting") and, like the earlier tenor patterns, is reiterated to melodic content which, often enough, is itself repeated, sometimes to reiterations of a new *talea.* Thus, in de Vitri's *Douce playsence—Garison—Neuma* this tenor pattern appears four times:

[17] CouS III, 191.   [18] CouS IV, 257.   [19] See GasMA, xxi, 49; BorS, 302f. (GasMA should be used in the light of G. de Van's review in Acta, XII [1940], 64ff.)   [20] Printed in GasMA, 139, 142.
   [21] Concerning the evidence for de Vitri's authorship, see BesS I, 188ff; BesS II, 192ff. The 4 definitely authentic pieces are printed in BesS I, 249; BesS II, 250; DTO XL, 4; GasMA, 49 (after the MS at Apt). Two of the other 3 Ivrea pieces are printed in BesS II, 245, 247 (= GasMA, 139, after Apt MS). Of the 4 *Fauvel* pieces, 3 are included in the WolfG, WolfO, and DTO XL transcriptions listed in footnote 10 (see also BesS II, 193 for a fragment). The WolfG and WolfO transcriptions are accompanied by transcriptions of the organ versions (*Firmissime—Adesto— Alleluia* being incomplete). The plans for VanM provide for a fascicle to be devoted entirely to de Vitri.

EXAMPLE 100.   ♩♩|♩♩|♩♩|- - -|o|o|o|o|∗|-|

Then the tenor has the following related pattern, also four times:

EXAMPLE 101.   ♩♩♩|♩♩|♩♩|-|

This is applied to exactly the same notes as those the tenor spread over the first four *taleae*. In another de Vitri motet, *Vos quid admiramini—Gratissima —Gaude gloriosa,* in which the tenor is again isorhythmic, the triplum also takes on isorhythmic character towards the end, with the following pattern, different from the tenor pattern:

EXAMPLE 102. Portion of Triplum of *Vos quid admiramini—Gratissima —Gaude gloriosa*—Philippe de Vitri (from BesS II, 252).

Dulcis est a-ma-si-a. Me-a spon-sa, que pia.   Rex ego sum, hec re-gina! Quid tam - - ta re-fe-ri - mus?

Nos, qui cuncta novimus, dig-nam pre - e-le-gi-mus   Et ut rosam hanc pre spi-na. Sur-gi-te   vos   i-gi-tur,

qui a tempus la-bi-tur Et mors vos per-sequi-tur! Huic servite, hanc vo- ca-te! Quod si neg- le - xe-ri- tis,

". . . sweet and loving is my bride, who is upright. A king am I, this a queen! Why do we utter words so many? We, who knew all things, have chosen the [one who is] worthy and like this rose before the thorn. Rise ye then, for time slips on and death pursues ye! Serve her, call her! For if ye will have failed to do so . . ."

An anonymous motet in the Ivrea MS, *Ha fratres—Rachel plorat* (DTO XL, 5), is, with minor exceptions, isorhythmic in all its parts, of which there are three. Each has its own six *taleae*—at first, one pattern three times in succession and, after that, another pattern similarly repeated (so that the piece falls into two sections). The second tenor pattern is the same as the first, except that the time-values are halved. (We shall find this kind of diminution again in the motets of Machaut.) Another anonymous motet in the same MS, the four-part *Apta caro—Flos Virginum—Alma Redemptoris Mater,* begins with an instrumental prelude, or *Introitus,* after which the tenor twice spreads Hermannus Contractus's melody (or, rather, so much of it as sets the first three words) over three *taleae,* so that upon its repetition the melody has a rhythmical shape different from the one it had at first (*cf.* p. 299). While

Prosdocimus de Beldomandis (Prosdocimo de' Beldomandi), writing at Padua early in the 15th century, tells us that 14th-century theorists were not unanimous in differentiating between *color* as the term for repetition of melodic material (*cf.* p. 306) and *talea* as the term for rhythmic repetition, he states that there was a school of thought that did make the distinction [22] —a convenient one, adopted in modern analyses of isorhythmic motets, thus:

EXAMPLE 103. Tenor of the Anonymous Motet (ca. 1360) *Apta caro—Flos Virginum—Alma Redemptoris Mater* (from BesM, 130).

In this motet, not only do the *taleae* and *colores* overlap in the tenor, but the three upper parts all repeat their own *taleae,* only minor variations occurring.[23] Where, as here, motets are isorhythmic in all their parts, they are "variations upon a rhythmical skeleton that remains unchanged throughout. In the entire history of music hardly an example is found in which the constructive energy of tectonics attained to such a degree of rigidity as in these compositions. Of their technical refinements, however, the hearer perceives nothing. For the composer possessed the art of clothing each variation number in a brand-new tone-weft, of continually bringing on new harmonic and melodic shades and intensifications of tone, so that an impression of inevitable consistency resulted."[24]

The isorhythmic motet continued alive as a form for new compositions for more than a century.[25] It is interesting to observe that we have here a second form which, like *cancrizans* writing, produces a unifying effect without its being possible for the listener to know at a first hearing how that effect results. Such forms are additional evidence for the trend towards subtlety discernible in the 14th century—towards an art intended for connoisseurs, an art existing more for its own sake than as a servant of religion. A single work is generally not unified by both isorhythms and the new sonority: on the contrary, between

22 CouS III, 226. See also SchneiderA, 34f; SartN, 143.
23 For the complete motet, see BesS II, 254ff. See also BesM, 129f.   24 FiG, 504.
25 Further concerning the isorhythmic motet, see BesS II, 210ff, 221ff.

these two means there is a sort of schism, and the line of demarcation becomes increasingly sharp as the century progresses.

The fourth voice of the *Apta–Flos–Alma* is a contratenor. Here we have an important 14th-century innovation—a voice which, as its name implies, functions as a counter to the tenor. It gradually becomes the standard third voice—in three-part pieces also—and plays a prominent role in motet construction.

CouS III contains four treatises ascribed to de Vitri. The authenticity of all has been held dubious,[26] but it now seems reasonably clear that the *Ars nova* is in fact his.[27] The fame of this tract rests chiefly on the new theory it expounds with respect to mensural notation, a theory enlarging upon the Franconian system. The other treatises are at least written under de Vitri's influence.

It is clear that the Pierre de la Croix style would eventually require the introduction into notation of smaller time-values than the semibreve. It is clear too that binary rhythm was bound, sooner or later, to demand its rights. Both these things happened in French music of the 14th century and also in that of the Italians. During this period Italy seriously competed with France for musical honors. Each country doubtless affected the other, and which was the first to introduce certain innovations will perhaps never be determined. It was once thought that the *Lucidarium* of Marchettus of Padua was written in 1274 and his *Pomerium* in 1309. On the basis of this belief, it was claimed that Italy led the way towards reform in notation, inasmuch as the *Pomerium* expounds a new doctrine in this field. Since it has now been proved,[28] however, that both treatises date from sometime between 1309 and 1343, and since de Vitri's *Ars nova* may date from between *c.* 1316 and 1325, it is impossible to establish the priority of either country. None of the French treatises of the time mention Italian theory, while Marchettus does cite Franco. But this may indicate nothing more than that the new developments in both countries were based, at least in part, on French music of the 13th century. The other chief theorist expounding Italian notation is Prosdocimus.[29]

To facilitate comparison, the improvements in notation produced in Italy will be touched on here (rather than as part of the discussion of Italian 14th-century music) immediately before a brief mention of the French *Ars nova* notation. In both, the old Franconian ligature theory survives, but a most striking and most important new feature is the means of notating binary rhythm.

According to Marchettus in the *Pomerium*,[30] the breve may be divided into three equal parts (this division being known as *ternaria*) and subdivided into six (*senaria perfecta*), nine (*novenaria*), and twelve (*duodenaria*) parts, or it may be divided into two equal parts (*binaria*) and subdivided into four

---

[26] RieG, 233f; MaP, 36. [27] BesS II, **192**. It is printed in CouS III, 13; a German translation is included in BohnV. [28] LudQ, 289.

[29] See his *Tractatus practicae de musica mensurabili ad modum Italicorum*, printed, after the MS at the Liceo Musicale in Bologna, in CouS III, 228 (*errata* list in SartN, 26ff) and, after the MS at the Bibl. Pubblica at Lucca, in SartN, 35.

[30] Printed in GerS III. 121ff.

(*quaternaria*), six (*senaria imperfecta*), and eight (*octonaria*) parts. It is worthy of note that while Marchettus vouchsafes the imperfect divisions a subordinate place in the system, the musical examples he gives show that in practice they were no less important than the perfect divisions.

The chief means of indicating the nature of the rhythmic divisions employed in a particular composition was the *punctus divisionis,* separating one measure from another and thus performing the same function as the modern bar-line. The Italians applied it more frequently than the French. Additional guides used by some writers to aid in the recognition of the reigning measure were the letters placed at the beginning of a composition, T (*ternaria*) for perfect measure and B (*binaria*) for imperfect measure. Other writers used the letters P (perfection) and I (imperfection), while Q (*quaternaria*), S.P. (*senaria perfecta*), S.I. (*senaria imperfecta*), O (*octonaria*), N (*novenaria*), and D (*duodenaria*) were also sometimes employed. These were in effect signatures. When the semibreves within a breve measure were more or less in number than the signature indicated, the first semibreves received their normal value and the last ones were shortened or lengthened, as needed, to fill the measure, the process being called *via naturae.* If the lengthening was wanted at some other part of the measure, a descending stem was added to any semibreve affected and the alteration was known as *via artis.*

At first all the divisions of the breve were indicated by means of the semibreve. Thus in the *duodenaria* twelve semibreves equalled one breve while in the *quaternaria* four semibreves equalled one breve. This led to confusion, and the desire for clarity gradually brought into use modifications of the written form of the semibreve to show its value in the different rhythmic divisions, as well as symbols for note-values smaller than that of the semibreve. The following are some of the principal forms of the semibreve, minim, and semiminim as they appear in Italian notation.[31]

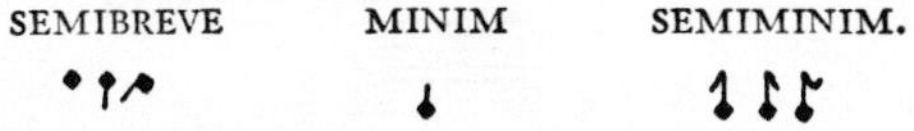
SEMIBREVE
MINIM
SEMIMINIM.

To illustrate, we give the values of these notes in the *senaria perfecta.*[32]

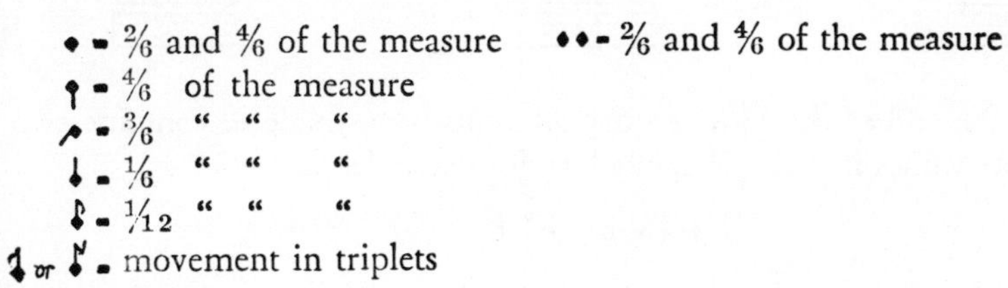
- 2/6 and 4/6 of the measure
- 2/6 and 4/6 of the measure
- 4/6 of the measure
- 3/6 " " "
- 1/6 " " "
- 1/12 " " "
or
- movement in triplets

[31] Many others may be found in 14th-century MSS. See WolfH, 311ff, 329. An account of Italian notation, in English, fuller than is here possible, may be found in EllinL, xxiff.

[32] For a complete table of comparative values in the various divisions see GaspA, 617.

Returning to our example of the *duodenaria,* in which at the beginning of
the 14th century twelve semibreves equalled one breve, we find that at the end
of the same century twelve minims equalled one breve, just as four minims
equalled one breve in the *quaternaria,* six minims equalled one breve in the
senaria, and so on.

EXAMPLE 104. The Opening of Jacopo da Bologna's *Un bel sparver* in
    the Original Notation [33] and in Transcription (after WolfG
    II, 65; III, 97).

Other dots applied were the *punctus perfectionis* (used to make sure that
a performer would understand the note it followed to equal 3 of the next
smaller value), the *punctus additionis* (a dot of augmentation, increasing the
value of a note by half, as in modern notation and thus, to a certain extent,
corresponding to the *punctus perfectionis—cf.* p. 290), and the *punctus demon-
strationis,* sometimes appearing in pairs, one dot being placed on each side
of the stem. This kind of point is of special interest, since it indicates a device
that was apparently new in the 14th century—*syncopation.*

The following are rests used in Italian notation:

Towards the end of the 14th century attempts were made to combine two
different note-values in a single symbol as, for example, in

$$\text{♩}=\text{♪♪♩} \quad or \quad \text{♩}=\text{♩♪♪}$$

---

[33] The original is written on a six-line staff. See, for a facsimile of the complete piece, plates
77 and 78 in WolfMS. The notes within brackets were taken from another MS and interpolated
here by Wolf. The O at the beginning of this excerpt is the symbol for the *divisio octonaria.*

These attempts were made at a time when Italian notation was fast declining and giving way to French *Ars nova* notation. French notation was already triumphant in Italy quite early in the 15th century but some 15th-century MSS written in Italian notation survive.

The Italians favored a six-line staff while the French preferred a staff of five lines. The flat is used much as it is today; the sharp to indicate both a semitone elevation and the cancellation of a previous flat.

The notation that came into use in answer to the demands of French *Ars nova* practice, while retaining the fundamental note-values of the Franconian system, recognized the independence of the minim, applied the principle of the old relationships between long and breve to smaller note-values, introduced some of the time-divisions employed also by the Italians, and fused the whole into a system that formed the basis of subsequent development. The new system contained as its most important elements the following symbols:

MAXIMA OR DUPLEX LONGA	◥	SEMIBREVIS	◆
LONGA	◣	MINIMA	♩
BREVIS	▪	SEMIMINIMA	♪

To the old division

MODUS (the term here applying to the division of the longa) [34]

PERFECTUS   IMPERFECTUS

were now added

TEMPUS (the term applying to the division of the breve)

PERFECTUM   IMPERFECTUM

and PROLATIO (the term applying to the division of the semibreve)

MAIOR OR PERFECTA [35]   MINOR OR IMPERFECTA

The "four prolations"—  —the invention of which is ascribed to Philippe in the 14th- and 15th-century treatises, became the principal measure-units of 14th-century mu-

---

[34] Apparently no opportunity was to be lost to give this long-suffering word as many different meanings as possible.

[35] In both editions of OH the minim is incorrectly given with descending tail. A lozenge with such a tail correctly represents a form of semibreve—one having, actually, a greater value than the lozenge without a tail (*cf.* p. 341, where the form is discussed in connection with Italian notation, to which, however, it is not confined).

sic and thus, in a way, occupied the position formerly held by the first three rhythmic modes.

The Franconian rule *"Longa ante longam perfecta"* was changed to the more general *"Similis, ante similem perfecta,"* that is, any note in a triple measure, from the long down to the semibreve, if followed by another note of the same species was perfect or tripartite. Just as a long preceded or followed by a breve became, in the old system, bipartite, so now did a breve when flanked on either side by a semibreve, or a semibreve by a minim. All the other rules that in the old system governed the relationship between long and breve were now applied to breve and semibreve, semibreve and minim. Thus "alteration," in which the second of two breves enclosed between two longs doubled its value, was now extended to the second of two semibreves between two breves and to the second of two minims between two semibreves.

Syncopation, which, as we have seen, now makes its appearance, is first actually defined in the *Ars perfecta secundum Philippum de Vitriaco*,[36] though it is in an English tract rather than in this one that we first encounter it (*cf.* p. 414). As explained by the medieval theorists, it is a complex and difficult matter. The principle seems to be that a shift in rhythm took place when a whole measure or part of a measure was interpolated between the unequal constituents of another measure. Thus ♦■■· ▪ o+o|o· . If the second breve is interpolated between the unequal parts of the first measure, we get ♦■·■ ▪ o+o͞|o+o . This is one of the simpler forms of syncopation as it appears in the MSS.[37]

The following six widely accepted special signatures are expounded in the *Ars perfecta,* attributed to de Vitri:

| modus perfectus | ▥ | tempus perfectum | O | prolatio maior | ⊙ |
| "   imperfectus | ▯ | "   imperfectum | C[38] | "   minor | ℂ |

These were modified according to need. Thus tempus perfectum with prolatio minor (■ ▪ ♦♦♦ ▪ ♩♩ ♩♩ ♩♩) was indicated by ⊙ or ⏀ , and tempus imperfectum with prolatio maior (■ ▪ ♦♦ ▪ ♩♩♩ ♩♩♩) was indicated by ℂ or ℂ . The desired symbol was written at the beginning of a composition and it frequently happened that a different signature was introduced during the course of a piece to indicate a change of the fundamental measure.

French 14th-century composers used the dot to indicate many different functions, a fact that gave rise to some confusion and that led Prosdocimus to point proudly to the clarity and simplicity of Italian usage. The names given to the dots by French writers help to show the nature of their several func-

---

[36] CouS III, 34.   [37] For an extended discussion of this difficult subject, see WolfG I, 132ff.

[38] The sign still in use today for ⁴⁄₄ time. These first 4 signatures appear in the *Ars nova* also. In the form in which this treatise is printed in CouS III, the shapes for the prolation signatures appear there too, but with a different significance. CouS, however, is in error (*cf.* WolfG I, 92).

tions: *punctus divisionis, perfectionis, imperfectionis, alterationis, syncopationis,* and *augmentationis.*

The rests already presented as appearing in Italian notation are among those used in French notation also.[39]

The use of colored notes to indicate a change in rhythm was not an *Ars nova* invention. They had already been so employed in the *Roman de Fauvel.* But Philippe de Vitri gives the most complete account of the varied uses to which colored notes were put. Red notes served sometimes (1) to indicate a shift in rhythm, (2) to differentiate between cantus planus and cantus mensurabilis, (3) to show that a melody was to be sung an octave higher, (4) to prevent a note's being measured as perfect, (5) to prevent, instead, its being measured as altered or imperfect, and, later on, (6) to indicate a tripartite value in binary rhythm and (7) to call for diminution (see below). "Vacant" (i.e. white) notes with black outlines were employed when red ink was not available, and because they were much more conveniently written they soon generally displaced red notes. (The use of red notes in some elaborate MSS survived, however, until well into the 15th century, especially in England. White notes were used for special purposes in Italian *trecento* notation also.) In the first part of the 15th century, white notes replaced black ones for all the values, from semiminim up; in the latter half, the semiminim lost its tail and became black and notes of shorter value—also black—appeared with increasing frequency, so that the same division as we have today, between white for everything from the minim up and black for everything from the semiminim down, became established.

Important in *Ars nova* theory and practice was the employment of *diminution* and *augmentation,* indicated in the parts by a special sign or number or, if diminution, by white notes with red outlines. By diminution was meant the performing of a part (usually the tenor) in the next smaller note-values than those in which it was written; for example the breves were performed as semibreves, and so on. None of the proportional relationships between the notes of the passage affected was altered; all these notes were simply reduced in performance by a third or a half of their value. The way in which the principle was applied may be seen in the *Vince con lena* of Bartolomeo da Bologna and the anonymous *Par le grant sens.*[40] In the Italian piece, diminution is used for want of any notes smaller than the semiminim, which are needed. The scribe's writing, dating from the 15th century, is of the white-note kind (except for such black notes as appear where red ones would have been used earlier). The diminution is indicated by a semicircle open at the

---

[39] For a table of the rests employed in more than 20 medieval treatises, see WolfH I, 336f. (Some of the rests tabulated there, but not actually occurring in the treatises to which they are accredited, are apparently supplied by Wolf through analogy.)

[40] Facsimile of the former on the last plate of the facsimile section of StaD; transcription on p. 60. Original notation of the latter in WolfG II, 46; transcription in WolfG III, 72.

left, the effect of which lasts until the reintroduction of the signature used at the beginning. (This is a circle enclosing one dot, the new signature for the major prolation.) In the French piece, each of the three parts offers examples of diminution, indicated sometimes by a semicircle open at the left (effective until "cancelled" by reintroduction of the initial signature for time imperfect), sometimes by "vacant" notes outlined in red. (The piece illustrates the use of filled-in red notes also.) In augmentation the notes were to be performed as if written in the shapes of the next larger values.

Not all the above mentioned 14th-century guides to the recognition of the measure were universally employed, but, on the other hand, the treatises of the time contain many other hints to the performer. These hints have been tabulated by Wolf and may be found in WolfG I, 150ff.

When we add that French 14th-century composers, like their Italian contemporaries, often availed themselves of flats and sharps to mark chromatic alterations of tones, it will be seen that, if Franconian notation provided the fundamental principles upon which our modern notation is based, *Ars nova* notation already included almost all the more important characteristics that give our system its varied scope. Even if the symbols were not all uniformly accepted in the 14th and 15th centuries and there was a great profusion of different signs for the same thing,[41] the approach to modern notation was there. It remained for succeeding centuries to prune away superfluous symbols and systematize the important ones.

If Jacques de Liége was a conservative, Jean de Muris (b. *c.* 1290; d. *c.* 1351) was an energetic advocate of the new art. He seems not to have composed. His *Ars novae musice* is an important work.[42] Its central idea is that in the mensural system the relations of a note of a given species to notes of the next larger and next smaller species ought to be precisely the same as the corresponding relations of a note of any other species. In other words, one ought not to have one set of rules for the relation of long to duplex long, another for the relation of breve to long, another for the relation of semibreve to breve; one set of rules should govern all these relations; the system should be a logical and consistent whole, consistent in its rules, in its signs, in its terminology. Among the other works attributed to him, a few additional writings are genuine (these include a letter to Philippe de Vitri),[43] but the ascription of the *Summa musicae* to him joins that of the *Speculum musicae* as unfounded. With the certainty that he did not write the *Speculum,* the contradiction between his character as a "modern" and the conservativeness of

---

[41] French 14th-century notation attained "the highest degree of complexity that notation has ever reached in the history of music." (LudG, 226.)

[42] This may be pieced together out of material in GerS III (see BesS II, 207). An English translation will soon appear in Oliver Strunk's book of readings in music history.

[43] *Cf.* BesS I, 183; II, 209.

that treatise has been removed. Also unfounded is the former identification of him as the man appointed rector of the Sorbonne c. 1350.[44]

The outstanding French musician of the 14th century, so far as we can judge in view of the little that survives by de Vitri, was Guillaume de Machaut, born c. 1300 in Champagne. He took holy orders at an early age and in 1323 became secretary to John, king of Bohemia and duke of Luxembourg. This adventurous figure, brother-in-law and devoted adherent of Charles-le-Bel of France, travelled much and warred much in many parts of Europe and in 1346 was killed at the disastrous battle of Crécy, in which he fought on the French side as an ally of Philippe VI, the successor of Charles. King John appears to have favored Guillaume considerably, obtaining several benefices for him and his brother from Pope John XXII, to whom we shall return presently, one of the line of Popes who, from 1309 to 1377, resided at Avignon. Guillaume finally became canon of Rheims. The king appears to have taken him along on many of his escapades over Europe, and it is possible to trace some of the poet-composer's travels—in Bohemia, Poland, Lithuania, Italy, etc.—in his writings: that is, in his poetry which, if somewhat artificial and strained, is nevertheless of historical importance. The French themselves compared him with his contemporary, Petrarch. Another contemporary of his, but a younger one, was Chaucer (1340–1400), whose "Legende of Good Women," which may have been suggested by Machaut's *Jugement dou Roy de Navarre,* at any rate interweaves phrases and lines derived from the French poet. After the death of King John, Machaut entered successively the service of several other high personages. In his latter years he entered into an amorous correspondence with a certain Péronne, and references in it to his work give us some insight into his attitude towards composition. In one letter, in which he avows that he writes only for Péronne, he includes the lines:

Qui de sentiment ne fait,   *Would one without true feeling sing,*
Son dit et son chant contrefait.   *His words and tune with discord ring.*

Guillaume must have been a fairly active, jolly, and worldly ecclesiastic. He died c. 1377.[45]

His compositions reach us in considerable quantity.[46] Certain of the MSS preserving them are of extraordinary beauty. One of the richest once belonged to Duke Jean de Berry (d. 1416), brother of Charles V. Miniatures in some

---

[44] For further facts concerning de Muris, see BesS I, 181ff.
[45] For a full-length biography, see MaG (1930), 425ff.
[46] A complete edition, MachM, was undertaken by Friedrich Ludwig. Although he completed the work of transcription etc. before his death (1930), the last volume (to contain the Mass, hocket, and *lais*) has not yet appeared.

of the MSS include portraits of Machaut himself.[47] Miscellaneous collections that contain pieces by him help to show the extent to which his influence spread: an Italian MS (now Paris Bib. Nat. n. a. fr. 6771), for example, contains seven of his compositions. Works of his are preserved in German and other MSS also.

Machaut's compositions belong to several *genres*. He seems himself to have settled the order in which they appear in the best of the collections devoted to him, since these have almost the same arrangement. The *lais* come first, then the motets, then the Mass (sometimes followed by a 3-voice hocket), then the *ballades notées* (so designated to distinguish them from *ballades* without music), then the *rondeaux*, and finally the *chansons balladées*.

The *Remède de Fortune*, a work almost didactic in its purpose, explaining, as it does, the style and construction of various lyric forms, contains, interspersed through the poem, one composition to illustrate each of seven forms: a *lai*, a *rondeau*, etc.

There are altogether 18 *lais*,[48] 16 monodic. With Machaut, indeed, the brighter days of one-line writing in art music may be said to come to an end. The polyphonic portions of the 2 exceptions are in three parts and are in canon. One of them actually bears the marking: *chace*. Machaut's *lai* differs in form from that of the 13th century, but the influence of the double-versicle sequence-type is still traceable. His typical *lai* (there are deviations) may be described thus: The work has 12 strophes, the first and last of which are alike in poetic form and have the same musical setting. Each of the other 10 strophes has a poetic form and musical setting of its own. Each strophe is divided into two sections, sung to the same melody; often each section is itself divided into two subsections, both sung successively to the same portion of the melody. Thus the immediate repetitions in pairs preserve some of the old *lai* character. There are *lais* in which the first subsection is provided with both *ouvert* and *clos* cadences.[49] The melodic style is sometimes quite simple, sometimes highly ornamented.[50]

---

[47] Ludwig, in MachM II, lists 37 MSS, some containing musical works of Machaut's, some containing poems written for musical settings. He describes the former group in detail. A MS in the J. P. Morgan Library, mentioned but not examined by Ludwig, contains the music of 4 works, printed in MachM after other MSS. These are: on fol. 213 ᵛ, the *ballade, De toutes flours* (lacking the triplum with which it is printed in MachM I, 35); on fol. 214, the *ballade, De Fortune me doy* (lacking the triplum and both versions of the contratenor with which it is printed in MachM I, 25); on fol. 214 ᵛ, the *rondeau, Se vous n'estes pour mon guerredon nee* (lacking the triplum and the 2 alternative contratenors with which it is printed in MachM I, 56) and the *rondeau, Tant doucement* (lacking the triplum and contratenor with which it is printed in MachM I, 58).

[48] For 1 complete *lai* in print, see MachM I, 93, or HoepM II, appendix, 1. (HoepM is a 3-volume edition of Machaut's poems, to which Ludwig contributed transcriptions of the 7 *Remède de Fortune* pieces.)

[49] All these traits are illustrated by the *lai* in MachM I, 93; all but the division into subsections, by the first 2 strophes of another *lai* printed in BesM, 137.

[50] The 2 styles are illustrated and contrasted by means of extracts in GéroM, 326f; there is another extract in simple style in GéroH, 369. Further concerning the *lais*, see MaG (1931), 329ff (in which exception is taken to the theory of the derivation of the *lai* from the sequence).

Amour Presents Doux Penser, Plaisance, and Esperance to Guillaume de Machaut. Miniature by the Maître aux Bouqueteaux in a MS Containing Machaut's Works

(Paris, Bib. Nat. fr. 1584. After Henry Martin, La Miniature française du XIIIe au XVe siècle)

Lady Playing Dulcimer. Harp and Portative Organ in the Foreground. Singers and Players on Recorder, Shawm, and Bagpipe, in the Background

From the early 16th-Century MS of the 14th-Century poem, Les Échecs amoureux, made for the instruction of the future François I

(Paris, Bib. Nat. fr. 143)

PLATE VII

There is only one example apiece with music, of the *complainte* and the *chanson royale,* both appearing in the *Remède de Fortune.*[51]

It is perhaps in his *rondeaux, virelais* (which he calls *chansons balladées,* without, however, successfully establishing the new designation for future use), and *ballades,* that we most clearly see a duality in Machaut's artistic character. The influence of the 14th-century innovations is plainly discernible, but Machaut, the retainer of the dashing John of Bohemia, looks back romantically at the 13th century—at the age of chivalry, now past. He emulates, after a fashion, the art of the trouvères, but it is wrong to call him the last of their number. The old, courtly chivalry survives in the 14th century only as a literary flourish. "Here for the first time, in art and in life, the schism, incapable of solution, between inherited, fate-imposed form and new, original experience, comes to light—the true sign of an old culture grown overripe." But "the poet-musician Machaut captured the sublimest moods and secrets of the old culture" in the music of his *rondeaux, virelais,* and *ballades.*[52] In his works there is an attempt at a restoration as well as a reaching out after the new.

Of the *chansons balladées* or *virelais,* 25 monodic examples are preserved, as well as 7 with instrumental tenor and one with an instrumental contratenor as well.[53] The 13th-century pattern is still valid (*cf.* p. 223). Machaut favors having three strophes, so that a complete *virelai* of his consists of a refrain, followed by a strophe (of which the first verses are set to a new melodic phrase, sung twice—the first time with an *ouvert,* the second time with a *clos*—; the last verses, to the melody of the refrain), refrain, strophe, refrain, strophe, refrain. Frequently—especially in polyphonic examples—there is melodic rhyme between the close of the refrain and the close of the repeated section of the strophe, recalling somewhat the melodic rhyme already referred to, in Chapter 7, as appearing in certain monodic *ballades.* The following piece, with its simple, attractive melody, has something of the old trouvère spirit. But it is in binary rhythm, thus departing (at least in the view of the adherents of the modal theory) from troubadour and trouvère custom. (Most of the *virelais,* however, are in ternary rhythm, and one is in the old second rhythmic mode almost throughout.) Syncopation is used strikingly if sparingly.

EXAMPLE 105. *Douce dame jolie*—Guillaume de Machaut (from MachM I, 71).

[51] For transcriptions, see MachM I, 96; for discussions, see MaG (1931), 333f.
[52] BesM, 137.
[53] All printed in MachM I, 70–92, 101.

fors vous seu-le - ment. I a. Qua - des sans tri-che - ri - e   chie - ri - e   vous ay et hum-ble-ment   ri - tein pen - se - ment.
ce   ne vous en prent. b toys les jours de ma - vi - e   ser - vi - e   sans
nul a - li - ge - ment. II a. Mais vo dou-ce mai-stri-e   mai-stri-e   mon cuer si du - re - ment   a - mours tel - le - ment
lan-gui lon-gue - ment. b quel-le le con-tra-li - e   et li - e   en   stes de mon tour-ment.
III a. Et quant ma ma-la - di - e   qa - ri - e   ne se - ra nul-le-ment
b sans vous, douce a-ne - mi - e,   qui li - e   e.

"*Sweet pretty lady, pray do not think that any one has signory over me save you alone,* [over me] who have without deceit cherished you always, and humbly serve you all the days of my life without evil thought. Alas! and I beg in my hope and anguish; since my joy is ended if you do not take pity on me. *Sweet pretty lady,* etc. But your sweet mastery masters my heart so forcefully that it is bound and bound again in love so much that it has no desire at all to be outside your domain; and will not bind itself to any allegiance except to your heart. *Sweet pretty lady,* etc. And since my sickness will never be cured without you, sweet enemy who are the cause of my torment, with joined hands I beg your heart to forget me, or straightway kill me, for too long I have languished. *Sweet pretty lady,* etc.

A cadence, such as we find in this example, with the final immediately preceded by the raised leading-tone (here called for by the rules of *musica falsa* —cf. measure 2 of Example 97 and pp. 380ff), does not exclude the possibility of a cadence in which what we today would call the 6th scale-degree is sounded between the leading tone and the final. The *virelai, Se je souspir,* contains the following:

EXAMPLE 106. (from MachM I, 89).

da - me   ne   voy

This type of cadence was once particularly associated by modern writers with Machaut's Italian contemporary, Landini, and the penultimate note was named the Landini sixth. But such a cadence is by no means peculiar to the Italian master and, in fact, was used in France before Machaut.

The *rondeaux,* of which there are 21 with music [54]—in two, three and four parts—likewise retain the 13th-century pattern (*cf.* p. 222). But the musical content is often highly sophisticated. In fact, it is most unlikely that the *rondeau* was danced to any longer. It is possible, however, that dancing occurred to *virelai* melodies, in connection with the *carole,* [55] as it certainly did to the *estampie* (*cf.* p. 218). Complexity in the *rondeau* reaches its height in the musico-poetic enigma, *Ma fin est mon commencement et mon commence-*

---

[54] Printed in MachM I, 52–69, 103.
[55] See on this point, MaG (1931), 337. Concerning the *carole* as distinguished from the *danse,* see SachsW, 269–75. Concerning the derivation of the term from *Kyrie eleison,* see Margit Sahlin's interesting philological thesis, *Etude sur la carole médiévale* (1940).

ment ma fin. Here, fittingly enough in view of the text, use is made of *cancrizans* writing. The top part, which is instrumental, has the same   melody as the tenor, but backwards, while the contratenor, also instrumental, is constructed in the same way as the antecedent in Example 99—that is, it is the same from the end backwards to the middle as from the beginning forwards to the middle, or, in other words, it reverses itself. It is the song itself, therefore, that is speaking in the poem. Such close relation between music and text as we find here and in Example 98, however, is not characteristic of 14th-century composition, although there are other exceptions, including market scenes. The piece, perhaps more playful than pedantic, makes frequent use of syncopation.

EXAMPLE 107. *Ma fin est mon commencement—Rondeau—*Guillaume de Machaut (after MachM I, 63).

(a) *the d is an emendation from WolfG III, 64-5.*

"*My end is my beginning and my beginning my end*, and [this] holds truly. *My end is my beginning*, My third song three times only reverses itself and thus ends [i. e. in a complete performance with all repetitions, the second half of the piece occurs three times, so that the "third song"—the contratenor—has the opportunity of reversing itself thrice; the last time it does this it brings the piece to its close]. *My end is my beginning and my beginning my end*." (For the rather amusing original notation of this piece, see WolfG II, 40, but in the light of MachM I, 64.)

Machaut has journeyed a long distance from the stage reached by Adam de la Halle.

Not only syncopation, as in Example 107, but triplets (*cf.* Example 104), freely inserted coloratura passages (*cf.* p. 361), and *ritardandi* and *rubati* actually written out, embellished the music of the period. Only the motet, yielding, as it did, to the novelty of isorhythmics, in comparison tended to resist the blandishments of these decorations.

Rondeaux are among the pieces occurring in different versions in different MSS (*cf.* footnote 47). Sometimes the variants give rise to changes in the harmony, a fact which may indicate that at this period the desire for definitely fixing a harmonization was not very strong—that with respect to harmony too there was a development, such as we have observed in connection with the psalm-tones and perhaps in connection with rhythm, in which interchangeability and flux characterized an early stage. Where several versions exist with varying numbers of parts, they very likely furnish evidence of the practice of performing works with such resources as might be available—with, let us say, in one place four musicians, in another, two. The growth away from interchangeability in the performance of a given part by a voice or by one of any number of different instruments was not to begin taking on imposing proportions until after the Renaissance. Where a piece by Machaut occurs in more than one MS, the general uniformity in the underlaying of the text may be connected with his double rôle as musician and poet and a consequent regard for the interrelation between words and music, rather than to any general objection against having adjustments between words and music variable.

The lack of stability, not only in music of the 14th century but also in much other old music, is obviously a serious handicap to us today, since we cannot be certain to what degree a MS faithfully represents the way in which a particular composition was actually performed. Differing versions of individual works seem to indicate that parts were added or omitted at will. It has been pointed out, in a special study of 14th-century music, that chime-bells are depicted in many miniatures of the period and are mentioned in literary sources, but that parts really suitable for chime-bells are not easily found; that we know drones to have been widely used, but find none notated. It would seem that, in periods when improvisation flourishes, the written com-position may, at least sometimes, be only the skeleton of the performed one.[56] There is some comfort, however, in the thought that certain 14th-century compositions are so complex that, if performers may have wished to modify them, they would hardly have wanted to elaborate them.

There are 42 *ballades notées* [57] by Machaut. One is monodic; the rest are in from two to four parts. Some of the polyphonic pieces have words in all parts, some apparently are intended for voice, or voices, with instrumental accompaniment. Machaut's *ballade* form agrees with the last of the three 13th-century *ballade* patterns described on p. 223. That is, there is no refrain at the beginning; the strophe consists of two main sections, the first of which is repeated, the second not; the refrain follows. (In Machaut, this often rhymes musically with the recurring section of the strophe—as it does twice in *Roman de Fauvel ballades*, i.e. in those in GennR I, 298, 302—; *cf*. the musical rhyme frequent in his *virelais* and the rather differently disposed use of such rhyme noted in some *ballades* in Chapter 7.) Like the *rondeau*, the *ballade* was no longer danced to in the 14th century. Among Machaut's works in this form, there is a double *ballade*. Machaut relates that a certain Thomas Paien sent him a *ballade* text with the refrain, *Je vois assez, puisque je vois ma dame* ("I see enough, since I see my lady") and that its receipt prompted him to write another *ballade* with the same rhymes and refrain and to make of the two poems a composition for two voices and two instruments. He sent the result to Péronne, with a letter stating that he had had the piece performed and that he had assured himself it was good.[58] There are also two triple *ballades*. In *De triste cuer*,[59] each of the three voices has its own text, the group having only the refrain in common. In *Sanz cuer m'en vois*,[60] each of the three voices again has its own text, but they all have the same melody—that is, the piece is in canon. The *ballades, Se quanque amours* and *Nes que on porroit* contain examples of imitation at the second and third respectively.[61] Machaut, however, uses imitation sparingly in this form, in which he cast some of his most lovely works. The style of the typical three-part *ballades*, in which the leading melody is in the highest voice and the two lower parts

[56] *Cf*. SchneiderA, 18. See also SachsW, 297f.   [57] Printed in MachM I, 1–49, 98.
[58] The piece is printed in MachM I, 40; LudG, 270.   [59] Printed in MachM I, 32.
[60] Printed in MachM I, 16. Concerning a possible error in the transcription, see FeinK, **13**.
[61] See MachM I, 22 and 38.

are instrumental supports, apparently enjoyed great vogue and, as we shall see, assumed considerable importance.

The 23 motets,[62] 19 in three parts and 4 in four parts, are remarkable for their isorhythmic features. In only 3 does Machaut fail to have at least the tenor isorhythmic. In 10 motets the tenor melody, after its complete statement in the original time-values, is repeated in diminution, with the values divided by 2 or 3 or (in motet 2) irregularly, the concluding sections of the works thus gaining a perceptible degree of animation. In several motets, the upper parts, while not isorhythmic throughout, are so to some extent. The contratenor as well as the tenor is isorhythmic in motets 22 and 23 (the numbers correspond to those in MachM), while, in motet 23, the other parts are free; in motet 22, the other parts contain some isorhythmic features, but are fairly free. Five motets begin with an Introitus, played before the entrance of the isorhythmic tenor. In motets 4, 7-9, 14, 19, and 22, the number of *taleae* and *colores* does not agree, so that there results the interesting kind of overlapping (investing a melody, upon its repetition, with new rhythms), mentioned on p. 339. One of these—motet 4—has upper parts that are isorhythmic throughout, so that this work is especially noteworthy for its display of technical features. The upper parts are almost entirely isorhythmic in motet 13. The tenor melody of motet 6, after being given forth in association with one reiterated *talea,* is then repeated in association with another *talea* that is not a mere diminution of the first. In all but 6 of the 23 pieces, at least one upper part has a secular French text.

Isorhythmic features appear not only in Machaut's motets, but in *ballade* 1 and *rondeau* 7. In fact, the motets and *ballades* have several stylistic traits in common. If, as in the troubadour and trouvère pieces, the poems of the *rondeaux, virelais,* and *ballades* dictated the form of the music, in the motets the independence of the music—which was the prime consideration—was complete. The theorist Aegidius de Murino, in giving directions for the composition of a motet, indicates that the music should be written first and the words set to it afterwards.[63] Notwithstanding, it is characteristic of the 14th-century motet that the different, simultaneously sung texts are related to one another in some way, and they are usually in the same language. Where the tenor is textless, it is probably intended for an instrument. The subjects of the motets vary—they may be lyrical, religious, moralizing, political. "The motet has now become the representative musical form *par excellence,* employed for the glorification of actions of the state, church, and court. We have motets on nearly all the French kings, on princes of the church and great lords, on political events that stir the soul . . . , on warlike undertakings. . . . But the theme of courtly love also continually reappears in the motet-literature." [64]

[62] Constituting the contents of MachM III.   [63] CouS III, 125.   [64] FiG, 502.

Machaut's motets contain some examples of imitation, and display certain weak points of the French school in using it. In *Dame je sui cilz,* what may possibly have been intended as a snatch of free imitation loses some of its force (if it actually was so intended) through the fact that neither voice enters after a rest or cadence.

EXAMPLE 108. (From MachM III, 42).

In *Bone pastor,*[65] the imitation is somewhat more effective: the second voice enters after a rest. Another imitation in *Dame je sui cilz* is obscured—although both parts enter after rests—by the prefixing, to the melody of the second voice, of a motive that does not belong to the phrase.

EXAMPLE 109. (From MachM III, 41).

The only work of Machaut's labelled as a hoquetus is his *David.* The hoquetus part and the triplum alternate with each other in characteristic hocket manner. The isorhythmic tenor uses two patterns, the first has 8 appearances, and these are applied to 3 appearances of the melody, so that we have 8 *taleae* and 3 *colores* overlapping and giving the melody a different rhythmic aspect each time it is performed. The fourth and last *color* is spread over 4 appearances of the second *talea.*[66] The piece seems to be instrumental. The chief motive is derived from the musical underscoring of the word *David* in the liturgical *Alleluia Nativitas . . . ex stirpe David* (= *Alleluia Solemnitas . . . ex stirpe David* in the present service), and it has

[65] MachM III, 65.
[66] The tenor is printed in SchneiderA. appendix, 4; the whole piece is published separately by the Editions de l'Oiseau Lyre.

been suggested that Machaut may have intended his piece to provide a continuation for Perotin's organum triplum based on that *Alleluia*. Hocketing reaches its zenith with Machaut and Vitri, who seem to place no deliberate restriction on the rhythms they use or on the number of notes they insert between two rests.

Machaut's Mass [67] is a work of great historical importance. It is the earliest known complete polyphonic setting of the Ordinary of the Mass by one man. The *Ite missa est* is added to the five usual main sections. In Machaut's composition, as in later strictly liturgical polyphonic Masses, the words *Gloria in excelsis Deo* and *Credo in unum Deum* are not set to part-music but continue to be sung in plainsong, as they are rendered by the celebrant.

The right of Machaut's Mass to priority as the first through-composed polyphonic setting is challenged only by the so-called *Messe de Tournai*,[68] dating, as a unit, from the first half of the 14th century. (Machaut's Mass has, on the basis of no particular evidence, been said to have been composed for the coronation of Charles V in 1364.) The *Messe de Tournai,* however, is not a homogeneous work and, in fact, seems to be a collection of individual compositions written at different periods. The Kyrie, Sanctus, and Agnus, are in older style. In the Gloria and Credo, however, the Gregorian melodies are in the highest voice and are elaborated,[69] this being an unusual practice for the period. Like the Machaut Mass, this probable compilation includes an *Ite missa est* (preserved also in the Ivrea MS). The setting of this part of the service, using a liturgical tenor, is in motet style, with a motetus written to a Latin text and a triplum to secular French words.

In the Machaut Mass, on the other hand, an effort is plainly made to bind the work together. The following motive

EXAMPLE 110. (From MaG, 407).

"may be regarded as the generating cell of this vast composition: not only does one encounter it in each of the sections, but in addition it gives rise to imitations, to fugal entries, to repetitions, to counter-melodies in long time-values (Kyrie), well proving that Machaut made of it the basic material of

[67] Not yet completely printed. The original notation and a transcription of the Kyrie may be found in WolfG II, 28, and III, 50; an improved transcription of the final Kyrie in LudB, 457 (WolfG is a work of first-line importance, but it should be used in conjunction with Ludwig's review of it in SIM, VI [1905], 597); the original notation of a brief fragment of the Gloria. in A. W. Ambros, *Geschichte der Musik,* II, 370; original notation and transcription of the Credo (incomplete) in WolfG II, 30, and III, 53; facsimiles of a portion of the Sanctus in GasP, 65, and GéroH, opposite p. 365; transcriptions of the first section of the Agnus in BesM, 149, and of the middle section in OH I, 245; transcriptions of portions of the Kyrie, Credo, and Agnus in GasV. Further concerning printed extracts, see MachM II. 5*.   [68] Printed in CouM.

[69] See FiK, 22, 40ff; also HandZP, 542, which likewise believes the chant-melodies to be paraphrased, but refers to Peter Wagner's article in *Gregoriusblatt* XLVIII, which disputes their presence.

his Messe Notre-Dame." [70] The Kyrie is written after the pattern aaa, bbb, ccd, which is that of the liturgical melody that is borrowed [71] but freely treated in the tenor. The Gloria is in conductus style. The absence of melismas in the Credo (perhaps because of the length of the text) makes the writing especially chordal. The plainsong melody is paraphrased in the motetus part.[72] There is a striking broadening of the time-values in the *Et incarnatus est* subsection at the words *Ex Maria Virgine*, the importance of which is thus impressively underscored. Such a broad treatment was destined to become standard for the whole *Et incarnatus est* in later Masses. After markedly consonant writing, Machaut introduces sharp dissonance on the word *Crucifixus*. But, on the whole, the Mass is not characterized by "expressive" treatment of the text. The stark majesty of Machaut's Credo is far removed from the elegant playfulness of some of the *virelais* and *rondeaux*. The Sanctus is based on the plainsong of Mass XVII in the Vatican Edition,[73] as is the Agnus Dei. The first invocation of the Agnus is set in isorhythmic-motet style, consisting, as it does, of an Introitus followed by two isorhythmic periods (with some liberties in the motetus and triplum). The whole Mass has, in fact, been designated by Curt Sachs as "basically a gigantic motet."

In the Machaut Mass we see arriving at a goal the experiments of the past in embellishing the Ordinary with organum and discant. This work, which was still performed in the 16th century, was destined to prove the ancestor of the polyphonic Masses of Josquin and Palestrina and even of those of Bach and Beethoven.

Outstanding as this Mass is, sacred music obviously constitutes a comparatively small part of Machaut's output. In this respect, he seems to be a true child of his century. In both French and Italian 14th-century MSS, secular music occupies the chief attention of composers. This is perhaps the result of the famous bull of Pope John XXII, issued in the year 1324/5 (not 1322) at Avignon, banning from the church service not only the addition of motetus and triplum parts to the plainsong but practically all kinds of polyphony.[74] It seems quite clear, however, that this bull did not fully achieve its ends over any wide area and that some historians have greatly exaggerated its influence. Composers continued to write polyphonic music for liturgical use.[75] But the edict may have acted as a partial check, if not as a complete one, thus diverting the main flow of musical creation into secular channels. In the vicinity of Avignon itself, the effect evidently did not last very long. The Ivrea and Apt MSS (the latter dating from late in the 14th century or even, perhaps, early in the 15th) both contain music for the Mass. If the bull did

---

[70] MaG (1931), 407. [71] From Mass IV in the Vatican Edition. See *Liber usualis*, 25.
[72] *Cf.* HandZP, 542f. [73] See *Liber usualis*, 61.
[74] Organum, if not too elaborate, is exempted from the general prohibition. The text of the document is conveniently available in both Latin and English in OH I, 294ff.
[75] See BesM, 148. For an article on the 14th-century polyphonic Mass, see LudD; also BorB.

cause composers to concentrate on the writing of secular music for a while, it thereby brought about the extraordinary result that, when they returned to the writing of music for the Mass, they wrote it in the popular *ballade* style. (The Machaut Mass, whenever it was written, made use rather, as we have seen, of motet and conductus style.) The Ivrea and Apt MSS preserve three-part settings of sections of the Ordinary, in which the highest part sings a dominating melody, untraceable to a plainsong source and apparently unborrowed, and in which the two lower parts serve as supports.[76] Friedrich Ludwig coined the term *"Ballade*-Mass" to designate such compositions. The Ordinary of the Mass was not destined to receive a setting individual in style until the 15th century. [77]

Nine hymns in the Apt MS have liturgical melodies, almost unaltered, in the highest voice; another has such a melody somewhat embellished in the contratenor. The nature of these settings has nothing to do with the *faux-bourdon* style, to be discussed in Chapter 14.

Among the composers represented in the MS are Tapissier and Baude Cordier [77a] who, as men known to have flourished about the turn of the century, help us date the MS. That Philippe de Vitri is represented in it also, testifies to the honor in which he continued to be held. He, Machaut, and Jean de Muris are all praised in a motet in the Ivrea MS (together with nine other musicians) and also in a motet in a much smaller MS, Paris Bib. Nat. Coll. de Picardie 67.

MS Chantilly 1047, dating from the turn of the 15th century, though itself of Italian provenance, is a copy of a French original of *c.* 1385. It adds to our knowledge of names of French 14th-century composers, a knowledge that is scanty, since the MSS on the whole give few names. Among the composers represented are Jean Cuvelier,[78] Jacques de Senleches, with a *ballade* in honor of Duke Jean de Berry, Pierre des Molins, the Italians A. and F. da Caserta,[78a] who composed to French texts, and two Parisians, Jean Vaillant and Pierre Tailhandier. Also represented in the MS is F. Andrieu, who set to music in four parts a double *ballade* written by the poet Eustache Deschamps on the death of Machaut, with the refrain: *La mort Machaut, le noble retorique.* This is the earliest known of the several late medieval and renaissance *Déplorations* lamenting in music the deaths of famous composers.[79] Andrieu's work, like many other compositions produced by the new generation, shows the vigorous survival of the influence of Machaut, "the

[76] For some examples, see GasMA, 19, 64, 74, 83, 119, 152, 159.
[77] Further concerning the *Ballade*-Mass, see LudB, 441f; BesS I, 202ff. [77a] *Cf.* BesM, 150.
[78] Example in BesM, 145. The mensural notation of Chantilly 1047 is most complicated; some of the problems it presents have not yet been solved (*cf.* MachM II, 23*). [78a] *Cf.* p. 362.
[79] The piece is printed in MachM I, 49–51. The above list of MSS makes no attempt at completeness. See BesS I; LudG.

greatest musical genius of 14th-century France." [80] Its *ballade* form—but as applied to a three-part composition with instrumental tenor and contratenor, rather than to a four-part piece as here—was not only a mainstay of French composers of the 14th century when writing secular and even sacred works, but was to retain its supremacy into the time of Dufay and later, the three-part *ballade* style affecting the *rondeau* and *virelai* also, the tenor and contratenor, which in the motet served as foundation, continuing in this style to be merely supports freely added. Not only the *ballade*, but also the motet was destined to survive, so that, paradoxically, 13th-century musical tradition was transmitted to the 15th century by the very men, belonging to the intervening century, whose period is somewhat loosely characterized as that of the *ars nova*, a fact that emphasizes to what an extent the time was really one in which innovations were engrafted upon a basically old stock—one ending the Gothic period in music—rather than a time of broadly and essentially original creativeness.

[80] LudG, 267.

Chapter 13: THE 14TH CENTURY: Italian, Spanish and German Music—*Musica Falsa*—Instruments

Italian Music

ALTHOUGH the Provençal troubadours travelled and sang in Italy in the 13th century, they seem not to have aroused in their hosts an immediate desire to emulate them in musical composition, all we have by way of wholly non-liturgical Italian *dugento* monody being the *laude*. And this is true even though the same century, as we have seen in Chapter 6, found Italy making such an important contribution to the repertoire of the sequence as the *Dies irae*. Few examples survive to show what she may have accomplished in the field of organum (*cf.* pp. 263f). The widespread supposition that Dante's friend, Pietro Casella, set to music a poem by Lemmo da Pistoia has no tangible foundation.[1] But in the 14th century musical Italy covered herself with glory. A group of MSS has come down to us containing a large and attractive collection, mostly of two- and three-part compositions, which, if they show French influence clearly, and possibly Provençal influence also, are sufficiently different from contemporary music in France to justify the statement that, while France was concluding the Gothic period in music, Italy, though not unbound to it herself, was looking forward to the Renaissance.

One of these MSS, British Museum Add. 29987, includes 15 one-line instrumental dances. Of these, 8 are *istampite* (Italian for *estampies*) with titles (*Cominciamento di gioia, Isabella,* etc.), 1 is a *trotto,* and 6 are *saltarelli,* 4 being so designated while the other 2 are entitled *Lamento di Tristano* and *La Manfredina.*[2] In this last pair, "the three parts of the main dance are followed by three parts of an appurtenant *rotta* . . . the Italian word *rotta,* from *rompere* = Latin *frangere,* 'to break,' is simply the *refractorium,* the refrain. . . ." The melodic motives of the three main-dance sections recur in the sections of the *rotta* and in the same order. But, whereas in the former the tunes are in triple time, in the latter they are in duple time;[3] sometimes, in the *rotta,* the motive is expanded, sometimes contracted. It is almost as

[1] See LudQ, 298; EllinO, 30.

[2] All transcribed (in whole or in part) in WolfT, 24ff.; 3 printed in ScherG, 20f. Concerning the *trotto* and *saltarello* as dances, see SachsW, 293-7.

[3] That is, they are basically so despite the notation, since in the first section there is a rhythm of 3 *battute* and in the second section a rhythm of 2. See SachsW, 293f, from which the quotation comes.

though we had three themes with variations. It has been suggested that the *rotta* sections were probably not played straight through after those of the *saltarello* proper, but alternated with them.

EXAMPLE 111. *Lamento di Tristano—Tertia pars* of the dance proper and the corresponding *rotta* (after WolfT, 41).

The *puncta* of most of the 15 dances make use of melodic rhyme (*cf.* pp. 107f, 226).

The great musical contribution of 14th-century Italy, a body of fresh, luminous polyphony, seems to derive chiefly from sources not specifically Italian. In it the melismatic style, favored in the past in the south of France and Provence, as is shown by the St. Martial organa and the melodies of the troubadours, finds wide application. This style, to be sure, might just as easily have come from plainsong. The melismas are especially prominent in the earlier stages when they are usually assigned to the upper of the two parts to which writing was then restricted, this part flowing along over a somewhat slower-moving tenor. The Italian music tends generally to be more florid than the contemporary French. Traces of the hocket technique are present also. But it is the conductus that chiefly affected Italian *trecento* music. Here, too, a newly composed tenor is preferred—creation, not borrowing, is the watchword of the day—and, almost without exception, one text is common to all the parts. But the main melody, which in the conductus was usually in the lower voice, in *trecento* music is as a matter of course on top. The melismas found in conducti before and after the main body of the phrase (*cf.* p. 307) have their Italian counterpart also. On the other hand, Italian taste seems not to have taken kindly to the French motet, with its combined texts and borrowed tenor.[4] In fact, *trecento* music shakes off the shackles of a *cantus firmus.*

---

[4] Brit. Mus. Add. 29987, however, contains a motet on the Latin tenor, *Sanctus Dominus Deus Sabbaoth,* with the 2 upper parts singing in Italian (*Cantano gli angioletti*). Concerning the origins of the *trecento* music, see LudG, 276f; BesM, 157; and, for a more extended consideration, EllinO.

The period of Italian *"trecento"* music does not actually coincide with the span of the 14th century: it begins about 1325 and ends about 1425. Leonard Ellinwood has, on the basis of the chronological order apparently followed in arranging the contents of the Squarcialupi Codex—one of the chief MSS of the period (*cf.* p. 372)—and on the basis of the type of notation devices employed by each composer, assigned a large number of the *trecento* composers to three different generations, thus:

The first generation: Giovanni da Cascia (= Giovanni da Firenze), Jacopo da Bologna, Bartolomeo da Padova (= Padua), Grazioso da Padova, Vincenzo d'Arimini (= Rimini), Piero.

The second generation: Francesco Landini (= Landino, 1325-97), Paolo tenorista da Firenze, Niccolo da Perugia, Ghirardello da Firenze, Donato da Firenze, Lorenzo da Firenze, Andrea da Firenze, Egidio, Guglielmo di Santo Spirito.

The third generation: Zacherie, a papal singer from 1420 to 1432, Matteo da Perugia, Giovanni da Genova (= Genoa), the Belgian Johannes Ciconia, Antonello and Filippo da Caserta, Corrado da Pistoia, Bartolomeo da Bologna.

The secular pieces of these men are written chiefly in three forms: the *madrigal, ballata,* and *caccia.*

The origin of the term *madrigale* has been traced with the help of a passage in an early 14th-century work by Francesco da Barbarino. He uses *matricale* (Latin for "belonging to the womb" or "matrix") in referring to a form of song. It is therefore held that *madrigale* originally denoted a poem in the mother tongue. Antonio da Tempo, writing in 1332, used independently the word *mandrialis* to designate a rustic kind of pastoral poem, popular at the time, this term being a fusion of the older term *madriale* (a dialectical use of *madrigale*) and *mandria* (Italian for "sheep-fold").[5] The form of the term as used in the MSS of *trecento* music undergoes considerable variation.

Although there were deviations from the norm, a typical 14th-century madrigal might be said to consist of one to four stanzas of three 7- or 11-syllable lines, each stanza being sung to the same music, and of a *ritornello* of two lines set in a contrasting rhythm and occurring at the end (the *ritornello,* then, not being a refrain).[6] The madrigal—in which the influence of both troubadour art and the *conductus* may be seen illustrated—is one of the two forms appearing in the earliest period of *trecento* music, when it flour-

---

[5] See E. H. Fellowes in WolfI, 28f, and in his "English Madrigal Composers," 42–8, and the publications by Leandro Biadene and O. Antognoni cited by him. See also WolfV, 55f.

[6] *Cf.* LudG, 278; SchneiderA, 50; etc. In EllinL, 11, 13, and 19, it is pointed out, in connection with 3 madrigals of Landini, that the MS Panciatichi 26 at the National Library in Florence gives first the music and text of stanza 1, then the text of stanza 2 (in none of the 3 instances are more than 2 stanzas given), then an indication that the *ritornello* is to follow, and then the music and text of the *ritornello*. This MS, therefore, does not, as is claimed elsewhere, indicate by means of these pieces that the *ritornello* is to be performed at the end of every stanza.

ishes as a two-part composition. Melodic embellishment, i.e. "coloration," is plentiful in the upper part, which tends to have more notes than the lower part. It will readily be seen that the *trecento* madrigal and the familiar 16th-century madrigal, two centuries apart in time, are widely separated from each other in character also. The text of the following example of the older type is a quaint allegory of the Conquest of Winter by Summer.[7]

EXAMPLE 112. *Di novo è giunt' un cavalier errante*—Jacopo da Bologna
(MS Florence Bib. Med. Laur. Pal. 87, ff. 11ᵛ–12ʳ).

"Once more has come a wandering knight on coursing steed rough-shod for ice, with crossbow-men who every open place assail. Some in the chest he's wounded,

7 It must have been rather popular, since it survives not only in the MS followed above but

others in the face. Whoso with strong armor is not provided should stay shut up within the gates. *Rit.* Until there come the maid of ardent summer heat, and by her wounded he needs must die." (Transl. M.V.—The Italian text is given as edited by Carducci, *Opere,* VIII, 380.) For a verse translation, see John Addington Symonds, *Sketches and Studies in Italy,* Chap. VII.

Influences from the past did not prevent the madrigal from giving voice to a new spirit. Whereas in 13th-century polyphony the individuality of the parts was paramount, in the 14th-century madrigal there is evident a greater desire for relationship between them. While this desire is also evident in the few surviving French *chaces* (closeness of relationship between parts can hardly exceed identity) and in the occasional use of triads, it is stronger in Italian music than in the French—which, on the whole and in the motet especially, adheres to the old preference for melodic strata—as is most convincingly shown by the much more frequent and more effective use of imitation and canon by the Italians.[8] Here is a snatch of imitation at the fourth from a madrigal by the provost Ser Niccolo da Perugia:

EXAMPLE 113. Extract from *Non dispregiar virtu*—Niccolo da Perugia (WolfG III, 129).

Such examples might be multiplied at length. Maestro Piero's two-part madrigal, *Cavalcando con un giovine,*[9] does not stop short at imitation: the first section (but not the *ritornello*) is actually written in canon. In the first section of Landini's three-part madrigal, *De dimmi tu,*[10] the two lower voices are actually in canon (an unusual disposition, the two upper voices being normally chosen where two voices in a three-part composition are in canon) while in the second section all three parts are in canon.[11]

Canon is the characteristic feature of the other form favored in the earliest

also in Brit. Mus. Add. 29987, in Paris Bib. Nat. f. it. 568 and f. fr. nouv. acq. 6771, and in Panciatichi 26. The music of all 5 MSS is in substantial agreement, more deviations from Bib Med. Laur. Pal. 87 occurring in Panciatichi 26 than in the other MSS.

[8] Besseler (BesM, 158) finds additional evidence for an inclination to link the parts in the supporting character of the tenor in some *trecento* music (*cf.* our Ex. 114), this part, according to him, now performing the rôle of bass for the first time. However, the freely composed tenor in the 14th-century French *ballade* sometimes supported the composition as effectively as does the tenor in *trecento* music, though it may be that in French music the tenor performed the bass function more sporadically.   [9] WolfF, 639; OH I, 265.   [10] EllinF, 210; EllinL, 22.

[11] For some transcriptions of additional examples of the madrigal, see 2 by Bartolino da Padova (WolfG III, 106, 109), 2 by Donato da Firenze (WolfF, 636, WolfG III, 114), 4 by Giovanni da Cascia (ScherG, 14; WolfF, 633; WolfG III, 92, or WolfH I, 297; WolfG III, 94), 3 by Jacopo da Bologna (BesM, 156; WolfG III, 97, 99—there are two versions of the latter), all of Landini's in EllinL, 4 being also elsewhere (LudG, 287; WolfF, 641, or OH I, 261; EllinF, 206, 207), 1 by Lorenzo da Firenze (WolfG III, 119), 2 by Niccolo da Perugia (WolfG III, 129, 131), 2 by Paolo da Firenze (WolfF, 644; WolfG III, 145), 1 by Vincenzo d'Arimini (WolfG III, 122), and 2 anonymous ones (WolfV, 67, 68). The original notation of all transcriptions in WolfG III, cited in this and other notes, may be found in WolfG II.

*Group of Singers with Musical MS
in Roll Format (Rotulus)*

(*From the Machaut MS, Paris, Bib. Nat.
fr. 9221. After E. Droz and G. Thibault,
Poètes et musiciens*)

*Miniature of Jacopo da Bo-
logna from the Squarcialupi
Codex*

(*Florence, Bibl. Medicea-Laurenziana, Pal. 87*)

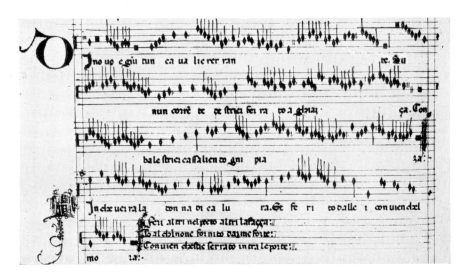

Jacopo da Bologna's Di novo è giunt' un cavalier errante *as it appears in the
Squarcialupi Codex*

(Cf. *Example 112*)

PLATE VIII

period of *trecento* music, the *caccia,* the Italian equivalent of the apparently older *chace.*[12] "What life in this *caccia!* Greatest motion everywhere in word and in music, one voice chasing the other. Here is a lively description of a chase with the calls of the beaters and the sound of the horns; there a vivid picture of a fire, and there an equally dramatic scene of the market-life with the cries of the sellers and the calls and questions of the buyers."[13] *Passando con pensier per un boschetto* by Niccolo da Perugia [14] includes a description of a sudden shower. Landini's *Cosi pensoso com' amor mi guida* [15] depicts a fishing scene and might therefore be called a *pesca.* The normal Italian *caccia* is in three parts, the upper two of which are in canon while the tenor is free, supporting the canon and adding to the euphony of the composition. The normal French *chace,* on the other hand, consists only of the two parts in canon. Canon as such, however, is not always treated in these manners. The madrigal of Maestro Piero, mentioned above, lacks (though Italian) a free tenor to support the section using the device, while in the French three-part composition, *Amour par qui,*[16] a two-part canon is reinforced by a free top voice. The *caccia* with few exceptions consists, like the madrigal, of two sections. the second being a *ritornello.* While the first (and longer) section is always in canon, the second, most often canonic also, may sometimes be homophonic or monodic, or even absent. Musically, all *cacce*—which tend to run to considerable length—are actually one-strophe madrigals, though obviously not all madrigals are *cacce.* There is a distinction, also, in the character of the texts.[17]

EXAMPLE 114. *Ritornello* of the Caccia *Da poi che'l sole* (Niccolo da Perugia) (MS Florence Bib. Med. Laur. Pal. 87, f. 83^r).

12 But not necessarily an outgrowth. See FeinK, 10ff.   13 WolfI, 20.
14 Printed in WolfS, 16. For an English translation, see Dante Gabriel Rossetti's *The Early Italian Poets,* where it is called "On a Wet Day."   15 EllinF, 204; EllinL, 35.   16 WolfG III, 75.
17 For some transcriptions of additional examples of the *caccia,* see 1 by Piero (WolfG III, 135), 1 by Ghirardello da Firenze (WolfF, 626), and 1 by Zacherio (WolfF, 268). The *caccia* from which our Example 114 is taken survives not only in Bib. Med. Laur. Pal. 87, but also in Brit. Mus. Add. 29987. The 2 MSS are in substantial agreement.—Since this book first appeared, MarrF has been published, a special study of the *caccia* with 20 transcriptions.

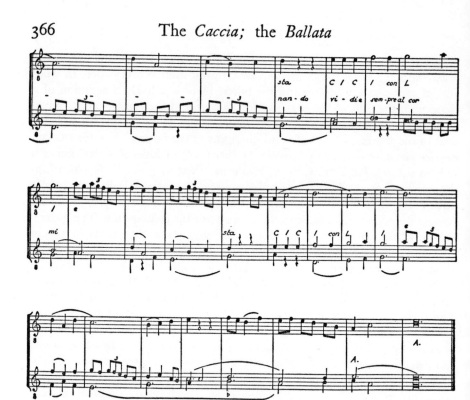

The first part of the *caccia* describes a fire at sunset. (This is the piece referred to above.) Here are some passages: "At the time when the sun hides its soft rays and the moon shows its splendor, I heard many people shouting, 'To the fire, to the fire! . . .' And then in a little while, 'Where is it? where is it?' 'Here.' . . . 'Oh, ring out, bellringer.' 'Don don, don don.' . . . 'Water, water. Hurry with the jugs.' . . . 'Oh, you with the horn, sound it.' 'Tatin, tatin.' . . . Some carried things back with them and some stole them. One poured water and another broke down the door with his axe. Every one makes haste to put out the fire and the sparks. The bells stopped ringing, when the leaders shouted . . . , 'Go home every one, for it is out!' " Ritornello: "On returning home I saw, and she is always in my heart, CICI with LI and A." (Transl. L.B.)

The *ballata* form—in which Landini is known to have written at least 141 works—is not the equivalent of the French *ballade,* but rather of the *chanson balladée*—that is, the *virelai.* The pattern is *AbbaA.* (This letter-series is not the same as that given for the *virelai* on p. 223, but the principle is the same, since, on that page, *A* and *B* [= *a* and *b*] are never separated from each other and, for purposes of repetition, are a single unit. The difference between Example 105, which fits the pattern of p. 223, and Example 115 is merely one of relative length of the musical units, the variation being caused by a difference in the number of lines, Example 105 having 16 per stanza [including both the introductory and concluding refrains] and Example 115 having 10. The numbers showing the order in which the musical sections are to be repeated in these two examples do not, of course, constitute a clue to the number of lines.) [18] Where there are enough stanzas, repetitions may, as in Example 115, continue along the same plan. The second section often has *aperto* (= *ouvert*) and *chiuso* (= *clos*) endings, which occur sometimes also at the end of the first section. Whether or not the artistic *trecento ballate* were danced to, the *ballata* was doubtless once used for dancing, as its name and apparent derivation from the *virelai* would indicate. It differs markedly from the madrigal in that the long first section and short *ritornello* of the madrigal are replaced by two sections of more nearly equal length and in the fact that the metric change from one section to another, common in the madrigal, does not occur in the *ballata*. Another distinguishing feature is that it is not unusual for a *ballata* to lack text in one or two of its parts, these doubtless being intended for instruments, so that it tends, like the French *ballade,* to be a song with instrumental accompaniment. Such a piece is the remarkably beautiful three-part *ballata* of Landini, *Gram piant' agli occhi.* On the other hand, each of the three parts of his *Perche* has a different text written under it.[19] It is not impossible, however, that the texts were intended to be sung successively rather than simultaneously, the music being repeated the requisite number of times—that is, the above pattern being extended by *bbaAbbaA.* The following *ballata* survives also in a two-part arrangement, no doubt for organ, in Paris Bib. Nat. fr. nouv. acq. 6771 [20] and arranged as a Kyrie in Munich MS 3232a.[21] In the organ version the original upper part is much embellished, coloration being as characteristic of keyboard arrangements of vocal music in the 14th century as it was to remain when Liszt transcribed Schubert *Lieder.* This *ballata* presents several examples of the so-called "Landini sixth" which, however, as stated on p. 350, does not deserve its name. Musical rhyme, such as in Chapter 12 we found frequent in the *virelais* and *ballades* of Machaut, is strikingly illustrated in the example by the seven-measure unit occurring at the close of each of the two sections.[22]

[18] There is some confusion concerning the *ballata* form in modern writings. But the above description, doubtless correct, agrees with EinSH, 419; EllinF, 196ff, etc.

[19] *Gram piant'* is printed in LudB, 459; EllinL, 222. In LudG, 279, Ludwig calls this "perhaps the most beautiful work of the century." *Perche* may be found in EllinL, 265.

[20] For a portion of the arrangement, in original notation and transcription, see WolfH II, 254; for a complete transcription, see Félix Raugel, *Quarante-six pièces pour orgue . . . d'anciens auteurs,* 5.

[21] *Cf.* LudG, 281.

[22] For some transcriptions of additional examples of the *ballata,* see 1 very expressive piece by Giovanni da Cascia (EinSH, 265, printed as anonymous), 1 by Arrigo (WolfG III, 138, 139—transcriptions after 2 MSS), all of Landini's in EllinL, 8 being also elsewhere (EllinF, 214, 215, 216; ScherG, 16 [but see EllinF, 197f]; WolfG III, 124, 125, 128; WolfS, 14), and 1 anonymous piece (WolfV, 68).

EXAMPLE 115. *Questa fanciulla*—Landini (after EllinL, 285).

"*This maiden, love, make her compassionate, because she hath wounded my
heart in thy manner*. Thou hast, oh maiden, so stricken me with love that I can
find rest only when thinking of thee. My heart from me thou hast removed,
with thy beautiful eyes and joyous face. Yet on thy servant, alas, have pity—
mercy I ask for my great distress. *This maiden etc.* If thou dost not help me
in my grievous pains, my heart will fail me, which thou hast taken, because my
life never feeleth at ease unless it gazeth at thy charming face. Since, maiden, thou
hast enwrapt me with love, I beg thee to be somewhat kind to me. *This maiden etc.*"

Whether owing to Pope John XXII's bull or not, Italian polyphony of this
period does not yield evidence of as great interest in sacred as in secular music.
Still, there are examples of it by members of all three generations. Just as, in
Chapter 12, we found French composers writing Mass settings in *ballade*
style, so, among the Italians, we find settings in the style of the madrigal
and *caccia*.[23]

[23] *Cf.* LudB, 442. For a collection of Ordinary and Benedicamus settings of the period, see
VanM I. Some later fascicles of VanM will contain additional liturgical music of the *trecento*, while
still others will be devoted to its secular music.

Occasionally a text though secular is not in Italian. Among several examples with French text is a madrigal by Bartolino da Padova, who is the composer also of a madrigal with a text mixing Italian, French, and Latin. The subjects treated in the *trecento* compositions cover a wide range. Some observations have already been made on this point in connection with the *caccia*. There is a madrigal of rejoicing by Paolo da Firenze on the subjection of Pisa by the Florentines.[24] Giovanni da Cascia has left us a madrigal beginning: "O my beloved science, my music." The *Un bel sparver* of Jacopo da Bologna (*cf.* p. 342) foretells, by means of a parable, the success the singer expects his love for his lady to achieve: One day he saw a beautiful white-feathered sparrowhawk flying high above a green meadow. Amor, "who never hides himself, if one serves him," told the singer to follow the bird, which would become gentle and tame. All day the singer sought to decoy the bird, until midnight, when he rested betwixt two grottoes.

*All' alba 'l giorno apparve ed io
  tornava:
E quell' in pugno allora mi vo-
  lava.*

*At daybreak I returned, the first ray
  sighting:
The bird flew down, upon my fist
  alighting.*

There is a great rhythmic richness in this *trecento* music, especially in the upper part. Triplets are mingled with two-beat groups, syncopation is not infrequent.

EXAMPLE 116. Extract from *O dolc' appresso*—Jacopo da Bologna (from WolfI, 20).

A   cui   di   fe - - - del cor   tut - to   mi   die - di

"To whom with a faithful heart I wholly gave myself . . ."

Occasionally there are changes in meter even at points other than that dividing the strophe and the *ritornello* in the madrigal. There are examples of melodic sequence: [25]

EXAMPLE 117. Extract from *Si, monacordo gentile stromento*—Donato da Firenze (from WolfI, 22).

[24] The beginning is printed in BesM, 164.   [25] See also WolfV, 62.

The melodic lines give evidence of a feeling for tonality, the music preceding the cadence in a phrase leading up relevantly to the concluding tone. A piece is even likely to have a higher-rank cadence that recurs more often than the others and draws them into a relationship with it. Ellinwood, in analyzing the 49 three-part *ballate* of Landini for their tonality characteristics,[26] has found the predominant finals to be D and C, and the other two finals used—G and F—to appear most frequently in compositions with a one-flat signature (that is, to be mere transpositions of D and C). An interesting feature is that, in the D (= G) tonality, the second section of the *ballate* bears a supertonic relationship to the first, while, in the C (= F) tonality, the relationship of the second section to the first is mediant as often as supertonic.

The prominence of tonality in the Italian music is quite independent of the triad technique found in some 14th-century French music (*cf.* pp. 333f). It appears, in fact, in two-part compositions even where the unison, fifth, and octave are the predominant harmonic intervals, as they generally are, especially before the middle of the century. With that turning-point there arrived, probably under French influence, an increase in three-part writing and with it a greater opportunity, which was not neglected, for triads.[27] At the same time, there was a tendency, evident especially in the *ballate,* towards greater moderation in the use of melismas. Here, too, French influence may have been at work.

Resemblances to the kind of conductus with melismas before and after the main body of the phrase (*cf.* p. 361) occur most frequently in the madrigals. But melismas appear also in other parts of the phrase and in other forms. There are some of such length that certain writers have felt that they were not sung but were instrumentally performed, even where the parts containing them have texts. Riemann felt that, where melismas opened and closed phrases, only the intervening relatively syllabic section was sung and the melismas were played on instruments.[28] Schering has proposed that the versions that have reached us are embellished organ arrangements of originally unornamented vocal melodies.[29] Both views have been vigorously attacked by Ellinwood.[30] There would seem to be no justification for the Schering view. Since, however, just as with French pieces (*cf.* p. 352), the practice doubtless prevailed of performing works with such resources as might be at hand, it is not impossible that, if an instrument doubled with a voice and the singer chanced not to be sufficiently expert, some of the melismas extraneous to the body of the phrases were performed by the instrument alone. (Adjustments to suit the occasion are attested by pieces sometimes appearing

[26] In EllinL, xxxviff.   [27] See further, BesM, 159.
[28] *Cf.* RieK and RieH I[2], on pp. 315ff of which the theory is applied to Jacopo da Bologna's *Un bel sparver.*
[29] ScherK; ScherS, 54ff. See also HaasA, 98ff.   [30] For the details, see EllinF, 201ff.

in one MS with words lacking where they are present in another, by a piece
that is inscribed in one tonality in one MS reappearing transposed in another,
etc.) But there is nothing in the mere presence of extended melismas—especially in Italian music—to rule out the likelihood that it was primarily vocal
execution that *trecento* composers had in mind. The lengthy florid sections
in Gregorian Chant, especially in the Alleluias, could have furnished the
composers with precedents, were any needed.[31] Moreover, their works were
art-compositions apparently intended not for popular entertainment but for
the elegant social circles of the day, where expert performers would probably
not be wanting. Especially convincing is the fact that, in Brit. Mus. Add.
29987, pains are frequently taken to show the sustaining of a vowel through
a melisma, by repeating the vowel or its succeeding consonant every few notes
until the next syllable is reached, as in *ra-a-a-a-a-ma, per-r-r-r-de*, etc. Only in
connection with an opening melisma are there grounds for feeling that a purely
instrumental execution may be intended as primary. Here it sometimes happens that the first syllable of text appears at the very beginning, possibly for no
better reason than to give the scribe an opportunity to draw a decorative initial,
and is then repeated after the introductory passage is over. (*Cf.* p. 324.) [32]

The full list of *trecento* composers was apparently a long one. The text of
Jacopo da Bologna's madrigal, *Uselletto selvaggio,* says that everybody is
writing *ballate,* madrigals, and motets, that all are blossoming forth as "Fili-
potti et Marchetti" (the ironic metaphor referring to Philippe de Vitri and
Marchettus of Padua). The poet Franco Sacchetti writes in a similar vein: [33]

Pieno è il mondo di chi vuol far rime ...	*The world is full of those who would be*
Così del canto avvien: senz alcun arte	*rhyming . . .*
Mille Marchetti veggio in ogni parte.	*And thus in song: on every hand beset us*
	A thousand unskilled doubles of Mar-
	chettus.

But there were clearly plenty who were not *"senz alcun arte."* Florence
was the great center of this activity. But, as the names of the musicians show,
contributions were made also by Bologna, Padua, Perugia, Rimini.

Little is known about the lives of most of these men. Giovanni da Cascia
was, in the first half of the century, organist at Santa Maria del Fiore and
closed his career at the court of Mastino II della Scala at Verona. It is his
creative force and that of composers of his generation—Jacopo da Bologna,
Piero, Lorenzo—that gave *trecento* music its native impetus. Jacopo was a

---

[31] Concerning the possible influence of the Chant on *trecento* music, see WolfV, 60.

[32] *Cf.* OH II, 320; WolfI, 25f (neither of which, however, subscribes to the Riemann theory
otherwise). See also WolfV, 63f. For a penetrating discussion of the instrumental renditions for
which some medieval music may have served, especially that of the *trecento* (though, according
to that discussion too, it was conceived primarily as vocal, with the exception of the dances mentioned at the beginning of this Chapter), see HandR, 31ff.

[33] See Giosuè Carducci, *Cantilene,* 264.

theorist as well as composer.[34] Sometime before 1351 he became the teacher of Francesco Landini. This is the man concerning whom we know most.[35] He was born at Fiesole in 1325 and went blind in childhood, apparently from smallpox. He became skilled as a player on several instruments, particularly the *organetto,* and himself invented a stringed instrument called the *serena serenorum.* There survives an interchange of letters in verse between Francesco and Franco Sacchetti. In 1364 at Venice Landini, although defeated at the organ by the organist of St. Mark's, Francesco da Pesaro, was awarded the laurel crown for his poetry by Peter the Great, king of Cyprus; Petrarch was a member of the jury. Landini's extant works, numbering over 150, constitute more than one-third of surviving *trecento* music—evidence of the popularity he enjoyed. He is mentioned in the *Romanza* written in 1389 by Giovanni da Prato: *Il Paradiso degli Alberti.*

> *In many ways this surpasses the* Decameron *of Boccaccio in giving us a clear picture of Florentine life, especially since da Prato uses real rather than fictitious characters. The narrative relates the daily activities among a group living at the* Paradiso—or lovely villa—of *the Alberti family. . . . Interspersed among the philosophic discussions, to which Francesco makes his own contributions, are stories, or* novelli, *told by various persons, including Francesco. . . . In one of the interludes of the third book, . . . Francesco plays his love verses so sweetly "that no one had ever heard such beautiful harmonies, and their hearts almost burst from their bosoms." On another occasion, when "a thousand birds were singing," Francesco was asked to play on his organ to see if their carolling would lessen or increase. At first, it is reported, the singing became hushed as the birds listened to the musician, but then grew louder than ever, while a single nightingale flew down and perched on a limb above Francesco's head.* (EllinF, 192.)

The composer died September 2, 1397, and was buried at San Lorenzo in Florence. The tombstone[36] shows him blind, holding his portative organ in his arm.

Landini is depicted also in the largest and most sumptuous of the MSS preserving *trecento* music. This belonged in the 15th century to the celebrated Florentine organist Antonio Squarcialupi (1417–80) and is therefore known as the Squarcialupi Codex. Here Landini and twelve other composers are portrayed in miniatures[37] at the beginnings of the sections devoted to their works. Since Zacherio, of the last generation, is among those represented and the MS must therefore be fairly late, the faithfulness of at least some of the portraits may be open to question. Landini is shown seated with his *organetto,*

---

[34] His treatise is printed (in Italian with German translation) in WolfJ.

[35] A few facts about composers may be found in WolfI, 27. Biographical information on Giovanni da Cascia is assembled in MoriniC. For much fuller accounts of Landini than the one here given, see EllinL; EllinF; MachM II, 26*.

[36] Photograph in KinsP, 49; EllinL, opposite p. xvi.

[37] All reproduced in GanI, tables vii–xix. The Landini portrait has been reproduced several times (LudG, 286; EllinF, opposite p. 196; BesM, opposite p. 168—in color).

and the decorative border contains pictures of still other instruments—a psaltery, three kinds of lute, and another small portative organ, played on by St. Cecilia.

The composition thus embellished is the madrigal *Musica son* which, like Landini's *ballata, Perche,* has the appearance of being tri-textual.[38] Music herself is singing. She laments

Veder gli effetti mie' dolci et perfecty	To see, for street-songs, fickle wits forsaking
Lasciar per frottol' i vagh' intellety.	The sweet and perfect sounds that I am making.

The high noon of the *trecento* art was soon to pass. But the *quattrocento* was by no means the sterile period in Italian music history that it was once thought to be. Zacherio was among those to pass the torch on to the new century. And the *frottole,* deplored by Madonna Musica, were destined, at the touch of Venetian genius, to yield some works of exquisite simplicity and charm.

Spanish Music

THE Las Huelgas MS, as already noted, testifies to native Spanish activity. But it also shows the continued forcefulness of French influence, perhaps not only by its inclusion of many Notre Dame pieces, but in a way that is associated with the 14th century, during the earlier part of which the MS was inscribed: four conducti contain passages that Anglès regards as capable of being interpreted in binary rhythm (though the notation does not unequivocally support such an interpretation), passages of the kind, to be sure, being in themselves nothing essentially new (*cf.* p. 309; also p. 398); but in one of the pieces the scribe has entered *"manera francesa"* in the MS where what may be binary rhythm begins and *"hespanona"* where a return may be intended to ternary rhythm, favored, it would seem, by the presumably more conservative Spaniards. According to Anglès, it looks as though the scribe, by *"manera francesa,"* was recognizing the existence in France of the impulse that was about to produce the *Ars nova* movement.

Music appears to have flourished with particular vigor in 14th-century Catalonia. The names have been found of approximately six hundred *joglars,* minstrels, and singers who, from *c.* 1290 through the 14th century, served at the court of Catalonia-Aragon.[39]

The musical contents of the *Llibre Vermell* ("The Red Book"), a 14th-century MS at Montserrat, the famous mountain monastery near Barcelona, have been held to show little definite trace of contemporary French influence. They reveal, in fact, some distinctiveness, but have been looked upon

---

[38] See, however, EllinF, 203. For the music, see LudG, 287; EllinL, 26. For an English translation of the text, see EllinF, 194.

[39] See AngD, 56.

as giving indications, through the presence of the *caça* (= *caccia*) and certain other technical features, of Italian influence. In view of the fact that political events had brought Italian literature into prominence in Catalonia, it would not be surprising if Italian influence was actually felt there in the field of music also. But it is by no means impossible that the *chace* rather than the *caccia* originally inspired the Catalonian counterpart. The *Llibre* includes the *Cants dels Romeus* ("Pilgrim Songs"),[40] pieces that were sung and danced by pilgrims going to the shrine on the eves of great festivals and performed the next day with greater magnificence, in order, it was maintained, "to refresh the weary pilgrims and stimulate them to religious fervor." These festive songs and dances were, no doubt, carried away by some of the pilgrims to other parts of Spain.

The pieces in the MS are short, most of them polyphonic. There are grounds for assuming that some of the melodies, around which the counterpoint is woven, are very old—that they are, in fact, folk-songs concealed under ecclesiastical trappings. Of the *caça,* there are three examples, differing, however, from the Italian type in having no free instrumental tenor (possible evidence of French influence?) and in being designated as performable as either two- or three-part canons. *Polorum regina,* another Pilgrim song, is a fine tune that two hundred years later was still popular in the neighborhood of Salamanca and was sung to the *villancico, Yo me iba, mi madre.* Salinas (*cf.* p. 375) included this song in his collection of folk-songs, stating that the melody, or one very like it, was still sung in some cathedrals. Other interesting survivals in the *Llibre Vermell* include *Inperayntz,* for two voices, each with its own text (in Catalan) after the manner of a motet, the two texts having rhyming phrase-ends. This piece survives also in a fragment at Tarragona, containing music by de Vitri (see AngL, 67). *Los set Gotxs* ("The Seven Joys of Mary"), a monodic piece, has its refrain included within an introduction, this having the form *aaB* and each stanza proper with its refrain having the form *aabbB* (the two *b*'s having the same text).

In some respects the most interesting composition in the *Llibre* is another monodic piece, the oldest known surviving example with music of a "Dance of Death," that curious and mysterious outgrowth of the period of the Black Death which ravaged Europe from 1347-48. All the arts contributed to the acknowledgment of the all-conquering power of Death, and this peculiar form of dance was apparently music's contribution to the common recognition. Wrapped in mystery as it is, this much at least seems clear, that the Dance of Death came direct from Spain—Spain the typical land of dance and song, where the dance has more significance than mere social enjoyment and where, as we have seen, the Council of Toledo had found it necessary, back

---

[40] For studies of them, with examples (including those here discussed), see SuñC and UrS. The former contains 12 facsimiles. Some examples are also in TreM. Concerning 2 other Spanish 14th-century MSS containing polyphonic pieces, see AngF, 163.

in the year 589, to lift its voice against the custom of dancing during the divine service.

EXAMPLE 118. Dance of Death (after SuñC, 191).

1, 5. Ad mor-tem fe-sti-na-mus pec-ca-re de-si-sta · · mus, pec·
4. Jam est ho-ra sur-ge-re a som-no mor-tis par · · vo.

2. Scri-be-re pro-po-su-i de con-temptu mun-da · · no:
3. Ut de-gentes se-cu-li non mul-cen-tur in va- · · ne:

"*We hurry towards death, let us desist from sin.* I have resolved to write concerning contempt of the earth, so that the living of the world may not be crushed in vain. Now is the hour to rise from the evil sleep of death."

Another source of Spanish 14th-century music is the wonderful collection of folk-songs, the oldest such collection known, *De Musica Libri Septem* ("The Seven Books of Music") by Salinas.[41] Two centuries later than the period we are considering, in 1513, Francisco de Salinas was born at Burgos. At the age of ten he lost his sight. He became known as an organist and teacher and acquired a great reputation for learning, eventually being nominated abbot of a monastery in the kingdom of Naples. It was a visit to Rome in 1538, where he was deeply impressed by the singing he heard in the streets of popular songs and ditties, that gave him the idea of collecting such tunes, an idea that flowered into his great book in 1557. Some of the tunes he collected were hundreds of years old, among them, as already pointed out, being the *Polorum regina* contained in the *Llibre Vermell* of Montserrat.

Another song in Salinas's collection is the tune, probably of Moorish origin and still in the 16th century sung to Arabic words (or at least to words sounding like Arabic), the much-discussed *Calvi vi calvi, calvi arabi,* which in Arabic would be *Qalbi bi qalbi, qalbi arabi* ("Heart, oh my heart, 'tis the heart of an Arab"). The song was well known in Spain with new Spanish words in the 14th century and is mentioned as *Calbi garabi* in the colorful work known as the *Libro de Buen Amor* by the not very saintly Archpriest of Hita (*cf.* p. 385).[42]

One of Spain's most ardent early patrons of music was King John I of Aragon (1350–96),[43] of whom it was written that he delighted "in inventing and setting to music *lais, virelais,* and *rondeaux."* Various letters from the king to his court-musicians and to his brother Martin mention works evidently of his own composition. King John's violent passion for books was

[41] See the interesting study of Salinas in TreC.
[42] Juan Ruiz, the Spanish counterpart of Chaucer. "The Book of True Love" (published, 1901, in an edition by Jean Ducamin and, 1913, in *Clásicos castellanos*) is, at bottom, an autobiography in verse.
[43] For an article on him as musician, see PedJ.

equalled only by his passion for music and musical instruments. Even though Catalonia could at that time supply numerous and good performers, John was not content but scoured Europe for others, bombarding kings and courts with requests for musicians, instruments, and exchanges of the same. He desired to possess every new instrument that was invented and sent his musicians all over Europe in quest of them and of people to play them.

German Music

IN German-speaking countries, monody continued to flourish in the 14th century as it had in the 13th. In fact, some of the figures mentioned in Chapter 8—e. g. Frauenlob and Witzlaw von Rügen—were active well into the 14th century, and, as pointed out in that chapter, the *Geisslerlieder* were linked with the plague of 1349.

The later representatives of the Minnesinger tradition belong to a period when the general decline of feudalism was penetrating even to Germany. Indeed, Frauenlob had already embodied the first beginnings of the burgher and didactic spirit which was to flourish increasingly with the rising prestige and importance of the towns.

The fact that Frauenlob's musical product was inferior to that of Adam de la Halle, who died when Frauenlob was twenty-eight years old, is one of the many striking indications of the lag that was to characterize the development of music in Germany for some time to come. A *Spruch* by Frauenlob, "in der grünen Weise"[44] shows stiffness and poverty of melodic grace in comparison with the work of the earlier Minnesinger. One must take into account, however, that, as pointed out in Chapter 8, the 15th-century Colmar MS, which preserves works of Frauenlob's (as does the related Donaueschingen MS), reveals conformity with the practice of the full-fledged Meistersinger, who may have "edited," and possibly distorted, Frauenlob's works in the versions there left to us.

The forms of the songs of the Minnesinger of the late 14th and early 15th centuries are strongly marked by experimentation, which shows that the period is, in Germany, one of transition. It has been neatly characterized by Moser[45] as the old-age of the Minnelied, the mature manhood of the Meistergesang, the youth of the Volkslied, and the childhood of polyphony.

Whereas previously the *Abgesang* had regularly been relatively long in comparison with the *Stollen,* the practice was now reversed, until at times the *Abgesang* was reduced to the slightest of appendages. There was likewise a tendency to restrict the number of stanzas, often to three, which was to become the rule in the 16th-century *Gesellschaftslieder.* Nevertheless, in

[44] ScherG, 14; DTO XX [2], 19, 67. [45] MosG I, 194.

spite of the incoming burgher style, the courtly tradition persisted, and its last musical representatives exhibited considerable gifts in their exposition of it.

In contrast to monody, German polyphony made little headway in the 14th century. A MS at Engelberg in Switzerland contains music illustrating 13th- rather than 14th-century style, as well as some in 11th-century style.[46] A canon has been found in a 14th-century MS now at Vienna (Nat. B. 4696). This is a three-part piece with German text, written in honor of St. Martin and bearing the superscription *Ain radel mit drein stymmen* ("A Round with Three Voices").[47] Some MSS at Erfurt contain further examples of early German polyphony, including several assignable to the 14th century.[48] In the latter part of the century some interesting attempts at polyphony were made by the later Minnesinger, among them the courtly Hermann der Münch (= Mönch) von Salzburg (fl. second half of the 14th century). Ascribed to him are about 50 one-line and 6 polyphonic selections, but the Münch's authorship of all of the former is not certain.[49] These works are best studied in the Mondseer Liederhandschrift.[50] The Münch's activities in profane music were particularly fostered by his attachment to the brilliant court of the art- and pleasure-loving Archbishop Pilgrim of Salzburg (d. 1396). Here his priestly character did not deter him from the expression of warmth and sensuous emotions in a mixture of the Minnesinger and folk-song styles. Thus one of his songs is a strophic love-letter,[51] *Dem allerlibsten schönsten weib im Freudensaal* ("To the Dearest and most Beautiful Woman in the *Freuden-saal* [which was the name of the Archbishop's pavilion]"). A more religious spirit is shown by his having, *c.* 1370, translated the psalm passages that serve as a grace at meals, into German verse as *Benedicite! Allmechtiger got,* destined to become famous. The Münch's polyphonic efforts are still stiff and primitive. In his *Nachthorn,* the lower part, which is for *"der pumhart"* (*cf.* p. 383), has almost nothing but the fundamental of the instrument and its fifth. But the *Tagelied* (*cf.* p. 233), of which the following is only the beginning, is more developed. The two lovers and the watcher all sing, but no more than two voices ever sing at once. There is a six-note introduction for trumpet: the first *"Hör"* is not sung. It is not unusual in 15th-century MSS, such as the Mondsee MS in which this piece is preserved, for the first syllable of a text to be repeated at the end of an instrumental prelude (*cf.* pp. 324, 371; also, concerning the rhythm, Chapter 11, footnote 56).

[46] For studies of this MS, see LudE and HandAP, which has an appendix of 26 musical examples.
[47] For a transcription, see MosG, I, 187.   [48] See HandEr.
[49] On this point and for a general musical discussion, see UrV II.
[50] Vienna MS 2856. Concerning the secular songs and for examples, see MayerM. For some consideration of the religious compositions, see RietschM. 10 pieces are printed in RunS.
[51] Printed in MosG I, 181.

EXAMPLE 119. Extract from the *Tagelied* of the Münch von Salzburg (after MayerM, Part II, 328).

Rubric: "That is called a trumpet and is also good for blowing"—Legends before staves: "The black is he, the red is she," [52] "That is the watcher to boot." Text: "He: Hark, dearest lady, to me thy slave. She: What means the long-held sound in the night? He: Nought else, lady, but what is good. Etc. Watchman: I will warn you, in truth, in the street, as I should, if I wish well the weal of both. Man holds care not in esteem . . ."

Count Hugo von Montfort (1357-1423) was a prominent figure in the political disturbances of his period. 13 of his works are preserved in the Heidelberg Cod. Pal. germ. 329.[53] In connection with the 10 songs in this MS that have melodies, one is confronted with a circumstance very unusual at the time: the music is definitely ascribed to a hand other than that responsible for the poetry. The musician named is Burk Mangolt, who was the Count's "minstrel." Although such joint authorship was possibly a frequent occurrence in actuality (*cf.* p. 213), the noble lord here specifically admits: "I did not make the tunes to the songs, I will not deceive you: another wrote them." Although the majority of these tunes is lacking in inspiration, one of the songs,[54] an argument between an ascetic knight and the sensuous Lady World (*Fro Welt ir sint gar hüpsch und schön*), is of considerable melodic charm. None of the Montfort-Mangolt pieces is polyphonic.

The most distinguished of this late group was Oswald von Wolkenstein (*c.* 1377-1445). It will be noted that the year of his birth was approximately that of Machaut's death, another indication—since with respect to the music of their own countries the two were counterparts, notwithstanding their inequality with respect to each other—of the slower progress of music in medieval Germany than in its western and southern neighbors. Two MSS, both of about 1425, contain a generous repertoire of monodic and polyphonic compositions by Wolkenstein.[55] His life was one of extraordinary adventures, which took him as far afield as Byzantium, Persia, Africa, Russia, and Spain. He was skilled in the intricacies of the mensural notation of his time, but his

---

[52] This refers to the notation. The lover's notes are in black, the lady's in red. The indications "Er" and "Sy" given in our example, therefore, are unnecessary in the original and do not appear there.
[53] They are printed in RunH.   [54] Printed in MosG I, 190.   [55] Printed in DTO IX.[1]

creative work is that of a gifted dilettante. The influence of folk-song is strong. His monodic pieces, from the standpoint of text, belong to the usual types— there are love songs, religious songs, bitter political *Scheltgedichte* (= *sirventes*). Three polyphonic pieces ascribed to him prove to be French works to which he merely set German texts. *Wolauff, gesell, wer jagen well* is *Fies de moy* (preserved in Prague Cod. XI E 9), the tenor of *Der may mit lieber zal* is marked *Per moutes fois* and the piece is derived from a *virelai* by Vaillant,[56] *Die Minne füget niemand* is really the French canon *Talent mes prus* (*cf.* Example 99). Wolkenstein, however, was probably the composer of the canon, *Gar wunnikleich*.[57] His various sojourns in Italy had a considerable effect on his development, and his style may be regarded as one of the first examples of the influence of Italian music on that of Germany. He was particularly fond of introducing instrumental *ritornelli*, especially in his polyphonic works. These range from simple songs with instrumental accompaniment to fairly developed three-part vocal compositions, which latter, however, because of technical shortcomings are usually less successful than the works in two parts.

The most celebrated of Wolkenstein's songs, a work on which a small literature exists,[58] is *Wach auff, myn hort*, printed below. It will be observed that the piece shows the continuance of the use of consecutive octaves (at the opening) and consecutive fifths (measures 12, 13, 21, and 22). In measures 3, 7, and 19, sevenths are expressively used as appoggiaturas.

EXAMPLE 120. *Wach auff, myn hort*—Oswald von Wolkenstein (after DTO, IX[1], 200).

"1. Awaken, my treasure, the bright day dawns in the East. Look through your eyelids, behold the glow, how, pure blue, the horizon of the sky blends with gray of just the right shade. I fear that soon the day will break. 2. I complain of death,

[56] *Fies de moy* is printed in KamF, 134ff. Gennrich has published the Vaillant piece and Wolkenstein's adaptation together in the *Zeitschrift für deutsche Bildung*, II, 550ff.
[57] Concerning 2 other canons of the period having German texts—the music of one being likewise borrowed from France—see FeinK, 16ff.
[58] MülleW; ScherS, 25; BaumD, 18f.

which I do not like. The birds are heard in the grove, with clear sound already singing. O nightingale, thy spying voice brings me distress, which I reward not; unceasingly must I sorrow. 3. I must away! The spear of your heart wounds me, since I may not tarry; the distress of parting saddens me. Your sweet red lips overpower me with longing. Bitter death would pain me less. Therefore must I despondent be."

It is from Wolkenstein's lifetime that the first monument of German organ music dates, but this was the beginning of a long development that lies beyond the scope of the present volume, as does any account of the growth of the movement of the Meistersinger.

In the first half of the 14th century, German influence had begun to be felt in Scandinavian music, which had previously been under the influence of French music, including that of the Parisian organa. But even so, in addition to the Latin songs that were still to be found in Sweden and Finland during the time of the Reformation, there remained in use, at that late period, pieces in the conductus and *Stimmtausch* style of the 13th century.

There is clear evidence that, in Holland, there was considerable activity in music during the 14th century at 's Hertogenbosch, but the music MSS mentioned in the records have disappeared.[59]

Musica Falsa

IF sharps and flats have been mentioned, as on p. 216, it has been stated also (*cf.* p. 335) that they were often not written where sharpening and flattening were actually wanted and that the rules of *musica falsa* then acted as guide. The writings of Johannes de Garlandia (both those ascribed to the 13th-century theorist and those assigned to a hypothetical 14th-century homonym) include mention of these rules: the *Introductio Musicae* defines *musica falsa* ("False music exists when we make a semitone of a tone, and *vice versa.*"); [60] the *De Musica Mensurabili* treats the subject but does not employ as a term either *musica falsa* or *musica ficta*. These terms—whether the adjective be "false" or "feigned" (in the archaic sense)—are synonymous.[61] The former is older than the latter but continued in use after the latter came into

[59] See Albert Smijers, *Music of the Illustre Lieve Vrouwe Broederschaps in 's Hertogenbosch*, Paper read Sept. 14, 1939, before the International Congress of the American Musicological Society, held in New York. Concerning music elsewhere in 14th-century Holland, see SillemA.

[60] CouS I, 166.

[61] Ficker's claim (in FiB) that the terms had different meanings, *ficta* involving transposition and *falsa* referring only to "accidental" sharps and flats, is to be found accepted in several later works. But it has been disposed of in LeviA, 182ff, which marshals numerous quotations from the theorists in GerS, CouS, etc. (as does also FiB). For translations of passages about *musica falsa*, see: OH I, 331f, for Fox Strangways's interpretation of an extract from the *De Musica Mensurabili*; SchlecD for German translations of extended passages from the *Tractatus de Contrapuncto* and *Libellus monochordi* of Prosdocimus (as well as a list of corrections of errors in CouS III).

being. The untransposed Guidonian hand produced *musica vera.* By the 15th century there was a further distinction: the *cantus* was *mollis* if there was one flat in the signature, *fictus* if transposed beyond that (it will be seen that the adjective thus eventually found application where sharps or flats were written down as well as where they were to be understood); music in its natural or untransposed position was *cantus durus.* Odington had recognized both B-flat and b-flat as indigenous to the scale, as well as the natural forms, but had designated all other chromatic tones as *extra manum* ("outside the hand"). It is apparently through drawing an analogy to the b♮–b♭ relation that the theorists formulated a doctrine accounting for the relationships, arising in practice, between the other diatonic and chromatic tones. For they sometimes write of arriving at a chromatic tone by means of the *synemmenon* (or, translating the Greek term into Latin, the *coniunctio*).

The early definitions of *musica falsa* show that it applied semitone alteration either *causa necessitatis* or *causa pulchritudinis* ("by reason of necessity" or "of beauty"). Marchettus, anticipating "chromatic," tried to substitute the term *colorati toni* for *falsi toni,* since some of the tones designated "false" were really "necessary."

Musica falsa was applied for both melodic and harmonic reasons. In the interval, F–B, to avoid a melodic tritone, B was flattened if, after it, the melody dropped; an extension of the principle led to the recognition of E-flat and A-flat. If, instead, the melody rose from F, the latter was sharpened. Flattening was applied also to a B between two A's. (*Una nota supra la semper est canendum fa.*) And, by a reversal of the principle, the idea of the *subsemitonium* took shape and alteration was applied at the lower end of the hexachord as well, so that an F between two G's was sharpened. Also, a G between two A's was sharpened, and a C between two D's.

There were several harmonic reasons for alteration. Ugolino d'Orvieto (fl. *c.* 1400),[62] who is only one of several theorists treating the subject, includes the following: (1) Fifths, octaves, and twelfths must be perfect. If they arise in the course of the counterpoint and would normally be diminished, they must be enlarged by a semitone and rendered perfect. (2) A third expanding stepwise to a fifth, or a sixth to an octave, should be major; a third contracting stepwise to a unison should be minor. If not naturally so, they should be rendered so by alteration. The enlarging of a minor sixth into a major interval before an octave has a clear relation to the development of the leading tone. Only in the Phrygian mode, with its naturally major sixth, F-d, would operation of the rule leave a subtonal rather than a subsemitonal leading tone in cadences using what we would today call dominant harmony. Perhaps a feeling for the leading tone helped to prompt the rule.

[62] Concerning him and for writings of his, see HabU, KornM, LafE, 116ff.

EXAMPLE 121.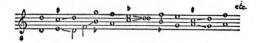

By the time of Prosdocimus, a complete chromatic scale is arrived at; but he states that D-sharp and A-sharp are rare.

Transposition was regarded as applying to hexachords (that is, it was not necessarily the composition that was actually transposed from a previously used pitch level; the scale elements out of which the piece was made could be looked upon by themselves as transposed), and as a result of the increasing recognition given it by theorists, the Englishman John Hothby (d. 1487) was able to erect hexachords even on F-sharp and D-flat. That transposition was bound to complicate solmisation is obvious. It was generally indicated by accidentals in the course of the music; in the signature, usually only if not more than one flat was required, though the 14th century knew the two-flat signature also.[63]

Ugolino bemoans the ignorance of the singers of his day. Formerly it was the performer's proud prerogative to apply the self-understood alterations. Now it was becoming necessary to notate them. The MSS of Landini's music contain many accidentals and require little application of the principle of *musica falsa* by the performer. This state of affairs, fortunate for the modern transcriber, did not, however, continue. The theorists warn against overuse of alteration, and it is by no means always clear whether a rule should be applied, so that *musica falsa* is a source of frequent embarrassment to modern transcribers.[64] That the composers were themselves no pedants is shown by their occasionally using accidentals where no rule would require them, simply to beautify the music, the theorists legitimizing the practice, as we have seen, by recognizing alteration *causa pulchritudinis*. In the 14th century, indeed, composers applied accidentals with a freedom so great that it was prejudicial to the purity of the church modes.

The *Ars Contrapuncti*, allegedly reporting theory according to Philippe de Vitri, mentions *"ficta musica quae instrumentis musicalibus multum est necessaria, specialiter in organis,"* and Johannes de Garlandia, the *Summa musicae* (*cf.* p. 346), and the *Speculum musicae* of Jacques de Liége are likewise among the sources referring to the close relation of *musica falsa* to *instrumenta*. It has been claimed that these passages indicate a closer relation of *musica falsa* to instrumental than to vocal music. But there is a strong possibility that *instrumenta* here includes, in the manner of Boethius, voices as well as instruments in the modern sense.[65]

---

[63] For an example, see WolfMS, no. 80, middle of 5th staff.

[64] Riemann much overused it. Hence the absence of his versions from the lists of printed madrigals, *ballate*, etc., given in the first portion of this chapter.   [65] This theory is developed in a

Instruments

The instruments whose functions included playing the wordless parts in 14th-century pieces were preponderantly such as might have counted among their duties the performing of tenors in motets, under what were apparently the usual conditions, in 13th-century compositions.

Machaut mentions instruments in several of his poems, long lists appearing in his *Prise d'Alexandrie* and *Remède de Fortune*. The latter names, among others, the psaltery, *canon, micanon,* lute, guitar, *citole,* rebec, monochord, *grant cornet d'Allemaigne* (the *zink*), *trompe petite, ele,* four kinds of bagpipes, cymbals, and *cromorne.*

The last of these, not mentioned in Chapter 11, is named also in the *Dit de la Panthère,* a 14th-century poem earlier than the *Remède.* This instrument (*krumphorn* in German) belonged to the reed-type. It had a wooden pipe, the lower part of which was bent, and six or seven holes. Another French name for it was *douçaine;* the Spanish name, *dulcaina.* Belonging to the same family was the *bombarde.* In 1376 Jean Lefevre de Ressons referred to *"grosses bombardes"* as *"nouvelles."* The instrument was adopted in Germany under the name of *bomhart,* which gave rise to several variants including the later *Pommer.*

Among the instruments mentioned in the *Prise d'Alexandrie* is the *"eschaquier d'Engleterre."* In 1360 Edward III of England had presented an *echiquier* to his captive, King John of France. The instrument was probably of English origin.[66] We have here an outgrowth of earlier experimentation towards applying keyboards to stringed instruments. The first attempts are accredited in some modern literature to the 13th century, possibly the 12th, but it would seem that no very definite evidence is to be found before the first half of the 14th, when Jean de Muris tells us [67] of a keyboard instrument of his which, even though he calls it a monochord, had nineteen strings. (The force of the prefix, mono-, seems to have been lost sight of well before the 11th century, for Theoger of Metz writes [68] of "monochords" with eight strings—apparently plucked—as having been in existence.) "It is commonly supposed that the name Echiquier . . . which also means a chessboard, refers either to the shape or to the decoration of the case. It is more likely . . . that it refers to the *jacks,* which, appearing in a row across the soundboard, suggested the idea of chessmen, which was enhanced by the action of 'checking' or repulsing the strings as they rose to pluck them . . . the

paper by Lloyd Hibberd to be published in MQ. The older view is set forth in HirschN, HaasA, 90f, and ScherS, 47f (which prints the 4 passages referred to above and draws upon them to support a rather far-fetched deduction on p. 49).
[66] An Arabic origin is suggested for the instrument, however, by H. G. Farmer in *The Journal of the Royal Asiatic Society of Great Britain and Ireland* for 1926, p. 239ff.
[67] GerS III, 283.   [68] GerS II, 183.

check of the Echiquier [became] the *jack* of the English Virginal." [69]
John I of Aragon especially favored the *exaquier* (=*echiquier*) and small
organs. Anyone who could play either or both was at once taken into his
service. Writing from Saragossa in 1388 to his brother-in-law, Philip the
Bold, Duke of Burgundy, John describes the *exaquier* as "like an organ
which sounds with strings," and he asks that not only should an instrument
be sent him but also a player who could perform both on it and on the small
organs. Other instruments beloved by King John were the *cornamusa,* the
xelamia (*chalemie,* shawm), and the *bombarde.* He also possessed a harp,
rote, and *orguens de coll,* a portative so small that it could be suspended from
the neck by a cord, being blown by the right hand and played by the left.

Machaut refers to the organ as "*de tous instruments le roi.*" To the improvements made in the 13th century, pedals were added *c.* 1300, their supposed inventor being Louis van Valbeke of Brabant (d. 1318). We learn that
King John of France, while in England, possessed an organ, that Charles V
of France had at least three, and that Philip the Bold had several also. In
the church the organ appears not to have accompanied the voices. Thus, a
passage [70] in *Il "Sollazzo"* ("The 'Bearer of Joy,' " the title being the sobriquet
of the musician whose skill the poem celebrates)—a work containing information concerning the use of many other instruments also—describes an occasion
when the organ, instead of accompanying the voices, alternated with them.
The great organ, the portative (as Landini's *organetto* shows), and the positive all remained in use in the 14th century. Artistic representations of portatives are more plentiful from England during the first part of the century,
from Italy during the latter part; French and Dutch examples are numerous,
German examples less so.

In the 14th century, possibly earlier, a long, narrow, one-stringed instrument,
about the height of a man, was played with a bow. Thus this instrument,
later called "marine trumpet" (German *Trumscheit*), was really a bowed
monochord.

A list of known 14th-century literary documents mentioning instruments
would run to considerable length. Boccaccio in the *Decameron,* in *Novella X*
of the first Day, has Dioneo playing a lute; in *Novella X* of the seventh Day,
he writes about dancing to a bagpipe; in *Novella VII* of the tenth Day he has
Minuccio performing an *istampita* on a viol ("*con una sua vivuola dolcemente
sonò alcuna stampita*").[71] Prodenzani relates that Il Sollazzo performed, on a
harp, works we still possess by Jacopo da Bologna, Giovanni da Cascia, and
others. Probably the extant versions were adapted for the purpose.[72] The same
poet tells us that Il Sollazzo played on the Flemish organs, among other

---

[69] GalpO, 121. See also GalpE, 103f. For another ingenious explanation, see GéroH, 408;
GéroM, 389.

[70] DebS, 171.   [71] For articles on Boccaccio and music, see GutD, BonaB.

[72] ScherS, 113f, notwithstanding.

pieces, *El molin de Paris,* which survives in the Ivrea MS, Prague MS XI
E. 9, etc.[73] A passage by the Archpriest of Hita [74] enumerates about thirty
different instruments—among them the *rabé gritador* ("shrill rebec"), *cin-
fonia,* rote, lute, harp, *guitarra morisca,* and *guitarra latina.* Froissart reports
the use of trumpets, clarions, and *"toutes manières d'instrumens"* upon a
special occasion at a church in Ghent in 1386, and mentions an organ *"mélo-
dieusement joué"* at a church at Orthez in 1388. The *Déploration* of Eustache
Deschamps on the death of Machaut refers to the transverse flute, rebec, lute,
viol, psaltery, and *symphonie.* And the anonymous *Échecs amoureux,* written
c. 1370–80 by a French dilettante, includes, among various items of musical
information, the names of many instruments.[75] One of the passages in it is
paraphrased in the following extract from the "Reson and Sensuallyte" of
John Lydgate (*c.* 1373–*c.* 1450).

> *For ther wer rotys of Almayne*
> *And eke of Arragon and spayne, . . .*
> *And Instrumentys that dyde excelle,*
> *Many moo than I kan telle:*
> *Harpys, fythels, and eke rotys,*
> *Wel accordyng with her notys,*
> *Lutys, Rubibis, and geterns,*
> *More for estatys than taverns,*
> *Organys, cytolys, monacordys.*
> *And ther wer founde noo discordys, . . .*
> *And for folkys that lyst daunce*
> *Ther wer trumpes and trumpetes,*
> *Lowde shallys and doucetes,*
> *Passyng of gret melodye,*
> *And floutys ful of armonye,*
> *Eke Instrumentys high and lowe*
> *Wel mo than I koude knowe,*
> *That I suppose, ther is no man*
> *That aryght reherse kan*
> *The melodye that they made:*
> *They wer so lusty and so glade.*

(Ernst Sieper, *Lydgates Reson and Sensuallyte,* I (1901), 146f.)

"Instrumentys high and lowe" refers not so much to pitch as to volume—
i. e. to loud and soft instruments.[75a] The loud instruments seem to have been
better suited to the spirit of the times than the soft ones. *Crescendi* and
diminuendi were still unobtainable on many instruments, so that, on the
whole, an unvarying volume was characteristic of instrumental music of the

---

[73] Printed in KamP, 145ff, after all the sources.   [74] Quoted in RiaC, 129.
[75] For an article on the musical esthetics of the poem, see AbE.   [75a] *Cf.* HertzS, 402.

period. The still simple organs, the recorders, sackbuts, cromornes, and varieties of oboe were incapable of much dynamic change.

Pictorial evidence furnishes some clues to the type of instrumental ensemble preferred. This shows a strong liking for contrast. Where two stringed instruments chance to form a group, one is almost certain to be bowed, the other plucked. If the group is larger, the additional instruments are likely to include aerophones, membranophones, or idiophones.[76]

It would seem that the new recognition of music as an independent art, as important to trained musicians in secular life as in the Church, redounded to the benefit of the development of instrumental music.[77]

[76] For an interesting table listing the instruments that appear on 40 different pictures and illustrating the principle of contrast, see SchneiderA, 27f. (The Coronation of the Virgin at Santa Croce in Florence, attributed by Schneider to Giotto, is really by Taddeo Gaddi.) See also LeiW.

[77] Further concerning instruments in the 14th century, see PirR; GennK; GéroH, Chap. XX; GéroM, Chap. XX; SachsMI; SachsR; ScherS; ParI.

Chapter 14: POLYPHONY IN THE BRITISH ISLES FROM THE 12TH CENTURY TO THE DEATH OF DUNSTABLE

S OME hints of what was happening in England in the 11th century and earlier in the field of primitive organum have been given in Chapter 9, some of these being based upon evidence supplied by John Scotus (Erigena) and by one of the Winchester tropers. An important bit of evidence concerning part-singing in Great Britain in the following century appears in the *Descriptio Kambriae* [1] of Giraldus Cambrensis (*c.* 1147–1220). Gerald de Barri—to give him his family name—was the son of a Norman nobleman and a high-born Welshwoman; he studied and lectured in Paris as a young man, and then returned to England to become, in 1184, Court chaplain to Henry II. In his lively "Description of Wales," Gerald, who was a cultured man, the friend of scholars in England, France, and Italy, writes:

> *In their musical concerts they do not sing in unison like the inhabitants of other countries, but in many different parts; so that in a company of singers, which one very frequently meets with in Wales, you will hear as many different parts and voices as there are performers, who all at length unite, with organic melody, in one consonance and the soft sweetness of B flat.[2] In the northern district of Britain, beyond the Humber, and on the borders of Yorkshire, the inhabitants make use of the same kind of symphonious harmony, but with less variety; singing only in two parts, one murmuring in the bass, the other warbling in the acute or treble. Neither of the two nations has acquired this peculiarity by art, but by long habit, which has rendered it natural and familiar; and the practice is now so firmly rooted in them, that it is unusual to hear a simple and single melody well sung; and, what is still more wonderful, the children, even from their infancy, sing in the same manner. As the English in general do not adopt this mode of singing, but only those of the northern countries, I believe that it was from the Danes and Norwegians, by whom these parts of the island were more frequently invaded, and held longer under their dominion, that the natives contracted their mode of singing as well as speaking.[3]*

Very elaborate theories have been based on this description,[4] but the passage only shows that in Wales there was singing in more than two parts—

[1] This work is dedicated to Stephen Langton, Archbishop of Canterbury (*cf.* p. 191).
[2] Various hypotheses have been advanced concerning the meaning of "the soft sweetness of B flat." See BukE, 114; OH I, 92; DaveyH, 18f.
[3] HoareG, 74f. For the original Latin, see DimK, 189f.
[4] Some of them are listed in DaveyH, 19.

no exact number being specified—and in Northern England singing in two parts.

What kind of music may this English two-part singing have been? That it may in some respects have differed from the various types of organum known to Continental Europe is deducible from Gerald's so definitely localizing it. And in fact a method of part-writing quite unlike anything in Continental music of that time is displayed in the one known composition that may be said in certain ways to fit Gerald's account of the Northern English music, since it not only is in two parts but seems to have been written in the Orkney Islands, which belonged to Norway for several centuries beginning with the 9th. This composition, *Nobilis, humilis,* found in a late 13th-century MS—Upsala C 233—is a two-part hymn in praise of St. Magnus (d. 1115), the patron of the Orkneys.[5] The voices proceed in thirds almost throughout the piece. It is possible that this is the kind of music Gerald had in mind. Or, since he was describing conditions prevailing about one hundred years before the date of the Upsala MS, it is perhaps more likely that he had in mind some kind of singing in parallel fifths in the manner of the Icelandic *Tvisöngvar,* which, as we have seen (pp. 270f), are still sung today in parallel fifths.[6]

Whether the parallel organum in thirds illustrated by this St. Magnus hymn was borrowed from the Scandinavians or was a spontaneous indigenous growth, evidence of a predilection for thirds is found in various English compositions dating from the end of the 12th or the beginning of the 13th century, for example: *Adjuva nos deus* and *Redit aetas aurea,*[7] the latter a conductus celebrating the accession of Richard the Lion-Hearted in 1189. This predilection often finds satisfaction not only in music in which the two voices proceed mostly in parallel thirds, as in *Nobilis, humilis,* but in music in which the voices vary such parallel motion by an occasional change in position, resulting from a passage in contrary and conjunct motion from a third, through a unison, to another third. Sometimes the two voices show a predilection for parallel sixths (varied by an occasional expansion, by contrary and conjunct motion, into an octave) rather than parallel thirds. (Simon Tunstede, in the *Quatuor principalia,* written in 1351, points out that singing in parallel sixths against plainsong melodies was practiced in neither France nor Rome—thus apparently implying that it was a specifically English practice.) This important type of part-writing—that is, two-part writing displaying frequent parallel successions of imperfect consonances—was employed in many English pieces of the 13th to the 15th centuries, but it was not until the 15th century that it was given a name in the MSS—*gymel* (from *cantus*

[5] First printed, with commentary, in KolT. Printed also in BesM, 175; LudG, 167.
[6] Cf. BukP, 33. Concerning the rhythm of this piece and its citation by Robert de Handlo. see Bukofzer in M&L, XXI (1940), 203.
[7] For a passage from the *Adjuva,* see HandE (1933), 702; for the *Redit,* see EinSH, 260.

gemellus, "twin song"; *cf. Tvisöngvar*). It is worthy of note that the style, which was in all probability that of popular music, early shows its influence in the conductus, with its often newly invented tenor, and displays it only much later in works having a borrowed tenor. Passages of gymel appear in the course of compositions partly written in the older technique, displaying chiefly the perfect consonances, and it was thus only one of several available methods of composition. An early example of gymel is *Jesu Cristes milde moder,* a polyphonic sequence of which we transcribe the first and tenth double versicles: [8]

EXAMPLE 122. First and Penultimate Double Versicles of *Jesu Cristes milde moder* (Brit. Mus. MS Arundel 248, after EEH facsimile).

The complete text is a translation of the *Stabat iuxta Christi crucem,* a sequence resembling the *Stabat Mater.* While the presence of English words may indicate a popular origin, it should be remembered that there is some evidence that the early English lyric was mainly fostered by Franciscans. Such an English song as this might have been actually used in the Church, for there is an early 14th-century Latin sermon that provides for the rendering of this very sequence in English, with impersonation of the Mother and Son, completely within the frame of the regular church service. Other early gymels include the sequence *Risum,* having, like *Nobilis, humilis,* a Latin text, and, with English texts, *Foweles in the Frith* and *Edi beo.*[9] These three pieces, like Example 122, date from the second half of the 13th century. The gymel style

[8] Facsimile in EEH I, pl. 35. Inaccurate transcription in EEH II, 75 (the transcriptions in EEH II are not consistently dependable); partial transcription in OH I, 308. *Quen of evene,* printed as an individual composition in OH I, 168, is actually the last double versicle of *Jesu Cristes milde moder;* it is transcribed also by F. Gennrich in *Internationale mittelalterlichen Melodien* in ZfMW, XI (1929), 262.

[9] For a transcription of a portion of *Risum,* see BukP, 37. Facsimile of *Foweles* in EEH I, pl. 7, StaE, I, pl. 6; transcription in OH I, 307, StaE II, 10. Transcription of *Edi beo* in BukG, 79. A translation of as much of the Middle English text as is given in the transcription may be found in BukG, 80. For the full Middle English text, see Carleton Brown, *English Lyrics of the XIIIth Century,* 1932, 116ff.

is employed also in the earliest known motet with English words, *Worldes blisce-Domino* (*c.* 1260). Here the upper of the two voices is supplied with an English text, while the tenor bears only the word *Domino.*[10] In *Edi beo* the lower part has a distinct *a a b a* form, while the upper part is free. It is therefore reasonable to assume that, in this piece, the main melody is in the lower voice. However, in a 13th-century two-part setting of *Angelus ad Virginem,*[11] the melody referred to in Chapter 8 appears, in slightly modified form, in the upper part. This setting illustrates progressions in sixths.

Even in the 13th century, attempts were made to fill out the gymel by adding a third part above the "twin" voices. The same MS as contains Example 122 preserves also a three-part *Salve virgo,* the two lower parts of which, taken by themselves, form a completely normal gymel. (There is no way of knowing which of these parts has the melody intended as the main one.) The uppermost voice has several earmarks of having been merely added to this two-part structure.[12]

That hocketing was practiced in England as well as in France in the 12th century, we know from Ailred's complaint (see pp. 321f). But there seem to have been objections to part-singing in general, at least in the performance of religious music. John of Salisbury wrote:

Could you but hear one of these enervating performances executed with all the devices of the art, you might think it a chorus of Sirens, but not of men, and you would be astonished at the singers' facility, with which indeed neither that of the nightingale or parrot, nor of whatever else there may be that is more remarkable in this kind, can compare. For this facility is displayed in long ascents and descents, in the dividing or in the redoubling of notes, in the repetition of phrases, and the clashing of the voices, while, in all this, the high or even the highest notes of the scale are so mingled with the lower and lowest, that the ears are almost deprived of their power to distinguish.[13]

What music might have been heard in the Celtic portions of the British Isles at this period is debatable. Literary references show that from very early times music occupied a position of great importance in Celtic life and was practiced by a highly trained bardic profession.[14] The bards did not, however, record their compositions in writing: in speaking of the Celtic bards on the Continent, Caesar had suggested that they did not wish to disseminate

[10] For a transcription and discussion of this work, see BukM.
[11] To be published in *English Gothic Music,* a collection for practical use, in course of preparation by Dom Anselm Hughes and Percy Grainger.
[12] *Cf.* BukG, 8of. (Facsimile in EEH I, pl. 36.) Further concerning gymel generally, see BukG.
[13] OH I, 290, footnote.
[14] For the Irish bards, see O'CurM. For literary references to the Welsh bards, see JoneM I, 1–122; and for a discussion of laws relating to them, see GwynB: this Welsh material is summarized in GwynnW, 3–43.

their craft too widely among the vulgar or to encourage their students to rely on the written record instead of the memory.[15]

There is in the British Museum a MS containing Welsh harp music (MS Add. 14905), reputedly of great antiquity. An 18th-century owner of it, Lewis Morris, believed that he had here the music of the ancient Welsh as codified under Gruffydd ap Cynan about 1100 A. D., together with, as he stated, "Some of the most antient Pieces of the Britains, Supposed to have been handed down to us from the British Druids." He accordingly drew up a title-page to that effect, and had it bound with the MS, along with about thirty pages of his own notes on early Welsh music.[16] Going even further than Morris in claiming antiquity for the MS, Arnold Dolmetsch wrote: "I doubt if [this music] could have originated at any date later than the eighth century." [17]

The music, written in alphabetical tablature, displays a comparatively modern type of perpendicular harmony, based upon the alternation of tonic and dominant chords in certain fixed patterns or "measures." Before some of the pieces, their particular measures are represented by a series of 1's and 0's (for tonic and dominant); and towards the end of the MS a list is given of the "24 measures of Welsh string music," together with their names. If the contents of the MS were as ancient as has been claimed, that fact would revolutionize both our notions concerning the development of music in medieval Europe and the general belief that the concept of harmony as a system governing musical combinations from the vertical standpoint did not make itself felt with any radically great strength until the 17th century. Disregarding what Morris wrote, we find that the original MS dates only from the 17th century; and that only a small section of it is indicated as having been copied from an earlier work, which in turn was only of the preceding century. From other sources we know that a King Gruffydd ap Cynan did rule in North Wales in 1100; [18] also, as "24 measures of Welsh string music" are referred to in more than one MS,[19] it is quite possible that the *idea* of them does go back to the 12th century or earlier,[20] and even some of the names that the scribe gives in his list of the measures may go back to the time of Gruffydd. But the measures

[15] Caesar, *Bellum Gallicum*, Bk. VI, Ch. xiv.
[16] The MS is sometimes called the Robert ap Huw MS, for Morris says on his title page: "This Manuscript was wrote by Robert ap Huw of Bodwigen in Anglesey, in Charles ye I[st]'s time." (LewM, vi, suggests that Morris was here in error, and that the scribe was the Robert ap Huw who was musician to James I.) The MS is also sometimes called the Penllyn MS, for Morris has indicated that 12 pages of it had been copied "out of Wm Penllyn's Book." (This may be the William Penllyn who graduated at the Eisteddfod of 1568.) A facsimile of the complete MS is given in LewM, and a sample page in GwynnW. The original notation has been reproduced in modern type in JonesM 1089–1204, and some of the material has been transcribed *ibid*. 1217–37 and 1243–47. Three pieces are transcribed in DolT I.
[17] DolC, 7.   [18] JonH; FloodH 47–50; GwynnW 30–35.
[19] E. g. MS Peniarth 62 (16th century); see GwynnW 30–34.
[20] The literary source from which Morris may have derived the impression that he had in his possession the authentically ancient "24 measures" appears in LewM, 8.

themselves (in their musical aspects) as given in this MS, and the pieces in turn based upon them, probably are of a late date that places them outside the scope of this chapter.

There is in existence one brief example of music actually written down in the 12th century, though probably older, and preserved in a MS from a Celtic portion of Britain. It is a two-part setting of *Ut tuo propitiatus*—the verse to the response *Sancte dei pretiose*—inscribed in the Cornish MS Bodley 572.[21] It is pentatonic in character, which (judging from traditional Celtic music recorded in the 18th and 19th centuries) would associate it more with Irish and Scottish than with Welsh music.[22] It is noted in a double row of letters, and is melismatic rather than syllabic. The two voices frequently move in contrary motion, and cross, producing all the intervals from unison to octave, but most frequently fourths and fifths. It is, with the Winchester pieces, among the earliest practical examples of contrary motion that we have.

Welsh music seems to have been influenced at an early period by Ireland.[23] King Gruffydd ap Cynan, for example, grew up in Ireland in exile, and after reclaiming his throne invited Irish harpers to Wales to help codify the music.[24] The fact that some of the "24 measures" have Irish names may be a reflection of this assistance from Ireland.

There were, however, differences between the music of the two nations even at that early period. Giraldus Cambrensis, after making a trip through Ireland in 1183, wrote in his *Topographia Hibernica* that he had been particularly impressed by the greater rapidity of movement in Irish than in Welsh music: he says that the Irish "play the little notes so sportively under the blunter sounds of the bass (*grossioris*) strings," and they play with "so discordant a concord, as if the chords sounded together fourths or fifths." [25]

Ireland affected not only Welsh music, but Scottish as well. Giraldus writes, in the same work, that "in the opinion of many, Scotland has not only equalled Ireland, her teacher in music, but has . . . surpassed her." Our knowledge of the actual music heard in Scotland at that time, however, is entirely hypothetical. We know that in the 12th century Anglo-Norman culture began to influence Scottish music, bringing in many new instruments from the South and encouraging the development of folk-music of a recreative character, in contrast to the older and more serious bardic compositions. In the 13th century Simon Tailler led a reform in Scottish church music, writing

[21] Facsimile in EEH I, pl. 1; transcription in EEH II, 1 and OH I, 51.

[22] *Cf.* FleiM, 428f. Concerning its status as processional music, see Handschin in Acta, IV (1932), 50.

[23] FloodH, 48–53. Certain Cambrians, however, deny or minimize this influence, e. g., GwynB, 236.

[24] JonH gives a full account of his life.

[25] Giraldus also included this passage in his later work, the *Descriptio Kambriae*. The Latin text can be found in DimH, 153ff, and DimK, 186f; the translation given here is from HoareG, 172.

four treatises, and making Scottish music (according to Dempster, who d. 1625 and whose testimony, even if it were not so obviously exaggerated, would therefore have to be taken with reservation) "the rival of Rome." Also dating from this early period is the most important MS that has come down to us from medieval Scotland—Wolfenbüttel 677 (cf. p. 297), of which more presently. James III of Scotland (d. 1488) endowed a Chapel Royal at Stirling, and sent musicians abroad to learn. The connections between Scotland and Flanders during the 15th century were very close; and Scotland not only enjoyed a "Golden Age" in all the arts at home during that period, but was also in contact with the flourishing centers of music on the Continent.[26] Some of this, however, takes us beyond the period here to be considered.

Though Wolfenbüttel 677, which comprises eleven fascicles, seems to have been written in Scotland (since it contains two responsories for St. Andrew's Day [27] and its history appears to point to a Scottish origin), most of the pieces in it are, as we have seen, French compositions that are found also in the other great Notre Dame collections. All the works in the 11th fascicle, however—consisting of two-part compositions for Mary Masses, including tropes for the Ordinary, Alleluias, sequences, Offertories, etc., as well as other Sanctus and Agnus tropes and certain other pieces [28] scattered through the rest of the MS—are composed in a style which, though closely related to that of Notre Dame in several fundamental ways, differs from it in others. This style is also discernible in the compositions in another MS that is probably of insular origin—Bib. Nat. f. lat. 15129.[29] It has been held that works in this style are insular compositions and that some of those in Wolfenbüttel 677 are contemporary with the Notre Dame repertoire, while others in it, and those in Bib. Nat. f. lat. 15129, are slightly younger.[30] (Following Handschin, we stretch the meaning of the word "insular" to describe works apparently originating in the British Isles, since few of them can with any certainty be identified as specifically English, Scottish, Welsh, or Irish.)

The general characteristics of this style have been described in Chapter 11 (cf. pp. 306, 319f) where we have called it "peripheral." Let us examine it in slightly greater detail. The Notre Dame organa embellished only the responsorial portions of the Mass. Early polyphonic tropes for the Ordinary are contained only in insular sources and are therefore thought to represent a species of composition peculiar to Great Britain, so that even such Wolfen-

[26] For a fuller account of early Scottish music, see FarmM.
[27] For a transcription of the verse of one of these (with facsimile of the whole piece), see HughH, 178, 181. For another (incomplete) transcription of the same piece and a discussion of both, see HandE, 699.
[28] These include, besides the two for the feast of St. Andrew, the 3-part organum *Haec Dies* (partly transcribed in HandE, 699).
[29] The 4 pieces in this MS have been transcribed by Handschin. Three of them are printed in HandH, 71ff, and the fourth in HandS, appendix, 6.
[30] HandE, 512; HandH, 61.

büttel 677 examples as appear before fascicle 11 have been regarded as insular.[31] These tropes and the contents of fascicle 11 contain features of both organum and conductus. "The ground melody, it is true, is a given one [in the 'insular' pieces of both parts of the MS] but in the sequences and tropes it is not a Gregorian tune; and . . . our compositions have this in common with the Choralbearbeitung [organum] and the Conductus, that they presuppose the simultaneous pronunciation of the text in all voices; which distinguishes them from the Motet." [32] Some of the Ordinary tropes in the 11th fascicle alternate with portions of the original chant sung purely as plainsong, as the Notre Dame organa alternated with pure plainsong. In other Ordinary tropes, however, not only is the troping polyphonic but the chant is itself set polyphonically also; as a result no chant remains to be sung monodically. Writing that is based on plainsong but entirely eliminates it in its pure form may at the time be specifically insular.[33] Another interesting peculiarity of these pieces is that while all of them are essentially in two parts, in some a third voice enters towards the end.[34]

Whatever the Sanctus and Agnus tropes of the main body of Wolfenbüttel 677 may have in common with the pieces in fascicle 11, they differ from these pieces in certain respects, a fact that has prompted the suggestion [35] that the two parts of the MS were written in different regions of Great Britain. Thus, the Ordinary tropes in the 11th fascicle are less melismatic and more simply constructed than some in the rest of the MS,[36] and show less of a predilection for the use of thirds.

The English compositions with metrical text also display points of difference when compared with similar pieces in the Notre Dame repertoire (cf. pp. 306ff). Whereas the latter are sometimes highly melismatic, those in fascicle 11 are either not melismatic or contain only short melismas. And while in the Notre Dame melismas all the voices generally sing the same rhythmical figure simultaneously, the English style prefers to write the tenor in longs, giving the smaller time-values to the upper voices. The English pieces with metrical text use borrowed melodies for the tenor, while the Notre Dame pieces of the same class, as we have seen, appear to employ melodies in the main especially created for the compositions in question.

In English organa as well as compositions with metrical text the melodically varied repetition of a phrase is rather more common than in Notre Dame pieces.[37] It is perhaps worth observing, although an English origin cannot be definitely claimed for the motet *Ave gloriosa mater*, the interestingly colored

---

[31] HandE, 697. [32] HandE, 512. [33] Example in HandS, appendix, 4.
[34] *Cf.* p. 243. For an example, see HandS, appendix, 3. [35] HandE, 511.
[36] An elaborate Agnus trope from fascicle 8 is printed in full in HandE, 701. For additional discussion of the English origin of this and some other pieces in the first 10 fascicles of Wolfenbüttel 677, see HandE, 512 and *passim*.
[37] Examples from the 11th fascicle of Wolfenbüttel 677 and Bib. Nat. f. lat. 15129 in HandZP, 515.

tenor of which has been mentioned on p. 320, that the oldest of the several MSS preserving the piece in one form or another is the famous English one, Harley 978 at the British Museum.[38] Coloration of the tenor has already been noted in the *Alle psallite cum luya,* in the Montpellier MS (p. 320), and this motet too appears in an English MS, with other words and in a fragmentary and somewhat different form.[39] This piece may exhibit also another English trait,[39a] for *Stimmtausch,* to which reference has frequently been made and which it employs, may possibly be of English origin. An early example of *Stimmtausch* technique is the two-part *Ad cantus laetitiae,* found in a Cambridge MS dating from the beginning of the 13th century.[40] Here the music for the first verse is repeated in the second, but in the third verse the two voices exchange melodies. This piece seems to have had a remarkable vitality: it appears also in 15th-century MSS at Berlin and Bamberg, a 15th- or 16th-century Dutch MS at Cologne, and in the Finnish collection *Piae Cantiones* (1582).[41] Among the theorists, *Stimmtausch* is described only by natives of the British Isles,[42] Johannes de Garlandia [43] and Walter Odington (*cf.* below), even though it appears also in Notre Dame compositions. It is very possible that English musicians may have taught French musicians as well as learned from them. Paris attracted a great many Englishmen in the 11th to 14th centuries; English students were numerous enough to form one of the four schools into which the University of Paris was divided. Among the visitors to Paris were Adelard of Bath (12th century), Robert Kilwardby (d. 1279), Roger Bacon (d. 1292), and perhaps Robert Grosseteste (who became bishop of Lincoln in 1235). Although these men were essentially philosophers or, like Bartholomaeus Anglicus (whose treatise dates from 1230–50), encyclopedists, they have left us writings on music.[44] As we have seen in previous chapters (in which we have encountered such other 13th-century English theorists as Johannes de Garlandia, pseudo-Aristotle, and Alfred), Garlandia and Anonymus IV also studied at Paris. Thus, it is not unreasonable to suppose that English music was performed in France and perhaps exerted some influence upon native composers.

A more elaborate form of *Stimmtausch* than that displayed by *Alle psallite cum luya* appears in a type of composition described by Odington—the *ron-*

---

[38] Facsimile in EEH I, pl. 20–21. Further concerning this piece, see LudQ, 275f, where, while it is conceded that Harley 978 is the oldest MS containing the piece, greater age is claimed for the form in which it appears in the Montpellier and Bamberg MSS.

[39] *Cf.* HughW, 71.   [39a] Further concerning English traits in the 13th-century motet, see TischE.

[40] Facsimile in EEH I, pl. 28.

[41] For transcriptions of the Cambridge, Bamberg, and *Piae Cantiones* versions, see Jacques Handschin, *Angelomontana polyphonica,* in *Schweizerisches Jahrbuch für Musikwissenschaft* III (1928), appendix, 22f.   [42] HandZP, 557.   [43] CouS I, 116.

[44] Concerning Grosseteste as a theorist, see Hermann Müller, *Zur Musikauffassung des Mittelalters,* in *Festschrift für H. Kretzschmar,* 1918, p. 96ff. For references to the literature on the other 4 men and to printed editions of their writings on music, see PietzschK, 26, 28, 31. See also WolfE.

dellus. According to him, two or three melodies are to be sung simultaneously by as many voices and all the voices are to sing each melody in turn.[45] In his example, which is in three parts, there are six melodies, arranged as follows:

Top voice	2	3	1	5	6	4
Middle voice	3	1	2	6	4	5
Lowest voice	1	2	3	4	5	6

It may be added that 6 is closely related to 3, 4 to 2, and 5 somewhat related to 1.[46] The *rondellus* is sometimes grouped with the *rota* and *rondeau,* the three being treated as different phases of the same thing. The *rota* (or "round") and the *rondellus* do resemble each other to the extent that, in each, identical melodic material is assigned to all the voices, but they are unlike in that they distribute this material differently. Thus, in the former—a true canon—the voices enter successively with the same melody, while in the latter the voices enter simultaneously with different portions of the common melodic material. The term *rondeau,* on the other hand, describes a musical or poetic form (*cf.* p. 222) and has no application to a *method* of part-writing, though polyphonic as well as monodic pieces may be cast in the form.[47]

The most famous rota and indeed one of the most celebrated medieval compositions that have come down to us is the so-called Reading Rota, *Sumer is icumen in,*[48] preserved in MS Harley 978 at the British Museum. This is a four-part canon over a two-part *pes* or tenor.[49] Dating from *c.* 1310,[49a] it is the oldest known ostensibly six-part composition. (Doublings at the unison reduce the apparent 6 parts, most of the time, to an actual 3.[50]) The identity of its composer and of the writers of the other 13th-century English polyphonic pieces is unknown.[51] Just possibly they included one or more of the musicians mentioned by Anonymus IV: "There were good singers in England, and they sang very delightfully, such as Master John *filius Dei,* Makeblite of

---

[45] CouS I, 246f (with ex.). For a translation of the passage in question and for a transcription of the example, see OH I, 171.

[46] The rondellus technique appears in 2 of the compositions printed in HughW (135, 141). A good example, of non-English origin, is an Agnus trope in WagG, 32. For other Continental examples, see F. Ludwig, *Die mehrstimmigen Werke der Handschrift Engelberg 314,* in *Kirchenmusikalisches Jahrbuch* XXI (1908), 48; GennF, 85 and 88; and both settings on p. 31 of H. Anglès, *El Còdex musical de las Huelgas,* 1931, Vol. III (analysis of the three-part setting and of a third setting—the trope just referred to as in WagG—in HandZP, 535).

[47] There seems to be no connection between the term *rondellus* as used by Odington and the same term as applied to the one-line Latin song (*cf.* p. 202).

[48] Facsimiles and transcriptions are too numerous and well known to require citations here.

[49] The use of the word *pes* instead of tenor seems to be confined to some English MSS of the 13th and 14th centuries. We shall encounter it again in Worcester compositions.

[49a] The generally accepted older view is that it dates from *c.* 1240. Since this book first appeared, however, M. F. Bukofzer has published '*Sumer is icumen in*': A Revision, in *University of California Publications in Music,* II (1944), 79. He adduces strong evidence to show that the piece dates from 1310-25 and has no demonstrable connection with Reading. At present (1946) this claim remains under dispute, but it is too well supported to be ignored.

[50] As has already been pointed out in BukP, 34.   [51] The MS of the rota is sometimes said to be in the handwriting of a monk of Reading Abbey called John of Fornsete (= Forncett, a village in Norfolk), but the attribution rests on very flimsy support, and in any case there is no evidence of the alleged scribe's having been also the composer. See HurryS, 19.

Winchester, and Blakesmit at the Court of lord King Henry the last." [52]
The skilful construction of *Sumer is icumen in* and the facts that a Latin text
appears under the English one and that the instructions for its performance
are written in Latin, have led some to believe that it is not an example of
folk or popular music, as is sometimes supposed, but the work of a trained
and expert musician; on the other hand, the presence of the Latin text and
directions has led others to the opposite conclusion, for the Latin is obviously
not the original text for the music, and the explicit directions for performance
might well indicate that they were needed by the learned users of the manuscript, this manner of singing in canon being unfamiliar to them. The origin
of the style of composition exhibited in *Sumer is icumen in* thus remains
largely an open question. We have seen traces of canon in works of the
Notre Dame school (*cf.* pp. 303ff), so that the *Sumer*-Rota is not as miraculous and as wholly unprecedented as it is sometimes said to be. But what is
really remarkable is that this canon should be so much more ambitious—at
least in its attempt to use 4 voices—than the 14th-century canons of France
and Italy.[53] The four upper voices are in rhythmic mode 1 while the two-
part *pes* is in mode 5, and the result of this combination, together with
the frequent thirds and sixths, is a fresh, dance-like effect. The piece moves
harmonically only between the chords of F and G.[54] The *pes*, which employs
the *Stimmtausch* technique, is repeated over and over, forming a kind of
ostinato.

An interesting *ostinato* effect is achieved in the three-part motet *Puellare
gremium.*[55] Here the wordless tenor consists of two lively phrases which are
repeated and alternated in this manner: AA BB AA BB AA BB, with a
remarkable rhythmical displacement amounting actually to a measure of $\frac{4}{1}$
plus a measure of $\frac{5}{1}$ for each A phrase and two measures of $\frac{4}{4}$ followed by a
measure of $\frac{2}{4}$ for each B phrase, while the upper parts have $\frac{4}{1}$ throughout.

The MS in which this motet appears is part of a collection of MSS, some
of which have been assembled from old bindings and wrappers in the Library
of Worcester Cathedral and others from fly-leaves of books in the Bodleian
Library at Oxford and in the British Museum.[56] At least a good part of the
compositions date from the beginning or first half of the 14th century.[57] They
indicate the existence at Worcester of a school of composers who seem to
have been influenced by older French music, but whose works, while on the

[52] Henry III (d. 1272). For the original Latin, see CouS I, 344.
[53] According to FloodH, 66, *Sumer* is "a harmonized arrangement of a phrase taken from"
an old Irish tune. But it is far from a mere harmonization; and the canon technique, which lends
it its special charm, has its known prototype only in French—not in Irish—music.
[54] Concerning the liking for an alternation of 2 harmonies in early insular music, see GeorE,
84. *Cf.* also p. 391 *supra*.
[55] Transcription in HughW, 100.
[56] A few of the compositions on these leaves have been reproduced in facsimile, and many of
them have been transcribed, in HughW.
[57] According to HandWM, 55. But see also various datings in HughW, *passim.*

whole old-fashioned in comparison with contemporary French compositions, contain some new elements that were to be developed by later Englishmen and through them were to influence the course of Continental music. Several pieces appearing in one or another of the Notre Dame MSS appear also, sometimes altered, in the Worcester MSS.[58]

The Worcester compositions include polyphonic settings of tropes for the Mass, motets, conducti, and rondelli. The motets, like those in the Notre Dame MSS, still have several texts and a borrowed tenor. Some of the compositions for the Ordinary of the Mass [59] display a merging of styles: the technique is that of the conductus, mostly note against note, although a chant melody is used. Here we see mixture of types under way, a process that was to continue for several centuries and that was to effect not only mergers of organum and conductus, as here, but other mergers also. Some of the pieces (e. g. *Puellare gremium*) have been transcribed in duple time. Odington has left us not only the retrospective passage which, as we have noted on pp. 273f, has been wrongly interpreted as indicating the use of binary rhythm during an early stage of the development of mensural music, but also statements showing that in his own day (which, let us remember, is as late as c. 1300, i. e., shortly before the appearance of de Vitri's *Ars nova*) binary rhythm was in use in art-music alongside ternary rhythm.[60] And it is claimed that these pieces are early specimens of that practice.[61] The conductus *Beata viscera* [62] is a perfect example of what is *commonly* called "fauxbourdon." Let us see what is meant by this term.

For many years an element of mystery surrounded the emergence of progressions of $\frac{6}{3}$ chords as a feature of medieval music. Until recently all early pieces using such harmony—the use of the word in this connection seems to be justified—have been called examples of fauxbourdon, regardless of how distinct they might be from one another in other respects. Both the time and the place of origin of this technique were formerly the subject of controversy, an amusing feature of which was that certain Continental scholars attributed the innovation to England,[63] while one of the leading English scholars [64] disclaimed the honor on the ground that the evidence for its English origin was inadequate. Our knowledge of the Worcester pieces, however, has greatly increased the amount of available evidence, and this has tended strongly to support the English origin of the general style.[65] Bukofzer,

---

[58] See HughW, 143f in conjunction with HandWM, 61.

[59] E. g., the Gloria in HughW, 39.   [60] CouS I, 245 (2 passages).

[61] For a discussion of the use of duple rhythm in connection with the Worcester MSS, see HughW, 14f and HandWM, 55.

[62] Transcriptions in HughW, 108 (*cf*. footnote 123) and Grove II, 209 (incomplete).

[63] See, for example, RieG, 111. Similar contentions were more zealously advanced by Victor Lederer, whose book (LedH), while it contains much of interest, is full of extravagant claims.

[64] Wooldridge in OH I, 91ff.

[65] For the first extended discussion of this evidence in this light, see HughO.

however, has contended [66] that there were two forms of this general style, one English and the other a Continental offshoot, these being alike in their use of thirds and sixths, but distinguished by the position of the *cantus firmus,* which in the English form is in the lowest voice and in the Continental form in the highest voice. He gives the name "English discant" to the English style, retaining that of "fauxbourdon" for the Continental style, in which the lowest voice, deprived of the *cantus firmus,* is in reality a "false support." [67]

Of the two methods, English discant is the older, as is proved by the dates both of the examples of it that have been preserved and of the theorists who standardized the rules governing its use. It came into being by the end of the 13th century, a Cambridge MS [67a] containing the earliest known specimen, of which the following is a transcription. The close of the Te Deum melody appears in the tenor which, it will be noted, treats its material in a manner strikingly different from the one that would be applied if this were a normal motet of the period.

EXAMPLE 123. *In te Domine speravi* (after BukE, Ex. 18).

"In Thee, Lord, have I trusted: let me not be confounded forever." The crosses over the tenor indicate the notes of the *cantus firmus.* (The date of this example would dispose of any claim to priority in the use of the general $\frac{6}{3}$ style in connection with such pieces as Landini's *El mie dolce sospir* [WolfS, 14].)

---

[66] In BukE, a monograph that is a complete and masterly elucidation of what was an obscure phase of musical history, and that should be made available in English.

[67] BukE, 1of. The terms will here be retained. Another scholar, working independently, has published a study based largely on the same sources (GeorE); he does not stress the distinction between the methods Bukofzer calls English discant and fauxbourdon, but seems inclined to consider the former "a Continental variant of the English fauxbourdon practice" (GeorE, 105, footnote), his conclusions concerning the part played by the English in the development of harmony consequently differing radically from Bukofzer's.

[67a] Gonville and Caius Coll. 334, consisting of two sets of fly-leaves. The first set (which preserves Ex. 123) is of the 13th century, while the second set is of the 14th century.

Salve rosa [68] may be bracketed with *Beata viscera* as a Worcester example of only slightly later date. The theory that these pieces have the main melody in the lowest voice is based on the fact that they are conducti, in which, as we have seen, Franco states the tenor melody is written before the others (*cf.* p. 308).[69]

English discant, of course, like gymel, was only one of several styles employed by Englishmen (indeed, the two were in use at the same time). Thus, despite the English liking for keeping the *cantus* in the tenor, we find that, strangely enough, the earliest known real composition in three parts that has the *cantus* in the top part is of English origin. This piece—a Sanctus in the same MS that contains Example 123—cannot properly, however, be called an example of fauxbourdon: it is written in the ordinary discant style and is not characterized by thirds and sixths.[70]

Even though Johannes de Garlandia had admitted both major and minor thirds as imperfect consonances (*cf.* p. 294), and although Anonymus IV had done so also, adding that "among the best *organistae* . . . in England, in the land called Westcuntre, they are called best consonances," [71] and although, besides legalizing thirds, Walter Odington had mentioned the common use of major sixths,[72] we have to wait until the last half of the 14th century for any clear statement of the rules governing English discant. (In discussing major and minor thirds, Odington had even wandered so far from Pythagorean doctrine as to observe that, if mathematically they were not quite consonant, their tuning brought them very close to the ratios $5:4$ and $6:5$, acceptable as the source of consonances, and that, in any event, human voices "lead them forth with subtlety into a sweet mixture." [73]) Many of the authorities are still later: Guilielmus Monachus, the Italian [74] monk whose notes—describing both the English and Continental practices but failing to differentiate between them—have been the source of both information and confusion, wrote, not about 1400, as was once supposed, but nearer 1480.[75] The English theorists [76]—who include the fine composer Leonel (Lyonel)

[68] HughW, 124.

[69] See also BukE, 116. It might be pointed out, however, that the top part of *Beata viscera* has more of the character of a spontaneous and independent melody than the tenor. (*Cf.* p. 308; also Yvonne Rokseth, *Le Contrepoint double vers 1248*, in *Mélanges de Musicologie*, 1933, 12, concerning the possibility that the main melody in a conductus may sometimes be in the top part.) But it should be borne in mind that a melody skilfully composed against a *cantus prius factus* may well sound more spontaneous than the *cantus* itself. Perhaps Franco's rule does find application here, but there are nevertheless grounds for concluding that it was not adhered to quite as universally as is sometimes taken for granted.

[70] See BukE, 115.   [71] CouS I, 358.   [72] CouS I, 198, 200.   [73] CouS I, 191, 198f.

[74] BukE, 77 gives reasons for believing that Guilielmus was Italian, in opposition to the view held by Wooldridge and others that he was an Englishman living in Italy. See also DaveyH, 51.

[75] See BukE, 59. For Guilielmus's Latin text, see CouS III, 273 (*errata* list in BukE, 153); for a German translation of the part of the treatise that deals with the $\frac{6}{3}$ technique, see AdlerS, 790.

[76] BukE quotes, in addition to Leonel Power, the following English theorists: Tunstede (*Quatuor Principalia*, in CouS IV, 200), Johannes Torkesey (*Declaratio Trianguli*), Richard Cutell, John Hothby, and anonymous authors represented in the Brit. Mus. MSS Add. 21455 and Lans-

Power, of whom more presently—in revealing the laws governing the practice of English discant, imply its popular origin and acceptance, for several of their treatises are in the vernacular. Refreshing is the attitude shown by theorists who can write that "this manner of singing is mery to the singer and to the herer," and that "the mo imperfit tones that a man synges in the trebyll the merrier it is." [77]

As regards the actual rules, the English writers list the perfect and imperfect concords that may be used and lay down the compass of each voice (tenor, mene, treble, and, in four-part singing, quatreble). Furthermore—and this is important—they make it clear that English discant was originally a method of improvisation that could be applied to any *cantus firmus* by means of the "sight" system. This was a method of transposition in which—to take a three-part example—the singers of the mene and treble begin a fifth and octave above the *cantus firmus* and then imagine themselves to be singing a third below it. They preserve the same distance against the imaginary line, however, as, at the outset, separated them from the *cantus*. Hence the mene actually sings a third above the notated line and the treble a sixth above it. The improvising singers end their phrases on an imaginary unison with the *cantus,* so that they actually once more sing at the distance of a fifth and octave from it. If rigidly followed, the "sight" system would, of course, produce simply an unbroken succession of parallel $^6_3$ chords (except at the beginnings and endings of phrases), but the upper voices were supposed to ornament their parts according to their skill, and the fully-composed examples of English discant that we possess naturally include not only such fairly strict pieces as Example 123 and *Beata viscera,* but also some that show a greater degree of freedom.[78] The method relied for its effect, however, mainly on the massive and vigorous impression made by the succession of $^6_3$ chords moving in the rhythm—frequently modal—of the tenor's *cantus firmus*.

It is clear that the sound of $^6_3$ chords was much liked for its own sake. Snatches of $^6_3$ progressions are sometimes present in pieces in which English discant seems not at all to be the basic structural device, these passages being introduced, apparently, with deliberate artistic intent. The four-part motet *Ave miles coelestis—Ave rex patrone patriae—Ave rex* (early 14th century), a piece apostrophizing St. Edmund (*c.* 840–70), king of East Anglia, contains such snatches, sometimes with the tenor at the bottom in the normal English discant way—mostly towards the beginning of the piece—, sometimes with

---

downe 763. He prints those that are not in CouS. MeechT prints and discusses 3 of the treatises in Lansdowne 763, including that by Power. Four of these treatises are printed also in GeorE. Both BukE, 53 and GeorE, 53, footnote, point out that Riemann's attribution to Chilston of the treatise in Lansdowne 763, No. 16, is erroneous. Owing to the attribution, however, the author of the treatise is now sometimes referred to as "pseudo-Chilston."

[77] The first quotation is from Lansdowne 763 (printed in BukE, 149; MeechT, 260); the second is from Brit. Mus. Add. 21455 (printed in BukE, 138).

[78] E. g. . . . *nos sceleres,* HughW, 113.

only the three upper voices participating, so that, the tenor being silent, what we have is definitely not English discant, but free use of the $\frac{6}{3}$ technique. Free use of $\frac{6}{3}$ chords (as well as of triads in root position) constitutes part of the new sonority mentioned in Chapter 12 as present in some 14th century French music. It occurs, for example, in the l'Escurel three-part *rondeau* (though not in the tenorless manner just described). Whether there is any connection between the appearance of this sonority in France and the development of English discant across the Channel, the current state of our knowledge does not permit us to say. It does seem, however, that no organized method of using $\frac{6}{3}$ material, comparable to the English discant method, appears in France at this time. To return to *Ave miles:* Occasionally while the two upper voices move in fourths, the two lower ones share between them a line that moves in parallel sixths with the top part, one lower voice resting while the other sings. In two interesting but quite brief passages, the two lower voices hocket, while the upper voices progress in fourths, in such a way that there results what we would today call an alternation of chords made of root, fifth, and octave, with $\frac{6}{3}$ chords. The piece makes considerable use of *Stimmtausch.*

EXAMPLE 124. Last Two-thirds of the Motet *Ave miles coelestis—Ave rex patrone patriae—Ave rex* (Oxford, Bodl. e Museo 7, ff. 10^v-11^r. The preceding third is transcribed in BesM, 172).

Transl. of the entire motet: Triplum—"Hail, soldier of the heavenly court, whom the honor of victory adorns! You live with God, enjoying rest after the manner of the heaven-dwellers. Now you are rejoicing with the citizens above, yet are not abandoning your people, whom you know to be devoted to you. Your deeds strengthen our faith in the report of them, the blind see, the dead arise. Strengthened by the approbation of so great a king, we devotedly bless God." Motetus— "Hail, King, protector of our native land, morning-light of Saxony, shining on us at mid-day, star of the English-born! O Edmund, martyr, bright above all others! By prayer you make the lame walk again; you heal lepers; you release captives. With upright mind you keep enemies away, and with gracious heart you spare your servants. Enable us, O martyr, at the end of life to render fitting praises to God." Tenor—"Hail, King, O Edmund, flower of martyrs! O light of the faithful! Utter psalms to God. *Euouae.*" (Transl. W. W.)

Four-part writing was of course no novelty *c.* 1300 (we have found it well before that in the works of Perotin); but its appearance in several English compositions (including some Worcester motets), when considered together with the attempt at six-part writing in *Sumer is icumen in* and a similar attempt, as well as some five-part writing, both to be mentioned presently (p. 421), seems to show a predilection on the part of the English for greater fullness of sound, a predilection that is attested also by the very fact that they developed the $\frac{6}{3}$ style. Our example, in its use of this style and of four-part writing (which, though old, was not the usual thing), illustrates progressiveness in English music of its period. In one respect, however, the piece illustrates conservatism, for the liturgical motet in which the upper voice tropes the text of the plainsong in the tenor is a type of motet that had ceased to be cultivated in France when *Ave miles* was written in England.

In another motet in the same MS, *Petrum Cephas Ecclesiae*,[79] there are again four parts, but one voice or another is always silent. In this piece there is considerable use of $^6_3$ progressions during pauses in the tenor. This part, which has a plainsong fragment, receives especially interesting treatment. Its melody occurs four times in succession but it is broken up by the introduction of rests, each time differently, so that at each of its appearances it presents a different rhythmical arrangement. Thus the last 6 tones of the tenor, to take a brief extract for purposes of illustration, are heard as follows (each dash represents a rest of one measure in the transcription): (1) G F E D C – – – – D; (2) G – – – – F E D C D; (3) G F – – – – E D C D; (4) G F E – – – – D C D. In this way the rhythmic form of the melodic fragment changes upon repetition through a means other than that of non-coinciding *taleae* and *colores* (*cf.* p. 339).

Progressions of $^6_3$ chords occur in profusion also, without English discant being present, in the three-part Gloria trope *Spiritus et alme*,[80] which dates probably from the first half of the 14th century and is well known to scholarly writing. It has been claimed that the pre-existent melody to the same text appears paraphrased in the middle voice (at times in the outer voices too) but, if this is so, that melody has been very highly colored. In any event, the tenor melody cannot be shown to be the main one. It would seem that, with so much "organizing" in $^6_3$ chords, the piece, notwithstanding the numerous thirds formed by the two lower voices, was conceived as in three parts from the outset and not, like *Salve virgo* (*cf.* p. 390), as a gymel with added part.

The same is true of a three-part setting of *Angelus ad Virginem*,[81] dating from the second half of the 14th century, in which the main melody is definitely in the middle voice. Wherever the lower voices have parallel thirds, the top part moves in sixths with the lowest one. It would seem sufficient to recognize in this version of *Angelus ad Virginem* further evidence of the popularity of the $^6_3$ technique, causing it to be used not only, as originally, in providing a setting for a main melody placed in the lowest voice, but, little by little, for other purposes. What may actually have caused the combination of $^6_3$ writing with the species of writing that has the main melody in the middle voice need not concern us here at any great length. There are several reasonable explanations. One of these is that the existence of the kind of expanded gymels that have main melodies in the middle voice may quite possibly

[79] Facsimile in StaE I, pl. 10–11; transcription in II, 24. The date there suggested for this piece (*c.* 1375) is too late by perhaps 50 to 75 years.

[80] Facsimile in CouH, pl. 33; transcription in HandZP, 544. This composition is taken from the so-called "Coussemaker Fragment," a MS of English origin, written in the second half of the 14th century. It once belonged to Coussemaker but disappeared after his death; it was recently rediscovered by Handschin.

[81] EEH I, pl. 46; transcription in EEH II, 111, a portion in OH I, 311.

have suggested the experiment of writing pieces with the melody there even
when they were originally conceived in three parts and when the influence
of gymel was not present in any more fundamental way than that. The $\frac{6}{3}$
technique, being popular and ideally suited to three-part writing, would then
have been a likely medium to suggest itself. That the charming *Angelus ad
Virginem* melody was popular in the 14th century is shown not only by this
three-part setting but by the mention of some version of the song by Chaucer
when writing about Nicholas, the "poore scholar":

And all above ther lay a gay sautrye,   *So swetely that al the chamber rang,*
On which he made a-nightes melodye,   *And Angelus ad Virginem he sang.*

The sixth in a group of Kyrie settings—also dating from the second half
of the 14th century—preserved in Brit. Mus. Arundel 14, a setting in which
the melody is again definitely in the middle voice, has been singled out as a
piece conceived in three parts from the outset. It is claimed, however, to have
been written under gymel influence, since the middle voice moves in thirds
sometimes with the lower voice, sometimes with the upper one. These thirds
are by no means always mere constituents of $\frac{6}{3}$ chords, and the gymel influence can therefore be much more readily regarded as present in a fundamental way here than in the *Angelus* setting. The third of the Kyrie settings
in Arundel 14 provides an example of fully composed English discant, showing, even more than the piece referred to in footnote 78, interesting elaboration of the $\frac{6}{3}$ technique.[82]
During the first twenty years of the 15th century English discant was to
begin to appear on the Continent and alongside of it the earliest examples of
fauxbourdon proper, with the *cantus firmus* in the highest voice.[83] The
majority of these early examples are by Dufay, and it was probably owing
to his initiative in seizing upon the harmonic style of the English and
applying it to the Continental tradition of discant singing, with the *cantus
firmus* in the highest voice, that the style took root in Europe with such extreme rapidity. While in England the English discant style kept spreading
with conservative slowness from conductus to psalmody, thence to the rest of
the Office and only at long last to the Proper and Ordinary of the Mass, the
Continental fauxbourdon style was to appear in every kind of church music
in less than a century.[84] It is named in 15th-century poetry; it is seized upon

[82] This piece (based on the *Kyrie de angelis; Liber usualis,* 37) is printed in BukE, Ex. 19
(comments on p. 117); a portion also in BesM, 173. For the other three-part Kyrie mentioned
(based on a Kyrie of the Sarum use; *Sarum Gradual,* 9*), see BukG, 83.
[83] Wooldridge's claim (OH I, 298f) that fauxbourdon arose out of a Continental attempt to
evade the provisions of the Bull of Pope John XXII (cf. p. 357) by writing the *cantus firmus*
in the tenor, where it belonged, but singing it an octave higher, loses much of its force in the light
of the fact that true fauxbourdon does not appear until about a century after the issuance of the
Bull.
[84] Even here, however, some time elapsed before the style was used in the Proper and Ordinary
of the Mass.

and standardized by the 15th-century theorists.[85] Finally, after becoming well established on the Continent, it was to cross the Channel to England —only to be looked on, at first, as an outlandish innovation! Certainly it differed markedly from the English discant style: the floreations and cadential phrases with which the *cantus firmus* was ornamented made any question of a "sight" system of singing an unfloreated tenor from the upper voice impossible. The MSS normally supply only the outer voices and indicate that the middle voice is to be supplied by the singer, the task of contriving a part in parallel fourths below the notated top part being obviously one of no great difficulty.

It may have been the methods of fauxbourdon that Tinctoris, writing *c.* 1480, had in mind when he hailed a "new art" of music, an art that "had its fount and origin among the English."[86] The fauxbourdon style was to remain the subject of experimentation, both in England and on the Continent, into the 16th century.

THE dance rhythms obvious in such vocal music as *Sumer is icumen in* had their counterparts in purely instrumental 13th-century music. The same MS that contains the Rota includes three two-part dances, which belong to the family of *stantipedes*. Sachs holds that *stantipes* is not Latin for *estampie* (*cf.* p. 226) and that the form was an instrumental offshoot of the *ballata*. Antonio da Tempo describes the *ballata* for dancing as consisting of four sections. The form was *a b b a,* and the two middle parts were popularly called *pedes*. The word *stantipes,* according to Sachs, is a compound of the Vulgar Latin *stantia* (actually meaning "delay") and *pes,* the new word indicating that the number of *pedes* was increased by the addition of supplementary parts of the same character. The term was used where there were six or seven *pedes* or *puncta* (*cf.* p. 226). Where there were three or four, the term *ductia* appeared; the four-period type could be called a *nota* also; and *stantipes imperfecta* is sometimes applied to either.[87] Of the three two-part dances in Brit. Mus. Harley 978, the first is a *stantipes,* the second is a *nota* or *ductia,* and the third, comprising five *puncta,* is probably a *stantipes imperfecta.*[88]

An English[88a] instrumental-music MS of special interest is the so-called Robertsbridge MS, Brit. Mus. Add. 28550. This document, dating from the first half of the 14th century, contains what is probably the earliest known tablature for organ (or *echiquier?*).[89] It includes six pieces, of which the

---

[85] BukE quotes—in addition to Guilielmus Monachus—Tinctoris, Adam von Fulda, and Franchino Gafori, representing Continental writers on fauxbourdon, and anonymous theorists in the Brit. Mus. MSS Lansdowne 763 and Add. 4911, representing British writers.

[86] CouS IV, 154.   [87] See SachsW, 290 and WolfT, 12.

[88] For facsimiles of these pieces, see EEH, pl. 18, 19; transcriptions are printed in WolfT, 19ff. See also Schral, 52ff.   [88a] Generally so held; but see W. Apel, *Notation* . . . , 384.

[89] Concerning what may just possibly be an earlier example, see HandU, 9, note 3. The organ transcription of Landini's *Questa fanciulla* is not notated in tablature. (Moreover, the MS containing it dates from the 15th century.)

first and last are incomplete. The first three are purely instrumental, while the other three are instrumental arrangements of vocal compositions. Of the former, the two that are complete are in *estampie* form; of the latter, the two that are complete are the transcriptions of *Roman de Fauvel* motets already mentioned (*cf.* p. 337).[90] The tablature represents a combination of mensural and alphabet notation. There are usually two voices, the upper voice being written in mensural notation on a five-line staff, while the lower voice is indicated by letters from a to g. Occasionally, at cadences or other important places, one or two additional voices enter. There is considerable use of chromaticism, and we find among the notes on staves F-sharp, G-sharp, b-flat, c-sharp, e-flat, f-sharp, g-sharp, ^b_b-flat, and ^c_c-sharp, while the letters sometimes have a special symbol added to them to indicate sharpening (there is no flattening, except on b) up to F-sharp, C-sharp, G-sharp, and D-sharp. Noteworthy in the transcriptions of vocal pieces is the coloration of the original melodies, which are decorated with instrumental embellishments. This treatment was to be characteristic of organ music of the next two centuries (it became almost a vice in German organ tablatures).

We have said a few words in Chapter 5 about instruments used in the British Isles in the early Middle Ages and shall now touch briefly upon their successors. A comprehensive treatment of the whole subject of instruments in the Isles is easily available in GalpO, on which the following discussion is largely based.[91]

Giraldus Cambrensis reports that the Irish play principally the *cithara* and *tympanum*. By *cithara* he apparently means the rote, not the triangular harp nowadays used as a symbol for Ireland. As identified by Galpin, the *tympanum* was another chordophone, probably a kind of psaltery or dulcimer that was called by the Irish *timpan* or *tiompan*. To the Welsh, Giraldus assigns the *cithara* and *chorus*. The Scotch, he says, also use these two instruments and the *tympanum*. Whether or not the Welsh and Scotch applied the bow to the rote in the time of Giraldus, the Irish and English did. The bowed instrument—*cruit* or *crot* in Irish, *crwth* in Welsh, *crowd* in English—can be traced to the 11th century. The *chorus* was apparently a small type of crowd.[92] The same name, as we have seen in Chapter 11, was also sometimes applied to a bagpipe.

Among the other chordophones most commonly used in England were the harp, rote, guitar (spelled gittern, gyttren, gythorn, geterne), citole, psaltery, dulcimer, symphony, echiquier, lute, crowd, viol, rebec, and rubebe.

[90] Facsimiles of the Robertsbridge MS are in EEH I, pl. 42–45; transcriptions (unreliable) in II, 89ff. The purely instrumental compositions are transcribed complete in HandU, 14, 16; fragments are transcribed in WolfO, 17 and WolfH II, 9. See also SchraI, 78.
[91] See also, with special reference to instruments used in Celtic portions of the Isles, O'CurM.
[92] The Latin text of the Giraldus passage appears in DimH, 154. For a detailed study of the crowd, see AndersB and SchlesP, but in the light of SachsHI.

The harp is frequently mentioned in Middle English literature. Chaucer's Friar evidently enjoyed singing to the instrument:

> And in his harping, when he had songe
> His eyen twinkled in his head aright,
> As don the sterres in the frosty night.

A passage from Robert de Brunne's paraphrase (begun in 1303) of the *Manuel de Peches* by Robert Grosseteste (*cf.* p. 395) shows that the harp was highly esteemed for its powers to ward off evil:

> He answered hym on thys manere
> Why he helde the harpey so dere.
> The vertu of the harpe thrughe skylle and ryght,
> Wyl destroy the fendes myght;
> And to the croys by god skylle
> Ys the harpe lykened weyle.[93]

On the other hand, the Pardoner in "The Canterbury Tales" speaks of harps as instruments of the devil:

> Wher-as with harpes, lutes and giternes
> They daunce and pleye at dees bothe day and night.

The guitar reached England in the 13th century and was popular for accompaniment before the introduction of the lute. It is mentioned by Chaucer when Absolon, the parish clerk, serenades the carpenter's wife.

There are several references to the psaltery in "The Canterbury Tales." To some form of psaltery in the 13th century the name *cembalo* or *cymbal* was given—these names being of some interest in view of the appearance in 15th-century Germany of the term *clavicembalum* for the early harpsichord.

The first reference in literature in English to the word "dulcimer" is found in the poem "The Squyr of Lowe Degre" (*c.* 1400). But it may be to a dulcimer (or psaltery) that reference is made in Latin when we are told that St. Dunstan (*cf.* p. 123) used to play "in timphano," for the *tympanum* (or *timphanum*), as has already been said, may be the timpan, or tiompan.[94]

The *echiquier* and the probability of its English origin have already been mentioned (*cf.* pp. 383f).

Although the lute does not appear in English carvings or illustrations until the late 15th century, it is mentioned in the list of instruments at the Feast of Westminster in 1306.

The viol, destined to become a special favorite in the manor houses of Tudor England, is illustrated in a MS written at Canterbury early in the 12th century. This illustration is among the earliest pictorial representations of the viol known, the oldest antedating it by a century, or perhaps a little

---

[93] Quoted in CuttsS, 288.   [94] GalpO, 67f.

more.[95] The term *fithele* or *fydel* is the usual English equivalent at this time for the French *vièle*. This instrument is mentioned, together with the citole etc., in the 14th-century romance *Lybeaus Desconus*:

> *Myche he couthe of game*
> *With sytole, sautrye yn same,*
> *Harpe, fydele and crouthe.*

The principal aerophones found in medieval England are the recorder, shawm, double whistle-flute, tabor-pipe; the horn, bugle, cornett, trumpet; the organ and bagpipe. Bagpipes, as we have seen (*cf.* p. 124), were known in England *c.* 1100, but seem not to have figured prominently in Scotland (strangely enough), Wales, or Ireland, until considerably later. The sackbut (a *buisine* furnished with a slide) makes its appearance in England by the 15th century.

An illustration of a recorder has been found dating from the 12th century, though the name does not appear in English literature until the 14th century. The shawm is represented in Norman carvings in England about 1200. It was used in connection with the waytes (watches) established in London by Henry III and it assumed the name of waygte or wayte pipe. Although there is little mention of the flageolet in England until the 17th century, a double whistle-flute was known in the 13th century, when, so it seems, the pipe and tabor spread from the Continent to enliven English greens.

Various instruments of the bugle type—the horn (sometimes *byme* or *beme*), the cornett, trumpet, clarion (a shorter form of the *buisine*), and sackbut—were used chiefly in connection with war, hunting, and state occasions. Trumpets and clarions were used by the English army at the Battle of Crécy in 1346, and are mentioned in an old ballad telling of the defeat of the Scots at Halidon in 1333:

> *This was done with merrie sowne*
> *With pipis, trompes and tabers thereto*
> *And loude clarionis thei blew also.*

The organ had been popular in England since the early Middle Ages (*cf.* p. 123). It is referred to in Chaucer:[96]

> *His voice was merier than the mery orgon*
> *On messe-days that in the chirche gon.*

Ailred, whose complaint about hocketing has been mentioned (*cf.* p. 321), objected also to the use of certain instruments in the Church, for we find him writing: "Why such organs and so many cymbals in the Church? What with the sound of the bellows, the noise of the cymbals and the united strains

[95] For further details, see GalpO, 86, and SachsHI.
[96] For articles on instruments etc., mentioned by Chaucer, see MontM and OlsonC.

of the organ pipes, the common folk stand with wondering faces, trembling and amazed."

OUR knowledge of English vocal polyphony is augmented with respect to the second half of the 14th century and is carried forward to *c.* 1450 chiefly by three main bodies of material, two of them English and the third Continental. The English materials are (1) a collection of MSS in the Bodleian Library at Oxford,[97] including documents representing the entire period, chief among them being Selden B 26, dating from *c.* 1450; and (2) the Old Hall MS, a collection of music for the Mass, interspersed with motets and polyphonic antiphons, which appears to have been in use at St. George's Chapel, Windsor, and is now in the Library of St. Edmund's College, Old Hall, near Ware.[98] The date of the Old Hall MS is a subject of debate.[99] Whether it was inscribed in the reign of Henry V (1413–22), as Bukofzer is inclined to believe,[100] or of Henry VI (1422–61), as the editors of RamsO believe, it is very likely that many of the pieces in it were originally composed at or before the turn of the century. The third group of works by English composers is spread among MSS belonging to libraries at Trent, Bologna, Modena, and elsewhere on the Continent.

The six Trent Codices, from which important collections of transcriptions into modern notation began to appear in 1900, consist of folio volumes containing 1585 pieces dating from *c.* 1420–*c.* 1480, by composers of various nationalities. These MSS were bought by the Austrian Government in 1891, but after the World War they became the property of Italy by the terms of the peace treaty. In 1920 a seventh codex was found, which brought the apparent total of compositions up to 1864, though there are actually fewer, since many of them appear in two or more versions. Most of the pieces in the volumes of transcriptions [101] are by Continental composers who are younger contemporaries of the Englishmen about to be discussed. The English pieces drawn by these volumes from the Trent Codices are supplemented by some additional English works derived from certain other Continental MSS, especially Bibl. Estense, A X I, 11, at Modena.[102]

We have the names of some English *notatores* of about the time of the Selden MS: John Hanboys mentions Robert Trowell, Robert of Brunham (not with complete approval), and a certain W. of Doncaster.

---

[97] Facsimiles and transcriptions of many of the compositions in these MSS in StaE I and II.
[98] The Old Hall MS was first described in SquireN. Three volumes of transcriptions of all the pieces in the MS except a few fragments have been published in RamsO.
[99] See RamsO III, Introduction, for a discussion of this problem.   [100] BukD, 105, footnote.
[101] DTO VII, XI¹, XIX¹, XXVII¹, XXXI, XL.
[102] The reader pursuing the study of this music further may welcome being forewarned that the MS referred to as Bibl. Est. A X I, 11 in DTO XL etc. is identical with the one called Bibl. Est. Cod. VI H 15 in StaiR etc. and Bibl. Est. lat. 471 in BukD etc. The library has from time to time changed the call-number of the MS. (It has also been called Modena 98.)

Very little is known about the English composers represented in any of these MSS. Selden B 26 contains an anonymous four-part *Ave Regina Celorum* [103] that appears also in a MS at Bologna, where it is attributed to Leonel,[104] as well as an anonymous three-part *Beata Mater* ascribed to Dunstable in versions at Modena and Munich.[105] The only composer named in the Bodleian MSS is one Childe, about whom nothing is known. The following composers are represented in the Old Hall MS: Cooke, Aleyn, Sturgeon, Burell, Damett, Roy Henry (there are two attractive pieces by him), Byttering (Gyttering), J. Tyes, Excetre, Leonel, Forest, Pycard, Rowland (Rowlard), Queldryk, Jervays, Fonteyns, Oliver, R. Chyrbury, W. Typp, Swynford, Pennard, Lambe, and Mayshuet. There is also an anonymous transcript of a motet by Dunstable. Damett, whose compositions are among the finest in the collection, may be the Thomas Damett who was a canon of Windsor from 1430–36.[106] John Aleyn may be the J. Alani who composed a motet, *Sub Arthuro plebs,* found in Chantilly 1047 (*cf.* p. 358), and also in Bologna Liceo musicale Cod. 37—a piece in which many otherwise unknown English composers are mentioned by name.[107] Alani has been identified with a Jean Alain who was in the service of the Duke of Lancaster in 1396.[108] Mayshuet may be the same as the Mayhuet de Joan represented in the Chantilly MS. If these last two identifications are correct, they would seem to indicate a close musical relationship, also at this period, between France and England.[109] Leonel is represented also in the Trent Codices, in Bologna Univ.-Bibl. Cod. 2216 and Liceo musicale Cod. 37, and in Modena Bibl. Est. A X I, 11; next to Dunstable he seems to have been the best-known English composer on the Continent; he was apparently older than Dunstable.[110] In addition to Leonel, Forest, and a number of Anonymi (Anglicus, Anglicanus, De Anglia), the Trent Codices mention the Englishmen Bedingham, Johannes Benet (also represented in Bologna Liceo mus. 37 and Univ.-Bibl. 2216), Standley (Sandley in Modena Bibl. Est. A X I, 11), Gervasius de Anglia (probably the Jervays of the Old Hall MS; also in Bologna Liceo mus. 37), Ricardus Markham, Sorbi, and, most distinguished of them all, John Dunstable.

[103] Facsimile in StaE I, pl. 42–43; transcription in II, 88.
[104] The composition also appears twice, anonymously, in the Trent Codices. A transcription based on the 3 Continental versions is printed in DTO VII, 210.
[105] Facsimile of the Selden B 26 version in StaE I, pl. 44; transcription in II, 98. Transcription after the Modena MS and one of the Trent Codices in DTO VII, 94. In the Trent MS, Dunstable's name is crossed out and Binchois's is substituted.
[106] RamsO III, xiif.
[107] For a facsimile of this motet, see WolfMS, pl. 30–31. It is transcribed in DTO XL, 9.
[108] *Chantilly. Le Cabinet des livres. Manuscrits, tome II,* 1900, 281. RamsO II, vii and III, xii footnote, suggest that John Aleyn the composer may have been the similarly named canon of Windsor who died in 1373.
[109] Further concerning such an interrelationship, see Handschin, *Zur Geschichte von Notre Dame,* in Acta, IV (1932), 52, footnote.
[110] KorteH, 23f, 41.

Some fifty-odd compositions,[111] two books from his library and two epitaphs, one of which gives the date of his death—these are all that remain to us of a composer whom his contemporaries ranked among their leaders. Conjecture has placed his birth as early as *c.* 1370.[112] The epitaph in the church of St. Stephen's Walbrook,[113] where apparently he was buried, shows that this musician who was also an astronomer and mathematician died in 1453. One of his precious astronomical books, the MS in St. John's College, Cambridge (the other, transcribed with his own hand, is in the Bodleian Library in Oxford), gives us almost the only other clue to the events of his life.[114] On the Cambridge MS is written "Iste libellus pertinebat Johanni Dunstable cñ duci Bedfordie musico." This, however, tells us much. It explains why the bulk of his surviving works is preserved in Continental MSS, for John, Duke of Bedford, became regent of France in 1422; on the death of his brother Henry V, married the Duke of Burgundy's sister in 1423; and remained in France until his death in 1435. It was under his regency that Joan of Arc was burned at the stake. If Dunstable was a member of the musical establishment which we know the Duke maintained in Paris [115] it would help to account for his wide renown and for the spread of his compositions. Significant, too, in the light of the Duke's Burgundian marriage, are the references to Dunstable in the poem "Le Champion des Dames," written about 1440 by Martin le Franc and dedicated to the Duke of Burgundy. The poet declares, with regard to the Burgundians Dufay and Binchois:

. . . *ilz* . . . . . . *ont prins de la contenance* *Angloise et ensuy Dunstable* *Pour quoi merveilleuse plaisance* *Rend leur chant joyeuse et notable.*[116]	*The English guise they wear with* *grace,* *They follow Dunstable aright,* *And thereby have they learned apace* *To make their music gay and bright.*

Notwithstanding this, the style of Dunstable's later works shows that he was not too proud to be in his turn influenced by the technique of his younger contemporary Dufay; indeed, the musical relationship between the two men has been compared to that between Haydn and Mozart.[117] Thus, in Dunstable's *Ave maris stella*,[118] there are passages definitely in fauxbourdon style.

---

[111] For a list of Dunstable's compositions, see the thematic catalogue in StaiR, 8 and its revision in BukD, 111. This catalogue includes a fairly large number of compositions which in some MSS are attributed to Dunstable but in others to Leonel. In fact, some writers have been inclined to believe that Dunstable is identical with Leonel (*cf.* FiK, 24). Bukofzer discusses this question (BukD, 105) and decides that he is not, partly on the grounds that Hothby, only slightly later, mentions both names as belonging to different men. See also KorteH, 41.
[112] EinSH, 50.   [113] Both epitaphs are printed in Grove II, 112 and MaclD, 235, 247.
[114] For what may be another, see FloodR, 227. *Cf.* also Grove II, 110ff.
[115] A. Pirro. *La Musique à Paris sous le règne de Charles VI*, 1930, 35.
[116] BorG, 85; etc.   [117] BukD, 106.   [118] WolfS, 36.

The insular motets dating from the last decades of the 14th century [119] retain the *cantus-firmus* technique of that century: the borrowed melody is again performed in longish tones in the tenor, which repeats the melody several times, occasionally varying the measure upon repetition (*cf.* p. 354).

The early 14th-century leaves preserving Example 124 and *Petrum Cephas Ecclesiae* are bound, in Oxford Bodl. e Museo 7, together with other matter, including several leaves of music inscribed in the second half of the century. These contain a few motets in which the strength of French influence on English music of the period is shown, not only by means of their musical style but, in two of them, through the combination of French and Latin texts. At this stage of English history, of course, the presence of a French text in an English MS would not necessarily mean that the work containing it was Continental and had merely been copied. There is evidence, however, that one of these two motets did actually appear in a French MS that has failed to survive.[120]

In the following example from the Old Hall MS, the manner of writing is so closely akin to that of the conductus that a modern scholar actually calls pieces of its type conducti.[121] The lowest voice flows along with the other voices, the form-producing device of tenor-repetition is lacking, and there is a single text. But *Beata progenies* is not actually a conductus, for it contains a borrowed melody (*cf. Sarum Antiphonal,* 518) in the middle voice (*cf.* p. 404). The piece is a noble one, however little progressiveness its general style may display.

EXAMPLE 125. *Beata progenies*—Leonel Power (after RamsO I, 156).

[119] Such as those printed in StaE and in RamsO III.
[120] *Cf.* BesS I, 222. Portions of the two motets are transcribed in StaE II, 32 and 37.
[121] BesS I, 225. The compositions in question are the polyphonic antiphons (including our Example 125) printed in RamsO I, where they are termed motets.

"Blessed progeny whence Christ was born. How glorious is the Virgin who gave birth to the king of heaven!"

In an attractive composition by Damett, contained in the same MS, *Beata Dei genetrix Maria*,[122] which also has a single text, we find a mixture—sometimes simultaneous, sometimes successive—of $\frac{6}{2}$ and $\frac{3}{1}$ rhythms (*cf.* p. 274), a mixture destined to become a popular device with composers, both insular and Continental, throughout the 15th and 16th centuries. This piece offers some interesting examples of syncopation. We have, of course, already found striking examples of syncopation in French 14th-century music, but the English seem to have made use of it at an early date, since, in theoretical writing, we encounter it for the first time in the treatise of Robert de Handlo, dating from 1326 (*cf.* p. 344).[123] Among the three-part pieces in Old Hall that have the main melody in the middle voice and show, like Example 125, the influence of the gymel tradition, is the antiphon *Regali ex progenie* by Fonteyns.[124]

Thus such English vocal polyphony, dating from roughly *c.* 1350–1425, as is preserved in English MSS reveals, in the main, no very striking structural advance over earlier French music. The English contribution, as shown by such polyphony, seems to consist largely in the invention of melodies more pleasing than the French to ears trained chiefly on 18th- and 19th-century music, and in the working out of smoother voice-leading—this last achieved by the characteristic progression of the parts in thirds and sixths.

A more advanced style, on the whole, appears in the motets (that is, both in motets in the old sense and in related works included under the same designation) attributed to English composers in Continental MSS. The full significance of the work of the English school on the Continent, however, can be understood only in relation to that of contemporary Continental composers, which we cannot discuss in this volume. These English pieces [125] perhaps date mainly from the second quarter of the 15th century.

In dealing principally with them (but also with some insular pieces), and particularly with the works of Dunstable, including his Mass movements and secular music as well as his motets, Bukofzer [126] has defined seven classes, of which the first five are already familiar to us through examples we have encountered in earlier music, English or Continental or both. These types are: (1) English discant, (2) the style with unborrowed melodies and with the top part dominating, (3) the style showing gymel influence, (4) the isorhythmic motet, (5) the motet that applies figuration to a borrowed melody in the top part,

---

[122] RamsO I, 165.
[123] CouS I, 398; *cf.* WolfG I, 132. The arresting syncopation in *Beata viscera* as transcribed in HughW, 108, however, seems not to be justified by the MS, which appears to warrant nothing more than a six-three chord, all the members of which move simultaneously to a root-fifth-octave chord.
[124] RamsO I, 159. The *cantus*, in the middle voice, may be found in *Liber Usualis*, edition of 1934, p. 1626.
[125] Most of those that are published are printed in DTO VII and XL.   [126] In BukJ, 22ff.

(6) the declamation motet, and (7) the double-structure style. (A single Dunstable example of fauxbourdon has already been mentioned.)

Type 1 is illustrated in Dunstable by an *Ascendit Christus* [127] (as well as some Mass items [128]). This consists of four sections alternately in two- and three-part writing. The tenor of the three-part sections has the melody (but not the text) of the *Alma Redemptoris Mater,* which is allowed to flow along naturally, without being subjected to the special rhythmic treatment normally applied to a motet tenor. The position and treatment of the *cantus* provide the only chief characteristic of English discant that remains intact, the schematic organizing in $\frac{6}{3}$ progressions now being abandoned in favor of a free flowing of the parts, although such progressions still appear occasionally. Compositions of this sort represent the height of the development of English discant.

We encountered type 2, with its *ballade* characteristics, for the first time in Chapter 12. In Dunstable this is represented by several Mass movements,[129] in a general way recalling the *ballade*-Mass settings in the Apt and Ivrea MSS.

The only example of type 3 in Dunstable is his *Crux fidelis.*[130] As in the *Ascendit Christus,* we find in this work contrast in the number of parts in different sections. Such contrast has been noted by us so often in insular works that its systematic use may well be of insular origin. It occurred in the dance in Bodley Douce 139 (*cf.* p. 243); shifting from two to three parts was found present in Wolfenbüttel 677, occurring at the end of some insular pieces (*cf.* p. 394); and such shifting may be observed also in the Worcester MSS.[131] It appears also in some secular pieces of the Dunstable period (*cf.* p. 422).

A fine example of type 4 is Dunstable's four-part motet *Veni sancte Spiritus,*[132] which carried his fame throughout Europe and is cited as late as 1496 by Gafori in his *Practica musicae.*[133] As texts Dunstable has used those of the hymn *Veni Creator Spiritus* and the sequence *Veni sancte Spiritus.* The *cantus firmus,* in the tenor, consists of the second and third phrases of the *Veni Creator Spiritus;* the top part sings the whole of the *Veni sancte Spiritus* text; the second part has a trope to it; and the countertenor sings all but the doxology-stanza of the *Veni Creator Spiritus* text. Musically the motet falls into three sections; in each the *cantus firmus* is given complete, the second phrase repeating the rhythmic scheme of the first; and the tenor time-values obtaining in the first section are reduced by one-third in the

[127] DTO XL, 53.
[128] E. g., the three-part sections of the Sanctus in DTO XXXI, 111; the Agnus in DTO XXXI, 113.
[129] E. g., DTO XXXI, 107; BukJ, 24.   [130] DTO VII, 183; see BukJ, 25.
[131] See, for example, HughW, 53. Other Dunstable examples are a *Salve Regina* (DTO VII, 191) and the Sanctus and Agnus mentioned in footnote 128. For an example by Benet, see WolfG III, 181.
[132] DTO VII, 203 (the interpolated rest is unnecessary; see BesS I, 236). This motet appears anonymously in the Old Hall MS (RamsO II, 66).
[133] *Lib.* 2, *Cap.* 7.

second section and by an additional third in the third section. Within each section the rhythmic repetition in the tenor in the second half goes hand in hand with a more or less exact repetition in the other parts of the rhythmic patterns they had in the first half, thus rendering the motet isorhythmic. The correspondence is most exact in the countertenor and least exact in the second voice, where it is only occasionally present in the middle section. In the top part it is fairly exact, but there are considerable divergences of detail.[134]

Type 5 is distinguished by the placing of the *cantus firmus* in the highest voice and the coloring of it by elaborate figuration—much the sort of thing we encountered in Chapter 12 in connection with the *Messe de Tournai*. This colored discant style was successfully developed in the early 15th century by Dufay, and it may be from him that Dunstable learned it. Of this type, in the latter's work, are his *Regina celi letare* [135] and *Ave regina celorum*.[136]

Some scholars have advanced the theory that motets in which no pre-existent melody can be traced may well contain borrowed melodies colored beyond recognition (in which event the compositions could belong to type 3 or type 5).[137] Among the motets in which no pre-existent melodies can be detected are one of Dunstable's two settings of the *Salve regina* text [138] and Forest's *Qualis est dilectus*.[139] These, however, seem to have actually been freely invented,[140] and they have, for this reason and because they display three other traits regarded as characteristic of type 6, been cited [141] as examples of it. These other traits are: musical rhythm strongly influenced by the declamation of the text; handling of the declamation in such a way that all the parts move together in chordal fashion; equal importance of all parts.

Another piece offered as an example of type 6 is Dunstable's *Quam pulchra es*.[142] There is, however, little except harmonic texture to distinguish a piece like this from an old conductus, so far as general character is concerned. The style is preponderantly note against note, there are melismas at the ends of several of the phrases (all the parts moving pretty much together), there is only one text, and there seems to be no pre-existent tenor. If this piece and the conductus-like works in the Old Hall MS that we have referred to

[134] For further analysis, see RieH II[1], 113; KorteH, 23. The latter analyzes also Dunstable's 3-part *Veni sancte Spiritus* (DTO VII, 201). Another isorhythmic motet by Dunstable that lends itself well to analysis is to be found in DTO XL, 36. There are, in all, 12 isorhythmic motets by Dunstable, 4 of which are in 4 parts.
[135] DTO XL, 49.   [136] DTO XL, 50.   [137] *Cf.* OrelE, 70.   [138] DTO, XL, 57.
[139] RamsO II, 77.
[140] Among features tending to raise the presumption that a borrowed plainsong is not the basis of a melodic line are: (1) wide melodic leaps, (2) frequent broken-triad passages, and (3) frequent immediate repetitions (unless the work is a Magnificat setting or some other work involving formulas of the psalm-tone type; while repetitions may sometimes occur in plainsong melodies not of this type—as on the word *surgere* in the *Alma Redemptoris Mater*—extensive use of them is not characteristic.)   [141] BukD, 107.
[142] Facsimile after Bologna Lic. Mus. 37 in EEH I, pl. 59–60; transcriptions in DTO VII, 190; ScherG, 29; Grove II, 112.

can properly be called motets at all—and it would seem that they may be, since in Bibl. Estense, A X I, 11, the line *"Hic incipiunt motetti"* is followed by a group of pieces that includes *Quam pulchra es* itself [143]—they would appear to indicate that, whereas in France the conductus style had declined during the 14th century when, as the Worcester pieces show, it continued alive in England, it eventually became merged in the latter country with the motet. If this is true, the English may have been responsible for the free motet, without polytextuality or a pre-existent *cantus firmus;* though as a result of a merger (*cf.* p. 398) that was perhaps in turn the result of their conservatism rather than of any venturesomeness. It is interesting to note that while, in the 14th century, it was possible for declamation of the text to receive attention in the top part of a *ballade* and in all the upper parts of a motet, it was only in the conductus that such attention could be given to all the parts. We may see here additional evidence of a merger, evidence showing that, if the English do indeed deserve credit for the declamation motet, the type took form under the influence of a precedent originating on the Continent.

Whatever may be the traits of pieces like *Quam pulchra es,* it is characteristic of most motets assigned to type 6 that all their voices display a greater degree of rhythmic independence. Perhaps it is not too much to conjecture that such more representative pieces show the results of the merger in the course of development. Polytextuality and borrowed tenor may be gone, but there is no faithful adherence in these works to the chordal style of the conductus. The polyphonic character of the motet is much in evidence, and the term "motet" is therefore not out of place for them. The impetus towards rich and rhythmically unhampered polyphony, which, as we have seen, was at least latent in 13th-century organum, has here reached a point where it needs only the addition of a highly developed technique, such as the Continental composers of the 15th century were to achieve, to blossom into the plastic style of the 16th-century motet.

Type 7 has the *appearance* of involving the simultaneous employment of *two* borrowed melodies in a single extended piece, one in the tenor and the other in the discant. Even should it never be possible to demonstrate conclusively that the unidentified discant melodies in question are pre-existent, a distinctive type is represented by the music under discussion, since we have here compositions in which *two* parts jointly form the substructure upon which the composition is built. The melodies of both parts may appear in one guise or another, in their respective voices, in various sections of the piece.[144] The tenor melody is normally taken from the plainsong repertoire; it is sometimes colored but more often not; and it proceeds in longish time-values. The origin of the discant melody is uncertain, but that it is pre-existent is indi-

---

[143] I am indebted to Dr. Bukofzer for this item of information.
[144] For further details, see FiK, 27ff.

cated, so Ficker claims, by the fact that the melody is capable of being repeated with variations—a treatment allegedly reserved to *cantus firmi*.[145] The same scholar suggests that the discant may be a colored development of a secular melody. The combination of two (or more) pre-existing melodies had been employed in the 13th-century motet (*cf.* p. 317), but it does not seem to have been used in compositions for the Mass before the 15th century, and, in any event, seems in the 13th century to have had no real structural significance but to have been a mere stunt. This double-structure technique may possibly have been invented by Dunstable himself. It became the leading technique of Mass composition in the 15th century.

Besides pieces falling definitely within one or another of the seven categories, there are others, having a special interest of their own, that combine features of more than one. Thus the three-part sections in the following *Alma Redemptoris Mater* are predominantly in *ballade* style but occasionally contain reminiscences of Hermannus Contractus's melody, producing a sort of free fantasia on fragments of it and, in the process, introducing the chief characteristic of type 5, present also in the *Duo* section. Dotted brackets call attention to snatches of imitation, one of them in three parts. The notes marked + are associated with the same words in the chant melody as they are here; those marked x are, in that melody, associated with slightly earlier words. It will be observed that the three parts do not all bear the same signatures. Different signatures in different parts are not rare in 15th-century music, but an examination of this point would be more appropriate in a discussion of such music generally rather than in one confined to English music.[146]

EXAMPLE 126. *Alma Redemptoris Mater*—Dunstable (after DTO XL, 51).

[145] For the arguments in favor of regarding these unidentified discants as *cantus firmi*, see FiK, 31. Of course, it might be contended *contra* that the very fact that this treatment is here accorded to unidentified melodies indicates that it was not, at least at this period, limited to *cantus firmi*.
[146] The reader might, however, refer to ApelP, among other writings on the subject.

For a translation see p. 128.

English polyphonic settings of the various movements of the Ordinary of the Mass—like English motets which, in this section, have thus far been our main concern—generally reveal conservatism on the part of the composers represented only in insular MSS. But venturesomeness of a sort is shown by some such settings in the Old Hall MS. Thus the first of Typp's four settings of the Sanctus [147] treats the plainsong [148] freely, not only by omitting notes here and adding them there, thus applying the time-honored English practice of varying the melody (cf. pp. 394f), but by not confining it to one voice. In fact, each of the three voices sometimes has the plainsong (this statement does not imply that imitation is present, but merely that a portion of the plainsong

[147] RamsO III, 4.   [148] To be found in *Liber Usualis,* edition of 1934, 21.

is now in one voice and another portion is later in another voice) and at one point a portion of the plainsong is even transposed up a fifth. An unusually elaborate composition is Pycard's ostensibly six-part Gloria.[149] The lowest part has an eight-note fragment of plainsong repeated in *ostinato*-fashion throughout the piece. The next two parts, jointly duplicating the lowest, divide the same theme in hocket. The fourth part from the bottom has its own short *ostinato* figure. The two top parts are much livelier than the others and contain many passages of canon. It will be noticed that the work is actually in only four parts. The canon over what is essentially a two-part *pes* recalls the *Sumer*-Rota. A Gloria by Leonel [150] is partly in two parts, partly in four, and partly in five. The old device of musical rhyme is found in Excetre's Sanctus.[151] The chromaticism illustrated in such pieces as Chyrbury's Benedictus and Agnus [152] by no means necessarily represents a spirit of "modernism": we have found chromaticism not only in 14th-century France and Italy but in the Robertsbridge MS (*cf.* p. 407). The c-natural immediately followed by c-sharp at the beginning of Chyrbury's Agnus, however, is decidedly arresting. Rhythmical variety is interestingly represented, but this, as the *Puellare gremium* (*cf.* p. 397) has shown us, is in itself nothing new.

Compositions for the Mass attributed to English composers in the Continental MSS, however, display new features in addition to the important one already mentioned in connection with our discussion of the seventh type exemplified in the works of Dunstable. Of especial interest are a Gloria and a Credo by this composer,[153] which, although they apply the old motet technique to the *cantus-firmus* in the tenor, also illustrate something new: both pieces are based on the same tenor (*Jesu Christe*). The borrowed melody is repeated once in each movement, thus appearing four times in all. This adaptation of the old motet technique to successive sections of the Ordinary doubtless indicates an attempt on the part of the composer to combine different sections of the Mass into a unified whole. Indeed Dunstable carried the process of unification still further, as did also Leonel.[154]

A distinctive feature of some English Gloria and Credo settings is the division of the text between the two upper voices. These voices sing different portions of the text simultaneously, the composer's aim apparently being to avoid too extended a composition in setting the longest texts in the Ordinary.[155]

English composers on the Continent were among the first to write poly-

---

[149] RamsO I, 92.
[150] RamsO I, 60.
[151] RamsO III, 90.   [152] RamsO III, 22, 116.
[153] DTO XXXI, 114ff.   [154] *Cf.* BukJ, 28.
[155] *Cf.* FiF, 40. For a discussion of later developments of this practice, see p. xxxiii of the introduction to the *Missa "O quam suavis,"* ed. by H. B. Collins, 1927.

phonic settings of the Magnificat; one by Dunstable survives in Modena Bibl. Est. A X I, 11.[156]

Insular MSS afford some idea of what the secular polyphony of the English was like at home. A parchment roll at Trinity College, Cambridge, dating from the first half of the 15th century, contains a group of carols and other short, secular compositions in two and three parts.[157] Among these is the famous *Deo gratias Anglia,*[158] written in celebration of the English victory at Agincourt (1415). This work, partly for two voices and partly for three, displays, in the three-part section, the English discant style. A survival of the conductus influence may be seen in the two-part song *I Have set my Hert so hye* (*c.* 1425),[159] in which passages of wordless music separate phrases that set text. Such melismas are found also in the three-part drinking song, *Tappster, dryngker, fylle another ale* (*c.* 1450) [160] and in other contemporary part-songs. In the very beautiful three-part song *Go Hert Hurt with Adversite* (*c.* 1450) [161] the top voice is the only one with a text; the two lower voices frequently cross and contain many thirds and sixths. The general style is that of the *ballade,* as is that of *Wel were hym that wyst,* preserved in the early 15th-century Cambridge MS Univ. Add. 5943.[162] The pieces in this MS show a marked preference for the form *abb.* (It obtains in *I rede that thou be, This Yule the beste red, Wel were hym that wyst, Pater noster most of might, Ave Maria I say to that blassyd mayde,* etc.) The MS contains 2 rounds, several French pieces, a partial setting of the Gloria, etc. The two-part *Glad and blithe mote ye be* (*c.* 1450) [163] is interesting as an English version of the 11th-century sequence *Laetabundus* (*cf.* p. 189). The Latin words are retained for the final lines of each stanza except the last two. The original melody is colored and placed in the upper voice.

Secular music that may be English is represented in Continental MSS, in part, by three 3-voice pieces attributable to Dunstable: *O Rosa bella,* which, appearing in seventeen MSS, seems to have been especially popular, *Durez ne puis,* and *Puisque m'amour.*[164] These are examples of the polyphonic *chanson,* i. e., of the pieces that continued the tradition of the polyphonic secular

---

[156] For a list of other early English polyphonic Magnificats, see IllM, *Chronologisches Verzeichnis,* 6f.

[157] Printed, with not wholly dependable transcriptions, in FullerC.

[158] FullerC, frontispiece (facsimile) and 14; for a slightly different version, found in a MS at Oxford, see StaE I, pl. 66 and transcriptions in II, 128 and OH II, 7.

[159] Facsimile in StaE I, pl. 20; transcription in II, 51.

[160] Facsimile in StaE I, pl. 96; transcription in II, 177.

[161] Facsimile in StaE I, pl. 32; transcription in II, 68.

[162] Facsimiles and transcriptions of the musical contents of this MS are included in MeyM.

[163] Facsimile in StaE I, pl. 70–71; transcription in II, 134.

[164] Although most modern scholars name Dunstable as the composer of *O Rosa bella,* it may be well to point out (as did Wooldridge) that it is attributed to him in only one MS—Bibl. Vat. Urbini lat. 1411. Fifteen other versions are anonymous, and the remaining one is attributed to Bedingham (this is not a reference to the *concordantiae,* to be mentioned presently). *Puisque m'amour* (ScherG, 30; DTO VII, 254) is also of questionable authenticity. It appears in 3 MSS but is attributed to Dunstable in only one. The other two versions are anonymous.

compositions of the 14th century (especially the French contributions), the new works mostly retaining the old formal characteristics of the *rondeau* and *ballade,* but differing, in content, as other 15th-century music differed from 14th-century music.[165] The chief early 15th-century examples of the polyphonic *chanson* were the work not of Englishmen but of Dufay and Binchois. The Italian text of *O Rosa bella* is by Leonardo Giustiniani. Although there is nothing to show that Dunstable ever actually set foot in Italy, there is more in the compositions ascribed to him than the mere use of an Italian text to indicate that he felt Italian influence to at least some extent. This influence, demonstrable in the career of Dufay, gave that composer's music a clarity of texture somewhat similar to that of the Italians—and of Dunstable—and contrasting with the texture of the compositions of Machaut and his followers. This clarity in the writing of both Dunstable and Dufay results from more than the English chordal tendency alone.

Perhaps the most interesting versions of *O Rosa bella* are the two that appear in Trent Codices 89 and 90. In each of these, three additional voices (*concordantiae*) are supplied together with the three voices attributed to Dunstable, the performers apparently being at liberty to make their own polyphonic combinations by adding to the original parts any or all of the three *concordantiae* in one set and a selection of one or two from the other. The three optional parts in Trent 89 seem to have come from the pen of Bedingham (they are marked *"concordantiae ut posuit Bedingham"*); the three in Trent 90 are called *Gimel* (here meaning only "second voice"), *alius Gimel,* and *secundus contratenor.*[166]

An anonymous three-part *chanson, Princhesse of youth,* is an example of a *chanson* with English text that has survived from the 15th century in a Continental MS (*Go Hert Hurt with Adversite* and *Wel were hym,* mentioned above as appearing in insular MSS and described as being in *ballade* style, are *ipso facto* in *chanson* style also), this being at the Escorial.[167] A MS probably of Burgundian origin contains three more English *chansons* of the period.[168]

[165] "Chanson," as used here in a generic sense, has no connection with the word, as used in a specific sense, on p. 229.

[166] All 9 parts are printed together in DTO VII, 229. The editors give as their belief that only one *concordantia* is to be added at a time. However, their transcription of the basic composition contains several errors (which may be found by comparison with the facsimile printed in the same volume) and the correction of these removes many difficulties standing in the way of satisfactory combinations. LedH, 359ff, gives a new transcription, correcting DTO errors not only in the basic piece but in the *concordantiae,* with the result that at least all the Bedingham *concordantiae* can be played simultaneously in combination with the original. For a discussion of this *chanson,* see StaiR. An energetic effort is made in RaphO, 170ff, to prove the piece a *ballata.* This effort is based on B. Wiese's reading of the text (reprinted also in StaiR, 6) which is at variance with the Trent MSS (*cf.* DTO VII, 285). According to information kindly supplied by Dr. Bukofzer, however, the piece is shown, in 2 earlier MSS, to have actually been conceived as a *ballata.*

[167] Transcription and discussion in BukC.

[168] The 3 *chansons* are described in Manfred Bukofzer, *An Unknown Chansonnier of the 15th Century* (the Mellon *Chansonnier* at Yale University), in MQ, XXVIII (1942) 24f; one *chanson* is printed on p. 42ff. Further concerning English vocal secular polyphony of the period, see OH II, 336.

424 Vitalizing Effect of English Harmonic Tendencies

The enormous influence exerted by English methods on Continental voice-leading is evident in the widespread adoption of the fauxbourdon style about the middle of the 15th century. The dissatisfaction with the old interval theory, felt when English discant was found pleasing, was now replaced by an apparently unconscious desire to bring some order into the progressions of chords, to relate them somehow to each other, as chords. It is possible to see, in English, as well as Continental compositions of the first half of the 15th century, the first attempts at what we should call functional harmony. If we regard simultaneously sounding tones of different pitch in this music as vertical phenomena (an attitude perhaps justified by the very nature of fauxbourdon) rather than as more or less accidental results of the combination of melodies, we notice here and there a succession of chords that seems to be governed by, or grouped about, some nodal harmony, generally that of the tonic or dominant. Such passages may be found, for example, in some of Leonel's pieces.[169] Dunstable's compositions, examined from the same standpoint, reveal a much more highly developed feeling for harmonic relationships.[170] Yet in no case, at this period, is there any question of a systematic approach towards harmony in the modern sense, or even of the awareness of the possibility of building such a system. Such relationships as may be found are of the simplest sort and seem entirely instinctive.

The vitalizing power of the English method of voice-leading and of the various other new technical elements, best exemplified in the works of Dunstable, makes his period one of the outstanding ones in the history of composition. The music of this period was in its time at least as much entitled to be called "new" as was, in its time, the music actually so designated early in the 14th century. When this younger music came, "and it came. . . not . . . from the followers, confined by formalism, of the great 14th-century Frenchmen and Italians, . . . but led by artistically fresh English forces, there began a new epoch of musical history; once more, as a somewhat later writer [Tinctoris], a leader in the field of theory, called it, an 'ars nova.' "[171]

[169] E. g., his hymn *Ave maris stella* (DTO XXVII, 78); see the analysis in KorteH, 7ff.
[170] See, for example, the harmonic analysis of *Veni sancte Spiritus* in KorteH, 23ff.
[171] LudG, 293f.

Bibliography

The bibliographies for individual chapters are presented in two parts—the first listing books and articles, the second listing music collections and facsimiles. When a chapter is divided into sections of any considerable length, each section has its own bibliography.

Usually when a work has on the whole no connection with the chapter in which it is mentioned and is referred to only incidentally (especially if it is not primarily about music), the footnotes give the complete title instead of a symbol and the work does not appear in the bibliography.

To conserve space, works with long titles do not appear in full in the bibliography of every chapter in which they are referred to, and, instead, the bibliography of a given chapter may refer to the bibliography of another chapter for the full title.

Symbols in bold type indicate important works. But the fact that the symbol of a work is not in bold type in the bibliography of a particular chapter may mean, not that the work is unimportant, but only that it is not important in that chapter.

PERIODICALS, SERIES, ENCYCLOPEDIC WORKS, ETC.

REFERRED TO BY SYMBOL THROUGHOUT THE BOOK, AS WELL AS IN THE FOLLOWING BIBLIOGRAPHIES FOR INDIVIDUAL CHAPTERS WITHOUT BEING SEPARATELY LISTED THERE

Acta	*Acta Musicologica.* Quarterly magazine of the International Society for Musical Research. 1928– .
AdlerF	*Studien zur Musik-Geschichte. Festschrift für Guido Adler zum 75. Geburtstag*, 1930.
H	Adler, Guido. *Handbuch der Musikgeschichte*, 1st Ed., 1924; 2nd ed. (2 vols.), 1929. Written by Adler with collaboration of outstanding specialists. References are to the 2nd ed.
AfMF	*Archiv für Musikforschung.* 1936– .
AfMW	*Archiv für Musikwissenschaft.* Oct. 1918–Sept. 1927.
DTO	*Denkmäler der Tonkunst in Österreich.* 83 volumes. Editor-in-Chief, Guido Adler. 1894–1938.
EC	*Encyclopédie de la musique et dictionnaire du conservatoire.* Ed. A. Lavignac and L. de la Laurencie. *Partie I: Histoire de la musique* appears in 5 vols.; *Partie II: Technique, pédogogie et esthetique*, in 6 vols.; *Partie III: Dictionnaire alphabétique* has not appeared, but a partial index has been compiled by Robert Bruce for the Music Library Association. (1913–31)
Grove	*Grove's Dictionary of Music and Musicians*, 1st Ed. 1879–89; 3rd ed. (5 vols. and supplement), 1928, edited by H. C. Colles. References are to the 3rd ed.
M&L	*Music & Letters.* 1920– .
MAn	*The Musical Antiquary.* Oct. 1909–July 1913.
MfMG	*Monatshefte für Musikgeschichte.* 1869–1905.
MQ	*The Musical Quarterly.* 1915– .
OH	*Oxford History of Music*, 7 vols. plus unnumbered Introductory Vol., 1901–34. Vols. 1 and 2 (*The Polyphonic Period*) are by H. E. Wooldridge. Vols. 3–7 lie outside of the range of the present book. 2nd ed. of Vol. 1 issued in 1929, and of Vol. 2 in 1932. Our references are to this edition.
PMA	*Proceedings of the Musical Association.* 1874– .
PubAMD	*Publikationen älterer Musik . . . der deutschen Musikgesellschaft.* 1926– .
RdM	*Revue de musicologie.* Originally entitled *Bulletin de la société française de musicologie.* 1917– .
RieF	*Riemann-Festschrift. Gesammelte Schriften . . . überreicht von Freunden und Schülern*, 1909.
RM	*Revue musicale.* 1920– .

SIM   *Sammelbände der internationalen Musikgesellschaft.* Quarterly magazine of the International Musical Society, Oct. 1899–Sept. 1914.
SzMW   *Studien zur Musikwissenschaft.* Issued under the editorship of Guido Adler, in conjunction with DTO.
TSG   *Tribune de St. Gervais.* Jan. 1895–Dec. 1922.
VfMW   *Vierteljahrsschrift für Musikwissenschaft.* 1884–94.
ZfMW   *Zeitschrift für Musikwissenschaft.* 1918–35.
ZIM   *Zeitschrift der internationalen Musikgesellschaft.* Monthly magazine of the International Music Society. Oct. 1899–Sept. 1914.

CHAPTER 1

BOOKS AND ARTICLES

ClosU   Closson, Ernest. *Une nouvelle série de hautbois égyptiens antiques,* in AdlerF (1930), 17.

─────   Engel, Carl. *Music of the Most Ancient Nations, particularly of the Assyrians, Egyptians, and Hebrews,* 1864.

─────   Farmer, Henry George. *The Organ of the Ancients from Eastern Sources (Hebrew, Syriac, and Arabic),* 1931.

FineM   Finesinger, Sol Baruch. *Musical Instruments in the Old Testament,* 1926. (Reprinted from the Hebrew Union College Annual, III, 1926)

GalpS   Galpin, Francis William. *The Music of the Sumerians and their Immediate Successors, the Babylonians and Assyrians,* 1937.

GasO   Gastoué, Amédée. *Les Origines du chant romain,* 1907.

Grove   *Grove's Dictionary* etc. (Article on Hebrew Music)

GuilS   Guillemin, M. and J. Duchesne. *Sur l'origine asiatique de la cithare grecque,* in *L'Antiquité classique,* IV (1935), 117.

HornS   Hornbostel, Erich M. von and Curt Sachs. *Systematik der Musikinstrumente,* in *Zeitschrift für Ethnologie,* XLVI (1914), 553.

IdJ   Idelsohn, Abraham Z. *Jewish Music,* 1929.

JE   *Jewish Encyclopedia,* 12 vols., 1901–06. (Articles on Cantillation, Music, etc.)

MaN   Machabey, Armand. *Notes de musicologie pré-médiévale,* in RM, XV (1934), 275.

MacH   MacCurdy, George Grant. *Human Origins,* 2 vols., 1926.

MendS   Mendel, Arthur. *Spengler's Quarrel with the Methods of Music History,* in MQ, XX (1934), 131.

─────   Pélagaud, Fernand. *Assyrie-Chaldée: La Musique assyro-babylonienne* (in collaboration with Ch. Virolleaud), in EC, *Partie I,* I, 35.

─────   Pélagaud, Fernand. *Syriens et Phrygiens,* in EC, *Partie I,* I, 49.

PulI   Pulver, Jeffrey. *Israel's Music-Lesson in Egypt,* in *The Musical Times,* LVI (1915), 404.

─────   Pulver, Jeffrey. *The Music of Ancient Egypt,* in PMA, XLVIII (1921), 29.

RosoM   Rosowsky, Solomon. *The Music of the Pentateuch,* in PMA, LX (1934), 38.

SachsA   Sachs, Curt. *Die Musik der Antike,* in Bücken's *Handbuch der Musikwissenschaft Series,* 1928.

B   Sachs, Curt. *The Mystery of the Musical Notation in Babylonia,* Paper read Sept. 14, 1939, before the International Congress of the American Musicological Society, held in New York. (To be published)

D   Sachs, Curt. *Die Musikinstrumente des alten Ägyptens,* 1921.

GW   Sachs, Curt. *Geist und Werden der Musikinstrumente,* 1929.

M   Sachs, Curt. *Altägyptische Musikinstrumente,* in *Der alte Orient,* XXI (1920), *Heft,* 3/4.

N   Sachs, Curt. *Die Namen der altägyptischen Musikinstrumente,* in ZfMW, I (1919), 265.

T   Sachs, Curt. *Die Tonkunst der alten Ägypter,* in AfMW, II (1920), 9.

Z   Sachs, Curt. *Zweiklänge im Altertum,* in WolfF (1929), 168.

─────   Sachs, Curt. *Musik des Altertums,* 1924.

SeeB   Seewald, Otto. *Beiträge zur Kenntnis der steinzeitlichen Musikinstrumente Europas,* 1934.

SpeiR   Speiser, E. A. Reports in *Bulletin of the American Schools of Oriental Research,* No. 64 (Dec. 1936), 4; No. 65 (Feb. 1937), 2; No. 66 (Apr. 1937), 2.

StaM   Stainer, Sir John. *The Music of the Bible;* new edition, containing additional illus-
        trations and supplementary notes by F. W. Galpin, 1914.
WagE   (See bibliography for Chapter 5)
WilP   Wilson, Thomas. *Prehistoric Art,* in *Annual Report of the Board of Regents of the
        Smithsonian Institution . . . for the year ending June 30, 1896* (Report of the
        U.S. National Museum, 1898), 325.

                                MUSIC COLLECTION

IdH   Idelsohn, Abraham Z. *Thesaurus of Hebrew Oriental Melodies,* 10 volumes, 1914–
        32.

CHAPTER 2

AbA   Abert, Hermann. *Antike* (revised by Curt Sachs), in AdlerH I, 35.
L   Abert, Hermann. *Die Lehre vom Ethos in der griechischen Musik,* 1901.
———   Abert, Hermann. *Gesammelte Schriften und Vorträge,* 1929. Includes several papers
        on music of Antiquity.
AudaM   Auda, Antoine. *Les Modes et les tons de la musique,* 1930.
———   Auda, Antoine. *Contribution à l'histoire de l'origine des modes et des tons grégoriens,*
        in *La Revue du chant grégorien,* XXXVI (1932), 33, 72, 105, 130.
BarryG Barry, Phillips. *Greek Music,* in MQ, V (1919), 578.
BédH   Bédart, G. *Note sur "l'Hydraulus,"* in *Le Monde musical,* XLIV (1933), 225.
BellA   Bellermann, Friedrich. *Anonymi Scriptio de Musica. Bachii senioris introductio artis
        musicæ,* 1841.
———   Bellermann, Friedrich. *Die Tonleitern und Musiknoten der Griechen,* 1847.
BelliP Belling, Karl Julius. *Plato's Position with Reference to Art, and in Particular to Music,*
        in *Music,* I (1892), 197, 317.
———   Boeckh, A. *De metris Pindari,* 1811.
BromP   Bromby, J. H. *The ΠΕΡΙ ΜΟΥΣΙΚΗΣ of Plutarch,* 1822.
BüchA   Bücher, Karl. *Arbeit und Rhythmus,* 1st ed., 1847; 6th ed., 1924.
BuryL   Bury, R. G. *Plato. The Laws.* 2 vols., 1926. (In *The Loeb Classical Library*)
CellO   Cellier, Alexandre. *L'Orgue hydraulique d'Aquincum,* in *Le Monde musical,* XLIV
        (1933), 190.
ClemI   Clements, E. *The Interpretation of Greek Music,* in *Journal of Hellenic Studies,*
        XLII (1922), 133.
———   Combarieu, Jules Leon Jean. *Histoire de la musique,* Vol. I, edition of 1930.
———   Daremberg, Charles and E. Saglio. *Dictionnaire des antiquités grecques et romaines.*
        5 vols. 1877–1919. (See articles on Syrinx, Tibia, etc., also ReinD and ReinL *infra*)
DavyL   Davy, Charles. *Letters . . . upon subjects of literature: including a translation of
        Euclid's Section of the canon; and his [recte, Kleonides'] treatise on harmonic; with
        an explanation of the Greek musical modes, according to the doctrine of Ptolemy,*
        1787.
DeiS   Deiters, Hermann. *Studien zu den griechischen Musikern. Ueber das Verhältniss
        des Martianus Cappella zu Aristides Quintilianus,* 1881.
DelN   Del Grande, Carlo. *Nuovo frammento di musica greca in un papiro del Museo del
        Cairo,* in *Aegyptus,* V (1936), 369.
———   Del Grande, Carlo. *Tentativi e possibilità di ricostruzione della musica greca antica,*
        1935.
———   Denniston, J. D. *Some Recent Theories of the Greek Modes,* in *The Classical Quar-
        terly,* VII (1913), 83.
DeubL   Deubner, Ludwig. *Die vierseitige Leier,* in *Mitteilungen des Deutschen Archäolo-
        gischen Instituts (Athenische Abteilung),* LIV (1929), 194.
T   Deubner, Ludwig. *Terpander und die siebensaitige Leier,* in *Berliner Philologische
        Wochenschrift,* L (1930), 1566.
DupuT   Dupuis, J. *Theon de Smyrne. Des Connaissances mathématiques utile pour le lec-
        ture de Platon,* 1892. Translation of HillerT.
DürH   Düring, Ingemar. *Die Harmonielehre des Klaudios Ptolemaios,* 1930.
K   Düring, Ingemar. *Porphyrios Kommentar zur Harmonielehre des Ptolemaios,* 1932.
P   Düring, Ingemar. *Ptolemaios und Porphyrios über die Musik,* 1934.
EB   *Encyclopaedia Britannica* etc. (Articles on Aulos, Cithara, Lyre, etc.)

EmG   Emmanuel, Maurice. *Grèce: Art gréco-romain*, in EC, *Partie I*, I, 377.
H   Emmanuel, Maurice. *Histoire de la Langue Musicale*, 2 vols., 1928.
FarmH   Farmer, Henry George. *Historical Facts for the Arabian Musical Influence*, 1930.
O   Farmer, Henry George. *The Organ of the Ancients from Eastern Sources (Hebrew, Syriac and Arabic)*, 1931.
———   Farmer, Henry George. *Greek Theorists of Music in Arabic Translation*, in *Isis*, XIII (1930), 325.
ForsP   Forster, E. S. *The Works of Aristotle*, Vol. VII, 1927. Contains "Problems Connected with Music."
———   Fortlage, K. *Das musikalische System der Griechen in seiner Urgestalt*, 1847.
FriedM   Friedländer, Paul. *Die Melodie zu Pindars ersten pythischen Gedicht*, 1934.
GevP   Gevaert, François Auguste. *Problèmes musicaux d'Aristote* (in collaboration with C. Vollgraff). 3 parts, 1899–1902. Contains Greek text, French translations, and commentary.
———   Gevaert, François Auguste. *Histoire et théorie de la musique de l'antiquité*. 2 vols., 1875–81. Important even though partly outdated.
GomG   Gombosi, Otto. *New Light on Ancient Greek Music*. Paper read Sept. 14, 1939, before the International Congress of the American Musicological Society held in New York. (To be published)
M   Gombosi, Otto. *The Melody of Pindar's "Golden Lyre,"* in MQ, XXVI (1940), 381.
S   Gombosi, Otto. *Studien zur Tonartenlehre des frühen Mittelalters*, I, in Acta, X (1938), 149.
T   Gombosi, Otto. *Tonarten und Stimmungen der Antiken Musik*, 1939.
GoodP   Goodwin, William W. *Plutarch's Morals translated from the Greek . . . corrected and amended by Wm. W. Goodwin.* 5 vols. Vol. I, 102–35. Contains *Concerning Music*, translated by John Philips.
———   Greif, Francisque. *Études sur la musique antique*, in *Revue des études grecques*, XX–XXIV, XXVI (1908–10, 1912).
GriesN   Grieser, Hans. *Nomos. Ein Beitrag zur griechischen Musikgeschichte*, 1937.
GuilS   (See bibliography for Chapter 1.)
GulD   Gulick, C. B. *Athenaeus of Naucratis. The Deipnosophists*, Vol. 6, 1937. (In *The Loeb Classical Library*)
HamiG   Hamilton, Edith. *The Greek Chorus, Fifteen or Fifty?* in *Theatre Arts Monthly*, XVII (1933), 459.
HarapS   Harap, Louis. *Some Hellenic Ideas on Music and Character*, in MQ, XXIV (1938), 153.
———   Headlam, Walter. *Greek Lyric Metre*, in *Journal of Hellenic Studies*, XXII (1902), 209.
HerG   Herbig, Reinhard. *Griechische Harfen*, in *Mitteilungen des Deutschen Archäologischen Instituts (Athenische Abteilung)*, LIV (1929), 164.
HillerT Hiller, E. Θέωνος Σμυρναίου τῶν κατὰ τὸ μαθηματικὸν χρησίμων εἰς τὴν τοῦ Πλάτωνος ἀναγνωσιν ά-έ, 1878.
HornT   Hornbostel, Erich M. von. *Tonart und Ethos*, in *Festschrift für Johannes Wolf*, (1929), 73.
HowA   Howard, Albert A. *The Aὐλός or Tibia*, in *Harvard Studies in Classical Philology*, IV (1893), 1.
M   Howard, Albert A. *The Mouth-Piece of the Aὐλός*, in *Harvard Studies in Classical Philology*, X (1899), 19.
HydeD   Hyde, Walter Woodburn. *The Recent Discovery of an Inscribed Water-Organ at Budapest*, in *Transactions and Proceedings of the American Philological Association*, LXIX (1938), 392.
JahnA   Jahn, Albert. *Aristidis Quintiliani de musica libri III*, 1882.
JanE   Jan, Karl von. *Die Eisagoge des Bacchius*, in *Lyceum zu Strassburg im Elsass: Beilagen zur Programmen für die Schuljahre 1889–90 und 1890–1.*
M   Jan, Karl von. *Musici Scriptores Graeci et melodiarum veterum quidquid exstat*, 1895; *Supplementum*. 1899.
———   Kralik, R. von. *Altgriechische Musik, Theorie, Geschichte, und sämtliche Denkmäler*, 1903.
LachmW   Lachmann, Robert. *Die Weise vom Löwen und der pythische Nomos*, in *Festschrift für Johannes Wolf* (1929) 97.
LalA   Laloy, Louis. *Aristoxène de Tarente et la musique de l'antiquité*, 1904.
MaE   Machabey, Armand. *Etudes de Musicologie pré-médiévale*, in RdM, XIX (1935), 65, 129, 213, and XX (1936), 1.

———— Machabey, Armand. *Notes de musicologie pré-médiévale*, in RM, XV (1934), 275.

MaasK   Maas, P. and J. Müller-Blattau. *Kircher und Pindar*, in *Hermes*, LXX (1935), 101.

MaclP   MacLean, Charles. *The Principle of the Hydraulic Organ*, in SIM, VI (1905), 183.

MacrH   Macran, Henry S. *The Harmonics of Aristoxenus*, 1902.

MarrouZ   Marrou, Henry Irénée. *Les Fragments musicaux de papyrus de Zenon, Musée du Caire No. 59532*, in *Revue de philologie, de littérature, et d'histoire anciennes*, XIII (1939), 308.

MeiA   Meibom, Marcus. *Antiquae Musicae Auctores Septem*, 2 vols., 1652.

MendS   (See bibliography for Chapter 1.)

MeyerH   Meyer, Bonaventura. 'APMONIA, *Bedeutungsgeschichte des Wortes von Homer bis Aristoteles*, 1931.

MonroM   Monro, D. B. *Modes of Ancient Greek Music*, 1894.

MorelA   Morelli, Jacopo. *Aristidis oratio adversus Leptinem, Libanii declamatio pro Socrate, Aristoxeni rhythmicorum elementorum fragmenta ex bibliotheca Veneta d. Marci*, 1785.

MounG   Mountford, J. F. *Greek Music in the Papyri and Inscriptions*, in J. U. Powell and E. A. Barber, *New Chapters in the History of Greek Literature*, Second Series (1929), 146. Supplement in Third Series (1933), 260.

H   Mountford, J. F. *The Harmonics of Ptolemy and the Lacuna in ii. 14*, in *Transactions of the American Philological Association*, LVII (1926), 71.

L   Mountford, J. F. *The Music of Pindar's "Golden Lyre,"* in *Classical Philology*, XXI (1936), 120.

M   Mountford, J. F. *Greek Music and its relation to modern times*, in *Journal of Hellenic Studies*, XL (1920), 13.

N   Mountford, J. F. *A New Fragment of Greek Music in Cairo*, in *Journal of Hellenic Studies*, LI (1931), 91.

P   Mountford, J. F. *The Musical Scales of Plato's "Republic,"* in *The Classical Quarterly*, XVII (1923), 125.

NagyA   Nagy, Lajos. *Az Aquincumi orgona*, 1934.

———— Pauly, A. F. and Georg Wissowa. *Real-Encyclopädie der klassischen altertumswissenschaft*, 2nd ed., 1894– . 22 vols. to 1936. (See VettP *infra*.)

———— Perrett, Wilfrid. *The Heritage of Greece in Music*, in PMA, LVIII (1932), 85.

———— Perrett, Wilfrid. *Some Questions of Musical Theory*. 2 vols. (1926–8).

PhilM   Phillips, R. C. *Mean Tones, Equal Tempered Tones, and the Harmonic Tetrachords of Claudius Ptolemy*, in *Memoirs and Proceedings of the Manchester Literary and Philosophical Society*, XLVIII (1904), Mem. No. 13.

RectP   Rector, Sergius. *Plato on the Education of the Young*, in *Music*, XXI (1902), 183.

ReinD   Reinach, Théodore. *Musica*, in C. Daremberg and E. Saglio, *Dictionnaire des antiquités grecques et romaines*, III Part 2, p. 2072.

L   Reinach, Théodore. *Lyra*, in C. Daremberg and E. Saglio, *Dictionnaire des antiquités grecques et romaines*, III Part 2, p. 1437.

M   Reinach, Théodore. *La Musique grecque*, 1926.

P   Reinach, Théodore. *Plutarque, de la Musique* (in collaboration with H. Weil), 1900.

RieL   Riemann-Einstein. *Musiklexikon*, etc. (Articles on *Griechische Musik*, etc.)

RomeO   Rome, A. *L'Origine de la prétendue mélodie de Pindare*, in *Les Etudes classiques*, I (1932), 3.

RuelA   Ruelle, Charles Emile. *Le Musicographe Aristide Quintilien*, in SIM, XI (1910), 313.

C   Ruelle, Charles Emile. *Collection des auteurs grecs relatifs à la musique: Alypius et Gaudence . . . Bacchius l'ancien*, 1895.

E   Ruelle, Charles Emile. *Sextus Empiricus contre les musiciens*, in *Revue des études grecques*, XI (1898), 138.

I   Ruelle, Charles Emile. *Collection etc.: Cléonide . . . Introduction harmonique*, 1884.

N   Ruelle, Charles Emile. *Collection etc.: Nicomachus . . . Manuel d'Harmonie et autres textes relatifs à la musique*, 1881.

P   Ruelle, Charles Emile, Hermann Knoellinger, and Joseph Klek. *Aristotelis quae feruntur Problemata physica*, 1922.

S   Ruelle, Charles Emile. *La Solmisation chez les anciens Grecs*, in SIM, IX (1907), 512.

SachsA   Sachs, Curt. (See bibliography for Chapter 1.)

D   Sachs, Curt. (See bibliography for Chapter 1.)

G   Sachs, Curt. *Die griechische Gesangsnotenschrift*, in ZfMW, VII (1924), 1.

HI   Sachs, Curt. *The History of Musical Instruments*, 1940.

SachsI   Sachs, Curt. *Die griechische Instrumentalnotenschrift*, in ZfMW, VI (1924), 289.

Mu   Sachs, Curt. *Musik des Altertums*, 1924.

R   Sachs, Curt. *Real-Lexikon der Musikinstrumente*, 1913. (Articles on Kithara, etc.)

SamoA   Samojloff, A. *Die Alypius'schen Reihen der altgriechischen Tonbezeichnungen*, in AfMW, VI (1924), 4.

SchäfA   Schäfke, Rudolf. *Aristides Quintilianus. Von der Musik.* Translation with commentary, 1937.

SchlesA   Schlesinger, Kathleen. *The Greek Aulos*, 1939.

G   Schlesinger, Kathleen. *The Greek Foundations of the Theory of Music*, in *The Musical Standard*, XXVII (1926), 23, 44, 62, 96, 109, 134, 162, 177, 197; XXVIII (1926), 31, 44.

N   Schlesinger, Kathleen. *Further Notes on Aristoxenus and Musical Intervals*, in *The Classical Quarterly*, XXVII (1933), 88.

P   Schlesinger, Kathleen. *The Precursors of the Violin Family* (Vol. II of *The Instruments of the Modern Orchestra and Early Records of the Precursors of the Violin Family*), 1910.

R   Schlesinger, Kathleen. *Researches into the Origin of the Organs of the Ancients*, in SIM, II (1901), 167.

——————   Schlesinger, Kathleen. *The Significance of Musical Instruments in the Evolution of Music*, in OH Int. (1929), 85.

SonnW   Sonnenschein, Edward Adolf. *What is Rhythm?* 1925.

StilesE   Stiles, Sir Francis Haskins Eyles. *An Explanation of the Modes or Tones in the Ancient Greek Music*, in *Philosophical Transactions of the Royal Society of London*, LI (1760), 695.

StumpfG   Stumpf, Carl. *Geschichte des Konsonanzbegriffes. 1. Die Definition der Consonanz im Altertum*, 1897, in *Abhandlungen der philosophisch-philologischen Classe der königliche Bayerischen Akademie der Wissenschaften*, XXI (1901), 1.

——————   Tillyard, H. J. W. *Instrumental Music in the Roman Age*, in *Journal of Hellenic Studies*, XXVII (1907), 160.

TorrG   Torr, Cecil. *Greek Music*, in OH Int. (1929), 1.

——————   Torr, Cecil. *On the Interpretation of Greek Music*, 1896.

VettA   Vetter, Walter. *Die antike Musik in der Beleuchtung durch Aristoteles*, in AfMF, I (1936), 2.

M   Vetter, Walter. *Musikalische Sinndeutung des antiken Nomos*, in ZfMW, XVII (1935), 289.

P   Vetter, Walter. *Musik*, in A. F. Pauly and G. Wissowa, *Real-Encyclopädie der klassischen Altertumswissenschaft*, 2nd ed., XVI 1, col. 823.

VincN   Vincent, Alexandre J. H. *Notice sur divers manuscrits grecs relatifs à la musique*, in *Notices et extraits des manuscrits de la bibliothèque du roi*, XVI, Part 2, 1847.

WallP   Wallis, John. *Claudii Ptolemaei harmonicarum libri III*, 1682. Greek text with Latin translation and appendix. Contained also in Wallis' *Opera Mathematica* (1693–9), III, with *Porphyrii in harmonica Ptolemaei commentarius; Manuelis Byrennii harmonica*.

WarmH   Warman, John W. *The hydraulic organ of the ancients*, in PMA, XXX (1904), 37.

WestA   Westphal, Rudolf. *Die Aristoxenische Rhythmuslehre*, in VfMW, VII (1891), 74.

F   Westphal, Rudolf. *Die Fragmente und Lehrsätze der griechischen Rhythmiker*, 1861. 3rd ed., 1885, as Vol. 1 (*Griechische Rhythmik*) of *Theorie der musischen Künste der Hellenen*, by August Rossbach and Westphal.

WinnA   Winnington-Ingram, R. P. *Ancient Greek Music: A Survey*, in M&L, X(1929), 326.

I   Winnington-Ingram, R. P. *Aristoxenus and the Intervals of Greek Music*, in *The Classical Quarterly*, XXVI (1932), 195.

M   Winnington-Ingram, R. P. *Mode in Ancient Greek Music*, 1936.

S   Winnington-Ingram, R. P. *The Spondeion Scale*, in *The Classical Quarterly*, XXII (1928), 83.

WmsA   Williams, C. F. Abdy. *The Aristoxenian Theory of Musical Rhythm*, 1911.

M   Williams, C. F. Abdy. *The Music of the Ancient Greeks*, 188–?.

R   Williams, C. F. Abdy. *The Aristoxenian Theory of the Rhythmical Foot*, in MAn II (1911), 200.

CHAPTER 3

1. *The Beginnings of Christian Sacred Chant*

BOOKS AND ARTICLES

AbD	Abert, Hermann. *Die Musikanschauung des Mittelalters und ihre Grundlagen,* 1905.
Ante-Nicene	Roberts, Alexander, and James Donaldson, Editors. *The Ante-Nicene Fathers. Translations of the Writings of the Fathers down to A.D. 325.* American ed., 10 vols., 1917–25.
BernS	Bernard, John H. *The Pilgrimage of Saint Silvia of Aquitaine to the Holy Places (circa 385 A.D.).* Transl. with introduction and notes, 1891.
CE	*Catholic Encyclopedia.* 17 vols. and index, 1907–22. (Articles on Cantor, Gnosticism, Manichaeism, etc.)
CouS	Coussemaker, Charles Edmond Henri. *Scriptorum de medii ævi nova series,* 4 vols., 1864–76. Facsimile ed., 1931.
———	Dickinson, Edward. *Music in the History of the Western Church,* 1927.
DuchC	Duchesne, L. M. O. *Christian Worship: its Origin and Evolution* (transl. by M. L. McClure), 5th ed., 1919.
EB	*Encyclopædia Britannica,* 14th ed., 1929. (Articles on Gnosticism, Manichaeism, etc.)
EdelM	Edelstein, Heinz. *Die Musikanschauungen Augustins nach seiner Schrift „De Musica",* 1929.
GerC	Gerbert, Martin. *De Cantu et musica sacra, a prima ecclesiae aetate usque ad praesens tempus.* 2 vols., 1774.
S	Gerbert, Martin. *Scriptores ecclesiastici de musica,* 3 vols., 1784. Facsimile ed., 1931.
GéroH	Gérold, Théodore. *Histoire de la musique des origines a la fin du XIVᵉ siècle,* 1936.
P	Gérold, Théodore. *Les Pères de l'Eglise et la Musique,* 1931.
HeraS	Heraeus, Wilhelm. *Silviae vel potius Aetheriae peregrinatio ad loca sancta,* 1908.
HuréA	Huré, Jean. *Saint Augustin musicien, d'après le De musica et différents pages de ses oeuvres,* 1924.
JamesA	James, Montague Rhodes. *The Apocryphal New Testament* (English translation), 1926.
KrepsN	Kreps, Joseph. *Le Nombre musical chez saint Augustin et au moyen âge,* in *Compte rendu du 1ᵉʳ Congrès du Rhythme* (1926), 21.
LipA	Lipsius, R. A. and Maximilian Bonnet. *Acta Apostolorum Apocrypha post Constantinum Tischendorf.* 3 vols., 1891–1913.
MackP	Mackenna, Stephen. *Plotinus on the nature of the soul, being the 4th Ennead, translated from the Greek,* 1924.
MelP	Melmoth, William. *Pliny, Letters.* 2 vols., 1915.
Migne	Migne, Jacques Paul. *Patrologiae cursus completus.*
G	*Series Graeca.* 166 vols., 1857–66.
L	*Series Latina.* 221 vols., 1844–55.
	The 1st vol. of an index (by Th. Hopfner) to the Greek Series appeared in 1928.
Nicene & Post-N	Schaff, Philip *et al.,* Editors. *A Select Library of the Nicene Fathers of the Christian Church.* English translations with notes. 28 vols. in 2 series, 1886–1900.
PerlA	Perl, Carl Johann. *Aurelius Augustinus Musik,* 1937.
PuseyL	Pusey, Edward Bouverie. *A Library of the Holy Catholic Church, anterior to the division of the East and West.* Translated by members of the English Church. [Edited by E. B. Pusey, J. H. Newman, J. Kable and C. Marriott.] 51 vols., 1838–85.
———	Quasten, Johannes. (See Section 2)
TalA	Taliaferro, R. Catesby (ed.). *St. Augustine on Music. Books I–VI,* 1939.
WachsU	Wachsmann, Klaus. *Untersuchungen zum vorgregorianischen Gesang,* 1935.
WagE	(See bibliography for Chapter 5, Section 1)
YongeP	Yonge, C. D. *The Works of Philo Judaeus.* 4 vols., 1854–55.

2. Syrian Chant

BOOKS AND ARTICLES

AbD   (See Section 1)

BesM   Besseler, Heinrich. *Die Musik des Mittelalters und der Renaissance*, 1931–35.

BonS   Bonvin, Ludwig. *On Syrian Liturgical Chant*, in MQ, IV (1918), 593.

BrooksJ   Brooks, E. W. *James of Edessa. The Hymns of Severus of Antioch and others*, in *Patrologia orientalis*, VI (1911), 1, and VII (1911), 595.

EurN   Euringer, Sebastian. *Die neun Töpferlieder des Simeon von Gêšîr*, in *Oriens Christianus*, New Series III (1913), 22.

GasB   Gastoué, Amédée. *Catalogue des manuscrits de musique byzantine de la Bibliothèque Nationale de Paris et des bibliothèques publiques de France*, 1907.

I   Gastoué, Amédée. (See Section 3)

M   Gastoué, Amédée. (See Section 3)

O   Gastoué, Amédée. *Les Origines du chant romain*, 1907.

GéroP   (See Section 1)

GomS II   (See Section 3)

HöegB   (See Section 3)

JeannC   Jeannin, Dom Jules Cécilien. *Le Chant liturgique syrien*, in *Journal asiatique*, Xme Série, XX (1912), 295, 389; XIme Série, II (1913), 65.

M   Jeannin, Dom Jules Cécilien. *Mélodies liturgiques syriennes et chaldéennes*, Vol. I, 1924; Vol. II, 1928. In collaboration with Julien Puyade and Anselme Chibas-Lassalle.

O   Jeannin, Dom Jules Cécilien. *L'Octoëchos syrien. Etude historique, étude musicale*, in *Oriens Christianus*, New Series III (1913), 82, 277. (In collaboration with Julien Puyade.)

JulD   Julian, John. *A Dictionary of Hymnology*, 5th ed., 1925.

MMB   (See Section 3, Music Collections etc.)

PetO   (See Section 3, Music Collections etc.)

QuasM   Quasten, Johannes. *Musik und Gesang in den Kulten der heidnischen Antike und christlichen Frühzeit*, 1930.

ThibM   (See Section 3)

VincN   (See Section 3)

WachsU   (See Section 1)

WagE   (See bibliography for Chapter 5, Section 1)

WelleB   Wellesz, Egon. (See Section 3)

D   Wellesz, Egon. (See Section 3)

G   Wellesz, Egon. (See Section 4)

O   Wellesz, Egon. *Die Struktur des serbischen Oktoechos*, in ZfMW, II (1919), 140.

WrightS   Wright, William. *Catalogue of the Syriac Manuscripts in the British Museum*. 3 vols., 1870–72.

MUSIC COLLECTION

The 2nd vol. of JeannM (listed above) contains a collection of melodies.

3. Byzantine Chant

BOOKS AND ARTICLES

The literature on this subject is large. For additional bibliographical information the reader is referred to TibyB, 11–20; WelleM, 74–7; PetO, 3–5; TillH, 9–11.

ChristA   Christ, Wilhelm and M. Paranikas. *Anthologia graeca Carminum Christianorum*, 1871.

FleiN   Fleischer, Oskar. *Neumen-Studien*, 3 vols., 1895, 1897, 1904. Vol. 3.

———   Gaisser, Dom Ugo. *Le Système musical de l'Eglise grecque*, 1901.

Gas—   Gastoué, Amédée. *Catalogue des manuscrits de musique byzantine de la Bibliothèque Nationale de Paris et des bibliothèques publiques de France*, 1907.

I   Gastoué, Amédée. *L'Importance musicale, liturgique et philologique du ms. Hagiopolites*, in *Byzantion*, V (1929–30), 347.

GasL   Gastoué, Amédée. L'Origine lointaine des huit tons liturgiques, in La Revue du chant grégorien, XXXIV (1930), 126.

M   Gastoué, Amédée. Moyen Age I (La Musique byzantine et le chant des églises d'Orient) in EC, Partie I, I, 541.

U   Gastoué, Amédée. Ueber die 8 Töne, die authentischen und die plagalen, in Kirchenmusikalisches Jahrbuch, XXV (1930), 25.

Z   Gastoué, Amédée. Le Chromatisme byzantin et le chant grégorien, in TSG, V (1899), 6.

GomS   Gombosi, Otto. (See bibliography for Chapter 6, Section 1)

HöegB   Höeg, Carsten. Le Théorie de la musique byzantine, in Revue des études grecques, XXXV (1922), 321.

N   Höeg, Carsten. La Notation Ekphonétique (Monumenta Musicae Byzantinae, Subsidia, Vol. 1, Fasc. 2), 1935.

JulD   (See Section 2)

LapB   La Piana, George. The Byzantine Theater, in Speculum. A Journal of Mediaeval Studies, XI (1936), 171.

———   Merlier, Melpo. Études de musique byzantine: Le premier mode et son plagal, 1935.

Neale   Neale, J. M. and S. G. Hatherly. Hymns of the Eastern Church with Music, 1882. (Useful for its English translations; the musical section is not authoritative.)

PitraH   Pitra, J.-B. Hymnographie de l'église Grecque, 1867.

RieL   Riemann-Einstein. Musiklexikon, etc. (articles on Byzantinische Musik, Psellos, etc.)

SwanM   Swan, Alfred J. Music of the Eastern Churches, in MQ, XXII (1936), 430.

———   Tardo, D. Lorenzo. Musica Bizantina e i Codici di Melurgia della Biblioteca di Grottaferrata, in Academie e Biblioteche d'Italia, IV (1931).

———   Tardo, D. Lorenzo. L'Antica melurgia bizantina, 1938.

ThibM   Thibaut, Jean-Baptiste. Monuments de la notation ekphonetique et hagiopolite de l'Eglise greque, 1913.

O   Thibaut, Jean-Baptiste. Origine byzantine de la notation neumatique de l'Eglise latine, 1903.

TibyB   Tiby, O. La Musica Bizantina, 1938.

TillA   Tillyard, H. J. W. A Musical Study of the Hymns of Casia, in Byzantinische Zeitschrift, XX (1911), 420.

B   Tillyard, H. J. W. Byzantine Music and Hymnography, 1923.

C   Tillyard, H. J. W. Signatures and Cadences of the Byzantine Modes, in The Annual of the British School at Athens, XXVI (1923–25), 78.

E   Tillyard, H. J. W. The Acclamation of Emperors in Byzantine Ritual, in The Annual of the British School at Athens, XVIII (1911–12), 239.

H   Tillyard, H. J. W. Handbook of the Middle Byzantine Musical Notation (Monumenta Musicae Byzantinae, Subsidia, Vol. 1, Fasc. 1), 1935.

L   Tillyard, H. J. W. The Morning Hymns of the Emperor Leo, in The Annual of the British School at Athens, XXX (1928–30), 86, and XXXI (1930–31), 115.

M   Tillyard, H. J. W. Mediaeval Byzantine Music, in MQ, XXIII (1937), 201.

N   Tillyard, H. J. W. Byzantine Neumes; The Coislin Notation, in Byzantinische Zeitschrift, XXXVII (1937), 345.

Z   Tillyard, H. J. W. Byzantine Music, in M&L, IV (1923), 269.

VilloD   Villoteau, Guillaume. Description de l'Egypte, XIV, 1826.

VincN   Vincent, Alexandre J. H. Notice sur divers manuscrits grecs relatifs à la musique, in Notices et extraits des manuscrits de la bibliothèque du roi, XVI, Part 2, 1847.

WallP   (See bibliography for Chapter 2)

WelleA   Wellesz, Egon. Das Alter der Melodien der byzantinischen Kirche, in Forschungen und Fortschritte (1932), 431.

B   Wellesz, Egon. Byzantine Music, in PMA (1932), 1.

D   Wellesz, Egon. Die byzantinische und orientalische Kirchenmusik, in AdlerH I, 126.

L   Wellesz, Egon. Die byzantinischen Lektionszeichen, in ZfMW, XI (1929), 514.

M   Wellesz, Egon. Byzantinische Musik, 1927.

———   Wellesz, Egon. Die Entzifferung der byzantinischen Notenschrift, in Oriens Christianus, New Series VII (1918), 97.

———   Wellesz, Egon. Die Rhythmik der byzantinischen Neumen, in ZfMW, II (1920), 617; III (1921), 321.

———   Wellesz, Egon. Der Stand der Forschung auf dem Gebiete der byzantinischen Kirchenmusik, 1936.

MUSIC COLLECTIONS ETC. (INCLUDING FACSIMILES)

MMB   *Monumenta Musicae Byzantinae.* Edited by Carsten Höeg, H. J. W. Tillyard, and Egon Wellesz. (For *Subsidia,* see separate entries under the names of Höeg and Tillyard.)

Monumenta

I   *Sticherarium. Codex Vindabonensis Theol. Graec. 181.* Facsimile, 1935.
II   *Hirmologium Athoum. Codex Monasterii Hiberorum 470.* Facsimile, 1939.

Transcripta

I   *Die Hymnen des Sticherarium für September.* Transcriptions by Egon Wellesz, 1936.
II   *The Hymns of the Sticherarium for November.* Transcriptions by H. J. W. Tillyard, 1938.

Lectionaria

I   *Prophetologium.* Edited by Carsten Höeg and Günther Züntz, 1939.
PetO   Petresco, J.-D. *Les Idiomèles et le Canon de l'Office de Noël,* 1932. After Greek manuscripts of the 11th–14th centuries. Preface by A. Gastoué.
WelleT   Wellesz, Egon. *Trésor de musique byzantine,* Vol. 1, 1934. (Transcriptions into modern notation with introduction.)

4. Armenian Music

BOOKS AND ARTICLES

———   Aubry, Pierre. *Le Système musical de l'église arménienne,* in TSG, VII (1901), 325; VIII (1902), 23, 72, 110, 320; IX (1903), 136, 287.
DayanM   Dayan, Leonzio. *Musica* (section of the article, *Armeni*), in *Enciclopedia Italiana,* IV (1929), 443.
———   Fortescue, Adrian. *The Lesser Eastern Churches,* 1913.
GasM   (See Section 3)
MaclerA   Macler, Frédéric. *La Musique en Arménie,* 1917.
WelleD   Wellesz, Egon. (See Section 3)
G   Wellesz, Egon. *Aufgaben und Probleme auf dem Gebiete der byzantinischen und orientalischen Kirchenmusik,* 1923.
MM   Wellesz, Egon. *Die armenische Messe und ihre Musik,* in *Jahrbuch der Musikbibliothek Peters,* XXVII (1920), 1.

MUSIC COLLECTION

ApcarM   Apcar, Amy. *Melodies of the apostolic church of Armenia,* 1897 (Calcutta).

5. Coptic and Ethiopian Music

BOOKS AND ARTICLES

ButlerC   Butler, Alfred Joshua. *Ancient Coptic Churches of Egypt,* 2 vols., 1884.
DerayE   Deray, A. *Le Chant liturgique en Éthiopie,* in *La Revue du chant grégorien,* XL (1936), 134, 182.
HerschA   Herscher-Clément, J. *Chants d'Abyssinie,* in *Zeitschrift für vergleichende Musikwissenschaft,* II (1934), 51, and 24 of musical examples section.
WelleB   Wellesz, Egon. (See Section 3)
D   Wellesz, Egon. (See Section 3)
G   Wellesz, Egon. (See Section 4)
K   Wellesz, Egon. *Studien zur äthiopischen Kirchenmusik,* in *Oriens Christianus,* New Series, IX (1920), 74.

MUSIC COLLECTION

BadetC   Badet, Louis. *Chants liturgiques des Coptes,* 1899.

CHAPTER 4

1. *Russian Chant*

BOOKS AND ARTICLES

—— Arnold, Yurii K. *Theory of Ancient Russian Church and Folk Singing Based on Historic and Acoustic Analysis* (in Russian), 1880.

BourR Bourdeau, Célestin. *Le Chant religieux de l'église orthodoxe russe*, in EC, *Partie II*, IV, 2355.

FindR Findeisen, Nikolai. *Sketches of the History of Music in Russia* (in Russian), 2 vols., 1928–29.

—— Koschmieder, E. *Die wichtigsten Hilfsmittel zum Studium des russischen Kirchengesanges*, in *Jahrbücher für Kultur und Geschichte der Slaven*, N.F. IV (1928), 49.

—— Makarii, Metropolitan. *History of the Russian Church* (in Russian), 12 vols., 1868–83.

MettR Mettalov, Vasilii Mikhailovich. *Survey of the History of Orthodox Church Singing in Russian* (in Russian), 4th ed., 1915.

Z Mettalov, Vasilii Mikhailovich. *The Eight Modes of the Znamenny Chant* (in Russian), 1889.

—— Mettalov, Vasilii Mikhailovich. *Liturgical Singing of the Russian Church in the Pre-Mongol Period* (in Russian), 1912.

—— Mettalov, Vasilii Mikhailovich. *Russian "Semeiography"* (in Russian), 1912.

—— Nikolsky, A. *Forms of Russian Church Singing* (in Russian), 1915.

PanóffA Panóff, Peter. *Altslavische Volks- und Kirchenmusik*, 1930.

PreobC Preobrazhensky, Antonin Viktorovich. *Cult Music in Russia* (in Russian), 1924.

—— Preobrazhensky, Antonin Viktorovich. *Dictionary of Russian Church Singing* (in Russian), 1896.

—— Preobrazhensky, Antonin Viktorovich. *On Church Singing. Survey of Books, Pamphlets, and Magazine Articles (1793–1896)* in Russian, 2nd ed., 1900.

—— Razumovsky, Dimitri Vasilyevich. *Church Singing in Russia* (in Russian), 3 vols., 1867–69.

—— Razumovsky, Dimitri Vasilyevich. *Concerning the Manuscripts of Staffless Notation of the Znamenny Chant of the Church* (in Russian), 1863.

RieseR Riesemann, Oskar von. *Russischer Kirchengesang*, in AdlerH I (1929), 140.

—— Riesemann, Oskar von. *Die Notationen des altrussischen Kirchengesanges*, 1909.

—— Sakharov, Ivan Petrovich. *An Investigation into Russian Church Singing* (in Russian), 1849.

SmolA Smolensky, S. *Alphabet of Znamenny Singing, 1668, edited by S. Smolensky* (in Russian), 1888.

—— Smolensky, S. *On the Old Russian Chant MSS in the Moscow Synodic School* (in Russian), 1899.

SwanR Swan, Alfred J. *The Nature of the Old Russian Liturgical (Znamenny) Chant*, in *Papers Read by Members of the American Musicological Society at the Annual Meeting Held in Washington, D.C., Dec. 29 and 30, 1938.*

Z Swan, Alfred J. *The Znamenny Chant of the Russian Church*, Parts I and II in MQ, XXVI (1940), 232, 365; Part III to appear shortly.

—— Swan, Alfred J. *Music of the Eastern Churches*, in MQ, XXII (1936), 430.

—— Undolsky, Vukol Mikhailovich. *Remarks on the History of Church Music in Russia* (in Russian), 1846.

—— Vosnessensky, Ivan Ivanovich. *About Singing in the Orthodox Church of the Grecian East from the Most Ancient to Recent Times* (in Russian), Parts I and II, 1896.

—— Vosnessensky, Ivan Ivanovich. *The Greater and Lesser Znamenny Chant* (in Russian), 2nd ed., 1889.

—— Vosnessensky, Ivan Ivanovich. *The Eight-Mode Chants of the Last Three Centuries in the Orthodox Russian Church (Pt. I. Kiev Chant; Pt. II. Bulgarian Chant; Pt. III. Greek Chant; Pt. IV. Examples of the Eight Modes in the Kiev, Bulgarian, and Greek Chants, with explanatory text)* (in Russian), 1899.

MUSIC COLLECTION
(See also Pt. IV of last item above)

Cycle   *Cycle of the Ancient Church Singing of the Znamenny Chant* (with commentary in Russian), 6 vols., 1884.

2. Ambrosian Chant

BOOKS

DrevesA   Dreves, Guido Maria. *Aurelius Ambrosius, der Vater des Kirchengesanges*, 1893.
GerC   Gerbert, Martin. *De Cantu et musica sacra, a prima ecclesiae aetate usque ad praesens tempus*. 2 vols., 1774.
HuréA   Huré, Jean. *Saint Augustin musicien, d'après le De musica et différents pages de ses oeuvres*, 1924.
JulD   Julian, John. *A Dictionary of Hymnology*, 5th ed., 1925.
MigneL   Migne, Jacques Paul. *Patrologiae cursus completus. Series Latina*. 221 vols., 1844–55.
MorinN   Morin, Dom G. *Nouvelles recherches sur l'auteur du Te Deum*, in *Revue Bénédictine* (of Maredsous), XI (1894), 49.
Nicene &   Schaff, Philip *et al.*, Editors. *A Select Library of the Nicene Fathers of the Christian
Post-N   Church*. English translations with notes. 28 vols. in 2 series, 1886–1900.
OrtD   Ortigue, Louis Louis d'. *Dictionnaire liturgique et théorique du plainchant*, 1854.
PothM   Pothier, Joseph. *Les Mélodies grégoriennes*, 1881.
WagE   (See bibliography for Chapter 5, Section 1)

MUSIC COLLECTIONS AND FACSIMILE

Antiphonale   *Antiphonale missarum juxta ritum Sanctae Ecclesiae Mediolanensis*, 1935.
(Ambro-
sian)
BasM   Bas, Giulio. *Manuale di canto ambrosiano*, 1929.
PM   *Paléographie Musicale.*
  V   *L'Antiphonaire Ambrosien*. Codex Add. 34209 of the British Museum. Facsimile. 1896–9.
  VI   *L'Antiphonaire Ambrosien*. Codex Add. 34209 of the British Museum. Transcription into modern plainsong notation. 1897–1900.

3. Mozarabic and Gallican Chant

BOOKS AND ARTICLES

AngE   Anglès, Higini. *El Codex musical de las Huelgas (Música a veus dels segles XIII-XIV)*, 3 vols., 1931. Vol. 1: Introduction.
R   Anglès, Higini. *La Musique aux Xe et XIe siècles. L'École de Ripoll*, in *La Catalogne à l'époque romane* (1932), 157.
BishM   Bishop, W. C. *The Mozarabic and Ambrosian Rites: four essays in comparative Liturgiology*, 1924.
DAC   *Dictionnaire d'archéologie chrétienne et de liturgie*, published by Dom Fernand Cabrol and collaborators, 1907– . (In progress)
DuchC   Duchesne, L. M. O. *Christian Worship: its Origin and Evolution* (Transl. by M. L. McClure), 5th ed., 1919.
GasCG   Gastoué, Amédée. *Le Chant gallican*, in *Revue du Chant grégorien*, XLI (1937), 101, 131, 167; XLII (1938), 5, 57, 76, 107, 111, 146; XLIII (1939), 7, 44. (Also published, 1939, in book form)
D   Gastoué, Amédée. *Le Graduel et l'Antiphonaire romains, histoire et description*, 1913.
G   Gastoué, Amédée. *L'Art grégorien*, 1911.
GerS   Gerbert, Martin. *Scriptores ecclesiastici de musica*, 3 vols., 1784. Facsimile ed., 1931.
GéroH   Gérold, Théodore. *Histoire de la musique des origines à la fin du XIVe siècle*, 1936.
LindE   Lindsay, W. M. *Isadori Hispalensis Episcopi Etymologiarum sive originum Libri XX* (2 vols.), 1911.

MigneL   (See Section 2)
PM   *Paléographie Musicale.*
I   *Le Codex 339 de la Bibliothèque de Saint-Gall (Xᵉ siècle): Antiphonale Missarum Sancti Gregorii,* 1889.
XIII   *Le Codex 903 de la Bibliothèque Nationale de Paris (XIᵉ siècle): Graduel de Saint-Yrieix,* 1925–30.
PradoM   Prado, Germán. *Mozarabic Melodics,* in *Speculum, A Journal of Mediaeval Studies,* III (1928), 218.
———   Riaño, Juan F. *Critical and bibliographical notes on early Spanish music,* 1887.
RojoC   Rojo, Casiano and R. P. Germán Prado. *El Canto Mozárabe, Estudio histórico-critico de su antiguedad y estado actual,* 1929.
SuñP   Suñol, Dom Gregory. *Introduction à la Paléographie musicale grégorienne,* 1935.
———   Trend, John Brande. *The Music of Spanish History to 1600,* 1926.
UrG   Ursprung, Otto. *Alte griechische Einflüsse und neuer gräzistischer Einschlag in der mittelalterlischen Musik,* in ZfMW, XII (1930), 193.
N   Ursprung, Otto. *Neuere Literatur zur spanischen Musikgeschichte,* in ZfMW, XII (1929), 93.
WagE   Wagner, Peter. (See bibliography for Chapter 5, Section 1)
K   Wagner, Peter. *Der mozarabische Kirchengesang und seine Überlieferung,* in *Spanische Forschungen der Görresgesellschaft, I. Reihe,* I (1928), 102.
L   Wagner, Peter. *Untersuchungen zu den Gesangstexten und zur responsorialen Psalmodie der altspanischen Liturgie,* in *Spanische Forschungen der Görresgesellschaft, I. Reihe,* II (1930), 67.

MUSIC COLLECTION

Liber   (See bibliography for Chapter 5, Section 1)

CHAPTER 5

The literature on Gregorian Chant is so extensive that only a small selection of especially useful material can here be given. Further references may be found in such works as SuñP, UrK, WaesM, RobI, etc. The reader wishing a *Daily Missal* with Latin and English texts will find editions by Cabrol and by Lefebure; for the Office, he will find, similarly provided, the Burns and Oates editions of the *Day Hours of the Church* and the *Vesperal.* Since the current pronunciation of Church Latin differs from that of classical Latin as taught in the schools, the reader may find use also for Michael de Angelis, *The Correct Pronunciation of Latin According to Roman Usage* (Revised ed.), 1939. The *Glossarium ad scriptores mediae et infimae latinitatis* of Charles du Cange (1678) and the *Medieval Latin Word-List* of James H. Baxter and Charles Johnson (1934) are invaluable aids to the student reading the medieval treatises.

1. *The History*

BOOKS AND ARTICLES

AbD   Abert, Hermann. *Die Musikanschauung des Mittelalters und ihre Grundlagen,* 1905.
———   Abert, Hermann. *Zu Cassiodor,* in SIM, III (1902), 439.
AmelM   Amelli, Ambrosio M. *Micrologus ad præstantiores codices mss. exactus,* 1904.
AudaE   Auda, Antoine. *L'École musicale liégeoise au Xᵉ siècle. Étienne de Liége,* 1923.
O   Auda, Antoine, *L'Office de Saint Trudon,* 1911.
———   Batifoll, Pierre. *Saint Grégoire le Grand.* 2nd ed., 1928.
BaurG   Baur, Ludwig, *Domenicus Gundissalinus. De Divisione philosophiae,* 1903, in *Beiträge zur Geschichte der Philosophie des Mittelalters* (Ed. Cl. Bäumker), Bd. IV, Hft. 2, 3.
BesM   Besseler, Heinrich. *Die Musik des Mittelalters und der Renaissance,* 1931–35.
BittH   Bittermann, Helen Robbins. *Hārūn Ar-Raschīd's Gift of an Organ to Charlemagne,* in *Speculum. A Journal of Mediaeval Studies,* IV (1929), 215.
O   Bittermann, Helen Robbins. *The Organ in the Early Middle Ages,* in *Speculum. A Journal of Mediaeval Studies,* IV (1929), 390. (To be used in the light of *Speculum* V, 217ff)

BohnO — Bohn, Peter. *Oddo's von Clugny Dialog*, in MfMG, XII (1880), **24, 39.**
BramR — Brambach, W. *Die Reichenauer Sängerschule*, 1888.
—— Brambach, W. *Gregorianisch. Bibliographische Lösung der Streitfrage über dem Ursprung des gregorianischen Gesanges*, 2nd ed., 1901.
—— Brambach, W. *Die Musiklitteratur des Mittelalters bis zur Blüthe der Reichenauer Sängerschule (500–1050 n. Chr.)*, 1883.
BronH — Bronarski, Ludwig. *Die Lieder der heiligen Hildegard*, 1922.
—— *Catholic Encyclopedia.* 17 vols. and index, 1907–22. (Articles on Plain Chant, etc.)
CouS — (See bibliography for Chapter 6)
—— *Dictionnaire d'archéologie chrétienne et de liturgie*, published by Dom Fernand Cabrol and collaborators, 1907– . (In progress.) (Articles on *Chant Romain et Grégorien*, etc.)
DorenE — Van Doren, Rombaut. *Étude sur l'influence musicale de l'Abbaye de Saint-Gall (VIIIᵉ au XIᵉ siècle)*, 1925.
—— Douglas, Winfred. *Church Music in History and Practice*, 1937.
EllinM — (See Section 2)
FarmH — Farmer, Henry George. *Historical Facts for the Arabian Musical Influence*, 1930.
O — (See bibliography for Chapter 2)
W — Farmer, Henry George. *Al-Farabi's Arabic-Latin Writings on Music*, 1934.
FortC — Fortescue, Adrian. *The Ceremonies of the Roman Rite Described*, 5th ed., 1934.
FoxT — (See bibliography for Chapter 9)
FrereP — Frere, W. H. *Plainsong*, in OH Int. (1929), 133.
FriedlB — (See Section 2)
GasD — Gastoué, Amédée. *Le Graduel et l'Antiphonaire romains, histoire et description*, 1913.
G — Gastoué, Amédée. *L'Art grégorien*, 1911.
J — Gastoué, Amédée. *Chant Juif et Chant Grégorien*, in Revue du Chant Grégorien, XXXIV (1930), 157; XXXV (1931), 9, 52, 70, 113, 115, 129.
M II — Gastoué, Amédée. *Moyen Age II (La Musique occidentale)* in EC, Partie I, I, 556.
O — Gastoué, Amédée. *Les Origines du chant romain*, 1907.
OH — Gastoué, Amédée. *Les Origines hébraïques de la liturgie et du chant chrétien*, in Revue du Chant Grégorien, XXXIV (1930), 64.
GerC — Gerbert, Martin. *De Cantu et musica sacra, a prima ecclesiae aetate usque ad praesens tempus.* 2 vols., 1774.
S — (See Section 2)
GéroP — Gérold, Théodore. *Les Pères de l'Église et la Musique*, 1931.
GevM — Gevaert, François Auguste. *La Mélopée antique dans le chant de l'église latine*, 1895.
O — Gevaert, François Auguste. *Les Origines du chant liturgique de l'église latine*, 1890.
GrutH — (See Section 2)
HermE — Hermesdorff, Michael. (See bibliography for Chapter 6, Section 1)
M — Hermesdorff, Michael. *Micrologus Guidonis de disciplina artis musicae, d.i. Kurze Abhandlung Guido's über die Regeln der musikalischen Kunst*, 1876.
HughT — Hughes, Dom Anselm. *Theoretical Writers on Music up to 1400*, in OH Int. (1929), 117.
IdG — Idelsohn, A. Z. *Parallelen zwischen gregorianischen und hebräisch-orientalischen Gesangsweisen*, in ZfMW, IV (1922), 515.
JohnG — Johner, Rev. Dom. *A New School of Gregorian Chant*, 1925. An English translation of *Neue Schule des gregorianischen Choralgesanges*, 1906.
KornT — Kornmüller, Utto, *Der Traktat des Johannes Cottonius über Musik*, in Kirchenmusikalisches Jahrbuch, XIII (1888), 1.
LambiE — Lambillote, Louis. *Esthétique, théorie et pratique du chant grégorien.* Posthumous work, ed. by J. Dufour, 1855.
MaN — Machabey, Armand. *Notes de musicologie prémédiévale*, in RM, XV (1934), 275.
MG — *Monographies Grégoriennes*
I — Dom Mocquereau. *L'Introit "In Medio,"* 1910.
II — Dom Mocquereau. *Verset alléluiatique "Ostende nobis,"* 1911.
III — Dom Mocquereau. *Le Chant authentique du Credo*, 1922.
IV — Dom Mocquereau and Dom Gajard. *La Tradition rythmique dans les manuscrits*, 1923.
V — H. Potiron. *L'Accompagnement du Chant Grégorien. Des rapports entre l'accent et la place des accords*, 1924.
VI — H. Potiron and Dom Desrocquettes. *La Théorie harmonique des trois groupes modaux et l'accord final des troisième et quatrième modes*, 1926.

VII	Dom Mocquereau. *Examen des critiques dirigées par D. Jeannin contre l'École de Solesmes*, 1926.
VIII	Dom Desrocquettes. *L'Accompagnement rythmique d'après les principes de Solesmes*, 1928.
IX	H. Potiron. *La Modalité Grégorienne*, 1928.
X	Dom Gajard. *La Musicalité du Chant Grégorien*, 1931.
XI	Dom Gajard. *Pourquoi les éditions rythmiques de Solesmes*, 1935.
XII	Dom Gajard. *Le "Nombre Musical Grégorien*," 1935.
XIII	Dom Murray. *Rythme Grégorien: Les Étapes d'un pèlerin*, 1938. (French transl. of MurG in Section 3)
MigneL	(See Section 2)
MosL	Moser, Hans Joachim. *Musiklexikon* (articles on *Gregorianischer Gesang*, etc.)
MülH	Müller, Hans. *Hucbalds echte und unechte Schriften über Musik*, 1884.
W	Müller, Hans. *Die Musik Wilhelms von Hirschau*, 1884.
MynorsC	Mynors, R. A. B. *Cassiodori Senatoris Institutiones LVI*, 1937.
PaulB	(See Section 2)
PietzschK	Pietzsch, Gerhard. *Die Klassifikation der Musik von Boetius bis Ugolino von Orvieto*, 1929.
M	Pietzsch, Gerhard. *Die Musik im Erziehungs- und Bildnungsideal des ausgehenden Altertums und frühen Mittelalters*, 1932.
PiperS	Piper, Paul. *Die Schriften Notkers und seiner Schule*, Vol. 1, 1882.
ReinU	Reinach, Théodore. *Un Ancêtre de la musique d'église*, in RM III, No. 9 (1922), 8.
RieG	Riemann, Hugo. *Geschichte der Musiktheorie im IX–XIX Jahrhundert*, 1898, 2nd ed., 1921. References are to the 2nd ed.
RobI	Robertson, Alec. *The Interpretation of Plainchant*, 1937.
SachsH	Sachs, Curt. *Handbuch der Musikinstrumentenkunde*, 1920.
SchlecG	Schlecht, Raimund. *Micrologus; Guidonis de disciplina artis musicae*, in MfMG, V (1873), 135.
M	Schlecht, Raimund. *Musica Enchiriadis von Hucbald*, in MfMG, VI (1874), 163, 179; VII (1875), 1, 17, 33, 49, 65, 81; VIII (1876), 89.
SchlesU	Schlesinger, Kathleen. *The Utrecht Psalter and its Bearing on the History of Musical Instruments*, in MAn II (1910), 18.
SchmidtgO	Schmidt-Görg, Joseph. *Ein althochdeutscher Traktat über die Mensur der Orgelpfeifen*, in *Kirchenmusikalisches Jahrbuch*, XXVII (1932), 58.
SchraD	Schrade, Leo. *Die Darstellungen der Töne an den Kapitellen der Abteikirche zu Cluni*, in *Deutsche Vierteljahrsschrift für Literaturwissenschaft und Geistesgeschichte*, VII (1929), 229.
SchubS	Schubiger, Anselm. *Die Sängerschule St. Gallens*, 1858.
SowaT	(See bibliography for Chapter 9)
SpittaM	(See bibliography for Chapter 9)
StegQ	Steglich, Rudolf. *Die Quaestiones in Musica; ein Choraltraktat . . . und ihr mutmasslicher Verfasser Rudolf von St. Trond (1070–1138)*, 1911.
UrG	Ursprung, Otto. *Alte griechische Einflüsse und neuer gräzistischer Einschlag in der mittelalterlichen Musik*, in ZfMW, XII (1930), 193.
H	Ursprung, Otto. *Die Gesänge der hl. Hildegard* in ZfMW, V (1923), 333.
K	Ursprung, Otto. *Die katholische Kirchenmusik*, 1931–33.
VivD	Vivell, Cölestin. *Direkte Entwicklung des römischen Kirchengesanges aus der vorchristlichen Musik*, in *Kirchenmusikalisches Jahrbuch*, XXIV (1911), 21.
	Vivell, Cölestin. *Vom Musik-Traktate Gregors des Grossen*, 1911.
WaesM	Van Waesberghe, Jos. Smits. *Muziekgeschiedenis der Middeleeuwen*, Vol. I, 1939.
WagD	Wagner, Peter. *Der gregorianische Gesang*, in AdlerH I (1929), 75.
E	Wagner, Peter. *Einführung in die gregorianischen Melodien*, 1st ed., 1895; 2nd ed., Part 1, 1901–05, 3rd ed. 1911, as *Ursprung und Entwicklung der liturgischen Gesangsformen bis zum Ausgange des Mittelalters*; Part 2, *Neumenkunde*, 1905, 2nd ed., 1912; Part 3, *Gregorianische Formenlehre; eine choralische Stilkunde*, 1921. Part 1 appeared in English, 1907, as *Introduction to the Gregorian melodies: Part I, Origin and development of the forms of the Liturgical Chant up to the end of the Middle Ages*. References to Part I are to the English ed.; to Part 2, to the 2nd.
M	Wagner, Peter. *Das Media vita*, in *Schweizerisches Jahrbuch für Musikwissenschaft*, I (1924), 18.
WantM	Wantzloeben, Sigfrid. *Das Monochord als Instrument und als System*, 1911.
WolkG	(See bibliography for Chapter 9)
WyattG	Wyatt, E. G. P. *St. Gregory and the Gregorian Music*, 1904.

MUSIC COLLECTIONS AND FACSIMILES

Antiphonale   *Antiphonale . . . pro diurnis horis*, 1912. (Typis Polyglottis Vaticanis)
Compendium   *Compendium Gradualis et Antiphonalis Romani*, 1924.
FrereG   (See Section 2)
GmelchK   Gmelch, Joseph. *Die Kompositionen der heil. Hildegard*, 1913.
Graduale   *Graduale Romanum*, 1924. (Desclée ed.)
Kyriale   *Kyriale seu Ordinarium Missae*, 1927. (Fischer ed.)
Liber   *Liber Usualis Missae et Officii pro Dominicis et Festis cum Cantu Gregoriano*, 1934. (Desclée ed.)
LiberE   *The Liber Usualis, with Introduction and Rubrics in English*, 1938. (Desclée ed.)
LiberM   *Liber Usualis Missae et Officii pro Dominicis et Festis cum Cantu Gregoriano . . . in recentioris musicae notalas . . .* (in modern notation), 1932. (Desclée ed.)
Officium   *Officium Majoris Hebdomadae et Octavae Paschae*, 1932. (Dessain ed.)
PM   (See Section 2)
UP   *Latin Psalter in the University Library of Utrecht . . . produced in facsimile by the . . . autotype process . . .* , 1873.
Vesperale   *Vesperale romanum*, 1924. (Desclée ed.)
WagT   (See Section 2)

2. The Notation of Intervals

BOOKS AND ARTICLES

——   Benedictine of Stanbrook. *Gregorian Music: An Outline of Musical Palaeography*, 1897.
——   *Catholic Encyclopedia*. 17 vols. and index, 1907–22. (Articles on Clovesho, Councils of; Neum; etc.)
CelM   Celentano, F. *La musica presso i Romani*, in *Rivista Musicale Italiana*, XX (1913), 513.
EbelA   Ebel, P. Basilius. *Das älteste alemannische Hymnar mit Noten . . .* (*XII. Jahrhundert*), 1931.
EllinM   Ellinwood, Leonard. *Musica Hermanni Contracti*, 1936.
FerM   Ferretti, Paolo. *I manoscritti musicali gregoriani dell'archivio di Montecassino*, in *Casinensia (Miscellanea di studi casinensi . . .)*, I (1929), 187.
FrereB   Frere, Walter Howard. *Biblioteca Musico-Liturgica. A . . . Handlist of the Musical and Latin-Liturgical MSS of the Middle Ages . . . in the Libraries of Great Britain and Ireland*, 2 vols., 1901, 1932.
FriedlB   Friedlein, G. *Boetii de institutione arithmetica libri duo; de institutione musica libri quinque*, 1867. Ed. by Friedlein.
GasC   Gastoué, Amédée. *Cours théorique et pratique de plain-chant . . .*
GerS   Gerbert, Martin. *Scriptores ecclesiastici de musica*, 3 vols., 1784. Facsimile ed., 1931.
GmelchV   Gmelch, Joseph. *Die Vierteltonstufen im Messtonale von Montpellier*, 1910.
GomS   Gombosi, Otto (See bibliography for Chapter 6, Section 2)
GrutH   Grutchfield, E. J. *Hucbald: A Millenary Commemoration*, in *The Musical Times*, LXXI (1930), 507, 704.
KunzT   Kunz, Lucas. *Die Tonartenlehre des Boethius*, in *Kirchenmusikalisches Jahrbuch*, XXXI–XXXIII (1936–38), 5.
Migne   Migne, Jacques Paul. *Patrologiae cursus completus.*
    L   *Series Latina.* 221 vols., 1844–55.
PaulB   Paul, Oskar. *Boetius. Fünf Bücher über die Musik*, 1872.
RieL   Riemann-Einstein. *Musiklexikon*, etc. (Articles on *Buchstabentonschrift*, etc.)
SidM   Sidler, Hubert. *Zum Messtonale von Montpellier*, in *Kirchenmusikalisches Jahrbuch*, XXXI–XXXIII (1936–38), 33.
SuñP   Suñol, Dom Gregory. *Introduction à la Paléographie musicale grégorienne*, 1935.
ThibO   (See bibliography for Chapter 3, Section 3)
VivQ   Vivell, Cölestin. *Studien über das Quilisma*, in *Gregorianische Rundschau* (1905).
WagB   Wagner, Peter. *Ein bedeutsamer Fund zur Neumengeschichte*, in AFMW, I (1919), 516.
    D   (See Section 1)
    E II   (See Section 1)
WolfH   Wolf, Johannes. *Handbuch der Notationskunde*, Vol. I, 1913; Vol. 2, 1919.
YasQ   (See bibliography for Chapter 6, Section 1)

FACSIMILES

BannM	Bannister, H. M. *Monumenti Vaticani di paleografia musicale latina*, 1913.
——	Briggs, H. B. *The Musical Notation of the Middle Ages*, 1890. (Contains facsimiles, 10th–16th centuries)
FrereA	Frere, W. H. *Antiphonale Sarisburiense*, 1901–25, Facsimile with Introduction, etc.
G	Frere, W. H. *Graduale Sarisburiense*, 1894. Facsimile of 13th-cent. MS with commentary and historical index showing development from Gregorian *Antiphonale Missarum*.
PA	*Pars Antiphonarii*, 1923. Facsimile of 11th-cent. MS at Durham. Introduction by Frere.
NichE	Nicholson, E. W. B. *Early Bodleian Music*. Vol. III. *Introduction to the Study of some of the Oldest Latin Musical Manuscripts in the Bodleian Library, Oxford*, 1913.
PM	*Paléographie musicale*. Begun under the editorship of Dom Mocquereau. Monumental contribution. Facsimiles, some transcriptions, commentary.
I	*Le Codex 339 de la Bibliothèque de Saint-Gall (Xe siècle): Antiphonale Missarum Sancti Gregorii*, 1889.
II	*Le Répons-Graduel "Justus ut palma."* First part. Plates 1–107, 1891–92.
III	*Le Répons-Graduel "Justus ut palma."* Second part. Plates 108–211, 1892–93.
IV	*Le Codex 121 de la Bibliothèque d'Einsiedeln (X^e–XIe siècle): Antiphonale Missarum Sancti Gregorii*, 1893–96.
V	*L'Antiphonaire Ambrosien*, Codex Add. 34209 of the British Museum. Facsimiles, 1896–99.
VI	*L'Antiphonaire Ambrosien*, Codex Add. 34209 of the British Museum. Transcription into modern plainsong notation, 1897–1900.
VII	*Le Codex H. 159 de la Bibliothèque de l'École de Médecine de Montpellier (XIe siècle): Antiphonarium Tonale Missarum* (commentary), 1901–05.
VIII	*Le Codex H. 159 de la Bibliothèque de l'École de Médecine de Montpellier (XIe siècle): Antiphonarium Tonale Missarum* (facsimile), 1901–05.
IX	*Le Codex 601 de la Bibliothèque capitulaire de Lucques (XIIe siècle): Antiphonaire monastique*, 1906–09.
X	*Le Codex 239 de la Bibliothèque de Laon (IXe–Xe siècle): Antiphonale Missarum Sancti Gregorii*, 1909–12.
XI	*Le Codex 47 de la Bibliothèque de Chartres (Xe siècle): Antiphonale Missarum Sancti Gregorii*, 1912–21.
XII	*Codex F. 160 de la Bibliothèque de la Cathédrale de Worcester (XIIIe siècle): Antiphonaire Monastique*, 1922–25.
XIII	*Le Codex 903 de la Bibliothèque Nationale de Paris (XIe siècle): Graduel de Saint-Yrieix*, 1925–30.
XIV	*Le Codex 10673 de la Bibliothèque Vaticane Fonds Latin (XIe siècle): Graduel Bénéventain*, 1931– .
Ser. 2, I	*No. 390–391 de la Bibliothèque de Saint-Gall (Xe siècle): L'Antiphonaire du B^e Hartker*, 1900–01.
Ser. 2, II	*Le Codex 359 de la Bibliothèque de Saint-Gall (IXe siècle): Cantatorium*, 1924–25.
WackG	Wackernagel, M. *Codex Gisle*, 1926. Facsimile of part of a Gradual of c. 1300.
WagT	Wagner, Peter. *Das Graduale der St. Thomaskirche zu Leipzig (14. Jahrhundert) als Zeuge deutscher Choralüberlieferung*. Vol. 1, 1930; Vol. 2, 1932. In *Publikationen älterer Musik* (of the *Deutsche Musikgesellschaft*), V, VII.

3. The Notation of Rhythm

BOOKS AND ARTICLES

AmelM	(See bibliography for Section 1)
AuD	Aubry, Pierre. *Le Rhythme tonique dans la poésie liturgique et dans le chant des églises chrétiennes au moyen-âge (Essais de musicologie comparée, I)*, 1903.
BesM	Besseler, Heinrich. *Die Musik des Mittelalters und der Renaissance*, 1931–35.
BonG	Bonvin, Ludwig. *Rhythm as taught by the Gregorian masters up to the twelfth century and in accordance with the Oriental usage*, in *The Messenger*, XLVI (1906), 465.
L	Bonvin, Ludwig. *Liturgical Music from the Rhythmical Standpoint up to the 12th Century*, in *Proceedings of the Music Teachers' National Association*, X (1915), 215.
M	Bonvin, Ludwig. *The "Measure" in Gregorian Music*, in MQ, XV (1929), 16.
——	Bovet, Joseph. *La Liberté relative du rythme dans le chant grégorien*, in *Compte rendu du 1er Congrès du Rythme* (1926), 10.

CserbaM   Cserba, Simon M. *Der Musiktrakat des Hieronymus Moravia O.P.*, 1935. (Cserba's dissertation was published without Jerome's treatise in 1934.)

DAC   *Dictionnaire d'archéologie chrétienne et de liturgie*, published by Dom Fernand Cabrol and collaborators, 1907–   . (In progress) (Articles on *Mora vocis* etc.)

DavidM   David, Dom Lucien. *Méthode pratique de Chant Grégorien*, 1922.

R   David, Dom Lucien. *Le rythme verbal et musical dans le chant romain*, 1933.

S   David, Dom Lucien. *Les signes rythmiques d'allongement et la tradition grégorienne authentique*, in *Revue du chant grégorien*, XLII (1938), 180; XLIII (1939), 1, 38, 78, 111, 142 (more to follow).

DechV   Dechevrens, Antoine. *Les Vraies Mélodies gregoriennes*, 1902.

FleiN   Fleischer, Oskar. *Neumen-Studien*, 3 vols., 1895, 1897, 1904. Vol. II.

FleuryG   Fleury, Alexandre. *The Old Manuscripts of Two Gregorian Schools*, in *The Messenger*, XLVI (1906), 344.

GerS   (See Section 2)

GietC   Gietmann, Gerhard. *Choralia*, in *Kirchenmusikalisches Jahrbuch*, XIX (1905), 53, and XX (1906), 1.

HoudR   Houdard, Georges Louis. *Le Rhythme du chant dit grégorien*, 1898.

JamG   Jammers, Ewald. *Der gregorianischen Rhythmus*, 1937.

JeannE   Jeannin, Dom Jules Cécilien. *Études sur le rythme grégorien*, 1926.

M   (See bibliography for Chapter 3, Section 2)

LafE   La Fage, J. Adrien L. de. *Essais de diphthérographie musicale*, 1864.

LindE   Lindsay, W. M. *Isadori Hispalensis Episcopi Etymologiarum sive originum Libri XX* (2 vols.), 1911.

MigneL   (See Section 2)

MocqL   Mocquereau, Dom André. *Le nombre musical Grégorien ou rythmique Grégorienne*. 2 vols., 1908, 1927.

N   Mocquereau, Dom André. *"Le Nombre musical grégorien," a Study of Gregorian Musical Rhythm*, Vol. 1—Part I, translated into English by Aileen Tone, 1932.

P   Mocquereau, Dom André. *Notules pratiques sur les incises mélodiques du type "Fiat mihi" de l'antienne "Ecce ancilla Domini,"* in *Revue Grégorienne*, III (1913), 160, and IV (1914), 16.

MurG   Murray, Dom Gregory. *Gregorian Rhythm: A Pilgrim's Progress*, in *The Catholic Choirmaster*, XX (1934), 111, 163; XXI (1935), 3, 55.

MynorsC   (See bibliography for Section 1)

SchmidtG   Schmidt, J. G. *Principal Texts of the Gregorian Authors concerning rhythm*, 1928 [?].

SowaQ   Sowa, Heinrich, *Quellen zur Transformation der Antiphonen, Tonar und Rhythmusstudien*, 1935.

SuñG   Suñol, Gregory. *Text Book of Gregorian Chant*, 1930. An English translation by G. M. Durnford of *Método completo de Canto gregoriano* (1st ed., 1905).

WaesC   Van Waesberghe, Jos. Smits. *Chant grégorien et castagnettes*, in *Revue du Chant grégorien*, XXXVI (1932), 39, 84, 111.

WagE II   (See Section 1)

WardG   Ward, Justine. *Gregorian Chant according to the principles of Dom André Mocquereau of Solesmes*. Catholic Education Series, Music—Fourth Year, 1923.

MUSIC COLLECTION AND FACSIMILES

Compendium   *Compendium Gradualis et Antiphonalis Romani*, 1924.

PM   *Paléographie musicale*. (See Section 2. Vols. II, III, IV, VII, and VIII all contain studies bearing on Gregorian rhythm.)

CHAPTER 6

1. *The Modes*

BOOKS AND ARTICLES

AmelM   (See bibliography for Chapter 5, Section 1)

AndrM   Andrews, Frederick S. *Mediaeval Modal Theory*, 1935. (Thesis, Cornell University, unpublished. Abstract printed, 1935.)

AudaC   Auda, Antoine. *Contribution à l'histoire de l'origine des modes et des tons grégoriens*, in *La Revue du chant grégorien*, XXXVI (1932), 33, 72, 105, 130.

AudaM   Auda, Antoine. *Les Modes et les tons de la musique*, 1930.
BalT   Balmer, Lucie. *Tonsystem und Kirchentöne bei Johannes Tinctoris*, 1935.
BarbP   Barbour, J. Murray. *The Persistence of the Pythagorean Tuning System*, in *Scripta Mathematica*, I (1933), 286.
BohnG   Bohn, Peter. *Glareani Dodecachordon*, translated into German; in *Publikationen der Gesellschaft für Musikforschung, Bd. XVI*, 1888–90.
BommW   Bomm, Urbanus. *Der Wechsel der Modalitätsbestimmung in der Tradition der Messgesänge im IX. bis XIII. Jahrhundert*, 1929.
CouS   Coussemaker, Charles Edmond Henri. *Scriptorum de Musica medii aevi nova series*, 4 vols. 1864–76. Facsimile ed., 1931.
DürH   Düring, Ingemar. *Die Harmonielehre des Klaudios Ptolemaios*, 1930.
P   Düring, Ingemar. *Ptolemaios und Porphyrios über die Musik*, 1934.
EllinM   Ellinwood, Leonard. *Musica Hermanni Contracti*, 1936.
FarmH   Farmer, Henry George. *Historical Facts for the Arabian Musical Influence*, 1930.
FrereK   Frere, William Howard. *Key-Relationship in Early Medieval Music*, in PMA, XXXVII (1911), 129.
FriedlB Friedlein, G. (See bibliography for Chapter 5, Section 2)
GerS   Gerbert, Martin. *Scriptores ecclesiastici de musica*, 3 vols., 1784. Facsimile ed., 1931.
GlarD   Glareanus, Heinrich Loris. *Dodekachordon*, 1547.
GmelchV Gmelch, Joseph. *Die Vierteltonstufen im Messtonale von Montpellier*, 1910.
GomS   Gombosi, Otto. *Studien zur Tonartenlehre des frühen Mittelalters*. I in Acta, X (1938), 149; II, Part 1 in Acta, XI (1939), 28, Part 2 in preparation.*
HaasA   Haas, Robert. *Aufführungspraxis der Musik*, 1930.
HawkH   Hawkins, John. *A General History of the Science and Practice of Music*, 5 vols., 1776. New ed., 3 vols., 1853, 1875. References are to the ed. of 1875.
HermE   Hermesdorff, Michael. *Epistola Guidonis Michaeli Monacho de ignoto cantu directa, d.i. Brief Guido's an den Mönch Michael über einen unbekannten Gesang*, 1884.
M   Hermesdorff, Michael. *Micrologus Guidonis de disciplina artis musicae, d.i. Kurze Abhandlung Guido's über die Regeln der musikalischen Kunst*, 1876.
JacC   Jacobsthal, Gustav. *Die chromatische Alteration im liturgischen Gesang der abendländischen Kirche*, 1897.
LangeZ   Lange, Georg. *Zur Geschichte der Solmization*, in SIM, I (1900), 535.
MG IX   (See Chapter 5, Section 1)
Migne   Migne, Jacques Paul. *Patrologiae cursus completus*.
L   *Series Latina*. 221 vols., 1844–55.
MühlA   Mühlmann, Wilhelm. *Die Alia Musica (Gerbert, Scriptores I) Quellenfrage, Umfang, Inhalt und Stammbaum*, 1914.
PaulB   Paul, Oskar. *Boetius. Fünf Bücher über die Musik*, 1872.
UrK   Ursprung, Otto. *Die katholische Kirchenmusik*, 1931–33.
VivC   Vivell, Cölestin. *Commentarius anonymus in Micrologum Guidonis Aretini*, 1917.
F   Vivell, Cölestin. *Frutolfi Breviarium de musica*, 1919.
WagD   Wagner, Peter. *Der gregorianische Gesang*, in AdlerH I (1929), 75.
E   Wagner, Peter. (See Section 2)
         Wagner, Peter. *Zur mittelalterlichen Tonartenlehre*, in AdlerF (1930), 29.
WolfC   Wolf, Johannes, *Anonymi cuiusdam Codex Basiliensis*, in VfMW, IX (1893), 408.
YasQ   Yasser, Joseph. *Medieval Quartal Harmony*, in MQ, XXIII (1937), 170, 333; XXIV (1938), 351. (Also published, 1938, in book form.)

MUSIC COLLECTIONS

Liber   *Liber Usualis Missae et Officii pro Dominicis et Festis cum Cantu Gregoriano*, 1934. (Desclée ed.)
Antiphonale (Ambrosian)   (See bibliography for Chapter 4, Section 2)

2. The Forms of Gregorian Chant and of Some Outgrowths

BOOKS AND ARTICLES

AbT   Abert, Hermann. *Die ästhetischen Grundsätze der mittelalterlichen Melodiebildung*, 1902.
AlbrF   Albrecht, Otto E. *Four Latin Plays of St. Nicholas*, 1935.

* Since this book first appeared, Part 2 of *Studie* II has become available in Acta, XI (1939), 128, while Part 3 has been printed in Acta, XII (1940), 21, and *Studie* III in Acta, XII (1940), 29.

AmelM   (See bibliography for Chapter 5, Section 1)
Analecta   *Analecta hymnica medii aevi.* 55 vols. (G. M. Dreves in collaboration with Clemens Blume and H. M. Bannister), 1886–1922.
AndrM   Andrews, Frederick Sturges. *Mediaeval Modal Theory.* Dissertation, 1935, unpublished. Abstract printed, 1935.
AngL   Anglès, Higini. *La música a Catalunya fins al segle XIII,* 1935.
    R   Anglès, Higini. *La Musique aux Xe et XIe siècles. L'École de Ripoll,* in *La Catalogne à l'époque romane* (1932), 157.
AuN   Aubry, Pierre. *La Musique et les musiciens d'église en Normandie au XIIIe siècle,* 1906.
AudaM   Auda, Antoine. *Les Modes et les tons de la musique,* 1930.
BenP   Benedictine of Stanbrook. *A Grammar of Plainsong,* 3rd ed., 1934.
BluV   Blume, Clemens. *Vom Alleluia zur Sequenz,* in *Kirchenmusikalisches Jahrbuch,* XXIV (1911), 1.
ChamM   Chambers, E. K. *The Mediaeval Stage,* 2 vols., 1903.
ChevR   Chevalier, Ulysse. *Repertorium Hymnologicum,* 6 vols., 1892–1921 (Vols. 3–4, 10, 15, 19–20, of Chevalier's *Bibliothèque liturgique*).
CouS   Coussemaker, Charles Edmond Henri. *Scriptorum de musica medii ævi nova series,* 4 vols., 1864–76. Facsimile ed., 1931.
DorenE   van Doren, Rombaut. *Étude sur l'influence musicale de l'Abbaye de Saint-Gall (VIIIe au XIe siècle),* 1925.
FerC   Ferretti, Paolo. *Il cursus metrico e il ritmo della melodia gregoriana,* 1913.
    E   Ferretti, Paolo. *Estetica gregoriana, ossia Trattato delle forme musicali del Canto gregoriano,* Vol. I, 1934. (Available also in French transl. by Dom A. Agaësse, 1938.)
FleiN   Fleischer, Oskar. *Neumen-Studien,* 3 vols., 1895, 1897, 1904. Vol. III.
FrereW   Frere, W. H. *The Winchester Troper* (Henry Bradshaw Society, Vol. VIII), 1884.
GaiS   Gaisser, Dom Ugo. *Le Système musical de l'Eglise greque,* 1901.
GasG   Gastoué, Amédée. *L'Art grégorien,* 1911.
    H   Gastoué, Amédée. *La Psalmodie traditionelle des huit tons,* in TSG, XIV (1908), 193, 227, 251, 268.
    O   Gastoué, Amédée. *Les Origines du chant romain,* 1907.
    ———   Gastoué, Amédée. *Cours théorique et pratique de plain-chant romain grégorien,* 2nd ed., 1917.
GautT   Gautier, Léon. *Histoire de la Poésie liturgique au Moyen Age. Les Tropes,* 1886.
GennF   Gennrich, Friedrich. *Grundriss einer Formenlehre des mittelalterlichen Liedes als Grundlage einer musikalischen Formenlehre des Liedes,* 1932.
    I   Gennrich, Friedrich. *Internationale mittelalterliche Melodien,* in ZfMW, XI (1929), 259, 321.
GerS   Gerbert, Martin. *Scriptores ecclesiastici de musica,* 3 vols., 1784. Facsimile ed., 1931.
GéroM   Gérold, Théodore. *La Musique au moyen âge,* 1932.
GevM   Gevaert, François Auguste. *La Mélopée antique dans le chant de l'église latine,* 1895.
GomS   (See Section 1)
HaapZ   Haapanen, T. and Arno Malin. *Zwölf lateinische Sequenzen aus den mittelalterlichen Quellen Finlands herausgegeben,* 1922.
    ———   Halbig, Hermann. *Kleine gregorianische Formenlehre,* 1930.
HammM   Hammerich, Angul. *Mediaeval Musical Relics of Denmark,* 1912.
HandU   Handschin, Jacques. *Über Estampie und Sequenz,* in ZfMW, XII (1929), 1, and XIII (1930), 113.
    W   Handschin, Jacques. *The Two Winchester Tropers,* in *The Journal of Theological Studies,* XXXVII (1936), 34, 156.
HughA   Hughes, Dom Anselm. *Anglo-French Sequelæ, edited from the papers of the late Dr. Henry Marriott Bannister,* 1934.
JeanJ   Jeanroy, Alfred. *Le Jeu de Sainte Agnès.* Music transcribed by Th. Gérold, 1931.
JohnG   Johner, Rev. Dom. *A New School of Gregorian Chant,* 1925. An English translation of *Neue Schule des gregorianischen Choralgesanges,* 1906.
    ———   Johner, Rev. Dom. *Wort und Ton im Choral,* 1940.
JulD   Julian, John. *A Dictionary of Hymnology,* 5th ed., 1925.
KunzU   Kunz, Lucas. *Ursprung und textliche Bedeutung der Tonartensilben Noeane, Noeagis,* in *Kirchenmusikalisches Jahrbuch,* XXX (1935), 5.
LiuV   Liuzzi, Fernando. *Le Vergini Savie e le Vergini Folli,* in *Studi medievali,* New Series III (1930), 82.

	Liuzzi, Fernando. *L'Espressione musicale nel dramma liturgico*, in *Studi medievali*, New Series II (1929), 74.
LudG	Ludwig, Friedrich. *Die geistliche nichtliturgische, weltliche einstimmige Musik des Mittelalters bis zum Anfang des 15. Jahrhunderts* in AdlerH I, 157.
MathS	Mathias, Franz Xaver. *Der Straszburger Chronist Königshofen als Choralist*, 1903.
Migne	Migne, Jacques Paul. *Patrologiae cursus completus*.
L	*Series Latina*. 221 vols., 1844–55.
MobergU	Moberg, C. A. *Über die schwedischen Sequenzen*, 1927.
RieH	Riemann, Hugo. *Handbuch der Musikgeschichte*. I, 1923; II ¹, 1920; II ², 1922; II ³, 1922. (Orig. ed.: I ¹, 1901; I ², 1905; II ¹, 1907; II ², 1911; II ³, 1913.) Vol. I.
SachsS	Sachs, Curt. *Anthologie Sonore*. Notes to the record albums. 4 albums, 1935–36.
SchubS	Schubiger, Anselm. *Die Sängerschule St. Gallens*, 1858.
SuñG	Suñol, Gregory. *Text Book of Gregorian Chant*, 1930. An English translation by G. M. Durnford of *Método completo e Canto gregoriano* (1st ed., 1905).
UrSS	Ursprung. *Das Sponsus-Spiel*. in AfMF, III (1938), 80, 180.
VilleO	Villetard, H. *Office de Pierre de Corbeil*, 1907.
WagE	Wagner, Peter. *Einführung in die gregorianischen Melodien*, 1st ed., 1895; 2nd ed., Part 1, 1901–05, 3rd ed., 1911, as *Ursprung und Entwicklung der liturgischen Gesangsformen bis zum Ausgang des Mittelalters;* Part 2, *Neumenkunde*, 1905, 2nd ed., 1912; Part 3, *Gregorianische Formenlehre; eine choralische Stilkunde*, 1921. Part 1 appeared in English, 1907, as *Introduction to the Gregorian melodies: Part 1, Origin and development of the forms of the Liturgical Chant up to the end of the Middle Ages*. References to Part 1 are to the English ed.
WelleD	Wellesz, Egon. *Die byzantinische und orientalische Kirchenmusik*, in AdlerH I, 126.
WolfMR	Wolf, Johannes. *L'Italia e la musica religiosa medievale*, in *Rivista Musicale Italiana*, XVI (1938), 269.
YoungD	Young, Karl. *The Drama of the Medieval Church*, 2 vols., 1933.

MUSIC COLLECTIONS AND FACSIMILES

Ancient & Modern	*Hymns Ancient and Modern: Historical Edition*, 1909.
Antiphonale	*Antiphonale . . . pro diurnis horis*, 1912. (Typis Polyglottis Vaticanis)
ClémentC	Clément, Félix. *Choix des principales sequences du moyen âge*, 1861.
CouD	Coussemaker, Charles Edmond Henri. *Drames liturgiques du Moyen Âge*, 1860.
FrereA	Frere, Walter Howard. *Antiphonale Sarisburiense*, 1901–25. Facsimile with Introduction, etc.
Graduale	*Graduale romanum*, 1924. (Desclée ed.)
Liber	*Liber Usualis Missæ et Officii pro Dominicis et Festis cum Cantu Gregoriano*, 1934. (Desclée ed.)
MissetP	Misset, E. and Pierre Aubry. *Les Proses d'Adam de Saint-Victor*, 1900.
Officium	*Officium Majoris Hebdomadae et Octavae Paschae*, 1932. (Dessain ed.)
PM	*Paléographie musicale*.
IV	*Le Codex 121 de la Bibliothèque d'Einsiedeln (X–XI⁰ siècle): Antiphonale Missarum Sancti Gregorii*, 1893–96.
IX	*Le Codex 601 de la Bibliothèque capitulaire de Lucques (XII⁰ siècle): Antiphonaire monastique*, 1906–09.
XII	*Codex F. 160 de la Bibliothèque de la Cathédrale de Worcester (XIII⁰ siècle): Antiphonaire Monastique*, 1922–25.
Ser. 2, I	*No. 390–391 de la Bibliothèque de Saint-Gall (X⁰ siècle): L'Antiphonaire du Bᵉ Hartker*, 1900–01.
ScherG	Schering, Arnold. *Geschichte der Musik in Beispielen*, 1931.
Vesperale	*Vesperale romanum*, 1924. (Desclée ed.)

CHAPTER 7

The Latin Songs—Jongleurs, Troubadours, and Trouvères

BOOKS AND ARTICLES

In addition to the following, certain writings of Romanic philologists that are constantly referred to by musicologists dealing with the troubadours and trouvères should be brought to the reader's attention: Karl Friedrich Bartsch, *Grundriss zur Geschichte der provenzalischen Literatur*, 1872; Friedrich Gennrich, *Die beiden neuesten Bibliographien altfranzösischer und altprovenzalischer Lieder*, in *Zeitschrift für romanische Philologie*, XLI (1921), 289; Gustav Gröber, *Grundriss der romanischen Philologie*. 3 vols., 1888–1901; Alfred Jeanroy, *Bibliographie sommaire des chansonniers français du moyen âge*, 1918; Alfred Jeanroy, *Bibliographie sommaire des chansonniers provençaux*, 1916; Emil Levy, *Provenzalisches Supplement-Wörterbuch*. 8 vols., 1894–1924; Gaston Raynaud, *Bibliographie des chansonniers français des XIIe et XIIIe siècles*. 2 vols., 1884; M. Raynouard, *Lexique roman ou dictionnaire de la langue des troubadours*. 6 vols., 1836–44; F. E. Godefroy, *Dictionnaire de l'ancienne langue française*. 10 vols., 1881–1902. The Bartsch *Grundriss* contains a catalogue of the Provençal poems in the *chansonniers* and the Raynaud *Bibliographie* of the French poems. The Jeanroy and Gennrich works supplement these catalogues. Trouvère pieces are frequently referred to in scholarly writings by their Raynaud numbers.

Analecta   (See bibliography for Chapter 6, Section 2)
AngE and L Anglès, Higini. (See bibliography for Chapter 8, Section 4)
   M   Anglès, Higini. *Les Melodies del trobador Guiraut Riquier*, in *Estudis Universitaris Catalans*, XI (1926), 1.
AppS   Appel, Carl. *Die Singweisen Bernarts von Ventadorn*, 1934.
AuI   Aubry, Pierre. (See bibliography for Chapter 8, Section 4)
   N   Aubry, Pierre. *La Musique et les musiciens d'église en Normandie au XIIIe siècle*, 1906.
   O   Aubry, Pierre. *L'Oeuvre mélodique des Troubadours et des Trouvères*, in *Revue musicale* (the one founded in 1901, not RM), VII (1907), 317, 347, 389.
   Q   Aubry, Pierre. *Quatre poésies de Marcabru, troubadour gascon du XIIe siècle*, in TSG, X (1904), 107.
   R   Aubry, Pierre. *La Rhythmique musicale des troubadours et des trouvères*, 1907.
   S   Aubry, Pierre. *Refrains et rondeaux du XIIIe siècle*, in RieF (1909), 213.
   T   Aubry, Pierre. *Trouvères and Troubadours*, 1914. An English translation by C. Aveling of *Trouvères et Troubadours*, 1909.
BeckM   Beck, Johann Baptist. *Die Melodien der Troubadours*, 1908. (Available also in Italian transl. by Gaetano Cesari, 1939.)
   R   Beck, Johann Baptist. *Der Takt in den Musikaufzeichnungen des XII und XIII Jahrhunderts, vornehmlich in den Liedern der Troubadours*, in RieF (1909), 166.
   T   Beck, Johann Baptist. *La Musique des troubadours*, 1910.
BédiC   Bédier, Joseph. *Les Chansons de Colin Muset*, 1912. (Contains transcriptions of the melodies by J. B. Beck.)
BesM   Besseler, Heinrich. *Die Musik des Mittelalters und der Renaissance*, 1931–35.
BreulC   Breul, Karl Hermann. *The Cambridge Songs*, 1915.
BrinE   (See bibliography for Chapter 8, Section 1)
ChabB   Chabaneau, Camille. *Les Biographies des troubadours en langue provençale*, 1885.
ChayT   Chaytor, Henry John. *The Troubadours*, 1912. On the troubadours as literary figures.
CouH   Coussemaker, Charles Edmond Henri. *Histoire de l'harmonie au moyen-âge*, 1852.
   S   Coussemaker, Charles Edmond Henri. *Scriptorum de musica medii ævi nova series*, 4 vols., 1864–76. Facsimile ed., 1931.
DentS   Dent, Edward J. *Social Aspects of Music in the Middle Ages*, in OH Int. (1929), 184.
EB   *Encyclopaedia Britannica*, etc. (Articles on Troubadours, etc.)
EmH   Emmanuel, Maurice. *Histoire de la Langue Musicale*, 2 vols., 1928.
FarJ   Faral, Edmond. *Les Jongleurs en France au moyen âge*, 1910.
FerM   (See bibliography for Chapter 5, Section 2)
FerandM   Ferand, Ernst. *Die Improvisation in der Musik*, 1938.
——————   Gastoué, Amédée. *Les Primitifs de la musique française*, 1922.
GasT   Gastoué, Amédée. *Three Centuries of French Mediæval Music*, in MQ, III (1917), 173.
GennA   Gennrich, Friedrich. *Die altfranzösische Rotrouenge*, 1925.
   F   Gennrich, Friedrich. *Grundriss einer Formenlehre des mittelalterlichen Liedes als Grundlage einer musikalischen Formenlehre des Liedes*, 1932.
   H   Gennrich, Friedrich. *Die altfranzösische Liederhandschrift London, Brit. Mus. Egerton 274*, in *Zeitschrift für romanische Philologie*, XLV (1926), 402.
   I   Gennrich, Friedrich. *Internationale mittelalterliche Melodien*, in ZfMW, XI (1929), 259, 321.
   L   Gennrich Friedrich. *Lateinische Kontrafacta altfranzösischen Lieder*, in *Zeitschrift für romanische Philologie*, L (1930), 187.

GennM   Gennrich, Friedrich. *Musikwissenschaft und romanische Philologie*, 1918.
   S   Gennrich, Friedrich. (See Chapter 8, Section 1)
   V   Gennrich, Friedrich. *Der musikalische Vortrag der altfranzösischen chansons de geste*, 1923.
   Z   Gennrich, Friedrich. (See Chapter 8, Section 1)
GéroL   Gérold, Théodore. *Monodie et Lied*, in EC, Partie II, V, 2757.
   M   Gérold, Théodore. *La Musique au moyen âge*, 1932.
HandU   Handschin, Jacques. *Über Estampie und Sequenz*, in ZfMW, XII (1929), 1, and XIII (1930), 113.
   V   Handschin, Jacques. *Die Modaltheorie und Carl Appels Ausgabe der Gesaenge von Bernart de Ventadorn*, in *Medium Aevum*, IV (1935), 69.
HilkaC   Hilka, Alfons and Otto Schumann. *Carmina Burana*. First 2 vols., 1930; still in process.
JarV   Jarcho, Boris I. *Die Vorläufer des Golias*, in *Speculum. A Journal of Mediaeval Studies*, III (1928), 523.
JeanJ   (See bibliography for Chapter 6, Section 2)
─────   Lommatzsch, Erhard. *Provenzalisches Liederbuch*, 1917. (Contains 100 texts, 16 melodies, some in several transcriptions, etc.)
KirbyT   Kirby, P. R., *A Thirteenth Century Ballad Opera*, in M&L, XI (1930), 163.
LudG   Ludwig, Friedrich. *Die geistliche nichtliturgische, weltliche einstimmige und die mehrstimmige Musik des Mittelalters bis zum Anfang des 15. Jahrhunderts* in AdlerH I, 157.
   Q   Ludwig, Friedrich. (See bibliography for Chapter 10)
   Z   Ludwig, Friedrich. *Zur "modalen Interpretation" von Melodien des 12 and 13 Jahrhunderts*, in ZIM, XI (1910), 379.
MigneL   (See bibliography for Chapters 4, 5)
MosS   Moser, Hans Joachim. *Stantipes und Ductia*, in ZfMW, II (1920), 194.
   Z   Moser, Hans Joachim. *Zu Ventadorns Melodien*, in ZfMW, XVI (1934), 142.
MüG   Müller, Hermann. *Zum Texte der Musiklehre des Joannes de Grocheo*, in SIM, IV (1902), 361.
NefG   Nef, Karl. *Gesang und Instrumentenspiel bei den Troubadours*, in AdlerF (1930), 58.
PruN   Prunières, Henry. *Nouvelle Histoire de la musique. I. La Musique du moyen âge et de la renaissance*, 1934.
─────   Restori, Antonio. *Per la storia musicale dei Trovatori provenzali*, in *La Rivista Musicale Italiana*, II (1895), 1, and III (1896), 231, 407.
RibC   (See bibliography for Chapter 8, Section 4, Music Collection)
RieB   Riemann, Hugo. *Die Beck-Aubry'sche "modale Interpretation" der Troubadourmelodien*, in SIM, XI (1910), 569.
   D   Riemann, Hugo. (See Chapter 8, Section 1)
   H   Riemann, Hugo. *Handbuch der Musikgeschichte*
         I, 1923; II ^{1}, 1920; II ^{2}, 1922; II ^{3}, 1922. (Orig. ed.: I ^{1}, 1901; I ^{2}, 1905; II ^{1}, 1907; II ^{2}, 1911; II ^{3}, 1913.)
   L   Riemann-Einstein. *Musiklexikon*, etc. (Articles on Troubadours, etc.)
Roh G   Rohloff, Ernst Franz. *Studien zum Musiktraktat des Johannes de Grocheo*, 1930.
SachsW   Sachs, Curt. *World history of the dance*, 1937. (English translation of *Eine Weltgeschichte des Tanzes*, 1933. References are to the translation.)
SmyT   Smythe, Barbara. *Troubadour Songs*, in M&L, II (1921), 263.
SpaA   Spanke, Hans. *Eine altfranzösische Liedersammlung*, 1925. Primarily a philological work, but contains music.
   C   Spanke, Hans. *Der Codex Buranus als Liederbuch*, in ZfMW, XIII (1931), 241.
   L   Spanke, Hans. *Das lateinische Rondeau*, in *Zeitschrift für französischer Sprache und Litteratur*, LIII (1929–30), 113.
   M   Spanke, Hans. *St. Martial-Studien*, in *Zeitschrift für französischer Sprache und Litteratur*, LIV (1930–1), 282, 385.
   S   Spanke, Hans. *Das öftere Auftreten von Strophenformen und Melodien in der altfranzösischen Lyrik*, in *Zeitschrift für französischer Sprache und Litteratur*, LI (1928), 73.
StreckC Strecker, Karl. *Die Cambridger Lieder*, 1926.
TierS   Tiersot, Julien. *Sur le Jeu de Robin et Marion*, 1897.
VerC   Verrier, Paul. *La "Chanson de Notre Dame" de Gautier de Coinci* in *Romania*, LIX (1933), 497.
VilleO   Villetard, H. *Office de Pierre de Corbeil*, 1907.

WagJ   Wagner, Peter. *Die Gesänge der Jakobusliturgie zu Santiago de Compostela,* 1931.
——   Wechssler, Eduard. *Das Kulturproblem des Minnesangs,* 1909.
WolU   Wolf, Ferdinand. *Über die Lais, Sequenzen und Leiche,* 1841.
WolfH   Wolf, Johannes. *Handbuch der Notationskunde.* Vol. 1, 1913; Vol. 2, 1919.
   M   Wolf, Johannes. *Die Musiklehre des Johannes de Grocheo,* in SIM, I (1899), 69. Contains the *Theoria* of J. de G. in the original Latin with a German translation.
   T   Wolf, Johannes. *Die Tänze des Mittelalters,* in AfMW, I (1918), 10.

MUSIC COLLECTIONS AND FACSIMILES

AdO   Adam de la Halle. *Oeuvres complètes du trouvère Adam de la Halle,* ed. by E. de Coussemaker, 1872.
AuA   Aubry, Pierre. *Le Chansonnier de l'Arsenal,* 1909–   . Facsimile ed. with transcriptions. Unfinished.
   C   Aubry, Pierre. *Les Chansons de croisade* (in collaboration with J. Bédier), 1909.
   E   Aubry, Pierre. *Estampies et danses royales: les plus anciens textes de musique instrumentale au moyen âge,* 1906.
   L   Aubry, Pierre. *Lais et descorts français du XIIIᵉ siècle* (in collaboration with L. Brandin and A. Jeanroy), 1901.
——   Aubry, Pierre. *Les plus anciens monuments de la musique française,* 1903. Contains 24 facsimiles.
BeckC   Beck, Johann Baptist. *Corpus Cantilenarum medii aevi.*
       Ser. 1 I. *Le Chansonnier Cangé.* Facsimile, 1927.
            II. *Le Chansonnier Cangé.* Transcriptions and commentary, 1927.
       Ser. 2 I. *Le Manuscrit du Roi.* Facsimile, 1938.
       (with Louise Beck) II. *Le Manuscrit du Roi.* Commentary, 1938.
   L   Beck, Johann Baptist. *Les Chansons de Colin Muset* (in collaboration with J. Bédier), 1912.
   P   Beck, Johann Baptist. *The Play of Robin and Marion,* 1928. With English translation by J. M. Gibbon.
GennR   Gennrich, Friedrich. *Rondeaux, Virelais und Balladen.* 2 vols.: I in 1921, II in 1927.
JeanC   Jeanroy, Alfred. *Le Chansonnier d'Arras,* 1925. Facsimile ed. issued by the *Société des anciens textes français.*
RayC   Raynaud, Gaston. *Le Chansonnier français de Saint-Germain des Prés* (in collaboration with P. Meyer). Vol. I (only one issued), 1892. Facsimile ed. issued by the *Société des anciens textes français.*
RoksM   (See bibliography for Chapter 11)

CHAPTER 8

1. *The Minnesinger*

BOOKS AND ARTICLES

AmbG   Ambros, August Wilhelm. *Geschichte der Musik,* 5 vols. (1st ed. 1862–78, 1882.) Completed by Hugo Leichtentritt. References are to the 3rd ed.
BesM   Besseler, Heinrich. *Die Musik des Mittelalters und der Renaissance,* 1931–35.
BrinE   Brinkmann, Hennig. *Entstehungsgeschichte des Minnesangs,* 1926.
——   Bützler, Carl. *Untersuchungen zu den Melodien Walthers von der Vogelweide,* 1940.
GennD   Gennrich, Friedrich. *Der deutsche Minnesang in seinem Verhältnis zur Troubadour- und Trouvère Kunst,* in *Zeitschrift für deutsche Bildung,* II (1926), 536, 622.
   F   Gennrich, Friedrich. (See bibliography for Chapter 7)
   S   Gennrich, Friedrich. *Sieben Melodien zu mittelhochdeutschen Minneliedern,* in ZfMW, VII (1924), 65.
   Z   Gennrich, Friedrich. *Zur Ursprungsfrage des Minnesangs,* in *Deutsche Vierteljahrsschrift für Literaturwissenschaft und Geistesgeschichte,* VII (1929), 187.
HagM   Hagen, Friedrich Heinrich von der. *Minnesänger.* 5 vols. plus an *Ergänzungs-Atlas.* 1838–61.
JamU   Jammers, Ewald. *Untersuchungen über die Rhythmik und Melodik der Melodien der Jenaer Liederhandschrift,* in ZfMW, VII (1925), 265.
LudG   (See bibliography for Chapter 7)

MolL   Molitor, Raphael Fidelis. *Die Lieder des Münsterer Fragments,* in SIM, XII (1911), 475.
MosD   Moser, Hans Joachim. *Die Entstehung des Durgedankens,* in SIM, XV (1914), 270.
  G   Moser, Hans Joachim. *Geschichte der deutschen Musik.* 3 vols. 5th ed., 1930.
──────   Moser, Hans Joachim. *Musikalische Probleme des deutschen Minnesangs,* in *Bericht über den musikwissenschaftlichen Kongress in Basel* (1925), 259.
MülleF   (See Section 2)
RieD   Riemann, Hugo. *Die Musik der deutschen Minnesinger.* A series of articles in the *Musikalisches Wochenblatt,* XXVIII–XXXVIII (1897–1907). The titles vary slightly.
  L   Riemann-Einstein. *Musiklexikon,* etc. (Articles on *Minnesänger,* etc.)
SchmiedN   Schmieder, Wolfgang. *Zur Melodiebildung in Liedern von Neidhart (von Reuental),* in SzMW, XVII (1930), 3.
──────   Sorensen, Margot. *Musik und Gesang im mittelhochdeutschen Epos,* 1939.
WustW   Wustmann, Rudolf. *Die Hofweise Walters von der Vogelweide,* in *Festschrift . . . Rochus Freiherrn von Liliencron* (1910), 440.

MUSIC COLLECTIONS (INCLUDING FACSIMILES)

DTO XX[2]   *Bd. 41. Gesänge von Frauenlob, Reinmar von Zweter und Alexander* (ed. by Heinrich Rietsch), 1913.
XXXVII[1]   *Bd. 71. Neidhart (von Reuental), Lieder* (ed. by W. Schmieder and E. Wiessner), 1930.
MH   *Die Manessische Handschrift,* 1925–27. (Six portfolios of facsimiles.) A supplement to this, *Die Manessische Lieder-Handschrift,* was published in 1929 by Rudolf Sillib, Friedrich Panzer, and Arthur Haseloff.
MüllP   Müller, K. K. *Phototypische Facsimile-Ausgabe der Jenaer Liederhandschrift,* 1893.
RunS   Runge, Paul. *Die Sangweisen der Colmarer Handschrift und die Liederhandschrift Donaueschingen,* 1896.
SarJ   Saran, Franz Ludwig. *Die Jenaer Liederhandschrift* (in collaboration with G. Holz and Ed. Bernoulli). 2 vols., 1902.
ScherD   Schering, Arnold. *Geschichte der Musik in Beispielen,* 1931.

2. Laude and Geisslerlieder

BOOKS AND ARTICLES

BertT   Bertoni, Giulio. *I Trovatori in Italia,* 1915. (On the troubadours as literary figures)
ChayT   Chaytor, Henry John. *The Troubadours,* 1912.
HandUL   Handschin, Jacques. *Über die Laude ("à propos d'un livre récent")* in *Acta,* X (1938), 14.
HübG   Hübner, Arthur. *Die deutschen Geisslerlieder,* 1931.
LiuB   Liuzzi, Fernando. *Ballata e Lauda,* in the *Annuario 1930–31* of the R. Academia di S. Cecilia, 1931.
  M   Liuzzi, Fernando. *Melodie italiane inedite del duocento,* in *Archivum Romanicum,* XIV (1930), 527.
  P   Liuzzi, Fernando. *Profile musicale di Jacopone,* in *Nuova Antologia,* CCCLVII (7th ser. CCLXXIX) (1931), Fascicle 1428 (September 16), 171.
LudG   (See bibliography for Chapter 7)
MosG   Moser, Hans Joachim. (See Section 1)
  T   Moser, Hans Joachim. *Tönende Volksaltertümer,* 1935.
MülleF   Müller-Blattau, Josef. *Zu Form und Überlieferung der ältesten deutschen geistlichen Lieder,* in ZfMW, XVII (1935), 129.
  G   Müller-Blattau, Josef. *Die deutschen Geisslerlieder,* in ZfMW, XVII (1935), 6.
RunL   Runge, Paul. *Die Lieder und Melodien der Geissler des Jahres 1349,* 1900.
  M   Runge, Paul. *Maria mûter reinû mait,* in RieF (1909), 256.
WolfMR   (See bibliography for Chapter 6, Section 2)

MUSIC COLLECTION (INCLUDING FACSIMILES)

LiuL   Liuzzi, Fernando. *La Lauda e i primordi della melodia italiana.* 2 vols., 1935. Contains facsimiles, transcriptions, and commentary.

3. *English Secular Monody*

BOOKS AND ARTICLES

BrownE   Brown, Carleton, *English Lyrics of the XIIIth Century*, 1932.
ChayE   Chaytor, Henry John. *The Troubadours and England*, 1923. (On the troubadours as literary figures)
EllisO   Ellis, A. J. *On Early English Pronunciation* (Chaucer Society), 1869–89. Part II is of special musical interest (Chaucer Society Publ., 2nd Ser., No. 4).
GennF   (See bibliography for Chapter 7)
I   (See bibliography for Chapter 7)
HandU   (See bibliography for Chapter 7)
PadelE   Padelford, Frederick Morgan. *Old English Musical Terms*, 1899.
RankH   Rankin, J. W. *The Hymns of St. Godric*, in *Publications of the Modern Language Association*, XXXVIII (1923), 699.
RegL   Reginald of Durham. *Libellus de Vita et Miraculis S. Godrici* (Surtees Society, Vol. 20), 1845.
SainH   Saintsbury, George. *History of English Prosody*, 1906.
SaltT   Saltmarsh, John. *Two Medieval Love-Songs set to Music*, in *The Antiquaries Journal*, XV (1935), 1.
SchraI   Schrade, Leo. *Die handschriftliche Ueberlieferung der ältesten Instrumentalmusik*, 1931.
TreE   Trend, J. B. *The First English Songs*, in M&L, IX (1928), 111.
WellsM   Wells, John Edwin. *A Manual of the Writings in Middle English 1050–1400*, 1926.
WolfH   (See bibliography for Chapter 7)
T   (See bibliography for Chapter 7)
WrR   Wright, Thomas. *Reliquiae Antiquae*, Vol. I, 1841.

MUSIC COLLECTIONS AND FACSIMILES

————   Baxter, J. H. *An Old St. Andrews Music Book, Codex Helmstadt 628* (St. Andrews Univ. Publ. No. XXX), 1931.
EEH   *Early English Harmony*. Vol. I (facsimiles, selected and with short notes by H. E. Wooldridge), 1897; Vol. II (transcriptions, with notes, by H. V. Hughes), 1913.
StaE   Stainer, Sir John. *Early Bodleian Music*, 3 vols., 1901.

4. *The Cantigas, etc.*

BOOKS AND ARTICLES

AngC   Anglès, Higini. *Les "Cantigas" del rei N'Anfós el Savi*, 1927.
E   Anglès, Higini. *El Còdex musical de las Huelgas (Música a veus dels segles XIII–XIV)*, 3 vols., 1931. Introduction, facsimiles, and transcriptions.
L   Anglès, Higini. *La música a Catalunya fins al segle XIII*, 1935.
AuI   Aubry, Pierre. *Iter Hispanicum*, in SIM, VIII (1907), 337, 517; IX (1907), 32; (1908), 157, 175.
ChayT   (See Section 2)
ColC   Collet, Henri. *Contribution à l'étude des "Cantigas" d'Alphonse le Savant*, in *Bulletin hispanique*, XIII (1911), 270. (With P. Villalba)
MitM   Mitjana y Gordón, Rafael. *La Musique en Espagne*, in EC, Partie I, IV, p. 1913.
PopeM   Pope, Isabel. *Mediaeval Latin Background of the Thirteenth-Century Galician Lyric*, in *Speculum. A Journal of Mediaeval Studies*, IX (1934), 3.
————   Reis, P. Batalha. *Da origem da música trovadoresca em Portugal*, 1931.
RiaC   Riaño, Juan F. *Critical and bibliographical notes on early Spanish music*, 1887.
RibA   Ribera y Tarragó, Julian. *La Música árabe y su influencia en la española*, 1927.
M   Ribera y Tarragó, Julian. *Music in Ancient Arabia and Spain*, 1929. An English translation by E. Hague and M. Leffingwell of commentary in *La Música de las Cantigas*, 1922. (See RibC, below)
T   Ribera y Tarragó, Julian. *La Música andaluza medieval en las canciones de Trovadores, Troveros y Minnesinger*. 3 vols., 1923–25.
TreA   Trend, John Brande. *Alfonso the Sage, and other Spanish Essays*, 1926.
M   Trend, John Brande. *The Music of Spanish History to 1600*, 1926.

UrA   Ursprung, Otto. *Um die Frage nach dem arabischen bzw. maurischen Einfluss auf*
           die abendländische Musik des Mittelalters, in ZfMW, XVI (1934), 129, 355.
VindS   Vindel, Pedro. *Las siete canciones de amor: poema musical del siglo XII*, 1915.

MUSIC COLLECTION (INCLUDING FACSIMILES)

RibC   Ribera y Tarragó, Julian. *La Música de las Cantigas: Estudio sobre su origen y*
           naturaleza. Contains facsimiles of the Madrid MS of the *Cantigas* (B.N. 10069),
           with transcriptions and commentary (see pp. 345ff *supra*), 1922. (See RibM, above)

CHAPTER 9

BOOKS AND ARTICLES

———   Adler, Guido. *Über Heterophonie*, in *Jahrbuch der Musikbibliothek Peters*, XV
           (1908), 17.
AmelM   Amelli, Ambrosio M. *Micrologus ad praestantiores codices mss. exactus*, 1904.
AppelT   Appel, Margarete. *Terminologie in den mittelalterlichen Musiktraktaten*, 1935.
BelF   Belaiev, Victor. *The Folk-Music of Georgia*, in MQ, XIX (1933), 417.
BukE   (See bibliography for Chapter 14)
CouH   Coussemaker, Charles Edmond Henri. *Histoire de l'harmonie au moyen-âge*, 1852.
   S   Coussemaker, Charles Edmond Henri. *Scriptorum de musica medii ævi nova series*,
           4 vols., 1864–76. Facsimile ed., 1931.
EllinM   (See bibliography for Chapter 6, Section 1)
FarmH   Farmer, Henry George. *Historical Facts for the Arabian Musical Influence*, 1930.
FeldQ   Feldmann, Fritz. *Ein Quintorganum aus einer Breslauer Handschrift des 16. Jahr-*
           hunderts, in *Kirchenmusikalisches Jahrbuch*, XXVII (1932), 75.
FerandH   Ferand, Ernst. *The "Howling in Seconds" of the Lombards*, in MQ, XXV (1939),
           313.
   M   Ferand, Ernst. *Die Improvisation in der Musik*, 1938.
FiO   Ficker, Rudolf. *Der Organumtraktat der Vatikanischen Bibliothek (Ottob. 3025)*,
           in *Kirchenmusikalisches Jahrbuch*, XXVII (1932), 65.
FoxT   Fox Strangways, Arthur Henry. *A Tenth Century Manual*, in M&L, XIII (1932),
           183.
FrereW   Frere, Walter Howard. *The Winchester Troper* (Henry Bradshaw Society, Vol.
           VIII), 1884.
GalpO   Galpin, Francis William. *Old English Instruments of Music*, 1910.
   S   Galpin, Francis William. (See bibliography for Chapter 1)
GasG   Gastoué, Amédée. *L'Art grégorien*, 1911.
   M   Gastoué, Amédée. *Moyen Age II (La Musique occidentale)*, in EC, Partie I, I, 556.
   PP   Gastoué, Amédée. *Paraphonie et Paraphonistes*, in RdM, IX (1928), 61.
GennF   (See bibliography for Chapter 7)
GerS   Gerbert, Martin. *Scriptores ecclesiastici de musica*, 3 vols., 1784. Facsimile ed., 1931.
———   Grutchfield, E. J. *Hucbald: A Millenary Commemoration*, in *The Musical Times*,
           LXXI (1930), 507, 704.
HammS   Hammerich, Angul. *Studien über isländische Musik*, in SIM, I (1900), 341.
HandB   Handschin, Jacques. *Ein mittelalterlicher Beitrag zur Lehre von der Sphärenhar-*
           monie, in ZfMW, IX (1927), 193.
   E   Handschin, Jacques. (See bibliography for Chapter 11)
———   Handschin, Jacques. *Gregorianisch-Polyphones aus der Handschrift, Paris, B.N. lat.*
           15129, in *Kirchenmusikalisches Jahrbuch*, XXV (1930), 60.
   L   Handschin, Jacques. *L'Organum à l'Église*, in *La Revue du Chant Grégorien*, XI
           (1936), 180; XLI (1937), 14, 41.
   M   Handschin, Jacques. *Die Musikanschauung des Johannes Scotus*, in *Deutsche Vier-*
           teljahrsschrift für Literaturwissenschaft und Geistesgeschichte, V (1927), 316.
   O   Handschin, Jacques. *Der Organum-Traktat von Montpellier*, in AdlerF (1930), 50.
   R   Handschin, Jacques. (See bibliography for Chapter 11)
   UU   Handschin, Jacques. (See bibliography for Chapter 11)
   W   Handschin, Jacques. *The Two Winchester Tropers*, in *The Journal of Theological*
           Studies, XXXVII (1936), 34, 156.
   Z   Handschin, Jacques. *Zur Geschichte der Lehre vom Organum*, in ZfMW, VIII
           (1926), 321.

HayesM   Hayes, Gerald R. *Musical Instruments and their Music, 1500–1700.* 5 vols. (1928–   ).

HornI   Hornbostel, Erich M. von. *Phonographierte isländische Zwiegesänge,* in Deutsche *Islandforschung,* II (1930), 300.

HughA   Hughes, Dom Anselm. *Anglo-French Sequelae, edited from the papers of the late Dr. Henry Marriott Bannister,* 1934.

H   Hughes, Dom Anselm. *The Origins of Harmony* in MQ, XXIV (1938), **176.**

T   (See bibliography for Chapter 5, Section 1)

JacC   (See bibliography for Chapter 6, Section 1)

KornT   (See bibliography for Chapter 5)

LafE   La Fage, Juste Adrien L. de. *Essais de diphtérographie musicale,* 1864.

LudG   Ludwig, Friedrich. *Die geistliche nichtliturgische, weltliche einstimmige und die mehrstimmige Musik des Mittelalters bis zum Anfang des 15. Jahrhunderts,* in AdlerH I, 157.

K   Ludwig, Friedrich. *Die mehrstimmige Musik des 11. und 12. Jahrhunderts,* in *Bericht über den III. Kongress der IMG 1909* (1910), 101.

MaH   Machabey, Armand. *Histoire et évolution des formules musicales du Ier au XVe siècle,* 1928.

MigneL   Migne, Jacques Paul. *Patrologiae cursus completus. Series Latina.* 221 vols., 1844–55.

MülH   Müller, Hans. *Hucbalds echte und unechte Schriften über Musik,* 1884.

W   Müller, Hans. *Die Musik Wilhelms von Hirschau,* 1883.

PulE   Pulver, Jeffrey. *The English Theorists,* in *The Musical Times,* LXXIV (1933), 892, 984; LXXV (1934), 26, 220, 408, 709, 804, 900.

RieG   Riemann, Hugo. *Geschichte der Musiktheorie im IX–XIX Jahrhundert,* 1898, 2nd ed., 1921. (References are to the 2nd ed.)

SachsH   Sachs, Curt. *Handbuch der Musikinstrumentenkunde,* 1920.

HI   Sachs, Curt. *The History of Musical Instruments,* 1940.

R   Sachs, Curt. *Real-Lexikon der Musikinstrumente,* 1913.

SchlesG   (See bibliography for Chapter 2)

SchneiderG   Schneider, Marius. *Geschichte der Mehrstimmigkeit.* 3 vols: Vol. 1, 1934; Vol. 2, 1935; Vol. 3, in prep.

SowaT   Sowa, Heinrich. *Textvariationen zur Musica Enchiriadis,* in ZfMW, XVII (1935), 194.

SpittaM   Spitta, Philipp. *Die Musica Enchiriadis und ihr Zeitalter,* in VfMW, V (1889), 443.

SteinZ   Steinhard, Erich. *Zur Frühgeschichte der Mehrstimmigkeit,* in AfMW III (1921), 220.

WagJ   Wagner, Peter. *Die Gesänge der Jakobusliturgie zu Santiago de Compostela,* 1931.

P   Wagner, Peter. *La Paraphonie,* in RdM, IX (1928), 15.

U   Wagner, Peter. *Über die Anfänge des mehrstimmigen Gesanges,* in ZfMW, IX (1926), 2.

WolfQ   Wolf, Johannes. *Eine neue Quelle zur mehrstimmigen kirchlichen Praxis des 14. bis 15. Jahrhunderts,* in *Festschrift zum 60. Geburtstage von Peter Wagner* (1926), 222.

WolkG   Wolking, Hubert. *Guidos "Micrologus de disciplina artis musicae" und seine Quellen,* 1930.

YasQ   Yasser, Joseph. *Medieval Quartal Harmony,* in MQ, XXIII (1937), 170, 333; XXIV (1938), 351. (Also published, 1938, in book form)

T   Yasser, Joseph. *A Theory of Evolving Tonality,* 1932.

MUSIC COLLECTIONS AND FACSIMILES

BannM   Bannister, Henry Mariott. *Monumenti Vaticani di paleografia musicale latina,* 1913.

LinR   Lineva, Yevgenija Eduardovich (Eugenie Lineff). *Peasant Songs of Great Russia as they are in Folk's Harmonization,* 2 series: Series I, 1905; Series II, 1912.

PM   *Paléographie musicale.*

I   *La Codex 339 de la Bibliothèque de Saint-Gall (Xe siècle): Antiphonale Missarum Sancti Gregorii,* 1889

IV   *Le Codex 121 de la Bibliothèque d'Einsiedeln (Xe–XIe siècle): Antiphonale Missarum Sancti Gregorii,* 1893–96.

ThorI   Thorsteinsson, Bjarni. *Islenzk Thjódlög,* 1906–09.

CHAPTER 10

BOOKS AND ARTICLES

AbD   Abert, Hermann. *Die Musikanschauung des Mittelalters und ihre Grundlagen*, 1905.

AngL   (See bibliography for Chapter 8, Section 4)

BesS II   Besseler, Heinrich. *Studien zur Musik des Mittelalters. II. Die Motette von Franko von Köln bis Philippe von Vitry*, in AfMW, VIII (1927), 137.

BohnP   Bohn, Peter. *Die Plica im gregorianischen Gesange und im Mensuralgesange*, in MfMG, XXVII (1895), 47.

CouA   Coussemaker, Charles Edmond Henri. *L'Art harmonique aux XIIᵉ et XIIIᵉ siècles*, 1865.

S   Coussemaker, Charles Edmond Henri. *Scriptorum de musica medii ævi nova series*, 4 vols., 1864–76. Facsimile ed., 1931.

GerS   Gerbert, Martin. *Scriptores ecclesiastici de musica*, 3 vols., 1784. Facsimile ed., 1931.

JacM   Jacobsthal, Gustav. *Die Mensuralnotenschrift des 12. und 13. Jahrhunderts*, 1871.

KromP   Kromolicki, Joseph. *Die Practica Artis Musicae des Amerus*, 1909.

KuhlM   (See bibliography for Chapter 11)

LudQ   Ludwig, Friedrich. *Die Quellen der Motetten ältesten Stils*, in AfMW, V (1923), 185, 273.

R   Ludwig, Friedrich. *Repertorium organum recentioris et motetorum vetustissimi stili, 1.Bd. Catalogue raisonné der Quellen*, 1910.

MichalM   Michalitschke, Anton Maria. *Studien zur Entstehung und Frühentwicklung der Mensuralnotation*, in ZfMW, XII (1930), 257.

T   Michalitschke, Anton Maria. *Die Theorie des Modus*, 1923.

———   Michalitschke, Anton Maria. *Zur Frage der Longa in der Mensuraltheorie des 13. Jahrhunderts*, in ZfMW, VIII (1925), 103.

MülA   Müller, Hans. *Eine Abhandlung über Mensuralmusik in der Karlsruhe Handschrift St. Peter pergamen 29ᵃ*, 1886.

NieL   Niemann, Walter. *Die abweichende Bedeutung der Ligaturen in der Mensuraltheorie der Zeit vor Johannes de Garlandia*, 1902.

———   Pulver, Jeffrey. *The English Theorists*, in *The Musical Times*, LXXIV (1933), 892, 984; LXXV (1934), 26, 220, 408, 709, 804, 900.

RieG   Riemann, Hugo. *Geschichte der Musiktheorie im IX–XIX Jahrhundert*, 1898, 2nd ed., 1921.

———   Riemann-Einstein. *Musiklexikon*, etc. (Articles on *Ligatur, Mensuralmusik, Mensuralnote, Modus, Perfectio, Proprietas*, etc.)

RibM   (See bibliography for Chapter 8, Section 4)

SchmiD   (See bibliography for Chapter 11)

SowaA   Sowa, Heinrich. *Ein anonymer glossierter Mensuraltraktat 1279*, 1930.

Z   Sowa, Heinrich. *Zur Weiterentwicklung der modalen Rhythmik*, in ZfMW, XV (1933), 422.

StainN   Stainer, J. F. R. *The Notation of Mensurable Music*, in PMA, XXVI (1900), 215.

———   Ursprung, Otto. *Die Ligaturen, ihr System und ihre methodische und didaktische Darstellung*, in Acta, XI (1939), 1.

WolfG   Wolf, Johannes. *Geschichte der Mensural-Notation von 1250–1460*, 1904. 3 vols. Vol. 1, Historical text; Vol. 2, Examples of Notation from the 13th to the 15th century; Vol. 3, Translations of the examples into modern notation.

H   Wolf, Johannes. *Handbuch der Notationskunde*. Vol. 1, 1913; Vol. 2, 1919.

M   Wolf, Johannes. *Die Musiklehre des Johannes de Grocheo*, in SIM, I (1899), 65.

MM   Wolf, Johannes. *Die Musiktheorie des Mittelalters*, in Acta, III (1931), 53.

MUSIC COLLECTIONS AND FACSIMILES

AuM   (See bibliography for Chapter 11)

BaxO   (See bibliography for Chapter 11)

HughW   Hughes, Dom Anselm. *Worcester Mediæval Harmony*, 1928.

RoksM   (See bibliography for Chapter 11)

CHAPTER 11

BOOKS AND ARTICLES

AdlerW   Adler, Guido. *Die Wiederholung und Nachahmung in der Mehrstimmigkeit*, in VfMW, II (1886), 271.

AngE   (See Facsimiles and Music Collections)

F   (See bibliography for Chapter 13)

L   (See bibliography for Chapter 8, Section 4)

AuM   (See Facsimiles and Music Collections)

BellerF   Bellermann, Heinrich. *Franconis de Colonia Artis Cantus Mensurabilis Caput XI, de Discantu et eius Speciebus, Text, Übersetzung, und Erklärung*, 1874.

BesM   Besseler, Heinrich. *Die Musik des Mittelalters und der Renaissance*, 1931–35.

S II   Besseler, Heinrich. *Die Motette von Franko von Köln bis Philippe von Vitry*, in AfMW, VIII (1927), 137.

———   Besseler, Heinrich. *Musik des Mittelalters in der Hamburger Musikhalle*, in ZfMW, VII (1924), 42.

BuhleB   Buhle, Edward. *Die musikalischen Instrumente in den Miniaturen des frühen Mittelalters I. Die Blasinstrumente*, 1903.

BukP   (See bibliography for Chapter 14)

ChomT   Chominski, Josef Michal. *Technika imitacyjna XIII i XIV wieku*, in *Kwartalnik Muzyczny*, XIX–XX (1933), 133.

CouH   Coussemaker, C. E. H. *Histoire de l'harmonie au moyen-âge*, 1852.

S   Coussemaker, C. E. H. *Scriptorum de musica medii ævi nova series*, 4 vols., 1864–76. Facsimile ed., 1931.

CserbaM   Cserba, Simon M. *Der Musiktrakat des Hieronymus Moravia O.P.*, 1935. (Cserba's dissertation was published without Jerome's treatise in 1934.)

Ein SH   Einstein, Alfred. *A Short History of Music*, 2nd ed., 1938.

———   Ellinwood, Leonard. *The French Renaissance of the Twelfth Century in Music*, Paper read Sept. 14, 1939, before the International Congress of the American Musicological Society, held in New York. (To be published)

FarmC   Farmer, H. G. *Clues for the Arabian Influence on European Musical Theory*, in *Journal of the Asiatic Society of Great Britain and Ireland*, for 1925, 61.

FeinK   (See bibliography for Chapter 13)

FiD   Ficker, Rudolf. *Die Musik des Mittelalters und ihre Beziehungen zum Geistesleben*, in *Deutsche Vierteljahrsschrift für Literaturwissenschaft und Geistesgeschichte*, III (1925), 501.

FiG   Ficker, Rudolf. *Polyphonic Music of the Gothic Period*, in MQ, XV (1929), 483.

GalpE   Galpin, F. W. *A Textbook of European Musical Instruments*, 1937.

O   Galpin, F. W. *Old English Instruments of Music*, 1910.

GasP   Gastoué, Amédée. *Les Primitifs de la musique française*, 1922.

———   Gastoué, Amédée. *Three Centuries of French Mediaeval Music*, in MQ, III (1917), 173.

GennF   Gennrich, Friedrich. *Grundriss einer Formenlehre des mittelalterlichen Liedes als Grundlage einer musikalischen Formenlehre des Liedes*, 1932.

T   Gennrich, Friedrich. *Trouvèrelieder und Motettenrepertoire*, in ZfMW, IX (1926), 8, 65.

GerS   Gerbert, Martin. *Scriptores ecclesiastici de musica*, 3 vols., 1784. Facsimile ed., 1931.

GéroH   Gérold, Théodore. *Histoire de la musique des origines à la fin du XIVᵉ siècle*, 1936.

M   Gérold, Théodore. *La Musique au moyen âge*, 1932.

GrönR   Gröninger, Eduard. *Repertoire-Untersuchungen zum mehrstimmigen Notre Dame-Conductus*, 1939.

HandC   Handschin, Jacques. *Zum Crucifixum in carne*, in AfMW, VII (1925), 161.

E   Handschin, Jacques. *A Monument of English Mediæval Polyphony: The Manuscript Wolfenbüttel 677*, in *The Musical Times*, LXXIII (1932), 510; LXXIV (1933), 697.

H   Handschin, Jacques. *Gregorianisch-Polyphones aus der Handschrift, Paris, B.N. lat. 15129*, in *Kirchenmusikalisches Jahrbuch*, XXV (1930), 60.

N   Handschin, Jacques. *Notizen über die Notre Dame-Conductus*, in *Bericht über den musikwissenschaftlichen Kongress zu Leipzig* (1925), 209.

HandND	Handschin, Jacques. *Zur Geschichte von Notre Dame,* in Acta, IV (1932), 5, 49.
NDS	Handschin, Jacques. *Was brachte die Notre Dame-Schule Neues?* in ZfMW, VI (1924), 545.
R	Handschin, Jacques. *Die Rolle der Nationen in der mittelalterlichen Musikgeschichte,* in *Schweizerisches Jahrbuch für Musikwissenschaft,* V (1931), 1.
S	Handschin, Jacques. *Eine wenig beachtete Stilrichtung innerhalb der mittelalterlichen Mehrstimmigkeit,* in *Schweizerisches Jahrbuch für Musikwissenschaft,* I (1924), 56.
UU	Handschin, Jacques. *Über den Ursprung der Motette,* in *Bericht über den Musikwissenschaftlichen Kongress in Basel, 1924* (1925), 189.
UV	Handschin, Jacques. *Über Voraussetzungen sowie Früh- und Hochblüte der mittelalterlichen Mehrstimmigkeit,* in *Schweizerisches Jahrbuch für Musikwissenschaft,* II (1927), 5.
ZB	Handschin, Jacques. *Die mittelalterlichen Aufführungen in Zürich, Bern und Basel,* in ZfMW, X (1927), 8.
ZP	Handschin, Jacques. *Zur Frage der melodischen Paraphrasierung im Mittelalter,* in ZfMW, X (1928), 513.
———	Handschin, Jacques. *Zur Notre Dame-Rhythmik,* in ZfMW, VII (1925), 386.
HickP	Hickmann, Hans. *Das Portativ,* 1936.
HusM	Husmann, Heinrich. *Die Motetten der Madrider Handschrift und deren geschichtliche Stellung,* in AfMF, II (1937), 173.
O	Husmann, Heinrich. *Die Offiziumsorgana der Notre Dame-Zeit,* in *Jahrbuch der Musikbibliothek Peters,* XLII (1936), 31.
———	Husmann, Heinrich. *Die dreistimmigen Organa der Notre Dame-Schule,* 1935.
KollerL	Koller, Oswald. *Der Liederkodex von Montpellier,* in VfMW, IV (1888), 1.
KuhlM	Kuhlmann, Georg. *Die zweistimmigen französischen Motetten des Kodex Montpellier, Faculté de Médecine H 196 in ihrer Bedeutung für die Musikgeschichte des 13. Jahrhunderts.* 2 vols., 1938.
LudB	Ludwig, Friedrich. *Musik des Mittelalters in der Badischen Kunsthalle Karlsruhe,* in ZfMW, V (1923), 434.
C	Ludwig, Friedrich. *Die 50 Beispiele Coussemakers aus der Handschrift von Montpellier,* in SIM, V (1904), 177.
G	Ludwig, Friedrich. *Die geistliche nichtliturgische, weltliche einstimmige und die mehrstimmige Musik des Mittelalters bis zum Anfang des 15. Jahrhunderts,* in AdlerH I, 157.
L	Ludwig, Friedrich. *Die liturgischen Organa Leonins und Perotins,* in RieF (1909), 200.
M	Ludwig, Friedrich. *Über die Entstehung und die erste Entwicklung der lateinischen und französischen Motette in musikalischer Beziehung,* in SIM, VII (1906), 514.
Q	Ludwig, Friedrich. *Die Quellen der Motetten ältesten Stils,* in AfMW, V (1923), 185, 273.
R	Ludwig, Friedrich. *Repertorium organorum recentioris et motetorum vetustissimi stili, 1. Bd. Catalogue raisonné der Quellen,* 1910. (Part 2 of this *1. Bd.* and also a portion of the *2. Bd.* were printed later, but copies are rare.)
U	Ludwig, Friedrich. *Über den Entstehungsort der grossen "Notre Dame-Handschriften,"* in AdlerF (1930), 45.
———	Ludwig, Friedrich. *Perotinus Magnus,* in AfMW, III (1921), 361.
	Meyer, Wilhelm. *Der Ursprung des Motets,* 1897.
MülleGF	Müller-Blattau, Joseph. *Grundzüge einer Geschichte der Fuge,* 1931.
NowakO	Nowak, Leopold. *Grundzüge einer Geschichte des Basso Ostinato in der abendländischen Musik,* 1932.
PanS	Panum, Hortense. *Stringed Instruments of the Middle Ages,* 1941.
RauO	Raugel, Félix. *Les Grandes Orgues des Églises de Paris et du Département de la Seine,* 1925.
RieG	(See Bibliography for Chapter 10)
RoksC	Rokseth, Yvonne. *Le Contrepoint double vers 1248,* in *Mélanges de Musicologie offerts à M. Lionel de La Laurencie* (1933), 5.
F	Rokseth, Yvonne. *Les Femmes musiciennes du XIIᵉ au XIVᵉ siècle,* in *Romania,* LXI (1935), 464.
RosM	Rosenthal, Karl August von. *Einige unbekannte Motetten älteren Stils aus Handschriften der Nationalbibliothek, Wien,* in Acta, VI (1934), 8.
SachsH	Sachs, Curt. *Handbuch der Musikinstrumentenkunde,* 1920.
HI	Sachs, Curt. *The History of Musical Instruments,* 1940.

SachsR　　Sachs, Curt. *Real-Lexikon der Musikinstrumente*, 1913.
SchlesI　　Schlesinger, Kathleen. *The Significance of Musical Instruments in the Evolution of Music*, in OH Int. (1929), 85.
　　P　　Schlesinger, Kathleen. (See bibliography for Chapter 2)
SchmiD　　Schmidt, Helmut. *Die drei- und vierstimmigen Organa*, 1933.
　　M　　Schmidt, Helmut. *Zur Melodiebildung Leonins und Perotins*, in ZfMW, XIV (1931), 129.
SchneiderG　　(See bibliography for Chapter 9)
　　H　　Schneider, Marius, *Der Hochetus*, in ZfMW, XI (1929), 390.
　　Z　　Schneider, Marius. *Zur Satztechnik der Notre Dame-Schule*, in ZfMW, XIV (1932), 398.
SowaZ　　(See bibliography for Chapter 10)
TrederM　　Treder, Dorothea. *Die Musikinstrumente in den höfischen Epen der Blütezeit*, 1933.
UrK　　Ursprung, Otto. *Die katholische Kirchenmusik*, 1931–33.
WolfH　　Wolf, Johannes. *Handbuch der Notationskunde*. Vol. 1, 1913; Vol. 2, 1919.
　　M　　Wolf, Johannes. *Die Musiklehre des Johannes de Grocheo*, in SIM, I (1899), 65.
　　MR　　Wolf, Johannes. (See bibliography for Chapter 6, Section 2)

MUSIC COLLECTIONS AND FACSIMILES

AdO　　(See bibliography for Chapter 7)
AngE　　Anglès, Higini. *El Còdex musical de Las Huelgas* (*Música a veus dels segles XIII–XIV*), 3 vols., 1931. Introduction, facsimiles, and transcriptions.
AuM　　Aubry, Pierre. *Cent Motets du XIIIe siècle*. 3 vols., 1908. Facsimile of the Codex Bamberg Ed. IV. 6, with transcriptions into modern notation and commentary.
BaxO　　Baxter, J. H. *An Old St. Andrews Music Book*, 1931. Facsimile edition of the MS Wolfenbüttel 677, with introduction.
FiS　　Ficker, Rudolf. *Musik der Gotik* (*Perotinus, Sederunt principes*), ed. by Ficker, 1930.
GennR　　Gennrich, Friedrich. *Rondeaux, Virelais und Balladen*. 2 vols. I in 1921; II in 1927.
HusD　　Husmann, Heinrich. *Die drei- und vierstimmigen Notre-Dame-Organa*, 1940.
RibC　　(See bibliography for Chapter 8, Section 4)
RoksM　　Rokseth, Yvonne. *Poylphonies du XIIIe siècle* (*Manuscrit H 196 de Montpellier*), 4 vols.: facsimile, transcriptions (2 vols.), commentary, 1935–39.
ScherG　　Schering, Arnold. *Geschichte der Musik in Beispielen*, 1931.
SchmiB　　Schmidt, Helmut. *3 Benedicamus Domino-Organa*, 1933.

CHAPTER 12

The 14th Century: French Music—French and Italian Notation

BOOKS AND ARTICLES

BesH　　Besseler, Heinrich. *Musik des Mittelalters in der Hamburger Musikhalle*, in ZfMW, VII (1924), 42.
　　M　　Besseler, Heinrich. *Die Musik des Mittelalters und der Renaissance*, 1931–35.
　　S　　Besseler, Heinrich. *Studien zur Musik des Mittelalters*.
　　I. *Neue Quellen des 14. und beginnenden 15. Jahrhunderts*, in AfMW, VII (1925), 167.
　　II. *Die Motette von Franko von Köln bis Philippe von Vitry*, in AfMW, VIII (1927), 137.
BohnV　　Bohn, Peter, *Philipp von Vitry*, in MfMG, XXII (1890), 141.
BorB　　Van den Borren, Charles. *Les Fragments de messe du manuscrit 222 C 22 de la Bibliothèque de Strasbourg*, in *Tijdschrift der Vereeniging voor Nederlandsche Muziekgeschiedenis*, XII (1928), 177, 236.
　　S　　Van den Borren, Charles. *Le Manuscrit musical M.222 C.22 de la Bibliothèque de Strasbourg* (*XVe siècle*) *brulé en 1870, et réconstitué d'après une copie partielle d'Edmond de Coussemaker*, in *Annales de l'Académie Royale d'Archéologie de Belgique*, LXXI. 7e Série, Tome I (1924), 343; LXXII. 7e Série, Tome II (1924), 272; LXXIII. 7e Série, Tome III (1925), 128; LXXIV. 7e Série, Tome IV (1927), 71. (Also published separately.)
BorgP　　Borghezio, Gino. *Poesie musicali latine e francese in un codice ignorato della Biblioteca capitolare d'Ivrea* (*Torino*), in *Archivum Romanicum*, V (1921), 173.

——— Brenet, Michel. *Musique et musiciens de la vielle France* (contains *Les Musiciens de Philippe le hardi*), 1911.

——— Chominski, Jósef Michal. *Technika imitacyjna XIII i XIV wieku*, in *Kwartalnik Muzyczny*, XIX–XX (1933), 133.

CouS   Coussemaker, Charles Edmond Henri. *Scriptorum de musica medii ævi nova series*, 4 vols., 1864–76. Facsimile ed., 1931.

——— Coussemaker, Charles Edmond Henri. *Les harmonistes du XIVe siècle*, 1869.

CovA   Coville, A. *Philippe de Vitri. Notes biographiques*, in *Romania*, LIX (1933), 520.

——— Droz, Eugénie and G. Thibault. *Un Chansonnier de Philippe le Bon*, in RdM, X (1926), 1.

EllinL (See bibliography for Chapter 13, Music Collections etc.)

FeinK   (See bibliography for Chapter 13)

FiG   Ficker, Rudolf. *Polyphonic Music of the Gothic Period*, in MQ, XV (1929), 483.

K   Ficker, Rudolf. (See bibliography for Chapter 14)

GasP   Gastoué, Amédée. *Les Primitifs de la musique française*, 1922.

GaspA   Gasperini, Guido. *L'Art musical italien au XIVe siècle*, in EC, Partie I, II, 611.

GerS   Gerbert, Martin. *Scriptores ecclesiastici de musica*, 3 vols., 1784. Facsimile ed., 1931.

GéroH   Gérold, Théodore. *Histoire de la musique des origines à la fin du XIV siècle*, 1936.

M   Gérold, Théodore. *La Musique au moyen âge*, 1932.

GrossS Grossmann, Walter. *Die einleitenden Kapitel des Speculum musice*, 1924.

HandND Handschin, Jacques. *Zur Geschichte von Notre Dame*, in Acta, IV (1932), 5, 49.

ZP   Handschin, Jacques. (See bibliography for Chapter 11)

HoepM   Hoepffner, Ernest. *Oeuvres de Guillaume de Machaut*, 3 vols., 1908–21 (the poetry).

KamP   Kammerer, Friedrich. *Die Musikstücke des Prager Kodex XI E 9*, 1931.

LangfR Långfors, Arthur. *Le Roman de Fauvel par Gervais du Bus*, 1914–19.

LudB   Ludwig, Friedrich. *Musik des Mittelalters in der Badischen Kunsthalle Karlsruhe*, in ZfMW, V (1923), 434.

D   Ludwig, Friedrich. *Die mehrstimmige Messe des 14. Jahrhunderts*, in AfMW, VII (1925), 417.

G   Ludwig, Friedrich. *Die geistliche nichtliturgische, weltliche einstimmige und die mehrstimmige Musik des Mittelalters bis zum Anfang des 15. Jahrhunderts*, in AdlerH I, 157.

L   Ludwig, Friedrich. (See bibliography for Chapter 11)

MM   Ludwig, Friedrich. *Die mehrstimmige Musik des 14. Jahrhunderts*, in SIM, IV (1902), 16.

Q   Ludwig, Friedrich. *Die Quellen der Motetten ältesten Stils*, in AfMW, V (1923), 185, 273.

MaG   Machabey, Armand. *Guillaume de Machault*, in RM, XI (1930), 425; XII (1931), 320, 402.

P   Machabey, Armand. *Notice sur Philippe de Vitry*, in RM, X (1929), 20.

NovatiC Novati, Francesco. *Per l'origine e la storia delle Caccie*, in *Studi medievali*, II (1906–07), 303.

——— Pirro, André. *La Musique à Paris sous la règne de Charles VI (1380–1422)*, 1930.

——— Quittard, Henry. *Notes sur Guillaume de Machaut*, in *Bulletin de la soc. française de musicologie*, I (1918), 91, 123.

RieG   Riemann, Hugo. *Geschichte der Musiktheorie im IX–XIX Jahrhundert*, 2nd ed., 1921.

——— Sachs, Curt. *Anthologie Sonore*. Notes to record albums III–IV, 1936.

SartN   Sartori, Claudio. *La notazione italiana del trecento in una redazione inedita del "Tractatus practice cantus mensurabilis ad modum Ytalicorum" di Prosdocimo de Beldemandis*, 1938.

SchneiderA Schneider, Marius. *Die Ars nova des XIV. Jahrhunderts in Frankreich und Italien*, 1930.

WolfG I Wolf, Johannes. *Geschichte der Mensural-Notation von 1250–1460*, Vol. 1, historical text, 1904.

H   Wolf, Johannes. *Handbuch der Notationskunde*. Vol. 1, 1913; Vol. 2, 1919.

O   Wolf, Johannes. *Zur Geschichte der Orgelmusik im vierzehnten Jahrhundert*, in *Kirchenmusikalisches Jahrbuch*, XIV (1899), 14.

——— Wolf, Johannes. *Die Tonschriften*, 1924.

MUSIC COLLECTIONS AND FACSIMILES

AuF   Aubry, Pierre. *Le Roman de Fauvel*, 1907.

P   Aubry, Pierre. *Les plus anciens monuments de la musique française*, 1903.

CouM   Coussemaker, Charles Edmond Henri. *Messe du XIIIe siècle*, 1861.

DTO XL   Bd. 76. *Sieben Trienter Codices. Sechste Auswahl*, 1924. Ed. R. Ficker.

GasMA   Gastoué, Amédée. *Le Manuscrit de musique polyphonique du trésor d'Apt (XIVe-XVe s.)*, 1936.

V   Gastoué, Amédée. *Concert vocal historique . . . 1re série*, 1930.

GennR   Gennrich, Friedrich. *Rondeaux, Virelais und Balladen*. 2 vols. I, 1921; II, 1927.

MachM   De Machaut, Guillaume. *Musikalische Werke*, ed. by Friedrich Ludwig. In PubAMD. Vol. 1 (Ballades, Rondeaux, and Virelais), 1926; Vol. 2 (Commentary), 1928; Vol. 3 (Motets), 1929. Vol. 4 (Mass and Lais), unpublished.

RoksM   (See bibliography for Chapter 11)

StaD   Stainer, Sir John, etc. *Dufay and his contemporaries*, 1898.

VanM   (See bibliography for Chapter 13)

WolfG II & III   Wolf, Johannes. *Geschichte der Mensural-Notation von 1250–1460*, Vol. 2, examples of notation from the 13th to the 15th century; Vol. 3, transcriptions of the examples into modern notation, 1904.

MS   Wolf, Johannes. *Musikalische Schrifttafeln*, 1923.

CHAPTER 13

The 14th Century: Italian, Spanish, and German Music—Musica Falsa—Instruments

BOOKS AND ARTICLES

AbE   Abert, Hermann. *Die Musikästhetik der Échecs Amoureux*, in SIM, VI (1905), 346.

AngD   Anglès, Higini. *Cantors und Ministrers in den Diensten der Koenige von Katalonien-Aragonien im 14. Jhdt.*, in *Bericht über den musikwissenschaftlichen Kongress in Basel, 1924* (1925), 56.

F   Anglès, Higini. *Die mehrstimmige Musik in Spanien vor dem 15. Jhdt.*, in *Beethoven-Zentenarfeier Kongressbericht* (1927), 158.

L   *La música a Catalunya fins al segle XIII*, 1935.

BaumD   Baumann, Otto A. *Das deutsche Lied und seine Bearbeitungen in den frühen Orgeltabulaturen*, 1934.

BesM   Besseler, Heinrich. *Die Musik des Mittelalters und der Renaissance*, 1931–35.

BonaB   Bonaventura, Arnaldo. *Il Boccaccio e musica*, in *Rivista musicale italiana*, XXI (1914), 405.

———   Chominski, Jósef Michal. *Technika imitacyjna XIII i XIV wieku*, in *Kwartalnik Muzyczny*, XIX–XX (1933), 133.

CouS   (See bibliography for Chapter 12)

DebS   Debenedetti, Santorre. *Il "Sollazzo,"* 1922.

———   Debenedetti, Santorre. *Il "Sollazzo" e il "Saporetto" con altre rime di Simone Prudenzani d'Orvieto* (*Giornale Storico della Letteratura Italiana, Suppl. No. 15*), 1913.

EinSH   Einstein, Alfred. *A Short History of Music*, 2nd ed., 1938.

EllinF   Ellinwood, Leonard. *Francesco Landini and his music*, in MQ, XXII (1936), 190.

O   Ellinwood, Leonard. *Origins of the Italian Ars Nova*, in *Papers read by members of the American Musicological Society at the Annual Meeting . . .* (1937), 29.

FeinK   Feininger, Laurence K. J. *Die Frühgeschichte des Kanons bis Josquin des Prez (um 1500)*, 1937.

FiB   Ficker, Rudolf. *Beiträge zur Chromatik des 14. bis 16. Jahrhunderts*, in SzMW, II (1914), 5.

GalpE   Galpin, F. W. *A Textbook of European Musical Instruments*, 1937.

O   Galpin, F. W. *Old English Instruments of Music*, 1910.

GennK   Gennrich, Friedrich. *Zur Musikinstrumentenkunde der Machaut-Zeit*, in ZfMW, IX (1927), 513.

GerS   (See bibliography for Chapter 12)

GéroH   Gérold, Théodore. *Histoire de la musique des origines à la fin du XIVe siècle*, 1936.

M   Gérold, Théodore. *La Musique au moyen âge*, 1932.

———   li Gotti, E. and N. Pirotta. *Il Sacchetti e la tecnica musicale del trecento italiano*, 1935.

———   Grion, G. *Delle rime volgari, Trattato di Antonio da Tempo*, 1869.

GutD   Gutman, Hanns. *Der Decamerone des Boccaccio als musikgeschichtliche Quelle*, in ZfMW, XI (1929), 397.

HaasA   Haas, Robert. *Aufführungspraxis der Musik*, 1930.

HabU   Haberl, Franz Xaver. *Bio-bibliographische Notizen über Ugolino von Orvieto*, in *Kirchenmusikalisches Jahrbuch*, X (1895), 40.

HandAP   Handschin, Jacques. *Angelomontana polyphonica*, in *Schweizerisches Jahrbuch für Musikwissenschaft*, III (1928), 64.

Er   Handschin, Jacques. *Erfordensia*, in Acta, VI (1934), 97.

R   Handschin, Jacques. (See bibliography for Chapter 11)

HertzS   Hertzmann, Erich. *Studien zur Basse danse . . .* , in ZfMW, XI (1929), 401.

HirschN   Hirschfeld, Robert. *Notizen zur mittelalterlichen Musikgeschichte (Instrumentalmusik und Musica ficta)*, in MfMG, XVII (1885), 61.

KamP   Kammerer, Friedrich. *Die Musikstücke des Prager Kodex XI E 9*, 1931.

KinsP   Kinsky, Georg. *A History of Music in Pictures*, 1930.

KornM   Kornmüller, Utto. *Musiklehre des Ugolino von Orvieto*, in *Kirchenmusikalisches Jahrbuch*, XX (1895), 19.

LafE   La Fage, Juste Adrien L. de. *Essais de diphtérographie musicale*, 1864.

LeiW   Leichtentritt, Hugo. *Was lehren uns die Bildwerke des 14.–17. Jahrhunderts über die Instrumentalmusik ihrer Zeit?* in SIM, VII (1906), 315.

LeviA   Levitan, Joseph S. *Adrian Willaert's Famous Duo: Quidnam ebrietas*, in *Tijdschrift der Vereeniging voor Nederl. Musiekgeschiedenis*, XV (1938), 166, 193. (Contains section on *musica falsa*.)

———   Liuzzi, Fernando. *Musica e Poesia del Trecento nel Codice Vaticano Rossiano 215*, in *Pontificia Accademia Romana di Archeologia*, XIII (1937), 59.

———   López-Chavarri, Eduardo. *Historia de la Música*. 2 vols., 3rd ed., 1929.

LudB   Ludwig, Friedrich. *Musik des Mittelalters in der Badischen Kunsthalle Karlsruhe*, in ZfMW, V (1923), 434.

E   Ludwig, Friedrich. *Die mehrstimmigen Werke der Handschrift Engelberg 314*, in *Kirchenmusikalisches Jahrbuch*, XXI (1908), 48.

G   Ludwig, Friedrich. *Die geistliche nichtliturgische, weltliche einstimmige und die mehrstimmige Musik des Mittelalters . . .* , in AdlerH I, 157.

Q   Ludwig, Friedrich. *Die Quellen der Motetten ältesten Stils*, in AfMW, V (1923), 185, 273.

———   Ludwig, Friedrich. *Die mehrstimmige Musik des 14. Jahrhunderts*, in SIM, IV (1902), 16.

MachM   (See bibliography for Chapter 12, Music Collections etc.)

MayerM   Mayer, F. Arnold and Hermann Rietsch. *Die Mondsee-Wiener Liederhandschrift und der Mönch von Salzburg*: Part I in *Acta Germanica*, III (1894), Heft 4; Part II in *Acta Germanica*, IV (1896).

MoriniC   Morini, Adolfo. *Un celebre musico dimenticato: Giovanni da Cascia*, in *Bolletino della regia deputazione di storia patria per l'Umbria*, XXVII (1924), 305.

MosG   Moser, Hans Joachim. *Geschichte der deutschen Musik*. 3 vols., 5th ed., 1930.

MülleW   Müller-Blattau, Joseph. *Wach auf, mein hort! Studie zur deutschen Liedkunst des 15. Jahrhunderts*, in AdlerF (1930), 92.

ParI   Parent, D. *Les Instruments des musiciens au XIVe siècle*, 1925.

PedJ   Pedrell, Felipe. *Jean I d'Aragon, Compositeur de Musique*, in *Riemann Festschrift* (1909), 229.

PirR   Pirro, André. *Remarques sur l'éxécution musicale de la fin du XIVe siècle au milieu du XVe siècle*, in *International Society for Musical Research, First Report, Liége, September 1–6, 1930, Report*, 55.

RiaC   Riaño, Juan F. *Critical and bibliographical notes on early Spanish music*, 1887.

RieH I²   Riemann, Hugo. *Handbuch der Musikgeschichte*, Vol I², 1905.

K   Riemann, Hugo. *Das Kunstlied im 14.–15. Jahrhundert*, in SIM, VII (1906), 529.

———   Riemann, Hugo. *Geschichte der Musiktheorie im IX–XIX Jahrhundert*, 1898, 2nd ed., 1921.

RietschM   Rietsch, Paul. *Der Mönch von Salzburg*, in *Musica Divina*, II (1914), 306.

SachsMI   Sachs, Curt. *Handbuch der Musikinstrumentenkunde*, 1920.

R   Sachs, Curt. *Real-Lexikon der Musikinstrumente*, 1913.

W   Sachs, Curt. *World History of the Dance*, 1937. (English translation of *Eine Weltgeschichte des Tanzes*, 1933. References are to the translation.)

ScherK   Schering, Arnold. *Das kolorierte Orgelmadrigal des Trecento*, in SIM, XIII **(1911)**, 172.

S   Schering, Arnold. *Studien zur Musikgeschichte der Frührenaissance*, 1914.

SchlecD   Schlecht, Raymund. *Ueber den Gebrauch der Diesis im 13. und 15. Jahrhundert*, in MfMG, IX (1877), 79, 99.

SchneiderA   (See bibliography for Chapter 12)

SillemA   Sillem, J. A. *Aanteekeningen omtrent muzikanten en muziek, uit XIV⁰ eeuwsche Noord-Nederlandsche bronnen*, in *Tijdschrift der Vereeniging voor Noord-Nederlands Muziekgeschiedenis*, VI (1900), 218.

SuñC   Suñol, Gregory. *Els Cants del Romeus (Segle XIV⁰)*, in *Analecta Montserratensia*, I (1917), 100.

TreC   Trend, J. B. *A Sixteenth Century Collector of Folksongs*, in M&L, VIII (1927), 13.

M   Trend, J. B. *The Music of Spanish History to 1600*, 1926.

UrS   Ursprung, Otto. *Spanisch-katalanische Liedkunst des 14. Jahrhunderts*, in ZfMW, IV (1921), 136.

V   Ursprung, Otto. *Vier Studien zur Geschichte des deutschen Liedes*, in AfMW, IV (1922), 413; V (1923), 11, 316; VI (1924), 262.

WessA   Wesselofsky, A. *Il Paradiso degli Alberti . . . di Giovanni da Prato*. 3 vols., 1867.

WolfF   Wolf, Johannes. *Florenz in der Musikgeschichte des 14. Jahrhunderts*, in SIM, III (1902), 599.

H   Wolf, Johannes. *Handbuch der Notationskunde*. Vol. 1, 1913; Vol. 2, 1919.

I   Wolf, Johannes. *Italian Trecento Music*, in PMA, LVIII (1931), 15.

J   Wolf, Johannes. *L'arte del biscanto misurato secondo el maestro Jacopo da Bologna*, in *Theodor Kroyer-Festschrift* (1933), 17.

T   Wolf, Johannes. *Die Tänze des Mittelalters*, in AfMW, I (1918), 10.

V   Wolf, Johannes. *Die Rossi-Handschrift 215 der Vaticana und das Trecento-Madrigal*, in *Jahrbuch der Musikbibliothek Peters*, XLV (1939), 53.

———   Wolf, Johannes. *Ein Beitrag zur Diskantlehre des 14. Jahrhunderts*, in SIM, XV (1914), 504.

MUSIC COLLECTIONS AND FACSIMILES

DTO IX¹   *Bd. 18. Oswald von Wolkenstein, Geistliche und weltliche Lieder*, 1902. Ed. J. Schatz and O. Koller.

XX²   (See bibliography for Chapter 8, Section 1)

EllinL   Ellinwood, Leonard. *The Works of Francesco Landini*, 1939.

GanI   Gandolfi, Riccardo. *Illustrazioni di alcuni cimeli concernanti l'arte musicale in Firenze*, 1892.

MarrF   Marrocco, W. Thomas. *Fourteenth-Century Italian Cacce*, 1942.

RunH   Runge, Paul. *Die Lieder des Hugo von Montfort mit den Melodien des Burk Mangolt*, 1906.

S   (See bibliography for Chapter 8, Section 1)

ScherG   Schering, Arnold. *Geschichte der Musik in Beispielen*, 1931.

VanM   Van, Guillaume de. *Les Monuments de l'Ars Nova. Fascicule 1, Morceaux liturgiques*

I   I, *Oeuvres italiennes*, 1939.

WolfG   Wolf, Johannes. *Geschichte der Mensural-Notation von 1250–1460*. Vol. 2, examples

II & III   of notation from the 13th to the 15th century; Vol. 3, transcriptions of the examples into modern notation, 1904.

MS   Wolf, Johannes. *Musikalische Schrifttafeln*, 1923.

S   Wolf, Johannes. *Sing- und Spielmusik aus älterer Zeit*, 1926.

CHAPTER 14

Polyphony in the British Isles
From the 12th Century to the Death of Dunstable

BOOKS AND ARTICLES

AdlerS   Adler, Guido. *Studie zur Geschichte der Harmonie*, in *Sitzungsberichten der phil.-hist. Klasse der kais. Akademie der Wissenschaften in Wien*, XCVIII Bd., III Heft (1881), 781.

ApelP   Apel, Willi. *The Partial Signatures in the Sources up to 1450*, in Acta, X (1938), 1; XI (1939), 40.

AndersB   Andersson, Otto. *The Bowed-Harp*, 1930.
BesM   Besseler, Heinrich. *Die Musik des Mittelalters und der Renaissance*, 1931–35.
   S I   Besseler, Heinrich. *Neue Quellen des 14. und beginnenden 15. Jahrhunderts*, in AfMW, VII (1925), 167.
BorG   Van den Borren, Charles. *The Genius of Dunstable*, in PMA, XLVII (1921), 78.
BukC   Bukofzer, Manfred. *The First English Chanson on the Continent*, in M&L, XIX (1938), 119.
   D   Bukofzer, Manfred. *Über Leben und Werke von Dunstable*, in Acta, VIII (1936), 102.
   E   Bukofzer, Manfred. *Geschichte des englischen Diskants und des Fauxbourdons nach den theoretischen Quellen*, 1936.
   G   Bukofzer, Manfred. *The Gymel. The Earliest Form of English Polyphony*, in M&L, XVI (1935), 77.
   J   Bukofzer, Manfred. *John Dunstable and the Music of his Time*, in PMA, LXV (1938), 19.
   M   Bukofzer, Manfred. *The First Motet with English Words*, in M&L, XVII (1936), 225.
   P   Bukofzer, Manfred. *Popular Polyphony in the Middle Ages*, in MQ, XXVI (1940), 31.
CouH   Coussemaker, Charles Edmond Henri. *Histoire de l'harmonie au moyen-âge*, 1852.
CouS   Coussemaker, Charles Edmond Henri. *Scriptorum de musica medii ævi nova series*, 4 vols., 1864–76. Facsimile ed., 1931.
CuttsS   Cutts, Edward L. *Scenes and Characters of the Middle Ages*, 1872.
DaveyH   Davey, Henry. *History of English Music*, 2nd ed., 1921.
Dim   Dimrock, James F. (editor). *Giraldus Cambrensis. Opera.*
   H   Vol. V. *Topographia Hibernica et Expugnatio Hibernica*, 1867.
   K   Vol. VI. *Itinerarium Kambriae et Descriptio Kambriae*, 1868.
DolC   Dolmetsch, Arnold. *Concerning my Recent Discoveries*, in *The Consort*, No. 3, June, 1934, 1.
EinSH   Einstein, Alfred. *A Short History of Music*, 2nd ed., 1938.
FarmM   Farmer, Henry George. *Music in Mediaeval Scotland*, 1927.
FiK   Ficker, Rudolf. *Die Kolorierungstechnik der Trienter Messen*, SzMW, VII (1920), 5.
   F   Ficker, Rudolf. *Die frühen Messenkompositionen der Trienter Codices* in SzMW, XI (1924), 3.
FleiM   Fleischer, Oskar. *Review in Vierteljahrsschrift für Musikwissenschaft*, VI (1890), 424.
FloodH   Flood, William H. Grattan. *A History of Irish Music*, 2nd ed., 1906.
   R   Flood, William H. Grattan. *Entries Relating to Music in the Patent Rolls of the Fifteenth Century*, in MAn, IV (1913), 225.
———   Flood, William H. Grattan. *The English Chapel Royal under Henry V and Henry VI*, in SIM, X (1909), 563.
———   Flood, William H. Grattan. *Gild of English Minstrels under King Henry VI*, in SIM, XV (1913), 66.
GalpO   Galpin, F. W. *Old Instruments of Music*, 1910.
GennF   Gennrich, Friedrich. *Grundriss einer Formenlehre des mittelalterlichen Liedes . . .*, 1932.
GeorE   Georgiades, Thrasybulos. *Englische Diskanttraktate aus der ersten Hälfte des 15. Jahrhunderts*, 1937.
GwynB   Gwynn Jones, T. *Bardism and Romance* in *Transactions of the Honorable Society of Cymmrodorion*, 1913–14, 205.
GwynnW   Gwynn Jones, T. *Welsh National Music and Dance*, 1933.
HandE   Handschin, Jacques. *A Monument of English Mediæval Polyphony: The Manuscript Wolfenbüttel 677*, in *The Musical Times*, LXXIII (1932), 510; LXXIV (1933), 697.
   H   Handschin, Jacques. *Gregorianisch-Polyphones aus der Handschrift, Paris, B.N. lat. 15129*, in *Kirchenmusikalisches Jahrbuch*, XXV (1930), 60.
   S   Handschin, Jacques. *Ein wenig beachtete Stilrichtung innerhalb der mittelalterlichen Mehrstimmigkeit*, in *Schweizerisches Jahrbuch für Musikwissenschaft*, I (1924), 56.
   U   Handschin, Jacques. *Über Estampie und Sequenz*, in ZfMW, XII (1929), 1; XIII (1930) 113.
   WM   Handschin, Jacques. Review of *Worcester Mediaeval Harmony*, in ZfMW, XIV (1931), 54.

HandZP Handschin, Jacques. *Zur Frage der melodischen Paraphrasierung im Mittelalter* in ZfMW, X (1928), 513.
HoareG Hoare, Sir Richard Colt (translator). Giraldus Cambrensis. *The Itinerary Through Wales. Description of Wales.* Everyman's Library, 1935.
HughH Hughes, Dom Anselm. *The Origins of Harmony* in MQ, XXIV (1938), 176.
O Hughes, Dom Anselm. *On the Study of Early Harmony*, in *Laudate* I (1923), 28, 144.
——— Hughes, Dom Anselm. *Old English Harmony*, in M&L, VI (1925), 154.
HurryS Hurry, Jamieson B. *Sumer is icumen in*, 1914.
IllM Illing, Carl-Heinz. *Zur Technik der Magnificat-Komposition des 16. Jahrhunderts*, 1936.
JonH Jones, Arthur (editor). *History of Gruffydd ap Cynan*, 1910.
JoneM Jones, Edward. *Musical and Poetical Relicks of the Welsh Bards*, 4th ed., 1825.
JonesM Jones, Owen et al. *The Myvyrian Archaiology of Wales*, 2nd ed., 1870.
KolT Kolsrud, Olaf and Georg Reiss. *Tvo Norrøne Latinske Kvaede Med Melodiar*, in *Videnskapsselskapets Skrifter. II. Hist.-Filos. Klasse 1912 No. 5*, 1913.
KorteH Korte, Werner. *Die Harmonik des frühen XV. Jahrhunderts in ihrem Zusammenhang mit der Formtechnik*, 1929.
LedH Lederer, Victor. *Über Heimat und Ursprung der mehrstimmigen Tonkunst*, 1906.
LudG Ludwig, Friedrich. *Die geistliche nichtliturgische, weltliche einstimmige und die mehrstimmige Musik des Mittelalters bis zum Anfang des 15. Jahrhunderts*, in AdlerH I, 157.
Q Ludwig, Friedrich. (See bibliography for Chapter 13)
MaclD Maclean, Charles. *The Dunstable inscription in London*, in SIM, XI (1910), 232.
MeechT Meech, Sanford B. *Three Musical Treatises in English from a Fifteenth-Century Manuscript*, in *Speculum. A Journal of Mediaeval Studies*, X (1935), 235.
MontM Montgomery, Franz. *The Musical Instruments in "The Canterbury Tales"* in MQ, XVII (1931), 439.
——— Müller, Hermann. *Der Musiktraktat in dem Werke des Bartholomaeus Anglicus De proprietatibus rerum*, in *Riemann-Festschrift*, 1909, 241.
——— Nagel, Wilibald. *Geschichte der Musik in England*, 2 vols., 1894–97.
O'CurM O'Curry, Eugene. *On the Manners and Customs of the Ancient Irish*, ed. W. K. O'Sullivan, 1873.
OlsonC *Chaucer and Music of the Fourteenth Century*, in *Speculum. A Journal of Mediaeval Studies*, XVI (1941), 64.
OrelE Orel, Alfred. *Einige Grundformen der Motettkompositionen im XV Jahrhundert*, in SzMW, VII (1920), 48.
PietzschK Pietzsch, Gerhard. *Die Klassifikation der Musik von Boetius bis Ugolino von Orvieto*, 1929.
——— Pulver, Jeffrey. *A Biographical Dictionary of Old English Music*, 1927.
RaphO Raphael, Alfred. *Über einige Quodlibete mit dem Cantus firmus "O rosa bella" und über dieses Lied selbst*, in MfMG, XXXI (1899), 161.
RieG Riemann, Hugo. *Geschichte der Musiktheorie im IX–XIX Jahrhundert*, 2nd ed., 1921.
SachsHI Sachs, Curt. *The History of Musical Instruments*, 1940.
W Sachs, Curt. *World History of the Dance*, 1937. (English translation of *Eine Weltgeschichte des Tanzes*, 1933. References are to the translation.)
SchlesP Schlesinger, Kathleen. *The Precursors of the Violin Family* (Vol. II of *The Instruments of the Modern Orchestra and Early Records of the Precursors of the Violin Family*), 1910.
SchraI Schrade, Leo. *Die handschriftlichen Ueberlieferung der ältesten Instrumentalmusik*, 1931.
SquireN Squire, William Barclay. *Notes on an undescribed Collection of English 15th Century Music*, in SIM, II (1901), 342.
——— Squire, William Barclay. *Notes on Dunstable*, in ZIM, V (1904), 491 (preceded by notes by C. W. Pearce).
StaiR Stainer, Cecie. *Dunstable and the various settings of O Rosa Bella*, in SIM, II (1900), 1.
TischE Tischler, Hans. *English Traits in the Early 13th-Century Motet*, in MQ, XXV (1944), 458.
WagG Wagner, Peter. *Geschichte der Messe. 1. Teil: Bis 1600*, 1913.
——— Walker, Joseph Cooper. *Historical Memoirs of the Irish Bards*, 1786.

WolfE   Wolf, Johannes. *Early English Musical Theorists*, in MQ, XXV (1939), **420.**
H   Wolf, Johannes. *Handbuch der Notationskunde*. Vol. 1, 1913; Vol. 2, 1919.
O   Wolf, Johannes. *Zur Geschichte der Orgelmusik in vierzehnten Jahrhundert*, in *Kirchenmusikalisches Jahrbuch*, XIV (1899), 14.
T   Wolf, Johannes. *Die Tänze des Mittelalters*, in AfMW, I (1918), 10.

MUSIC COLLECTIONS AND FACSIMILES

AuM   Aubry, Pierre. *Cent motets du XIIIe siècle.* 3 vols., 1908.
DolT   Dolmetsch, Arnold. *Translations from the Pennllyn Manuscript of Ancient Harp Music,* 1937.
DTO VII   *Bd.14&15. Sechs Trienter Codices. Erste Auswahl,* 1900. Ed. G. Adler and O. Koller.
XI [1]   *Bd.22 Sechs Trienter Codices. Zweite Auswahl,* 1904. Ed. G. Adler and O. Koller.
XIX [1]   *Bd.38. Sechs Trienter Codices. Dritte Auswahl,* 1912. Ed. O. Koller and others.
XXVII [1] *Bd.53. Sechs Trienter Codices. Vierte Auswahl,* 1920. Ed. R. Ficker and A. Orel.
XXXI   *Bd.61. Sieben Trienter Codices. Fünfte Auswahl,* 1924. Ed. R. Ficker. *Cf. Sieben* with *Sechs* (in the 4 vols. above). The change was caused by the discovery of another codex.
XL   *Bd. 76. Sieben Trienter Codices. Sechste Auswahl,* 1933. Ed. R. Ficker.
EEH   *Early English Harmony.* Vol. I (facsimiles, selected and with short notes by H. E. Wooldridge, 1897; Vol. II (transcriptions, with notes, by H. V. Hughes), 1913.
FullerC   Fuller-Maitland, J. A. *English Carols of the Fifteenth Century,* 1891.
HughW   Hughes, Dom Anselm. *Worcester Mediaeval Harmony,* 1928.
LewM   Lewis, Henry. *Musica B.M. Add. Ms. 14905,* 1936. Facsimile of the Welsh Harp MS with introduction.
MeyM   S.L.M. [Meyer, S. L.] *Music, Cantelenas, Songs, Etc., from an early Fifteenth Century Manuscript,* 1906.
RamsO   Ramsbotham, Alexander. *The Old Hall Manuscript,* transcribed and edited by Alexander Ramsbotham, completed by H. B. Collins and Dom Anselm Hughes. Vol. I, 1933; II, 1935; III, 1938.
RieH   Riemann, Hugo. *Handbuch der Musikgeschichte.* Revised ed. I, 1923; II[1], 1920; II[2], 1922; II[3], 1922.
ScherG   Schering, Arnold. *Geschichte der Musik in Beispielen,* 1931.
StaE   Stainer, Sir John (editor). *Early Bodleian Music. Sacred and Secular Songs.* Vol. I, facsimiles; Vol. II, transcriptions by J. F. R. and C. Stainer, 1901.
WolfG   Wolf, Johannes. *Geschichte der Mensural-Notation von 1250–1460,* 1904. 3 vols. Vol. 1, Historical text; Vol. 2, Examples of notation from the 13th to the 15th century; Vol. 3, Translations of the examples into modern notation.
MS   Wolf, Johannes. *Musikalische Schrifttafeln,* 1923.
S   Wolf, Johannes. *Sing- und Spielmusik aus älterer Zeit,* 1926.

Record List

WHEN one disc has on it two or more pieces that appear in this List, the reader is warned in a footnote, so that he will not order the same record more than once. The footnotes also indicate when a record is part of a set in an album, so that the reader can order either the individual disc or the set. Where only a publisher's name appears in the column headed "Printed Transcriptions," the piece in question is printed separately by the publisher named. The following abbreviations are used:

An. Son. —Anthologie Sonore
Col. —Columbia (domestic)
Eng. Col.—English Columbia
Fr. Col. —French Columbia
H.M.V. —Gramophone (English)—His Master's Voice
O.L. —Oiseau Lyre
Vict. —Victor

CHAPTER 1

SINCE, so far as we know, none of the recorded Hebrew Chant available through the usual commercial channels is demonstrably ancient, no records of Hebrew Chant are listed here. The interested reader will have no difficulty in finding a sizeable repertoire of Synagogue Chant listed in the catalogues of the large recording companies. He may welcome the information that there are some private collections of recordings preserving what are believed to be traditional cantillations and songs. One of these is the Mailamm collection, housed in the Music Library at 121 East 58th St. in New York and available for study on the premises on special application. These records were made by Salomo Rosowsky. A collection of about 800 discs was assembled by Robert Lachmann and is now in the Hebrew University at Jerusalem. See the *Palestine Review*, June 18, 1937, p. 173f.

CHAPTER 2

TITLE AND COMPOSER	PRINTED MUSIC	RECORDING ARTISTS	RECORD NO.
Epitaph, Seikilos	P. 115 *supra;* see also Chap. 2, footnote 90	Hans Joachim Moser	Decca 20156 [1]
Ditto			
First Delphic Hymn to Apollo, Anon. (2nd cent. B. c.)	See Chap. 2, footnote 90; also Novello (*Hymn to Apollo*)	J. E. Butt	MSS 54 [2]

TITLE AND COMPOSER	PRINTED MUSIC	RECORDING ARTISTS	RECORD NO.
Ditto		Palestrina Choir	Victor 20896 [3]
Hymn to Kalliopeia,[4] Anon. (1st cent. B. C.–1st cent. A. D.)	See Chap. 2, footnote 90	J. E. Butt	MSS 54 [2]
Hymn to the Sun, Mesomedes	See Chap. 2, footnote 90	Hans Joachim Moser and Chorus	Decca 20156 [1]

[1] From album, *2000 Years of Music.* Appears once more in this list.

[2] Appears once more in this list. This record is issued by the Educational and General Services, Ltd., 37 Golden Square, London, W. 1. The transcriptions used are those in ReinM. The record gives only those sections of the *Delphic Hymn* which ReinM labels A and B.

[3] Appears also in list for Chaps. 5 and 6. This recording of the *Hymn* (sung in English) follows the Novello publication, which gives a reading by Reinach that is earlier than the one in ReinM (and which fills in the *lacunae* differently). Sections A and B as these are labelled in the Novello print are recorded. These equal most of C plus A of the ReinM version, so that, between them, the 2 records listed above present almost all of the Hymn that survives.

[4] This is No. 11 (i.e. one of the two Hymns to the Muse) listed on p. 49 *supra.*

CHAPTER 4

TITLE, BODY OF CHANT	PRINTED MUSIC	RECORDING ARTISTS	RECORD NO.
Credo, Ambrosian	Antiphonale (Ambrosian 611)	Ambrosian School of Sacred Music, Milan	Decca G.20419 [1]
Gloria I, Ambrosian	Antiphonale (Ambrosian 604)	"	Decca G.20418 [2]
Gloria IV, Ambrosian	Antiphonale (Ambrosian 610)		
O Sacrum convivium (Psallenda), Ambrosian	Antiphonale (Ambrosian 639)	"	Decca G.20420 [2]
O Salutaris (Hymn), Ambrosian	Antiphonale (Ambrosian 641)	"	Decca G.20418 [2]
Sanctus I, Ambrosian	Antiphonale (Ambrosian 614)	"	Decca G.20419 [1]
Tantum ergo (Hymn), Ambrosian	Antiphonale (Ambrosian 641)	"	Decca G.20420 [2]
Te laudamus (Transitorium), Ambrosian	Antiphonale (Ambrosian 81)		
Vexilla Regis (Hymn), Ambrosian	Antiphonale (Ambrosian 642)	"	Decca G.20419 [1]

[1] Appears twice more in this list.   [2] Appears once more in this list.

CHAPTERS 5 AND 6

FOR practical reasons the following list has been arranged slightly differently from the lists for the other chapters. Only records that present chants performed without accompaniment are included. The list makes no claim to completeness, even with respect to such items. Many excellent records are omitted (for example those in the Christschall series) which are now obtainable only as collectors' items. An album issued by Lumen contains a number of fine specimens of the Chant (sung by the Maîtrise de la Cathédrale de Soissons, Cond. H. Dogen) that are not recorded elsewhere. Unfortunately it has been impossible to obtain a copy of this album in time to check its contents for the purposes of this list. The music on most of the records in the list may be found in one or another of the standard chant-books. For more complete listings, the reader is referred to R. D. Darrell's *Encyclopedia of Recorded Music*, the *List of Gramophone Records* issued by the Plainsong and Mediaeval Music Society, Nashdom Abbey, Burnham, Bucks, England, and *Gregorian Chant Discography* by Dom Adelard Bouvilliers (McLaughlin & Reilly Co., Boston, Mass.).

TITLES, ARTISTS, ETC.   RECORD NO.

Collections:

Gregorian Chants sung by the Monks Choir of Saint-Pierre de Solesmes Abbey, Cond. Dom J. Gajard	Victor Album M – 87 [1]
Kyrie, Agnus Dei, Gloria, Sanctus—all from Vat. Ed. Mass No. I	7341
Requiem aeternam (Introit), *Absolve Domine* (Tract), *Domine Jesu Christe* (Offertory)—all from Mass for the Dead	7342
Christus factus est (Gradual), *Hoc corpus* (Communion), *Qui sedes, Dirigatur oratio mea* (Graduals)	7343
Alleluia: Justus germinabit, Memento verbi tui, Quinque prudentes virgines, Pascha nostrum (Communions)	7344
Ad te Domine levavi, Meditabor (Offertories), *Montes Gelboe* (Antiphon), *Custodi me* (Offertory)	7345
Ecce quomodo moritur justus, Tenebrae factae sunt (Responsories)	7346
Sanctus, Agnus Dei—both from Vat. Ed. Mass No. IX, *Adoro te* (Hymn), *Salve Regina* (Antiphon, simple tone)	7347
Spiritus Domini (Introit), *Spiritus Sanctus docebit vos, Spiritus qui a Patre* (Communions), *Da pacem* (Introit), *Kyrie*—from Vat. Ed. Mass No. X *ad lib.*	7348
Precatus est Moyses, Jubilate Deo (Offertories)	7349
Descendit (Responsory), *Alleluia: Ascendit Deus, Alleluia: Assumpta est Maria*	7350

Collections:

Media vita, Christus resurgens (Responsories), *Alleluia: Lapis revolutus est, Alleluia: Quem quaeris mulier, Alleluia: Noli flere Maria* (Antiphons)   7351

Urbs Jerusalem, Virgo Dei genitrix, O quam glorifica (Hymns)   7352

Gregorian Chants sung by the Venray Monastery Choir, Cond. Dr. Eliseus Brüning.   without album

Dominus dixit (Introit), *In splendoribus* (Communion), *Puer natus est* (Introit)   Dutch Col. DH 42

Spiritus Domini (Introit), *Veni Sancte Spiritus* (Sequence)   Dutch Col. DH 43

Rorate caeli (Introit), Second *Kyrie*—from Vat. Ed. Mass No. XVII, *Rorate caeli . . . ne irascaris Domine*   Dutch Col. DHX 6

Ecce lignum Crucis (Antiphon), *Quia eduxi* (Verse), *Agios o Theos* (Trisagion),[2] *Christus factus est pro nobis obediens* (Gradual), *Plange* (Respond)   Dutch Col. DHX 7

Haec dies (Gradual), *Victimae paschali* (Sequence), *Alleluia: Confitemini Domino, Alleluia: Laudate Dominum* (Antiphon), *Vespere autem Sabbati* (Antiphon)   Dutch Col. DHX 8

Requiem aeternam (Introit), *Kyrie eleison, Lux aeterna* (Communion), *In Paradisum* (Antiphon), *Ego sum resurrectio* (Antiphon)—all from Mass for the Dead   Dutch Col. DHX 9

Individual Discs:

Asperges me (Antiphon), *Kyrie*—from Vat. Ed. Mass No. IX, *Per omnia saecula saeculorum* (Responses to the preface, solemn tone), *Sanctus*—from Vat. Ed. Mass. No. IX, *Salve Regina* (Antiphon, simple tone)   HMV C 2087
    Sung by the Schola of Ampleforth Abbey, Cond. J. B. McElligott

Alleluia: Veni Sancte Spiritus, Veni Sancte Spiritus, et emitte caelitus (Sequence), *Ecce nunc* (Antiphon and Psalm), *Te lucis* (Hymn), *Ave Regina coelorum* (Antiphon, simple tone), *O Salutaris Hostia*   HMV C 2088
    Sung by the Schola of Ampleforth Abbey, Cond. J. B. McElligott

TITLES, ARTISTS, ETC.   RECORD NO.

Individual Discs:

Misit Dominus verbum suum (Gradual)   Decca 20157 [2]
    Sung by the choir of the Gregorian Society of the Berlin
State Academy of Church and School Music, Cond. H.
Halbig

Altera autem die (Gospel tone for Palm Sunday), *Alle-*
luia: Ascendit Deus, Alleluia: Dominus in Sina, Requiem   Eng. Col. DX 638
aeternam (Gradual)—from Mass for the Dead
    Sung by the Nashdom Abbey Singers, Cond. Dom An-
selm Hughes

Dies Irae, Sanctus—both from Mass for the Dead   Vict. 21621
    Sung by the Palestrina Choir, Cond. N. A. Montani

Ut queant laxis (Hymn)   Vict. 20897 [4]
    Sung by the Palestrina Choir, Cond. N. A. Montani.

Veni Creator Spiritus (Hymn), *Te Deum laudamus*   Vict. 20896 [5]
(Hymn)
    Sung by the Palestrina Choir, Cond. N. A. Montani.

Adiuvabit eam Deus (Gradual), *Alleluia: Pascha nostrum*   An. Son. 34 [6]
immolatus est
    Sung by Agop Agopian and Les Paraphonistes de St.
Jean des Matines, Cond. Guillaume de Van.

Hosanna filio David (Antiphon), *Passer invenit sibi*
domum (Communion), *Alleluia: Pascha nostrum immola-*   Fr. Col. DF 102 [7]
tus est
    Sung by Artists of the Schola Cantorum, Paris, Cond.
Amédée Gastoué.

Vexilla Regis (Hymn)   Eng. Col. D 40118 [8]
    Sung (in English) by The Winchester Music Club.

---

[1] The original French booklet accompanying this set contains the complete music. Although the American edition translates the explanatory text, it unfortunately omits most of the music.

[2] *Ecce lignum Crucis* is sung three times, on each repetition a degree higher than before. For an explanation of this procedure see Lefebvre's *Daily Missal*, p. 817. The verse, *Popule meus*, is omitted.

[3] From album, *2000 Years of Music*. Appears also in list for Chap. 9.

[4] Appears also in list for Chap. 9.

[5] Appears also in list for Chap. 2.

[6] From Album IV. The individual rhythmical interpretation is that of the conductor.

[7] Appears also in list for Chap. 7.

[8] Appears also in list for Chap. 14.

CHAPTER 7

TITLE AND COMPOSER	PRINTED TRANSCRIPTIONS	RECORDING ARTISTS	RECORD NO.
Agniaus douz (*rotrouenge*) Anon. (13th cent., French)	GennA, 65; GennR I, 254 [1]	Yves Tinayre	Lumen 32017 [2]
Ainsi doit entrer en vile (*rondeau*), Anon. (13th cent., French)	AuS, 219; GennR I, 272	La Psallette Notre Dame	Lumen 30058 [3]
A l'entrada del tems clar (*ballade*), Anon. (12th cent., Provençal)	Variously transcribed: AuT, 47; GennF, 85 (PruN, 62); GéroM, 148; OH II, 282. Recorded transcription by Gastoué (?)	Artists of the Schola Cantorum, directed by Gastoué	Fr. Col. DF 102 [4]
A l'entrant d'esté (*laisegment*), Blondel de Nesles	BeckC II, 17; GennF, 226	Max Meili	An. Son. 18 [5]
Beata viscera (*conductus*), Perotin	LudG, 187	Yves Tinayre	Lumen 32011 [6]
Ce fut en mai (*laisegment*), Moniot d'Arras	Ex. 55 *supra*	Mlle. Pironnay	Fr. Col. DF 103 [7]
Danse (Instrumental) (*ductia*), Anon. (13th cent., French)	AuE, 14	M. Debondue (musette) and M. Clayette (drum)	An. Son. 16 [8]
En mai la rousée (*laisegment*), Anon. (13th cent., French)	BesM, 119	Mairy Kuhner with medieval harp	An. Son. 91 [9]
Estampie (Instrumental), Anon. (13th cent., French)	AuE, 19	M. Crunelle (piccolo) and M. Clayette (drum)	An. Son. 16 [8]
Gaite de la tor, Anon. (13th cent., French)	AuT, 72; OH II, 280	Artists of the Schola Cantorum, directed by Gastoué	Fr. Col. DF 102 [4]
Je nuns hons pris (*rotrouenge*), Richard the Lion-Hearted	BeckC II, 144; GennA, 20	Max Meili	An. Son. 18 [5]

TITLE AND COMPOSER	PRINTED TRANSCRIPTIONS	RECORDING ARTISTS	RECORD NO.
Kalenda maya (*estampie*), Reimbautz de Vaquieras	RieH, I, Bk. 2. 234	Hans Joachim Moser	Decca 20158 [10]
Planctus Karoli: A solis ortu usque ad occidua (Lament for Charlemagne), Anon. (9th cent.)	Naumann (see chap. 7, *supra*, footnote 2)	Reinald Werrenrath	Victor 55072-B [11]
Pois preyatz me, senhor (*lai*-segment), Bernart de Ventadorn	Ex. 49, *supra*	Hans Joachim Moser	Decca 20158 [10]
Por conforter ma pesance (*ballade*), Thibaut de Navarre	Ex. 54, *supra*	M. Deniau	Fr. Col. 103 [7]
Prendés-i-garde S'on nous regarde (*rondeau*), Guillaume d'Amiens	AuS, 221; GennF, 64; GennR I, 38	La Psallette Notre Dame	Lumen 30058 [8]
Quand voi an la fin d'estey (*ballade*), Perrin d'Angincourt	BeckC II, 274	Max Meili	An. Son. 18 [8]
Reis glorios (*ballade*), Guiraut de Bornelh	Ex. 50, *supra*	M. Deniau	Fr. Col. DF 103 [7]
Robins m'aime (from *Le Jeu de Robin et Marion*) (modified *rondeau*), Adam de la Halle (as adapter of a folksong ?)	Ex. 53, *supra*	Mme. Gastoué	
Vous n'alez mie (*rondeau*), Anon. (13th cent., French)	GennR I, 84	La Psallette Notre Dame	Lumen 30058 [8]

[1] Gennrich's transcriptions follow a MS different from the one followed by the unpublished transcription recorded. His version, accordingly, lacks one line of text, printed in the notes accompanying the album.

[2] In *Sept Siècles de musique sacrée*, album II. Appears also in list for Chap. 11.

[8] Appears twice more in this list; also in list for Chap. 11. Three pieces named here are designated merely *Suite de rondeaux populaires* on label and are sung in alphabetical order. *Prendés-i-garde* preceded by "restored" introduction for rebec; *Vous n'alez mie* accompanied

by bells. Discrepancies between the printed and recorded versions are due to differences in the interpretation of MS Bibl. Nat. fr. 25566 (in which these pieces are preserved) on the part of Gennrich and M. Chailley, conductor of the Psallette. Of *Vous n'alez mie*, only the refrain of the printed version is recorded, but it is sung twice.

[4] Appears once more in this list; also in list for Chaps. 5 and 6. Music here named performed with "restored" acc. for *vielle* (i. e. a type of hurdy-gurdy, not a *vièle*).

[5] From album II. Appears twice more in this

list; also in list for Chap. 8. *Quand voi* and *Ja nuns hons pris* preceded by "restored" introductions for viol. The rhythms differ from those of Beck and of Gennrich, who, for *A l'entrant d'esté*, follows a MS different from the one followed on the record.

[6] In *Sept Siècles de musique sacrée*, album I. Appears also in list for Chap. 11.

[7] Music performed with "restored" acc. A *viola d'amore* is used, which, however, is not a 13th-cent. instrument.

[8] From album II. Appears also in lists for Chaps. 8, 13, 14. The drum part is added.

[9] Appears also in lists for Chaps. 11, 12, 13.

[10] From album, *2000 Years of Music*. Appears once more in this list; also in list for Chap. 8. *Kalenda maya* is sung in binary rhythm, used also in RieH I[2], 234; for transcriptions in ternary rhythm, see AuT, 43; GennF, 164; LudG, 190; for a transcription partly ternary, partly binary, see ScherG, 6.

[11] Discontinued, but special pressing obtainable on order.

CHAPTER 8

TITLE AND COMPOSER	PRINTED TRANSCRIPTIONS	RECORDING ARTISTS	RECORD NO.
Dance (Instrumental), Anon. (13th cent., English)	WolfT, 22	M. Crunelle (piccolo) and M. Clayette (drum)	An. Son. 16 [1]
Deich von der guoten schiet (*lai*-segment), Friedrich von Hûsen (poet)	GennS, 90–2	Hans Joachim Moser	Decca 20158 [2]
Der kuninc Rodolp minnet got (modified *chanson*), "Der Unvürzaghete" ("The Dauntless One")	Ex. 58, *supra*		
Gloria in cielo (*virelai = ballata*), Anon. (14th cent., Italian)	GennF, 74; LiuL II, 30; LudG, 211	Max Meili	An. Son. 8 [3]
Nu alerst leb' ich mir werde (rounded *chanson*), Walther von der Vogelweide	Ex. 57, *supra*	Hans Joachim Moser	Decca 20158 [2]
Ditto *Ob aller mynne* (rounded *chanson*), Rumelant	SarJ II, 33	Max Meili	An. Son. 18 [4]
Sancto Lorenço, martyr d'amore (*virelai = ballata*), Anon. (14th cent., Italian)	LiuL II, 258; LudG, 211	Yves Tinayre	Lumen 32018 [5]
Wê, ich han gedacht (reduced strophic-*lai*), Witzlaw von Rügen	GéroM, 218; MosG I, 170; SarJ II, 47	Hans Joachim Moser	Decca 20158 [2]

¹ From album II. Appears also in lists for Chaps. 7, 13, 14. The drum part is added. The recording gives a shortened version, the polyphonic section mentioned on p. 243 being omitted as well as some repetitions.

² From album, *2000 Years of Music*. Appears twice more in this list; also in list for Chap. 7. The melody of *Deich von der guoten schiet* is that of *Pois preyatz me* (see Chap. 7),

adapted by Gennrich to the German poem in accordance with the probable intention of von Hûsen.

³ From album I. Appears also in list for Chap. 13.

⁴ From album II. Appears also in list for Chap. 7.

⁵ In *Sept Siècles de musique sacrée*, album II. Appears also in list for Chap. 11.

Eng. Col. RO 50, included in the lists for Chaps. 9 and 14, contains also, sung monodically, the main melody of the 3-part setting (*cf.* Chap. 14) of *Angelus ad virginem* (rather than the unaltered melody of the 1-part setting) with a modern English version of the text by Michael Austen (rather than the Middle English version).

CHAPTER 9

TITLE AND COMPOSER	PRINTED TRANSCRIPTIONS	RECORDING ARTISTS	RECORD NO.
Congaudeant Catholici (*Benedicamus*-trope), Anon. (12th cent., from Santiago de Compostela)	Ex. 71, *supra*	Choir of the Gregorian Society of the Berlin State Academy of Church and School Music, Cond. H. Halbig	Decca 20157 ¹
Jubilemus omnes (sequence), Anon. (12th cent., Anglo-French)	HughA, 99	Monks of Nashdom Abbey, Cond. Dom Anselm Hughes	Eng. Col. RO 50 ²
Mira lege, miro modo (organum), Anon. (12th cent., from St. Martial)	OH I, 53	Choir, Cond. Sir Richard Terry	Col. 5710 ³
Tu Patris sempiternus and *Sit gloria Domini*, Anon. (9th cent., from the *Musica Enchiriadis*) (Examples of organum at the fourth and fifth respectively)	See Exx. 67 and 66, *supra*	Palestrina Choir, Cond. Nicola A. Montani	Vict. 20897 ⁴
Verbum bonum et suave (discant), Anon. (early 12th cent., French)	OH I, 80 ⁵		

¹ From album, *2000 Years of Music*. Appears also in list for Chaps. 5 and 6.

² See p. 251 *supra*. This record was issued for The Plainsong and Mediaeval Music Society. It is not listed in the regular English Columbia Catalogue. It appears also in list for Chap. 14.

³ In *Columbia History of Music*, Vol I.

⁴ Appears also in list for Chaps. 5 and 6.

⁵ See also p. 270 *supra*.

CHAPTER 11

TITLE AND COMPOSER	PRINTED TRANSCRIPTIONS	RECORDING ARTISTS	RECORD NO.
Alle Psallite cum luya —*Alleluia*, Anon. (13th cent.)	RoksM II, 256; OH I, 219	La Psallette Notre Dame	Lumen 32027 [1]
Anima mea—Descendi in ortum—Alma Re- demptoris, Anon. (13th cent.)	RoksM III, 148	Mm. Anspach, Jacquier, and Mertens	An. Son. 91 [2]
Ave virgo Regia—Ave gloriosa mater— Domino, Anon. (13th cent.)	RoksM II, 125	Yves Tinayre and La Psallette Notre Dame	Lumen 32018 [3][4]
Bien doy joye deme- ner—In Domino (*motet* in *rondeau* form), Anon. (13th cent.)	GennR I, 19	Yves Tinayre with strings in unison playing the tenor	Col. 70700-D [10]
Bone amourette me tient gai (*rondeau*), Adam de la Halle	GennR I, 67	La Psallette Notre Dame	Lumen 30057 [5]
C'est lajus par dessous l'olive—Quia com- cupivit rex (*motet* in *rondeau* form), Anon. (13th cent.)	GennR I, 21	Yves Tinayre with strings in unison playing the tenor	Col. 70700-D [10]
Crucifixum in carne (organum), Leonin	HandC, 161 [11]	Yves Tinayre with strings in unison playing the tenor	Col. 70700-D [10]
Deum time (orga- num), Leonin	Unpublished	Yves Tinayre and La Psallette Notre Dame	Lumen 32017 [3][6]
Diex, coment pourroie (*rondeau*), Adam de la Halle	GennR I, 66	La Psallette Notre Dame	Lumen 30057 [5]
Diex soit en cheste meson (*ballade*), Adam de la Halle	GennR I, 69	La Psallette Notre Dame	Lumen 30057 [5]

TITLE AND COMPOSER	PRINTED TRANSCRIPTIONS	RECORDING ARTISTS	RECORD NO.
En mai—L'autre jour —He! resvelle-toi Robins, Anon. (13th cent.)	RoksM III, 116	La Psallette Notre Dame	Lumen 30058 [7]
Fines amourettes ai (*virelai*), Adam de la Halle	GennR I, 57	La Psallette Notre Dame	Lumen 30057 [5]
Gaude super omnia— Descendi in ortum —Alma Redemptoris, Anon. (13th cent.)	AuM II, 51	La Psallette Notre Dame	Lumen 32027 [1]
Haec dies (organum), Leonin	LudG, 217	Yves Tinayre with strings in unison playing the tenor	Lumen 32011 [6] [8]
Hareu li maus d'aimer (*rondeau*), Adam de la Halle	GennR I, 57	La Psallette Notre Dame	Lumen 30057 [5]
Ille (melisma), Anon. (13th cent.)	RoksM III, 68 [9]	Yves Tinayre with English horn	Lumen 32013 [8]
Li jalous—Tuit cil— Veritatem, Anon. (13th cent.)	RoksM II, 295; AuM III, 27	La Psallette Notre Dame	Lumen 30058 [7]
Mout me fu griés— Robins m'aime— Portare, Anon. (13th cent.)	AuM II, 182	La Psallette Notre Dame	Lumen 30058 [7]
Or est Bayars (*rondeau*), Adam de la Halle	GennR I, 63	La Psallette Notre Dame	Lumen 30057 [5]
Ditto		Yves Tinayre with strings	Col. 70700-D [10]
Virgo (organum), Perotin (?)	RoksM II, 9	La Psallette Notre Dame	Lumen 32027 [1]

[1] Appears twice more in this list.

[2] Appears also in lists for Chaps. 7, 12, 13.

8 In *Sept Siècles de musique sacrée*, album II.

4 Appears also in list for Chap. 8.

5 Appears in this list five more times.

6 Appears also in list for Chap. 7.

7 Appears twice more in this list; also in list for Chap. 7.

8 In *Sept Siècles de musique sacrée*, album I.

9 The version here printed after the Montpellier MS is more elaborate than the one re-

corded, which follows Paris Bib. Nat. f. lat. 15139.

10 In Columbia Masterworks Set M-431. Appears in this list three more times.

11 Handschin transcribes the version preserved in Pluteus 29.1 at Florence and also that in Wolfenbüttel 677. His rhythmic interpretation often varies from that of the transcription recorded (by Yvonne Rokseth, unpublished), which is a composite of both versions.

Announced by L'Oiseau-Lyre, but not yet released at the time of the preparation of this list, were the following:

a) *Posui adiutorium* (Perotin); b) *Deus in adiutorium;* c) *Balam inquit vaticinans;* d) *Huic ut placuit tres magi*   O.L. 90
a) *Radix venie—Ave Maria;* b) *Mors a primi Patris—Mors que stimulo—Mors amorsu;* c) *Hui maiu, au doz;* d) *Trois serors, sor rive mer;* e) *J'ai mis toute ma pensée—Je rien puis, mais.*   O.L. 91
All these pieces are printed in RoksM.

CHAPTER 12

TITLE AND COMPOSER	PRINTED TRANSCRIPTIONS	RECORDING ARTISTS	RECORD NO.
A vous, vierge de dou-çour—Ad te virgo clamitans venio (iso-rhythmic), Anon. (middle 14th cent.)	L'Oiseau-Lyre	J. Archimbaud and R. Bonté with viol	O. L. 2 [1]
De ce que fol pense (*ballade*), Pierre de Molins	WolfH I, 357; E. Droz and G. Thibault, *Poètes et musiciens,* 21	H. Guérmant with lute, alto viol, tenor re-corder	An. Son. 59 [2]
Hoquetus David, Guillaume de Ma-chaut	L'Oiseau-Lyre	Foveau (trum-pet), Lafosse (bass trumpet), and Tudesq (trombone)	O. L. 3 [3]
Je voi douleur—Fauvel nous a fait present—Fauvel autant, Anon. (14th cent.)	WolfG III, 19	Mm. Bonté, De-niau, and Rous-selon	An. Son. 91 [4]
Mass, Guillaume de Machaut			
Credo	WolfG III, 53 (incomplete)	Les Paraphonistes de St. Jean des Matines and brass ensemble, Cond. Guil-laume de Van	An. Son. 31 [5]
Sanctus	Unpublished		
Agnus Dei I and II	BesM, 149; OH I, 245		An. Son. 32 [5]
Ite missa est	Unpublished		

TITLE AND COMPOSER	PRINTED TRANSCRIPTIONS	RECORDING ARTISTS	RECORD NO.
Or sus, vous dormés trop (*virelai*), Anon. (last half of 14th cent.)	L'Oiseau-Lyre	J. Archimbaud with brass trumpet and trombone	O. L. 3 [3]
Plourés, dames (*ballade*), Guillaume de Machaut	MachM I, 37	Yves Tinayre with strings	Col. 70701-D [6]
Se je chant mains que ne suel (*chace*), Anon. (14th cent.)	BesS I, 251	F. Anspach and E. Jacquier	An. Son. 59 [2]

[1] Appears also in list for Chap. 13.
[2] From Album VI. Appears once more in this list; also in list for Chap. 13.
[3] Appears once more in this list.

[4] Appears also in lists for Chaps. 7, 11, 13.
[5] From Album IV.
[6] In Columbia Masterworks Set M-431.

CHAPTER 13

TITLE AND COMPOSER	PRINTED TRANSCRIPTIONS	RECORDING ARTISTS	RECORD NO.
Ad regnum opulentum—Noster cetus, Anon. (14th cent., Swiss)	HandAP appendix, 16	Mm. Bousquet and Rousselon	An. Son. 91 [1]
Ave Mater, Anon. (14th cent., Venetian)	WolfH I, 318	Yves Tinayre with strings	Lumen 32019 [2]
Benche ora piova (*ballata*), Francesco Landini	EllinL, 50; WolfG III, 128	Carl Weinrich (organ)	Musicraft 1047 [3]
Congaudeant turba fidelium (*Benedicamus*-trope), Anon. (14th cent., Swiss)	HandAP appendix, 6	Mm. Bousquet and Rousselon	An. Son. 91 [1]
Fenice fu (madrigal), Jacopo da Bologna	BesM, 156	H. Guermant and E. Jacquier with lute and alto viol	An. Son. 59 [4]
Gloria in excelsis, Matteo da Perugia	To be published in VanM	J. Archimbaud and R. Bonté with bass trumpet	O. L. 1 [5]

TITLE AND COMPOSER	PRINTED TRANSCRIPTIONS	RECORDING ARTISTS	RECORD NO.
Io son un pellegrin (*ballata*), Giovanni da Cascia	EinSH, 265	Max Meili with viol	An. Son. 8 [6]
Ita se n'era (madrigal), Vincenzo d'Arimini	WolfG III, 122	Max Meili with viol	
Il Lamento di Tristano, Anon. (14th cent., Italian)	ScherG, 20; WolfT, 41	Debondue (musette) and Clayette (drum)	An. Son. 16 [7]
Lux purpurata radiis —Diligite justiciam, Jacopo da Bologna	To be published in VanM	J. Archimbaud and R. Bonté with trombone	O. L. 2 [8]
Non al suo amante (madrigal), Jacopo da Bologna	To be published in VanM	J. Archimbaud and R. Bonté	O. L. 1 [5]
Questa fanciulla (*ballata*)—organ transcription, Francesco Landini	Félix Raugel, *Quarante-six pièces pour orgue . . . d'anciens auteurs,* 5 [9]	André Marchal (organ)	Fr. Pathé PAT 63 [10]
Tosto che l'alba (*caccia*), Ghirardello	WolfF, 626	F. Mertens and E. Jacquier with trombone	An. Son. 59 [4]

[1] Appears once more in this list; also in lists for Chaps. 7, 11, 12.
[2] In *Sept Siècles de musique sacrée,* album II.
[3] In *Early Organ Music,* Vol. 1.
[4] From album VI. Appears once more in this list; also in list for Chap. 12.
[5] Appears once more in this list.

[6] From Album I. Appears also in list for Chap. 8.
[7] From album II. Appears also in lists for Chaps. 7, 8, 14. The drum part is added.
[8] Appears also in list for Chap. 12.
[9] See also Ex. 115, *supra,* with comments before it.
[10] In *Trois Siècles de musique d'orgue.*

CHAPTER 14

TITLE AND COMPOSER	PRINTED TRANSCRIPTIONS	RECORDING ARTISTS	RECORD NO.
Ad cantus laetitiae, Anon. (14th cent.)	See Chap. 14, footnote 41	Monks of Nashdom Abbey, Cond. Dom Anselm Hughes	Eng. Col. RO 50 [1]

TITLE AND COMPOSER	PRINTED TRANSCRIPTIONS	RECORDING ARTISTS	RECORD NO.
Alleluia psallat—Alleluia concinet, Anon. (14th cent.)	HughW, 83	Monks of Nashdom Abbey, Cond. Dom Anselm Hughes	Eng. Col. RO 50 [1]
Beata Dei Genetrix Maria (motet), Nicholas Damett	RamsO I, 164	The Nashdom Abbey Singers, Cond. Dom Anselm Hughes	Eng. Col. DX 581 [2]
Beata viscera (conductus), Anon. (14th cent.)	HughW, 108	Monks of Nashdom Abbey, Cond. Dom Anselm Hughes	Eng. Col. RO 50 [1]
Credo, Anon. (late 14th or early 15th cent.)	RamsO II, 8	The Nashdom Abbey Singers, Cond. Dom Anselm Hughes	Eng. Col. DX 582 [3]
Deo gratias Anglia (Hymn after Agincourt—incomplete), Anon. (early 15th cent.)	See Chap. 14, footnote 158	The Winchester Music Club	Eng. Col. D 40118 [4]
Gloria in Excelsis, King Henry VI (or V?)	RamsO I, 34	The Nashdom Abbey Singers, Cond. Dom Anselm Hughes	Eng. Col. DX 581 [2]
Pleni sunt coeli (from the *Sanctus*), John Benet	WolfG III, 182	Yves Tinayre with English horn	Lumen 32020 [5]
Salve porta paradisi (motet), Nicholas Damett	RamsO I, 166	The Nashdom Abbey Singers, Cond. Dom Anselm Hughes	Eng. Col. DX 581 [2]
Sanctus, King Henry VI (or V?)	RamsO III, 1	The Nashdom Abbey Singers, Cond. Dom Anselm Hughes	Eng. Col. DX 582 [3]
Stantipes, Anon. (13th cent.)	WolfT, 19	Crunelle (piccolo) and Debondue (musette)	An. Son. 16 [6]

TITLE AND COMPOSER	PRINTED TRANSCRIPTIONS	RECORDING ARTISTS	RECORD NO.
Sumer is icumen in (rota), Anon. (*c.* 1240)	OH I, 185	The St. George's Singers	Col. 5715 [7]
Virgo pudicitiae (conductus), Anon. (13th cent.)	Unpublished	Monks of Nashdom Abbey, Cond. Dom Anselm Hughes	Eng. Col. RO 50 [1]

[1] This record was issued for The Plainsong and Mediaeval Music Society. It is not listed in the regular English Columbia Catalogue. It appears twice more in this list; also in list for Chap. 9.

[2] Appears twice more in this list.

[3] Appears once more in this list.

[4] Appears also in list for Chaps. 5 and 6.

[5] In *Sept Siècles de musique sacrée*, album II.

[6] From album II. Appears also in lists for Chaps. 7, 8, 13.

[7] In *Columbia History of Music*, Vol. I. Though less easily obtained, the recording of this rota by the Winchester Music Club (Eng. Col. D 40119) is also recommended.

ADDENDA

Since the above list was drawn, Victor has issued the album, *Medieval and Renaissance Choral Music,* containing records made by the Choir of the Pius X School of Liturgical Music. The contents include the following items (the fourth and sixth of which are listed above in other recordings).

CHAPTER ILLUSTRATED	TITLE AND COMPOSER	PRINTED TRANSCRIPTIONS [1]
8	*Maria, muoter reinû mait* (*lai*-segment), Anon. (14th cent., German)	Ex. 61 *supra*
8	*Todolos benes que nos Deus* (modified *virelai*) *Cantiga* of Alfonso the Wise	AngC, 28; GennF, 77
9	*Alleluia: Angelus Domini* (organum), Anon. (11th cent., French)	LudG, 175
11	*Haec dies* (organum), Leonin	LudG, 217
11	*O miranda Dei caritas—Salve, mater salutifera—Kyrie,* Anon. (13th cent.)	AuM II, 188
14	*Alleluia psallat—Alleluia concinet,* Anon. (14th cent.)	HughW, 83
14	*Puellare gremium—Purissima Virgo,* Anon. (14th cent.)	HughW, 100
14	*Quam pulchra es* (motet), John Dunstable	See Chap. 14, footnote 142

On Victor 18413, played by Joseph Bonnet

13	*El molin de Paris,* Anon. (14th cent.)	KamP, 145 [2]

[1] The first 8 pieces are reprinted also in Georgia Stevens, *Medieval and Renaissance Music,* 1940 (pp. 69, 24, 2, 4, 9, 10, 5, 19).

[2] Also in Bonnet's *An Anthology of Early French Organ Music,* p. 3. Both there and on the record-label the piece is assigned to the 15th cent.; but see KamP, 28, 56. (See also KamP, 57f, concerning the possibility that the title by which the piece has come to be known is really a corruption of the composer's name.) The same record contains an *Organum Triplex* by Perotin (printed on p. 1 of the *Anthology*). This is part of the vocal *Alleluia Posui adjutorium,* but with the rhythm misinterpreted; *cf.* the transcriptions mentioned in Chap. 11, footnote 29; also the facsimile in RoksM I.

Index

Figures in bold type after titles of pieces indicate musical illustrations; after other items they indicate extended discussions of those items.

(Page references to medieval theorists indicate only where they are named; for references to their writings, see also pages given under names of modern editors—Gerbert, Coussemaker, etc.)